BOUND TO PLEASE

ALSO BY MICHAEL DIRDA

An Open Book

Readings: Essays and Literary Entertainments

BOUND TO PLEASE

AN EXTRAORDINARY ONE-VOLUME
LITERARY EDUCATION

ESSAYS ON GREAT WRITERS AND THEIR BOOKS

Michael Dirda

W. W. Norton & Company
New York London

Photographs courtesy of the Library of Congress

For information about permission to reproduce selections from this book, write to
Permissions, W. W. Norton & Company, Inc., 500 Fifth Avenue, New York, NY 10110

Manufacturing by Quebecor World, Fairfield
Book design by Blue Shoe Studio
Production manager: Amanda Morrison

Library of Congress Cataloging-in-Publication Data

Dirda, Michael.
Bound to please : an extraordinary one-volume literary education : essays on great writers
and their books / Michael Dirda.
p. cm.
Includes bibliographical references.
ISBN 978-0-393-32963-6
1. Best books. I. Title.
Z1035.A1D57 2004
081—dc22
2004054719

ISBN 978-0-393-32963-6 (pod)
W. W. Norton & Company, Inc., 500 Fifth Avenue, New York, N.Y. 10110
www.wwnorton.com

W. W. Norton & Company Ltd., Castle House, 75/76 Wells Street, London W1T 3QT

1 2 3 4 5 6 7 8 9 0

For my colleagues, past and present,
at *The Washington Post Book World*

What should we be without the sexual myth,
The human revery or poem of death?

Castratos of moon-mash—Life consists of
Propositions about life.

—*Wallace Stevens*
from "Men Made Out of Words"

CONTENTS

VII. CRITICAL OBSERVERS 263

VIII. LOVERS, POETS, AND MADMEN 303

IX. MAGICIANS OF THE WORD 337

CONTENTS

XII. PERFORMING SELVES 465

CODA 501

INTRODUCTION

Bound to Please intentionally resembles a cocktail party more than a work of criticism: it's meant to be entertaining, sometimes provocative, above all a way to catch up with old friends and make new ones. In these pages you'll be introduced to lots of writers and books, and I hope you'll be intrigued enough by what I say to spend an evening with some of them on your own.

During the past quarter century I've worked as a writer and editor at *The Washington Post Book World*, much of that time as a weekly columnist. Every Sunday my name appears on page 15 above a longish piece, usually a book review but sometimes a more personal essay (for a sampling of the latter, see my previous collection, *Readings: Essays and Literary Entertainments*). All my writing, in other words, has been aimed at the semimythical common reader, and usually one who is sleepily flipping through the newspaper while sipping coffee on Sunday morning.

By only the loosest definition, then, can the contents of *Bound to Please* be regarded as criticism. Instead, think of these articles as old-fashioned appreciations, a fan's notes, good talk. My primary goal is to describe a work accurately, to quote frequently when sentences are clever or memorable, and to convey something of each book's particular magic, strength, or excitement. By preference, I usually hint at the whole arc of a writer's career, or provide brief introductions to a life and work. Hence the pages that follow tend to be brisk, fact-filled, and anecdote-rich, sometimes stylistically playful (buried allusions, low-keyed puns) and enthusiastic about a wide variety of creative "makers." As an old newspaperman counseled me long ago, "writing that isn't fun to read doesn't get read."

Let me briefly describe how I wrote these pieces. For the past fifteen years or so *Book World* has granted me two days of each week away from my usual editorial duties to produce my column. Much of that home time is actually needed just to turn all the pages of any novel or biography under review—I'm really quite a slow reader, still moving my lips and sounding out every word.

My kind of essay—one that employs a new title as a springboard to reflect on a writer's general achievement—also requires me to poke around my bookshelves, visit the branch library, and delve into this and that. I enjoy such research. I like to know things.

While reading and browsing, I gradually accumulate notes and anecdotes and facts and even "thoughts," all of which are duly set down in one of those bound composition notebooks with black-and-white speckled covers. To mark key passages I pencil vertical lines in the margins of that week's "uncorrected page proofs," those preliminary versions of new books with generic green, light blue, or cranberry covers. Sometimes I'll scribble an idea on the endpapers, or make a list of pages to refer back to. In every way possible, I contrive to make my encounter with a book a relatively slow, deliberative enterprise, one during which I look for the salient arguments, linger over the author's style, take issue with his conclusions or storytelling. My goal, that of all good book reviewers, indeed of all good readers, is the one expressed in Henry James's celebrated dictum, "Try to be one on whom nothing is lost."

Being a *Post* staffer allows me to choose the books I write about. If a collection of stories or a work of history simply doesn't deliver the goods, of whatever kind, I can usually assign it to someone else who may be more sympathetic. Now and again, I will write a negative piece—always great fun, though bad for the character, according to W. H. Auden—but haven't included any here. All the books in *Bound to Please* are worth your time.

Unlike an academic critic, a literary journalist seldom enjoys the leisure to reread a novel or spend hours untangling its intricacies while tramping through field and stream, a faithful Labrador at his side. My 1,500 to 1,800 words are due every seven days. Over the years those weekly deadlines have nonetheless permitted me to range far and wide in literature and intellectual history—and without them I might never have written at all. It's always time to make the donuts, and my personal motto is "Hurry."

Of course, I wasn't always a journalist. So perhaps some biography may be in order.

Readers of my memoir *An Open Book* know that I grew up in a working-class Ohio steel town and spent much of my childhood and adolescence escaping into comics, adventure stories, mysteries, science fiction, and eventually more "grown-up" books. After receiving a scholarship to Oberlin College (thirteen miles away), I there pursued, after some missteps, a classic liberal arts curriculum, one emphasizing pre-twentieth-century English and French literature and European history.

After earning a B.A., I took off the following year to work as an "assistant" in a French lycée in Marseille, soaking up fiction and structuralist criticism during long Provençal evenings. Then, throughout much of the 1970s, I found myself in school again, mainly as a rather uncentered graduate student in comparative literature at Cornell. In fact, I spent four years just taking seminars, mainly in medieval studies, European Romanticism, and literary theory.

My dissertation ultimately focused on the French writer Stendhal as an autobiographer. But while still typing up its timeless pages I moved to Washington, only to earn the usual adjunct's pittance by teaching in the literature departments of American University and George Mason University. About this same time, largely because our nation's capital then boasted any number of interesting shops and annual sales, I began to collect books in a serious way. I cannot emphasize enough how much my literary education owes to both browsing through secondhand bookstores and actually possessing my own hardback copies of great works of literature and scholarship.

As it happened, I turned down the few rather dull academic jobs offered to me after I'd been awarded a Ph.D., preferring to reinvent myself as a freelance editor, translator, and technical writer for a small computer company.

So it came about that only when nearly thirty years old did I turn to book reviewing. The slippery slide began with a piece for the *Chronicle of Higher Education*—800 perspicacious words on Matthew Bruccoli's *The Last of the Novelists*, a study of F. Scott Fitzgerald's *The Last Tycoon*. Shortly afterward, I persuaded *The Washington Post Book World* to give me a try.

One Friday night a messenger dropped off a book for review: *In the Suicide Mountains*, a kind of moral fable by John Gardner (he of *Grendel* fame). *Book World* wanted only a brief notice, a mere 200 words. But for some reason I couldn't quite figure out when this little review was due. I had, however, seen movies about newspapers—never having worked for one—and knew that speed was absolutely critical. Reporters were always going on about deadlines or hurrying into phone booths where they would call up the city room and shout, "Stop the presses" or "Get me rewrite, sweetheart."

So I sped through Gardner's book that Friday night and spent all day Saturday penning my two or three short paragraphs. No prose since that on Trajan's column has been so carefully chiseled. Then came my true masterstroke. From my art-conservator girlfriend (and eventual wife) I appropriated a couple of sheets of thick, creamy, Italian paper, the kind of bond that imagines it's really vellum or parchment. I inserted a crisp black ribbon into my Hermes manual typewriter and, after a couple of failures, generated a brief notice you could mat and frame. Naturally I dashed off a seemingly nonchalant, fountain-penned thank-you to the editor, hoping that the enclosed would do.

Around 10 PM I drove downtown to the main post office, which was open until, I think, midnight. My copy reached *The Washington Post* on Monday morning.

Everyone at *Book World* was impressed, first of all, by the turnaround time. The book had been messengered on Friday and my mini-masterpiece received back on Monday. Usually reviewers are allotted several weeks, and then they will generally telephone to beg piteously for an additional three or four days. The entire staff enthusiastically claimed to admire my write-up, and the art director, Francis Tanabe, used my suggested illustration. But most important of all, the editor of *Book World*, Bill McPherson, loved the paper. "Where can I buy some of this?" he asked me. I wouldn't tell him. Instead I hinted that he just might be given a ream as a present, were a few more assignments to come my way. A little quid pro quo. I might be a provincial kid from Ohio, but I hadn't been living in Washington for nothing.

Over the following five or six months, I reviewed a novel called *Subway to Samarkand*, a collection of essays by the poet Howard Nemerov, Paul Monette's screwball gay novel *Taking Care of Mrs. Carroll*, a volume of very bad, late stories by William Saroyan, and anything else that turned up in my mailbox from *The Washington Post*.

Eventually, I was invited to lunch with Bill and his deputy, Brigitte Weeks. Was there any chance that I'd be interested in a job? Figuring that computers were never likely to amount to anything, I answered that I was in fact very interested. Brigitte then asked me to try out at the section for a week, to see how well I meshed with the others in the very small office (two assistant editors besides Bill, Brigitte, and Francis, a copy aide, and our beloved and redoubtable secretary for many years, Ednamae Storti). On May 1, 1978, I officially joined the staff of *Book World* as an assistant editor.

Let us now fast-forward a quarter century, passing over, in whizzing March of Time fashion, the usual traumas, crises, failings, pay raises, and honors that mark the life of a journalist. As we slow down, it is a Thursday morning, and a mild-mannered columnist for *Book World* is just settling into a seat on the subway from Silver Spring, Maryland, ready for a quiet twenty-five-minute ride. By now I will have studied my notebook entries for that week's review and reread all the marked passages in the book itself. I will be thinking—in my usual vague, desultory way—about what kind of piece to write. Some reviews call for lots of quotation; others—usually those of nonfiction—are built on summaries and paraphrase. For either sort, I prefer to fade somewhat into the background, but on occasion do decide on a larger, more forceful personal presence. It's all a matter of balance, rhetorical intent, tone.

After finishing my editorial work for the day, at 6 PM I pick up a sandwich in the *Post* cafeteria and bid good night to most of my *Book World* colleagues. On my computer screen I then wearily type in the title of the work under review, its author, publisher, number of pages, and price. I don't need to include my byline because, for a columnist, it appears at the top of the page in pleasingly big type. At that point everything often grinds to a halt. For the next ten minutes or two hours I will attempt one opening sentence after another, delete it, then try another until finally one of them sounds halfway right.

Unlike natural-born writers, if any actually exist, I lack what used to be called "the divine afflatus." None of my words simply flow onto the page. I possess no flair for simile or metaphor—nothing ever reminds me of anything else—and my sentences tend inevitably toward a certain Shaker plainness. To compensate for that missing razzle-dazzle, I work hard at word choice, balance, and rhythm. At its best my prose will be simple and clear as rainwater (oops, a simile), but given a shot of color by a literary allusion or an unexpected epithet. I write slowly, by methodical, almost geological accretion, setting down one sentence at a time, saying it over to myself, then adding another. I go back repeatedly to the opening paragraph and read down to where I've temporarily paused, each time changing an adjective, improving a turn of phrase, always listening to the sound of the words. By the time the review is finished, I will have silently mouthed its sentences scores of times. When I can read through the piece without making an alteration or when my fixes start to seem of doubtful merit, then I finally know it's time to stop. In general, I want the prose to unfold effortlessly. But I don't mind slowing it down occasionally for a flourish, digression, or sidenote that will somehow inject a bit more personality or pizzazz.

In my hot youth I could sometimes print out my work before 10 PM, though these days I'm usually racing down darkened L Street for the last, 12:07 AM subway train leaving from Farragut North station. The next morning I glance blearily over my printout, make a few more improvements (usually a matter of cutting things, sometimes for space), *et voilà*! Time to start reading the next book.

In principle, none of this engineering and text assembly shows in the end product. To anyone other than their author, my words simply sashayed nonchalantly into the newspaper. Loving all this labor, I've been blessed to have somehow made a career out of literary journalism—even if occasionally, now in middle age, I find myself wondering about the various roads not taken. After all, it must be agreeable to be called professor and hold an endowed chair of the humanities at a good university in a warm climate, not too far from the sea. Besides reading and writing, I spend a lot of time daydreaming.

A few words about the organization of *Bound to Please*. I hesitated over whether the pieces ought to appear chronologically or be shuffled around to assure a pleasing variety. In the end, I've settled for a loose historical structure. That is, the collection opens with essays about antiquity and the Middle Ages and then dallyingly progresses through the Renaissance up to the present. But within some sections I've mixed in appropriate fiction with the nonfiction. For instance, Thomas Pynchon's *Mason & Dixon* appears in the pages largely about the eighteenth century. A few of the categories are purely thematic—for instance, "Lovers, Poets, and Madmen" and "Performing Selves." Please do not regard the groupings as sacrosanct or anything but organizational conveniences.

Bound to Please will, I hope, encourage its readers to look beyond the boundaries of the fashionable, established, or academic. No cultivated person today should be hamstrung by unthinking prejudices about fantasy, crime fiction, or the literature of other times and places. For that reason, I decided to leave out many of the modern masters familiar to most English-speaking readers. Though I've written about Henry James, Philip Roth, Gabriel García Márquez, Angela Carter, and a dozen others equally well known, you won't enjoy those pieces here. Instead, I've deliberately emphasized terrific writers from around the world who are insufficiently read and known in the United States—among them, Fernando Pessoa, Raymond Queneau, Machado de Assis, Flann O'Brien, Marguerite Yourcenar, Mikhail Bulgakov. I've also included a good many "rediscoveries" of neglected authors: Cornell Woolrich, Vernon Lee, Avram Davidson.

Bound to Please represents about 20 percent of the reviews and essays I've contributed to *The Washington Post Book World*. In general, only longer biographical pieces permit a glance at an author's entire oeuvre, and for that reason you'll search in vain for my shorter reviews (often of art books), or my multi-title roundups of poetry and children's literature (for ten years I produced a monthly column called "Young Bookshelf"). I've also, with regret, set aside several essays on titles that address somewhat demanding or arcane topics—for instance, Anthony Grafton's exhilarating studies of Renaissance scholars and numerous other examples of intellectual history. But I have retained a long piece on the Bible to represent my ongoing fascination with serious academic research. Last, some favorite authors discussed in *Readings* don't reappear here—Murasaki Shikibu (author of *The Tale of Genji*), Max Beerbohm, Guy Davenport, Lord Dunsany, E. F. Benson.

Everything, by the way, appears virtually unchanged since it was first printed in *Book World*, with the date of original publication indicated at the end of each essay. Factual errors, when recognized, have been corrected, but I stand by my original opinions, for good or ill.

Let me repeat that *Bound to Please* is intended to convey the excitement of reading and to express my own gratitude for having had the chance to enjoy so many wonderful books. I hope that my essays will encourage you to try at least some of these works and writers yourself.

—Michael Dirda
Washington, D.C.

READING BEYOND THE
BEST-SELLER LIST:
A POLEMIC AND A PLEA

As *Bound to Please* was nearly ready to go to press, the National Endowment for the Arts issued its report "Reading at Risk: A Survey of Literary Reading in America." In its preface, Dana Gioia—a distinguished poet and critic, as well as director of the NEA—announced, with justifiable sadness, that our society is undergoing a "massive shift toward electronic media for entertainment and information" and that "less than half the adult population now reads literature."

According to the report, all of "one in six people reads 12 or more books in a year," and the majority of United States citizens don't look at anything literary, ever. This is, obviously, just pathetic. Yet how many times have I walked through elegant homes where I found lavish entertainment centers, walls of DVDs, state-of-the-art computer systems—and not a single book, with the debatable exception of Leonard Maltin's guide to movies on video?

Still, at least one in six people reads something between bound covers each month, and I suppose we should be grateful for this saving remnant. Alas, however, what the NEA report fails to note is that virtually all of those people have chosen the very same 12 books, starting, in 2004, with *The Da Vinci Code*, followed by (a) the latest movie tie-in and (b) whatever Oprah Winfrey has recommended lately.

To my mind, the real literacy crisis has less to do with the number of people reading than with the narrowing range of literary and intellectual works that Americans actually read. More and more, we have been straitjacketed and brainwashed by the books of the moment, the passing moment. Publishers know that they can promote almost any title to best-sellerdom. Glittery names and hot topics guarantee big sales, and so former presidents, like so many presidents before them (who now remembers *RN: The Memoirs of Richard Nixon?*), turn out their bricklike apologiae, even as former Hollywood celebrities and graying rock divas produce glitzy children's picture books (though no writing is harder to do well). Simultaneously, most of the nonfiction titles—and half the fiction titles, too—currently seem to be about terrorism, homeland security or the ongoing crisis in the Middle East.

By "literary" reading, the NEA report means almost any work that isn't a textbook or business report. So the category embraces mysteries, chick-lit, adventure novels, westerns, fantasy and science fiction, spy thrillers, possibly even children's books (this isn't clear). In short, almost everything.

Now, although I enjoy trolling in nearly all of fiction's genres—even, on occasion, checking out Harlequin romances, whose fans probably account for most of the people who get through a dozen or more titles a year—I still don't think of these books as, for the most part, serious reading, as literary reading. Let me stress that "for the most part." Any genre is capable of producing work of high artistic merit. James Crumley's *The Last Good Kiss* stands as a heartrending masterpiece of the modern private-eye novel, just as A. S. Byatt's Booker Prize–winning *Possession* is fundamentally, as its subtitle announces, "a romance." As for fantasy and science fiction, few works of contemporary American fiction can match John Crowley's *Little, Big* and Gene Wolfe's *The Book of the New Sun*, while Elizabeth Hand's brilliant *Mortal Love* deserves all the readers it can get. In truth, the world is full of good, as well as great, books, and *Bound to Please* will tell you about dozens of them.

By contrast, most of the best-seller list tends to be innately ephemeral— jumped-up magazine articles, journalistic dispatches in disguise, self-help manuals, and commercial novels that are essentially screenplays-in-waiting, heavy on plot, shock, and spectacle. Such works can hardly be called literary reading. They are at best entertainments, little more than 250-page TV shows and documentaries.

A true literary work, no matter what its genre, is one that makes us see the world or ourselves in a new way. Most writers accomplish this through an imaginative and original use of language, which is why literature has been defined as writing that needs to be read (at least) twice. Great books tend to feel strange. They leave us uncomfortable. They make us turn their pages slowly. We are left shaken and stirred.

But who now is willing to put in the time or effort to read a real book? People count on printed matter to be easy. Too often, we expect all pages to aspire to the condition of television, and to just wash over us. But those who really care about literature nearly always sit down with a pencil in their hands, to underline, mark favorite passages, argue in the margins. The relationship between a book and reader may occasionally be likened to a love affair, but it's just as often a wrestling match. No pain, no gain.

This is why the NEA report shows that poetry is suffering most of all. Poets keep their language charged, they make severe demands on our attention, they cut us no slack. While most prose works the room like a smiling politician at a fund-raiser, poetry stands quietly in the dusty street, as cool and self-contained as a lone gunfighter with his serape flapping in the wind. It's not glad-handing anybody.

Of course, we need ordinary English, aiming at a glasslike transparency, for business, journalism, and day-to-day discourse. But literary prose and poetry —art, in other words—draws attention to itself, sometimes subtly, often dramatically. We smile at a sentence by Jane Austen or savor an epithet by James Joyce because their words cause the scales to drop from our eyes. Suddenly we see the world afresh.

"Reading at Risk" is right to lament the decline of what I will forthrightly call bookishness. As the report implies, the Internet seems to have delivered a possibly knockout punch. Our children now can scarcely use a library and instead look to the Web when they need to learn just about anything. We all just click away with mouse and remote control, speeding through a blur of links, messages, images, data of all sorts. Is this reading? As Gioia reminds us, "print culture affords irreplaceable forms of focused attention and contemplation that make complex communications and insights possible. To lose such intellectual capability—and the many sorts of human continuity it allows— would constitute a vast cultural impoverishment."

Yes, the Internet has allowed fans of *Finnegans Wake* and Dorothy Sayers and the English ghost story to gather and share their knowledge. Web sites and chat rooms do encourage people from around the world to form digital communities. But the computer must seem a far more ambiguous gift to anyone who has ever faced screenfuls of spam, or discovered that hours are eaten up just answering email, or found their colleagues drooling over pixellated lovelies, or noticed that their children had stopped going outside to play because they were unable to tear themselves away from bloody, digitized battles, or simply realized that they themselves felt incomplete when not online every minute of the day—and half the night. In other words, virtually all of us recognize that that flat-screen monitor before our eyes casts an insidious spell, and all too often it seems that the best minds of the next generation—and more than a few of our own—are being lost to its insidious, relentless ensorcellments. Who now among the young aspires to be cultivated and learned, which takes discipline, rather than breezily provocative, wise-crackingly "edgy"?

Americans can still be smart and creative, but the pressure of the times is oriented toward quickness—we want instant messaging, live news breaks, fast food, mobile phoning, and snap judgments. As a result, we are growing into a shallow people, happy enough with the easy gratifications of mere speed and spectacle in all the aspects of life. Real books are simply too serious for us. Too slow. Too hard. Too long. Now and again, we may feel that just maybe we've shortchanged our better selves, that we might have listened to great music, contemplated profoundly moving works of art, read books that mattered, but instead we turned away from them because it was time to tune into *Law and Order* reruns, or jack into a WarCraft game on our home computer, or get back to the latest made-for-TV best seller. Sometimes nonetheless, late at night or when faced with one of life's true crises, we will surprise in ourselves what poet Philip Larkin called the hunger to be more serious.

Come the dawn, though, and our good intentions usually evaporate. Why persist with Plutarch or George Eliot or Beckett or William Gaddis when you can drop into a chat room or line up at the multiplex for this week's timeless Hollywood blockbuster? Of the making of many movies one doesn't need to see, there is no end. Instead of actually reading Tocqueville or Henry Adams, we just check out the latest political blogs. In short, we turn toward the bright and shiny, the meretricious tinsel, the strings of brightly colored beads for which we exchange our intellectual birthright as for a mess of pottage. For all too many twenty-first-century Americans, only the unexamined life is worth living.

Perhaps I exaggerate, and maybe I'm even wrong. (As Cromwell said, in one of my favorite sayings, "I beseech you, in the bowels of Christ, think it possible you may be mistaken.") Literature, or at least storytelling, will certainly survive, gradually take on new forms. Maybe hypertext will even reemerge as a viable literary genre. As every college freshman knows, art does need to make it new, else it shrivels to a dry husk.

Still I hate to think about how many great poems, stories, and plays are slowly dropping out of our general consciousness because so few people read them anymore. It's heartbreaking. All of us—even professional reviewers— need to explore more widely and deeply the truly wonderful books of the past. And there are so many. How is it that I've never looked at Samuel Richardson's *Clarissa*, the first great English novel, never read Freud's *Interpretation of Dreams*, and, aside from a few poems, hardly engaged with Chinese literature at all? Corny as it sounds, I believe that unless we try to familiarize ourselves with the best that human beings have thought and accomplished, we doom ourselves to be little more than mindless consumer-wraiths, docile sheep waiting to be shorn by corporation or government, sad and confused dwellers on the threshold of a palace we never enter. It's one reason why I've written so much about the magnificent and troubling writers you will discover in *Bound to Please*. They will open the door, they are the door, to a life of consequence, passion, and self-exploration.

Long ago, Thoreau said we should read the best books first, or we might simply never get the chance to read them. Life's days go by very quickly. Thoreau himself died at forty-four. *Carpe diem* is thus good advice for readers as well as hedonists (not, by the way, mutually exclusive categories). So, please, do your bit for real literacy: Pick up something serious you know you should have grappled with long ago. You could do worse than find a copy of *Walden* or any of the novels, poems, and stories I discuss in *Bound to Please.* As for me, I'll soon be breaking out my edition of *Clarissa*—in eight volumes. Time is passing, after all, and I'm not getting any younger.

July 25, 2004

OLD MASTERS

I

People sometimes ask teachers or critics, "Which books should I read to become educated?" The short answer is either "As many as you can" or "A small handful that you study to pieces." But a better question might be this one: "Which books should I read first?"

The answer to that is "The great patterning works of world literature and culture, the poems and stories that have shaped civilization."

Without a knowledge of the Greek myths, the Bible, ancient history, the world's folktales and fairy tales, one can never fully understand the visual arts, most opera, and half the literature of later ages. Homer tells us about Ulysses in The Odyssey; then Dante, Tennyson, James Joyce, Wallace Stevens, and Eudora Welty add to, enrich, and subvert that story in great works of their own. The classics are important not because they are old but because they are always being renewed.

In this first section of Bound to Please I touch on several of these touchstones and proffer some guidance to them. Years ago, I did once plan to become a medievalist, and so immersed myself in late antiquity, Old and Middle English, Middle High German, medieval French, and the writings of the church fathers. But just when I should have begun work on my dissertation, I decided that I would never be a good enough Latinist (one of those self-fulfilling prophecies). So I switched to the study of European Romanticism, taking two more years of graduate courses. This means that even though I've spent my career writing about contemporary books, I've never formally studied twentieth-century literature. But my reading in the great books of the past has laid a foundation upon which I've always been able to build and rely. Not only that. As Italo Calvino once said, "The classics are books which, upon reading, we find even fresher, more unexpected, and more marvelous than we had thought from hearing about them."

So here are reflections on Herodotus and Ovid, The Arabian Nights and the

Bible, as well as early Christian thinkers and Renaissance overreachers. Readers who wonder why I include nothing about, say, the Greek dramatists, Vergil, or Saint Augustine should bear in mind that opportunities somehow haven't arisen for me to write about these works or authors—at least not so far. This general caveat should be borne in mind throughout Bound to Please.

HERODOTUS: THE HISTORIES

Translated from the Greek by Robin Waterfield

Doubtless people do read history for instruction, to learn—as Santayana recommended—from the example of the past how to address the uncertainties of the present. Alas, I am not made of such noble clay. No, I read history strictly for pleasure, and regard former ages as a playground for the imagination, two and a half millennia of witty repartee, great deeds, and weary heroes fighting in narrow places against insuperable odds. Mine is an unashamedly epicurean approach to the past, spiced with a liking for what the Greeks called *tisis,* Fate's assurance that the biter is ultimately bitten and that, in the end, comeuppance will be delivered to the overconfident and the cruel.

For such a taste the key books have long been Plutarch's *Lives,* Saint-Simon's *Memoirs* (of the court of Louis XIV), Gibbon's *Decline and Fall of the Roman Empire,* and—earliest of all and, in some ways, the best—Herodotus's *Histories.* For a long time, though, the "father of history" (Cicero's phrase) was seriously undervalued. Even in antiquity Herodotus endured a steady barrage of criticism: the stern Thucydides suggested that his older contemporary was factually unreliable, Plutarch attacked the *Histories* for "malignity" and bias against certain groups (e.g., the Corinthians), and many readers regarded the historian from Halicarnassus as more traveling storyteller than ace reporter.

But over the past several decades classical scholarship, taking the retributive role of *tisis,* has largely redressed the balance. For with his Proust-like flair for artfully structured digression, Herodotus doesn't merely present a cast-of-thousands account of the Greco-Persian War (fifth century BC); he also relates the entire history of the known world. Moreover, his fascination with social mores, religion, sexual customs, statistics, and myth has rightly established him as godfather of the *Annales* school and of "history from below," just as modern archaeological discoveries have tended to support many of his hitherto suspect assertions. Once dismissed as a farrago of tall tales, Herodotus's "inquiries" or "researches" (the original meaning of *historie*) are now deemed not only an exemplary work of history but even the prose analogue of Homer's two great verse epics.

If people know any portion of Herodotus, they almost certainly know the story of Croesus, the immensely rich king of the Lydians, who asked the oracles at Delphi whether he should go to war against the Persians: "The answers both oracles gave to the question were perfectly consistent with each other: they told Croesus that if he made war on the Persians, he would destroy a great empire." Thus reassured, Croesus attacked and was utterly routed: the empire he would destroy was his own.

Herodotus provides a treasure chest of such stories and of what he calls *thomata,* or wonders. He tells us about temple prostitutes in Babylon, the Scythians' use of cannabis to get high, fathers inadvertently feasting on the flesh of their own sons; he shows us the oases of North Africa (the Ethiopians, he says, "are the tallest and most attractive people in the world"), giant ants that bring up gold from underground, and Amazons who must first kill a man before they can marry; we even glimpse a highborn Persian who cuts off his nose and ears to accomplish a daring undercover military operation, a circumnavigation of Africa, and a foolish king so infatuated with his wife's beauty that he insists that one of his counselors see her naked. With his usual charm, Herodotus notes that there are so many aromatic spices in Arabia that the entire country "gives off a wonderfully pleasant smell." His book's famous second chapter alone, a long excursus on Egypt, describes the use of mosquito netting, how to hunt a crocodile, the legend of Helen in Egypt, the building of pyramids, and three ways to embalm a corpse. After the mortuarial details, he gruesomely adds, "When the wife of an eminent man dies, or any woman who was particularly beautiful or famous, the body is not handed over to the embalmers straight away. They wait three or four days before doing so. The reason for this is to stop the embalmers having sex with the women."

Most of the first half of the *Histories* fills in the deep background to the Persian war against Greece. Books 5 through 9 take up the campaigns of Darius and Xerxes and build to the great battles of Marathon, Thermopylae, and Salamis. Even now, in this degraded age, the *kleos* (glory, renown) of these ancient names still thrills. Certainly, there are few more inspiring instances of military valor than that of the few thousand Greeks who hold off the Persian army in the pass at Thermopylae. When the Greeks are finally betrayed, their leader Leonidas sends most of the army away, remaining only with his 300 Lacedaemonians and 700 Thespians. They fight to the last man. In the end, "the Greeks defended themselves with knives, if they still had them, and otherwise with their hands and teeth, while the Persians buried them in a hail of missiles." The memorial inscription for the 300 Spartans—appropriately laconic and heartbreaking—says simply, "Stranger, tell the people of Lacedaemon / That we who lie here obeyed their commands." Herodotus informs us that the bravest Spartan of all was a wit named Dianeces. Before the battle he was warned that so many were the Persians that when they fired their bows, the arrows would block out the sun. "All to the good," observed Dianeces. "If the Persians hide the sun, the battle will be in shade rather than sunlight."

The Greeks ultimately triumph in this unequal war, but Herodotus is too smart to give them all the good lines. In a book swirling with strange tales and marvels, among the most haunting is Xerxes' review of his massed troops, almost one and three-quarter million men. Near the sea the Persian king sits on a dais of white stone high up on a hill and looks down at his navy and land army. "The sight of the Hellespont completely covered by his ships, and the coast and plains of Abydus totally overrun by men first gave Xerxes a feeling of deep self-satisfaction, but later he began to weep." When asked why he wept, Xerxes replied, "I was reflecting on things and it occurred to me how short the sum total of human life is, which made me feel compassion. Look at all these people—but not one of them will still be alive in a hundred years' time."

This is only one of the *Histories'* many observations on life's meaning and the nature of happiness—the Athenian lawgiver Solon, in particular, famously reminded a heedless Croesus that the gods play with our destinies and that no man knows his end. In his pages Herodotus spins a web of interconnections, and almost any conversation or anecdote is likely to be part of a pattern, the fulfillment of a prophecy, or an example of the instability of fortune; the great will fall, the apparently insignificant will rise. A Greek doctor tricks Cyrus and escapes to his homeland; as a result, the Persian king's wrath is ignited against Greece, and over the next three generations hosts of men will die. Out of little, big.

Four basic translations of Herodotus are available: the classic nineteenth-century version of George Rawlinson, the Penguin paperback by Aubrey de Sélincourt (recently revised with new notes by John Marincola), David Grene's lightly annotated edition for the University of Chicago, and now Robin Waterfield's for Oxford. I've read de Sélincourt and Waterfield entire, listened on audio tape to Rawlinson, and dipped into the Grene: scholars may fault each of them (and do), but none seems to me an unworthy investment. There is also a Norton Critical Edition—selections only (translated by Walter Blanco) but with much scholarly commentary and background material. On the whole, a new reader on a budget might happily plump for the $10.95 Penguin—de Sélincourt is a genial, easygoing stylist, and Marincola's notes are excellent.

But this new Oxford edition is still my current choice: Waterfield's prose is clear and straightforward (though slightly lacking at moments of grandeur), while his colleague Carolyn DeWald's introduction is lengthy and her end notes expansive, full of interesting matter, and illuminating. Moreover, Oxford has created an extremely handsome volume, bound in its trademark blue cloth, with a pleasant heft. It feels like a book to read and reread. If you come to love Herodotus, and you will, you might eventually wish to look for Aubrey de Sélincourt's useful *The World of Herodotus* or pick up James Romm's introductory volume on the historian in the fine Hermes series from Yale. But don't wait. Read the *Histories*—written, after all, "to prevent the traces of human events from being erased by time"—and reflect on human folly and grandeur as you stroll along the beach this summer while the waves gradually wash away your footprints.

July 12, 1998

THE BIBLE TELLS US SO

People read the Bible for myriad reasons, discovering in its pages consolation, religious instruction, moral example, and even the pleasures of mere literature. Some scholars look upon the book as "the great code" to Western art and literature, a glossary of myths and metaphors; others see it as a (flawed) work of history or a polemical tract justifying Judaism or Christianity; for many of the devout it remains quite simply the Word of God and its human redactors little more than the instruments, the quill pens, of its true Author.

Still, there can't be many people who have read the Bible not for the love of God or good prose but for the love of money. Filthy lucre. Cold cash. Some thirty years ago my father, not himself a religious man, though a shrewd one, offered his fourteen-year-old son a hundred dollars to go through the Bible from cover to cover. It took nearly six months, but I did it, and my dad, to my mind, certainly received his money's worth. Of course, without quite realizing it then, I got even more.

Like a grounding in the classics or a thorough knowledge of baseball, familiarity with the Bible invests life, whether one is a believer or not, with a kind of ballast, steadying one through moments of crisis, providing words or stories of such gravity and soul-shaking power that they become formative experiences, like running away from home or falling in love. Everyone will have his or her favorites: the aged, long-barren Sarah laughing to herself when told that she would bear a son. Abraham's near-sacrifice of his beloved Isaac ("Where is the lamb for a burnt offering?" "My son, God will provide himself a lamb"). Saul, that tragic king, confronting the witch of Endor. David's secret order to place Bathsheba's husband at the head of a battle where he is sure to be killed. The lamentations of Jeremiah ("The harvest is past, the summer is ended, and we are not saved"). The existential despair of Ecclesiastes. Job confronting the voice of God in the whirlwind.

Those are from the Hebrew Bible or, with its books rearranged, the Old Testament. Unlike most sequels, however, the New Testament keeps to an equally high standard: John the Baptist saying, "After me comes he who is mightier than I, the thong of whose sandals I am not worthy to stoop down and untie." Any of Jesus's parables—of the Good Samaritan, the Sower and the Seed, the Prodigal Son—or such miracles as the raising of Lazarus or the exorcism of the Gadarene demoniac ("My name is Legion: for we are many"). Think of Jesus's sad words to Peter, "Verily I say unto thee, that this night, before the cock crow, thou shalt deny me thrice"—and Peter's horror at their fulfillment. Or Pontius Pilate—that representative modern man—asking "What is truth?" and literally washing his hands of the whole Passion. And finally, John of Patmos after the breaking of the last seals: "And I saw a new heaven and a new Earth: for the first heaven and the first Earth were passed away, and there was no more sea."

They don't write sentences like that any more, but they sure do write about them. During the past decade there has been a remarkable revival in Bible studies, as literary critics, poets, and cultural historians have begun to venture where both fools and angels have often feared to tread. Even though the Reformation was based, in part, on the notion that people should be allowed to confront God and his Word directly, Luther probably didn't foresee the arcana of nineteenth- and early twentieth-century scriptural study, from Julius Wellhausen's discovery of the multiple authors of the Pentateuch (known as E, J, P, and D) to the exacting form studies of Rudolph Bultmann. Reading even snippets of these immensely learned scholars, Germans for the most part, can require the wisdom of Solomon and the patience of Job.

Of course, the church fathers, Origen in particular, had long ago built up elaborate systems for interpreting scripture, allegorizing nearly every element in the Old Testament as a prefiguration (or type or figure) of something in the New. (It has been said that the entire New Testament is symbolically embedded in the Old.) Jonah's being spit out of the belly of the great fish after three days and nights obviously symbolized Jesus's descent into hell and his resurrection. A tome like Gregory the Great's *Moralia in Iob*, a several-thousand-page study of Job, must rank among the seven wonders of creative misinterpretation: "For whoever is exalted with pride, whoever is tortured by the longings of covetousness, whoever is relaxed with the pleasures of lust, whoever is kindled by the burnings of unjust and immoderate anger, what else is he but a testicle of Anti-christ?"

Besides the typological extravagances of the Christian fathers and the orderly researches of the German scholars, biblical study has also been pervaded by the enthusiasms of the American true believers. Do airwave evangelists still invite you to place one hand on your Bible and the other on the radio, so that you can feel the healing power?—after which, you will of course be asked to place both hands deep into your pockets and give generously. Even an undoubted classic like the twelve-volume Interpreter's Bible sounds this note: "The reader should confront the fact that a professor erudite in the Scriptures may miss salvation, while the lowly saint on his knees before the Book may know the presence and almost feel the Hand." Any of us might envy the editor George Buttrick his faith, and even admire the rhythms of his prose, but still want a little less fervor.

LITERARY VIEWS OF THE BIBLE

W. H. Auden, like T. S. Eliot and C. S. Lewis, criticized those "who read the Bible for its prose." But for many nonbelievers, that is the only way the book can be approached at all, which accounts for the continued popularity of the seventeenth-century Authorized Version (aka King James Version) over more accurate contemporary translations.

Nearly all modern literary interpretations of the Bible look back to a seminal essay by Erich Auerbach, "Odysseus' Scar," which became the first chapter of *Mimesis* (1948). In that piece Auerbach contrasted the Homeric and biblical methods of representing reality, the former bringing everything into a uniformly illuminated foreground, the latter dwelling on "the decisive points of the narrative" while what lies between remains in the dark, virtually nonexistent, but generating an immensely suggestive power. The Old Testament, according to Auerbach, is "fraught with background."

In the 1950s and 1960s the poet Robert Graves put forth various obsessive views of Jesus in essays and his novel *King Jesus* (psychedelic mushrooms, Christ never died on the cross); the critic Kenneth Burke offered a characteristically elaborate schema for "the first three chapters of Genesis"; and the poet-critic William Empson virtually ruined his critical reputation by the vehemence of his attacks on God, the torturer of his Son. Since then a more sober line of literary scholars has come along. In *The Genesis of Secrecy* (1979) Frank Kermode uses biblical texts, especially Mark, to address various problems of interpretation, at one point comparing the young man who loses his shirt at the arrest of Jesus (traditionally Mark himself) with the mysterious man in the mackintosh in Joyce's *Ulysses* (in some views, Joyce himself). Similarly, Robert Alter, a professor of Hebrew and comparative literature at Berkeley, has written a trilogy about understanding the Hebrew Bible: *The Art of Biblical Narrative* (1981), *The Art of Biblical Poetry* (1985), and the recent *The World of Biblical Literature* (1992). All three books are suffused with a calm studiousness, whether Alter analyzes narrative allusiveness or Hebrew poetry's bent for repetition and parallelism. Eschewing the "excavative" endeavors of scholars who focus on Ugaritic loanwords and the like, he emphasizes "the complex means used by biblical writers to lock their texts together, to amplify their meanings by linking one text with another." In the most recent book, for instance, Alter explicates the rape of Tamar and finds echoes of Joseph's attempted seduction by Potiphar's wife. Amnon and Mrs. P. both use the same Hebrew words for "lie with me," while Tamar and Joseph are the only characters in the Old Testament to wear "a coat of many colors." This unexpected confluence adds depths to Tamar's victimization, as well as taking up the important biblical leitmotif of family strife.

Alter and Kermode combined their efforts to edit *The Literary Guide to the Bible* (1987), a massive compendium that includes work by such scholars as Meir Sternberg, Carol Newsom, and Bernard McGinn, as well as the general editors. Many approaches are represented. The structural anthropologist Edmund Leach, for instance, judges the Bible as simply "a corpus of mythology which provides a justification for the religious performances of believers." In his essay he proceeds to link the wanderings in the desert with the halfway stage in a rite of passage. "In this Other World everything happens in reverse. The heavenly bread falls from the sky like rain; the heavenly water does not fall like rain but emerges from a rock." Eventually he builds up to a stunning analysis of the fish imagery surrounding Jesus, reminding us that Joshua was generally perceived as a prefiguration of Christ (the two names are virtually the same), that Joshua is called the "son of Nun," and that the word Nun can mean fish.

Such linkages and parallels have long been the purview of Northrop Frye, who capped his distinguished career with *The Great Code: The Bible and Literature* (1982) and *Words with Power* (1990). The first of these books opens with an elaborate, nearly impenetrable bramble of fifty pages about the nature of language, and Frye will probably lose many readers in these thistles. But later in the book, and throughout *Words of Power*, he explores the unifying imagery of the entire Bible. For instance, Frye considers the virgin birth as mythically necessary, the closing of a loop: "The counternatural creation of woman [Eve] from a more or less male body leads to the fall"; therefore "redemption would be symbolized by another miraculous act reversing the perversion of sex at the Fall, which for the NT is the myth of the Virgin Birth, the begetting of God from a female body." Sections elaborate, with familiar virtuosity, such archetypal structuring images as the mountain, the garden, the cave, and the furnace.

Perhaps the most congenial of recent books is Gabriel Josipovici's *The Book of God: A Response to the Bible* (1988). Josipovici, a British scholar of modern literature as well as a novelist, stresses reading—reading again and again—as the heart of his critical method. Rather than worry about the genesis of scripture, all its strands and threads, Josipovici, like Alter and Kermode, actually prefers to confront the final, seemingly seamless text. He talks about everything from the look of childhood Bibles to the paradox of treating scripture as seriously as literature, reminding us that Dostoevsky and Eliot can change our lives too. At times Josipovici's Bible resembles a modernist classic, sometimes even a postmodernist one.

While Josipovici subtly traces his response to the Bible, Harold Bloom sweeps the reader up with his trademark razzmatazz. In *The Book of J* (1990) Bloom notoriously proposes that J—one of the four main authors of the Torah, aka Pentateuch—was a woman. Bloom enthuses, belabors, and soliloquizes with impressive patriarchal fervor, but has to admit that his theory relies almost entirely on his gut instinct as a strong reader. Unfortunately this time out Bloom, despite characteristically provocative insights, strikes many informed readers as not so much strong as muscle-bound. In Robert Alter's review of *The Book of J* for *Commentary* magazine (now a chapter of *The World of Biblical Literature*), his still, small voice—pointing out linguistic, historical, and interpretive errors—quite overwhelms Bloom's whirlwind.

Besides these major works, several quirky, appealing literary books take up biblical matters. Translations, for instance: Marcia Falk's edition of *The Song of Songs* (1990) arrives with Barry Moser illustrations, Hebrew original on left-hand pages, Falk's ripe poetic versions on the right, and a long, thoughtful section of notes. I find Falk's poems sexy and successful; they do, however, ride a fine line balancing lush and gush: "Between my breasts he'll lie, / Sachet of spices, / Spray of blossoms plucked / From the oasis." More daring is Stephen Mitchell's *The Gospel of Jesus* (1991), which aims to present only Christ's genuine words, sans the gospeler's accretions. A dozen pages of wisdom, parables, and observations float on a hundred pages of commentary that frequently associates Jesus with other religious masters, especially Mitchell's beloved Buddhist and Taoist sages. This apparent lèse-majesté also includes speculation about Jesus's "illegitimacy," his callousness in the Gospels toward his mother, the crucial importance of the episode with the woman taken in adultery (most scholars consider this a later addition to John)—and suggests that it is no accident that Jesus's last spoken word in Aramaic was "Abba," father. Admirers of Mitchell's work should also look for his fine, and more critically restrained, version of *The Book of Job* (1987).

Readers who enjoy freestyle interpretation might relish two good anthologies, *Congregation: Contemporary Writers on the Hebrew Bible* (1987), edited by David Rosenberg, and *Incarnation: Contemporary Writers on the New Testament* (1990), edited by Alfred Corn. In these one can read, say, the poet John Hollander reflecting on the Psalms (quite dazzling), Isaac Bashevis Singer on Genesis, or any number of other fine writers from Anthony Hecht, Cynthia Ozick, and Howard Moss to John Updike, Annie Dillard, and Richard Howard. Most of the pieces are endearingly autobiographical, none of the writers is a specialist in biblical scholarship, a few are atheists, and some, like Guy Davenport, even agree with Trollope "that a strong interest in religion is a prelude to insanity."

THE BIBLE AND HISTORY

Any of the various college texts used in Bible courses will offer a sound grounding in basic history, archaeology, geography, and like matters. I'm fond of Joseph B. Tyson's *The New Testament and Early Christianity* (1984); it summarizes vast learning without flourish but in fascinating detail.

Much the same can be said of Richard Elliot Friedman's *Who Wrote the Bible?* (1987), which actually adumbrated, albeit with proper tentativeness, Bloom's theory of J as a woman. Friedman attempts to answer such seemingly impossible questions as why Aaron made the golden calf. Why Aaron? Why a calf? The answer has to do with political gripes against King Jeroboam, whose temple to Yahweh sported a throne supported by golden calves. In another notable incident in the OT, Moses announces he plans to marry a Cushite; Cush was ancient Ethiopia, which suggests that the lawgiver's intended might be black. When Aaron and Miriam criticize his decision—perhaps an early form of racism—it becomes ironically appropriate that Yahweh punish Miriam by turning her skin leprously white.

Valuable as these books are, they pale before the relentless, blistering scholarship of Robin Lane Fox's *The Unauthorized Version: Truth and Fiction in the Bible* (1992). Augustine used to emphasize that all Bible study should lead to love of God or neighbor; Lane Fox instead proposes truth as the proper aim. Writing with a Gibbonian irony and a soft Voltairean malice (he refers to Yahweh as Number One, calls early Christianity "a harmless cause"), this young Oxford don proffers no comfort for believers, and his thorough study of biblical contradiction, uncertainty, and fabrication will leave a lot of shaken souls in its wake. Who killed Goliath, "the shaft of whose spear was like a weaver's beam"? If you think it was David, how do you explain Elhanan, to whom the deed is also attributed in 2 Samuel? Loaded with odd facts (e.g., Dido was the great-niece of Jezebel), *The Unauthorized Version* is essentially a work of synthesis, though Lane Fox has his own convictions, among them that Nehemiah and John were eyewitnesses to the events they write about and that Jesus died in March 36, when he was in his mid to late forties. Here is Lane Fox at his most succinctly provocative: "The book [of Daniel] has the formulaic ingredients of a biblical success story: its hero probably never existed, he was credited with visions he never saw and actions he never did; the book itself arose from two separate sources, arriving joined into one, while its dates and kings are incorrect and its setting is a fiction posing as history."

Paul once wrote, "If Christ was not raised, your faith is empty." Two recently published biographies take up the issue of the historical Christ: John P. Meier's *A Marginal Jew: Rethinking the Historical Jesus* (1991) and John Dominic Crossan's *The Historical Jesus: The Life of a Mediterranean Jewish Peasant* (1991). By their titles and subtitles ye shall know them, and these are clearly not your penny-catechism lives of Christ. Both writers are distinguished scholars: Meier's book, the first of four volumes, treats the social background and private years of Jesus; it is written with considerable zest, has lots of scholarly notes (these are frequently reviews of past scholarship and at least as interesting as the main text; see the notes about Ben Panthera, the Roman soldier sometimes claimed to be Jesus's "real" father), and sticks closely to biblical and historical sources. As a Catholic, Meier occasionally butts up against the dogma of the church; after presenting the arguments over, say, the virgin birth or whether Jesus had brothers and sisters, he backs away from any conclusions. Similarly, he notes that he will not deal at all with the resurrection, as this is a matter that one can, finally, affirm only by faith. Crossan is more daring, drawing on sociology and anthropology to illuminate his subject and his society, formulating a list of genuine Jesus sayings (à la Stephen Mitchell), and making extended comparisons between the life of a carpenter in Nazareth and the life of a weaver in Egypt. His notes, however, are sparse (though scholarly references are woven into the text). Sometimes Crossan's prose also betrays an overfamiliarity with modern social science: "We have, then, it would seem, three stages in this movement from commensality to salary." Neither scholar believes Jesus was born in Bethlehem, but the amount of evidence they accumulate leaves no doubt that he did live, preach, and suffer death by crucifixion. On the whole, I prefer the careful Meier to the more speculative Crossan (who once brought out an interesting book comparing the parables of Jesus with those of Borges), but both strike me as having written very good books about this hero of the Good Book.

EDITIONS AND COMMENTARIES

Anyone starting on a concerted plan to study the Bible should consider acquiring or borrowing the various volumes of the Anchor Bible; they vary in quality, but most are the standard references. Of course, it's fine to read good one-volume editions, like the Annotated Revised Standard Version, the Jerusalem Bible, or the recent Oxford Study Bible (1992), based on the revised New English Bible. But for serious work you should turn to the best. In the Anchor series (as in the older Interpreter's Bible), each book of scripture gets a fresh translation, long introductions, and extensive notes, all by respected scholars.

The four Gospels also receive splendid annotations in the paperback *Pelican New Testament Commentaries*. A fat Norton Critical Edition of *The Writings of St. Paul* (1972), edited by Wayne A. Meeks, offers 150 annotated pages of Paul's epistles, followed by 300 pages of essays on his life and thought by distinguished thinkers from Kierkegaard to Kristin Stendhal. Paul generally gets a bad press as the guy who institutionalized sweet Jesus's message; a good corrective to this oversimplification is the volume on Paul by E. P. Sanders in the Past Masters series from Oxford.

All these works can be relied on, along with such useful, somewhat dated books as *Twentieth Century Biblical Commentary*. One would, however, hardly call the *The Women's Bible Commentary* (1992) dated; it is perhaps all too up-to-date. On the one hand, it presents work by leading women biblical scholars; on the other, it takes with exceeding seriousness a feminist platform that some readers may find upsetting—or liberating. For instance, in her preface Sharon Ringe (the volume's coeditor with Carol A. Newsom) writes, "In the Christian confession that Jesus of Nazareth is the Christ, clearly the reference is to a human male. That fact itself presents problems for many feminist interpreters, for whom the idea that women are ultimately dependent on a male for their relationship to God is unacceptable. . . ." Elsewhere we are told that Luke may be "the most dangerous [text] in the Bible" because it shows women as "models of subordinate service." The fairy-tale Esther receives similar treatment: "By working within the power structure of her environment (the Persian harem system) she moves from a completely powerless position into the relatively more powerful one of queen." In a critique of Hosea the commentator faults the book for failing to consider actual battered wives.

Such remarks, as I have said, may seem all too politically current (or correct), and yet it should be evident that the Bible speaks with so much power—of all kinds—that the best readings will, in some way, resist its authority. It is a source of unending paradox: as with any book, we need to humble ourselves to receive its message, but can never be truly blessed until we struggle mightily with the text, perhaps remembering how Jacob once wrestled all night with God.

April 19, 1992

TALES FROM OVID

By Ted Hughes

An old tale's best for winter, and very few are older or better than those in Ovid's great poem the *Metamorphoses*. For most of the past two thousand years—and especially from the twelfth through the eighteenth centuries— writers, painters, and composers found in its witty, dexterous verse a kind of secular scripture, a source book for the most evocative and disturbing myths of the ancient world. Even today, many readers will recognize at least some of its more than two hundred stories: The rape of Proserpina. Actaeon devoured by his own hunting dogs. Phaëthon and the uncontrollable horses of the sun. The weaving contest between Arachne and Minerva. Ajax and Ulysses contending for the armor of Achilles. Often just a name suffices to call to mind a story first heard in childhood: Midas, Pygmalion, Narcissus, Orpheus.

Though best known for these accounts of how various nymphs and heroes found themselves transformed into beasts and flowers, rivers, constellations, or natural landmarks, Publius Ovidius Naso (43 BC–AD 17) first made his reputation as the author of erotic elegies, in particular the youthful *Amores* (Loves) and the once scandalous *Ars Amatoria* (The Art of Love: *Casta est quam nemo rogavit*—"Only she is chaste whom none has invited"). But just after completing the *Metamorphoses,* Rome's most fashionable and esteemed poet was suddenly "relegated" by the emperor Augustus to the Black Sea town of Tomis. No one knows precisely why, though in his poems of exile (*Tristia*, or Sorrows) Ovid alludes to a mysterious "error": over the centuries guesses about the nature of this indiscretion have ranged from an affair with the promiscuous imperial daughter Julia to involvement in political intrigue. Despite his best efforts, including some rather fawning verses of supplication, Ovid died in Tomis—though there later arose a legend that he was finally recalled to Rome, only to be crushed and suffocated by the crowd welcoming him back.

Among Latin poets, Vergil and Horace tend to hog most of the official laurels, but neither can match Ovid in actual influence: allegorized (i.e.,

Christianized) in the Middle Ages, he survived to become the favorite classical author of Chaucer ("Venus' clerke Ovyde"), Shakespeare, Molière, and Goethe. Virtually every Shakespeare play reveals some Ovidian allusion or echo (most pervasively, the bloody revenge tragedy *Titus Andronicus* and the wonder-filled *Midsummer Night's Dream*); seemingly half the operas ever written (*Dafne, Orfeo, Semele,* etc.) take their plots from the *Metamorphoses*; and many of the best-known works of Titian and Guido Reni, Bernini and Poussin, can be thought of as illustrations to this prodigal, graceful poet. All the principal eighteenth-century Augustans, Dryden with particular brilliance, translated some Ovid, and in our own time Ezra Pound went so far as to call Arthur Golding's Renaissance version of the *Metamorphoses* "the most beautiful book in the language." Even more recently, one can discern an Ovidian lightness and exuberance in such playful creators as Jean Cocteau and Italo Calvino.

Still, I don't think one would immediately think of Ted Hughes as an admirer of Ovid. Where the Roman is smooth, flippant, and wanton, the Englishman is angular, gritty, and brutal. But then one pauses, recalling Hughes's longtime passion for nature and animals, especially trickster figures like the hero of *Crow*; his Robert Graves–like obsession with mythic, psycho-sexual conflict in Shakespeare; a fascination with the grotesque and shamanistic; and even his Ovid-like artistic facility: official verse as England's poet laureate, modern fairy tales for children (*The Iron Giant*), literary journalism, and, not least, his own serious poetry, most recently—and unexpectedly—in a volume devoted to his near-legendary first wife, Sylvia Plath (*Birthday Letters*).

However one accounts for it, Hughes's *Tales from Ovid* is certainly one of the most enchanting books of poetry in many a year. Hughes writes short-lined free verse, relatively faithful to the Latin original in meaning without aiming to replicate its regular hexameters. He relates only a couple of dozen of the major stories—leaving out, for instance, Baucis and Philemon, the Cave of Sleep, Perseus and Andromeda, the tales of Medea and Orpheus—and he blithely ignores the original order of the myths in the poem. Ovid expended much care on his transitions, embedding tales within tales and contriving links between transformations, but most of this cohesive artistry has been jettisoned. Occasionally, Hughes also opts for modern diction ("a medicinal blocker") with a consequent jolt of either readerly pleasure or annoyance. (He also echoes, now and again, various other poets: I noticed little touches of Frost, Williams, Dante, Graves, Stevens, and Yeats.)

Yet, these limitations aside, *Tales from Ovid* is as sun-dappled, clear, and refreshing as those quiet pools that regularly—and sometimes fatally—attract the poet's nymphs and mortals. Not least, this is a manageable book: the complete *Metamorphoses* is longer than the *Aeneid*, and apt to discourage many would-be fans.

Hughes's extracts emphasize, as he says in a preface, "human passion in extremis—passion where it combusts, or levitates, or mutates into an experience of the supernatural . . . the peculiar frisson of that event, where the all-too-human victim stumbles out into the mythic arena and is transformed." Here the nymph Echo, who can only repeat what others say, glimpses and falls in love with the beautiful boy Narcissus:

It so happened, Narcissus
Had strayed apart
From his companions.
He hallooed them: "Where are you?
I'm here." And Echo
Caught at the syllables as if they were precious:
"I'm here," she cried, "I'm here" and "I'm here" and "I'm here."

Narcissus looked around wildly.
"I'll stay here," he shouted.
"You come to me." And "Come to me,"
Shouted Echo. "Come to me,
To me, to me, to me."
Narcissus stood baffled.
Whether to stay or go. He began to run,
Calling as he ran: "Stay there." But Echo
Cried back, weeping to utter it, "Stay there,
Stay there, stay there, stay there."
Narcissus stopped and listened. Then, more quietly,
"Let's meet halfway. Come." And Echo
Eagerly repeated it: "Come."

But when she emerged from the undergrowth
Her expression pleading,
Her arms raised to embrace him,
Narcissus turned and ran.
"No," he cried, "no, I would sooner be dead
Than let you touch me." Echo collapsed in sobs,
As her voice lurched among the mountains:
"Touch me, touch me, touch me, touch me."

Being a storyteller as well as a poet, Ovid is most affecting when quoted at length. But Hughes is also good at the haiku-packed phrase: Scythia, we learn is "a barren country, leafless, dreadful: / Ice permanent as iron, air that aches." Hercules, his body on fire from the poison of Nessus's cloak, cries out, "I have become a leaf in a burning forest." After Zeus transforms the hero into a constellation, "Atlas grunted under the new weight." As Atalanta races, "her running redoubled her beauty. / The ribbon-ties at her ankles / Were the wing-tips of swallows. / The ribbon-ties at her knees / Were the wing-tips of swifts." Arethusa, pursued by the river god Alpheus, hides in some tall weeds, feeling "what the lamb feels when the wolf's jaws / Are ripping the edge of the shed door. / Or what the hare feels / Peering through the wall of grass blades / When the circling hounds lift their noses."

Among the writers of antiquity Ovid was perhaps the shrewdest psychologist, with an exceptional sympathy for the feelings of women caught up in forbidden passions. (He had a particular fascination with Medea, about whom he wrote a much acclaimed play, now lost.) Hughes here chooses to include the gruesome account of the overrational Pentheus torn apart and devoured by the frenzied Bacchantes, as well as Procne's agonizing decision to butcher her son to revenge the rape and mutilation of her sister Philomela by her own husband. Still, the most powerful and pathetic of all these stories must be that of Myrrha's incestuous desire for her own father, Cinyras. The young girl's internal monologue, filled with Hamlet-like wavering, shows how insightful—and dramatic—Ovid can be:

Myrrha felt the stirring secret
Serpent of her craving and the horror
That came with it.
"What is happening to me?" she whispered.
"What am I planning?"
She prayed to the gods: "You watchers in heaven,
Help me to strangle this.
I pray
By the sacred bond between child and parent
Let me be spared this.
Do not permit this criminal desire
To carry me off—if it is criminal.
Is it criminal?
Is it unnatural?
For all the creatures it is natural—
When the bull mounts the heifer, his daughter,

Neither feels shame. . . .
How lucky they are, those innocents
Living within such liberties.
Man has distorted that licence—
Man has made new laws from his jealousy
To deprive nature of its nature. . . .
. . . What am I doing?
Thoughts are running away with me.
I must not let such hopes roam so freely.
And yet, by every contract and custom,
Cinyras owns my love.
It would be a crime indeed to withhold it.

And so the young girl gradually persuades herself, using all the tricks of classical rhetoric, to do what she knows is wrong. As for so many of us when tempted, she can say (with Medea), *Video melora proboque deteriora sequor:* "I see and approve the better course, yet choose the worse." Her fate is terrible. Dryden himself judged the story of Myrrha more moving than that of Vergil's Dido.

Ovid concluded the *Metamorphoses* with the prediction that his name would live as long as Roman power—and implicitly the Latin language—held sway over the world. Happily, because of poets like Ted Hughes, and wonderful books like this one, he will live even a little longer than that.

February 1, 1998

POSTSCRIPT: Ours is a great age for fine new translations of the classics. See, for example, David Ferry's fluent version of the odes of Horace:

Delighting you more than Pholoe did, the shy
Or Chloris, whose shoulders are so beautiful,
White as the moonlight shining on the sea.

THE RISE OF WESTERN CHRISTENDOM: TRIUMPH AND DIVERSITY, A.D. 200–1000

Second Edition
By Peter Brown

In a celebrated analysis of *Beowulf*, the great medievalist Robert Kaske once charted instances in the life of its warrior protagonist that demonstrated *sapientia* and *fortitudo*. These qualities—wisdom and fortitude—were long ascribed to heroes as their characteristic virtues. I couldn't help being reminded of "sap and fort"—as graduate students sometimes call them—while reading this encyclopedic survey of Christianity during late antiquity and the early Middle Ages. Much expanded from its original 1996 version, *The Rise of Western Christendom* is unquestionably a work of profound *sapientia* and measured thoughtfulness, as well as the synthesis of researches undertaken during a distinguished academic career of nearly forty years, but it will nonetheless requite a certain *fortitudo* on the part of many modern readers.

It repays the effort. Peter Brown writes clearly and succinctly, he artfully employs anecdotes and quotations to point up his arguments, and his narrative steps right along. What makes the book demanding is simply our lack of familiarity with this world. The years between AD 200 and 1000 were long discounted as simply the period of the Roman Empire's sad decline due to barbarian invasion and theological schism. In short order, Europe sank into "the dark ages" during which an oppressive monkish culture gradually extinguished any flicker of antiquity's sweetness and light. Only around 800, with the dawn of the Carolingian Renaissance, did intellectual life finally start to perk up a bit, though you had to wait for the twelfth century before there was any real sunshine.

Horace Walpole vividly summed up our fuzzy sense of the early Middle Ages when he spoke about getting bogged down in Gibbon during the historian's accounts of the fifth and sixth centuries: "Then having both the Eastern and Western Empires in his hands at once, and nobody but imbeciles and their eunuchs at the head, one is confused with two subjects, that are quite alike, though quite distinct, and in the midst of this distraction enters a deluge of Alans, Huns, Goths, Ostrogoths and Visigoths, who with the same features and characters are to be described in different terms, without any substantial variety, and he is to bring you acquainted with them when you wish them at the bottom of the Red Sea." Somehow, Walpole overlooked the Vandals.

Setting aside this gloomy folk view, modern historians proffered, at least until recently, a brighter take on this period: the Pax Romana was gradually replaced by a new cultural unity under a Christian imperium. "It was through the insubstantial but tenacious bonds created by the Catholic Church that the broken unity of Roman Europe was recreated," as Brown sums up this interpretation. From such an angle, Charlemagne "brought to an end the four centuries of aimless fragmentation" following the sack of Rome in 410. Alas, after the Frankish empire's own disintegration, one had again to tarry a while until the advent of an all-encompassing Latin Christendom under the medieval papacy.

This narrative, particularly attractive to Catholic historians, long dominated academic study. But in 1967 the young Peter Brown published his much lauded biography *Augustine of Hippo* and with it ushered in renewed scholarly interest in the years 200–1000. His subsequent essays and books—*Society and the Holy in Late Antiquity, The Making of Late Antiquity, The Body and Society: Men, Women, and Sexual Renunciation in Early Christianity*—coupled with the the work of disciples and colleagues (Ian Wood, Averil Cameron, G. W. Bowersock, Robert Markus, and many others) has led to a vigorous reappreciation of the "dark ages," currently one of the hottest areas in historical studies: the stone that the builders refused has become the headstone. In this period, alien as it remains, scholars now detect the origins of many of the cultural attitudes, social institutions, and religious dogmas that shaped the West, for good or ill.

To sum up much of this intensive, ongoing work of reclamation, Brown has amplified and reworked his highly praised first edition of *The Rise of Western Christendom*. One might justly call this new book, then, an example of *correctio*—a refocusing that allows an even deeper understanding of the era's "triumph and diversity."

First of all, Brown's increased scope and detail convey a real sense of the dynamism of these centuries. He starts by noting that the famous Pirenne thesis—the claim that the empire hadn't been destroyed by the barbarians but that prosperous commerce and city life continued to flourish along the Mediterranean as always—has been undermined by archaeological evidence: "By the year 600, much of western Europe was in a state of almost total economic 'involution.' " From here, he goes on to emphasize how much the world of late antiquity lacked a clearly defined center, being made up instead of many "Micro-Christendoms." Irish monks, for instance, looked not to the actual Rome for guidance but to an inner Rome based on their study of the Bible and the church fathers. Throughout, Brown underscores the centuries-long fluidity of contact between the northern realms and Christian civilization; the barbarians didn't so much invade as gradually seep into the empire—and they were more often "displaced agriculturalists" than warrior-nomads, many of them already Romanized or amenable to "religious experimentation."

Possessing a long-standing interest in social psychology, Brown analyzes the intricate gift relationships that spring up between clerics (whether missionaries, abbots, or bishops) and the local secular authorities (whether Roman, Celtic, or Germanic): these last "would endow and protect monasteries and convents in return for having a powerhouse of prayer in their midst." He almost amusingly notes the different ways tribes and nations converted to Christianity (through missionary fervor, bloody kingly fiat, election, and even, in the case of Iceland, shamanistic vision), then analyzes how such conversions were subsequently mythologized. Indeed, he concludes that monks helped create for the barbarians a usable sense of their pre-Christian past. Drawing on his own researches (and earlier publications), he tracks the sociological impact of Egyptian holy men (like the Syrian Simeon Stylites) as examples (Irish and Saxon monks re-created the austere life of the "desert" in the bleak offshore islands of Iona and Lindisfarne), reflects on the growing cult of the saints, traces the emerging concept of purgatory, and analyzes "tariffed penances," set down in penitentials, not just as part of the growing practice of confession (at first practiced only by the deeply pious) but also as a means of gaining insight into private life: "A single Penitential can range from explosive cases of perjury and bloodshed to the most intimate details of sexual behavior. Fornication by a bishop is mentioned alongside intercourse with animals, masturbation, intercourse with one's wife 'from behind, in the manner of dogs,' and sexual play by small children."

Though Brown can shift speedily from the Ireland of Saint Patrick to the Germany of Boniface to the Middle East of Justinian and Theodoric, he slows down for a more sustained look at some major figures: Pope Gregory the Great (whose Rule for Bishops created a "Europe-wide language of power"); Columbanus, who left his Irish home to work among the Franks and became the model for later monk missionaries; the notable eighth-century historian Bede (author of the Ecclesiastical History of the English Nation); and, not least, the family of Charlemagne (the Carolingian empire, we're told, produced "the first technocrats of Europe"). While emphasizing a kind of "inner history" that seeks to understand social and religious belief systems, as well as their practical institutions, Brown never fails to provide telling anecdotes. Parchment, for example, was essential to book production and the monks had to keep vast flocks of sheep: "The skins of over 500 sheep were required to make one large Bible. Altogether, by modern standards, book production involved an immense outlay of labor and resources. To write a book was the equivalent of putting up an entire building. To assemble a library was a crushing investment. . . . To copy the four Gospels took up to eight months."

Best of all, *The Rise of Western Christendom* pays much more than cursory attention to the Middle East. The Eastern Roman Empire (at Constantinople) is studied in detail—from the spread of Monophysite Christianity to the controversy over icons, which, though seemingly trivial, was at heart an argument about how one conceived of God's presence in the world. Most strikingly, two long chapters take up, with much detail and sympathy, the triumph of Islam and the way it incorporated Christians within its empire. Here, Brown speaks warmly of the beauty of Arabic, "the richest language of the Near East," later adding, with even more enthusiasm, that "nothing which happened in barbarian western Europe equaled the energy with which the Muslims around 700 mobilized a sense of their own Arabian past. The creation of an Arabic historical tradition was one of the great intellectual achievements of the early Middle Ages."

Such eloquent touches frequently light up Brown's sentences. Inhabitants of the Celtic fairy kingdom, usually referred to as "the other side," are "untouched by sadness." In his last chapter, "*In Gear Dagum*" (that is, "in days of yore"), our guide evokes the world of *Beowulf*—noting that the poem as it now stands "assumed a reader's knowledge of at least 20 similar legends"—before concluding his book with a quick précis of the conversions of Scandinavia and Iceland around the year 1000. From this time on, all Europe was officially Christian.

Throughout these 600 densely thoughtful pages, Peter Brown finds that our tendency to reduce this period to sharp contrasts—Rome and the barbarian hordes, classical past and Christian present, East and West, invisible and visible, desert and city, center and periphery—should be largely, if not always, resisted. Early Christian Europe's history, especially its "inner history," was in every way far more nuanced, variegated, mongrel. In *The Rise of Western Christendom* Peter Brown, yet again, restores much of the richness and color to what once seemed a dull, monochrome age.

July 13, 2003

POSTSCRIPT: Most of *Bound to Please* concentrates on literary subjects, but I confess to a nearly equal obsession with European intellectual history, though it is only weakly represented in these pages. Besides Peter Brown's book, I've included John Hale's study of the Renaissance, Jenny Uglow's history of the "Lunar men" of the eighteenth century, and Peter Washington's account of the followers of Madame Blavatsky. But essays on many other engaging, yet scholarly, works had to be left out. Readers with a liking for history should try the new translation of Jacob Burckhardt's *The Greeks and Greek Civilization*, Richard Fletcher's *The Barbarian Conversion*, Marcia Colish's *Medieval Foundations of the Western Intellectual Tradition*, Diarmaid MacCulloch's *The Reformation*, John Brewer's *The Pleasures of the Imagination*, Roy Strong's *Flesh in the Age of Reason*, Philip Mansel's *Paris between Empires*, A. N. Wilson's *The Victorians*, and Peter Conrad's *Modern Times, Modern Places*. Each of these is practically a seminar on its particular subject, and I recommend them all.

THE ARABIAN NIGHTS:
A COMPANION

By Robert Irwin

Like the Bible, *The Arabian Nights* is a book that people think they know, at least sort of, even if they've never read it. Also like the Bible, it ranks among the most influential books of all time: What non-European literary title has had more impact on modern Western culture? Ever since the Frenchman Antoine Galland made these astonishing stories available to Europe early in the eighteenth century, *The Thousand Nights and a Night* (the English translation of the Arabic *Alf Layla wa-Layla*) has been tantalizing the West with its vision of a realm of lavishness and gratified desire. *The Decameron* is often just a collection of naughty escapades, and *The Canterbury Tales* is an enduring monument of English poetry and dramatic characterization; but *The Arabian Nights* has become an aspect of the imagination.

Scheherazade, magic rings, caves of wonder, jinn, Sinbad, flying horses, cities of brass, automatons, wicked sorcerers, kismet—all these have often served as the trappings, the gaudy orientalizing backdrop of films (*The Thief of Baghdad*), spectacles (the Diaghilev production of Rimsky-Korsakov's *Scheherazade*), and fiction (from William Beckford's perverse *Vathek* to John Barth's playful *Chimera*). More fundamentally, though, the *Nights* managed to enlarge our imagination by democratizing the strange and magical. No longer did you have to travel to exotic climes or be a prince or knight, saint or learned scholar, to encounter the marvelous; it might simply irrupt into a dull life while you were busily doing something quite ordinary, like catching fish or going to the market. In several tales a storekeeper, literally minding his own business, glances up to see a mysterious woman examining his stock. Before you can say *shazam*, the tradesman finds himself (1) infatuated and (2) caught up in some amazing adventure. By its end he may find himself a vizier or just another victim of a kohl-eyed *belle dame sans merci*.

Robert Irwin's *The Arabian Nights: A Companion* is one of those superlative works of scholarship that survey a fascinating, if slightly arcane, subject with enviable authority and stylishness. Irwin lays out everything you might care to know about the *Nights*—the mysteries surrounding its origins, the history of its translations (Lane, Burton, Galland), what it reveals about medieval Arab life, how people have interpreted the tales, their influence on later English and American literature. He does, however, shun any deliberate literary criticism, preferring to show how early Arabic social history can illuminate the *Nights* and vice versa. This is, in short, just the sort of relaxed, informative book that Edmund Wilson might have written had he grown interested in the Middle East and its early literature.

In his *Companion*, Irwin—a novelist as well as an Arabist—discloses his own liking for the seamier side of history, proffering anecdotes about medieval criminals, acrobats, storytellers, jugglers, beggars, and con men. "When the Emir Qusun was condemned to be crucified, street vendors cashed in by selling lollipops in the shape of the crucified victim." (Today, they'd be hawking T-shirts.) The *Nights* revel in a similar bitter humor. A king executes, unjustly, a clever sorcerer who leaves behind a magic book, *The Secret of Secrets*, to tantalize his killer. "When the king opened the book, he found the pages stuck. So he put his finger in his mouth, wetted it with his saliva, and opened the first page, and he kept opening the pages with difficulty until he turned seven leaves. But when he looked in the book, he found nothing written inside. . . . The king opened some more pages but still found nothing, and while he was doing this, the drug spread through his body—for the book had been poisoned—and he began to heave, sway, and twitch."

Most of us, I suspect, know *The Arabian Nights* only from the simplified, bowdlerized versions found in the nursery. So to read the unexpurgated tales can be a revelation. First of all, they are quite exceptionally gripping. Two illicit lovers try desperately to convince a murderous demon that they are strangers to each other. The monster turns to the man and says, " 'Take this sword and strike her head off, and I will believe that you do not know her and let you go free.' I replied, 'I will do it,' and I took the sword and sprang toward her." End of the forty-fifth night. Tune in tomorrow evening.

Yet not only suspenseful, the *Nights* are also steamy with a hothouse sexuality (and more than a touch of misogyny). Consider, for instance, "The Porter and the Three Ladies," with its hint of lesbianism, incidents of sadomasochism (the bizarre beating of the dogs who turn out to be metamorphosed sisters), naughty games about private parts, and tales of incest and nymphomania. In the end, marriages rather than an orgy take place, but there's no mistaking those tickles of the pornographic.

Above all, the *Nights* display the entire bazaar, colorful and noisy, of modern narrative techniques, including "early and exotic examples of framing, self-reference, embedded references, hidden patterns, recursion and intertextuality." Irwin illustrates one aspect of this intricacy with "The Tale of Attaf":

The caliph Harun al-Rashid "visits a library, consults a volume at random, falls to laughing and weeping and dismisses the faithful vizier Ja'afar from his sight. Ja'afar, disturbed and upset, flees Baghdad and plunges into a series of adventures in Damascus, involving Attaf and the woman whom Attaf eventually marries. Returning to Baghdad, he reports back to Harun, who takes him into the library. Now Ja'afar is allowed to consult the book which caused his master such grief and mirth, and in it Ja'afar finds the story of his own adventures with Attaf, those same adventures which were provoked by Harun's reading of the story in the book." Mirrors within mirrors.

To enter *The Arabian Nights* is like being lost in a funhouse. Stories are telescoped inside stories to a vertiginous degree, and since most of them sport vague, generic titles (e.g., "The Third Dervish's Tale"), it's hard to find one's way around in the book. At one point Scheherazade starts telling the sultan that "the tailor told the king of China that the barber told the guests that he said to the caliph . . ."

Dizzying yes, but the prose itself can be as crisp as a sultan's command. The body of a beautiful young woman, hacked to pieces, has been discovered in a trunk dragged from the river. Two men, one young, one old, come forward. " 'Which of you killed the girl and threw her into the river?' The young man replied, 'I murdered her,' and the old man said, 'None killed her but I.' Then the caliph said to Ja'afar, 'Hang them both.' "

Robert Irwin proves a wonderful, genial guide to all these worlds of wonder, and any page of his *Companion* offers plenty of its own *ajib* (marvels). Of recent translations of the *Nights*, he particularly recommends that of Husain Huddawy, based on a scholarly edition of the original core collection of stories, which means that many of the later, better-known standards, like those of Aladdin and Ali Baba, are missing (though they can be found in his companion volume, *Arabian Nights II: Sindbad and Other Stories*). Yet whatever the version read, it's nearly impossible to resist the spell of Scheherazade when she starts telling one of her tales that "help everyone to forget his cares and banish sorrow from the heart."

The story, we can be sure, will be a strange one.

October 9, 1994

POSTSCRIPT: The versatile Robert Irwin has also compiled *Night and Horses and the Desert: An Anthology of Classical Arabic Literature*. Not merely a collection of poems and stories, it also provides interstitial commentary by Irwin on the themes, genres, and major figures of a thousand years of Arabic writing. Throughout Irwin reminds us that it is all too easy "to underestimate the degree to which Arabic culture, and more specifically its literature, was the natural heir to the Hellenistic civilization of late Antiquity."

THE NAME OF THE ROSE

By Umberto Eco
Translated from the Italian by William Weaver

It is a dark time for church and empire. Europe is rotten with heresy; the false pope John XXII reigns in Avignon; Holy Roman Emperor Louis of Bavaria pursues the consolidation of his power in Italy. In north and south charismatic messiahs preach poverty, or debauchery, or revolution. Bogomils, Albigensians, Cathars, Dolcinians, Fraticelli, Spiritual Franciscans, Jews—all are vilified, hunted down, tortured, burned by the Inquisition. It is widely believed that the trumpets of the Apocalypse are about to sound, the Seven Seals be opened. Was not the Emperor of the Last Days already born and perhaps even now in power at Avignon or Rome? For surely the world has turned upside down, surely the time of Antichrist has come around at last!

Such is the ominous backdrop of Umberto Eco's medieval thriller, *The Name of the Rose,* a novel of murder, politics, and ideas that has rightly become an acclaimed European best seller.

Late in 1327 a Franciscan, William of Baskerville, accompanied by the novice Adso of Melk, journeys to an unnamed Benedictine monastery to arrange a meeting of détente between representatives of Pope John and Emperor Louis. Just as master and disciple arrive at the abbey, a young monk commits suicide under suspicious circumstances. The worldly abbot asks the Sherlock Holmes–like Franciscan—a disillusioned inquisitor and former pupil of Roger Bacon—to investigate the shadowy affair. To this end, William is granted free run of the establishment—except for the library, the finest in all Christendom. Malachi, the librarian, and his assistant prohibit any direct access to the fragile illuminated manuscripts. And if a man were to try to enter the locked tower rooms? "No one," replies the abbot, "even if he wished, would succeed. The library defends itself, immeasurable as the truth it houses, deceitful as the falsehood it preserves. A spiritual labyrinth, it is also a terrestrial labyrinth. You might enter and you might not emerge."

Ah, now that's the kind of demonic book room that Jorge Luis Borges might imagine. And indeed, William and Adso soon meet the ancient blind monk Jorge de Burgos, whose name and bookishness recall the Argentine fabulist (as does the novel's learned preface about how the author researched Adso's manuscript). Such homage whispers, sub rosa, that Eco's novel aims to be modernist as well as medieval, to reflect both the time of its action and the time of its telling. William, for example, embodies a spirit of tolerance and scientific inquiry, that of the approaching Renaissance; he consequently appears a relatively modern man surrounded by religious fanatics, many of these actual historical figures. In the course of his detecting, this relentless bloodhound of Baskerville meets, for instance, the mystic Ubertino of Casale, the inquisitor Bernard of Gui, the general of the Franciscans, Michael of Cesena, and followers of the Italian leveler Fra Dolcino. Each of these believes he possesses the Truth; yet their voices and vociferations resonate in twentieth-century ears with the stridency of born-again evangelicals, fascists, corporation climbers, Marxist fellow travelers.

The mirroring of now-in-then seems peculiarly appropriate in *The Name of the Rose*, for such a technique mimics the figural or typological thinking common to the Middle Ages. The Old Testament Job, in this view, is both himself and a type of the New Testament's suffering Christ; the offerings of the priest Melchisedek are historical yet also prefigure the bread and wine of the Last Supper. So too, this novel can be read as a poetic synthesis of the early fourteenth century, and as oblique commentary on the excesses of the twentieth. Adso, for instance, learns about the various cults that take fire from Joachim of Flora's vision of an earthly paradise, but modern readers also learn timeless character and appeal of a revolutionary ideology. Such rich, implicitly ironic textuality might be expected from Eco, a professor of semiotics at the University of Bologna; yet even his seemingly ultramodern academic discipline finds its roots in monastic learning and patristic exegesis. The Bible and the universe are God's two great scriptures, and in them we may read his message to the world—though their intricate symbols must first be properly understood on several levels, including the anagogical and eschatological.

Especially the eschatological. For like the theological thrillers of Charles Williams, *The Name of the Rose* returns obsessively to John's vision of apocalypse. The various heresies that the monks practice or discuss—and this is a talky novel, in the vein of Mann or Murdoch—all derive from a chiliastic foreboding that traditional hierarchies are being upset by new ideas, new ways. The theme of the world turned upside down occurs pervasively: in allusions to the topsy-turvy realms of Cockaigne, Saturnalia, the *Coena Cypriani*, and Carnival, in unnatural love between monks, in the leveling character of the various heretical movements, in the triumph of inductive reasoning over a priori reliance on received authority, in Aristotle deposing the church fathers, even in the newfangled inventions that William makes passing mention of: gunpowder, the compass, spectacles, paper, the sextant, flying machines. All the signs suggest that breakup of the great chain of being which will herald the Last Days. Slyly, even the novel's preface alludes to such millennial fantasies, for Eco tells us that he "translated" this manuscript in 1968—at the very time a youthful revolutionary populism was overturning the old order, hoping to forestall a fiery Armageddon and establish the new Jerusalem.

In his investigations William comes to realize that the secret of the abbey is somehow intertwined with the biblical revelation to John. After the first death, there is a second, and a third; the murderer's modus operandi seems to derive from, almost to copy religiously, the opening of the Seven Seals. Even more disquieting, behind all the ritual killings looms a book, a book to rival the Ark of the Covenant in its awesome power. But to find that dread manuscript, William and Adso must penetrate the forbidden library, solve its riddles, and find their way to a hidden *sanctum sanctorum*.

Such gothic hugger-mugger—part Borges, part John Dickson Carr—lightens Eco's operatic gravity, especially when the reader might begin to weary of visionary rapture or philosophical and theological wrangling. Number symbolism, alchemical secrets, the language of gems, pagan love charms, a linguistic Quasimodo, and the clockwork of a life ordered by the Benedictine rule further enhance the supernatural atmosphere. So too does the religious imagery, and the interlacing of vernacular and Vulgate. When Adso braves the library at night and surprises a beautiful girl, he is unsure whether she is the Whore of Babylon, the Woman Clothed with the Sun, or the devil in the flesh. When he gives way to her nakedness, his ecstasy elicits the delirious language of the Song of Songs.

In its range, *The Name of the Rose* suggests an imaginative summa, an alchemical marriage of murder mystery and Christian mystery. It conveys remarkably the desperation of a dying culture, while at the same time touching on perennial issues of love, religion, scholarship, and politics. Even an occasional reliance on coincidence and fortuitous revelation strengthen its medieval aura, its convincing re-creation of a way of life now lost. As Adso writes at the end of his chronicle—quoting a twelfth-century poem about the passing of Babylon and Rome—*Stat rosa pristina nomine, nomina nuda tenemus.* The rose of yore is but a name, mere names are left to us. Yes and no, for through Umberto Eco's prodigious necromancy some of those names quicken and live again.

June 19, 1983

THE CIVILIZATION OF EUROPE
IN THE RENAISSANCE

By John Hale

There's nothing petty about the Renaissance. Even a contract, that loving home to the qualification, waiver, and escape clause, can actually escape the bonds of the niggling and lawyerly. "I, Jacopo Gallo, promise his very reverend lordship [the cardinal of St. Denis] that the said Michelangelo shall finish the said work in the space of one year and that it shall be the most beautiful work in marble in Rome, and that no living master shall be able to make one as beautiful." In due course, the *Pietà* appeared. Contract fulfilled. To the letter.

"Everyone his own Tamburlaine"—so the English art historian Michael Levey once summed up the swagger, the boundless self-confidence, of the European Renaissance. "Is it not passing brave to be a king / And ride in triumph through Persepolis?" One condottiere owned armor inscribed, with chilling simplicity, "The enemy of God, of pity, and of mercy." Certainly the most celebrated Renaissance portraits memorialize imposing, personal power: Verrocchio's equestrian statue of the armored warlord Bartolomeo Colleoni; the silky, almost sacerdotal authority of Bellini's painting of the Venetian doge Leonardo Loredano; Dürer's hypnotic self-portrait, in which he vaingloriously likens himself to Christ; Donatello's calmly self-assured Saint George. A similar, albeit feminine mystique irradiates those serenely wistful beauties, Botticelli's Venus, sorrowful at "the thought of the whole long day of love yet to come," and Leonardo's Mona Lisa, "older than the rocks among which she sits."

John Hale's *The Civilization of Europe in the Renaissance*, the crowning achievement of one of the great historians of early modern times, leisurely surveys "the long sixteenth century," that period running from the mid-1400s to the early 1600s. Hale calls his 600-page masterwork a "guidebook for time travelers," implying that readers should not expect a textbook history. Instead Hale emulates Jakob Burckhardt's famous *Civilization of the Renaissance in Italy* and proffers an essay, an "investigative impression." But while the nineteenth-century Swiss historian emphasized individuality as the defining character of the Italian *cinquecento*, Hale avoids any obvious thesis mongering, preferring to show, in as many ways as he can, how the medieval world changed into the modern. This focus permits him to take up such diverse matters as Europe's discovery of itself, the exploration of new lands, humanism and the rediscovery of antiquity, the ideal of civility, the new importance of cash, nationalist politics, the rise of vernacular literatures, religious reform, and, as is appropriate to this age of energy and exuberance, much, much more.

Like any good tourist manual, Hale's "guidebook" shines in its details. "Italian princes imported falcons from Iceland." Rosso Fiorentino was the first known artist to commit suicide (because of—wouldn't you know it?—litigation troubles; not everyone could be Michelangelo). Henry VIII "played the lute and virginals, sang from scores at sight and composed masses and songs." Cardinals used to meet in the Vatican privies to barter votes during papal elections. The twenty-nine-year-old courtesan (and poet) Veronica Franco charged two ducats for her intimate attentions. "By the late 15th century doctors had come to discriminate between twenty varieties of colour and density in urine, and the same number for faeces."

Complementing this flair for the striking factoid, Hale also writes a generally vivid, even poetic prose. "Skies," he says of a medieval manuscript illumination created for the duc de Berry, "were never so piercingly blue, nor castles quite so lofty, so raised as though by wizards rather than masons, as these before which peasants carried out their tasks or fashionable men and women rode out in festival guise to the sound of trumpets." The nostalgia for a golden age, he notes, "drew on the vision of medieval millenarianism: a world of restored simplicity in which man, naked amidst the ruins of his pomps and institutions, awaited judgement." Hale can even toss off a snappish witticism, describing the ancient physician Galen, for instance, as "one of those men whose intellectual tediousness wins acclaim because of the importance of his subject." Now and again he constructs a prose couplet: "For some, then, self-grooming for success could suppress the animal in man only to turn him into an ape of his betters."

Still, what most readers will take away from *The Civilization of Europe in the Renaissance* is how much the long sixteenth century can sound like our own. There's unemployment in the cities, ethnic and religious "cleansing," inflation and financial scandal. "Jacques de Beaune, from a modest merchant family, was able to lend the French crown 240,000 livres in 1518. In 1523, richer than ever, he was appointed chief financial officer of the kingdom. In 1527 he was hanged for peculation." Then as now, everybody grumbles about something.

People near the London theaters complain about the traffic when the plays let out. Parents complain "about the expense of buying revised education primers." William Harrison complains, in 1547, "that what with ear-ringed men and doubletted women" he has become confused about which sex is which. Even the French poet Ronsard complains, in verse, that his mistress exhausts herself with a dildo.

Familiar social problems abound. The warden of an orphans' home abuses a nine-year-old girl. Convicted, he is executed, but his "contaminated" victim is driven from the town. Smoking, it is said, leaves the veins "covered in soot like a chimney." Ten percent of the English population perishes in 1471 from the Black Death, the original plague. Young men without jobs frequently run wild in the streets; and urban violence grows endemic, even among artists: Michelangelo broke his nose in a fight, Mantegna hired bravos to rough up his rivals, Christopher Marlowe was murdered in a tavern, Ben Jonson killed a man in a brawl. For quieter fun, the Renaissance could also play its own Monopoly-like board game, with one of the squares labeled "Your patron dies"; it sent you immediately back to Go.

Though fine in most of the ways that matter, *The Civilization of Europe in the Renaissance* occasionally seems a little rough-hewn and rambling. Hale suffered a stroke after completing the manuscript and needed to rely on others, chiefly his wife and scholarly colleagues, to prepare the book for publication. A few sentences read strangely: "In 1538 the city council of Basel agreed to continue to pay most of Holbein's salary to his widow during his prolonged stay at the court of Henry VIII. . . ." The risen Christ met two disciples, not five, on the road to Emmaus. And, ironically, a person would be "haled," not "hailed"—as is written here—before the privy council.

Certainly these textual blemishes are partially redeemed by the book's plentiful, often unexpected illustrations (though some are printed so darkly that details mentioned in the text cannot be verified). For instance, Bartholmaeus Spranger's innocent-sounding *Triumph of Wisdom*—actually a portrait of a helmeted beauty, with bare breasts and provocative wisps of armor—looks rather like the cover for a sword-and-sorcery paperback: SheRa or Red Sonya, as painted by a sixteenth-century Boris Vallejo. The silver plaquette of Paulus van Vianen's *Mercury and Argus* reveals a beautiful reclining youth, languorously nude, an epicene's dream. Of course, the first great depiction of existential despair could hardly be left out: Masaccio's fresco showing the expulsion of Adam and Eve from paradise, he despondently burying his face in his hands, she staring up in anguish while covering her breasts and genitals.

During the Middle Ages fallen man and woman might hope for a celestial paradise after death. But with the Renaissance, people, even Christians, realized that this world could be more than just a testing ground for heaven. Great personal achievement gradually replaced holiness as an ideal, begetting the striving and competition, the anxiety and glory, of the modern age. Perhaps, as religious thinkers and Marxist historians tend to believe, this hurly-burly ethos has been a mistake, a spiritual or moral blight. Others, like Hale himself, counter by pointing to the Renaissance ideal of civility, displayed in beautiful penmanship and ingratiating manners as well as harmonious art and well-organized government. In either case, *The Civilization of Europe in the Renaissance* reminds us, through its vivid detail and scholarly authority, that we are still living out the perhaps ambiguous legacy of the long sixteenth century.

August 14, 1994

POSTSCRIPT: See the coda of this book for "A Renaissance Reading List."

WILLIAM TYNDALE:
A BIOGRAPHY

By David Daniell

When I was a child, I thought as a child and firmly believed that the Bible was literally written, or at least dictated, by God: the Creator, in the voice of Orson Welles, gravely intoned, "Let there be light," and an enraptured priest or prophet set down the words on some kind of parchment. Having put away childish things, if only for the moment, I now know that the author of the Bible was in fact a man named William Tyndale.

For most of us the words of God and the prophets, Jesus and his disciples, resound most powerfully in the Authorized or King James Version of the scriptures. Generally acclaimed as the greatest work ever produced by a committee, this 1611 Bible in fact builds largely on the work of William Tyndale (1494–1536), the first translator, into English, of the New Testament from the Greek and of about half the Old Testament from the Hebrew. In a broad way, historians and theologians have long recognized Tyndale's importance, but, according to the Renaissance scholar David Daniell, they have unconscionably failed to honor him sufficiently. Here, after all, is the man who gave us such phrases as "Am I my brother's keeper?," who made Christ speak an English of sublime simplicity—"Blessed are the poor in spirit: for theirs is the kingdom of heaven"—and who established prose rhythms that stir us to our very marrow: "But the serpent was subtler than all the beasts of the field which the Lord God had made, and said unto the woman. . . ."

William Tyndale: A Biography is thus a work of reparation, the portrait of an underappreciated genius. It follows, logically enough, upon Daniell's sumptuous editions (also from Yale) of Tyndale's New and Old Testaments. To his zealous, impassioned biographer Tyndale took the language used by ordinary people "at slightly heightened moments" and translated God's words at that level, employing "a neutral word-order and English rather than Latin forms." Thus where the AV prissily writes, "Thou hast now done foolishly in so doing,"

Tyndale says plainly, "Thou wast a fool to do it." Having reread the Gospel of Matthew according to Tyndale, I can confirm the power of his work: neither the Revised Standard Version nor the Authorized Version ever seemed quite this heartfelt, forceful, and exciting. Since Tyndale lies behind both later translations, there are naturally many similarities, but Tyndale's original rhythms often seem more haunting, his language quicker and tighter (if occasionally a tad alien). These are disputable matters, of course, made all the more complex because Jesus's sublime eloquence seems capable of surviving even the most leaden modern renderings.

Yet it is wrong to mock, however gently, the contemporary attempts to make the Bible more easily understood by ordinary people. For this was in fact Tyndale's own goal: as the story goes in Foxe's *Book of Martyrs*, a young Tyndale was disputing with a learned man and, in vexation, protested, "If God spare my life, ere many years I will cause a boy that driveth the plough shall know more of the Scripture than thou dost." Repeatedly, Daniell asserts and shows by quotation that "what is characteristic of Tyndale, and what matters, is his clarity, his determination to put nothing in the way of being understood." "When now Moses stretched forth his hand over the sea, the Lord carried away the sea with a strong east wind that blew all night...." What could be plainer or more beautiful?

In some of the strongest sections of his book Daniell analyzes the subtly elusive qualities of Tyndale's English. Besides clarity and simplicity, Tyndale excels at narrative drive. "He went down and slew a lion in a pit in a time of snow." He can evoke sheer heartbreak by daring to repeat, again and again, a simple phrase. King David has learned that his rebellious son Absalom is dead. "And the king was moved and went up to a chamber over the gate and wept. And as he went thus he said: my son Absalom, my son, my son, my son Absalom, would to God I had died for thee, Absalom my son, my son." The King James Version is similar, but stiffer and more formal, with superfluous O's interjected, and lacking one of the repetitions of "my son" that does so much to evoke David's inconsolable grief.

William Tyndale was probably born in 1494, though "there is no documentary evidence of him until he took his Oxford B.A. in his late teens." In truth, very little factual evidence survives about Tyndale, outside the prefaces to his theological tracts and translations. Daniell tries to make up for this lack by speculating when necessary or by describing the milieu in which the young scholar probably moved. The early sixteenth century in England was a period of continual religious strife and anxiety. The Catholic Church had fallen into a period of decadence, with a widespread loss of authority as it unduly stressed outward observances (indulgences, sacraments, good works) and failed to satisfy

a more general spiritual hunger. Luther flourished in Germany, and his translations of the Bible (sometimes used by Tyndale) emphasized a straightforward
approach to the sacred text. "No fine words," was the arch-Protestant's motto,
producing a Bible in German that aimed to be understood literally and his-
torically, without any need for the fourfold allegorizing characteristic of
the church fathers, what Tyndale once scorned as the church's reliance on the
"chopological."

This doctrine—*Sola Scriptura*, the Bible alone—was obviously a danger to
the church: much of its dogma was based on deep readings of every biblical
sentence, and on imaginative interpretations thereof: think of Christ calling
Peter the rock upon which he would build his church and to whom he would
give the power to loose and bind in heaven. For Catholics the passage provides
much of the scriptural foundation for the papacy and all its consequent trappings. But to arrive at this understanding one must extrapolate beyond the literal meaning. As Daniell writes, rather overheatedly, "The Church would never
permit a complete printed New Testament in English from the Greek, because
in that New Testament can be found neither the Seven Sacraments nor the
doctrine of purgatory, two chief sources of the Church's power."

By the time Tyndale arrived in London, he had apparently already resolved
to translate the Bible and hoped to win official approval. When this was not
forthcoming, he traveled to Germany and there began his work in earnest. His
first New Testament appeared in 1525, followed by the Pentateuch in 1530,
then Jonah in 1531, and finally a revised NT in 1534. Most of these translations
were smuggled into England; when found, the books were burned and sometimes their readers were burned as well. Tyndale's greatest enemy proved to be
John Stokesby, the bishop of London, who in his own youth had been accused
of "numerous crimes and misdemeanours, ranging from disobedience to the
President [of his Oxford college] to adultery with the wife of the organist and
baptizing a cat in order to discover a treasure by magic." Stokesby probably
masterminded the plot by which Tyndale was seized by the authorities in
Antwerp and eventually tried for heresy and condemned. The still-young
scholar died at the stake in 1536, his last words being "Lord, open the King of
England's eyes."

All this makes for a fascinating story, in which appear Erasmus (who
brought out the Greek New Testament used by Tyndale); Thomas More, who
composes almost insane polemics, marked by recurrent excretory imagery,
against "this captain of our English heretics"; Henry VIII, the Defender of the
Catholic Faith who would found his own church; and Miles Coverdale, who
very likely used Tyndale's unpublished translation of the later historical books
of the Old Testament (Joshua to Nehemiah) in the so-called Matthew's Bible

of 1537. By the end of *William Tyndale: A Biography* one has traversed forty of the most intellectually tempestuous years in European history.

Yet for all his book's merits, Daniell mars his claims for this intellectual hero by an egregious stridency. He repeatedly portrays the Catholic Church as the Whore of Babylon, speaking of "the pointlessness of a religion based only on outward observances," calling ritual "something fostered by the Church simply for its own profit." He even identifies certain sources as "Catholic historians."—How does he know? As for his subject, he is constantly defensive, worrying about "those (and they have been many) who have wanted to deny Tyndale any stature at all." In fact, Tyndale, in his panegyrist's mind anyway, "might have gone on to be the architect of a new, more English, Reformation theology with the profoundest effect on the arriving Church of England."

Though this is still in most respects an important and useful book, David Daniell (or his editors) should have tried harder to be a little more like the oft-scorned Laodiceans, those who in Revelation are "neither cold nor hot." There's a clear line between passionate advocacy and polemical excess. A more even-tempered view of Tyndale's opponents, especially, would make the translator's merits seem uncontestable. In truth, all anyone really need do to be convinced of William Tyndale's rightful claim to greatness is to read his versions of the Old and New Testaments. "If any man will follow me, let him forsake himself, and take up his cross and follow me. For whosoever will save his life, shall lose it. And whosoever shall lose his life for my sake, shall find it." For such sentences as these, and many others, nothing but hosannas will do.

December 25, 1994

A DEAD MAN IN DEPTFORD

By Anthony Burgess

The two greatest Elizabethan dramatists were both born in 1564, but William Shakespeare outlived Christopher Marlowe by more than two decades. Yet so precocious was Marlowe's talent that before his violent death at age twenty-nine he had written at least six plays, among them *Dr. Faustus* and *Tamburlaine*, perhaps the most famous lyric poem of his generation ("Come live with me, and be my love") and two parts of a gorgeous and erotic mini-epic, *Hero and Leander*: "Where both deliberate, the love is slight; / Whoever loved, that loved not at first sight?"

One might think that this was enough for a literary career that lasted little more than half a dozen years. But there was also another, darker side to "Kind Kit Marlowe" (as his fellow playwright John Marston once dubbed him). Sometime while at Cambridge in the late 1580s, Marlowe was recruited into the Elizabethan secret service, almost certainly to work as a courier and probably as a kind of double agent in England's shadow war against Spain and Catholicism. In these circles he met such unsavory types as Robert Poley, Nicholas Skeres, and Ingram Friser—all associated with espionage or petty crime—who in 1593 invited him to a little party at the house of the widow Eleanor Bull in Deptford, just outside London. The four spent a quiet day together, but in the evening an argument reportedly broke out over the bill—"le recknynge"—and when the dust cleared "the gentle Shepherd" (Shakespeare's phrase) was dead, stabbed to the quick through the right eye. As Marlowe himself wrote prophetically, "Cut is the branch that might have grown full straight / And burned is Apollo's laurel bough."

Such is the background for Anthony Burgess's *A Dead Man in Deptford,* a fictionalization of Marlowe's firecracker life. First published in England in 1993 for the quatercentenary of its subject's death, the novel makes a companion piece to Burgess's superb 1964 re-creation of the young Shakespeare, *Nothing like the Sun*. But where that small masterpiece possessed a rollicking, picaresque raciness—as WS loves not wisely nor too well, becoming amorously entangled with the earl of Southhampton, finding himself cuckolded at home by his brother Richard and finally catching syphilis from his Dark Lady (the black Fatimah)—this new book moves at a somber, more philosophical pace. There are discussions of religion, politics, playmaking, free speech, homosexuality, and many other such matters, featuring a dramatis personae that includes several of the major figures in Elizabethan literature: Thomas Kyd, Sir Walter Raleigh, Robert Greene, Thomas Nashe, and Shakespeare, as well as the actor Edward Alleyn, the spymaster Sir Francis Walsingham, and some notable Catholic recusants. One needn't be an expert on this swashbuckling period to enjoy *A Dead Man in Deptford*, but—as always with Burgess—one may need to stretch a little to enjoy his allusions, lip-smacking vocabulary, and quicksilver style.

For example, when some Catholic conspirators go on the run, Burgess wryly observes that they were captured in St. John's Wood, obviously "unprotected by either the Precursor or the Beloved Disciple." Kit notes that "we are but the guests of life, we begin aghast and end a ghost." Walsingham's "fine Spanish chair all knobs and curlicues" should have been "wooden heresy" to this rabid anti-Catholic. Much of the novel is in fact made up of "quotations" from history. "One week later the Queen of Scots, given but a day's warning, was beheaded in a late sunrise of winter, and her little dogs trotted out from under her skirts to lap her blood." When the unnamed actor narrator—whose identity turns out to be a sly self-reference—talks about Thomas Kyd's Hamlet play, he adds that it was so poor that "if the script was lost to the future it would be no hardship." (Virtually all that scholars now know of this precursor to Shakespeare's masterpiece is that in it the ghost utters the chilling command "Hamlet, revenge!") Punsters will enjoy the allusion to Marlowe's savage drama about the duke of Guise, for whom "Paris is worth a massacre."

Throughout, Burgess regularly alludes to famous lines and opinions: we see Thomas Nashe working on the wording of "Brightness falls from the air," Marlowe noticing that a raging November sunset "streams in the firmament" (which in *Dr. Faustus* becomes "See, see where Christ's blood streams in the firmament!"). Above all, Burgess allows Marlowe to overhear from others— spies, courtiers, scientists—the heterodox views associated with his name: e.g., that Christ may have lain with both Mary Magdalen and the beloved disciple John; that anyone should be able to coin money; that the alchemist Thomas Hariot could perform greater miracles than Moses. When Marlowe glimpses the sinister Friser, a line pops into his head (later used in *Edward II*): "I learn'd in Naples how to poison flowers." Building toward the horrific finale, there are repeated eye references: "eye to eye knowledge," Kit nearly being poked in the eye by a sycamore branch, assertions like "we know the world to exist only by our seeing it. You shut eyes in a man's death and in a sense you kill the universe."

But who in fact killed Christopher Marlowe? And why? Burgess presents a plausible scenario, not unlike that suggested by Charles Nicholl in his suspenseful exposition of Marlowe's espionage connections, *The Reckoning*. In both books Marlowe dies largely because of his association with Sir Walter Raleigh and his radical views (though Burgess keeps matters ambiguous, hinting that a traitorous friend might also wish the "voiding" of a man who knows too much). George Garrett speculates about other factors to the killing in his own first-rate historical novel, *Entered by the Sun*. Calvin Hoffman notoriously maintained that Marlowe didn't die, but that his homosexual lover had him spirited away and that he later went on to write the plays commonly attributed to William Shakespeare. The archivist William Urry, in his careful biographical study *Christopher Marlowe and Canterbury*, concludes for the most traditional view: "There is no need to invent a plot to put Marlowe out of the way. He was a victim of his own temperament," reminding us that the playwright-poet was involved in at least four crimes of violence and well known for his "sudden privy injuries to men." As Harry Levin wittily observed, Christopher Marlowe—atheist, homosexual, freethinker, tobacco smoker, spy, brawler, and poet—was "the embodiment of all the proscribed excesses."

In Burgess's view, though, Marlowe is chiefly a great artist, "the Muse's darling," one who soaks up experience and transmutes it into imperishable verse. Shakespeare, he tells us in a brief afterword, "may have outshone him but he did not contain or supersede him. That inimitable voice sings on." It can rise to the shout of a brutal conqueror: "Is it not passing brave to be a king, / And ride in triumph through Persepolis?" Or it can be of ethereal sensuousness: "Shadowing more beauty in their airy brows / Than has the white breasts of the queen of love." It can be cynical: "Thou hast committed— / Fornication: but that was in another country / And besides, the wench is dead." And it can be racked with the deepest anguish, as in the last hour in the life of a scholar who has traded away his soul: "The stars move still; time runs; the clock will strike; / The devil will come, and Faustus must be damned. . . . Adders and serpents, let me breathe a while! / Ugly hell, gape not. Come not, Lucifer! / I'll burn my books. Ah, Mephistopheles!"

Anthony Burgess died shortly after completing *A Dead Man in Deptford*, and so this fine novel should serve as a memorial not only to a great poet but also to a distinguished, consistently surprising modern writer. A Renaissance man in every sense, Burgess turned his hand to fiction, biography, screenplays, musicals, symphonies, poems, criticism, and autobiography. He also possessed a fierce appetite for drink, sex, and living with gusto. Like Tamburlaine, like Christopher Marlowe, he was by instinct an overreacher, at work to the very end:

> Nature, that framed us of four elements
> Warring within our breasts for regiment,
> Doth teach us all to have aspiring minds:
> Our souls, whose faculties can comprehend
> The wondrous architecture of the world
> And measure every wand'ring planet's course,
> Still climbing after knowledge infinite
> And always moving as the restless spheres,
> Wills us to wear ourselves and never rest. . . .
> (*Tamburlaine,* act 2, scene 7).

May 28, 1995

THE COMPLETE WORKS
OF FRANÇOIS RABELAIS

Translated from the French by Donald M. Frame

Readers have never been quite sure about François Rabelais (1494?–1553). On the one hand, he has been called the most difficult of all French writers, a sly social critic, and a Renaissance James Joyce pushing language beyond the brink of sense. On the other, actually reading *Gargantua and Pantagruel* is a lot like going to a Slovak or Ukrainian wedding in an Ohio steel town, where you pay a dollar to dance with the bride, eat way too much kielbasa and stuffed cabbage, drink yourself silly, and spend half the evening listening to somebody's red-cheeked uncle tell dirty jokes and tall tales. A lot of fun, but a little of it goes a long way.

For Rabelais—monk, physician, humanist—nothing succeeds like excess. His giant heroes and their hard-living cronies wallow in the socially, aesthetically, and politically incorrect. They're sexist, gluttonous, profane, bellicose, cruel, childish, ingenious, disputatious, and completely vulgar. You wouldn't want them for neighbors, but they'd be great on your side in a fight.

In 1532 an anonymous work about the "enormous giant Gargantua" appeared to an inevitably colossal success, and François Rabelais decided to cash in on its fame. The next year he brought out *Pantagruel,* which relates the fabulous and sometimes fabliaux-like exploits of Gargantua's son, focusing on his education in Paris, his friendship with the roguish normal-sized Panurge, and their epic battle against the rebellious Dipsodes. Imagine, if you can, Paul Bunyan on his junior year abroad. In 1535 this was followed by Rabelais's own prequel: *The Very Horrific Life of the Great Gargantua, Father of Pantagruel,* again chronicling the upbringing, friendships, and wars of its hero. It concludes with the establishment of the renowned Abbey of Thélème, a kind of proto–liberal arts college where the only monastic rule is "Do what you will."

In general, *Gargantua* and *Pantagruel* comprise the most celebrated episodes in all Rabelais. Consider, for example, Gargantua's laborious research to establish that for certain intimate needs nothing can compare with a soft downy gosling. Or the account of "how Gargantua was taught by Ponocrates in such a regimen that he did not waste an hour of the day"—a classic early instance of the overscheduled child. Then there is Pantagruel's encounter with the Limousin student who speaks entirely in Latinate gobbledygook and frankly admits that for "venerean ecstasy" he and his pals like to "inculcate our veretes into the most recondite recesses of the pudenda of these most amiable meretricules." And admirers of Borges and Escher will naturally pounce on the discovery—by the anagrammatic narrator and "abstractor of quintessence," Alcofribas Nasier—of an entire world inside Pantagruel's mouth.

Like Dickens, like Joyce (who, despite affinities, probably never read him), Rabelais revels in the way people talk. He can make us hear a sophistical schoolman or a coarse peasant; he can be as rarefied as a troubadour or as grimly and precisely anatomical as William Burroughs. One chapter of *Gargantua* merely sets down unidentified snatches of conversation, while another describes a philosophical debate conducted entirely in sign language "for the matters are so arduously difficult that human words would not suffice to explain them." In his own, relatively quiet narrative voice, Rabelais can conjure up a Brueghel painting with a single sentence: "After dinner, they went pell-mell to the Willow Grove, and there, on the sturdy grass, they danced to the sound of joyous flutes and sweet bagpipes, so gaily that it was heavenly fun to watch them sport."

For a book about giants, Rabelais's "veracious history" manages to be remarkably encyclopedic. Where else would you find the answer to the lascivious riddle "Why is it that a lady's thighs are always cool?" Or learn of the rewarding books in the Library of Saint Victor, among them *The Mustard Pot of Penitence*, *The Apparition of Saint Gertrude to a Nun of Poissy in Labor*, and even the untranslatable but suggestive *Antipericatametanaparbeugedamphicribrationes merdicantium*. Of course, all these pale before the testimony in a law case that renders "Jabberwocky" a model of lucidity: "The tailors wanted to make, out of the pilfered leftovers, a sackbut to cover the Ocean Sea, which for the time was pregnant with a potful of cabbage, in the opinion of the hay balers; but the doctors said that from its urine they recognized no evident sign, in the bustard's step, of eating axes with mustard, unless the Gentlemen of the Court gave a command in B-flat to the pox not to go gleaning after the silkworms. . . ." At times you'd swear you were reading *Alice's Adventures at Finnegans Wake*.

Most of these tomfooleries and language games have been cagily interpreted by the Russian scholar Mikhail Bakhtin as aspects of the carnivalesque, those interludes in life when people let themselves go in feasting and saturnalia, when the world is turned upside down. By contrast, the next two volumes of

Rabelais, the unimaginatively titled *Third Book* (1546) and *Fourth Book* (1552), display a more talky, intellectual character and have been glossed, with awe-inspiring scholarship, by Michael Screech, as reflections of the religious and philosophical skirmishes of Renaissance humanism. *The Third Book*, in particular, offers a series of bachelor conversations modeled partly after Plato and Lucian; in one episode Panurge squanders all his money, then expounds—with a paradoxical logic worthy of W. C. Fields—an entire cosmology based on universal debt.

Thematically, this third volume rapidly zeroes in on Panurge's itch to get married and his fears that he may then be cuckolded. What to do? Marry or burn? He consults a doctor, a jurist, a philosopher, a fool, a witch—and keeps getting ambiguous answers. And some not so ambiguous, like the ribald story of Hans Carvel's ring. Panurge lyricizes longingly about "the little business, performed on the sly, between two closed doors, across the stairs, behind the tapestry, on a pile of loose kindling" and then compares it to the even greater joys of wedded bliss "under precious canopies, between golden curtains, at long intervals, to one's heart's content, using a crimson flyswatter, and chasing away the flies with a brush of Indian feathers, and the female picking her teeth with a little bit of straw that she had meanwhile plucked out from deep down in the straw mattress." Wonderful stuff.

Unable to resolve his marital dilemma, Panurge finally sets sail with his friends, in an obvious parody of the Arthurian quest for the Holy Grail, to consult the Divine Bottle. Rabelais's *Fourth Book* relates the company's Gulliverian adventures among strange peoples as they journey toward the oracle. They encounter pygmies, a sausage-like race called the Chitterlings, the Papimaniacs, who have made the pope their god, and even the Gastrolators, who worship the belly. The book ends with their quest still unfulfilled.

And then Rabelais died. Nine years later, however, there unexpectedly appeared a *Fifth Book*. Most scholars reject it as a fake; others, like Frame, accept the possibility that it may be based on Rabelais's rough drafts. All editions print it regardless, for it concludes with the questers reaching the Divine Bottle, where they receive its message: *Trinch*. Or, less succinctly, drink life to the lees and savor every minute, the very definition of what has been called Pantagruelism. According to the scholar Erich Auerbach, this attractive ism "represents a grasp of life which comprehends the spiritual and the sensual simultaneously, which allows none of life's possibilities to escape."

There were several English editions of Rabelais before Donald Frame's, all of them with merit. In the seventeenth century Sir Thomas Urquhart translated the first three books into a vinously purple prose that often found more in Rabelais than was there. It is a half classic of English literature. In our time the best-known translations have been Samuel Putnam's—abridged in the Viking Portables series—and J. M. Cohen's capable Penguin. In 1989 Burton Raffel came out with a smooth and expert version; currently a Norton paperback, it lacks notes and scholarly apparatus but insinuates some of this matter into the text.

The great virtue of Donald Frame's translation lies in its fidelity to the French, extensive annotations (crucial, I think, in reading a writer as topical and allusive as Rabelais), and an exceptionally large glossary of proper names. All of these come backed by the authority of Frame, for years the leading American scholar of French Renaissance prose. Still, where Frame's earlier translation of Montaigne seemed an uncannily exact re-creation, here the Columbia professor—who died before he was fully satisfied with his work—sometimes sounds insufficiently musical and a tad low-keyed for his often florid, manic original. Even though Rabelais makes for hard reading in French—Chaucer's Middle English is a rough equivalent—he well repays the effort since the humor of his puns and portmanteau wordplays tends to elude translation. Frame's version of the *Complete Works*, beautifully produced by the University of California Press, is certainly the one to acquire (all my quotations are from it), but any version will convey some of the earthy, sourdough flavor.

Reading through Rabelais one is consistently amused by the grotesque misadventures, by the satire of contemporary history, by scraps of classical learning. Little wonder that his books should have influenced Swift, Voltaire, and Fielding and even such distinctive modern novelists as Robertson Davies and Steven Millhauser (see *The Rebel Angels* and *From the Realm of Morpheus*). But Rabelais remains more than a kind of rowdy vaudeville comedian. Because he presses everything to the limit—language, acceptable behavior, taste, narrative technique, scholarship—he stands among the world's most provocative and subversive writers, a perennial disturber of the peace, a carnival in himself. To read the man's work is to climb onto the literary equivalent of a county-fair tilt-a-whirl. You laugh, you get dizzy, you lose your bearings or even your lunch. But what a ride!

February 16, 1992

PROFESSIONALS
AT WORK

II

The highest compliment one can pay almost anyone in almost any line of work is to say, "He's really professional." Professionals know their jobs, meet deadlines, produce their best day in, day out. They may be artists, but they also use their art to pay the rent and support their families.

Is this mercantilization of the Renaissance spirit a bad thing? Hard to say. Writers, for instance, need time to explore their genius, and then more time to transform their obsessions and observations into art. Where will the money for this come from? Patrons, family wealth, the state, grants of one sort or another—all these can provide the wherewithal needed to underwrite those periods of curious leisure that precede the intensity and hard labor of making a poem or picture.

Balzac once asserted, "Constant work is the law of art as it is of life." Artists who enter into the marketplace know that they must be prepared not only to work hard but also to please the public. To the high-minded this may suggest "selling out"; but in most cases this really means producing art that fits the temper and taste of the age. Professionals usually can't afford to be visionaries if they must put money in their pockets. There are exceptions, of course. Picasso once said of himself, "I am merely an entertainer who has understood his time."

All but one of the titles covered in "Professionals at Work" are biographies—there will be many more—largely because such books give one a chance to think about the entire life and oeuvre of the glorious dead. Does this mean that I, like Samuel Johnson, love the biographical part of literature most? Not quite. What I really enjoy in any kind of writing is simply a distinctive style, an idiosyncratic diction, the sound of a voice on the page.

VERMEER:
A VIEW OF DELFT

By Anthony Bailey

In the arts a gaudy excess is usually a sign of genius. Bach doesn't compose just one cantata, he composes dozens of them. Balzac turns out sixty or seventy novels, and long ones at that. Picasso could almost certainly fill the National Gallery—and the Met as well—with just his own work. Such fecundity results from a kind of inner exuberance, the ceaseless overflow and shaping of personal energy characteristic of the artistic temperament at its most glorious. Shakespeare never blotted a line, because he was already scribbling the next one. Haydn didn't agonize over which notes should come next in a symphony or a string quartet: whatever occurred to him was bound to be just fine. Only amateurs worry about perfection.

Except, it would seem, in a few cases. Flaubert spent five years making *Madame Bovary* perfect. Were you to turn over any of Jane Austen's six novels, and shake it hard, nothing would fall out. Such books—*The Great Gatsby* and *The Good Soldier* are others—stay in our minds because of their calm and absolute rightness of design; they register less as transcriptions of sordid love affairs or hesitant courtships than as pieces of sustained verbal music, the melody of their witty or pitiless sentences supported by their closely harmonized plots. When a work of art seems without flaw, whether a lyric by A. E. Housman or a ballad like "The Way You Look Tonight," what we really mean is that every element contributes to the creation of aesthetic bliss within us, a readerly sense of "luxe, calme et volupté."

Over the past hundred years Jan Vermeer (1632–1675) has gradually replaced Raphael—whose Madonnas now seem oversweet and close to kitsch—as the most serenely perfect of all great painters. In particular, we harried moderns are drawn to his meditative stillness, to the intense feeling of mystery and Mystery in his work, to his depiction of light and air and domestic warmth, to his refusal of all visual grandiloquence. In *The Art of Painting—*

apparently Vermeer's own favorite among his pictures—he shows us an artist before an easel studying a young woman in blue made up as Clio, the muse of history. But just as Moses was only vouchsafed a glimpse of God's backside, so we can view this elusive creator only from behind, his face forcefully turned away from us. Long ago, Proust named the *View of Delft* an aesthetic touchstone, and that depiction of Vermeer's hometown must now rank as just about everyone's favorite landscape. Similarly, *The Girl with a Pearl Earring* has become as familiar as the *Mona Lisa*, and to twenty-first-century eyes far more alluring. If I myself could own any painting in the world, I would pick Vermeer's *The Little Street*—hardly more than a building, a door, and an alley, but together they elicit . . . what? It sounds corny to say a feeling of blessedness. But for a moment, while peering at these patched-up walls and dark or closed passageways, one's normally troubled heart feels hushed, peaceful, refreshed.

Though such exquisite masterpieces might seem the pictorial analogues to Mozart's exquisite music, the Dutch painter had nothing of that composer's easy genius. Vermeer was a professional artist, registered with the local guild of Saint Luke in Delft, a man who theoretically made his living by his brush, and yet he apparently finished only two or three paintings a year. And kept some of them for himself. When he died at forty-three, he left only thirty-five or thirty-six known works. How did so unproductive, so costive a painter manage to live?

Not much is known about the man, who throughout his oeuvre seems tantalizingly close but just beyond our view. There are no self-portraits as such. We can't say with whom or where he learned his consummate skills. We can only guess that his wife or daughters might have modeled for the demure and buxom women in his portraits. No one is sure what he died from (possibly a stroke). What we do know tends to be official: betrothal to Catharina Bolnes in 1653, births of fifteen children (and the deaths of at least four), enrollment in various guilds and civic groups, ownership of property, including an inn that belonged to his mother. From the evidence Vermeer was able to take up a middle-class or even patrician lifestyle, largely because he was supported by his well-to-do mother-in-law. He may also have worked as an art dealer and gotten a little revenue from the family inn. But when the soft money dried up, Vermeer couldn't repay his debts, stopped painting, took ill, and "in a day and a half . . . had gone from being healthy to being dead." His widow was forced to sell all his paintings, but they didn't earn her enough to escape bankruptcy and penury.

Anthony Bailey—for thirty-five years a *New Yorker* staff writer and author of two studies of Rembrandt—relates Vermeer's sketchy life in a leisurely and expert fashion. He surrounds the paucity of facts with some cautious speculation, an occasional poetical flourish, brief analyses of the paintings, and a series of vignettes about life in seventeenth-century Delft. William the Silent, tulipo-mania, the wars with England and France, Anton van Leeuwenhoek's discoveries with the microscope, tile making, the artistic use of the camera obscura—all these give heft and context to the intelligent guesses about Vermeer's life, career, and painting practices. In his last two chapters Bailey traces the fortunes of Vermeer's later reputation, touching on market values, the notorious Van Meegeren forgeries, and Proust's beatification of the painter in *A la Recherche du Temps Perdu*.

Though his focus is historical rather than art historical, Bailey rises periodically to a kind of impressionistic criticism, often rounding off a chapter by re-creating verbally, as in the following passage, some of the quiet intensity of Vermeer's extraordinary tableaux: "The painter thwarts our incessant demands for a story-line by freezing the action, by bringing time to a stop for an instant or two while contemplation exercises its power. The passivity or stillness he creates, reflecting his own nature, is in its way more dramatic, more active, than any action. So the young woman with a metal water jug pauses, one hand on the jug, one hand on the frame of the casement window which she seems about to open further, and the earth for a moment ceases to spin on its axis. So the woman in blue's downcast gaze travels along the lines of the letter she has received, word by word by word, over and over. Vermeer seizes the moment and it repeats itself indefinitely. And in the same way his milkmaid, his figure of Fortitude, tips her jug and the milk falls from it in a silent stream forever."

April 29, 2001

POSTSCRIPT: Washingtonians are spoiled, in more ways than one. We can take in wonderful art exhibitions—of Watteau and Vermeer, Van Gogh and Stanley Spencer, to name only some past favorites—at the National Gallery, Hirshhorn, and other museums in town. For many years I was indulgently allowed to write up exhibition catalogs and biographies of painters and printmakers for our special holiday issue of *Book World*. As usual, book reviewers educate themselves in public, and I learned a great deal just from turning those glossy pages and looking hard at what I saw.

SAMUEL PEPYS:
THE UNEQUALLED SELF

By Claire Tomalin

Samuel Pepys (1633–1703) kept his celebrated diary for only nine years, from 1660 to 1669, starting when he was twenty-six. Written in shorthand—with the racier episodes related in a potpourri of languages ("mi mano was sobra her pectus, and so did hazer with grand delight")—the book wasn't transcribed into readable English until the nineteenth century and wasn't commonly available in its unbowdlerized entirety until 1970. Despite a history of puritanical editing, the diary quickly established a reputation as one of those naughty literary classics, like Chaucer's "Miller's Tale," Defoe's *Moll Flanders*, and Wycherley's *The Country Wife*.

Pepys, though married to the strong-willed, tempestuous, half-French Elizabeth, herself a beauty, does in fact regularly interfere with pretty serving girls, ladies' maids, tavern wenches, mainly by squeezing their breasts and pinching their bottoms. But there's nothing particularly erotic or even bawdy about his accounts of seventeenth-century sexual harassment. He records a tumble with Betty Lane with the same strict accuracy as he does his pleasure in a production of *Hamlet* or the purchase of a keg of oysters. In every sense, Pepys is very much a man of accounts, in his work as a secretary to the Naval Board, in his close attention to his household funds and in his depiction of his own life. Little wonder, then, that his days, no matter how full and varied, always seem to balance: a variant on "Up betimes and to the office" opens most of the entries, just as some form of the famous "And so to bed" closes them. Everything in between is noted in precise factual sentences: even when printed as regularized English, the prose sounds like shorthand. Pepys may sometimes confess that he's sad or out of sorts, but he doesn't go maundering on and on about it, or larding his reflections with Latin quotations, as Montaigne or Sir Thomas Browne might. Instead he's a pointillist, quickly daubing in the elements of his daily life as a young careerist on the make in Restoration England.

Though watchful of the world around him and especially attentive to the miens of the men who might advance his career, Pepys also possesses an irrepressible gusto for life itself, and he works his hedonism hard: music making, theatergoing, flirting, drinking, paying social calls, reading, conversing and disputing with his wife. They're all scribbled down in his quicksilver jottings, a nonstop barrage of data, like individual frames of film that the reader joins together to achieve a cinematic sense of life zipping along at fast-forward.

No page of Pepys ever seems mediated or deliberative—he's essentially a "facts, just the facts" kind of writer. But even as the rapid notation and his run-on style ("And . . . and . . .") give his diary vivacity, they also sometimes frustrate: one hungers for expansiveness, quotation, detail, all those matters at which discursive prose normally excels. He keeps you wanting just a bit more than he delivers—one of the secrets, perhaps, of his perennial fascination. Just what, for example, were those erotic tricks by which Barbara Villiers, aka Mrs. Palmer, aka Lady Castlemaine, ensnared the king?

Not that Pepys, that ardent playgoer, didn't possess a flair for the dramatic or an eye for a well-put-together scene. The at first halting, uncertain progress of the Great Fire is underscored by his own tentativeness and confusion, succeeded by a burst of frenetic activity. He closely observes the understated drama of the royal barges landing at Whitehall, the king stepping ashore with the queen, and Lady Castlemaine watching and everybody pretending to ignore one another. Best of all may be the series of diary entries that recounts the aftermath of Pepys's involvement with Deb, his wife's maid. As Claire Tomalin says in her fine and engrossing biography, "I know of no other account of marital rage and jealousy to match this one." It opens with a mournful flourish in the middle of Pepys's write-up for October 25, 1668: "And at night W. Batelier comes and sups with us; and after supper, to have my head combed by Deb, which occasioned the greatest sorrow to me that ever I knew in this world; for my wife, coming up suddenly, did find me imbracing the girl con my hand sub su coats. . . . I wast at a wonderful loss upon it, and the girl also; and I endeavoured to put it off; but my wife was struck mute and grew angry, and as her voice came to her, grew quite out of order; and I do say little, but to bed; and my wife said little also, but could not sleep all night; but about 2 in the morning waked me and cried."

During the next weeks, Pepys's life becomes so hellish that he grows afraid to go home at night. Oddly, though, in spite of all the accusations and denials and general despair, the errant husband and his wronged wife have sex "more times since this falling-out then in I believe twelve months before—and with more pleasure to her then I think in all the time of our marriage before." Such are the strange byways of passion.

Because Pepys's diary spotlights his young manhood so brilliantly, it is easy to forget about his impoverished youth or the last thirty-odd years of his public life. Though Tomalin admires the diarist as an almost inadvertent genius ("the most ordinary and the most extraordinary writer you will ever meet"), she frames his self-portrait within the context of the times and his entire public career. To explain how a tailor's son rose to power as, roughly, a cabinet minister in charge of naval affairs, she must describe the civil war, Cromwell, the machinations to restore Charles II, and the impact of the plague. She details the system of patronage, bribes, and quid pro quo that kept the Restoration's merry world spinning along. She shows how the older Pepys survived the Popish Plot—in which he was accused of being a Catholic rebel—and she discusses his interactions with the great men of the period: kings, aristocrats such as his patron the earl of Sandwich, industrial magnates, and eminent scholars (Robert Hooke, Christopher Wren, Hans Sloane). Not least, Tomalin reminds us of Pepys's physical stoicism: he endured painful and delicate surgery for kidney stones at twenty-five, with a fair possibility of death, and worried for years that he was going blind. Because reading and writing eventually caused him such ocular distress, he abandoned his diary.

Not only an able biographer in the lively English style of Richard Holmes, Michael Holroyd, and Victoria Glendinning, Claire Tomalin also possesses a particularly graceful and pleasing diction, a proper sense of measure (by no means is her subject a wholly admirable, let alone a heroic, figure), and a piquant willingness to express her own views: we are left in no doubt as to how reprehensible she finds Pepys's sophomoric groping and pursuit of young girls, or how tough-minded his wife and his later "companion" Mary Skinner must have been to put up with him.

In itself highly agreeable reading, *Samuel Pepys: The Unequalled Self* should also lead one to either start on or return to this most irresistible, this most addictive, of English diaries. Expect a good time: "It is strange what weather we have had all this winter; no cold at all, but the ways are dusty and the flyes fly up and down, and the rosebushes are full of leaves; such a time of the year as never was known in this world before here. This day, many more of the fifth monarchy men were hanged."

December 15, 2002

BOSWELL'S PRESUMPTUOUS TASK:
THE MAKING OF THE LIFE
OF DR. JOHNSON

By Adam Sisman

Fans of Boswell's *Life of Johnson* (1791)—the greatest of all biographies and probably the most entertaining book in English literature—have had much to huzzah about lately. Early in 2001 Peter Martin brought out a new scholarly life of James Boswell. More recently, Liza Picard's *Dr. Johnson's London* provided a guide to, as its subtitle has it, eighteenth-century "coffee-houses and climbing boys, medicine, toothpaste and gin, poverty and press-gangs, freakshows and female education," and a gallimaufry of much else, all related with a gusto worthy of "the Great Cham" himself. Even Beryl Bainbridge's much admired historical novel *According to Queeney* is set in Johnsonian circles.

To such plenty, we may now add this lively chronicle of how a naive and lusty, sometimes melancholy and frequently drunk Scots lawyer came to write the life of England's most formidable man of letters. Adam Sisman brings an amateur's zeal and a novelist's flair to *Boswell's Presumptuous Task*, but he makes clear that his narrative is based almost entirely on the research of others. Over the past five or six decades the so-called "Boswell factory"—with corporate headquarters at Yale—has edited and published Boswell's correspondence, a dozen hefty volumes of his journals (the first installment, *Boswell's London Journal*, became a 1950s best seller, largely because of its Pepys-like frankness about its author's amorous exertions), and numerous works of biography, criticism, and history. Though the main work has been completed, revised editions and ever more subtle works of scholarship continue to emerge from New Haven even now.

Not so long ago, James Boswell (1740–1795) was regarded as little more than a kind of idiot-savant who managed to remember and record what his betters said over beverages at the Mitre or around dinner at the Thrales.

Macaulay, as Sisman reminds us, first fixed this phantasmic image of the biographer in a celebrated essay review (1831); as late as 1910 this article was still being used as the entry for Johnson in the *Encyclopaedia Britannica*. But the discovery of the Boswell manuscripts—journals, drafts, memoranda—at Malahide Castle in the 1920s started a scholarly revolution. As Boswell's writing was studied more and more, it became increasingly evident that the author of the *Life of Johnson* possessed a genius all his own.

But what you gain on the straightaways, you lose on the roundabouts. Just as Boswell was starting to earn a little respect, some Johnsonians began to attack his work for what one might call its biographical hegemony: the *Life* was wonderful, yes, but it presented a skewed, partial image of its subject. In particular, Boswell overemphasized the older Dr. Johnson, the blustery literary autocrat of the tea table. In fact, it was claimed, the Samuel Johnson who really mattered could be found mainly in his writings: in poems like "London" ("Slow rises worth by poverty depress'd"), the moral essays in *The Rambler*, the brilliant criticism embedded in the biographical *Lives of the Poets* ("Whoever wishes to attain an English style, familiar but not coarse, and elegant but not ostentatious, must give his days and nights to the volumes of Addison"). These works, previously dismissed as prolix, Latinate, and ponderous, were reinvigorated through new editions (from Yale). Popular biographies, by Walter Jackson Bate and John Wain, as well as the somewhat later *Dr. Johnson and Mr. Savage*, by Richard Holmes, also magnified the Johnson before or without Boswell: young Sam as a Grub Street hack, "Dictionary" Johnson as a man combating demons (physical tics, partial blindness, melancholy, the failure of his play *Irene*, fear of death, "toil, envy, want, the patron and the jail"), all in all, a far more conflicted and humane figure than the boldly assertive soliloquist that Boswell knew. Donald Greene went so far as to claim that the *Life* should be regarded as autobiography, an account of its author's particular infatuation with an intellectual father figure. After all, scholars have calculated that the duo met on only some four hundred days over the last twenty-two years of Johnson's life.

What Sisman offers the aficionado of the Augustan Age—once romantically described by George Saintsbury as "a place of repose and refreshment"—is a sprightly and touching portrait of Boswell as he prepares for, labors over, and finally brings to a triumphant conclusion his great work. His autocratic father, a high court judge, wanted Jamie to stay in Scotland and practice his lawyering, then expand the family estate at Auchinleck. Boswell, however, was infatuated with celebrity—early on he studied with David Hume and Adam Smith at Edinburgh—and eventually talked the laird into supporting him on annual trips to London. There he hobnobbed with Johnson and the eminences of his circle—the actor David Garrick, painter Joshua Reynolds, politician Edmund Burke, historian Edward Gibbon, and Shakespeare scholar Edmond Malone (this last served as Boswell's goad and editor when he came to write the *Life*). Required to study abroad, Boswell managed to pay his respects to such Enlightenment grandees as Frederick the Great, the Corsican leader Pascal Paoli, and the philosophes Voltaire and Rousseau (even—the randy scamp— enjoying the favors of Jean-Jacques's common-law wife).

From all accounts, young Boswell radiated boyish, almost feckless charm, a naturalness that made him endearing (or sometimes annoying) in this age of perukes and royal levees. He blithely chased after prostitutes—and confessed his transgressions to his wife, who was understanding, if hardly sympathetic, given that her husband was prey to periodic bouts of venereal disease. He also answered to the beck and call of the monstrous Lord Lonsdale, a kind of Augustan equivalent to a Tammany Hall political boss, in the vain hope of gaining a seat in Parliament. He endured periodic depression. Vacillated over the least little things. Drank. Toadied. Even after the *Life* became a best seller (second only to Burke's *Reflections on the Revolution in France*), Boswell managed to slide back into poverty and despair. He died, of kidney failure, at the age of fifty-four, in his own mind a sot and a failure.

All of which goes to remind us, yet again, of that sometimes immense gulf between the artist who creates and the man who suffers. For all the tribulations and sorrows of its author, the *Life of Johnson* ranks as one of the most high-spirited books in the world. Out of inveterate journal keeping, Boswell developed an easy, conversational style. What's more he aimed, as much as possible, to organize his book into scenes, investing it with a dramatic, even theatrical flavor. Yet how did he manage to capture so much of his major star's personality on the page? Apparently the young lawyer trained his mind to remember any conversation's give-and-take, to jot some rough notes as soon afterward as possible, and then over the next few days to expand these into detailed journal entries. As he spent more and more time with Johnson, so he learned to emulate his hero's turns of phrase. Thus, when people related rough anecdotes or half-remembered stories, he was able to recast them, when necessary, into Johnsonese.

The *Life of Johnson* was a great success from the first, though some contemporaries complained that its author was a ferrety little upstart with no sense of the proprieties. Up till then most biographies, after all, had tended to be idealized portraits à la Plutarch. Hadn't Boswell violated the laws of hospitality in recording private conversations? A few salons actually shunned him out of fear he would record the drunken palaver. But, as Boswell protested, without Johnson around, why would he bother?

In the end, one takes away from Sisman a sharp sense of the contingency of literary work—at any moment, Boswell might have just given up. Consider: he has no regular employment; his debts are enormous and never stop growing; one of Johnson's executors, John Hawkins, produces a biography before him; his beloved wife grows sick and dies; their four children start to run wild; he not only drinks to intoxication but also gets arrested for it. Yet still Boswell persists. He has pitched his life upon a cast, and he means to stand the hazard of the die. The *Life of Johnson* will justify his existence. And it does.

If you've never read Boswell, Adam Sisman offers an ingratiating introduction to his masterpiece (as well as his *Tour of the Hebrides*). I'm halfway through my latest reading, and as soon as I finish typing these words I plan to settle back and lose myself again in that world of coffeehouses and repartee: "Were it not for imagination, Sir, a man would be as happy in the arms of a chambermaid as of a Duchess. . . . Sir, I have two very cogent reasons for not printing any list of subscribers;—one, that I have lost all the names,—the other, that I have spent all the money. . . . Politics are now nothing more than a means of rising in the world. . . . Claret is the liquor for boys; port for men; but he who aspires to be a hero must drink brandy." Who would wish to stop? When a man is tired of Boswell's *Life of Johnson*, he is tired of life.

August 19, 2001

MASON & DIXON

By Thomas Pynchon

Shortly after *Gravity's Rainbow* appeared in 1973, Thomas Pynchon reportedly signed a contract for two future books. One was tentatively titled "The Japanese Insurance Adjuster"; Pynchon scholars such as Edward Mendelson have speculated that parts of this book may have been cannibalized for *Vineland* (1990). When that serio-goofy California novel appeared, many readers felt more or less disappointed: for all its merits, *Vineland* just couldn't be the awesome masterwork that Pynchon fans were patiently awaiting. Obviously, it was a breather, the analogue to the novella-length *Crying of Lot 49* (1967), which the reclusive author brought out between his ambitious first book, *V.* (1963), and his youthful summa of modern history and culture, *Gravity's Rainbow.*

The other novel, envisioned nearly a quarter of a century ago, was at that time called "The Mason-Dixon Line." Did Pynchon, nearly sixty, then know how many years he would devote to this project? Did he, as rumor has it, actually walk the entire line, the boundary between Maryland, Delaware, and Pennsylvania established in the 1760s by the astronomer Charles Mason and the surveyor Jeremiah Dixon? He certainly must have spent considerable time in libraries, mastering the arcana of surveying and early modern science, picking up the contemporary lingo of sailors, fops, Quakers, Dutch businessmen, preachers, Indians, slaves, colonial farmers, whores, and Philadelphia lawyers, gathering folktales and historical anecdotes, above all, sucking in the flavor of eighteenth-century speech, acquiring a bone-deep feel for its sentences.

The long-anticipated result, *Mason & Dixon*, proves a dazzling work of imaginative re-creation, a marvel-filled historical novel, set largely in colonial America, but with extended side trips to England, South Africa, and the island of St. Helena. In its pages Pynchon sets the reader down in a bustling world where bewigged men of science believe in ghosts and magic, where geometry may butt up against ancient myth, where dogs talk and golems stride through the wilderness and Jesuit agents are masters of guile and disguise. There are thrilling escapes, melodramatic revelations, glimpses of the great (Ben Franklin, Samuel Johnson), much reflection on death, dozens of songs (a favorite Pynchon device), and the steady growl of colonial complaint against King George and his rule. Not least, though, *Mason & Dixon* is a paean to friendship, a buddy book about an English Don Quixote and a Scots Sancho Panza at large in the New World, a 1760s *On the Road*.

Though daunting in appearance—the text is stippled with capitalized nouns and strange words—the novel is in fact fairly accessible and exceptionally funny, ever the saving grace of big demanding novels. Pynchon's humor takes many forms: puns, anachronisms, mimicry, in-house jokes, pastiche. Two ships, for instance, are named the HMS *Inconvenience* and HMS *Unreflective*. "You know of the *Ecole de Piraterie* at Toulon? Famous," says one character, adding that the notorious St. Foux "has lately been appointed to the Kiddean Chair." Elsewhere Pynchon mentions a seaman named O'Brian, old Pat being the best storyteller in the navy, with an unrivaled knowledge of complicated rigging.

Deftly mixing past and present, Pynchon frequently takes familiar proverbs and gives them a periphrastic, neoclassical spin: "this island . . . not ev'ryone's Brochette of Curried Albacore, is it?"; "Inexpensive Salvo"; even the Laurel and Hardyesque "Another bonny gahn-on tha've got us into. . . ." There are the usual funny names—the Reverend Wicks Cherrycoke, the Redzinger family—and an aunt who tells her nieces and nephews tall tales about her wild youth: " 'Twas given me by the Sultan. Dear Mustapha, 'Stuffy,' we called him in the Harem chambers, amongst ourselves. . . ." At one point a spooky clockwork duck hopes to attend a performance of the opera *Margherita e Don Aldo* (recall that a Margherita is a daisy, then think Disney). At a hanging, young aristos critique the condemned man's clothes: " 'Hideous suit,' remarks one of the Fops, '—what's that shade, some kind of Fawn? altogether too light for the occasion.' " Pynchon also periodically drops in a bad pun: " 'Sari,' corrects Mason. 'Not at all Sir,—'Twas I who was sarong.' " Of course, there are numerous more recondite literary jokes too: " 'Couldn't believe it,' reported the room-steward Mr. Gonzago, 'like watching Hamlet or something, isn't it?' " (The dumb show in Shakespeare's play is called "The Murder of Gonzago.")

In general, *Mason & Dixon* follows the actual events of its heroes' professional lives pretty faithfully—but makes sure that the duo bump up against a steady parade of eccentric, Monty Pythonesque characters, most with stories to tell. The Thermos bottle, pizza, shopping malls, and the self-winding watch make their American debuts. And Pynchon's flair for shoptalk proves an especial joy. For instance, here a colonial huckster starts his pitch: "Scandinavians!

yes, the famous Swedish Loggers, each the equal of any ten Axmen these Colonies may produce. Finest double-bit Axes, part of the Package, lifetime Warranty on the Heads, seventy-two-hour replacement Policy, customiz'd Handle for each Axman, for 'Bjorn may not swing like Stig, nor Stig like Sven,' as the famous Timothy Tox might say,—Swedish Steel here, secret Processes guarded for years, death to reveal them, take you down a perfect swathe of Forest, trimm'd and cleared, fast as you're likely to chain at the distance.—Parts of a single great machine,—human muscle and stamina become but adjunct to the deeper realities of Steel that never needs Sharpening, never rusts. . . ."

As it happens, miles into the wilderness, the survey team and its axmen encounter a case of—" 'Kastoranthropy,' Professor Voam shaking his head, 'And haven't I seen it do things to a man. Tragick.' " Seems that people suffering from this malady turn into giant beavers during the full moon. Naturally, the wife of the Were-Beaver soon instigates a contest between her husband and blond Stig to determine who can fell the most trees during a moonlit night. Huge bets are placed. Alas, the astronomers fail to remember the scheduled lunar eclipse, with disastrous consequences. About this time they also learn that Stig is not really a Swede but a mysterious Northern being who has mastered the subtle art of "impersonating a Swede." "Is ours not the Age of Metamorphosis, with any turn of Fortune a possibility?"

No Thomas Pynchon novel is authentic without its dollop of paranoia. Mason and Dixon speculate constantly about whether they are being manipulated by their superiors in Britain, or by Providence, or by other, stranger forces. The Indians speak of ancient Guardians; Dixon finds himself spirited away for a visit to the gnomelike creatures who inhabit the Hollow Earth; there are hints of aliens from outer space and a time when people could fly. At one point the British East India Company is referred to as the Company in solemn tones that suggest an eighteenth-century CIA. Obviously, the colonists are meeting secretly in taverns, talking sedition, and there is occasional fear of Kabbalists, Illuminati, and Freemasons. But a greater danger than any of these lurks behind the world's paper-thin stage scenery: the Jesuits and—shades of *Lot 49*'s secret postal system—their so-called Telegraph, made up of giant balloons and beams focused on parabolically perfect mirrors: "As expected of a Jesuit invention, timing and discipline are ev'rything. It is rumor'd that the Fathers limit themselves to giving orders, whilst the actual labor is entrusted to the Telegraph Squads, elite teams of converted Chinese, drill'd, through Loyolan methods, to perform with split-second timing the balloon launchings, to learn the art of aiming the beam, and, its reflection once acquir'd, to keep most faithfully fix'd upon it,—for like the glance of a Woman at a Ball, it must be held for a certain time before conveying a Message."

Adds the magus-like Ben Franklin, "If we could but capture one Machine intact, we might take it apart to see how it works. . . . Yet, what use? They'll only invent another twice as fiendish,—for here are conjoin'd the two most powerful sources of Brain-Power on Earth, the one as closely harness'd to its Disciplin'd Rage for Jesus, as the other to the Escape into the Void, which is the very Asian Mystery. Together, they make up a small Army of Dark Engineers who could run the World. The Sino-Jesuit conjunction may prove a greater threat to Christendom than ever the Mongols or the Moors."

Division, boundaries, chains, lines—such visible and invisible constraints provide the central metaphor of the novel. The melancholy Mason is obsessed with his dead wife, Rebekah, whose spirit occasionally crosses "that grimly patrolled Line, the very essence of Division." Slaves, in South Africa and America, are circumscribed in every aspect of existence; Dutch girls live constantly reminded "of the Boundaries there to be o'er stepped." While surveying, Mason and Dixon divide future states, at one point even run the line through a farmhouse and separate a man from his wife. Their unswerving path, we learn, violates the *sha* or spirit of the land, may even be "a conduit of Evil." In their own lives the pair constantly suffer from the barriers of class and ethnic prejudice, Dixon being from a Scots coal-mining family, Mason the son of a baker: both are denied membership in the Royal Society, and the coveted post of Astronomer Royal goes to a well-connected booby. Throughout these pages traditional distinctions are also deliberately blurred: between the organic and the mechanical, the past and the present, the fabulous and the historical. Moreover, since many of the jokes and allusions make sense only from a modern perspective—a kind of reversed palimpsest—one must, so to speak, always read between the lines.

This blurring takes its most dramatic effect two-thirds of the way through the book. The Reverend Cherrycoke has been relating the adventures of his friends Mason and Dixon as a Christmas treat, twenty years after the fact. During the evening two cousins vie for the attention of the beautiful Tenebrae, who eventually retires to peruse, secretly, an installment from a gothicky serial called *The Ghastly Fop*. In this sensationalist pulp a young wife is captured by savages and transported to a Jesuit redoubt in Quebec, where she is prepared, à la *The Story of O*, to become a Widow of Christ, i.e., part of an international network of pliant, selfless courtesans. When she and a Chinese acolyte escape from Father Zarbazo, the Wolf of Jesus, the couple eventually reach the safety of the Mason-Dixon camp. Smoothly the "fictional" Eliza and Captain Zhang slide right into Cherrycoke's "factual" narrative. Matters grow even more complicated when Zhang—in order to elude his nemesis—alters his appearance so that he looks exactly like Father Zarbazo, a master of disguise. But then, perhaps, he has been the insidious *El Lobo de Jesus* all along?

Along with its japery and playful artifice, *Mason & Dixon* conveys a real sense of felt life, of the years slowly rolling by: the two heroes only gradually recognize their affection and need for each other, and both ultimately discover that their fondest dreams will never be fulfilled. By comparison with Pynchon's trademark flash and narrative density, this new book seems unusually serene, almost mellow, avoiding both dramatic tension and serious erotic content. There are wonderful descriptive passages, however: at his worktable the aged Dixon "erases his sketching mistakes with bits of Bread he then keeps in a Pocket, not wishing to cast them where Birds might eat the Lead and come to harm." Still, I doubt that *Mason & Dixon* will attract the computer freaks, science fiction fans, and Gen-Xers who look upon *Gravity's Rainbow* as a kind of modern scripture (as little read, I suspect, as the ancient one). In truth, the novel will probably appeal most to the people who first celebrated Pynchon, the 1960s generation that is now entering its own late middle age.

At the book's climax, Mason and Dixon glimpse the edge of the Old America, a world of Indian mounds, magical Warrior Paths, giant vegetables, Telluric power sources, and invisible "Protectors." This experience of the "rapture of the west" never quite leaves them. It is, of course, an old dream: the prospect of an Edenic garden where the Fall never took place, the inviting legend of the Big Rock Candy Mountain, the recurrent sense that once, on these shores, mankind might have escaped some of the bonds and charters and boundaries that confined human beings elsewhere. *Mason & Dixon* transports us to the period when that mythic, natural geography—the realm of Vineland the Good—was first fading away, as surveyors divided the land and astronomers charted a sky across which there will all too soon come a certain hideous screaming.

Still, one mustn't end a review of this dark carnival of a book on a melancholy note. After all, Mason first meets his beloved Rebekah when he is nearly crushed to death by a gigantic cheese. When Dixon offers a toast "To the pursuit of happiness," a young man with red hair wonders whether he would mind "if I use the Phrase sometime?" A politically incorrect colonist asserts, "Bodices are for ripping, and there's an end upon it." Even a colonial sampler reads EXPECT INDIANS. In the strangest of all his jokes, Pynchon actually turns George Washington's manservant into a black-Jewish comedian, with a taste for terrible Borscht Belt shtick. " 'You see what I have to put up with,' groans Col. Washington. 'It's makin' me just mee-shugginah.' " In the pages of *Mason*

& Dixon humor may surprise you anywhere: when Dixon angrily frees some slaves, he decides to whip, maybe even kill, their swaggering, foul-mouthed exploiter, who immediately crumples and pleads, "No! Please! My little ones! O Tiffany! Jason! . . . Scott!"

Clearly there are still no boundaries to Thomas Pynchon's genius.

April 27, 1997

BLAKE

By Peter Ackroyd

William Blake (1757–1827) may be the most perplexing major figure in English literature. On the one hand, "The Tyger" is—according to William Harmon in *The Top 500 Poems*—the single most popular short lyric in our language. Young children learn to chant its haunting singsong in elementary school: "Tyger, Tyger, burning bright / In the forests of the night." A dozen of Blake's other poems—including "London," "The Mental Traveller," "The Chimney Sweeper"—are nearly as well known, and a great many of his lines will be familiar even to people who seldom read poetry: "To see a world in a grain of sand. . . . Oh, rose, thou art sick. . . . Sooner murder an infant in its cradle than nurse unacted desires. . . . Every harlot was a virgin once." Set to music by Parry, some of the poet's words about "chariots of fire" have even become a thrillingly patriotic hymn: "I will not cease from Mental Fight / Nor shall my Sword sleep in my hand / Till we have built Jerusalem / In England's green & pleasant land."

That's the one hand. On the other, we have the Blake of the long "prophecies"—*The Four Zoas, Europe, The Song of Los, Milton,* and, greatest of all, *Jerusalem.* These are among the most recondite poems in English. One scholar figured, in 1961, that the number of people "who have read *Jerusalem* . . . with substantial understanding must be less than a hundred." Certainly that number has grown, for there has been a great blossoming of Blake studies during the past thirty-five years, but, aside from graduate students in early Romantic poetry, most readers still find these declamatory epics daunting, confusing, and tedious. "Giant forms" with names like prescription drugs—Urizen, Enitharmion, Urthona—battle and seduce each other; there is much talk of Spectres and Emanations; and the poetry itself careers from prosaic lists reminiscent of Leviticus to a visionary excess that would give pause even to the author of Revelation. And yet, throughout these apocalyptic dithyrambs one discovers lines as moving as any in the *Songs of Innocence*:

What is the price of Experience?
do men buy it for a song?
Or wisdom for a dance in
the street? No, it is bought
with the price
Of all that a man hath,
his house, his wife,
his children. . . .

In a very general way, there are two schools of modern Blake criticism, not necessarily antagonistic (though Blake himself notes that "without contraries is no progression"). S. Foster Damon, Northrop Frye, and Harold Bloom aim to clarify the language and grammar of Blake's symbolism, to make poetic sense of what seem like mere farragoes of mystical blather. David Erdman, Mark Schorer, and, most recently, E. P. Thompson approach Blake's work from a historical perspective and reveal how deeply the prophecies are informed by contemporary politics, a long antinomian tradition in English working-class circles, and incidents from the author's life. As it happens, both these approaches tend to be strongly text-oriented. Yet Blake stands almost alone among the great poets in also being a great artist, one whose words truly can't be divorced from the illustrations that surround them: when Blake speaks of Orc or Los one needs to see these despondent and powerful figures, for all the world like Michelangelo nudes condemned to some metaphysical hell. As a result, current researches now focus on the poet-artist's actual engraved and colored pages, and the most important Blake works of the 1990s are undoubtedly the six volumes of facsimiles published by Princeton as *The Illuminated Books of William Blake.*

But where should an ordinary reader, enchanted by the simpler poems or the sardonic proverbs of *The Marriage of Heaven and Hell* ("Prudence is a rich, ugly old maid courted by Incapacity"), go to begin exploring Blake's complex universe? Peter Ackroyd's new biography provides just the right starting place. Without being pedantic, it covers the basic facts of Blake's life, offers dozens of superb reproductions (including "The Ancient of Days," that famous dorm-room poster of God dividing up the cosmos with a compass), and blithely eschews lengthy analyses of the verse. Instead Ackroyd emphasizes Blake the visionary Londoner, like Turner or Dickens, and convincingly relates the poet's work to the social upheavals of his time. A novelist (*Hawksmoor*) as well as a biographer (of T. S. Eliot and Dickens), Ackroyd writes with clarity and ease: his book is consistently intelligent, entertaining, and affectionate. One closes its pages full of admiration for

Blake and eager to study his pictures and read his poetry. In short, a good popular life.

That shouldn't sound like faint praise: nowadays we often employ biographies as the means to gaining a basic understanding of a writer. After all, only the most eager and determined will turn the densely packed pages of Frye's *Fearful Symmetry*, Damon's *A Blake Dictionary*, or Erdman's *Prophet against Empire* (still the three most useful general works of Blake criticism). As it is, in under 400 pages Ackroyd gives unity and drama to a relatively uneventful life, building on the most illuminating anecdotes, quoting the most famous poetic touchstones. For instance, Ackroyd reminds us that Blake's London—"a Human awful wonder of God"—swarmed with New Age religions (such as Swedenborgianism), radical thinkers (like Tom Paine), and visionary artists: the poet Cowper went insane because he knew, beyond a doubt, that he was irrevocably damned; the satirical artist Gillray had to be committed when he started to imagine that he was Rubens; and Henry Fuseli—who could swear in nine languages—shocked the genteel public with his still highly disturbing *Nightmare*, in which a lecherous imp squats on a swooning woman's breast. Blake, we learn, read trashy gothic novelists and often sat in the audience at schlocky melodramas; but he also got up each morning, laid the fire and made tea for his wife, Catherine; worked every day at his copper engraving and completed 580 commercial plates; spent his last years in utter poverty; and died singing.

Above all, Ackroyd makes Blake live for the modern reader. He shows us an artist who draws dirty pictures and mocks the great ("a ha to Doctor Johnson / Said Scipio Africanus / Lift up my Roman petticoatt / And kiss my Roman Anus"). He stresses the poet's startling and liberated sexual philosophy: "In a wife I would desire / What in whores is always found / The lineaments of gratified desire." Not surprisingly, the creator of the "proverbs of Hell" can be casually caustic: of the esteemed academic painter Joshua Reynolds, he once wrote, "This man was hired to depress art." As an adult this same Blake—who had virtually no education other than training as a painter and printmaker—taught himself, with relative ease, to read Latin, Greek, French, and Italian; his casual annotations in a wide range of books "prove, if nothing else, what an instinctively intelligent man he was."

Like all serious scholars, Ackroyd rejects the common nineteenth-century view that Blake was mad, aptly observing that madness is frequently "an analogue for religious belief in an increasingly secular and deistical world." Blake's prophecies, he stresses, blazoned forth during an Industrial Revolution fueled by the forces of separation, exclusion, and reification; like William Morris a century later, the revolutionary Blake wrote in the hope of restoring his world to a lost spiritual unity, one that he associated with ancient Albion. Though hardly certifiable, Blake nevertheless did unnerve acquaintances when he claimed to converse with spirits and glimpse angels: "What it will be Questioned When the Sun rises do you not see a round Disk of fire somewhat like a Guinea?" "O no no I see an Innumerable company of the Heavenly host crying Holy Holy Holy is the Lord God Almighty." Blake was always a poet of eternity as well as of the eighteenth century.

In his old age, after a life's work largely unnoticed and by then nearly forgotten, Blake ruefully observed, "What is fortune but an outward accident, for a few years, sixty at the most, and then gone?" As he lay calmly dying, he added, "I cannot consider death as anything but a removing from one room to another." In this accepting spirit he passed his last hours sketching his wife's portrait, displaying a serenity that is almost too saintlike. I prefer to think of Blake as a short, red-haired, and pugnacious Cockney, a man who worked with his hands every day and whose fierce motto should be that of every true artist: "I must Create a System or be enslaved by another Man's. / I will not Reason and compare: My business is to create."

May 12, 1996

THE LUNAR MEN: FIVE FRIENDS WHOSE CURIOSITY CHANGED THE WORLD

By Jenny Uglow

"In the time of the Lunar men science and art were not separated: you could be an inventor and designer, an experimenter and a poet, a dreamer and an entrepreneur all at once." Lunar men? Is this some science fiction vision—à la Edgar Rice Burroughs or Olaf Stapledon—of humankind's future evolution? To the contrary. Jenny Uglow's magnificent group history chronicles a last great upsurge of the all-embracing Renaissance spirit, when a few amateurs and tinkerers of genius ushered in, ironically enough, the gloomy Age of Machinery and Specialization.

In the final third of the eighteenth century, in Birmingham, England, of all places, in the middle of a region long known for its potteries, metal works, and refineries, a handful of friends with lively, wide-ranging minds formed a philosophical and scientific association. While Samuel Johnson lounged in fashionable London cafés, trading quips and drinking tea with members of the Club, the Lunar Society's founders simply met once a month to discuss chemistry, geology, and metallurgy, to carry on experiments, to exchange ideas and daydreams. Along the way, the group slowly "changed the world." They invented and promoted the steam engine, discovered oxygen and digitalis, soda water and laughing gas, speculated fearlessly about fossils and the earth's strata, categorized plants and identified minerals, built gigantic factories, dug canals, and wrote best-selling poems against slavery, as well as epics inspired by Linnaeus, tracts on education, and a novel for children that went through 140 editions in ninety years.

They also supplied the world with cups and saucers and buttons and hooks and new coins and buckles and delicate vases and heavy-duty mining equipment. And all the while they fiddled around with contraptions and homemade "gimcracks"—primitive copy machines, eight-legged wooden horses, new carriage designs, hydrogen balloons, sidereal clocks, horizontal windmills, pyrometers, even speaking machines. Provincials these men may have been, but they took all knowledge for their province. And not only knowledge. As James Boswell wrote of one, "I shall never forget Mr. Boulton's expression to me: 'I sell here, Sir, what all the world desires to have—Power.'"

But just who were these "Lunatics" who met when the moon was full over Birmingham? In rough order of importance—there were a few more than just the five of Uglow's subtitle—they included the immensely fat physician Erasmus Darwin; the swashbuckling manufacturer and businessman Matthew Boulton; the one-legged master potter Josiah Wedgwood; the multitalented and virile (twenty-two children) Richard Edgeworth; the scientist, dissenting minister, and revolutionary thinker Joseph Priestley; the depressed and hypochondriacal "mechanic" James Watt (inventor of the steam engine); the romantic millionaire Thomas Day; the chemist and glass expert John Keir; and, not least, William Small, who joined the group after returning from America, where he had been Thomas Jefferson's teacher (meeting Small, said Jefferson, "probably fixed the destinies of my life"). All these became close friends and business partners, shared their enthusiasms and discoveries, and together crackled with a creative synergy that our modern think tanks can only dream of and envy.

The Lunar Men is a grand story—imagine a kind of historical version of *Atlas Shrugged* set in eighteenth-century England (and minus Ayn Rand's tendentious economic didacticism). Of course, here James Watt, with the help of the industrialist Boulton, starts, rather than stops, the engine of the world. Like Rand's heroes, these overreachers—several of whom began their careers as boy apprentices—were not merely gifted; they were determined and indefatigable. Wedgwood, for instance, carried out five thousand trials before he figured out how to produce "jasperware," the Wedgwood china celebrated to this day. He brought this same resolve to his personal life. When he found himself unable to walk because of osteomyelitis in one of his legs, he consulted doctors, who gravely informed him that the only treatment was to have the limb amputated. This in an age before anesthesia, the age of unstoppable hemorrhages and gangrene. Drugging himself with laudanum, Wedgwood observed the entire operation and survived. He would later use his wooden leg to smash substandard pots.

Then there was John Keir, chemist, classicist (he translated Polybius), and inventor of a cheap industrial process to produce the alkali used in the manufacture of soap. This made his fortune: in fact, Uglow suggests that the decline in mortality rates at the end of the eighteenth century may owe as much to the increasing use of Keir's soap as to any medical advance. While a young man, Keir himself fell ill with yellow fever in the West Indies: "From his porthole in the hospital ship he watched sharks tear the bodies of fellow soldiers who had died of the disease until 'the sea was tinged with blood, and their mangled limbs were seen floating on the surface.' He gradually weakened, unable to speak or move, until the army surgeon declared 'he has gone too,' but just as a man arrived to throw him overboard he managed to scrawl a note asking for antimony, an unusual medicine, although long ago recommended by Paracelsus. This was granted 'only from the persuasion that his case was hopeless' and to the surprise of all he recovered."

"Knowledge is important," declared Keir, "but whether the discovery is made by one man or another is not deserving of consideration." (He did, however, take the secret of his alkali process with him to the grave.) Joseph Priestley didn't care about making money from his discoveries, but he did want credit. Remembered as a great chemist, Priestley was born the son of a Yorkshire cloth dresser, and soon orphaned. As a boy he studied Latin, Greek, and Hebrew, then taught himself French, German, and Italian well enough to act as a translator. He eventually became a dissenting minister, composed standard textbooks like *The History and Present State of Electricity*, nearly sailed with Captain Cook around the world (his appointment was blocked), grew to rival Tom Paine as an advocate for political liberty, and speculated with uncanny insight into the true nature of things: "He saw matter as made up of points, centres of force in perpetual motion governed by attraction and repulsion—our feeling of 'solidity' was simply resistance to force."

Generous with his scientific knowledge, courageous in his political convictions, and personally kindhearted and likable, Priestley may be the most sheerly admirable of all the Lunar Men. Consequently Uglow's most dramatic chapter, near the end of her book, describes in horrific detail the smashing of Priestley's church, house, library, laboratory—everything he had lived for—by a rampaging anti-Jacobin mob. "All Priestley's instruments were destroyed—his mortars made by Wedgwood, his retorts, his flasks, his machines." This was, writes Uglow, "a riot against intellectualism, and its abiding image is of book-burning. One witness remembered that 'the highroads for full half a mile of the house were strewed with books, and that on entering the library there was not a dozen volumes on the shelves, while the floor was covered several inches deep with the torn manuscripts.' " On the walls of Birmingham a slogan was chalked: "No philosophers—Church and King Forever."

That last phrase takes us into a world we recognize as very much our own, and reminds us again of all that the Lunar Men fought against. As Erasmus Darwin eloquently insisted, ignorance and credulity had long "misled and enslaved mankind," while philosophy or experimental science "has in all ages endeavoured to oppose their progress, and to loosen the shackles they had imposed: philosophers have on this account been called unbelievers, unbelievers of what? Of the fictions of fancy, of witchcraft, hobgoblins, apparitions, vampires, fairies; of the influence of the stars on human actions, miracles wrought by the bones of saints, the flight of ominous birds, the predictions from the bones of dying animals, expounders of dreams, fortune-tellers, conjurors, modern prophets, necromancy, cheiromancy, animal magnetism, metallic tractors, with endless variety of folly? These they have disbelieved and despised, but have ever bowed their hoary heads to Truth and Nature."

Little wonder that the Lunar Men, for all their business sense, were also "radicals, educators and firm believers in the democracy of knowledge." Shortly after the riots, the aging Priestley emigrated to America.

My own favorite Lunatic—and I think Uglow's too—is Erasmus Darwin, author of *The Loves of the Plants*, advocate of evolution long before his grandson Charles, a man of such Falstaffian girth that he cut a semicircle out of his dining room table to fit his belly, a botanist who could announce that the shrub *Kalmia*—which he'd never seen—"has precisely the colours of a seraph's wing," and a lover who, despite being middle-aged and pock-marked, stuttering and limping, was able to win the affections of the young and beautiful Elizabeth Pole and then to marry her after the death of their respective spouses. Darwin traveled all over the county treating patients (the poor for free), scribbling away in his carriage—a casebook on disease (*Zoonomia*), a translation of Linnaeus, epic verse about the natural world. Horace Walpole called *The Loves of the Plants* the "most delicious poem on earth," while Coleridge found it nauseating, though still proclaimed that "Dr. Darwin possesses, perhaps a greater range of knowledge than any other man in Europe." Imagine a British Benjamin Franklin—with a touch of Saint Nicholas. What a man! He even coined the beautiful word "iridescent."

Darwin wasn't always a good doctor, though, tending to overprescribe opium, which led to the addiction and death of his friend Wedgwood's son Tom. But his medical reputation grew nonetheless. Uglow relates this perhaps apocryphal story: "A mysterious gentleman arrived from London, to consult him 'as the greatest physician in the world, to hear from you if there is any hope in my case.' Darwin examined him and declared the issue hopeless, then asked why, if he came from London, had he not seen the famous Richard Warren, the senior royal physician? 'Alas, doctor,' came the reply, 'I am Dr. Warren.'"

Like a good historical novel, *The Lunar Men* bustles with colorful minor characters: Rudolph Eric Raspé, "geologist, gem expert, probable spy and anonymous author of *The Adventures of Baron Munchausen*"; John Baskerville, creator of the very type in which Uglow's book is printed; William Hamilton,

who sent Wedgwood vases from Italy; the chemist Humphry Davy; the novelist (and Lunar daughter) Maria Edgeworth; the sculptor John Flaxman; the
great painters Joseph Wright of Derby and George Stubbs; a young Richard
Trevithick, the engineer who will build the steam locomotive. And many others.

Have I made clear that *The Lunar Men* is a book you can live in for a
month or longer, especially in these dark times? Start reading some evening
when the moon is full.

November 3, 2002

ROMANTIC DREAMERS

III

Writers of a classical bent tend to follow the ideals and examples of earlier art, often from antiquity, while romantics instead look within themselves for the springs of creativity. But this is a generalization, for all poets and novelists must start by learning from the past. Even that arch-modernist Ezra Pound, who told writers to "make it new," also pointed out that "the tradition is a beauty which we preserve and not a set of fetters to bind us."

With the nineteenth century, we enter into a realm of emotional and erotic surfeit. A little too much is just enough for the burgeoning Romantic sensibility. This is the world of what Rimbaud called "the disordering of all the senses," of haunted poets like Baudelaire and saintly murderers like Raskolnikov, of titans of the imagination such as Victor Hugo and Flaubert. Nearly all of them are mad, bad, and dangerous to know.

When we usually think about the Romantics, most Americans call to mind Byron and Shelley and Keats ("that trio of lyrical treats," as Dorothy Parker dubbed them). But I focus here largely on the edgier Europeans, drawn more to revolution than to skylarks or Grecian urns. The classic guide to this world is Mario Praz's exciting, even overexcited, study The Romantic Agony (1933). Where else would one find chapter titles like "The Beauty of the Medusa," "The Metamorphoses of Satan," and "The Shadow of the Divine Marquis"?

To some modern cultural critics all the woes of the modern age can be traced back to the Romantic Age. Do your own thing. Pleasure before duty. The culture of narcissism. Certainly, modern adolescence is now, more than ever, a period of licensed romanticism. But, as the philosopher Nietzsche reminded us, attempts to impose an Apollonian view of life—cool, ordered, and rational—will always be overturned, eventually, by the Dionysian impulse, the periodic need for carnival. Dostoevsky's Underground Man pointed out, "Too much consciousness is a disease, a positive disease." In the Romantic sensibility we see not only the return of the repressed but its sometimes dubious apotheosis.

PUSHKIN: A BIOGRAPHY

By T. J. Binyon

This astonishingly detailed life of Alexander Pushkin (1799–1837) reveals yet again the vast gulf that looms between the creative spirit and the personal life. Almost universally acknowledged as the supreme Russian poet, the author of *Eugene Onegin* and "The Bronze Horseman" also displayed, with equal mastery, nearly every youthful failing. He drank like a frat boy, treated and spoke of women as whores, alternately rebelled against and toadied to the tsar, reduced his family to penury by addictive gambling, and typically allowed his usually dirty fingernails to grow long and clawlike. Once he arrived at a formal dinner "wearing muslin trousers, transparent, without any underwear." He could be utterly thoughtless of others' feelings but was himself "morbidly sensitive to . . . appearing comic" and quickly roused to anger, jealousy, and spite. Though he could be courageous and witty, and though he valued honor above all, it's no exaggeration to say that Pushkin all too often conducted himself like a lout and a vulgarian.

Except, of course, in his writing. The verse novel *Eugene Onegin* possesses the sparkle of Byron's *Don Juan* (its partial model, along with *Childe Harold*), coupled with *Tristram Shandy*–like digressions on life and literature, as well as a melancholy love story just as sad as Fitzgerald's in *Tender Is the Night*. (The poem, according to Russian scholars, doesn't translate well, though I have enjoyed the versions by Charles Johnston and James Falen, generally regarded as the best in English; Nabokov's edition shines mainly in its extensive notes— e.g., a long excursus on the code of dueling.) Throughout this biography T. J. Binyon quotes bits of Pushkin's verse, and even in his deliberately plain English, one can feel the wistful beauty of the lyrics:

> I loved you: love still, perhaps,
> Is not quite extinguished in my soul,
> But let it no longer alarm you;

I do not want to distress you in any way.
I loved you silently, hopelessly,
Tortured now by shyness, now by jealousy;
I loved you sincerely, so tenderly,
May God grant you be so loved by another.

Other poems are bawdy ballads (one describes two different women being brought to orgasm), or evoke a Horatian sense of *tempus fugit*. Pushkin's great poetic gift lay in his versatility and skill in mixing tenderness and irony, a Romantic appreciation of nature, and a worldly nonchalance: "He plays with his readers, teasing them and subverting their expectations."

In truth, the fickle Muses showered this minor aristocrat with gifts, for the poet also wrote some of the best stories of his time, and helped establish the norms of modern Russian prose. "The Queen of Spades," for instance, ranks as one of the world's great tales of the supernatural (or of madness, depending on your point of view). In it a young guardsman discovers an infallible system for winning at the card game Faro, but in gaining the secret he kills its possessor, an old woman. The cards avenge her. "The Captain's Daughter" is a melodramatic but enthralling love story set during the bloody Pugachev rebellion, a time when a Cossack peasant claimed to be the rightful heir to the throne of all the Russias.

T. J. Binyon, a professor of Russian at Oxford, is probably best known to common readers as an expert on crime fiction. For many years he reviewed mysteries for the *Times Literary Supplement*, eventually producing a study called *Murder Will Out* and two whodunits of his own. In his reviews Binyon disclosed an encyclopedic knowledge of detective fiction. He brings the same breathtaking command of detail to this biography, as he virtually re-creates Pushkin's daily life. This will surely become the standard account of the poet in English.

That said, despite an eminently readable, clean, dry style, Binyon's book can easily overwhelm. His pages are a veritable *Almanach de Gotha* of Russian nobility. So many names! It's hard to keep straight the Ekaterinas and Sofias and Mariyas. Readers who, like myself, love facts will relish such abundance, but others will suspect Binyon of surrendering to some compulsion to show off the range of his knowledge: for instance, during Napoleon's invasion of Russia he mentions that "many of the books of the imperial public library were crated and sent up the Neva." A nice detail, though hardly a necessary one. However, he then adds, in an asterisked footnote at the bottom of the page, "The brig carrying them wintered on the Svir River, between Lakes Ladoga and Onega: on its return most of the books were found to be spoilt by water." Such interesting, even amusing clutter as this seems the very definition of a scholarly factoid.

Alexander Pushkin was descended on his mother's side from Gannibal, an African given to Peter the Great as a gift, but a man of such talents that he rose to the rank of general in the Russian army. His great grandson was quite proud of his "Negro" blood, and none of his contemporaries appeared to think twice about it (other than as a way to account for Pushkin's dark features and thick lips). Like Mozart, the poet displayed his genius early on, producing accomplished verse while still a teenager in a Russian academy.

Like many other intellectuals of the time, the youthful Pushkin joined various secret or semisecret clubs, including the delightfully named Arzamas Society of Unknown People and the Green Lamp. Both these lighthearted sodalities, created for discussion, drink, and debauchery, lent several members to the violent Decembrist revolt of 1825, an insurrection as doomed as the Easter uprising of 1916 chronicled by another great poet. But like Yeats, Pushkin avoided being involved in open rebellion, and thus escaped prison or even execution.

But some impolitic verses caught the government's attention, and the young aristocrat was exiled for three years to Kiev and the Caucasus region, where he spent his time flirting with local matrons, writing sacrilegious verse like "The Gabrieliad" (Mary confesses to having had to service Satan, an archangel, and God all on the same day), and producing important poems such as "The Prisoner of the Caucasus," in which a Circassian maiden saves the life of a young Russian and then commits suicide because he rejects her love. Eventually ordered to his parents' small estate to serve out his term of exile, Pushkin promptly impregnated the bailiff's nineteen-year-old daughter.

After Pushkin petitioned his way back into the tsar's favor, he was finally allowed to return to Moscow, and there found himself acclaimed as the premier poet of Russia. Unfortunately, the sovereign now insisted on approving all his future publications. At times a twentieth-century reader is reminded of Soviet writers like Mikhail Bulgakov forced into an accommodation with Stalin.

Approaching thirty, the poet decided he needed to marry and settle down. But after being refused by several celebrated beauties, he fell into despondency:

There is no goal before me
The heart is empty, the mind idle,
And the monotonous sound of life
Oppresses me with melancholy.

But this lachrymose mood soon passed, as Pushkin was drawn to the social whirl, attending "routs," losing vast sums at cards, frequenting brothels, publishing his verse in magazines. He encountered the young novelist Nikolai Gogol, listened to the music of Mikhail Glinka, read Walter Scott, translated Chateaubriand. When Natalya Goncharova finally accepted his offer of marriage, he noted in a letter to a friend that she would be his 113th love.

For a man already given to gambling and extravagance, marriage to Natalya turned out to be an expensive proposition. She was high-maintenance, attending balls almost nightly, requiring a household of over a dozen servants, keeping her husband from the "spiritual tranquillity" he needed to write. And writing was one of the few ways open to Pushkin to increase his income. For when he could find the right quiet and solitude, he could be amazingly productive: "In under six weeks, between 1 October and 9 November, Pushkin finished the *History of Pugachev* and wrote *The Bronze Horseman*, possibly his masterpiece; a short story, *The Queen of Spades*; *Angelo*, a re-working, as a narrative poem, of Shakespeare's *Measure for Measure*, . . . two imitations of the verse folktale, *The Tale of the Fisherman and the Fish*, and *The Tale of the Dead Tsarevna and the Seven Heroes*; two translations of ballads by Mickiewicz; and a handful of short poems, including . . . the great lyric 'Autumn (A Fragment)'. . . ."

But such leisure was harder and harder to come by. Soon the poet had three and then four young children, a mountain of debts and unending social and financial obligations. Binyon aptly sums him up at this time: "When pressures upon him . . . became unendurable, he did not, as others might, lapse into apathetic resignation, but, in the grip of a kind of sullen rage, became incapable of rational thought or action, and lashed out indiscriminately at anyone or anything, caring little—on the contrary rather hoping—that he might, like Samson at Gaza, bring the whole edifice of his life crashing about him."

In 1836–37 a young Frenchman named Georges d'Anthès started paying increasingly indiscreet attention to Pushkin's beautiful wife. Rumors, probably untrue, began to circulate. Then one day Pushkin received an anonymous note enrolling him in a society of cuckolds. He immediately issued a challenge to d'Anthès, but their rencontre was averted through the machinations of friends; indeed, the Frenchman even married Natalya's sister Ekaterina as a way of defusing the situation. But the sense of dishonor festered in Pushkin and eventually flared up again. More letters were exchanged, and the two men finally met on the field of honor: Pushkin wounded d'Anthès slightly but was himself shot in the abdomen. There was nothing the doctors could do. Binyon tells us that the same pair of pistols used by d'Anthès was later employed in a duel in 1840 that left dead the poet Mikhail Lermontov, author of *A Hero of Our Time*.

Binyon's careful account of the d'Anthès affair makes for exciting reading

(Serena Vitale provides an even more leisurely re-creation of the bloody business in *Pushkin's Button*). After the poet's death his friends discovered that Pushkin was roughly 100,000 rubles in debt and that he could hardly have sustained his financial house of cards for more than a few more months. One wonders whether the poet might not have been half in love with easeful death as a way of solving his unsolvable money problems. But Binyon doesn't speculate, just as he eschews any extended interpretation of the poems and stories.

As the poet lay dying in his library, he told his friend Dahl—later the compiler of the great four-volume Russian dictionary beloved by Nabokov—that he had just been dreaming that the two of them "were climbing high up these books and shelves." A few minutes later Alexander Pushkin was dead at only thirty-seven, but in the library of the world's literature he has since climbed very high indeed.

November 16, 2003

THE MANUSCRIPT FOUND IN SARAGOSSA

By Jan Potocki
Translated from the French by Ian Maclean

Sometime in the early eighteenth century a Dutch soldier by the name of Alphonse van Worden is journeying on horseback through the desolate Spanish ranges of the Sierra Morena, a territory inhabited chiefly "by smugglers, bandits and some gypsies who were said to murder travellers and then eat them." In the valley of Los Hermanos, which he has been particularly warned to avoid, van Worden happens upon a gibbet from which hang the rotting corpses of two bandit brothers; a third brother, Zoto, the most fearsome of all, has supposedly escaped from prison and the noose. As night begins to fall, the young Dutchman finally reaches an inn, the Venta Quemada, which turns out to be deserted; indeed its former owner has posted a notice entreating all travelers, no matter how weary, to continue on their way "and not to spend the night here, for any reason."

But van Worden is hungry and exhausted, his two guides have abandoned him, and he prides himself on his courage. After searching the inn, without luck, for a bit of food, the soldier eventually settles down to sleep, though feeling strangely ill at ease. Unexpectedly, at precisely midnight, he hears a bell toll, and out of the darkness glides a bare-breasted woman holding a torch in each hand: "Senor caballero, you are invited to partake in the supper of two foreign ladies who are spending the night at this hostelry. Please be so good as to follow me." Van Worden soon finds himself before a banquet table presided over by two exotically beautiful sisters.

After their repast, Emina and Zubeida confess that they are daughters of a powerful and highly secretive family of Muslims called the Gomelez. They teasingly allude to bizarre realms beneath the earth and esoteric rites. On the last Friday of every month, for instance, the clan's sheikh has always "shut himself up in an underground part of the castle where he stayed immured until the following Friday. . . . Some said that the sheikh was conversing with the twelfth imam, who we believe will reappear at the end of time. Others believed that the Antichrist was kept chained in the cellars of the castle. Yet others thought that the seven sleepers of Ephesus were resting there. . . ." The two women hint at many other mysteries, as well as their own sapphic love for each other, and grow increasingly affectionate—until they notice the fragment of the true cross that van Worden wears around his neck and which he has promised his mother never to remove. Clearly frustrated, Emina and Zubeida promise their young "cousin" that they will nonetheless come to him in his dreams. That night van Worden feels himself transported "into the midst of African harems. . . . I revelled in vague and wanton fancies, never leaving the company of my beautiful cousins. I fell asleep on their breasts and awoke again in their arms."

But when the morning light actually rouses van Worden, he discovers himself lying on the ground between the loathsome corpses of Zoto's brothers: "I had apparently spent the night with them."

And so, with a Grand Guignol flourish, Alphonse van Worden is launched into one of the strangest and most structurally complex novels of the nineteenth century, the almost legendary gothic extravaganza called *The Manuscript Found in Saragossa*. Before van Worden comes to understand the meaning of the night he has passed in the Venta Quemada, he will encounter a host of strange beings, among them, a Kabbalist who aspires to immortality; a wonder-working hermit; the dreaded bandit Zoto; a gypsy chief with an adventure-filled past; the learned daughter of a great magus; a geometer who reduces everything, including love, religion, and storytelling, to mathematical propositions; and even the Wandering Jew.

All these people, and others, promptly relate the stories of their lives: monomaniacal fathers grow obsessed with honor or the making of perfect ink, young boys vow lifelong revenge for minor slights, an autodidact sums up all the world's knowledge in one hundred volumes only to have his work destroyed by rats. There are tales of vampires and night spirits, memories of life at the time of Christ, bawdy and touching accounts of sexual jealousy. An old man proposes, sight unseen, to the infant daughter of the woman he has adored and lost; young lovers marry after many obstacles and find that their passion has turned to dust; a sorcerer hopes to mate his children with angelic beings. One meets a dwarf automaton, the suavely diabolical tempter who calls himself Don Belial de Gehenna, a wild child, and a doomed beauty who dwells in eternal splendor with six skeletal retainers. There are court intrigues in Spain, Mexico, Italy, Austria, and the Middle East, inexhaustible seams of pure gold, and intimations that obscure adepts have pulled the strings of history. Emina and Zubeida regularly reappear to entice van Worden with their undeniable charms and to tempt him to renounce Christianity for Islam. And, eventually, behind everything, even the most casual utterance, one begins to glimpse the long reach of the Gomelez.

At its most magical *The Manuscript Found in Saragossa* reads like *The Arabian Nights*, at its most Italianate like something from *The Decameron* or Elizabethan revenge tragedy. A few of the weirder tales will remind readers of gothic fiction such as *Melmoth the Wanderer*, while the allusions to a secret brotherhood may even call to mind the sinister paranoia of *Foucault's Pendulum*. The book's fugal structure describes an elaborate interlaced pattern of tales within tales within tales, nearly all of which gradually illuminate van Worden's own experiences and confusions. Whom, wonders the young soldier, can he trust? Is he the prey of vampires or the plaything of even more bizarre forces? Whenever anybody sleeps in the Venta Quemada, he or she invariably, uncannily awakes beneath the gallows next to the hanged men.

Thematically, Potocki suggests a constant tension between "natural instincts" and "the dictates of religion," while the tales themselves can be, by turns, lascivious, farcical, scary, or neatly sardonic: the gypsy chief announces that his life "comprises quite humdrum events" and then goes on to relate a series of utterly fantastic exploits. But Potocki can also rise to thrilling prose arias: in Hebrew, the Kabbalist proclaims, "every letter is a number, every word a learned combination of signs, every phrase a terrible formula, which, when correctly pronounced with all the appropriate aspirates and stresses, could cause mountains to crumble and rivers to dry up. I do not need to tell you that Adonai created the world by the Word and then made himself into a Word."

As it happens, many of Potocki's own words actually disappeared for more than 150 years. No one knows for sure when this Polish adventurer and scholar (1761–1815) conceived *The Manuscript Found in Saragossa*, originally composed in French, but he appears to have worked on it all the latter part of his life. Until recently, however, only the first third or so of the book was available to most readers. In 1989, though, French scholars managed to collate several manuscripts to produce a full text, which provides the basis for this new English translation.

Ian Maclean details all these matters in his intelligent and useful introduction to this masterwork of European Romanticism. He also tantalizes with a brief account of its creator, that mysterious polymath Jan Potocki: educated in Geneva and Lausanne, the young Pole "spent some time on a galley as a novice Knight of Malta" and was "among the first to make an ascent in a balloon (in 1790)." As a political activist he consorted with "patriots in Poland, Jacobins in France and the court of Alexander I in Russia." Eventually the restless Potocki traveled throughout Europe, into Turkey and Russia and as far away as Mongolia. He published scholarly works in history, ethnology, and linguistics, married twice, and had five children: "There were rumours of incest." In his mid-fifties, suffering from political despair or depression or chronic pain, no one knows for sure, Potocki supposedly hand-forged a silver bullet, had it blessed by the chaplain of his castle, and then used it to blow out his brains in his library. Such a life with such a death could easily make up one last story for *The Manuscript Found in Saragossa*.

July 9, 1995

VICTOR HUGO

By Graham Robb

Genius often reveals itself as a kind of superior energy, a creative exuberance that overflows the boundaries of the conventional and earns its possessor a reputation as a troublemaker, immoralist, or crazed visionary. Blake, Tolstoy, Wagner, Picasso—such titans can hardly contain their sheer fecundity, and their personal lives are . . . messy. They glimpse angels, sleep with milkmaids, argue aesthetics with philosophers, regularly embarrass their friends, join revolutions, and dream of establishing the New Jerusalem, the brotherhood of man or the Bayreuth Music Festival. In between times, they somehow manage to dash off things of beauty by the dozen. There is, after all, no single great masterpiece by Dickens or Colette or Mozart or Michelangelo: instead every work, big or little, contributes its part to a distinctive, irreplaceable landscape of the imagination.

Even when we know all this, the subject of Graham Robb's authoritative, almost swashbuckling biography still remains extraordinary. "Victor Hugo," said Jean Cocteau, "was a madman who thought he was Victor Hugo." A shrewd joke, but Cocteau didn't take it quite far enough. As Robb points out, the most famous writer of his time also managed to convince the entire world that he was Victor Hugo.

But who precisely was that? To modern Americans, Hugo wrote the book behind a highly successful musical (*Les Misérables*), provided the original for a Disney cartoon (*The Hunchback of Notre Dame*), and fathered the schizophrenic heroine of François Truffaut's movie *Adèle H*. High school French students should certainly recognize two classic elegies about the author's older daughter, Léopoldine, who drowned in a boating accident: "A Villequier" and "Demain, dès l'aube." Some college lit majors may even recall André Gide's famous reply, when asked to name the greatest French poet: "Victor Hugo, alas."

Alas, nothing. For sixty years Hugo (1802–1885) utterly dominated French literature and politics. Today, a plaque actually commemorates the blessed spot—high up on Donon Mountain—where this multitalented genius was conceived by a brutal Napoleonic general upon a woman who later conspired against the emperor. Their offspring's life was appropriately both revolutionary and defiantly anti-imperial. In his early years young Victor lived all over Napoleonic Europe—France, Spain, Corsica—but eventually he and his two brothers settled in Paris with their mother; there he discovered an almost preternatural knack for turning words into poetry. Even as a teenager, observes Robb, Hugo could dash off alexandrines with "that gorgeous orotundity which makes it almost impossible to read them silently or sitting down. This is poetry in search of a context—ideally, a large crowd cheering at the end of each stanza."

By the time he was in his mid-twenties Hugo was the leader of the French Romantics. He wrote political articles for newspapers, delivered the official ode for the coronation of Charles X, prefaced his play *Cromwell* (1827) with "the most influential aesthetic treatise of the century" (one that called for a new art that embraced the grotesque as a kind of beauty), and, best of all, set off an opening-night riot with his 1830 drama *Hernani*. As an ambitious literary hotshot, Hugo strip-mined information and inspiration from everyone around him, including some of the best-known figures of nineteenth-century French literature: the antiquarian and ghostly storyteller Charles Nodier, the exquisite poet and novelist Théophile Gautier (notorious for the scarlet vest he wore at the *Hernani* premiere), and, in particular, the critic Sainte-Beuve, who in the Gallic way soon embarked on a secret love affair with his friend's wife, Adèle. It was, according to Cyril Connolly, the revenge of talent upon genius.

Hugo soon forgave both wife and disciple, in part because he himself possessed, along with consummate literary and political virtuosity, his own irrepressible sexual appetite. At one point, Adèle and two kept mistresses were all living within two hundred yards of each other. As he grew older, Hugo hired prostitutes, groped the servants, fondled society grandes dames, enjoyed casual sex with the daughters of old friends (e.g., Judith Gautier), slept with his own son's girlfriend, and may even have impregnated the actress Sarah Bernhardt. During the siege of Paris, Hugo—a year short of seventy—had forty partners in five months, averaging almost one sexual encounter a day. By then he was so famous that groupies would wait outside his doorway at night, pleading with him for a baby. Still later, his stepson-in-law used to catch the octogenarian creeping downstairs in his slippers and vest: "Where are you off to, you disgusting old man? Leave the cook alone!"

Hugo brought a similar over-the-top extravagance to his writing, in particular his fiction. He composed a gothicky novel about an evil Icelandic dwarf

(*Han d'Islande*, 1823), chronicled a slave rebellion in Haiti (*Bug-Jargal*, 1826), and related the tragic exploits of the Laughing Man (*L'Homme Qui Rit*, 1869), an English nobleman's son, kidnapped as a baby, whose face is fixed into a permanent grin so that he can be sold as a carnival freak. In *The Last Day of a Condemned Man* (1829) Hugo sets down a searing novella-length interior monologue, the swirling, agonized thoughts of a prisoner awaiting execution (and a likely influence on Camus's *The Stranger*). *Toilers of the Sea* (1866) builds to a heart-pounding, hand-to-tentacle combat with a squidlike monster that ingests its victims whole: "Beyond the horrific—being eaten alive—there is the unspeakable: being drunk alive." And, of course, in his two world-renowned masterpieces, *Notre Dame de Paris* (1831) and *Les Misérables* (1862), the visionary-realist creates gigantic, encyclopedic works that include disquisitions on history, architecture, Waterloo, language, and much else, as well as unforgettable scenes of beggar armies attacking a cathedral and desperate men splashing through the sewers of Paris.

What with all this writing, fooling around with women, and official duties as France's top literary lion, any lesser mortal would have found life pretty full. Not Hugo. Come the revolutions of 1830 and 1848, he was there in the streets. In 1848 the champion of the people temporarily espoused the reactionary side, led assaults against barricades (and could, conceivably, have been shot by Baudelaire, who was manning one with his new rifle), and briefly joined a provisional government. But after Louis Napoleon seized power and duly crowned himself Napoleon III, Hugo stood up as the tyrant's chief political enemy, choosing to live in exile on the Channel islands of Jersey and Guernsey—for nineteen years. "When freedom returns," he proclaimed, "so shall I." In 1870 the Germans invaded France, thus shutting down the reign of the man Hugo derided as "Napoléon le Petit." Immediately the exiled dissident packed his bags and—against all common sense—made his way to the French capital, arriving just in time for the siege of Paris. For the next few months, in between sexual romps and patriotic speeches, he dined on dog and rat.

Like other French intellectuals (Voltaire, Chateaubriand, Malraux), Hugo identified his own fortunes with those of *la patrie*. And not unreasonably. At several times in his life, this *pair de France* and people's friend might have used his popularity to become president of the country. As its unofficial king over the water, he welcomed to Jersey both revolutionaries and poets, crackpots and journalists, fans and spies. He answered 150 letters a week, worked hard to abolish the death penalty, defended John Brown, embraced pacifism, conducted seances with the illustrious dead, wrote while standing up, and spoke regularly to his only equal on earth, the Ocean. Rhetorical grandeur characterizes much of Hugo's life and writing, and to appreciate his genius one must share a taste for such flourishes (many modern readers do not). The great man could be ludicrously self-important and faintly ridiculous much of the time, but also extremely impressive, as in this early and eerily predictive speech about censorship: "Today, my freedom as a poet is taken by a censor; tomorrow, my freedom as a citizen will be taken by a policeman. Today, I am banished from the theatre; tomorrow, I shall be banished from the land. Today, I am gagged; tomorrow, I shall be deported. Today, a state of siege exists in literature; tomorrow, it will exist in the city."

Such heightened language usually works best as verse, and it is in poetry that Hugo remains incontrovertibly a verbal magician. In the pyrotechnical "Les Djinns," stanzas gradually lengthen as the demonic horde approaches— and then shrink back as they depart: "Tout passe; / L'espace / Efface / Le bruit." In the haunting poem "Conscience" Cain desperately tries to escape the all-seeing eye of God, going so far as to have himself immured underground, but even there "the eye was in the tomb and was looking at Cain." The great historical mini-epic "L'Expiation" opens with Napoleon's retreat from Moscow, repeating like hammer blows the phrase "Il neigeait" ("It snowed"), as the Grande Armée gradually falls apart, its soldiers eventually wandering through a frozen wasteland like figures in a dream, lost in shadow and mist. In "A Villequier"—the French equivalent to "Adonais" or even "The Wreck of the Deutschland"—Hugo beseeches God, humbly trying to understand the sudden death of his beloved daughter: "I know that fruit falls with the wind that shakes it, / That the bird loses its plumage and the flower its perfume, / That creation is a great wheel / That cannot move without crushing someone. / Months, days, the currents of the sea, eyes that weep, / Pass beneath the blue sky; / It is neccessary for grass to grow and for children to die, / I know it, my God." These lines are powerful enough in my prosaic English; in French they are devastating.

When Hugo was seventy-nine, the Third Republic declared a national holiday, and the parade in the poet's honor took all day to march by his window. This for a man who would ride the public omnibus to visit his young mistress and scribble poems as he bounced along. Even back in his years of exile, admirers would save the pebbles Hugo had trod upon while walking along the beach. At his death in 1885 the funeral procession to the Panthéon numbered two million, more than the ordinary population of Paris. Some forty or so years later a Vietnamese cult actually made the Frenchman a saint. Little wonder that Victor Hugo thought he was Victor Hugo.

Graham Robb tells the complicated story of this colossal life with authority and sympathy, well aware of his subject's numerous flaws (lack of humor, complacent megalomania). Though sometimes a little too colorful, Robb's own lively prose can be neatly wry: "A society in which Victor Hugo was the voice of reason had obviously reached an unhealthy state of extremes." As an expert on nineteenth-century literature (he is the author of well-received books on Balzac, Mallarmé, and Baudelaire), Robb speaks up passionately for Hugo's fiction, especially the lesser-known works, and winningly loses all scholarly equilibrium in his ardent enthusiasm for *Les Misérables*, calling it "the most lucid, humane and entertaining moral diagnosis of modern society ever written." For some reason, though, he seems rather cool about my own favorite, *Notre Dame*, that apotheosis of the grotesque and arabesque. I would also have welcomed a little more detailed attention to the poetry, though he is quite good on the biographical context of the famous romantic lyric "La Tristesse d'Olympio."

Cavils aside, this is, unquestionably, a magnificent biography, filled with grand exploits, terrible deaths, and occasional comedy. Here is Balzac calling Hugo's daughter Adèle "the greatest beauty I shall ever see" and Heine defining "Hugoiste" as "the superlative form of egoiste." Sainte-Beuve fights a duel while holding an umbrella, "quite prepared to go to the grave 'shot dead but not soaking wet.' " Before the coup d'état, notes Robb with a quick jab, Louis Napoleon "left Hugo with a signed copy of his book on artillery (one of History's little jokes)." Swinburne so admired the French master that he actually made a rhymed bibliography of his oeuvre. Among Hugo's lesser-known works are several thousand superb Mervyn Peake–like drawings as well as unproduced plays featuring a talking stone and—shades of Beckett—a hundred-year-old woman in a sack.

"Victor Hugo, alas?" After reading Graham Robb one is more likely to shout, even if with one or two misgivings, "Victor Hugo, hurrah!"

February 22, 1998

LES FLEURS DU MAL

By Charles Baudelaire
Translated from the French by Richard Howard

No one surpasses Baudelaire in portraying spiritual desolation. He is the Ancient Mariner of poetry; when those eyes fix you from the photographs of Nadar or Carjat, when the hypnotic voice rises from his stanzas—the reader, like Coleridge's Wedding Guest, cannot choose but hear. "Souvenirs? More than if I had lived a thousand years! . . ." In *Les Fleurs du Mal* (The Flowers of Evil) Baudelaire ponders his wretched past and broods—on the flight of time, the shocks of city living, the clamorings of desire, all the desperate ways of forgetting that "soon cold shadows will close over us / and summer's transitory gold be gone. . . ."

Baudelaire's own story is one of a slow grinding down by disease and despair. As a young dandy in his early twenties he became saddled with lifelong debts that were impossible to throw off, caught the syphilis that was to kill him, became enthralled by a mulatto actress-prostitute who soaked him for money and probably betrayed him with the postman. Later, he was laughed at as a buffoon by the literary giants of the day, found his poems condemned, then suppressed, as obscene, his art and music criticism relatively ignored, and nonentities elected to positions he dreamed of. In his last illness he became paralyzed and aphasic, capable of uttering only two words, "Sacré nom." When he died in 1867, at the age of forty-six, all his work was out of print.

Yet even then Baudelaire's rejection was slowly giving way to recognition, even renown. In 1866 the twenty-three-year-old Mallarmé and the twenty-one-year-old Verlaine each wrote tributes to his genius. In Britain Swinburne composed his greatest elegy, "Ave atque Vale." And, a generation later, Arthur Symons provided a seemingly extravagant summary of his achievement, but one that nobody today would disagree with: "Of the men of letters of our age he was the most scrupulous. He spent his whole life in writing one book of verse (out of which all French poetry has come since his time), one book of prose in which prose becomes a fine art, some criticism which is the sanest, subtlest, and surest which his generation produced, and a translation which is better than a marvellous original."

That translation is of Poe (whom Baudelaire idolized, promoted, and partly emulated). The criticism includes dazzling reviews of three Salons shows, studies of Delacroix and Constantin Guys, advocacy of Wagnerian opera. The art prose appears in *Le Spleen de Paris*, the collection that established the *poème en prose* as an artistic form. But above them all, of course, is that pilgrimage through the soul's dark night, a journey of Dantesque visionary power and Racinian elegance: *Les Fleurs du Mal*.

Such a legendary book—a Sacred Text of modern poetry—has naturally been much translated: in part by Edna St. Vincent Millay, Roy Campbell, Richard Wilbur, and Robert Lowell, among others. Now Richard Howard, generally esteemed as the finest American translator from the French of the postwar era, offers a new version of this masterpiece. Let me hasten to say, before a few cavils, that it is indubitably the English edition to acquire (although it might be supplemented with Marthiel and Jackson Matthews's selection from the best translations of the past). Howard deftly captures the modal music, the sickly-sweet fragrance, the startling modernity of Baudelaire; and being a poet, as well as a translator, he also manages to come up with English phrases comparable in power to the originals. Even those who know the French will be able to read Howard with pleasure: these are poems, not ponies.

What's more, Howard hopes that his translation, being the work of a single intelligence, will convey some of the "hidden architecture" of *Les Fleurs* (which Baudelaire always claimed was a unity). So the first half of the book presents the translations only; the second half provides the French originals. Unlike Baudelaire, Howard chooses to forgo rhyme, successfully using assonance, alliteration, and other prosodic effects to make up for its lack. Literalists, however, will notice that absolute fidelity is sometimes sacrificed for poetic ends: Howard misses important effects, at times leaves out an image or allusion, occasionally rearranges the order of lines, inserts extraneous names or figures, switches tenses or person, alters titles. With a bit more ingenuity and care these misjudgments might have been avoided. Still, they only mar an otherwise brilliant job.

Although the individual poems were written at various times, *Les Fleurs du Mal* is so organized that it traces the life of the poet—and, by extension, that of our old friend alienated modern man—in an unstable, unhappy world. Reviled by family, society, and lovers, the poet undergoes spiritual and sexual crises, searching in vain for serenity. ("All is order there, and elegance / pleasure, peace, and opulence.") Along the way, he describes city life, teeming, refuse-laden, horrible, seductive; an artist, he naturally identifies with other outsiders—especially criminals and sexual outcasts. In periodic despondency he seeks relief in wine, debauchery, travel, and opium, though nothing helps for long. The passage of time permits no permanence—except that of the torment within: "I am the knife and the wound it deals." Finally, only death awaits.

Howard's mastery of this familiar urban universe is evident from the very first poem, "To the Reader":

> Stupidity, delusion, selfishness and lust
> torment our bodies and possess our minds,
> and we sustain our affable remorse
> the way a beggar nourishes his lice.
>
> Our sins are stubborn, our contrition lame;
> we want our scruples to be worth our while—
> how cheerfully we crawl back to the mire:
> a few cheap tears will wash our stains away! . . .
>
> But here among the scorpions and the hounds,
> the jackals, apes and vultures, snakes and wolves,
> monsters that howl and growl and squeal and crawl,
> in all the squalid zoo of vices, one
>
> is even uglier and fouler than the rest,
> although the least flamboyant of the lot;
> this beast would gladly undermine the earth
> and swallow all creation in a yawn;
>
> I speak of Boredom which with ready tears
> dreams of hangings as it puffs its pipe.
> Reader, you know this squeamish monster well,
> —hypocrite reader,—my alias,—my twin!

In this proem Howard captures just the right tone of dry, slightly mocking self-dramatization mingled with genuine horror. He fails only in the beginning of the last stanza. Baudelaire leads up to the revelation of his ultimate monster quietly, gradually, and then screams its name: "C'est l'Ennui!" Howard's "I speak of Boredom" is slack by comparison, far too polite.

This occasional limpness appears as Howard's most common fault. Take the lines "L'amoureux pantelant incliné sur sa belle / A l'air d'un moribond caressant son tombeau." This becomes "The pining lover for his lady swoons / like a dying man adoring his own tomb." This is not bad; the *l* alliteration and the *i* and *o* assonance make for tightly knit lines, but Howard sacrifices a highly charged image for one that seems almost statuelike or allegorical. "Pining" suggests unfulfillment, "swoons" the epicene rather than the ecstatic, and "adoring his tomb" a prayer in a graveyard. The whole effect seems rather feminine, languid. In fact, the French is more graphic, sexual, and macabre. *Pantelant* means panting or shuddering; this becomes precise with the next phrase, "incliné sur sa belle," imaging the lover stretched out on top of his mistress. Then, as is typical with Baudelaire, the following line transforms the woman from sexual icon to object of disgust (compare "Carrion" or "To a Madonna"): the ecstatic sighs become a dying man's gasp; the woman beneath the man becomes his own sarcophagus. Love and death blur.

It is easy to pick holes in any translation; the best the translator can achieve is a selection from the effects inherent in the original. Not too surprisingly then, Howard proves least satisfying in transposing Baudelaire's richest, most atmospheric phrases. "La langoureuse Asie et la brûlante Afrique" becomes "torpid Asia, torrid Africa"—nice alliteration, but the short line and clipped adjectives lose the languorous liquids and open vowels of the French.

But Howard can be terrific on less familiar verses: "My heart! that palace ransacked by a mob / of drunken maenads at each other's throats. . . ." Or "And thighs that once were lithe with unconcern" (a particularly nice effect there: thighs and lithe being near aural anagrams). He achieves delightful effects too with emjambement:

Tonight the moon dreams still more languidly:
as if some beauty on her pillowed couch
were brushing with a half-unconscious hand
the contour of her breasts before she fell

asleep. . . .

In another vein, Howard expertly captures the city's mysteriousness in the quietly evocative openings of "The Seven Old Men" and "The Little Old Women":

Swarming city—city gorged with dreams,
where ghosts by day accost the passer-by. . . .

In murky corners of old cities where
everything—horror too—is magical. . . .

Baudelaire originally intended to call his book *Les Lesbiennes*—Lesbians—and it is the sexual aspect of his poetry that caused early readers such consternation. The hothouse flavor of the three lesbian poems especially requires just the right mixture of sympathy and sadness. In "Lesbos" the women are Warhol-like groupies:

> Lesbos, where on suffocating nights
> before their mirrors, girls with hollow eyes
> caress their ripened limbs in sterile joy
> and taste the fruit of their nubility. . . .

But "Damned Women: Delphine and Hippolyta" takes a more chilling view of sexuality: "I cringe each time you call me 'angel,' yet / I feel my mouth long for you." (The French is more active: "Je frissone de peur quand tu me dis: 'Mon ange!' / Et cependant je sens ma bouche aller vers toi"—the girl's mouth instinctively, involuntarily, moves toward her lover.) Such vampirism prevails in nearly all sexual relations; Woman may offer the poet temporary self-forgetfulness, but she is voracious, merciless, terrible:

> The woman, meanwhile, writhing like a snake
> across hot coals and hiking up her breasts
> over her corset-stays, began to speak
> as if her mouth had steeped each word in musk:
> "My lips are smooth, and with them I know how
> to smother conscience somewhere in these sheets.
> I make the old men laugh like little boys. . . ."

But, of course, no person, no drug, can dissipate life's relentless actuality: "oases of fear in the wasteland of ennui." Though Baudelaire may dream of "days where it is always afternoon," he still knows that "each instant snatches from you what you had, the crumb of happiness within your grasp," that "Paris changes . . . But in sadness like mine / nothing stirs." Finally all that remains is to embark on the last, the greatest adventure:

> Death, old admiral, up anchor now,
> this country wearies us. Put out to sea!
> What if the waves and winds are black as ink,
> our hearts are filled with light. You know our hearts!

Pour us your poison, let us be comforted!
Once we have burned our brains out, we can plunge
to Hell or Heaven—any abyss will do—
deep in the Unknown to find the new!

There is more, much more, to Baudelaire's poetic universe—evocations of autumn days, sunlit memories, dejection alternating with ecstasy, complex literary structures (especially in "The Swan" and "The Voyage"), satire and black humor, jagged surreal imagery, Debussy-like musical effects. Whether mirroring a fallen world or sounding the soul's depths, *Les Fleurs du Mal* remains an incomparable, yet very human, masterpiece.

August 1, 1982

CRIME AND PUNISHMENT

By Fyodor Dostoevsky
Translated from the Russian by Richard Pevear
and Larissa Volokhonsky

To Thomas Mann he was "the Pale Criminal." Nietzsche thought him "the only psychologist from whom he had anything to learn." Freud ranked his imagination with Shakespeare's. As the creator of "novel tragedies," he composed the most harrowing scene in all fiction (the suicide of Kirilov in *The Devils*, 1871–72), invented the classic existentialist antihero known as the Underground Man ("I am a sick man, I am a spiteful man"), and imagined that deeply upsetting philosophical soliloquy, the Legend of the Grand Inquisitor, wherein Christ returns to earth and is condemned to be burned at the stake by his own church.

Fyodor Dostoevsky's life (1821–1881) would seem excessively melodramatic even in one of his novels. Father murdered by serfs. First work of fiction, *Poor Folk* (1845), acclaimed a masterpiece. Shortly afterward arrested for revolutionary activity and sentenced to death. Reprieved moments before execution and exiled to Siberia for nearly ten years. Bouts of epilepsy. In 1864—the year before he started *Crime and Punishment*—his wife, brother, and close friend all die. To fulfill a contract he writes his novel *The Gambler* (1865) in less than a month and then marries his stenographer. Incessant poverty. Eventually, however, he becomes an immensely popular, politically conservative Slavophile journalist. Some forty thousand people attend his funeral.

Not surprisingly, Dostoevsky's novels depict the world as a battlefield for the soul of man. His heroes resemble fallen angels; his meek, hand-wringing characters seem like early Christian martyrs; and his villains might be demiurges. *The Brothers Karamazov* (1880) ranks as his greatest achievement, but *Crime and Punishment* (1866) stands as his most perfect in pacing and structure. There is no more gripping novel in the world.

First translated in 1886, the book became famous in the West in Constance

Garnett's 1914 English version, which helped create a vogue for Dostoevsky among intellectuals. In recent years, however, Garnett has suffered potshots as being too smooth, too Edwardian. Currently the most used editions of *C and P* have been those in the Norton Critical Edition (Jessie Coulson's translation) and the Penguin Modern Classics (David Magarshack's). There have also been versions by Michael Scammell (best known for his biography of Solzhenitsyn), Sidney Monas, and, recently, David McDuff, this last a Viking hardcover that will, apparently, replace Magarshack as the standard Penguin paperback.

Good as all these earlier translations are, scholars have already welcomed this new one by Richard Pevear and Larissa Volokhonsky as the best currently available. This edition's virtues start with its sturdy binding and large legible type (neither to be despised); as with the Pevear/Volokhonsky *Brothers Karamazov*, the translation itself aims for an especially faithful re-creation of Dostoevsky's rough-edged prose, jerky with a coiled-spring kinetic energy. *Crime and Punishment* is, however, a story with a power that bursts through any English version. It is also a novel that might easily be set in, say, contemporary Washington, a city as artificial and dream-filled as old St. Petersburg.

A young man of twenty-three has dropped out of school because he can't pay his tuition. He lives in what amounts to a closet and, being in arrears on his rent, is afraid of running into his landlady. Everywhere he wanders in his ghetto neighborhood people are out on the pavement begging, whoring, or drinking. One pathetic drunk buttonholes him and confesses how he sent his own daughter out on the streets. "Do you understand," he implores, "do you understand, my dear sir, what it means when there is no longer anywhere to go?" Revolutionary ideas fill the air, and this rather sullen intellectual finds them attractive. Sometimes, though, he thinks of throwing himself into the river.

And why not? His father is long dead. His fervently religious mother has been reduced to taking in sewing to save some money for her son's "university education." Even his attractive, hot-tempered young sister has accepted a menial job in a rich household. After narrowly avoiding seduction by the priapic husband, she has recently agreed to marry a considerably older and utterly crass businessman who can hardly wait to get her into bed. Our hero realizes that both his mother and his sister are sacrificing their lives for him.

Now, an old witchlike pawnbroker lives nearby, venal, usurious, and cruel; she treats her own sister like a slave. Why should such an insect flourish while others suffer? Think what could be done with all her money. An ambitious self-starter could finish his law degree, grow wealthy, divert funds back into his community, build parks, relieve the poor and addicted, achieve great things. Surely, the life of a miserable "louse" is next to nothing compared with all these good deeds. "One death for hundreds of lives—it's simple arithmetic."

And so Dostoevsky's ambiguous hero Raskolnikov—for it is he, not some kid in a modern big-city slum—feverish, despondent, half sick from malnutrition, starts to toy with the idea of murder, to rehearse it over and over in his mind, but only, he tells himself, as a kind of mental game. Then late one afternoon he inadvertently learns that at 7 PM the next day the old moneylender will be alone.

Will he do it? Should he? Can he? Raskolnikov wavers for a moment; then the life of Alyona Ivanova is bludgeoned out of her in a single chilling sentence: "The moment he brought the ax down, strength was born in him." Shortly thereafter, the pawnbroker's unfortunate sister returns home early.

Against all odds Raskolnikov manages to escape the scene of his double murder. He is safe. No one, absolutely no one, can touch him. We are on page 86, end of part 1, and *Crime and Punishment* has only just begun to accelerate.

Already sicklied o'er with the pale cast of thought, Raskolnikov (his name suggests schism or split) finds that his crime has cut him off from humanity. As Leskov wrote of a "Lady Macbeth of Mtsensk District" and Turgenev of a "Lear of the Steppes," so Dostoevsky creates a "Hamlet of St. Petersburg," suffering his doubts and uncertainties when it is too late. He insults his friends, refuses to see his mother and his sister, Dunya, reviles the latter's self-satisfied fiancé, falls sick, acts drunk, appears mad. At the police station he faints over a routine matter, drawing unneeded suspicion to himself. Gradually, he also grows entangled with the Marmeladov family, especially the old drunkard's consumptive, half-crazed widow and his prostitute daughter Sonya.

To increase its sense of nightmare, *Crime and Punishment* takes place mainly in cramped stuffy rooms; footsteps echo down the hallways; outside the weather is humid, the streets crowded. Raskolnikov perceives everything through a mist, his mind blurry with fever and fatigue. Strangers suddenly appear and argue vociferously with him about ideas, religion, the need for suffering. It's as though Captain Ahab, King Lear, and Mother Courage were to start debating life's meaning in a garret during a thunderstorm. This is a "polyphonic" novel (Mikhail Bakhtin), oppressively, irresistibly gregarious, abuzz with talk and debate. Do the ends ever justify the means? Is suffering the basis of religion? Does crime stem from the soul or the environment? What is the relationship between impulse and reason? (Raskolnikov's natural bent seems to be toward benevolence, while his calculating mind leads him to sin: his is, in a vivid phrase, "a heart chafed by theories.") Under what conditions is suicide permissible? How much do we live in dreams? Above all, why did Raskolnikov kill—and why does he apparently never feel remorse?

In Russian the word *prestuplenie* (the novel's title is *Prestuplenie i nakazanie*) means transgression, as well as crime, and Dostoevsky plays riffs off this image of stepping over or across. For instance, Raskolnikov—like many young intellectuals—believes that world-historical figures such as Napoleon step through blood and over petty murders without a second thought or a look back. Indeed, one of the more than half dozen differing explanations he offers for why he committed murder is simply that he wished to discover whether he might be just such an extraordinary person. As he intuited beforehand, he isn't—for he finds himself ridden with legitimate paranoia. He comes to exemplify Dostoevsky's critique of pure reason as a basis for living.

Nudging him, steadily, relentlessly, toward an admission of guilt is the novel's remarkable detective, the fat and unprepossessing Porfiry Petrovich, the ancestor of (and a reported model for) television's Columbo. Porfiry nips at the jumpy Raskolnikov with enigmatic winks, quiet chuckles, repeated talk of Napoleon and axes. He describes his investigative technique as a kind of art, unbound by protocols. The murderer, he tells Raskolnikov, will "keep on making circles around me, narrowing the radius more and more, and—whop! He'll fly right into my mouth."

With all its naturalistic detail, *Crime and Punishment* may look like a realistic novel, but it possesses a disorienting hall-of-mirrors artificiality. Prophetic dreams and uncanny coincidences reinforce a sense of fatedness to every action. The most unlikely people turn out to be neighbors. Scenes resembling paintings by La Tour or Le Nain open on dying figures in bare rooms lit by a single candle, or on a harlot and a murderer reading together the story of the resurrection of Lazarus (a tableau derided by Nabokov for its sentimentality). Sentences bristle with foreboding hints—"afterwards," "later on." The color yellow, hats, an old shawl, a drunkard's uneven walk, a leap from a belltower—all become emblems of death and transfiguration.

And then, midway through this urban gothic thriller, Svidrigailov appears. First mentioned as the would-be seducer of Dunya, Svidrigailov is the consummate amoralist, beyond good and evil, a murderer and sexual predator, repeatedly suffering—that key word again—from an inescapable boredom. This satanic dandy feels no regrets for his sins; indeed he performs acts of charity as well as evil with equal nonchalance. "I see," he says, that "I may actually strike people as a romantic figure." He is in fact electrifyingly attractive.

In one amazing chapter Svidrigailov traps Dunya in an empty apartment, far from help, and calmly explains to her that he intends to rape her and that if she breathes a word to anyone he will tell the police what he has learned about her beloved brother. I won't say more, except to add that the scene crackles with a palm-sweating sexual current to which Dunya is not immune.

Raskolnikov may bend to kiss the foot of the pitiable harlot, but Svidrigailov burns to kiss the hem of Dunya's dress because he can no longer bear the excitement of its constant "rustling."

I first read *Crime and Punishment* (in Constance Garnett's translation) some thirty years ago when my mother had to tear the book from my grasp to send me to bed. I've reread the novel three more times since, and in this fine translation by Pevear/Volokhonsky it is better than ever.

March 15, 1992

POSTSCRIPT: After this piece appeared, I began to write regularly about old books in new translations (e.g., Eça de Queirós's *The Crime of Father Amaro*, Cervantes's *Don Quixote*) and about minor classics, usually from the nineteenth century: George Meredith's sonnet sequence *Modern Love*, Sheridan Le Fanu's sensational *Uncle Silas*, Bulwer-Lytton's witty *Pelham*, Thomas Love Peacock's even wittier *Crotchet Castle*, and many other terrific books, now too often forgotten.

THE LETTERS OF GUSTAVE FLAUBERT, 1830–1857

Selected, edited, and translated from the French by Francis Steegmuller

I have sometimes thought about the books a kindly uncle ought to put into the hands of a young person who wishes to become a writer. Naturally, any aspiring writer should study the Bible, Shakespeare, and other such classics. But the books I mean are those that hint at the actual processes of the imagination, or strip away the tweed jacket and pipe to reveal the writer for what he is—a blacksmith of language, forging sentences with hard, painstaking labor. In such instances James's prefaces and notebooks always come to mind, as do Virginia Woolf's diaries, James Agee's letters to Father Flye, Trollope's autobiography, and any good life of the supreme hack Samuel Johnson. But for me the correspondence of Gustave Flaubert soars above all other works in setting forth the proper ideals and accompanying rigors of art.

To most Americans Flaubert is probably little more than a patchwork memory of *Madame Bovary*, the *Silas Marner* of introductory college French lit courses. But should Flaubert be more than a name, it is in large part due to the efforts of Francis Steegmuller, who now caps his career as a Flaubertiste with a translation of *The Letters of Gustave Flaubert*. Those readers familiar with Steegmuller's "double portrait," *Flaubert and Madame Bovary* (first published in 1939) or his more recent compilation, *Flaubert in Egypt*, know how extensively he has drawn on the letters—and how well he has already translated many of them in these earlier works. This thoughtful selection from the correspondence renders every phrase exactly and memorably, as befits the martyr of the *mot juste*, this anchorite of the religion of art. From its forthright Englishing of Flaubert's bawdy to the gracefulness of Steegmuller's connecting commentary and the handsomeness of the book's general design, *The Letters of Gustave Flaubert* is a treasure.

This first (of two volumes) focuses on Flaubert's growing obsession with writing, his travels in the Near East, and the composition of *Madame Bovary*.

Flaubert was early caught up in the fervor of a vision, which he proselytized to his correspondents and which he tried to realize in his work. "I envision a style," he wrote at the outset of his career, "a style that would be beautiful, that someone will invent some day, ten years or ten centuries from now, one that would be rhythmic as verse, precise as the language of the sciences, undulant, deep-voiced as a cello, tipped with flame: a style that would pierce your idea like a dagger, and on which your thought would sail easily ahead over a smooth surface, like a skiff before a good tail wind."

He spent his life pursuing that almost chimerical ideal, and in the process transformed novel writing from an amusement into a vocation. His letters chronicle his nightly devotions—"Last week I spent five days writing one page"—and have been justly called the bible of art for art's sake. André Gide kept a collection of them by his bedside; Henry James spoke reverently of their author as *the* novelist.

Born in 1821, Gustave Flaubert was the son of a highly respected Rouen surgeon, whose wise investments ensured that his son would never have to live by his pen. From an early age the boy wrote easily, turning out plays, stories, and short novels, all of them vaguely romantic and effusively lyrical. (The best early work, *Novembre*, treats a young man's love for a prostitute.) For a while Flaubert halfheartedly studied law in Paris, but following what appears to have been an epileptic seizure, he abandoned any thought of a worldly career for the more contemplative life of art.

His first novel that he thought publishable was *La Tentation de Saint Antoine*, a gaudy, phantasmagoric prose poem, based on a Brueghel painting that depicted the various temptations of the ascetic hermit. Flaubert's two best friends advised him to throw it into the fire. (He didn't: he was to return to *La Tentation* twice more, seeing in the saint's life a reflection of his own.) Depressed and uncertain of his vocation after this setback, Flaubert accompanied one of these friends, Maxime Du Camp, on an eighteen-month trip through the Near East.

In the "Orient" the young writer discovered an oasis of erotic satisfaction, a land of "*luxe, calme et volupté*." In letters home he describes the waters of the Red Sea caressing his body like "a thousand liquid breasts"; he watches a famous courtesan perform the erotic Bee dance and then sleeps with her amid the cockroaches. He even claims to have sodomized an Egyptian bath boy. "It made me laugh," he wrote his other friend Louis Bouilhet, "that's all. But I'll be at it again. To be done well, an experiment must be repeated." But even while sexually distracted the would-be novelist records the smallest details—a dancing girl's bad incisor, a speck of sand in the eye of a young whore.

When Flaubert returned from Egypt, the now thirty-year-old writer took up again with his mistress Louise Colet, a Parisian woman of letters, and soon afterward plunged into the four-and-a-half-year composition of *Madame Bovary* (whose plot was suggested by a provincial case of adultery and suicide).

In his almost daily letters to Louise, scribbled in the morning after a night of writing and revision, the young novelist hammers out his philosophy of art. "There are no noble or ignoble subjects," he writes. "From the standpoint of pure Art one might almost establish the axiom that there is no such thing as subject—style in itself being an absolute manner of seeing things." Louise, as a poet, counters with the claims of romanticism, that art should be an outpouring of strong, personal emotion. Flaubert answers disdainfully that "an author in his book must be like God in the universe, present everywhere and visible nowhere."

When not discoursing about the impersonality of art, Flaubert dwells on sex, the other great theme of the letters. "I wish to gorge you with all the joys of flesh," he writes to his mistress, "until you faint and die. I want you to be astonished by me, to confess to yourself that you had never even dreamt of such transports." (Despite this gusto, he becomes as fearful as an adolescent when "the redcoats" fail to arrive on time.) The correspondence constantly documents the close relationship, often antithetical, between sex and art, between the urge to procreate and the wish to create. A night of writing resembles a stretch of violent lovemaking. Spending his energies on a woman takes away his energies for art. Although he tells Louise that he dreams of the roundness of her breasts, instead of traveling to Paris for a rendezvous, he pumps her for information about the reading of romantic young girls, using her as a source for his heroine's psychology as Joyce would use his wife, Nora, for Molly Bloom's. "Love," he wrote, "is only a superior kind of curiosity."

While staving off the sexual demands of Louise, Flaubert spent his nights with *Madame Bovary*, taking three months to compose one scene, shouting out his phrases over and over, testing their balance. "A good prose sentence should be like a good line of poetry—unchangeable, just as rhythmic, just as sonorous." Even the alteration of a single word, he explains in one letter, disrupts the unity of several pages. Each Sunday his friend Bouilhet would go over the week's work with him, criticizing epithets, pointing out deficiencies in the dialogue (Flaubert much preferred indirect discourse), compelling him to rework his outline, in all ways playing Max Perkins to his Gallic Thomas Wolfe. Within a short while Flaubert loathed the book, began to label it a mere exercise. His niece Caroline, then a little girl, believed that "Bovary" was a synonym for work, since her uncle always gave a sigh and kept saying that he had to get back to his Bovary.

Yet even as he grew disgusted, he refused "to hurry by a single second a sentence that isn't ripe." His former traveling companion Du Camp founded a magazine, *La Revue de Paris,* and began to urge on him the idea of becoming established, of "making it." Literature, in Du Camp's view, was a product and one sells what the marketplace desires. Flaubert rejected this argument outright: "It may well be that from a commercial point of view there are "'favorable moments,' a ready market for one kind of article or another. . . . Let those who wish to manufacture those things hasten to set up their factories: I well understand that they should. But if your work of art is good, if it is authentic, its echo will be heard, it will find its place—in six months, six years, or after you're gone. What difference does it make?"

This faith in the ultimate recognition of good art is one that has consoled many writers since. Having been tested in these early years against the pulls of both romanticism and expedience, Flaubert continued to defend a disinterested, impersonal aesthetic throughout his career, in later years most vigorously against his friend George Sand's view that art should be socially useful and committed (see *The George Sand–Gustave Flaubert Letters*). Unfortunately, like many a founder of a sect, Flaubert also grew more intolerant and strident in later life: soon after this volume of letters closes with the publication of *Madame Bovary* (1856) and its successful defense against charges of obscenity, Flaubert will begin to rage obsessively about his nausea for the bourgeois. His future books will be drier, more clinical, whether portraying the sensual carnage of *Salammbô,* the bitter ironies of *L'Education Sentimentale,* or the black humor of *Bouvard et Pécuchet.*

Nearly everyone agrees that Flaubert might have become an even greater novelist had he been less the rigorous writing machine and more a human being. Yet his fanatical devotion to exactness and form make him the best of all writing teachers, as Maupassant, Proust, and Joyce all knew. "It takes more genius to say, in proper style: 'close the door,' or 'he wanted to sleep' than to give all the literature courses in the world." *The Letters of Gustave Flaubert* should both inspire and discourage writers of any age.

March 30, 1980

THE POSTHUMOUS MEMOIRS
OF BRÁS CUBAS

By Joaquim Maria Machado de Assis
Translated from the Portuguese by Gregory Rabassa

DOM CASMURRO

By Joaquim Maria Machado de Assis
Translated from the Portuguese by John Gledson

Machado de Assis (1839–1908) is Brazil's greatest novelist, and ranks high among the most appealing writers in the world. Machado started out with every disadvantage: he was epileptic, severely myopic, born to the most complete poverty; his father was a mulatto in a Brazil that still held slaves, his mother died young, and he had almost no formal education. Yet this short, unattractive boy taught himself to write while working at a typesetter's and rose to become the president of the Brazilian Academy of Letters. At his death he was given an official state funeral.

Though he lived mainly in the nineteenth century, Machado possesses an almost postmodern sensibility—playful, ironic, and tricky. He writes in one- or two-page chapters, loves digressions, and frequently addresses the reader, making him a part of the novel's action. That action often begins with a satirical portrayal of upper-class society but usually ends with some sort of disillusionment—the taste of ashes. One of the Brazilian's first English translators, William L. Grossman, called Machado "the most disenchanted writer in occidental literature."

Yet like Samuel Beckett or Thomas Bernhard, Machado covers his pessimism with a cloak of high spirits—the kind touched with gallows humor and an Olympian resignation before the sheer foolishness of mankind. In one of his best short stories, "The Psychiatrist," a doctor in a small provincial town gradually commits most of its population to his new insane asylum. However, the zealous medical man eventually frees all the inmates when he realizes that a person needs to be insane to survive in a crazy world. On the other hand, if this is true . . . In due course, the doctor recognizes that he himself possesses "wisdom, patience, tolerance, truthfulness, loyalty, and moral fortitude—all the qualities that go to make an utter madman." With perfect logic, he ends his life as the only patient in his own mental hospital.

In *The Posthumous Memoirs of Brás Cubas* (1881) Machado opens with the death of the main character. At sixty-four Brás Cubas imagines "a sublime remedy, an antihypochondriacal poultice, destined to alleviate our melancholy humanity." Unfortunately, while researching this elixir, he neglects his health, so much so that he falls mortally ill. On his deathbed, Brás finds himself plagued by the well-meaning, including "a fellow who would visit me every day and talk about exchange rates, colonization, and the need for developing railroads, nothing of greater interest to a dying man." Alas, our hero soon succumbs, and the real story begins, for after his "transition" Brás decides to relate the highlights of his exceptionally ordinary life: first love with a clever gold digger, university days in Portugal, years of idleness, a long-term affair with the woman who spurned him to marry an ambitious politico, and ultimately his own election to the Brazilian parliament. There, in his single address to that august body, Brás passionately urges the government to reduce the size of the hats called shakos worn by the national guard: "The impressions made by the speech were varied. As regards the form, the quick eloquence, the literary and philosophical part, the opinion was unanimous. Everyone told me it was perfect and that no one had ever been able to extract so many ideas from a shako. But the political part was considered deplorable by many. . . . I added that the need to reduce the size of the shako was not so great that it couldn't wait a few years and, in any case, I was ready to compromise in the extent of the cut, being content with three quarters of an inch or less."

The Posthumous Memoirs of Brás Cubas is a book that alternately recalls Sterne and Voltaire; in fact, its most appealing character is the philosopher Quincas Borba (who also appears in the novel translated as *Philosopher or Dog?*). Borba ardently espouses Humanitism, which reverses many of the traditional vices and virtues; he dies insisting that pain is an illusion and that "Pangloss, the calumnied Pangloss was not as dotty as Voltaire supposed." In another chapter, Brás actually complains in Shandean fashion: "I'm beginning to regret this book. Not that it bores me. I have nothing to do and, really, putting together a few meager chapters for that other world is always a task that distracts me from eternity a little. But the book is tedious . . . because the main defect of the book is you, reader. You're in a hurry to grow old and the book moves slowly. You love direct and continuous narration, a regular and fluid style, and this book and my style are like drunkards, they stagger left and right, they walk and stop, mumble, yell, cackle, shake their fists at the sky, stumble, and fall. . . ."

While *Brás Cubas* remains a highly original, bittersweet comic novel, *Dom Casmurro* (1900) is a heartbreaking masterpiece. Indeed, Helen Caldwell, a leading translator and critic of Machado, calls it "perhaps the finest of all American novels of either continent." Exaggeration? Yes, I suppose, but not by much. In *Dom Casmurro* young Bento Santiago falls for the vivacious, irresistible Capitu, but his mother has promised God that he will become a priest. After much effort and contrivance, not to mention the help of his good friend Escobar, Bento eventually frees himself from this vow and marries his beloved. Following a long wait, a son is born. From here on, life becomes a torture for Bento because he convinces himself that the child looks precisely like Escobar.

Dom Casmurro inexorably moves from the light of first love to the darkening penumbra of jealousy and obsession. It abounds with echoes of *Othello*. Yet the story is far more subtle than it may seem at first. For generations Brazilian critics assumed that Capitu was guilty of adultery—but is she? Caldwell and some other modern interpreters see the narrator's jealousy as entirely delusional. The soul of the affectionate Bento ("blessed") is gradually usurped by the bitter Hyde-like Casmurro ("a moody, wrong-headed man"). Which interpretation is correct? But need one, or even can one, decide? After all, ambiguity and uncertainty lie at the cankered heart of all jealousy. As Proust shows throughout *In Search of Lost Time*, no proofs of fidelity are ever enough. One can never really know.

In another of his nine novels, *Esau and Jacob*, Machado explains how he should be read: "The attentive, truly ruminative reader has four stomachs in his brain, and through these he passes and repasses the actions and events, until he deduces the truth, which was, or seemed to be, hidden." Certainly *Dom Casmurro* is one of those books that deepen the second time through. When does Bento's corruption—or Capitu's—start? Very early in their love the narrator observes, "As you see, Capitu, at the age of 14, already had some daring ideas, though much less daring than others she had later." On a first reading one may slide right past this remark; upon reflection it foretells the whole novel. In a sense *Dom Casmurro*, like *Brás Cubas*, may be considered a posthumous memoir, in this case by one of the living dead, a mere husk. The boy who once called Capitu his "vocation" has become a warped and embittered man, his pitiful existence devoted to casual affairs and a proposed history of the suburbs of Rio de Janeiro.

These two novels, newly translated, inaugurate Oxford's Library of Latin

America. I had hoped to welcome the series unreservedly but can't. John Gledson's *Dom Casmurro* seems excellent, as good as Helen Caldwell's classic 1953 version. But the *Brás Cubas* is—at least in its first edition—a disgrace. Never have I seen more typographical errors in one short book: letters are transposed ("htis"), left out ("short skits" becomes "short skis"), added (carved figures resemble "statutes"); words are broken up ("in vented") and syntax scrambled, "Put that in name small caps, OBLIVION"; the possessive *s* is regularly dropped from words, and inadvertent coinages proliferate, among them Erasmus's *The Praise of Polly*. That last is nearly as funny as "two souls the post encountered in Purgatory" and ideas "fluttering in my bran," not to mention the "single qua non" instead of sine qua non. I suppose many of these mistakes result from overreliance on computers, but Oxford really shouldn't boast about the novel's being "superbly edited." Rabassa's actual translation strikes me as slightly more precise but also more stilted than William Grossman's 1952 version (known as *Epitaph of a Small Winner*).

One expects Oxford to correct these errors in future printings. But will the publisher commission new afterwords as well? Those to both these wonderful novels are pretentious examples of almost unreadable academese. They represent just the sort of fustian, overblown rhetoric that Machado de Assis always loathed. Best to ignore them entirely and stick with the quicksilver prose of *Brás Cubas* and *Dom Casmurro*.

November 23, 1997

VISIONARIES
AND MORALISTS

I deeply admire the Victorians. They could churn out novels, tracts, poems, plays, and witticisms, while also ruling the empire, building fortunes, and translating Greek in their spare time. In private libraries one still sometimes glimpses sets of their complete works, thirty, forty, or fifty leather-bound volumes, with hubbed spines. They stare down at us with a kind of self-sufficient grandeur, disdaining the need for actual readers.

Yet, really, how could figures like Ruskin, Trollope, and Shaw actually write so much—and so brilliantly? They were not only Artists, they were also passionate about society, politics, culture. Perhaps the best—and most thrilling—summary of their character is still Lytton Strachey's description of Florence Nightingale in Eminent Victorians: *"It was not by gentle sweetness and self-abnegation that order was brought out of chaos; it was by strict method, by stern discipline, by rigid attention to detail, by ceaseless labor, by the fixed determination of an indomitable will."*

What follows is really a picture gallery, one in which experts have cleaned and properly illuminated the old portraits. One moves along the exhibition from that American Victorian eminence Ralph Waldo Emerson through William Morris and Oscar Wilde to A. E. Housman and Madame Blavatsky. Alas, I still await my chance to write on some of my favorite nineteenth-century writers—Jane Austen, in particular—and two of my favorite British novels, Vanity Fair *and* Middlemarch. *I have also, with regret, left out of this section some essays on minor masterpieces of the era:* Eothen, *A. W. Kinglake's account of his travels in the Middle East during the 1830s; the great boys' adventure story* Moonfleet, *by John Mead Falkner. I herewith recommend them.*

One last point: be prepared to discover that the Victorians led lives and thought thoughts far more unexpected, original, and disconcerting than commonly believed.

EMERSON: THE MIND ON FIRE

By Robert D. Richardson Jr.

Robert D. Richardson Jr.'s critical biography *Emerson: The Mind on Fire* is one of those exciting books that flash bolts of lightning across an entire intellectual era and up and down modern history. Earlier in this century Ralph Waldo Emerson (1803–1882) had been reduced, by some, to little more than an advocate of aggressive optimism, and his doctrine of "self-reliance" distorted into an apology for go-getting American Babbitry—"Hitch your wagon to a star." But more recently Emerson's essays and example have again been recognized for their decisive influence on much of this country's literature, philosophy, and religious thought. "The mind of Emerson," the critic Harold Bloom declares, "is the mind of America."

Following the approach adopted for his award-winning study of Thoreau, Richardson focuses on the shaping forces in Emerson's life: the family he loved, the friends he admired and argued with, and, above all, the books he eagerly skimmed and then carefully studied. Nothing of importance to American thinkers in the first half of the nineteenth century escaped Emerson's attention: he read and reread Plato, seventeenth-century divines, Persian poets, Goethe, theories of scientific classification, guides to the cultivation of fruit trees, *Leaves of Grass*, abolitionist tracts, Hindu epics, and every kind of biography and history.

Through all these influences Richardson carefully traces the growth of a fearless speculative mind as Emerson progresses from Harvard student to Unitarian minister to transcendental philosopher, gradually achieving renown as a controversial essayist and Lyceum lecturer (some five hundred talks in four decades) and ultimately concluding his life as the national sage. Along the way, this angular, steely-eyed New Englander listens to Coleridge soliloquize, earns the friendship of Thomas Carlyle, entertains John Brown, talks on the same platform with Susan B. Anthony, and meets everyone from Lincoln and Ruskin to John Muir and Brigham Young. When it counts, Emerson invariably stands up for the right causes: speaking out forcefully against the evils of slavery, proclaiming the genius of Walt Whitman and Henry Thoreau, supporting the rights of women.

As has long been recognized, Emerson's genius as a prose writer is aphoristic, gnomic. His essays loosely link sentences of fine-hammered steel, drawn largely from his journals (some 263 volumes altogether, elaborately cross-indexed). To read any of his better-known essays is like reading *Hamlet*: the pages crackle with "quotations." "We are always getting ready to live, but never living. . . . A foolish consistency is the hobgoblin of little minds. . . . In every work of genius we recognize our own rejected thoughts; they come back to us with a certain alienated majesty." Even Emerson's poems proffer a treasury of the familiar: "Things are in the saddle, / And ride mankind." "Here once the embattled farmers stood / And fired the shot heard round the world."

Some of these lines have lost luster only because they are so well known (though the power of "Self-Reliance" and "Experience" remains electrifying for anyone discovering them for the first time). But there subsists a good deal of wonderful strangeness throughout Emerson. Consider this Blakean parable: "I dreamed that I floated in the great Ether, and I saw this world floating also not far off, but diminished to the size of an apple. Then an angel took it in his hand and brought it to me and said, 'This must thou eat.' And I ate the world."

Nor should we overlook the essayist's Yankee shrewdness and humor. "That which we call sin in others is experiment for us." "The reason why the world lacks unity and lies broken and in heaps, is because man is disunited with himself." "The louder he talked of his honor, the faster we counted our spoons." And surely this journal entry should refute Henry James's view that Emerson possessed no awareness of "the dark, the foul, the base": "Now for near five years I have been indulged by the gracious Heaven in my long holiday in this goodly house of mine, entertaining and entertained by so many worthy and gifted friends, and all this time poor Nanny Barron, the madwoman, has been screaming herself hoarse at the Poorhouse across the brook and I still hear her whenever I open my window."

In fact, Emerson was a man all too well acquainted with earthly sorrows. His first wife, the beautiful Ellen Tucker, died at nineteen (from tuberculosis). Of his four brothers—Ralph Waldo was thought to be among the least promising of the Emerson boys—one proved retarded, another suffered a mental breakdown while studying in Germany, and the two most obviously gifted died in their late twenties (also from tuberculosis). Emerson and his second wife, Lidian, doted on their son Waldo—until the little boy caught scarlatina and succumbed suddenly at age five. Emerson's greatest intellectual counterweight, Margaret Fuller, with whom he carried on a platonic affair that periodically threatened to get out of hand, drowned on the ship bringing her back from Italy. She was only a few rods from the American shore and had just turned forty. Of course, Emerson pronounced the funeral elegy—Richardson compares it to "Lycidas" for its somber beauty—of the prickly eccentric he always regarded as his best friend, Henry David Thoreau, dead at only forty-four. In short, if Ralph Waldo Emerson built a doctrine of self-reliance and optimism, he built it over the abyss. "Great men, great nations, have not been boasters or buffoons," he writes, "but perceivers of the terror of life." And for the mature Emerson not even religion could offer any consolation: "Other world? There is no other world; here or nowhere is the whole fact."

About Robert Richardson's biography it is hard to be temperate. He sets forth complex matters—Neoplatonism, Transcendentalism, Hegelian thought —with conciseness and a light touch; each chapter is only five or six pages long. He quotes frequently from his subject, draws the occasional analogy with contemporary thinkers or writers (Eudora Welty, Simone de Beauvoir), and likes a whiff of dry wit: in one youthful journal Emerson "listed several references, then wrote, 'I shall resume this subject when I have more to say,' to which he added, evidently at some later date, 'Spare us.' "

In Richardson's own pages we discover that the philosopher ate pie for breakfast, preferred translations to texts in the original Greek or German, and cultivated more than one hundred different kinds of fruit trees. As a young man he once thought of writing an essay on the evils of imagination. Throughout Richardson convincingly emphasizes the contributions of several remarkable women to Emerson's mental development, starting with his mystical, deeply introspective Aunt Mary Moody Emerson, who, according to her obituary, "was thought to have the power of saying more disagreeable things in half an hour than any person living." He also shows us the nine-year-old Louisa May Alcott come to inquire after the sick five-year-old Waldo, only to be met at the door by the grief-stricken father who tells her, "Child, he is dead." We learn that Emerson was the second choice to deliver the Phi Beta Kappa address "The American Scholar," which Oliver Wendell Holmes later dubbed "our intellectual Declaration of Independence." Always Richardson makes clear how much Emerson borrowed and adapted from others—the Quaker's "inner light or still small voice," for example, lies behind the moralist's insistence that "no law can be sacred to me but that of my nature." "The universe," as he says elsewhere, "is the externalization of the soul."

Near the end of his book, Richardson lists some basic tenets of Emersonianism (e.g., "every day is the day of judgment," "the powers of the soul are commensurate with its needs"), then follows with a summarizing paragraph that displays his own considerable powers as a writer: "The public consequences of such convictions for Emerson were a politics of social liberalism, abolitionism, women's suffrage, American Indian rights, opposition to the Mexican War, and civil disobedience when government was wrong. The personal consequence of such perceptions was an almost intolerable awareness that every morning began with infinite promise. Any book may be read, any idea thought, any action taken. Anything that has ever been possible to human beings is possible to most of us every time the clock says six in the morning. On a day no different from the one now breaking, Shakespeare sat down to begin *Hamlet* and Fuller began her history of the Roman revolution of 1848. Each of us has all the time there is; each accepts those invitations he can discern. By the same token, every evening brings a reckoning of infinite regret for the paths refused, openings not seen, and actions not taken."

Emily Dickinson once called Emerson's *Representative Men* "a little granite book you can lean on." Just so, *Emerson: The Mind on Fire* is a book you can lean on, return to, live with. It can be dense, it can be repetitive (at least three times we are told that the *Heimskringla* is the Homeric epic of the North), but it is above all a book of impassioned and humane scholarship. It will send you on or back to a writer who will make you think about, well, almost everything—from art to religion to citizenship to fate. Of course, Emerson himself best summed up all these matters: "What," asks this great moralist, "is the end of human life? It is not, believe me, the chief end of man that he should make a fortune and beget children whose end is likewise to make a fortune, but it is, in few words, that he should explore himself."

April 9, 1995

LEWIS CARROLL: A BIOGRAPHY

By Morton N. Cohen

Near the beginning of this painstakingly researched and altogether engrossing biography of Lewis Carroll (1832–1898), Morton N. Cohen remarks that the two Alice books and the great nonsense poem *The Hunting of the Snark* are the most quoted literary works in English, excepting only Shakespeare and the Bible. Once that might have meant something, but who today knows Shakespeare and the Bible? In Wonderland, the Mock Turtle tells Alice, children learn "Reeling and Writhing," followed by "Ambition, Distraction, Uglification, and Derision." Not so long ago that was funny. Now it sounds . . . all too true.

Humor requires context. The two Alice novels constantly play against rigid Victorian commonplaces, expectations, and ideals—many of which, like the Baker, have "softly and suddenly vanished away." How can Wonderland seem quite as wonderful to a child who has lived all his life among electronic marvels? Can even the Jabberwock—"the jaws that bite, the claws that catch"—hold any fears in the era of *Alien* and *Predator*? More and more we really do need Martin Gardner's *Annotated Alice*, along with a fine biography like this one, to detect the jokes, appreciate the parodies, or simply get the point. Morton Cohen maintains that the Alice books have hitherto been so universally popular because they mirror the anxieties of all children (the arbitrary-seeming injunctions of teachers and parents, the confusions of body image, changing size, etc.). He may be right, but I suspect that today's kids seldom actually read the stories—the Disney movie is what they know—and Carroll has become the preserve of nostalgic or scholarly grown-ups. If this is true, I wish that Cohen had stressed more fully Carroll's true glory: a perfectly cadenced prose, chock-a-block with imaginative wordplay. Almost anything the man wrote—letters to child-friends, reports as the curator of an Oxford common room, an essay on how to compose a letter—mingles cleverness and kindliness in one of English literature's most engaging styles.

In this admiring life Cohen portrays Carroll, born Charles Lutwidge Dodgson, as a Victorian hero: set apart by a passion for little girls, burdened with the sense that he has failed to live up to his father's dreams, fussbudgety in his habits, and religious to the bottom of his soul, Dodgson needed huge reservoirs of will power to create and then maintain a life of decorum and achievement. Who knows? Without this self-discipline he might have been destroyed like Oscar Wilde. Cohen takes pains to emphasize that the ardent admirer of eleven-year-old Alice Liddell and the sometime portraitist of eight-year-old female nudes never in life crossed the thin line that took Humbert Humbert into the arms of his Lolita. In dreams and fantasies, however, Dodgson may have acted out forbidden desires: hence the feelings of sinfulness and the pleas for divine forgiveness that recur in his diaries, especially during the years of his infatuation with the winsome Alice. (One does wonder, however, about various missing volumes and pages: Just what did they reveal?) Still, Cohen has studied his man for thirty years, edited the letters, and mastered the historical record: he concludes, with a slight defensiveness, that Dodgson kept his relations with his child-friends flirtatious yet strictly honorable. To many in this age of Oprah and Geraldo—fit cousins to the Queen of Hearts and the Caterpillar—that kind of self-control may seem incredible, even sick in its own way.

The Reverend Charles Dodgson spent virtually his entire adult life at Christ Church, Oxford, squirreled away in a sumptuous ten-room nest above Tom Quad, the very model of a nineteenth-century minor cleric (he was a deacon in the Church of England) and bachelor mathematics don. Except for periodic trips to London for the theater (he adored Ellen Terry), vacations near the sea at Eastbourne, and a single train trip to Russia with a clergyman friend, the author of *Alice in Wonderland* lived as uneventful and unruffled an existence as one could imagine. He spent hours answering letters, liked to entertain child-friends in his study with mechanical toys and mathematical games, took sides in petty university debates, and published work in his field: little guidebooks to Euclid, a volume on symbolic logic.

To keep up a modern reader's interest, Cohen shrewdly organizes his work thematically so that he constantly circles back to the Alice books: he shows how Dodgson made his immortal story incorporate aspects of an actual little girl (Alice Liddell), elements of Oxford society, universal experiences of childhood, and, deepest of all, a kind of allegorical working out of its author's own inner angst. At the biography's center, though, there always glows that golden afternoon—July 4, 1862—when the three Liddell sisters and Dodgson went rowing on the river and he first imagined the underground realm of the White Rabbit and the Cheshire Cat.

Throughout these 500 pages Cohen reiterates the crucial importance of the young scholar's association with the Liddell family. Alice's father was coauthor of the Liddell-Scott Greek lexicon, the fashionable dean of Christ Church, and one of the most powerful men in Oxford. He and Dodgson disagreed about virtually everything. The imperious and ambitious Mrs. Liddell was even more difficult. Cohen asserts, after marshaling the evidence and making a number of guesses, that the thirty-one-year-old Charles may have hinted to Mrs. Liddell that at some future date he might ask for the hand of young Alice. After all, his own brother Wilfred had recently proposed to a fourteen-year-old (whom he married a few years later). Dodgson was probably delicately tentative, but Mrs. Liddell apparently found the suggestion either obscene or unwanted: she intended her girls to wed the highborn and wealthy. As it turned out, the grown Alice and Queen Victoria's son Leopold fell in love, but this time the young man's even more imperious mom insisted that he could marry only a real princess (which he eventually did). A class system can cut both ways.

Cohen devotes a half dozen excellent pages to Dodgson's notorious "nudities," his photographs of unclothed prepubescent girls (four examples survive). How, Cohen asks, did he manage to convince straitlaced, upper-class mothers to allow him to take such pictures? Dodgson's subtle, shrewd technique for achieving his desired end—his avowal of a purely artistic interest in the nude, the hints that other children had been photographed in this way, his expressed wish that the mother or another adult remain nearby during the photo session—reveal a sly, manipulative streak to his character that Cohen tends to downplay.

Dodgson's photography—he is second only to Julia Cameron as a Victorian portraitist—gave him access not only to children but to many English notables. He visits Tennyson and finds the poet laureate mowing his lawn. He takes some pictures of a little girl who becomes the once popular novelist Mrs. Humphry Ward, still others of the mother of Nancy Mitford, the actress grandmother of Sir John Gielgud, the sisters of Bloomsbury's Clive Bell. At one point Dodgson nearly collaborates with Arthur Sullivan (of Gilbert-and- fame) on an Alice operetta. In a scene that could make a steam-punk short story, the master of nonsense even visits Charles Babbage, the great pioneer of the computer, in the hopes of acquiring one of his "analytical engines." Girlish of face, dressed always in black, Dodgson, said one contemporary, "always appeared to have emerged from a hot bath and a band box."

Any book about Lewis Carroll is bound to be filled with examples of his wit: "Long and painful experience has taught me one great principle in managing business for other people, viz., if you want to inspire confidence, give plenty of statistics. It does not matter that they should be accurate, or even intelligible, so long as there is enough of them." He creates a four-line poem in which each line is an anagram of the hated prime minister, William Ewart Gladstone: "I, wise Mr. G., want to lead all. / A wild man will go at trees. / Wild agitator! Means well. / Wilt tear down all images?" Still, this is not a compendium of japes or jokes; it properly regards its subject as a major author who merits a serious, scholarly life. Personally, I wish there had been more discussion of the two Sylvie and Bruno books, those strange mixtures of Victorian realism and fairy tale that most people, including Cohen, tend to dismiss as pious failures. Cohen also insists that *The Hunting of the Snark* makes its best sense on the aural level rather than the semantic, reversing the view of the Duchess that if you "take care of the sense," then "the sounds will take care of themselves."

This year has been an excellent one for Victorian biography, and Morton N. Cohen's *Lewis Carroll* belongs on the shelf next to Denis Donoghue's *Walter Pater*, Juliet Barker's *The Brontës*, and Fiona MacCarthy's *William Morris*. Together they sound like the guest list for a more than slightly mad tea party.

December 3, 1995

JOHN RUSKIN: THE EARLY YEARS

By Tim Hilton

JOHN RUSKIN: THE LATER YEARS

By Tim Hilton

Of all the Victorian sages, John Ruskin (1819–1900) may be the least read nowadays. Carlyle, Arnold, Pater, Newman, and a few other exemplars of moral authority or refined aestheticism linger on as wraithlike and wispy presences, occasionally glimpsed out of the corner of one's eye in surveys of nineteenth-century British literature. But unlike most of these rather dour humanists, Ruskin wasn't really a literary eminence at all. He started out as a kind of art historian, metamorphosed into a wide-ranging social critic, grew increasingly visionary and utopian, and finally ended his life as a gentle, white-bearded madman.

A hundred years after his death in 1900, Ruskin is remembered, mainly, for the poetry of his prose and for the oddities of his personal life. The Library Edition of his complete works—one of those imposing scholarly monuments comparable to the *Oxford English Dictionary* and the *Dictionary of National Biography*—runs to thirty-nine hefty volumes, but most people have read nothing of this displaced titan other than his sometimes beautiful book titles: *Sesame and Lilies, The Queen of the Air, The Stones of Venice, Unto This Last, The Ethics of the Dust.* Only his late memoir, *Praeterita,* continues to find new admirers (as it should), though a few years back Knopf published an abridged edition of *Modern Painters,* the early magnum opus that starts off as a defense of the great English artist J. M. W. Turner and topsily grows into a study of landscape, a paean to nature, and a sermon on the purpose of life. Alas, too few readers seem to have noticed or cared about the reissue.

Still, Ruskin has never lacked for advocates, from the reverential Proust (who translated Ruskin's *The Bible of Amiens*) and the revolutionary Gandhi to the sleekly civilized Sir Kenneth Clark. That much-missed connoisseur actually went so far as to compile *Ruskin Today*, an anthology of passages originally chosen, he tells us, so that he might easily reread those "which had given me particular pleasure." The result ranks high among the world's ideal bedside books. Consider, for instance, this tender reminiscence—and probably the last sentences written before the memoirist's mind utterly collapsed. Ruskin is recalling a visit to Siena, in the company of the Harvard professor Charles Eliot Norton. The Latin means "More than her gates, Siena opens her heart to you":

"How things bind and blend themselves together! . . . Fonte Branda I last saw with Charles Norton, under the same arches where Dante saw it. We drank of it together, and walked together that evening on the hills above, where the fireflies among the scented thickets shone fitfully in the still undarkened air. How they shone! moving like fine-broken starlight through the purple leaves. How they shone! through the sunset that faded into thunderous night as I entered Siena three days before, the white edges of the mountainous clouds still lighted from the west, and the openly golden sky calm behind the Gate of Siena's heart, with its still golden words, 'Cor magis tibi Sena pandit,' and the fireflies everywhere in sky and cloud rising and falling, mixed with the lightning, and more intense than the stars."

"Fine-broken starlight"—has there ever been a more apt description of fireflies on a summer's night?

Much of Ruskin's descriptive prose—gorgeous, oratorical, ceaselessly streaming along as his consciousness remembers or free-associates—may make today's reader slightly impatient. We no longer have much taste for such opulence and biblical majesty, or much sympathy for unchecked, if glorious, incoherence. But in the right mood, or to those of a receptive sensibility, Ruskin's sentences will take your breath away. Not for nothing did Rossetti—admittedly a disciple—consider Ruskin's early style the best in the world. After all, this was a man who could announce, with Thoreau-like boldness, "There is no wealth but life"; who could tell us, as a godfather of the Arts and Crafts movement, that "in order that people may be happy in their work, these three things are needed: They must be fit for it. They must not do too much of it. And they must have a sense of success in it." Clearly persuasive and direct when he wanted to be, Ruskin is nonetheless at his most Ruskinian when letting out all the organ stops, as in this description of the serpent. It is long, but marvelous: "But that horror is of the myth, not of the creature. There are myriads lower than this, and more loathesome, in the scale of being; the links between dead matter and animation drift everywhere unseen. But it is the strength of the base element that is dreadful in the serpent; it is the very omnipotence of the earth. That rivulet of smooth silver—how does it flow, think you? It literally rows on the earth, with every scale for an oar; it bites the dust with the ridges of its body. Watch it, when it moves slowly:—A wave, but without wind! a current, but with no fall! all the body moving at the same instant, yet some of it to one side, some to another, or some forward, and the rest of the coil backwards; but all with the same calm will and equal way—no contraction, no extension; one soundless, causeless march of sequent rings, and spectral procession of spotted dust, with dissolution in its fangs, dislocation in its coils. Startle it;—the winding stream will become a twisted arrow;—the wave of poisoned life will lash through the grass like a cast lance. . . ."

Ruskin's other claim to common memory lies in his mysterious sexual nature. In 1847 he married Effie Gray, but for the six years of their marriage the couple never once engaged in sexual intercourse. Why? Or rather why not? All that we know for sure is what Effie later wrote, "He had imagined women were quite different to what he saw I was, and that the reason he did not make me his Wife was because he was disgusted with my person the first evening." Explanations for this disgust have ranged from the belief that Ruskin was shocked by the existence of female pubic hair to the possibility that Effie was menstruating. But perhaps the young husband was simply extremely innocent and shy? Certainly, he had been highly protected by his adoring parents—his mother even moved to Oxford to be near her only child while he attended university. Eventually, the Ruskins' marriage was annulled; Effie then wed the painter Millais and bore him eight children.

Many men might have been humiliated by this publicity, but Ruskin not only survived it but went on to love again—with comparable misfortune. In his forties he fell irremediably for a barely pubescent girl named Rose La Touche; the (probably) anorexic preteen grew into a sickly religious fanatic, who died at twenty-seven. But for fifteen years she was the center of Ruskin's emotional life, even during the six years when they were forbidden to meet. That he still managed to produce so much writing, travel extensively around Europe, copy and study the great masters of the Renaissance, and teach courses as the first Slade Professor of Fine Art at Oxford attests to his energy and determination. But there is no question of Ruskin's rapt obsession with this frail childlike beauty, and he belongs to the unhappy ranks of Victorian literature's Humbert Humberts, along with Hazlitt (whose misery over a young serving girl is chronicled in *Liber Amoris*) and Lewis Carroll. Interestingly, Ruskin knew the three Liddell sisters but much preferred the eldest, Edith, to Alice, the intrepid explorer of Wonderland.

All these matters, and much, much else, are illuminated in Tim Hilton's superb and capacious two-volume biography. *John Ruskin: The Early Years* first appeared in 1985 and has recently been reprinted in paperback; there one will

VISIONARIES AND MORALISTS

find an absorbing narrative of the writer's indulged childhood, insights into his prodigious talents as a graphic artist, geologist, and naturalist (as well as a minor poet—Ruskin beat out Arthur Hugh Clough to win Oxford's Newdigate Prize), and a detailed account of his unfortunate marriage. *The Later Years*, just published, is more than twice as long as the first installment, and may daunt all but those who have been eagerly awaiting it. In particular, Hilton hopes that his formidably researched and gracefully written life will win readers over to *Fors Clavigera*, the collective title for the monthly letters—monographs, actually, about anything and everything—that Ruskin ostensibly addressed to the workingmen of Britain. "My hope," confesses Hilton dreamily, "is that the present biography will help to give Ruskin's longest book a role within English literature, by which I mean a place on the shelves of those who like reading books and talking about them."

To those of us who know our Ruskin mainly from snippets, Hilton provides welcome guidance and encouragement. That awesome intellect and endearing personality met nearly everybody: Wordsworth, Darwin, Carlyle (a spiritual father as well as close friend), Gladstone, the Pre-Raphaelite painters (lukewarmly championed), Lewis Carroll, the linguist Max Müller, Cardinal Manning, the young Oscar Wilde. All of them, as well as numerous servants, acolytes, and hangers-on, here earn thoughtful paragraphs or pages. Oddly enough, though, Ruskin never encountered Walter Pater, with whom he is sometimes linked as a theorist of beauty, nor Whistler, who sued him for libel after the critic described his work as a pot of paint flung in the public's face. As one would expect, the first part of *The Later Years* chronicles the torturous love for Rose La Touche, while the second half records the activities of the rather vaguely constituted Guild of St. George—a sodality dedicated to civic reformation—and the great man's gradual descent into depression, madness, and silence. A brief postscript describes the history and current state of Ruskin scholarship.

Still, can any biography, no matter how fine and authoritative, repair the crumbled edifice that is John Ruskin? Perhaps not. But true scholarship needs no justification from bookstores. It is its own reward. Tim Hilton has obviously spent much of his maturity in the study of Ruskin's life and work; his 1,000 pages will be honored and consulted after most of this year's fast-moving best sellers have been long forgotten. He tells, moreover, as enthralling a story as any triple-decker Victorian sensation novel, especially for anyone who has ever loved hopelessly or suffered debilitating depression while trying to get on with his daily work. Above all, Hilton leaves the modern reader convinced that John Ruskin's quicksilver mind deserves our admiration; he seems almost a Victorian Leonardo. How could any one person create a classic children's story

("The King of the Golden River") as well as bring out a basic guide to drawing, then write so brilliantly about everything from the paintings of Turner and Botticelli to antique coins, glaciers, Venetian architecture, and flowers? Ruskin even started a tea shop, led Oxford undergraduates in the building of a road, taught at a girls' school, self-published his own books, and frequently sent letters composed entirely in baby talk.

John Ruskin, writes his biographer, "was out of step with his times; he respected no literary genre; his interests were recondite; he very seldom wrote to entertain; he had few followers, if any; and his methods of publication were so unusual as to limit circulation of his work." Who wouldn't want to know more about such a man? And in Tim Hilton's two-volume life, we have the means and the opportunity to do so. Seize them.

May 28, 2000

AN AUTOBIOGRAPHY

By Anthony Trollope

Anthony Trollope (1815–1882) is hardly a neglected novelist these days, though for a time the author of *Barchester Towers* and *The Way We Live Now* was relegated to the vast dust heap of Victorian period fiction. Vast indeed. For who now spends an evening with Mrs. Humphry Ward or Charles Reade's *The Cloister and the Hearth*?

But Trollope is another matter. Over the past fifteen years, four or five substantial biographies have appeared, nearly all of his fifty or so books are available in paperback, and a finely printed collected works is under way. As in the past, people eagerly turn to the chronicler of Barsetshire because he writes easygoing, plainspoken prose, creates vivid characters, and somehow knows how to tell a long story that just carries one happily along. That he is as wise about human nature as Jane Austen—and often as deliciously comic, too— makes him the ideal novelist for those of middle age or beyond. Fiction, he has written, "should give a picture of common life enlivened by humour and sweetened by pathos."

His autobiography, however, should be read by any would-be author, for it reveals, better than almost any other work in English, that a writer is a man (or woman) who sits down at a desk each morning . . . and writes. To Trollope, the creation of fiction may occasionally rise to Art, but there's no nonsense about awaiting inspiration or a timely visit from the Muse. For most of his adult life this amazing Victorian worked a full day as an administrator for the British postal service (he instituted the street-corner mailbox). He also rode to hounds two or three times a week, enjoyed playing whist in the evening at the Garrick Club, journeyed frequently on business—all around Ireland, to the West Indies, Egypt, America, Australia. Yet nearly every morning he woke promptly at five-thirty, drank a cup of coffee, and sat down before a quire of paper, pen in hand:

"When I have commenced a new book, I have always prepared a diary, divided into weeks, and carried on for the period which I have allowed myself for the completion of the work. In this I have entered, day by day, the number of pages I have written, so that if at any time I have slipped into idleness for a day or two, the record of that idleness has been there, staring me in the face, and demanding of me increased labour, so that the deficiency might be supplied. According to the circumstances of the time—whether my other business might be then heavy or light, or whether the book which I was writing was or was not wanted with speed,—I have allotted myself so many pages a week. The average number has been about 40. It has been placed as low as 20, and has risen to 112. And as a page is an ambiguous term, my page has been made to contain 250 words; and as words, if not watched, will have a tendency to straggle, I have had every word counted as I went. In the bargains I have made with publishers . . . I have prided myself on completing my work exactly within the proposed dimensions. But I have prided myself especially on completing it within the proposed time,— and I have always done so."

Impressive yes, but there's more: How long did Trollope actually work each morning, year after year? He tells us: "All those I think who have lived as literary men,—working daily as literary labourers—will agree with me that three hours a day will produce as much as a man ought to write. But then, he should so have trained himself that he shall be able to work continuously during those three hours,—so have tutored his mind that it shall not be necessary for him to sit nibbling his pen, and gazing at the wall before him, till he shall have found the words with which he wants to express his ideas. It had at this time become my custom, . . . to write with my watch before me, and to require from myself 250 words every quarter of an hour."

So a thousand words an hour, three hours a day makes 3,000 words. A fair-sized modern novel clocks in at 90,000 to 120,000 words. *The Great Gatsby* is only about 50,000 words. Trollope would have written it in less than a month. He goes on: "But my three hours were not devoted entirely to writing. I always began my task by reading the work of the day before, an operation which would take me half an hour, and which consisted chiefly in weighing with my ear the sound of the words and phrases. I would strongly recommend this practice to all tyros in writing. . . . By reading what he has last written, just before he recommences his task, the writer will catch the tone and spirit of what he is then saying, and will avoid the fault of seeming to be unlike himself. This division of time allowed me to produce over ten pages of an ordinary novel volume a day, and if kept up through ten months, would have given as its results three novels of three volumes each in the year."

Perhaps the only mild critique one might make of *An Autobiography* lies in just this faintest hint of smugness when Trollope describes his working methods.

Why, he seems to suggest, if somebody of such small talent as myself can write two or three long novels a year, anyone should be able to do it—provided he or she possesses the self-discipline. Perhaps the most astonishing sentence in this astonishing book occurs halfway through: "While I was in Egypt, I finished *Doctor Thorne*, and on the following day began *The Bertrams*." One might add that Trollope disdained rewriting and outlines as "a waste of time." "If a man knows his craft with his pen, he will have learned to write without the necessity of changing his words or the form of his sentences." Alas, some of us can't set down one new word without changing two others.

Trollope's early years instilled a realistic modesty about the literary life. His father was a dreamy, irritable man who spent years working on an *Encyclopedia Ecclesiastica*—"it was his ambition to describe all ecclesiastical terms, including the denominations of every fraternity of monks and every convent of nuns, with all their orders and subdivisions. . . . When he died, three numbers out of eight had been published by subscription; and are now, I fear, unknown, and buried in the midst of that huge pile of futile literature, the building up of which has broken so many hearts." Trollope's mother, Frances, began to write only after the age of fifty "for the sustenance" of her impoverished family—keeping to her publishing schedule even when nursing a consumptive son, daughter, and husband. "I have written many novels under many circumstances," Trollope tells us, "but I doubt much whether I could write one when my whole heart was by the bedside of a dying son." Husband and daughter also died. "It was about this period of her career," recalls Trollope with awe, "that her best novels were written." By the time of her own death, Frances Trollope had written more than one hundred books.

Young Trollope, being poor, was mocked at school, displayed no academic prowess, and was lucky to land a clerkly job in the post office. First published only in his early thirties, his initial novels were utter failures and went completely unremarked by the public. Indeed, Trollope tells us that he wrote for twelve years before making any income to speak of from fiction. Yet money was clearly important to him: he frankly discusses his contracts, even listing the exact amounts he was paid for each of his works: "It is a mistake to suppose that a man is a better man because he despises money. Few do so, and those few in doing so suffer a defect. Who does not desire to be hospitable to his friends, generous to the poor, liberal to all, munificent to his children, and to be himself free from the carking fears which poverty creates? The subject will not stand an argument;—and yet authors are told that they should disregard payment for their work, and be content to devote their unbought brains to the welfare of the public. Brains that are unbought will never serve the public much."

In many ways *An Autobiography* will surprise readers by such instances of authorial frankness—Trollope, for instance, admits, "I have always had before my eyes the charms of reputation." Above all, he is surprisingly harsh about his own creations. Take those two novels mentioned above, *Doctor Thorne* and *The Bertrams*. The first soon ranked among his most popular titles; the other long lay among his most ignored. Yet, says their author, "I myself think that they are of about equal merit, but that neither of them is good." His own favorites among his books are those about the politician Plantagenet Palliser, especially *The Prime Minister*—which the critics damned. *Orley Farm*, he observes, possesses his best plot, but "taking it as a whole," *The Last Chronicle of Barset* is "the best novel I have written." Elsewhere, of *The Small House at Allington* and *Can You Forgive Her?*, he writes, "I do not think I have ever done better work," even defensively asserting that neither would have been improved had he spent more time on them ("I have rushed at the work as a rider rushes at a fence which he does not see"). Though readers may speak tenderly of the characters in all these books, Trollope himself regards them with a surgeon's cold eye. The revered Lily Dale (of *Small House*) he contentiously calls "somewhat of a female prig." Once, when he overheard two clergymen complain that the celebrated Mrs. Proudie of the Barsetshire novels had grown tiresome, he went up and told them that she would be dead within the week. And so she was.

Trollope proffers one chapter on his contemporaries, judging Thackeray the major novelist of the day, followed by George Eliot (a more daring choice for the time). Dickens he thinks sloppy, stagey, and melodramatic and his style "jerky, ungrammatical." Wilkie Collins's work is overly contrived and plot driven. A serious reader, Trollope accumulated a private library of five thousand volumes, "dearer to me even than the horses." The greatest novels in English, in his considered view, are Thackeray's *Henry Esmond*, Jane Austen's *Pride and Prejudice*, and Walter Scott's *Ivanhoe*. In adulthood he took the trouble to teach himself to read Latin with ease, eventually bringing out a study of Caesar's *Commentaries* and a life of Cicero. At what seems a hardly decrepit fifty-five, some of his friends told him he was too old to go on fabricating "love-stories."

Trollope finished this memoir of his literary career at just past sixty and lived another half dozen years, long enough to turn out thirteen and a half more novels. When *An Autobiography* was published posthumously (in 1883), as was always intended, readers were said to be horrified at its mercantile tone, and Trollope's reputation sank. In truth, his books were beginning to suffer critical disparagement even before then. But nowadays one would be hard put to name a more sheerly enjoyable Victorian novelist than Anthony Trollope. Or one who, in this engaging, no-nonsense autobiography, offers greater insight into the maddening, incomparable profession of letters.

July 20, 2003

WILLIAM MORRIS:
A LIFE FOR OUR TIME

By Fiona MacCarthy

Quite possibly the greatest of all Renaissance men lived during the second half of the nineteenth century. Almost nothing, it would seem, lay beyond the creative powers and hands-on craftsmanship of William Morris (1834–1896), "the ablest man of his time," according to the multitalented John Ruskin; "one of those men whom history will never overtake," in the words of the historian E. P. Thompson.

Virtually any high Victorian might dash off a bit of verse or translate the classics, a few might also lecture on politics or even run a fashionable business, but only William Morris could also weave tapestry by hand, cut woodblocks, fabricate stained-glass windows, do needlework and embroidery, create intricate wallpapers, paint murals, edit a radical newspaper (*Commonweal*), travel to the interior of Iceland, found the Socialist League, and marry Jane Burden, the most hauntingly beautiful of the Pre-Raphaelite "stunners."

And all that's just for starters. Morris blithely composed lyrics for revolutionary marching songs, authored major works of sword-and-sorcery (e.g., *The Well at the World's End*, with its wonderfully evocative title), scornfully dubbed Queen Victoria the Empress Brown, penned some 1,500 pages of exquisite calligraphy (one of several old arts he largely revived), helped design the architecturally influential Red House, and oversaw the production of that most sumptuous of all fine press books, the Kelmscott Chaucer, for which he made the type, borders, and ornaments. He also managed to stay close friends with both the great painter and society favorite Sir Edward Burne-Jones and the legendary Russian nihilist Sergius Stepniak.

And even that isn't all. One can hardly talk about Morris's myriad achievements; one can simply list a few of them, from his successful fabric and interior design business, Morris and Co., which set a new standard for home decoration, to the vastly influential Kelmscott Press. Morris's four-volume poem, *The*

Earthly Paradise, was a major Victorian best seller (said by the critic George Saintsbury to be the best thing of its kind since Dryden). His translations virtually introduced Icelandic sagas into English. After the death of Tennyson, he refused an offer of the laureateship. Though Morris's verse can be, occasionally, as lulling as his flowered textiles, it can also be surprisingly erotic. His finest short poem, the sorrowful and psychologically strange medieval drama "The Haystack in the Floods," opens, "Had she come all the way for this / To part at last without a kiss?" and closes with the heroine's lover slain beside "the haystack in the floods." Some of his most famous lines are limpidly beautiful:

Of Heaven or Hell I have no power to sing,
I cannot ease the burden of your fears,
Or make quick-coming death a little thing,
Or bring again the pleasure of past years,
Nor for my words shall ye forget your tears,
Or hope again for aught that I can say,
The idle singer of an empty day.

Idle singer? Hardly. He accomplished, as his physician remarked, "more work than most ten men." Fiona MacCarthy's superb biography—a book that one can live in for weeks—reminds us that William Morris may now be somewhat underrated as a poet (we no longer read a lot of narrative verse about Volsungs and Nibelungs), but the man's ideas and ideals concerning art, society, craftsmanship, preservation, and much else continue to inspire educational reformers and radical politicians, hand bookbinders and environmentalists. His political writing has lost none of its rhetorical punch. "Apart from the desire to produce beautiful things, the leading passion of my life has been and is hatred of modern civilization." Morris frankly loathes "the swinish luxury of the rich" and thinks no better of the middle classes: "It is their ambition and the end of their whole lives to gain, if not for themselves yet at least for their children, the proud position of being obvious burdens on the community." In his best-known work, *News from Nowhere*, an otherwise lyrical vision of a future golden age, the Houses of Parliament have been converted into storerooms for manure. Elsewhere he prophesies our shoddy world of computers and concrete: "Was it all to end in a counting-house on the top of a cinder heap?" *The Communist Manifesto* aside, there can be few more stirring social tracts than Morris's "How We Live and How We Might Live" and "Useful Work versus Useless Toil."

In this latter, after blasting "the puffery of wares, which has now got to such a pitch that there are many things which cost far more to sell than they do to make," Morris addresses the real nature of wealth: "Wealth is what Nature gives us and what a reasonable man can make out of the gifts of Nature for his reasonable use. The sunlight, the fresh air, the unspoiled face of the earth, food, raiment, and housing necessary and decent; the storing up of knowledge of all kinds, and the power of disseminating it; means of free communication between man and man; works of art, the beauty which man creates when he is most a man, most aspiring and thoughtful—all things which serve the pleasure of people, free, manly, and uncorrupted. This is wealth."

Throughout his writings (twenty-four volumes in the standard edition) Morris hammers away at the simple point that "the chief source of art is man's pleasure in his daily necessary work, which expresses itself and is embodied in that work itself." "Have nothing in your house," he also pleads, "that you do not know to be useful, or believe to be beautiful." Once called in by a duke to offer his views on the furnishings in the nobleman's palatial home, Morris suggested burning everything in it on a huge bonfire.

William Morris: A Life for Our Time takes up, with an enthusiasm that can be electric, all these aspects of Morris's achievement, in particular "the way that he revealed to so many different people on different social levels such previously unimagined possibilities of life." MacCarthy frequently points out modern legatees of Morris's ideas, from the dress designer Laura Ashley to Green activists to contemporary feminists (Morris championed the sexual and political rights of women). Occasionally, her fascination with the sexual—focused here mainly on Jane Morris's affairs with the painter Dante Gabriel Rossetti and the notorious Victorian rake and poet Wilfrid Scawen Blunt—can seem a bit prurient. But, in general, her biography provides an amazingly rich conspectus of Victorian culture. A manager of Morris and Co. married Madeline Smith, the notorious Edinburgh poisoner who charmed a jury into delivering a verdict of "not proven." Daughter May Morris entered into a "Mystical Betrothal" with the young Bernard Shaw. When Gladstone and Morris spoke at the first national conference of the Eastern Question Association, listeners included Charles Darwin, Robert Browning, John Ruskin, and Anthony Trollope. The artist's model Marie Spartali, who looked a bit like "Janey," was once called "Mrs. Morris for beginners."

MacCarthy is especially good in showing how Morris progressed from one "saturation subject" to another, whether it was founding the Society for the Protection of Ancient Buildings, learning to dye cloth, perfecting his street-corner oratory, mastering old Icelandic, or simply practicing his cookery (Morris prepared the food for boating journeys, picnics, and northern treks). She offers amusing vignettes of Morris's associates, both political and artistic. Burne-Jones, for instance, liked gothic tales and frequently threatened to relate the story to end all stories. "He who tells that story often goes mad in the telling it, and he who hears it always does." She has a way with a phrase, neatly alluding to Newman's "radiant austerities." Besides sixty-four pages of photographs (of textiles, paintings, buildings, and people), her text offers at least a dozen Burne-Jones and Rossetti caricatures of the short and portly "Topsy" (Morris's nickname to close friends). Naturally, as the author of a study of British design, as well as a life of Eric Gill, MacCarthy displays extensive knowledge of the Arts and Crafts movement—not to mention a historian's understanding of the intricate workings of turn-of-the-century socialist politics. Surely this deeply impressive book belongs next to those modern biographical classics, by Richard Ellmann and Michael Holroyd respectively, devoted to two of Morris's most colorful admirers, Oscar Wilde and Bernard Shaw.

In fact, let Shaw have the last word (as he usually did): reviewing an early biography of this "phenomenon," he wrote, "I feel nothing but elation when I think of Morris. . . . You can lose a man like that by your own death, but not by his. And so, until then, let us rejoice in him." Let us rejoice, yes, but continue to learn from him as well.

September 24, 1998

OSCAR WILDE

By Richard Ellmann

On February 28, 1895, the author of *The Importance of Being Earnest*, London's newest hit comedy, scribbled in pencil an anguished note to his friend Robert Ross. "Dearest Bobbie, Since I saw you something has happened. Bosie's father has left a card at my club with hideous words on it. I don't see anything now but a criminal prosecution. My whole life seems ruined by this man. . . . I don't know what to do."

"Bosie" was the pretty and amoral Lord Alfred Douglas; his father the bellicose marquess of Queensberry, who had established the rules for boxing. On the calling card—left ten days earlier at the Albemarle Club—were the words, with the now famous misspelling, "To Oscar Wilde posing as a somdomite."

The fate of Oscar Wilde (1854–1900), who like a hero of classic tragedy plummeted from the heights of fame to utter ruin, has attracted many biographers, among them that prince of liars Frank Harris and the resolutely anecdotal Hesketh Pearson. Lively as their books are, they cannot compete with this capacious, deeply sympathetic, and vastly entertaining new life by Richard Ellmann. Ellmann, who died last year, spent most of his distinguished career studying the Irish literary renaissance: two early books on Yeats are standard references, and his *James Joyce* is generally regarded as the best literary biography of our time. In that book Ellmann focused on an exile who endured poverty, censorship, blindness, and family tragedy to emerge the saint of modernism, the most admired writer of the century. In *Oscar Wilde* Ellmann's tale is very nearly the opposite: a figure of showy splendor, "refulgent, imperial," quickly conquers London and then, through hubris, romantic infatuation, and indecision, loses everything—family, reputation, possessions—to end a wraithlike specter cadging drinks on the grand boulevards of Paris, eventually suffering a gruesome death in a cheap hotel room.

In the past Wilde's fall usually appeared a cautionary tale. Homosexuals revered him as a martyr to "the love that dare not speak its name." (The phrase occurs in a poem by Douglas.) Evangelists called him an unclean beast, the subject of more than seven hundred sermons in the United States alone between 1895 and 1900. In the popular memory he spoke entirely in epigrams and witticisms: "I can resist everything except temptation. . . . The English country gentleman galloping after a fox—the unspeakable in full pursuit of the unedible. . . . It is only an auctioneer who should admire all schools of art. . . . In old days men had the rack; now they have the Press. . . . At twilight nature becomes a wonderfully suggestive effect, and is not without loveliness, though perhaps its chief use is to illustrate quotations from the poets." To modern readers, though, Ellmann among them, Wilde appears chiefly as a fearless artist and social critic who, like a kamikaze pilot, used himself as the bomb to explode the bourgeois values, pretensions, and hypocrisies of late Victorian society.

Oscar Fingal O'Flahertie Wills Wilde was born in Ireland on October 16, 1854. Both parents were remarkable, his father the most distinguished ear and eye doctor in Britain, his mother—known as Speranza—an Irish nationalist, German translator, and celebrated hostess. Their second son grew up to be six feet three inches tall, tending to fat, with blubbery lips; the photographs show a plump, rather bland face, with kindly eyes.

At Oxford he nevertheless cut a dashing figure, casting off his Irish brogue, traveling on holidays to Italy and Greece, finding himself torn between the moralism of Ruskin and the paganism of Pater. Throughout these years he toyed with becoming a Roman Catholic, all the while attending the meetings of an Oxford Freemason lodge. He made stupid remarks, worthy of any sophomore; he once called Mrs. Browning's *Aurora Leigh* "much the greatest work in our literature." He also made stupid mistakes, probably catching syphilis from a local prostitute.

And yet he was insufferably brilliant from the beginning. At a key examination he was asked to construe some lines of Greek from the New Testament about Christ's betrayal and passion. When after a moment, he was asked to stop translating, Wilde held up an admonitory finger: "Hush, hush, let us proceed and see what happened to the unfortunate man." (Another time he casually referred to the Twenty Commandments.) Before he left Oxford, Wilde managed to win the Newdigate poetry prize and take a rare double first degree. Had he tempered his excesses he might have become one of the great scholars of the age.

But not Oscar. "I'll be a poet, a writer, a dramatist. Somehow or other, I'll be famous, and if not famous, notorious." As Ellmann notes, "Wilde's life is as full of tragic prolepses as an Ibsen play." In London the graduate set himself up as a poet and man of letters, a latter-day Pre-Raphaelite. His poems were decadent, inspired by Gautier and Baudelaire; one described a young man's love-making with a statue, another the passion of a nymph for a corpse. Soon, though, Wilde was trading quips with the painter James Whistler and establishing his reputation as the leading young aesthete, a position confirmed when he was parodied in Gilbert and Sullivan's *Patience* ("Walk down Picadilly, with a poppy or a lily in your medieval hand"). This new fame led to an unusual offer: a speaker's bureau wished to send him to America to lecture on the aesthetic movement, rather a mystery to homespun Yankee spectators of the Gilbert play.

Wilde's tour began in New York, where he "had nothing to declare but his genius," and led him around the country on a grueling schedule. He shocked his audience by appearing in knee breeches (an outfit, Ellmann tells us, he took from the initation ceremonies of the Freemasons). Besides the aesthetic movement, he also talked about "The House Beautiful." Once a woman asked him how she should arrange some decorative screens; Wilde answered, "Why arrange them at all? Why not let them occur?" The lecturer met Ulysses S. Grant, Jefferson Davis, Walt Whitman, and Henry James. (The repressed novelist and the flamboyant showman never got along, in later years partly because Wilde's plays were so fabulously successful and James's such dismal failures.) In Colorado he went down a mine and swigged whisky with the toughest miners. When he left America he was famous.

After his return to England, Wilde decided to get married. Earlier he had flirted seriously with a pair of women: Florence Balcombe, who wed Bram Stoker (later the author of *Dracula*), and Violet Hunt, who became the companion of the novelist Ford Madox Ford. But rumors were now flying about his increasingly epicene mannerisms and pronouncements; marriage would silence them. Wilde's bride, Constance Lloyd, appears to have been a sweet, intelligent, and understanding woman, who loved her husband and deserved a better one. They had two sons in rapid succession—Cyril and Vyvyan—but while Constance was occupied with the children Oscar went off to visit Oxford and was seduced by the seventeen-year-old Robbie Ross. Soon thereafter, he met the blond and beautiful Alfred Douglas.

From here on Wilde dallied with self-destruction. In his writing he had always preached a flouting of Victorian values but now in his private life he lived closer and closer to the dangerous edge. Douglas piloted him into a world of expense and excess—opulent dinners at Willis's restaurant, hotel suites, boy prostitutes, sordid *maisons de passe*. In a celebrated phrase, Wilde said it was like "feasting with panthers." Ellmann mentions precisely what Wilde liked to do with "renters," as male pickups were called, but goes to some pains to defend his subject. "What seems to characterize all Wilde's affairs is that he got to know the boys as individuals, treated them handsomely, allowed them to refuse his attentions without becoming rancorous, and did not corrupt them."

Of course, this was not how the marquess of Queensberry came to see his son's intimate companionship with Wilde. Bosie hated his macho father, and clearly egged Wilde into defying him, promising the support of his brother and mother. Angry and frustrated, Queensberry eventually tried to disrupt the opening night of *The Importance of Being Earnest*. When he failed, he consulted his solicitors, and then wrote his famous accusation. Apparently, he was advised that it would be easier to prove that Wilde acted like a sodomite than that he actually was one; hence the wording.

From the very moment he received the card, Wilde was doomed. Repeatedly in his biography Ellmann emphasizes the peculiar fatality that shadowed Wilde. In his children's stories, like "The Happy Prince" and "The Birthday of the Infanta," most of the characters die for love. The "poisonous" relationship between Lord Henry Wotton and Dorian Gray in *The Picture of Dorian Gray* uncannily prefigured the Wilde-Douglas association a few years later. A famous palmist found Wilde's left hand that of a king, "but the right that of a king who will send himself into exile," around his fortieth year.

Wilde went to his solicitor and assured him there was no truth to Queensberry's charge. A. C. Humphreys consequently advised him to sue for libel. Ellmann finds the lawyer naive in not realizing the truth; but he avoids admitting that Wilde lied to his counselor. At any event, the trial began, with Wilde showing off and Sir Edward Carson being brilliant in his cross-examination. (Ironically, the two had known each other as boys; Wilde said Carson attacked him "with all the ferocity of an old friend.") Letters to Bosie were produced, filled with passionate language addressed to "My Dear Boy," and several male prostitutes presented damaging testimony. In the end, Wilde lost his suit; therefore Queensberry's accusations were true. Indeed, the evidence suggested that Wilde was doing more than "posing." Under the law covering sexual offenses, the government had no choice but to issue a warrant for his arrest.

He might have gotten away. There was time to catch the boat train to France. But at a time when decisive action was needed, Wilde hesitated. Bosie wanted him to fight, as did his mother; Frank Harris, Ross, and others urged flight. He couldn't make up his mind. So he sat in the Cadogan Hotel, calling for hock and seltzer, a half-packed suitcase on his bed, until the burly policemen knocked at the door. After he was booked, his friends made bail; but no hotel in London would have him. He had to beg his brother to take him in. "Willie, give me shelter or I shall die in the streets." He got a small camp bed in a corner. (When Willie went around town defending Oscar, Wilde said, "My poor, dear brother, he would compromise a steam engine." One thing Willie reportedly said, as vindication of Oscar's character, was that you could leave any woman alone with him and she would be safe.)

Eventually, Oscar found his way to the house of Ada Leverson, widely known by her nickname, the Sphinx. This time he was given the bedroom of her young son who was away on holiday. "So among the rocking horses and dollhouses," writes Ellmann with quiet eloquence, "he received his solicitors and friends, gathering the threads of destitution and disgrace."

At his first trial the jury couldn't come to a decision; in the next Wilde was found guilty and given the maximum sentence: two years. This may not sound like much, but meant six hours a day on a treadmill, a diet of water and starches, a plank for a bed, a bucket for a toilet. The first year almost killed him. But Wilde suffered his greatest humiliation when he was transferred to Reading Prison and had to wait in handcuffs on the platform at Clapham Junction in the rain: a jeering crowd gathered and a man spat at him. At Reading he encountered the wife murderer who was to become the subject of his last literary work, *The Ballad of Reading Gaol*, with its haunting refrain "Each man kills the thing he loves."

In prison Wilde apparently tried to kill his love for Douglas. He wrote a long letter—never sent—explaining himself, excoriating Bosie for having caused him to waste his life, for bankrupting him with extravagances, for causing his destruction at the hands of Queensberry. But as Ellmann tells us, the thing to remember about *De Profundis*, as this book-length *cri de coeur* is known, is that it is a love letter. It ends with a call for a meeting and a reconciliation.

After prison Wilde never saw his wife or sons again. He went to live in France; he found he had no talent left; the gods had abandoned him. "I spend my evenings reading *The Tentation* by Flaubert. I don't think I shall ever write again: *la joie de vivre* is gone and that with will-power, is the basis of art." He began to borrow money from friends, promising plays he knew he would never finish. He went back to Bosie, and to a spendthrift's life in Italy—until the money ran out. Eventually he found himself, like so many others, down and out in Paris. "I have discovered," he wrote in a letter, "that alcohol taken in sufficient quantity produces all the effects of drunkenness." The actress Ellen Terry glimpsed him "looking into the window of a pastry shop, biting his fingers." Once Sir Edward Carson almost pushed a man into the gutter when, "about to apologize, he recognized him as Wilde." Obviously, his life over, Oscar Wilde was simply waiting for the final curtain. "How evil it is to buy love, and how evil to sell it! And yet what purple hours one can snatch from that grey slow-moving thing we call Time."

Wilde's end, most likely from cerebral meningitis (though there is still much debate), finally came in a dingy hotel bed, where at the moment of dying fluids exploded from every orifice of his body. He had just turned forty-six.

In one of his essays Cyril Connolly imagines that Wilde never received Queensberry's card. Instead the playwright grew rich and ladened with honors, was knighted, and came, in the fullness of years, to be one of the most venerated literary figures in England. It might have happened. Richard Ellmann's brilliant life makes clear that it should have.

September 25, 1988

A. E. HOUSMAN:
A CRITICAL BIOGRAPHY

By Norman Page

In 1892 a higher division clerk in the Trade Marks Registry applied for the professorship of Latin at University College, London. The clerk, in his early thirties, had spent over ten years at his patent office job, where he was known to be thorough, amiable, and hardworking. Admirable qualities no doubt, but the low-level bureaucrat frankly admitted that he had failed to pass the classical honors exams at Oxford years before; indeed, he had failed disastrously, not even answering many of the questions. On paper there seemed no reason in the world to consider seriously the candidacy of this unimportant government functionary. But in England they order these matters better than here, and the board of examiners wisely appointed Mr. A. E. Housman (1859–1936) to the vacant chair.

Really, they had no choice. As Norman Page's brisk, compact biography tells us, Housman's application came accompanied by seventeen testimonials—from classicists all over the world—confirming his brilliance as a Latin and Greek scholar. From the time he left Oxford in 1881 the young man had spent all his free hours at the British Museum library, researching manuscript minutiae, making careful emendations to Ovid and Propertius, publishing some twenty-five important papers in the scholarly journals. And this industry didn't flag once Housman began to lecture at University College: instead he settled on his life's work—the editing of the astronomer-poet Manilius, a task that would take him the next thirty years. Before his death, in 1936, the erstwhile clerk was to assume the Kennedy Professorship of Latin at Cambridge and come to be recognized as the greatest textual critic since Richard Porson, perhaps even since Richard Bentley. More incidentally, along the way he also refused the Order of Merit, half a dozen honorary degrees, and the laurels showered on him as the most beloved lyric poet of his day.

There was a time, not too distant, when *A Shropshire Lad* (1895) was regarded as just the book to introduce a young person to poetry. According to Housman, poetry aimed "to harmonize the sadness of the universe" and the young favor just such melancholy views: "I, a stranger and afraid / In a world I never made." In fact, *A Shropshire Lad* was the first book of poetry that this reviewer ever read voluntarily—and to this day he sometimes recites at parties "When I was One-and-Twenty" or the even shorter and more bitter-sweet poem that goes:

> With rue my heart is laden
> For golden friends I had,
> For many a rose-lipt maiden
> And many a lightfoot lad.
>
> By brooks too broad for leaping
> The lightfoot boys are laid;
> The rose-lipt girls are sleeping
> In fields where roses fade.

To tell the truth, I still love Housman's poems, old-fashioned and rose-bowered though they be. Their Debussy-like wistfulness, their accounts of eros deferred or defeated, their careful simplicity can readily touch hearts jaded by Ezra Pound or Charles Olson. Consider, for instance, this four-line elegy for the dead of the Boer War:

> Here dead lie we because we did not choose
> To live and shame the land from which we sprung.
> Life, to be sure, is nothing much to lose;
> But young men think it is, and we were young.

Despite his accomplishments as a minor poet, Housman's prose and scholarly example have gradually overwhelmed *A Shropshire Lad* and *Last Poems* (1922). Anyone who reads the letters (edited by Henry Maas) or the little volume of selected prose (gathered by John Carter) will discover a sly wit, a master of irony, and a scourge of sloppy scholarship. Better to suffer the slings and arrows of John Simon or Marvin Mudrick than the cool, rapier thrust of Housman.

At one point, Page tells us, Housman the textual critic was reviewing an edition of Fronto, a very minor Latin poet. "In style and diction the translation does not often fall below mediocrity nor often rise above it; if it did, it would rise above Fronto." Kipling's *The Jungle Books* Housman labeled "a tract in wolf's clothing." He observed that a certain writer's "self-love is a great passion squandered on an unworthy object." He could also be gentler but just as witty. A friend remembers showing the learned professor around his garden. "Over there I have a *Phallus amorphus*, but it hasn't come up yet. 'Perhaps modesty forbids?' (Housman) conjectured in his attractive thin mandarin voice." Yet this same poet-don could quietly confess, after a lecture on Horace's ode "Diffugere nives" and just before hurrying from the hall, "That I regard as the most beautiful poem in ancient literature."

Norman Page's biography is not the first devoted to Housman; there have been at least a half dozen of varying lengths, from the invaluable sketch by A. S. F. Gow (a colleague at Cambridge) to the detailed life by Richard Perceval Graves of a few years' past. Page's virtues are moderation—in length and psychologizing—coupled with an engaging style and careful shaping of his narrative. Unlike some earlier writers, Page refuses to indulge in what he deems unsupported speculation. No doubt the young Housman fell in love with his fellow undergraduate Moses Jackson, but whether the older scholar sought male sexual companionship on his annual trips to France and Italy remains conjectural (if likely).

Similarly, Page offers several possible explanations for Housman's redounding failure at his honors exams. The future textual scholar disliked Oxford's syrupy approach to the classics, with its emphasis on ancient philosophy. Instead of studying Plato's thought, he preferred to spend his time annotating Propertius. Coupled with this lack of preparation, a few days before the exam Housman learned that his father was dangerously ill. During this time he must also have come to realize that his love for the inveterately heterosexual Moses Jackson was doomed to be one-sided—and that he might never see his friend again after graduation. Moreover, with his innate passion for precision, it is likely that Housman would refuse to parrot back any half-baked answers. What is admirable, and Page emphasizes this, is that with all his hopes dashed the young Housman could then go out into the world, find a job, and through relentless effort earn the recognition that had been denied him.

To his students and colleagues the later Housman became an inspiring example of academic integrity. The textual critic, as Page describes him, "is engaged in the pursuit of truth and the banishment of error. . . . The perpetuation and multiplying of errors as texts are transmitted over a long period is not a bad image or paradigm for human delusion and deterioration in general: we say of texts, as of men and ideas, that they become corrupt. To determine what an ancient author actually wrote is, in a small but significant way, to repossess a lost certainty, to be enabled once again to see things as they really are."

Housman took this doctrine to its limit, choosing to edit Manilius because he needed a text with problems susceptible of solution; the Latin poet himself, he admitted, was dull and not worth reading. Throughout his career—and in his few public addresses, such as "The Application of Thought to Textual Criticism"—Housman repeatedly emphasized knowledge as its own end.

Page's biography, though otherwise scrupulous, in its second half is marred by a number of misprints that would have caused Housman to shudder. Nonetheless, it remains an extremely pleasant and enjoyable study, one to put on the shelf next to other books that picture the donnish life: Humphrey Carpenter's *The Inklings*, the George Lyttelton/Rupert Hart-Davis correspondence, Geoffrey Madan's notebooks, Aubrey's *Brief Lives* and Anthony à Wood's Oxford gossip, the stories of M. R. James, the biography of James Murray *Caught in the Web of Words*, memoirs of scholars like George Saintsbury, Eric Partridge, F. J. Furnivall. For those of a certain turn of mind, such compilations and biographies offer a peculiar refreshment and repose. All men desire to know, said Aristotle, and a good proportion of them would be scholars if they could.

March 27, 1988

BERNARD SHAW
VOLUME 2, 1898–1918:
THE PURSUIT OF POWER

By Michael Holroyd

When we last glimpsed George Bernard Shaw (1856–1950)—in the final pages of *The Search for Love*, the opening volume of Michael Holroyd's "biographical trilogy"—he was hobbling around on crutches preparing to marry the Irish millionairess Charlotte Payne Townshend. As he informed a friend, he proposed "to make her my widow."

In that year, 1898, Shaw was already forty-two, a well-known Fabian socialist, a vegetarian who sported all-wool Jaeger suits, author of such monographs as *The Quintessence of Ibsenism* and *The Perfect Wagnerite*, a spellbinding open-air speaker, and the best music and theater critic in London. "I could make deaf stockbrokers read my two pages on music," he rightly claimed. When he finally retired from drama reviewing, he even dubbed his successor, none other than Max Beerbohm, as "the incomparable Max"—who, in the way of critics ever and always, naturally used his first column to knock a Shaw play.

But the not so young GBS was used to shaking off far worse blows, beginning with an alcoholic father and a mother who ran off with a singing teacher. He'd already spent years in genteel poverty, studying Marx and music at the British Museum, writing five novels, one after the other rejected by publishers, composing play after play after play, all of them turned down or produced only in small, experimental theaters.

Marriage to Charlotte happily freed the author and civic activist from financial worries, but Shaw by then had acquired the monk's habit of constant work, and it never released him. In the years showcased here he scribbles on trains, buses, ships; plays or essays are composed on the run, between social and speaking engagements. "I never have a moment of leisure," he once confessed, "only an occasional pause from exhaustion":

"Throughout the year [1907], more than fifty of his articles, statements, interviews and letters appeared in the newspapers on such wide-flung topics as financial aid following an earthquake in Jamaica, the imprisonment of Egyptians after the Danshawaii affair and the suppression of Richard Strauss's *Salome* by the Metropolitan Opera House in New York. There was Shaw on disarmament in the *Evening Standard*, on polygamy in *The Times* and on diet in the *Daily Mail*. His most common subjects were marriage, censorship, theology and women's suffrage. But readers of the *Daily Graphic* could pick up what he had to say on 'the imperfections of phrenologists'; and *Clarion* subscribers could learn about 'the Gentle Art of Unpleasantness,' a social exercise in three parts. He wrote about old age pensions, women typists' salaries, corporal punishment and the railway strike."

No matter how fast or how much Shaw wrote, his sentences always came out clear, fresh, and "direct as a ray of light." Inveterately humorous, even on a soapbox, he sometimes let his jokes get in the way of his points; in Beerbohm's words, he was "a comedian whose frivolity, vampire-like, sucked the seriousness from his work." Still, Shaw's remains one of the best expository styles in English, forceful and epigrammatic. "Martyrdom is the only way a man can become famous without ability." "The truly damned are those who are happy in hell." When he wants to underline the shortcomings of contemporary novelists, he parodies the final scene of *Macbeth*, rewriting it in the lyrical style of Arnold Bennett or John Galsworthy: "What was the use of killing? Duncan, Banquo, the Macduff people: he had waded through their blood; and how much better would it not be if it were all a dream and they were alive and kind to him? How the martins were singing! Banquo, always a bit of a fool, had been sentimental about the martins. . . ."

And so on, for another perfect three pages. GBS would just toss these things off, a deadline journalist as well as a playwright who could compare himself to Shakespeare, to the latter's disadvantage.

Still, in the beginning, Shaw couldn't get his plays produced, so he carefully published them himself—*Plays Unpleasant, Plays Pleasant, Three Plays for Puritans*—and, by adding prefaces elaborating their ideas, managed to create a kind of total artwork. For instance, in *Man and Superman*, he not only tells us that the hero—John Tanner, MIRC (Member of the Idle Rich Class)—brought out a revolutionist's handbook; he appends the entire book. Even his stage directions crackle; one character's apparel "includes a very smart hat but with a dead bird in it."

During the years covered by *The Pursuit of Power* Shaw composes his major plays (up to *Androcles and the Lion*); argues against H. G. Wells, who hoped to speed up the gradualist Fabian Society; spars amicably with G. K.

Chesterton about nearly everything (GKC's book on GBS, he announces, "is the best work of literary art I have yet provoked"); shamelessly sends advice to Tolstoy about religion and God; models for a bust by Rodin (while the sculptor's secretary, the poet Rilke, looks on); and brings about a revolution in the theater with the help of the actor-director Harley Granville-Barker, who is whispered to be his natural son—shades of Shakespeare and Davenant! Much of this volume describes play production, a matter about which Shaw was, as in everything, meticulous. He once told an actress, "From the moment you come in you must make the audience understand that you live in a small town in the provinces and visit a great deal with the local clergy; you make slippers for the curate and go to dreary tea-parties." Her single line in the scene was "How do you do?"

In *The Search for Love*, Shaw found himself involved with a series of actresses, but those relations were mainly paper passions or passing fancies. (The children's author E. Nesbit, with whom Shaw flirted, once complained, "You had no right to write the Preface if you were not going to write the book.") In these middle years he becomes deeply entangled with Mrs. Patrick Campbell (the first Eliza Doolittle in *Pygmalion*). Confident that he could resist her charms, Shaw visited the middle-aged beauty at home. "Taking his hand she touched his fingers against her bosom and by this 'abandoned trick' he was undone." They kissed and cooed, but ultimately she couldn't persuade him to leave his wife and he couldn't persuade her to sleep with him.

Shaw's love life, odd already, becomes exceedingly original when you realize that he and Charlotte deliberately abstained from sexual relations after, but not before, their marriage.

The Pursuit of Power concludes with a litany for the British dead of World War I. "Every promising young man I know has been blown to bits lately, and I have had to write his mother." Shaw himself has been vilified by old friends and the reading public for his attempts to write "Common Sense About the War," to find a balance between jingoism and pacifism. Though famous, he nonetheless feels neutralized as a political force and almost neutered in his romantic life. By 1914 he has also buried his mother and sister and begun his long, long old age as the stand-up comic of the Western world, half Methuselah, half Mr. Punch. Appropriately, Michael Holroyd's next and final volume will be titled *The Lure of Fantasy*.

Holroyd's biography has already been much acclaimed and, when complete, will certainly become the standard life of Shaw, replacing earlier, though still valuable, books by St. John Irvine, Hesketh Pearson, and the Shavian pack rat Archibald Henderson. Holroyd—biographer of Lytton Strachey and the painter Augustus John—here brings to bear fifteen years of research but also considerable verbal flair: for instance, he smoothly refers to the flower girl's transformation into a lady (in *Pygmalion*) as the deflowering of Eliza. His Beatrice Webb—ever obsessed with sexual goings-on within the Fabian Society—ranks among the great comic creations of modern biographical literature. And every sentence he writes is thoughtful, clear, and, I am sure, well documented (though we will have to wait to check references and footnotes).

Less welcome to this reader, Holroyd also generally prefers analysis over narration, ideas rather than wit, the intellectual to the anecdotal. He never forgets to present a play's ideas, but he sometimes fails to give its plot. Notwithstanding an abundance of quotation, *The Pursuit of Power* is also surprisingly undramatic, favoring Shaw "the good man fallen among Fabians"— Lenin's description—to the Shaw who wrote plays with the sparkle of Mozart. The result, as Holroyd once remarked of Quentin Bell's life of Virginia Woolf, is to make his biography "curiously muffled," without narrative urgency or personal feeling.

Bernard Shaw is still a very good book, perhaps even the classic biography that the dust jacket brazenly trumpets. At the very least, it should send readers back to plays like *Man and Superman*, to Shaw's unrivaled music journalism, to his magnificent correspondence.

September 24, 1989

MADAME BLAVATSKY'S BABOON:
A HISTORY OF THE MYSTICS, MEDIUMS, AND MISFITS WHO BROUGHT SPIRITUALISM TO AMERICA

By Peter Washington

Isis Unveiled, The Astral Plane, The Coming of the World Teacher, Invisible Helpers, The Fourth Way, and, best of all, *The Secret Doctrine*—at the very least the Theosophists and their spiritualist rivals had a way with book titles. Such writings seem to promise the weary soul a glimpse into the very meaning of the universe, as well as hinting that one may, through effort, gain the power of the magus and the tranquil wisdom of the sage. Who, after all, would not wish to rend the curtain of illusion, receive communiqués from the hidden masters of history, integrate all one's vital forces, and secure a favored place in the elaborate hierarchy of the afterlife?

Compared with the evil or dopey pseudo-religions of today, the Theosophists seem a kinder, gentler cult. They exhibit an old-fashioned looniness, like G. B. Shaw's faith in the healthful effects of Jaeger all-wool suits, and their practices often sound more kitsch than kabbalistic. We can even read about their activities with an ironic smile—"What fools these mortals be!"— and dismiss Madame Blavatsky and Gurdjieff as mere light-opera charlatans. But the unceasing popularity of Theosophy's offshoots should alert us that, amusing though their antics are, these self-appointed gurus and mahatmas were clearly onto something. For many people traditional Christianity fails to satisfy some gnawing, inner hunger, while modern rationalism too often dismisses the spiritual altogether as gaseous maunderings or Freud's "oceanic" feeling. Yet the general condition of humankind appears to be an incessant yearning for completion, a desire for something more from life than what it seems to offer.

Among many other books about heterodox belief systems (such as James

Webb's fine surveys *The Occult Underground* and *The Occult Establishment*), *Madame Blavatsky's Baboon* excels in its anecdotal vivacity, tempered sympathy, and relatively sharp focus. There's little here about the Rosicrucians and Illuminati, let alone the tarot: instead Peter Washington looks at Theosophy and its descendants as relatively serious attempts to enhance the spiritual dimension of human life.

Not that Helena Blavatsky isn't a hoot. Born in 1831 in Russia, at seventeen she married a vice-governor of a province in the Caucasus, ran away a few weeks later, and never looked back. No one is quite sure how much of her biography is propagandistic myth. She "claimed to have ridden bareback in a circus, toured Serbia as a concert pianist, opened an ink factory in Odessa, traded as an importer of ostrich feathers in Paris, and worked as interior decorator to the Empress Eugenie." There may have been lovers, aristocratic and otherwise. The official outline of her life also includes "meetings with Red Indians in Canada and the United States in 1850 and 1851, a covered wagon journey across the Middle West of America in 1854; fighting with Garibaldi's army in the Battle of Mentana (1867), when she was wounded by both sabre blows and bullets; and shipwrecked at Spetsai off the Greek coast in 1871. . . . Between these events she is said to have dealt with cabbalists in Egypt, secret agents in Central Asia, voodoo magicians in New Orleans and bandits in Mexico." At times she sounds like Young Indiana Blavatsky.

But this fat, blowsy, vulgar woman possessed undoubted charisma. When she claimed to be in touch with ancient adepts, with names like Morya and Koot Hoomi, nobody laughed. In fact, she won over Colonel Henry Olcott, onetime member of the committee charged with investigating Lincoln's assassination. In 1875, in New York, this odd couple founded the Theosophical Society, devoted to collecting and diffusing "knowledge of the laws which govern the universe," later moved its headquarters to India, and eventually evangelized far and wide.

This was accomplished through public meetings, mammoth treatises like *Isis Revealed*, and regular messages from the Masters, usually sent in black envelopes and sometimes written in an unknown language called Senzar. Naturally, the society attracted the dreamy, the mad, and the scandalous. When HPB (as Blavatsky was called) traveled to Europe, her entourage included Mohini Mohandas Chatterjee, "who caused the worst trouble when he became entangled with a Miss Leonard who bared her breasts at him as they walked together through a wood near Paris." Not long after this contretemps, Chatterjee journeyed to Ireland, where he "converted" a young poet named W. B. Yeats.

Following the deaths of its two founders, leadership of the increasingly contentious movement fell to the vibrant Annie Besant, a former Fabian and women's rights activist with a love for pomp and ceremony: she created scores of theosophical clubs, such as the Order of the Star of the East and the Temple of the Rosy Cross. Besant's chief lieutenant—some might say her Mephistopheles—was the redoubtable Charles Webster Leadbeater, priest, pederast, and spiritualist politico par excellence. It was Leadbeater who, in February 1909, "noticed an extraordinary aura" surrounding a dirty, unkempt Indian boy frolicking at the beach near the movement's headquarters in Adyar. Leadbeater announced that this child, whom many thought half-witted, would become a very great teacher.

As it happens, he proved absolutely right, for the little boy was none other than Jiddu Krishnamurti. The Theosophical Society enthusiastically took over the future World Teacher's education, in the process alienating him from his family and country. (At one point Krishna's father, hoping to regain custody of his son, brought a lawsuit against Leadbeater that included "charges of deification and sodomy.") Although *Madame Blavatsky's Baboon* contains the stories of many men and women, that of Krishnamurti—a tale of great loneliness, vast spiritual authority, and accusations of personal scandal (sexual and financial)—is probably the most central, extending as it does from the early days of the society to this international guru's death in 1986.

Still, it's pretty clear that Peter Washington finds the outrageous G. I. Gurdjieff almost as irresistible as did his disciples, among them the African-American novelist Jean Toomer and the short-story writer Katherine Mansfield. (The tubercular Mansfield passed her last days at Gurdjieff's "monastery," the Prieuré; there she spent hours each day in the stable, kneeling on a special platform from which she inhaled the supposedly life-restoring aroma of cow manure.) Gurdjieff came from Central Asia, looked like Fu Manchu, and possessed remarkable personal magnetism. His mere presence made P. D. Ouspensky, himself an important spiritualist thinker, want to laugh, shout, and sing as though he "had escaped from school or from some strange detention." In later years "an American woman unknown to the Master felt that even his gaze from an adjacent restaurant table stirred her 'sexual centre' more than she had ever known."

As Washington notes, while the Theosophists might be associated with the League of Nations and social democracy, Gurdjieff represents the more contemporary fascination with barbarism, primitivism, and strife. Breathing exercises, dance, and other forms of movement, aiming for "the integration of all the vital forces," made up much of the Master's teaching. But his "basic pedagogical principle was contradiction: do what you hate, whatever seems hostile. Do the impossible; then do more of it, or work at two impossible tasks together."

Gurdjieff once commanded A. R. Orage—editor of the most influential English literary magazine of its day—to spend week after week digging holes. At the Prieuré near Paris "intellectuals were forbidden to read, while sensitive souls mucked out byres and slaughtered animals." Through such suffering and obedience, asserted the Master, we are able "to wake up to reality and stay awake." Part of Gurdjieff's charm, for a reader at least, derives from his tongue-in-cheek attitude toward himself and his followers; these latter he blithely referred to as "sheep to be shorn."

Later chapters of *Madame Blavatsky's Baboon* depict the spiritual adventures of the California writers Aldous Huxley, Gerald Heard, and Christopher Isherwood, touch on a number of recent gurus and movements (Idries Shah, the Aetherius Church), and describe the often sad later years of various would-be adepts and onetime disciples. All in all, Peter Washington has written a wonderfully engaging and useful book. My only cavil is that he gives somewhat short shrift to the actual dogma espoused by the various teachers whose lives and careers he so amusingly chronicles. I would have welcomed a few more quotations from the writings of, say, Rudolf Steiner and Blavatsky. Still, the interested can always go directly to *The Fourth Way* or *The Influence of Lucifer and Arhriman.* Carrying along, I hope, a large canister of salt.

January 29, 1995

WE MODERNS

V

For most of my life, the "modernist movement" defined the twentieth-century artistic enterprise, at least for Anglo-American readers. These are the writers—building on the achievements of Baudelaire and Flaubert—who first aimed to capture in words the jagged, largely urban, modern sensibility.

Proust is simply our greatest twentieth-century novelist—In Search of Lost Time is an amalgam of Balzac's Human and Dante's Divine Comedy. His Irish coeval James Joyce should be here, but isn't, only because I have held off from writing about him for years. Of all the books in my own library the Joyce section is the largest—multiple editions of Ulysses, all the major commentaries, and many of the minor ones. To paraphrase Lincoln, I have prepared myself and someday my chance will come. But I do include an essay on Joyce's Triestine friend, Italo Svevo, author of the much loved masterpiece Confessions of Zeno, and one on Flann O'Brien, who possessed an equal gift for gab and Irish blarney.

Sometimes dismissed as merely a campy humorist, Ronald Firbank strikes me as another great original and innovator, the writer who taught people how to leave things out: without him and Hemingway, we might still be writing like Dickens or Henry James. T. S. Eliot we now recognize as not only the wounded Fisher King of modern poetry but also as a very flawed human being, religiose, hypocritical, sometimes surprisingly vulgar, and in his youth anti-Semitic. "How unpleasant to know Mr. Eliot!" But his achingly beautiful verses will echo through the rose garden and the waste land so long as people care for poetry at all.

For me, many of these books may be characterized, somewhat melodramatically, by this entry from Kafka's diaries: "The books we need are of the kind that act upon us like a misfortune, that make us suffer like the death of someone we love more than ourselves, that make us feel as though we were on the verge of suicide, or lost in a forest remote from all human habitation—a book should serve as the ax for the frozen sea within us."

MARCEL PROUST: A LIFE

By Jean-Yves Tadié
Translated from the French by Euan Cameron

MARCEL PROUST:
SELECTED LETTERS, VOLUME 4, 1918–1922

Edited by Philip Kolb
Translated from the French by Joanna Kilmartin

PROUST'S WAY:
A FIELD GUIDE TO "IN SEARCH
OF LOST TIME"

By Roger Shattuck

REMEMBRANCE OF THINGS PAST

Abridged and read by Neville Jason

Reading the 3,000 pages of *A la Recherche du Temps Perdu* (In Search of Lost Time) is always a surprisingly personal adventure. Even now, the memory of the autumn more than thirty years ago, during which I first lost and found myself in Proust, can still overwhelm me with an unassuaged yearning. For what? For an impossible love, for happiness and success, for something out of life that has already passed, unseen. Back then, I discovered in this most seductive of great novels an image of my own interior self. Had I not, like Swann, been shredded with jealousy over an elusive, tantalizing young woman, one whose beauty, like Odette's, was so striking that strangers compared her to the strawberry blondes in Botticelli paintings? Did I not daydream, like the Narrator, of awakening some morning a real writer? Was I not burdened, even at twenty, with an inescapable feeling of disillusionment, never quite satisfied with the present, always nostalgic for a rosy past or eager for an even rosier future?

During that gray and rainy fall of my junior year in college, I read Proust steadily for five, six, eight hours a day. To those who respond to his sinuous prose—and many people don't—there is no more powerful hypnotic drug in all literature. *In Search of Lost Time* is no mere novel; it is a world, a universe that alternately expands into every layer of society and then contracts back into the Narrator's consciousness. Its author once compared his masterpiece to *The Arabian Nights*. But the book might also be likened to a modern *Metamorphoses*, for it depicts both public and personal life as restless, uncertain, and disheartening, a domain of constant transformation, of unceasing flux and shocking revelation. The disdained drawing master, M. Biche, who frequents the boorish Madame Verdurin's dinner parties, turns out to be the youthful Elstir, later the greatest painter of his day. One afternoon the Narrator suddenly recognizes the imperious mistress of his friend, the dashing Saint-Loup, as the popular Jewish whore at a brothel he visited when young. In a particularly shocking scene, an unnamed lesbian friend urges Mlle Vinteuil to desecrate her dead father's photograph; yet that same girlfriend later spends years reconstructing Vinteuil's most beautiful work, his septet (with its haunting "little phrase"). Most surprisingly, the awful Madame Verdurin unexpectedly reappears in the closing pages of *Time Regained* as none other than the new Princesse de Guermantes, having attained the apogee of Parisian social success by marrying the widowed prince.

Some people complain about the length of *In Search of Lost Time*. This is a little like saying that one's life is too long. Proust needs all his pages not only because he's presenting a panorama of society—from the glittering Duchesse de Guermantes to the earthy cook Françoise, from the predatory homosexual Baron Charlus (arguably his greatest creation) to the nosy provincial gossip Aunt Léonie—but also because only the steady accumulation of events and the recurrence of familiar patterns will allow him to convey the crushing passage of time. In plot, the novel traces a young dilettante's search for a vocation, and ends with the Narrator's realization that he can finally write the book we have just finished. But for the sensitive reader, who lives through all these pages, all these years, the *Recherche* grows into an analogue of his or her own memory. When the Narrator meets Mlle de Saint-Loup near the novel's end, he, like the reader, sees not just a pretty little girl but the daughter of Robert de Saint-Loup and his first childhood love, Gilberte Swann, the granddaughter of the cocotte

Odette de Crécy and the connoisseur Charles Swann, the coming together of myriad paths and bloodlines. So well have we come to know all these people that our own lives may actually seem slightly less real than theirs.

The last couple of years have been good ones for Proustians. Malcolm Bowie's *Proust among the Stars* offers a superb analysis of the novel's major themes (self, time, sex, etc.). Of the novel's "desolate pattern of recurrence," Bowie sorrowfully notes, in full Proustian voice, "All love affairs fail, and fail in the same way. All journeys end in disappointment. All satisfactions are too little and too late." William Carter has recently brought out a fine narrative biography, and Penguin will soon be publishing a wholly fresh translation of the *Recherche*, by divers hands. There's even a new movie, based on the novel's last section, *Time Regained.*

For me, though, the most welcome recent publication isn't a book at all. Over the past month I've listened to Neville Jason reading his own abridgment of *Remembrance of Things Past* (most scholars now use the more exact title, *In Search of Lost Time*, adopted by D. J. Enright when he revised the Kilmartin/Scott-Moncrieff translation). I've reached the halfway point, *Sodom and Gomorrah*, and may slow down soon: Jason has yet to record the last two volumes. In general I prefer unabridged readings, but Jason's intelligent cutting, amazing command of accents and tones (listen for his bumbling Bloch, his cockney Françoise, his unctuous Charlus), and choice of musical interludes make these Naxos CDs irresistible. Jason can transform the mere enunciation of a syllable into a *moment bienheureux*, a madeleine-like feeling of bliss. For anybody who's been daunted at the prospect of starting Proust, these recordings (there are twenty-seven CDs so far) provide an ingratiating alternative.

Proust's Way, by Roger Shattuck, a leading scholar of twentieth-century French literature, supplies a comparable critical overview of the novel's ways and means. This is a good, if slightly ramshackle, book—good in that it reprints sections of Shattuck's National Book Award winner, *Marcel Proust* (e.g., "How to Read a Roman Fleuve"), and several pages on the metaphorical use of optics from his even earlier study, *Proust's Binoculars*. Other chapters draw on lectures and reviews, in particular a critique of the recent translations and French editions of Proust's masterpiece. Certainly, all of this is worthwhile, even if it feels a bit of a hodgepodge. At the heart of Shattuck's view of the novel lies what he calls "Soul error" or "Proust's complaint"—"the incapacity to give full value or status to one's own life and experience." Any goal actually achieved thus ends in disappointment and the taste of ashes. As Proust himself writes, "The only true voyage, the only Fountain of Youth, would be found not in traveling to strange lands but in having different eyes, in seeing the universe with the eyes of another person, of a hundred others, and seeing the hundred universes each of them sees, which each of them is." Of course, Proust's novel allows its readers an experience of just such plenitude.

Plenitude also characterizes Jean-Yves Tadié's massive life of the novelist. As the editor of the recent Pléiade recension of the *Recherche* (in four volumes), Tadié possesses an unrivaled knowledge of Proustian manuscripts and source material. He structures his own biography almost as a kind of "Encyclopedia Proustiana," offering potted lives of seemingly everyone the novelist knew and cared about, along with brief essays on Proust's themes and influences. I spent ten days poring over this tightly written, relentless book and have no doubt that it is a monumental piece of scholarship. Tadié tells or reminds you that Proust never uses the word "legally"; that he wrote about music halls under the pen name Bob; that he might wear three overcoats at once; that his uncle and his father probably shared the favors of the courtesan Laure Hayward (a partial model for Odette); that Proust, though exceptionally erudite, never kept many books and (like Joyce) considered himself to lack imagination; that he read *Wuthering Heights, Crime and Punishment,* and *Jude the Obscure*; that he loved to gamble and play the stock market; that Wyndham Lewis almost painted his portrait and that the surrealist André Breton proofread *Le Côté de Guermantes*—very badly. There's even occasional humor, as when Pierre Loti, asked if there were any sailors in his family, answers, "Yes, I had an uncle who was eaten aboard the raft of the *Medusa.*" I noticed only a couple of typos—Montesquiou on an occasion when Montesquieu is meant, the drama critic James Agate referred to as John Agate—but this is otherwise a work of the most meticulous scholarship.

Still, most casual readers are likely to feel overwhelmed by Tadié's detail and slack narrative drive. Ronald Hayman's popular life or Carter's more scholarly one might be better choices for anybody who just wants a solid biography of Proust. Of course, it's worth consulting any of these lives to be reminded of the dinner party given by Sydney Schiff on May 18, 1922, at which the invited guests included Proust, Joyce, Diaghilev, Stravinsky, and Picasso. Now that's an A-list.

In *Contre Sainte-Beuve* Proust emphasized that a writer's social, personal character could be dramatically different from his deeper creative self. For many readers, Proust's letters are a demonstration of just that: they are primarily bread-and-butter notes, acts of verbal flattery or sycophancy, business memos, all of them lacking the mournful wisdom displayed in the *Recherche.* Still, this fourth and final volume of *Selected Letters*—gleaned from Philip Kolb's much admired twenty-one-volume French edition—makes a good adjunct to Tadié's biography. Proust can be witty here too: answering a critic who complains about one of the novel's long and meandering sentences, he writes, "But I think you are over-generous when you suggest that it becomes clear on a third reading; speaking for myself, I find it incomprehensible." Besides these well-annotated letters, this volume includes a touching memoir of its (American!) editor, who spent sixty years of his life working on Proust's correspondence.

In August of 1909 a young man about town wrote to Madame Emile Straus, "I have just begun—and finished—a whole long book." By this scholars have concluded that Proust composed his opening pages and his closing pages together, and then over the next thirteen years filled in the middle, allowing his book to grow, a bit like Topsy (though always sure of its inner architecture). Beyond any doubt, then, *In Search of Lost Time* is, for all its length and occasional longueurs (chiefly in some of the pages about the Narrator's obsession with Albertine), a carefully structured work of art. Its concluding pages, when the Narrator realizes that he can redeem the wasted years of his life, must rank among the most stirring in all literature. Yet *In Search of Lost Time* is more than just a work of semi-autobiographical fiction: to its admirers, it remains one of those rare encyclopedic summas, like Chaucer's *Canterbury Tales*, the essays of Montaigne or Dante's *Commedia*, that offer insight into our unruly passions and solace for life's miseries. That it is also a great comic masterpiece goes without saying.

August 27, 2000

MEMOIR OF ITALO SVEVO

By Livia Veneziani Svevo
Translated from the Italian by Isabel Quigley

In 1907 a Triestine businessman named Ettore Schmitz, whose company man-
ufactured paint for ship's hulls, decided to perfect his broken English by taking
private language lessons. For his teacher he chose a young Irishman, a lanky
would-be writer whom he described as "very shortsighted." He "wears strong
glasses that make his eyes look enlarged . . . and they gaze with a look of ceaseless curiosity matched with supreme coldness."

James Joyce—who else could it be?—quickly grew fond of both his forty-
six-year-old pupil and his wife, Livia (whose name and blond tresses were later
borrowed for Anna Livia Plurabelle in *Finnegans Wake*); he even read aloud to
them from the manuscript of "The Dead." One day Schmitz confessed that he
too, in his youth, had been a writer and presented his new friend with copies
of two novels: *A Life (Una Vita,* 1892) and *As a Man Grows Older (Senilità,*
1898), the second published under the pen name Italo Svevo. Joyce read the
books and, according to this lovely memoir, announced "that some pages of *As
a Man Grows Older* could not have been better done by the great masters of the
French novel." After leaving Trieste for Paris and his never-doubted destiny,
Joyce would always speak of Svevo as "the only modern Italian novelist who
interested him."

From this chance encounter the urge to write was slowly rekindled in this
hypochondriacal, cigarette-addicted Austro-Italian-Jewish paint manufacturer. Some fifteen years later Svevo brought out a third and last book, his comic
masterpiece of psychological fiction, *Confessions of Zeno (La coscienza di Zeno,*
1923). For many readers it is the greatest Italian novel of the century, a proto
Portnoy's Complaint, but subtler, gentler. Svevo himself died in a car accident
five years after it was published, but lived just long enough to see his earlier
work revived and to hear his praises sung by the avant-garde young, among
them the poet Eugenio Montale.

This reminiscence of her husband by Livia Veneziani Svevo first appeared in Italy in 1950; the Marlboro Press's beautifully presented translation comes with both an important preface by P. N. Furbank, who wrote a groundbreaking study of Svevo, and, as an appendix, the complete text of a 1927 talk on Joyce by his old pupil. Clearly this is a book that any fan of *Confessions of Zeno* will want to read.

I say fan because Svevo (1861–1928) inspires intense affection. This is largely due to the appeal of his alter ego, the bumbling, health-obsessed, psychologically sensitive Zeno Cosini. (His first name recalls the pre-Socratic philosopher best known for his logical paradoxes, including the one about a footrace against a tortoise that Achilles can never win.) Zeno's life consists of a stream of broken resolutions to stop smoking, a never-ending flow of self-analysis, a repeated yearning for a good night's sleep, a vast medicine chest of pills for his real and imaginary illnesses, and a knack for somehow coming out all right in the end. He also has a way with words: "Accountants are by nature a race of animals much inclined to irony"; "Life lacks the monotony of museums." An early critic once described Zeno as Charlie Chaplin in Trieste; another called his creator the Italian Proust. Neither is quite right, but *Confessions of Zeno* somehow manages to blend both in a series of slapstick meditations and mishaps that seem uncannily faithful to the way people actually think and feel and worry. Especially worry.

At one point, for instance, Zeno commits himself to a high-security hospital to cure his need for cigarettes, but as the door clangs shut, he notices—or rather thinks he notices—the doctor in charge glancing admiringly at his wife. Aha! Almost certainly he has been tricked into entering this clinic so that the guilty couple can more safely indulge their illicit passion. To escape his locked cell Zeno must bribe and half seduce his nurse, only to run home and discover —as he knew deep in his heart—that his plain and stolid wife is completely innocent.

In a subsequent chapter we learn that Zeno proposed to Augusta only after being refused by her two beautiful sisters. All three proposals took place, moreover, on a single evening of romantic cross-purposes, starting with a caress received by the wrong sister during a seance in the dark. As always happens for Zeno, the unwanted Augusta turns out to be a perfect wife, while his first choice, Ada, loses her looks and makes an unhappy marriage with the shallow but grossly vital Guido.

Pleasingly, the novel relates, among other matters, the eventual, unlikely triumph of the hypochondriacal over the healthy. (Zeno, looking in a mirror: "I saw that I was very pale, which for me is sufficient grounds for becoming paler still.") When Zeno keeps a mistress—an impoverished singing student—

the unsuspecting Augusta finds her conscience-nipped husband all the more affectionate at home; when Guido quietly takes up with the secretary at his office, Ada immediately grows suspicious. Guido's whole life goes gradually downhill, ending in a phony suicide attempt that inadvertently succeeds. Afterward Zeno works furiously to recoup his late brother-in-law's financial losses, surprisingly succeeds—and then joins the wrong funeral procession and misses poor Guido's burial. But what else would you expect from an obsessive who, upon learning that there are fifty-four muscles employed in walking, immediately finds it impossible to control his legs and limps along painfully for days afterward?

Confessions of Zeno is nearly always in print, as it should be, but Svevo's earlier classic, *As a Man Grows Older*, is regrettably somewhat more elusive. P. N. Furbank has called it "one of the solidest masterpieces of 19th-century fiction," but I think it's even better than solid. The middle-aged Emilio Brentani falls for a beautiful working-class girl named Angiolina; their relationship is amorous but chaste; he hopes to become her lover but first wants to form and educate her. Meanwhile, Emilio's dowdy sister nurses an unspoken passion for his best friend, a handsome sculptor and ladies' man named Balli. Svevo gradually leads this foursome through most of love's mysteries from the nearly sacred to the definitely profane. If you like Ford Madox Ford's *The Good Soldier* or the novels of Jean Rhys, this is a book for you.

Svevo's oeuvre is small enough that it is worth reading entire, including the stories in *Short Sentimental Journey* and the fragments collected posthumously as *Further Confessions of Zeno*. "This Indolence of Mine," for instance, relates the sixty-seven-year-old Zeno's disastrous final love affair, with a tobacconist, undertaken like his marriage for hygienic reasons: he calculates that Death will leave him alone if he continues to act like a randy young man.

When Svevo himself lay dying, he asked his physician nephew for a cigarette and was refused. He then mumbled, à la Zeno, "That would have been the last cigarette." For his funeral he requested that it be "without any ostentation of any kind, even of simplicity." Who can resist such a charming, all-too-human human being? Any reader of this memoir or his fiction will understand why scholars have long suspected that Svevo is a model, almost the model, for Joyce's great everyman, Leopold Bloom.

As an introduction to this appealing author, one whose personality seems to match pretty closely that of his major characters, this concise *Memoir* cannot be bettered: it is affectionate, informative, and a pleasure to read.

September 30, 1990

THE LETTERS OF T. S. ELIOT
VOLUME 1, 1898–1922

Edited by Valerie Eliot

ELIOT'S NEW LIFE

By Lyndall Gordon

During his lifetime T. S. Eliot (1888–1965) bestrode the literary world like a colossus. From the publication of *The Waste Land* in 1922 until his death in 1965 he was the chief literary pooh-bah of England and America; in 1956 over fourteen thousand people jammed into a stadium in Minnesota to hear him— or, more accurately, simply to see him; literary histories spoke reverently of "The Age of Eliot."

After all, he was the author of the most admired poem of the century, generally regarded as the greatest literary critic in English, and hearkened to as a social visionary and religious prophet. He received the outward signs of success too: the Nobel Prize, the Order of Merit, and a hit on Broadway (his play *The Cocktail Party*). He even became a (posthumous) pop star of sorts when his children's verse was turned into the musical *Cats*.

Which just goes to show that nothing fails like success. During the past twenty years T. S. Eliot's reputation has taken a beating on all fronts. He has been called a fascist and anti-Semite, a wife abuser, a repressed homosexual. In terms of poetic influence Wallace Stevens and William Carlos Williams divide contemporary American poetry between them. Virtually all of Eliot's literary judgments have been overturned or strongly qualified. Modern verse drama came and went. Critics talk of "The Pound Era."

There's always a swing downward in literary reputation after the death of a giant. But then matters even out as scholarship starts to strip away the veneer of the smiling—or in Eliot's case, sad-faced—public man. In his centennial year (he was born on September 26, 1888) Eliot is currently enjoying, some might say enduring, that process. Memoirs, biographies, the discovery and publication of the *Waste Land* manuscript, and now his letters are altering our image of the Anglo-Catholic royalist and classicist into something much richer and stranger. Those are pearls that were his eyes.

The first volume of the Eliot letters begins in 1898, when Eliot was ten, and ends in 1922, the year of *The Waste Land* and the establishment of *The Criterion*, the intellectual quarterly he was to edit for seventeen years. In her introduction Valerie Eliot, the poet's widow, mentions that she had originally intended the first volume to go up to the end of 1926, that is, up to the moment of Eliot's religious conversion. This would have allowed a neat continuity with Lyndall Gordon's superb *Eliot's New Life*, which focuses on the poet's spiritual biography from 1927 till his death. But the years between these two books are in fact their hidden focus: the dissolution of Eliot's marriage to his first wife, Vivienne, and the reblossoming of his love for the girl he left behind, Emily Hale. It is the revelation of this human drama which is largely responsible for the recent image of Eliot as a confessional poet, somewhere between Baudelaire and Robert Lowell.

Admittedly, it is sometimes hard to find the human being in Eliot's correspondence. Letter writing, as Lyndall Gordon observes, "was his least distinctive mode. He wrote hundreds of reserved letters; one might say he was adept at the reserved letter. . . ." Eliot simply is not in the class of his poet friends Conrad Aiken and Ezra Pound, who made their lively correspondence an extension of their personalities and their poetic platforms. Happily, Valerie Eliot includes a few letters from these friends, as well as from Jean Verdenal, the mysterious dedicatee of *Prufrock and Other Observations*, who was killed in World War I. There was speculation at one time that he and Eliot were homosexual lovers; but Verdenal's letters are merely affectionate and nostalgic. However, some of the correspondence with Aiken, Pound, and other old friends displays a locker-room bawdiness: there are several excerpts from the obscene King Bolo poems, and lots of verbal towel-snapping about private parts and even more private acts.

Most of the time, though, these London letters show us Eliot the son (at times the mama's boy), the nurse-husband to his neurotic wife, Vivienne, and the ambitious young urban professional. In the early notes home Eliot stresses his accomplishments; only to his friends does he talk of emptiness and acedia, of the hollow man within: "In Oxford I have the feeling that I am not quite alive—that my body is walking about with a bit of my brain inside it, and nothing else."

This "aboulie," as Eliot calls it, may offer one reason why he suddenly and rashly married Vivienne Haigh-Wood—"the awful daring of a moment's surrender / Which an age of prudence can never retract." Emily Hale had not, apparently, made her feelings clear to Eliot before he left for England. While abroad on his Oxford scholarship he met Pound, that showman of modern letters, who urged him to pursue a poetic career in London. Vivienne was vivacious, available; like characters in Henry James, they mistook each other's true selves. The result was a nightmare marriage: Vivienne constantly ill, drugging herself with one nostrum after another, suffering from migraines, shortness of breath, dizziness, abscessed teeth, colitis, various neuroses. More often than not, Tom suffered too: mostly exhaustion from trying to earn a living (first schoolmastering, then banking, along with lectures, reviews, and—seemingly last of all—poems), but he also complains about his nose, teeth, and feet. "My nerves are bad tonight. Yes bad."

And yet, throughout this litany of woes, Eliot keeps saying things like "The present year has been, in some respects, the most awful nightmare of anxiety that the mind of man can conceive, but at least it is not dull. . . ." One senses that the young Eliot's fear of the void within himself was so great that only by suffering and constant work could he keep it at bay. Eventually, I think, the ceaseless activity—both professional and social—became the workaholic's typical means of avoiding an impossible home-life.

Readers looking for Eliot the critic and poet in these pages will need to be highly imaginative. There are prefigurations of famous critical or poetic formulations—"I like to feel that a writer is perfectly cool and detached, regarding other people's feelings or his own, like a god who has got beyond them . . ." —but such tidbits are few and never developed. No one reading these pages would believe that their author was at work on the critical pieces that would make *The Sacred Wood* a touchstone in the history of literary theory.

What is true of the essays is even more true of the poems. Eliot never talks about "The Love Song of J. Alfred Prufrock" or "Gerontion" except as products—as poems to sell to *Poetry* or *The Dial*. Even when dealing with his benefactor John Quinn he seems more a literary agent than an author. There is literally more here about Eliot's underwear and pyjamas—about which Vivienne is strangely obsessed—than about his poetry. Only once do the letters seem to illuminate the poems directly: Eliot, looking through a picture album, notes "it gives one a strange feeling that Time is not before and after, but all at once, present and future and all the periods of the past"—very nearly the opening lines of "Burnt Norton."

Even though Eliot's letters give us no direct glimpse into his poetic workshop, they do relate some telling and touching moments. The pathos of Eliot writing his mother, when he learns of his father's death, that he wants to hear her "sing The Little Tailor to me." The probably unconscious double entendre of a note to Bertrand Russell, who has taken Viv on a little vacation: "I am sure you have done everything possible and handled her in the very best way—better than I" (Russell almost certainly slept with her). The personal plea behind the letter to *The Athenaeum* urging that the British Museum library stay open in the evenings for people who had jobs during the day.

There are, of course, occasional signs of the "bad" Eliot. He refers callously to "our servant" and almost never calls her by name; he mentions "Siegfried Sassoon (semitic)"; he cuts old friends, including "Conrad Aiken, stupider than ever." And all the while he is smiling at the right people, keeping his name in the news, managing his literary career with Rommel-like cunning.

These letters leave us at the end with Eliot on the verge of his greatest success. He has finished *The Waste Land* (while on leave from Lloyd's bank for nervous exhaustion) and has inaugurated *The Criterion*. He has every reason to be proud, perhaps a little too proud: "There is a small and select public which regards me as the best living critic, as well as the best living poet, in England. . . . I really think that I have far more influence on English letters than any other American has ever had, unless it be Henry James."

He was right, of course, despite the snooty tone. But Lyndall Gordon's *Eliot's New Life* shows in part how little that public success came to mean to him. By 1925 Vivienne Eliot's neurasthenia started to pass over into delusional madness. In 1928 Eliot converted to the Church of England, eventually going so far as to make a private vow of chastity. Soon thereafter he began to live apart from his wife, keeping his whereabouts secret, sneaking out of his office when she appeared, dodging her in public and private. She wouldn't sign a deed of separation.

Lyndall Gordon's *Eliot's Early Years* (1977) tried to understand Eliot's treatment of Vivienne, often taking her part against received history. *Eliot's New Life* chronicles the poet's "search for salvation," but focuses closely on the place of women in that search: the gnawing guilt over leaving Vivienne, the promise of renewed happiness with Emily Hale. Eliot wrote over one thousand letters to Hale—all of them locked up at Princeton until the year 2020—and spent many springs and summers in her company. She was simply a New England–born schoolteacher, with an interest in drama, but she represented for Eliot an ideal love, his own lost innocence and purity. Ultimately she served as Beatrice to his Dante—and then was cruelly cast aside.

For the Eliot of the 1930s and 1940s was a man with immortal longings in him, and the *Four Quartets*—"Burnt Norton," "East Coker," "The Dry Salvages," and "Little Gidding"—depict his quest for the perfected life. Emily Hale was, as Gordon emphasizes, "vital to Eliot's new life because she had the power to stir a dream of beatitude through their mutual memory of pure love."

It was in her company that the poet visited Burnt Norton, and saw the rose garden that was to figure so prominently as a symbol of unfulfilled happiness: "Footfalls echo in the memory / Down the passage which we did not take / Towards the door we never opened / Into the rose-garden."

In her brilliant analysis of the *Quartets*—a companion piece to the "autobiographical" reading of *The Waste Land* in her earlier book—Gordon links Eliot's spiritual search with that of his puritan forebears. Building on the celebrated studies by F. O. Matthiessen (who had stressed Eliot's connection with the classic American moralists) and Helen Gardner (whose sacramental readings of his poems gained Eliot's own approval), Gordon interprets the *Four Quartets* as a full-fledged spiritual autobiography—an attempt to understand how to live a religious life in a fallen world, how to achieve sanctity. These same highly personal themes recur in the plays of this era, not least *The Cocktail Party* with its submerged homage to Emily Hale as Celia, whom the hero does not marry and instead sends to her martyrdom.

Which is what Eliot finally did. His family assumed that he and Emily would eventually wed; but when Vivienne died in 1947, after years in an asylum, Eliot looked within and found that all his desire for marriage had died too. Never healthy in his attitudes toward women—the hyacinth girl on the one hand, Mrs. Porter on the other—he preferred his poetic dreams of the past and the lone path of the religious ordeal, divesting himself of everything in his quest to know God.

"What Eliot needed," elaborates Gordon, "was not love in the usual sense, passion or care, but love's transforming power, the idea of a momentous drama, partly on the model of Dante and Beatrice, partly a subtle Jamesian drama of buried sensibilities." Like most readers, Gordon finds this attitude easier to understand than to condone, especially when it resulted in a broken heart and blighted life for an admirable woman.

After such knowledge, what forgiveness? In his later years Eliot slept on a simple bed under a heavy iron cross. He took the bus every day to church, recited his prayers quietly in the crowded tube. He expected to retire to an abbey. As a lecturer he had gradually become something of a spiritual authority, talking about life and society, religion and literature, with a voice beyond time, beyond place. And then, at age sixty-eight, he married his thirty-year-old secretary, Valerie Fletcher.

This may seem almost a joke, the renunciation of a lifetime's habits. But this second marriage found Eliot surprised by joy, and his final years were, by all reports, extremely happy. He had journeyed from the inferno of his youth through the purgatory of his maturity to find an unexpected paradise in his last years.

For all his gifts and accomplishments, T. S. Eliot was for most of his life a haunted man, racked with a sense of sin, always yearning for "the peace that passeth understanding." In his self-obsession he sometimes treated others cruelly; he was often a holy prig; but knowing of his own purgatorial burning humanizes and transforms his poems, so perfectly beautiful, so terribly personal. Still, to read *The Waste Land* now is to hear the cries of Vivienne, as well as Philomel; and even though the end of "Little Gidding" may triumphantly unite the fire and the rose, it is hard to forget Emily Hale, ultimately left standing alone by the door that never opened.

March 17, 1991

POSTSCRIPT: No further volumes of Eliot's letters have yet appeared (2004).

FORD MADOX FORD

By Alan Judd

Mothers, don't let your children grow up to be writers. If your fresh-cheeked college grad announces that he or she plans to be a novelist, an essayist, or even a poet, immediately place Alan Judd's enthralling new biography of Ford Madox Ford (1873–1939) into the innocent one's hands. It's guaranteed to make law school or an M.B.A. look mighty attractive. Though not quite the saddest story—that epithet belongs to another tale—Ford's life is still quite sad enough. The author of *The Good Soldier, Parade's End*, and rather too much else was the greatest all-around literary man of his time, yet when he died in 1939, at age sixty-six, he was virtually penniless, with most of his books out of print and his reputation fading fast.

Though structured like a biography, Judd's *Ford Madox Ford* is more precisely a defense of its subject, a meditation on his topsy-turvy career, and a succinct intepretation of his lasting achievements as a novelist, editor, and—surprise!—poet. Scholars looking for all the facts will still need the monumental, often unsympathetic life by Arthur Mizener, but ordinary readers should find Judd's book just the right mix of swift-moving prose, lively storytelling, and solid scholarship tempered by affection and common sense. In fact, it's such a fine book that libraries and bookshops should prepare for a run on Ford's *Fifth Queen* trilogy, his several volumes of reminiscences, and even such late novels as *The Rash Act*.

On the other hand, maybe they shouldn't bother. Every generation rediscovers "Fordie," but somehow the man just won't stay rediscovered. Partly this is because he simply wrote way too fast and far too much— eighty-two books, at least half of them potboilers, with the second-rate tending to overwhelm the superb. Oddly enough, even success has worked against him. *The Good Soldier*—with its famous opening line "This is the saddest story I have ever heard"—has been applauded by Allen Tate and Anthony Burgess, among others, as the greatest British novel of the century.

Its heartrending, time-twisting minuet of betrayal and violent death is now such a staple of Modern British Fiction 101 that almost nobody reads anything else by Ford. Not even *Parade's End*—the equally anguished story of Christopher Tietjens, the last gentleman—which many regard as an even greater work. Of the other underread novels, William Gass has written with his customary panache in praise of *The Fifth Queen,* a three-part chronicle about Henry VIII and Katharine Howard, pointing out its cinematic qualities, its amazing pictorial economy, and the sheer gorgeousness of its sentences. Gass also remarks that Ford was essentially a nineteenth-century writer and that in his three major works he brought to their "final and most complete expression" the Jamesian study of fine consciences, the panoramic Victorian social novel, and the historical romance inaugurated by Sir Walter Scott.

Perhaps the main problem, though, in canonizing Ford derives from the messiness to every aspect of his life. His writing career cannot be slotted into any single literary period. He has been viewed as a womanizer in his private life, a snob and egotist in his conversation, and a liar in his memoirs. T. S. Eliot even called him a "parasite of letters." One of Judd's tasks is to dispel this penumbra of the unsavory and to reveal Ford as sensitive, hardworking, admirable, and as much a victim as a victimizer.

He was born Ford Hermann Hueffer (pronounced Hoofer) in 1873 into a Pre-Raphaelite family, with various Rossetti uncles, aunts, and cousins. He published his first book, the children's story *The Brown Owl,* at age eighteen, later ruefully noting that it sold more copies than anything else he ever wrote. In his early twenties he fell in love and eloped with teenaged Elsie Martindale. The young couple settled in the vicinity of Romney Marsh, where the neighbors included Joseph Conrad, Henry James, Stephen Crane, and H. G. Wells. Ford soon joined this "ring of conspirators" bent on overthrowing British fiction, becoming the close friend and ten-year collaborator of Conrad: the two worked on three novels together, and Ford even composed one of the chapters of Conrad's masterwork *Nostromo.*

All this time the young writer cranked out books—a biography of his painter grandfather, Ford Madox Brown, novels, studies of England's coastal towns, appreciations of London, a life of Holbein. Then in 1909 he became the founding editor of the *English Review,* which during his tenure he made the best literary magazine ever. In the very first issue Ford printed Thomas Hardy's poem "A Sunday Morning Tragedy," Constance Garnett's translation of Tolstoy's *The Raid,* James's "The Jolly Corner," the opening of Wells's *Tono-Bungay,* and some of Conrad's reminiscences. But Fordie wasn't content with just publishing the established figures of the day. In short order he discovered and launched the careers of D. H. Lawrence, Wyndham Lewis, and Norman Douglas. Eventually he also showcased work by Yeats, Ezra Pound, E. M. Forster, G. K. Chesterton, and virtually everyone else now safely ensconced in *The Norton Anthology of Modern Literature*. He also kept up with his own writing: in 1914 Pound declared "On Heaven" by "Forty Mad-dogs Hoofer" to be the "best poem yet written in the twentieth century fashion."

Unfortunately, while Ford was busy establishing himself as the compleat man of letters, he was also carrying on an affair with his wife's sister, an impropriety that may have provoked his father-in-law's suicide. Still, Elsie was willing to overlook this familial infidelity but not his growing passion for Violet Hunt, a well-known novelist more than a decade his senior but of considerable sex appeal: at various points in her career she turned down a marriage proposal from Oscar Wilde, dallied with Somerset Maugham, and resisted the besotted advances of the lesbian Radclyffe Hall. (Ah, the literary life!) In what may have been a desperate attempt to regain her husband's affection, Elsie subsequently accused the chief backer of the *English Review* of trying to take liberties with her. To no avail. In revenge for being abandoned, Elsie denied Ford a divorce, refused to let him see their two daughters, and managed to queer various desperate attempts to make Violet his legal wife. Worst of all, the scandal led to his losing control of the *English Review*.

Broke, his occupation gone, his marriage over, Ford began to write *The Good Soldier* on his fortieth birthday, putting into it, he later said, everything he knew about the art of fiction. With Conrad he had discussed method for ten years: point of view, the time shift (i.e., telling a story out of chronological sequence), *progression d'effet* (the notion that a novel should speed up as it approaches its end), the importance of surprise, "which in the end is the supreme quality and necessity of art." All these, along with his torturous love life and a conviction that "the heart of man is a dark forest," went into the crucible of this anguished, beautifully achieved masterpiece, "the greatest French novel in English."

It should have established him forever. Unfortunately, *The Good Soldier* appeared just after World War I broke out, so it was largely buried by world events. Nothing daunted, the patriotic Ford enlisted in the infantry and saw service in France, where he was shelled and gassed. For several years after the war he felt disoriented, suffered memory loss, thought himself washed up. Partly to escape the past, he changed his name from Ford Madox Hueffer to Ford Madox Ford. One day Ezra Pound introduced him to the young Australian painter Stella Bowen—and Violet joined the chorus of women who felt themselves wronged by Ford.

Soon the new couple shifted operations to Paris and Provence. With memories of the *English Review* leading him on like a will-o'-the-wisp, Ford invested what little money he had left in starting a new magazine, the *Transatlantic Review*. This time out he published Ernest Hemingway, Gertrude Stein, and James Joyce (sections of *Finnegans Wake*), admiring "the peculiar, hieratic quality of Mr. Joyce's mind." (To show his appreciation Joyce became godfather to Ford and Bowen's daughter Julia.) In these years he also wrote *Parade's End*, and fell into a brief affair with Jean Rhys, whom he encouraged to write. Her novel *Quartet* chronicles, with acid and irony, that strange, bitter interlude.

The affair with Rhys helped end Ford's relationship with Bowen, who was eventually replaced with another painter, Janice Biala. There was something, as Judd remarks, about this fat, soft-voiced, epicurean walrus that women found irresistible. By the 1930s Ford began to spend more and more time in America. He became friends with Allen Tate and Caroline Gordon, encouraged the early work of Robert Penn Warren, Robert Lowell, and Jean Stafford, tried to find a publisher for the young Eudora Welty, and recommended an editor friend to "get hold of Djuna Barnes who is another one of my babies." As he once said, "I am forever meddling with the young." During these years he also wrote delightful, rambling, self-centered "memoirs and impressions" of the literary greats he had known—they remind me of Stendhal's books on Italy—that later proved to be more creatively than faithfully remembered. More and more people started to call Ford a liar, "the helpless victim of his own imagination," as well as a womanizer and sentimental egotist.

In his final years, the old walrus managed to get a teaching job at . . . Olivet College in Michigan. By then he surely must have wondered at the strangeness of life. There, "an old man mad about writing," he completed *The March of Literature*, his garrulous idiosyncratic paean to the great writers he loved. Huffing and wheezing, altogether worn out, he fell ill on his way to France in 1939 and died at Deauville. Only three people attended his funeral.

Both during his life and afterward many of the writers Ford admired or promoted turned against him with unexpected vitriol. Wyndham Lewis described him as "a flabby lemon and pink giant who hung his mouth open as though he were an animal at the zoo inviting buns." Most notorious of all, in *A Moveable Feast* Hemingway—for whom Ford composed a superb and generous introduction to *A Farewell to Arms*—went so far as to say the old man smelled.

Still, for every detractor Ford has always had a passionate advocate. Alan

Judd is one of his best and most judicious. Maybe he can finally gain for "everybody's warrior" (Edward Dahlberg), this "scamp of literature" (Graham Greene), his rightful place among the masters of twentieth-century prose. As he says of one Ford book after another, so might it be said of his own biography: it should be read, it must be read.

March 17, 1991

POSTSCRIPT: There is now an exhaustive, two-volume life by Max Saunders.

THE COMPLETE SHORT STORIES

By Ronald Firbank
Edited by Steven Moore

In "Lambert Orme," one of the semifictional profiles in *Some People*, Harold Nicolson memorializes a figure closely modeled after the young Ronald Firbank. "It would be impossible, I feel, to actually be as decadent as Lambert looked." His walk "was more than sinuous, it did more than undulate: it rippled." He "seemed a walking-talking Max Beerbohm version of himself," one of "the rotted rose leaves of the Yellow Book."

To this day the name Ronald Firbank too often provokes a snicker or a giggle when it is recognized at all. For many, he is only an all-too-gay writer, fiction's pastry chef, the author of airy-fairy tales of randy prelates, creamy altar boys, and upper-class matrons who yearn to have their pet dogs baptized or their faces enshrined in the stained-glass windows of a cathedral. The very titles of his finest books suggest the fey and the fatuous: *Vainglory* (1915), *The Flower beneath the Foot* (1923), *Prancing Nigger* (1924), *Concerning the Eccentricities of Cardinal Pirelli* (1926).

In fact, Firbank (1886–1926) should be honored as a great master of twentieth-century literature, one whose books taught narrative economy, lightness of touch, and speed to a generation of writers, among them Evelyn Waugh, Henry Green, and Anthony Powell. As an innovator and stylistic influence he stands to later English fiction precisely as early Hemingway does to American. "My writing," asserted Firbank, and this hardly sounds like some epicene pipsqueak, "must bring discomfort to fools since it is aggressive, witty and unrelenting." Firbank's work may glisten like spun sugar but turns out to be as strong as chrome steel.

This frankly swishy dandy, constantly on the move (Lisbon, Cairo, Rome, Constantinope, Havana), possessed the iron will and drive of his railroad ties-to-riches grandfather. Over ten years he published a half dozen small masterpieces, with so little intelligent appreciation that the earth might have been deserted. But in that time he ushered in a literary revolution—and he did it by simply cutting the dull stuff out of his books. He discarded leisurely descriptions, stripped dialogue of its "he saids" and "she saids," subordinated plot to language, and made his characters, those absurd and ingratiating puppets with names like Mrs. Shamefoot and Madame Wetme, into vehicles for social satire and joyful, imaginative extravagance. Surprisingly, he did this not through some programmatic literary radicalism, but at least partly in the name of realism. For instance, to evoke accurately a crowded cocktail party (in *Valmouth*, 1919) he set down mere snatches of conversation, just the bits that might be overheard by someone wandering a little hazily around the room with a glass of sherry in his hand:

"Heroin."
"Adorable simplicity."
"What could anyone find to admire in such a shelving profile?"
"We reckon a duck here of two or three and twenty not so old. And a spring chicken anything to fourteen."
"My husband had no amorous energy whatsoever; which just suited me, of course."
"I suppose when there's no room for another crow's-foot, one attains a sort of peace."
"I once said to Doctor Fothergill, a clergyman of Oxford and a great friend of mine, 'Doctor,' I said, 'oh, if only you could see my——' "
"Elle était jolie! Mais jolie . . . C'était une si belle brune . . . !' "
"Cruelly lonely."
"Leery . . ."
"Vulpine."
"Calumny."

And so forth, funnier and funnier. As Aldous Huxley wrote—"Aldous—always my torture," lisped Firbank once—of a character similar to the author of *Inclinations* (1916) and *Caprice* (1917): "My life . . . is not so long that I can afford to spend precious hours writing or reading descriptions of middle-class interiors." Instead Firbank's nine slender novels—available from New Directions in two omnibus editions—are awash in white space, mosaics of sentence fragments, dashes, italics, ellipses. "I think nothing of filing fifty pages down to make a brief, crisp paragraph or even a row of dots." For Firbank unheard music was nearly the sweetest of all.

Firbank's pointillism, his soap-opera storylines, his wit, and even his silliness all helped to aerate the weighty fiction of eminent Victorians and earnest

Edwardians, and, in particular, allowed him to slice through the Gordian knot-tiness of a Henry James, who aimed to say everything in his novels, and took his own sweet time about it too. The iconic moment must have come when the young Firbank met the late James in 1907 at the twenty-first-birthday party of Vyvyan Holland, Oscar Wilde's son. The old world and the new, as the master himself might have observed.

Still, classic or no, Firbank remains unremittingly, gloriously campy. This is a given, like Beckett's gloom and Borges's scholasticism, and a real reader wouldn't have him any other way. A Miss Missingham, author of *Sacerdotalism and Satanism*, remarks that the towers of a cathedral at twilight resemble "the helmets of eunuchs at carnival time." Another character's overelaborate dress calls to mind "a St. Sebastian with too many arrows." Lady Georgia Blueharnis observes that the hills near her estate "would undoubtedly gain if some sorrowful creature could be induced to take to them. I often long for a bent, slim figure to trail slowly along the ridge, at sundown, in an agony of regret." Even throwaway lines show genius, as when Firbank evokes the "eternal she-she-she of servants' voices" or mentions a tapestry curtain that depicts "The Birth of Tact, in which Taste was seen lying on a flower-decked couch amid ultra-classic surroundings."

Perhaps the acme of Firbankian repartee occurs in his play *The Princess Zoubaroff* (1920), when two characters are introduced:

NADINE: My husband.
BLANCHE [genially]: I think we've slept together once?
ADRIAN: I don't remember.
BLANCHE: At the opera. During *Bérénice*.

Every word of this is perfect, but Blanche's stage direction strikes me as even more drily brilliant than Adrian's reply.

Not unexpectedly, only a small amount of this topnotch work appears in the *Complete Short Stories*, which is made up entirely of juvenilia, most of it written while Firbank was in his teens, much of it labeled "Not to be published." (Dalkey Archive Press unrepentantly embosses its binding with this phrase in Firbank's hand.) About half the stories are pastels in prose, saccharine bits of wispy fluff like "Odette D'Antrevernes," in which a young girl redeems a fallen woman, or fin-de-siècle fairy tales such as "The Singing Bird & the Moon," which recalls the most sentimental of Oscar Wilde's children's stories. The best pieces—several previously published in the late posthumous volume, *The New Rythum* (1962)—do provide the genuine Firbank tang: "Her weekends were a noted success. She arranged a circle of deck chairs under the lime trees on her lawn and everyone slept" ("When Widows Love"). And no Firbank admirer should miss the moment in "A Study in Opal" when a society woman learns that her new husband, a bishop, has "passed on." " 'You cannot mean he is dead?' Lady Henrietta gasped. Her fingers wound about her jeweled crucifix. Surely a stone was missing. She bent her eyes to see."

Ronald Firbank's books, blessed with insouciance and daring, may not be for everybody, but they do possess one of the true elements of a classic: they can be read again and again with ever-deepening pleasure. In the right mood they are very nearly the most amusing novels in the world.

December 16, 1990

THE SELECTED PROSE OF
FERNANDO PESSOA

Edited and translated from the Portuguese by Richard Zenith

Fernando Pessoa (1888–1935) is generally regarded as Portugal's greatest writer of the twentieth century. Some critics would even leave off that last qualifying prepositional phrase. Be that as it may, he is certainly one of the most appealing European modernists, equal in command and range to his contemporaries Rilke and Mandelstam. But while most writers strive mightily to discover their individual and distinctive authorial voice, Pessoa refused to narrow himself this way: instead he invented a series of poets and essayists, gave them names, literary styles, and philosophies, and then composed pages of verse and prose by Alberto Caeiro, Ricardo Reis, Alvaro de Campos, Antonio Mora, Bernado Soares. In some instances, he even wrote as Fernando Pessoa. That the word *pessoa* means "person" in Portuguese is almost too perfect.

Richard Zenith—who sounds as if he himself might be one of Pessoa's several dozen known "heteronyms"—has made himself into the Portuguese master's most energetic translator and advocate. In 1998 he brought out *Fernando Pessoa & Co.*, a selection of poems by Caeiro, Reis, Campos, et al. In general, I find translated poetry rather a bore, but Pessoa's work—like that of Cavafy and Yehuda Amichai—seems to carry something of its magic into English. At least I couldn't stop reading these lyrical meditations. At times they recall a slightly restrained Whitman:

> I salute all who may read me,
> Tipping my wide-brimmed hat
> As soon as the coach tops the hill
> And they see me at my door.
> I salute them and wish them sunshine,
> Or rain, if rain is needed,
> And a favorite chair where they sit

At home, reading my poems
Next to an open window.

Much of Pessoa's verse adopts a pagan outlook—his ur-heteronym, Alberto Caeiro, espoused a philosophy grounded in the senses—with a classical emphasis on life's fleetingness, the inexorablity of fate, the wisdom of stoicism:

Day after day life's the same life.
All that happens, Lydia
In what we are as in what we are not,
Happens all the same.
Picked, the fruit withers; unpicked
It falls. Destiny is
The same, whether we seek or wait
For it. Our lot today,
Our fate from always, and in either form
Beyond us and invincible.

A similar, albeit more urban, melancholy suffuses Pessoa's greatest and best-known work, *The Book of Disquiet*, the journals kept by Bernardo Soares, "a nondescript assistant bookkeeper for a fabric warehouse," who "having nowhere to go and nothing to do, nor friends to visit, nor any interest in reading books" was "in the habit of spending nights inside, in his rented room, writing." Zenith includes a chunk of that masterpiece in this *Selected Prose*, but back in 1996 he translated the entire work (Carcanet; a revised and amplified version is scheduled this year from Penguin). More accurately, he translated one of the reconstructions or proposed arrangements of *The Book of Disquiet*, for Pessoa never finished this lifelong project. Indeed, Zenith tells us that ideally its various fragments should be sold in a loose-leaf binder, so that the reader could shuffle the contents into whatever order suited.

The incomplete and fluid nature of *The Book of Disquiet* fits the modern taste and makes it a proto-postmodernist text—if one wants to regard it in that way. Most of us will simply enjoy Soares's mini-essays and moody reflections, their tone a blend of the wistful, sardonic, and self-pitying:

My destiny, which has pursued me like a malevolent creature, is to be able to desire only what I know I'll never get. If I see the nubile figure of a girl in the street and imagine for the slightest moment, however nonchalantly, what it would be like if she were mine, it's a dead certainty that ten steps past my dream she'll meet the man who's obviously her husband or lover. . . .

My ideal would be to live everything through novels and to use real life for resting up—to read my emotions and to live my disdain for them. For someone with a keen sensitive imagination, the adventures of a fictional protagonist are genuine emotion enough, and more, since they are experienced by us as well as the protagonist. No greater romantic adventure exists than to have loved Lady Macbeth. . . .

Having seen how lucidly and logically certain madmen justify their lunatic ideas to themselves and to others, I can never again be sure of the lucidness of my lucidity. . . .

To be a retired major seems to me ideal. It's a shame one can't have eternally been nothing but a retired major. . . .

Even writing has lost its appeal. To give expression to emotions and to refine sentences has become so banal it's like eating or drinking, something I do more or less with care but not much interest, always a bit detached and distracted, without enthusiasm or brilliance.

At times Pessoa's introspection verges on the sentimental or even maudlin—though he would naturally attribute any bathos to the repressed clerk Soares. More often, *The Book of Disquiet* or the pages of *The Selected Prose* provoke troubling questions about sincerity and authenticity. How essential is it to believe that a writer is speaking from the heart? Can one put faith in any statement by Pessoa? Or is everything provisional? Do the heteronyms underscore the importance of the author or his relative unimportance? As Pessoa paradoxically observed, "In the theater of life, those who play the part of sincerity are, on the whole, the most convincing in their roles."

Zenith's excellent introduction and headnotes to the *Selected Prose* give a brisk account of Fernando Pessoa's largely uneventful life: a childhood in South Africa, where he learned to write perfect English; a return to Lisbon as a teenager and a career there translating business documents; no known sexual activity (however, masturbation is used as a frequent metaphor in the prose); the founding of a couple of short-lived magazines and schools of poetry (sensationism, intersectionism); and constant writing, without much publication. Most of Pessoa's reputation, like Kafka's, is in fact posthumous: he left a trunk full of manuscripts—essays, poems, fragments of all sorts—and these have gradually been winnowed and published over the past forty years.

As one might expect, *The Selected Prose* showcases its author's fecundity and range. Under his several heteronyms Pessoa cranked out literary polemics (reminiscent of Wyndham Lewis's *Blast* or some of the surrealist manifestos);

accounts of occultism (in which he mildly believed); short stories (in "The Anarchist Banker," a cigar-smoking plutocrat argues that he is in fact the only true follower of anarchism); messianic political tracts about the coming Portuguese renaissance; defenses of paganism; rules for daily living ("Organize your life like a literary work, putting as much unity into it as possible"); commentary on favorite books (*The Pickwick Papers*) and on troubling authors (Shakespeare); vivid descriptions of weather and city sights; and aphorisms of all sorts: "A great painting means a thing which a rich American wants to buy because other people would like to buy it if they could. . . . Blank verse is the ideal medium for an unreadable epic poem. . . . The central thing about really great geniuses is that they are not forerunners." There's even a remarkable "static drama" called *The Mariner* that might be Samuel Beckett rewriting, with his usual elliptical pauses, Synge's *Riders to the Sea*:

> FIRST WATCHER: But is it really a good idea for you to continue? Should every story have an end? But keep talking anyway. . . . It matters so little what we say or don't say. . . . We keep watch over the passing hours. . . . Our task is as useless as Life. . . .

Having just begun reading Pessoa, I find myself utterly caught up by his melancholy wit and congenial temperament. Yet I instinctively speak as if he were a single author when he is, in fact, a whole library: if you don't care that much for Ricardo Reis, you may still like Alberto Caeiro or Alexander Search. And if you've never read Fernando Pessoa at all or have only heard a little about his remarkable genius, you may find, as I have, that he is one of those writers as addictive, and endearing, as Borges and Calvino. Certainly adventurous readers will want to explore this astonishing life's work.

July 22, 2001

NO LAUGHING MATTER:
THE LIFE AND TIMES OF FLANN O'BRIEN

By Anthony Cronin

Flann O'Brien (1911–1966) has never wanted for admirers, even though he remains too little known outside of Ireland. His first novel, *At Swim-Two-Birds*, was published on the recommendation of Graham Greene, who praised it as "a book in a thousand." Samuel Beckett later gave this whimsical masterpiece to James Joyce, who though nearly blind managed to read it—almost certainly the last novel he ever did read—and who pronounced it "a really funny book." On this side of the Atlantic, S. J. Perelman named O'Brien simply "the best comic writer I can think of."

Born in 1911 into a middle-class Catholic family in Strabane, a small town on the border of County Tyrone and County Donegal, Brian O'Nolan—aka Flann O'Brien, Myles na gCopaleen, and a dozen other pen names—spoke Gaelic as his first language. When he was eleven, the family moved to Dublin, where O'Nolan eventually won honors at University College Dublin as a student—and notoriety as a speaker at the Literary and Historical Society's stormy meetings. At UCD he also "laid faultlessly the foundation of a system of heavy drinking" and discovered that he "could always be relied upon to make a break of at least 25 with even a bad cue."

Upon graduation O'Nolan and several friends started a satirical magazine called *Blather*, and there he found his comic voice:

> Carruthers McDaid is a man I created [for a novel] one night when I had swallowed nine stouts and felt vaguely blasphemous. . . . McDaid, starting off as a rank waster and a rotter, was meant to sink slowly to absolutely the last extremities of human degradation. Nothing, absolutely nothing, was to be too low for him. . . .
>
> I shall never forget the Thursday when the thing happened. I retired

to my room at about six o'clock, fortified with a pony of porter and two threepenny cigars, and manfully addressed myself to the achievement of Chapter Five. McDaid, who for a whole week had been living precariously by selling kittens to foolish old ladies and who could be said to be existing on the immoral earnings of his cat, was required to rob a poor-box in a church. But no! Plot or no plot, it was not to be.

"Sorry, old chap," he said, "but I absolutely can't do it."

"What's this, Mac," said I, "getting squeamish in your old age?"

"Not squeamish exactly," he replied, "but I bar poor-boxes. Dammit, you can't call me squeamish. Think of that bedroom business in Chapter Two, you old dog."

"Not another word," said I sternly, "you remember that new shaving brush you bought?"

"Yes."

"Very well. You burst the poor-box or it's anthrax in two days."

Before long all of O'Nolan's characters have risen up in rebellion, and by the end of the sketch they are planning to murder him.

This is, in miniature, the Pirandellian plot device that powers *At Swim-Two-Birds*, a novel with a dizzying number of narrative planes. The first level describes the mildly sordid life of a laze-about university student, forever in conflict with an uncle who wonders whether he ever opens a book. In fact, this unnamed student-narrator is composing a novel about a novelist named Dermot Trellis, who is, in his turn, writing a novel. All of them are, of course, part of a book by "Flann O'Brien," who is really Brian O'Nolan.

"A satisfactory novel," we are instructed by the narrator, "should be a self-evident sham to which the reader could regulate at will the degree of his credulity. It was undemocratic to compel characters to be uniformly good or bad or poor or rich. Each should be allowed a private life, self-determination and a decent standard of living. . . . Characters should be interchangeable between one book and another. The entire corpus of existing literature should be regarded as a limbo from which discerning authors could draw their characters as required, creating only when they failed to find a suitable existing puppet. The modern novel should be largely a work of reference."

Despite this aesthetic bill of rights (adopted by several later authors), Trellis insists on being despotic and unscrupulous. He creates the beautiful Sheila Lamont and rapes her. He loses the respect of his entire dramatis personae, who secretly begin to defy him. Whenever Trellis sleeps they are able to lead independent lives, sometimes talking wistfully about the other, more respectable fiction that they've been in. Eventually, Trellis's puppets place him on trial and torture him for his sins—until a housemaid accidentally burns his novel's manuscript.

While all this is going on, *At Swim-Two-Birds* is also interweaving a high-falutin' (and rather tiresome) retelling of the ancient Irish poem about the madness of Sweeney, the fey adventures of the Good Fairy and the Pooka MacPhellimey, some incidents from the career of the legendary giant Finn MacCool, a parodic cowboy story, extracts from "A Conspectus of the Arts and Sciences," selections from the poems of the workingman poet Jem Casey ("A pint of plain is your only man"), periodic stage directions, an occasional synopsis of the novel's action so far, and even authorial comments ("The latter statement follows my decision to abandon a passage, . . . the passage being, by general agreement, a piece of undiluted mediocrity"). O'Nolan's prose ranges as needed from the pseudo-archaic to the plainspoken to the quietly poetic: "On the window-ledge there was a small bakelite clock which grappled with each day as it entered his room through the window from Peter Place, arranging it with precision into twenty-four hours."

All in all, *At Swim-Two-Birds* remains a showstopping performance, especially for a writer in his midtwenties. Such promise so brilliantly realized was naturally to hang like an albatross around its author's neck.

In 1935 O'Nolan joined the civil service. Shortly thereafter his father died, leaving him the main support of his mother and his five siblings. For the next eighteen years all his writing was produced in his spare time, much of it typed up on Sunday afternoons at the family dining room table, usually after a demanding week both as the private secretary to various government ministers and as a regular visitor to the public houses of Dublin.

After *At Swim-Two-Birds* finally appeared, in 1939, Brian O'Nolan, already given to sending mock letters to the newspapers, inaugurated a humor column called "Cruiskeen Lawn" ("the little overflowing jug") for the *Irish Times*. Written, sometimes in Gaelic, under the pen name Myles na gCopaleen, it would make O'Nolan a local celebrity, a mixture of H. L. Mencken, S. J. Perelman, and Dave Barry.

Consider the indispensable Myles na gCopaleen book-handling service. The newly wealthy often acquire libraries wholesale to impress their friends, but never take time to actually read the books. So Myles patents a service to "alter a book in a reasonably short time so that anybody looking at it will conclude that its owner has practically lived, supped and slept with it for many months." There are various degrees of book-handling, leading up to "Le Traitement Superbe." At that level every volume is guaranteed to be

> well and truly handled, first by a qualified handler and subsequently by a master-handler who will have to his credit not less than 550 handling hours; suitable passages in not less than fifty per cent of the books to be underlined in good-quality red ink and an appropriate phrase from the following inserted in the margin, viz . . .
> Yes, but cf. Homer, Od., iii, 151.
> Well, well, well.
> Quite, but Bossuet in his Discours sur l'histoire universelle has already established the same point and given much more forceful explanations. Nonsense, nonsense!
> A point well taken!
> But why in heaven's name?
> I remember poor Joyce saying the very same thing to me.

This is, of course, not all. "Not less than six volumes to be inscribed with forged messages of affection and gratitude from the author of each work." Myles then proffers half a dozen examples, including this one: "Dear A.B.— Your invaluable suggestions and assistance, not to mention your kindness, in entirely re-writing chapter 3, entitles you, surely, to this first copy of 'Tess.' From your old friend T. Hardy."

Over the next twenty years O'Nolan was to create dozens of regular features that he would spread out over his thrice-weekly (later daily) columns of 500–600 words. There was his escort service, which employed ventriloquists who would make their companions look brilliant by secretly carrying on both sides of witty conversations. The tales of Keats and Chapman that always built up to a dreadful pun. Lists of bores and clichés ("And of what nature is his loss? Well nigh irreparable"); inventions like alcoholic ice cream; the bus-stop tales of the Brother and the voice of the Plain People of Ireland; parodies of westerns, prison movies, romances; delicious impersonations of various obsessives and eccentrics ("The fact is I supported poppet valves at a time when it was neither profitable nor popular") and judicial mumbo-jumbo about matters like "the inseisinment of freebench copyholds" that "must stand in feoffment pending escheat of all incorporeal rent-charge bars."

Usually O'Nolan's tone as Myles is one of cool irony, often self-directed: "I have several plays (opens drawers, points in, hastily covers half-exposed bottle, slams drawer shut). . . ." Sometimes he is humorously savage, as in an argument over the spelling of "judgment," or is it "judgement"? "If you take the trouble to look up any dictionary, you will find that either form is admissible, you smug, self-righteous swine." Occasionally he is wistful: "Do engine drivers, I wonder, eternally wish they were small boys?" And sometimes just silly: "When I was taking a bath last night (fearful job disconnecting the taps and getting the thing out through the window). . . ."

A lot of this comic inventiveness appears in O'Nolan's other novels. Just after *At Swim-Two-Birds* he wrote *The Third Policeman*, an allegorical fantasy about a man who commits a murder and then finds himself in a surreally empty landscape, where he encounters monstrous policemen obsessed with bicycles and dentists, discovers the path to eternity, and relates various bizarre theories of the savant de Selby. According to de Selby, darkness is only a kind of black air, caused by eruptions of a volcanic material too fine to be seen by the naked eye, and sleep is "a succession of fainting fits brought on by semi-asphyxiation." The novel was so disorienting that no one would publish it, and O'Nolan spread the story that he'd lost the manuscript. It was brought out only in 1967, after his death.

His other books include a novel in Gaelic, *An Beal Bacht* (1941), a kind of Irish *Cold Comfort Farm* (translated as *The Poor Mouth* in 1973 by Patrick C. Powers); *The Hard Life* (1962), about a Mr. Collopy, who is obsessed with getting papal approval for public lavatories for women; a play called *Faustus Kelly* (1943), in which a small-time politician sells his soul for election to the Irish parliament; and a final short "exercise in derision," written when he was dying, *The Dalkey Archive* (1964). In it an elderly James Joyce, living in hiding, entirely disavows *Ulysses*, maintaining that the whole thing was a fraud perpetrated by its publisher Sylvia Beach. "I was shown bits of it in typescript. Artifical and laborious stuff, I thought. I just couldn't take much interest in it, even as a joke by amateurs."

Most of these works appeared after O'Nolan had been forcibly retired from the civil service in 1953 for making fun of the government once too often. As interesting as they are, none is a masterpiece to compare with *At Swim-Two-Birds*. In the late 1950s "Cruiskeen Lawn" also started to grow stale, a bit heavy-handed, oversavage. Although he spoke of his books as having "precision and occasionally the beauty of jewelled ulcers," O'Nolan also claimed to have written, pseudonymously, schlocky Sexton Blake mysteries for quick cash. He was spending more and more time in pubs (for a while he toted around a small machine to measure the proof of his whiskey), drinking into the early afternoon and then going home to his patient wife and spending the rest of the day in bed. In his last years our man suffered from myriad illnesses requiring "blood transfusions and other boons," received the last rites at least a dozen times, and eventually died of cancer at age fifty-five in 1966. On April Fool's Day.

Anthony Cronin's biography *No Laughing Matter* provides a well-written, sympathetic yet objective view of Brian O'Nolan and his times by one who knew him fairly well. Any admirer of its subject will want to read it. It is, as the title suggests, an often sad life, befitting one who gradually learned that humor is "the handmaid of sorrow and fear." Those new to O'Nolan/O'Brien/Myles should look first for *The Best of Myles* and *At Swim-Two-Birds* before going on to the other, and even odder, work of this funny, surprising, and altogether addictive writer.

August 11, 1991

COLLECTED FICTIONS

By Jorge Luis Borges
Translated from the Spanish by Andrew Hurley

Once, says Borges (1899–1986) in perhaps my favorite of his shorter stories, the king of Babylonia constructed a labyrinth "so confused and so subtle that the most prudent men would not venture to enter it, and those who did would lose their way." Alas, the king of the Arabs came to visit, and "to mock the simplicity of his guest," the Babylonian monarch bade him enter the maze, in which he wandered "humiliated and confused" until evening when Allah finally showed him the doorway out. Surprisingly, the king of the Arabs never complained but merely told his host that he too possessed a labyrinth and someday, Allah willing, he would show it to the Babylonian king.

As soon as he returned home, the Arab gathered his armies, attacked Babylonia, and razed its castles. After capturing his rival, he tied him across a camel and led him into the desert for three days. Then he spoke:

> "In Babylonia didst thou attempt to make me lose my way in a labyrinth of brass with many stairways, doors, and walls; now the Powerful One has seen fit to allow me to show thee mine, which has no stairways to climb, nor doors to force, nor wearying galleries to wander through, nor walls to impede thy passage."
>
> Then he untied the bonds of the king of Babylonia and abandoned him in the middle of the desert, where he died of hunger and thirst.

This suggestive story, "The Two Kings and the Two Labyrinths," appears in Borges's collection *The Aleph* (1949) and may be read as a farewell to the kind of "*ficciones*" that, translated into English and other languages, brought the Argentine writer world renown in his blind old age. In fact, from the 1960s until his death, Borges often pooh-poohed his most famous works, referring to himself as having become "a kind of factory producing stories about mistaken identity, about mazes, about tigers, about mirrors, about people being some-body else, or about all men being the same man or one man being his own mortal foe.... [T]here's no reason why I should go on doing it."

Instead he pressed the claims of his poetry, of prose poems like "The Maker" (a meditation on Homer discovering his vocation), and of naturalistic tales of Buenos Aires low-life (especially the early "Man on Pink Corner") and the late parables of gaucho violence such as "The Interloper." In this last, two brothers, finding their lives upset by their growing rivalry for the woman they share, kill her to restore fraternal harmony.

Yet as much as one honors the aesthetic of simplicity, and as much as one would like to point to some neglected masterpiece in the second half of this nearly 600-page book, the great Borges stories remain those of the period 1938 to 1952, those of *Fictions* (1944) and *The Aleph*. In these antiquarian fairy tales and mysteries, one finds that distinctive style in which, as Borges once observed, "every detail is an omen and a cause." During a dozen or so years this shortsighted, mother-coddled librarian managed to turn metaphysics into a branch of fantasy.

In "Tlön, Uqbar, Orbis Tertius"—generally regarded as his greatest story—"the conjunction of a mirror and an encyclopedia" leads to the discovery of an alien world, one that seems to be gradually contaminating the earth with its artifacts and culture. In "Funes, His Memory" Borges tells us about the unfor-tunate Funes, who, following an accident, discovers that he can no longer for-get anything. In some instances, even a story's title shimmers with a sinister attractiveness: "The Garden of Forking Paths," "The Lottery in Babylon," "The Immortal." To explain the character of these often essaylike fictions, their cre-ator asserted that it was madness to compose a vast book, to set out "in five hundred pages an idea that can be perfectly related orally in five minutes. The better way to go about it is to pretend that those books already exist, and offer a summary, a commentary on them." So, in "Pierre Menard, Author of the Quixote," a somewhat obnoxious scholar simply presents a brief memoir, with bibliography, of a minor French writer who decides to rewrite—no, re-create!—Don Quixote word for word.

Borges is sometimes compared to Kafka (whom he translated). But where the Prague fabulist evokes an ominous sense of claustrophobia—the door will never open, the trial will never take place—the Argentine prefers to induce a sudden feeling of vertigo. In the basement of a pedantic, self-important buf-foon, Borges discovers the Aleph, a small, shining sphere in which one can see everything that exists. The cursed Zahir, in the story of that name, takes the form of a common twenty-centavo coin which the narrator learns is utterly unforgettable; it will gradually drive out every idea from a person's mind until nothing is left but the image of the Zahir. Similarly, one shudders before the overwhelming sensual overload suffered by Funes, who "could continually perceive the quiet advances of corruption, of tooth decay, of weariness. . . . He was the solitary, lucid spectator of a multiform, momentaneous, and almost unbearably precise world." Finally, in a particularly vertiginous flourish, at the very end of "A Survey of the Works of Herbert Quain"—the account of an experimental writer obsessed with mathematical regression—we are told by Borges that from (the imaginary) Quain's "The Rose of Yesterday" he was "ingenious [sic]" enough to extract "The Circular Ruins," a real story that can be found "in my book *The Garden of Forking Paths*." Yet that is the very book we are now reading. And it also contains "A Survey of the Works of Herbert Quain." Surprisingly, Borges probably never saw the pictorial work of M. C. Escher.

The first collections of Borges in English appeared in 1962—*Ficciones*, translated by Anthony Kerrigan, and *Labyrinths*, a selection of stories and essays, translated by Donald A. Yates and James E. Irby. These books, particularly the latter, soon became standbys of college campuses. In the 1970s, though, Borges took a shine to a young scholar named Norman Thomas di Giovanni, and the pair embarked on a series of translations together, first of the poetry, then of old and new works. The most important of these was certainly *The Aleph and Other Stories*, which appeared with a substantial autobiographical essay. That volume and its companions were intended to provide definitive English versions, but Borges unexpectedly fell out with his zealous American translator.

Then, just before his death in 1986, Borges married a young Japanese-Argentine woman named Marie Kodama, to whom he left control of his entire estate. A controversial figure, Kodama has since established a Borges foundation and entered into an agreement with Viking to publish, in three volumes, her late husband's major works. *Collected Fictions* is the first installment. Borges enthusiasts hoping for an English equivalent to the French Pléiade edition of the writer, which brims with notes, bibliographical information, appendices, and other scholarly aids, will be disappointed. This is basically a reader's edition, with only a few clarifying endnotes chosen seemingly at random. Hurley will tell you, for instance, that Leopoldo Lugones is a famous Latin American poet, but he expects everyone to remember that Josef Korzienowski is the Polish name of Joseph Conrad.

Mario Vargas Llosa has said that Borges demonstrated that Spanish could avoid its tendency to baroque excess and become an instrument of precision and conciseness. In an afterword to the *Collected Fictions*, Hurley—a professor of English at the University of Puerto Rico—reminds us that Borges nonetheless often uses odd-sounding adjectives, sometimes to emphasize their Latinate roots. For example, the first sentence of "The Circular Ruins" is, in Hurley's version, "No one saw him slip from the boat in the unanimous night. . . ." That use of "unanimous," we eventually realize, should make us think of words like anima (soul) and animate (enliven), both central to this story. I think that Hurley is exceptionally attentive to such nuances. When reading "The Aleph," I paused at this sentence: "He holds some sort of subordinate position in an illegible library in the outskirts toward the south of the city. . . ." I checked the Spanish original and indeed the phrase is "una biblioteca ilegible." Di Giovanni's version is similar, though he recasts the sentence in the past tense and adds a bit of clarifying detail: "He held a minor position in an unreadable library out on the edge of the Southside of Buenos Aires."

Still, there are some oddities in Hurley, recognizable even for those of us with minimal Spanish. When Borges sets down in "El Muerto" ("The Dead Man") the phrase "atributos o adjetivos" why does Hurley translate "attributes (adjectives)," which looks like a mistake, instead of using "or"? In his version of "The Immortal" Hurley writes "With the depraved water of the watering holes others drank up insanity and death," while Irby, in *Labyrinths*, renders this "in the corrupted water of the cisterns others drank madness and death." The Spanish actually reads "en el agua depravada de las cisternas otros bebieron la locura y la muerte." So Hurley keeps the odd-sounding "depraved" rather than smoothing it to the more sensible "corrupted," but how did the cisterns become watering holes? And in "The Zahir," a story from the 1940s, would a person really say "tackiness"?

Serious students of Borges must obviously still learn their Spanish, but the rest of us can be reasonably satisfied with Hurley's *Collected Fictions*. Yet I wish it had been a fuller, more scholarly book, its versions more convincingly definitive and superior to earlier ones. That said, it nonetheless contains the major work of probably the most influential Latin American writer of the century, from the early tales of "iniquity" to such classics as the subtly humorous "Death and the Compass" and the blatantly despairing "Library of Babel" to all the very last stories. If you haven't ever read them, here's your chance.

September 27, 1998

DJUNA:

THE LIFE AND WORK OF DJUNA BARNES

By Phillip Herring

NIGHTWOOD:

THE ORIGINAL VERSION AND RELATED

DRAFTS

By Djuna Barnes
Edited by Cheryl J. Plumb

As it happens, a friend of mine lives in Patchin Place, the little courtyard in Greenwich Village where Djuna Barnes (1892–1982) spent the last forty-some years of her amazing life. Two decades ago, when Barnes was still alive, I used to think of ringing her doorbell and genuflecting or kissing her hand or presenting her with a bottle of scotch: after all, she was one of the last surviving giants of twentieth-century literature, author of the legendary novel *Nightwood,* and a woman who counted James Joyce among her drinking buddies and T. S. Eliot among her admirers. Make that fervent admirers: Eliot kept her picture above his desk (next to that of Yeats), addressed her as "dearest" in letters, and once extravagently declared her the greatest living writer.

Eliot was hardly alone in his enthusiasm. Dylan Thomas used to read from *Nightwood* on his speaking tours of America. Samuel Beckett, whom Barnes scarcely knew, sent her part of the royalties from *Waiting for Godot.* Even Dag Hammarskjöld, secretary-general of the United Nations, valued her work so highly that he helped translate her verse drama, *The Antiphon,* into Swedish. Rumor has it that he was pulling strings to get her the Nobel Prize when his plane was shot down over Africa.

I never saw her, and doubtless she would have growled at me to go away even if she had bothered to open the door. For most of her life Barnes was essentially a "cult" author, esteemed by a small coterie that kept *Nightwood* in print, savored the brocaded prose of her early autobiographical novel, *Ryder*, and guffawed over the Rabelaisian lesbians of *Ladies Almanack* (its various ribald characters were based on Parisian notables like the salonkeeper Natalie Barney, the journalist Janet Flanner, and the poets Romaine Brooks and Renée Vivien). In recent years, however, feminist scholars have begun to mine Barnes's work—the University of Maryland, which houses her papers, held a major conference a few years back. (Unfortunately, those talks, reprinted in a special issue of the *Review of Contemporary Literature*, are, for the most part, dully academic when comprehensible.) It is, thus, clearly the right time for both a good new biography and a modestly priced scholarly edition of Barnes's greatest prose work.

Phillip Herring, a Joyce expert by training, provides a straightforward chronological account of this once neglected writer's family, friends, and career. By comparison with the ill-organized, highly anecdotal 1983 life produced by Andrew Field (oft vilified—sometimes justly—for his early biography of Nabokov), Herring's work seems a little pedantic, the product of a sabbatical rather than the spillover from a passion. The phrase "thoroughly sound" comes irresistibly to mind and might normally be enough to sink the book, except for one small fact: if the soaps ever need any new plotlines, Djuna Barnes's life and work will supply plenty of naughty ideas.

For starters, Barnes's father, Wald, lived with wife, mistress, and mother, not to mention assorted offspring, in a big, unhappy family. As a believer in the freest sorts of free love, Dad either raped the teenaged Djuna and/or gave her as a present to an elderly neighbor to deflower. Through most of her childhood the future author slept in the same bed with her grandmother and would seem to have engaged in some level of sexual play with the older woman (surprisingly graphic letters exist). At seventeen she was even talked into a common-law marriage with a fifty-two-year-old soap peddler. It lasted only a few months.

Not surprisingly, Barnes was happy to escape from her family to New York, where in the years just before and after World War I she became a well-paid, sought-after young journalist (and occasional illustrator, all too obviously in thrall to Aubrey Beardsley). In one stunt piece she described the ordeal of being force-fed through a tube shoved down her throat, a then common method for preserving the life of fasting suffragettes. Soon she was hanging out with the Provincetown Players, where she came to know Eugene O'Neill, John Reed, and other bohemian notables. But, eventually, like so many of the artistically ambitious, the would-be novelist hied herself to Paris and the Left Bank, where she got to know . . . everybody, including Pound, Stein, Hemingway, and Joyce—or Jim, as she was allowed to call him.

In her youth Barnes was a striking, if somewhat severe auburn-haired beauty, attractive to both men and women. Although most of her affairs were heterosexual, she always called Thelma Wood the central passion of her life. "I'm not a lesbian. I simply loved Thelma." The liaison lasted eight or so years, and when it was over, Barnes memorialized her lost love in a great work of lamentation, *Nightwood*. In prose of haunting musicality and splendor, she describes the havoc wreaked by Robin Vote, i.e., Wood, on the people who care for her. Here is the book's august and intricately wrought opening sentence: "Early in 1880, in spite of a well-founded suspicion as to the advisability of perpetuating that race which has the sanction of the Lord and the disapproval of the people, Hedvig Volkbein, a Viennese woman of great strength and military beauty, lying upon a canopied bed, of a rich spectacular crimson, the valance stamped with the bifurcated wings of the House of Hapsburg, the feather coverlet an envelope of satin on which, in massive and tarnished gold threads, stood the Volkbein arms,—gave birth, at the age of forty-five, to an only child, a son, seven days after her physician had predicted that she would be taken."

Barnes doesn't always write with such oracular, slightly humorous gravity; she can also be quite vulgarly funny, as when a character describes another "whipped with impatience, like a man waiting at a toilet door for someone inside who had decided to read the *Decline and Fall of the Roman Empire*." In fact, most of the novel's grandest rhetorical flights belong to Dr. Matthew O'Connor, a drunken Irish Tiresias and adviser to the disconsolate, at once swishy, witty, and pitiful. As O'Connor explains, "just being miserable isn't enough—you've got to know how." When Nora, the Barnes stand-in, complains about her loneliness, the doctor quickly one-ups her: "A broken heart have you! I have falling arches, flying dandruff, a floating kidney, shattered nerves *and* a broken heart." O'Connor is quite unforgettable, as are the book's startling final pages: Robin, always associated with beasts, is glimpsed in an abandoned chapel, down on her hands and knees, making strangely sexual overtures to her former lover's pet dog.

Shocking, confusingly structured, lyrical, and haunting, *Nightwood* didn't precisely sell itself to prospective publishers. Indeed, Cheryl Plumb provides an enthralling account of its publishing history in her introduction to the novel's "original version," crediting Barnes's friend Emily Coleman with astute editorial advice and great cleverness in persuading T. S. Eliot to read the manuscript. Eliot, then working as an editor for the British publishers Faber and Faber, insisted on some thirteen pages of cuts, which are here restored. In general, his editing "blurred sexual, particularly homosexual, references and a few points that put religion in an unsavory light. However, meaning was not changed substantially, though the character of the work was adjusted, the language softened." Besides presenting Barnes's original vision of her masterpiece, Plumb's edition also provides useful textual and explanatory notes, as well as reproductions of the surviving typescript pages.

Soon after *Nightwood* appeared in 1936 Barnes's life fell apart: she started to drink heavily, love affairs went sour, money nearly dried up. Back in New York she rented a small apartment on Patchin Place and settled down to years of crankiness, alcohol, and writer's block. Perhaps not the normal kind of block, for she composed reams of poetry and worked sporadically on various projects, but it wasn't until 1957 that she was able to finish *The Antiphon*, a play that virtually no one could understand. Written in a kind of Elizabethan blank verse and reminiscent, by turns, of *Waiting for Godot*, *The Family Reunion*, and *Long Day's Journey into Night*, this sorrowful drama builds on its author's unresolved anger toward her family, her persistent sense of betrayal and sexual exploitation. It ends with a mother crushing the skull of her Barnes-like daughter.

Barnes thought *The Antiphon* her masterpiece. Maybe. Sometimes it seems brilliantly Shakespearean in its diction, rhythm, and syntax; at other times, it seems as kitschy as Ronald Firbank. In either case, I find it quite irresistible. What's a little thing like meaning compared to such word music as this:

> Yet corruption in its deft deploy
> Unbolts the caution, and the vesper mole
> Trots down the wintry pavement of
> the prophet's head.
> In the proud flesh of the vanished eye
> Vainglory, like a standing pool,
> Rejects the thirsty trades of paradise.
> The world is cracked—and in the breach
> My fathers mew.

Elsewhere Barnes evokes her father "flanked by warming-pans, bassoons and bastards" and gives her murderous brothers these conspiratorial lines: "We'll never have so good a chance again; / Never, never such a barren spot, / Nor the lucky anonymity of war." I think a production of *The Antiphon* could be a triumph. Or a hoot.

Djuna Barnes died in 1982 one week after her ninetieth birthday. Even now, I wish that I had had the courage to ring her doorbell at no. 5 Patchin Place. Real creators, no matter how wayward their genius, deserve our thanks and homage.

November 12, 1995

DAMNED TO FAME:
THE LIFE OF SAMUEL BECKETT

By James Knowlson

Following the massive heart attack that was to kill him, Samuel Beckett's father was heard to murmur "fight, fight, fight." Such spirit, even in the face of mortality, seems peculiarly appropriate to this hardworking, well-to-do Irish businessman. But these were not his actual last words. As Bill Beckett lay dying, he sighed, for all the world like one of his son's resigned and bleakly humorous characters, "What a morning."

Such stoic comedy crops up repeatedly in the life of Samuel Beckett (1906–1989). One spring the author of *Waiting for Godot* was visiting England, where he was going to spend a beautiful, sky-blue afternoon watching cricket. A friend remarked, as they walked along through the sunshine, "On a day like this it's good to be alive." To which Beckett immediately answered, "I wouldn't go as far as that."

It has, of course, always been easy to mythologize Beckett. Just look at his face in photographs—the bristly hair, the piercing blue eyes, a profile like an Aztec eagle, according to one critic. Or consider his legendary generosity. Once Beckett was drinking in a bar, late at night, when a bum admired his coat. Without a word, he gave it to him, never even bothering to empty the pockets. All around Paris the writer was known as an easy touch. After he received the Nobel Prize ("What a catastrophe," exclaimed his wife, Suzanne), he donated all the money—some to his alma mater, Trinity College, Dublin, but most to needy writers, artists, and actors. With the royalties from his plays, he paid the bills when family members fell ill or needed tuition money. He even established a trust fund for an ex-convict. At the same time, he himself lived in utter simplicity: a single brown suit, pants bought at thrift shops, an old beret. He might almost be one of his tramps, Vladimir (Didi) or Estragon (Gogo). (And yet this moody, reclusive artist was quite irresistible to women. Susan Sontag called him the sexiest man she'd ever met.)

As James Knowlson's fine biography makes clear again and again, kindness to others and hatred of cruelty and suffering were Beckett's defining personal characteristics. He loathed apartheid in South Africa and the artistic censorship in Eastern Europe (and once composed a short play for the imprisoned Václav Havel). During his last months, the fragile, undernourished writer was obliged to enter a nursing home:

"He kept biscottes in his dressing-gown pocket to give to the pigeons," remembers a friend. "What was noticeable was that he could easily have thrown the crumbs to them while standing up. But, unsteady on his feet as he was, he had to risk falling over by bending down to feed them almost out of his hand."

If James Joyce sometimes appears the great hero of modern letters, the introspective Beckett almost seems its saint. And not only of literature. Beckett served in the Resistance during World War II—processing, translating, and passing on clandestine information, a valuable member of a famous unit: Gloria SHS (run by the amazing twenty-six-year-old Jeannine Picabia). When the group was betrayed, he narrowly escaped capture and had to flee to the south of France, where he picked fruits and vegetables, worked on his novel *Watt* (in part to escape into his Irish past), and eventually joined another guerrilla group. After the war Beckett received the Croix de Guerre from a grateful nation. Yet until his previous biographer, Deirdre Bair, delved into his wartime activities, virtually none of his later friends and associates knew about his dangerous Resistance work. He simply never mentioned it.

Damned to Fame, the first authorized life of Samuel Beckett, has been long and eagerly awaited. Its author, James Knowlson, oversees the Beckett Archive at the University of Reading and is the general editor of Beckett's Theatrical Notebooks; he was also a close friend of his subject for twenty years. Not unexpectedly, the new biography is thorough, meticulous, sometimes revelatory (particularly on the late plays and prose), always readable. Without being vituperative, it offers corrections to many of Deirdre Bair's errors (her 1978 account has been much criticized by the Beckett establishment) and generously credits her when appropriate (e.g., Knowlson calls her chapter on the war years "excellent"). *Damned to Fame* immediately becomes the single basic source for anyone interested in Samuel Beckett's life and career. At 800 pages, in smallish type, the book is, however, immensely long and detailed, and some readers may feel that its second half pays excessive attention to the writer's involvement with the staging and direction of his plays. Apparently Knowlson hopes to establish Beckett as not only an important playwright and novelist but also a significant force in modern theater production. He largely succeeds, but the ordinary Beckett fan may feel his spirits starting to sag, as Beckett's eventually did, when hearing about yet another German production of *Endgame.* Anyone seeking a reliable and very brief life, with lots of illustrations, should look to Enoch Brater's *Why Beckett.*

While Beckett is universally honored as a dramatist (even in restrooms, where one still occasionally sees the graffito "Back in five minutes—Godot"), his prose remains something of a specialist taste. This is a pity, for much of the early fiction remains perfectly accessible to anyone with a liking for verbal clowning or learned humor. Just as Yeats memorized "Whoroscope," Beckett's long poem based on the life of Descartes, so Joyce learned by heart substantial portions of *Murphy.* The 1938 novel, Beckett's first, hums with literary wordplay ("night's young thoughts") and Zen-like aperçus ("Who knows what the ostrich sees in the sand?"), as well as neatly turned sentences with a wry Irish lilt: "And between going mad and having the rest of his life poisoned by the thought of having once worked for a week for nothing, Ticklepenny found little to choose." Above all, with its cast of philosophers and prostitutes and madmen and seekers after transcendence, the novel combines Rabelaisian gusto with slapstick erudition: "Murphy on the jobpath was a striking figure. Word went round among the members of the Blake League that the Master's conception of Bildad the Shuhite had come to life and was stalking about London in a green suit, seeking whom he might comfort."

As with Joyce, not enough people read Beckett simply for pleasure. His texts have been ivied over with tendrils of critical articles and a jungle of explications. Beckett himself always stressed the perils of overinterpretation: "If Godot had meant God I would have said God and not Godot." "No symbols where none intended," he even announced at the end of *Watt.* Much of this second novel—ostensibly a critique of rationalism—is as hilarious as S. J. Perelman or Flann O'Brien. "Watt had watched people smile and thought he understood how it was done." "The title of his dissertation I well remember was The Mathematical Intuitions of the Visicelts, a subject on which he professed the strongest views. . . ." "Lady McCann, coming up behind, thought she had never on the public road, seen motions so extraordinary, and few women had a more extensive experience of the public road than Lady McCann."

But the wry or gallows humor of the Beckettian universe is hardly restricted to the author's published oeuvre. When in the 1930s the shy young writer was perfecting his German, he observed, "How absurd, the struggle to learn to be silent in another language." For a while, the manuscript of *Watt* was in the hands of a literary agent named Watt. The first performance in America of *Waiting for Godot* took place in Florida, where it was described as the "laugh hit of two continents"; more than 40 percent of the audience left at the intermission. (Commenting on his own austere vision of his plays, Beckett admitted, "If they did it my way, they would empty the theater.") At one point, Buster Keaton and Marlon Brando (!) were lined up to play Gogo and Didi on Broadway. While in hiding in Roussillon during the war, Beckett read—attention, dissertation seekers—*Gone with the Wind*. (In later years, he also read, with admiration, *The Catcher in the Rye, Slaughterhouse-Five*, and *Humboldt's Gift*.) When a young woman asked the famous writer if he was offended that she had named her dog after him, Beckett answered, "Don't worry about me. What about the dog?" Once, out of sheer desperation, the young Beckett almost applied for a lectureship in English at the University of Buffalo. Just imagine! Some forty years later Buffalo was the site of a major Beckett festival. Because of his athletic prowess as an undergraduate—he played cricket for Ireland against England—Beckett is the only Nobel laureate listed in *Wisden*, the bible of cricket history.

Knowlson's biography, soon to be the bible of Beckett enthusiasts, sprinkles such tidbits throughout its pages, interspersing them with a solid history of an artist and his vocation. Beckett specialized in French and Italian at Trinity College Dublin, taught for a year at the Ecole Normale Supérieure, wrote important early essays on Proust and Joyce. Famously, he helped the near-blind novelist with research for "Work in Progress," aka *Finnegans Wake* (and much later referred to his own writing as "work in regress" and "ruins in prospect"). An enamored Lucia Joyce, the novelist's disturbed daughter, used to sing "You're the cream in my coffee" to Beckett, her imagined beau. In 1938 the young expatriate was stabbed late at night in the Paris street by a pimp; besides Joyce, hospital visitors included Suzanne Deschevaux-Dumesnil, who became his life companion.

During the marvelous years 1946–50 the middle-aged Beckett, in a frenzy of activity, a "whey of words," produced nearly all his greatest work: *Waiting for Godot, Molloy, Malone Dies, The Unnameable, Texts for Nothing*, three short stories, and a novella, *First Love*, as well as several other works, all of them in French. (He switched to French, he claimed, because it was easier to "write without style" and avoid prettiness and cheap rhetorical tricks.) Later, of course, he was to translate his works back and forth between his two main languages (he also knew German, Italian, Latin, and enough Portuguese to read Agatha Christie in it); in general his prose is slightly more vulgar and colloquial in French, tighter and bleaker in English. In either, what holds the reader, as Hugh Kenner has written, "is in part the unquenchable lust to know what will happen in the next ten words."

James Knowlson once wrote that there was a time he found "biography to be of little help in understanding the work of Samuel Beckett." No more. His own researches show how deeply Beckett draws on scenes from his past to energize even his most enigmatic and wispy texts. Knowlson also reveals Beckett's extensive use of painting and music: *Godot* probably got its start from a romantic picture by Caspar David Friedrich depicting two people looking up at a full moon. Of course, much of the action in that play draws on its author's wartime experiences, especially while on the run: the fearful waiting, sleeping in ditches, recurrent hunger, the threat of beatings. Starving Lucky tied to a fat Pozzo with his whip has frequently struck viewers as an image appropriate to a Nazi concentration camp (and Didi, we know, was originally called Levy). But of course, Beckett drowns these personal and historical elements beneath the play's flood of music-hall cross talk, circus clowning, and street mime, all of which give the action, or rather inaction, its timeless, metaphysical feel.

Northrop Frye once observed that a text like *The Unnameable* could "readily be called a tedious book, but its use of tedium is exuberant." Certainly Knowlson's accounts of Beckett's last works—plays like *Not I, Ohio Impromptu,* and *Footfalls,* prose poems like *Company* and *Ill Seen Ill Said*—make these brief, gloomy works (of, to use Watt's words, "great formal brilliance and indeterminable purport") sound compelling and exciting. In this regard, *Damned to Fame*'s emphasis on the Beckett of the 1960s and 1970s may gain new readers for these minimalist texts, woven from silence as much as sound. When Beckett finally did get to direct his plays, he always emphasized their careful choreography, the patterns of movement, the antiphonal echoes between voices, as something takes its course, usually in fits and starts. Of all his later works Beckett might say, adopting a remark of another of his crippled heroes, "Yes, my progress reduced me to stopping more and more often, it was the only way to progress, to stop."

"Rest then," says the voice in *How It Is,* "my mistakes are my life," adding "that yes a panting in the mud to that it all comes in the end." Perhaps so. But Beckett's life provides a moving lesson in artistic integrity—just as he himself provides the best of all artistic mottos in *Worstward Ho*: "No matter. Try again. Fail again. Fail better." He loved his friends, family, and colleagues and was loved in return. One can hardly ask for more from any life, let alone one so unswervingly devoted "to the well-built phrase and the long sonata of the dead."

October 13, 1996

SERIOUS
ENTERTAINERS

VI

Over the years I've written frequently about the great masters and masterpieces of popular fiction—reflections on Sherlock Holmes for the Baker Street Journal, a 9,000-word essay on John Dickson Carr and the locked-room mystery, an afterword to an edition of Jules Verne's Journey to the Center of the Earth. A number of my closest friends work in fantasy and science fiction. I truly love the league of extraordinary gentlemen (and ladies) who write the sort of books we read mainly for fun.

After all, as C. S. Lewis once observed, "To interest is the first duty of art; no other excellences will even begin to compensate for failure in this and very serious faults will be covered by this, as by charity."

I say all this because of my uneasiness about categorizing—ghettoizing?—these writers as entertainers. Many of them are also mythmakers, disturbing visionaries, important novelists. Still, one turns to their books first of all for their storytelling. Literary fictions are typically studies of character; genre fiction is primarily plot-driven. On the one hand, we watch the effects of adultery on Madame Bovary; on the other, we turn the pages breathlessly to see how James Bond will escape certain death.

That said, I've chosen "serious" entertainers for this section. Robert Aickman's uncanny stories may leave one puzzled about exactly what did happen in them, but they also leave one shaken, as from an encounter with the numinous. Vernon Lee's ghost stories obliquely chronicle sexual repression and its explosion in late nineteenth-century Italy and England. Though commonly regarded as a silly twit, like his narrator Bertie Wooster, P. G. Wodehouse possessed a flair for original similes that awed even such fastidious novelists as Evelyn Waugh ("He drank coffee with the air of a man who regretted it was not hemlock"). In the jazzy, absurdist tales of two African American detectives their creator, Chester Himes, describes Harlem and the insidious ways of racism. Avram Davidson, given to a leisurely, digressive prose that recalls oral storytelling, depicts Jewish and immigrant life in

America—while also spinning out tall tales of golems in New Jersey and dentists kidnapped by aliens.

From Edgar Rice Burroughs and Cornell Woolrich to K. C. Constantine and Terry Pratchett, these are all amazing artists, men and women who know how to tell a story, to create a world on the page that is darker, funnier, or more exciting than the one we know ourselves. Such brilliant gifts ought to be celebrated.

HAUNTINGS

By Vernon Lee

In his introduction to *The Supernatural Omnibus* (1931) Montague Summers—a name to conjure with, at least among aficionados of ghost stories—says this about the stories of Vernon Lee (the pen name of Violet Paget, 1856–1935): "*Hauntings* is a masterpiece of literature, and even Sheridan Le Fanu and M. R. James cannot be ranked above the genius of this lady." In fact, like David G. Rowlands, editor of the recent and essential Ash-Tree Press edition of Lee's complete supernatural writings (also called *Hauntings*), I would probably name her classic "Amour Dure" as my favorite uncanny tale of all time. It's at least the equal of such better-known anthology pieces as Charlotte Perkins Gilman's "The Yellow Wallpaper," Oliver Onions's "The Beckoning Fair One," and Robert Aickman's "Ringing the Changes."

"Amour Dure" takes the form of a diary kept by a young Polish scholar named Spiridion Trepka who travels to the Italian town of Urbania to explore its archives. A romantic, he reveres the energy and overreaching passion of the Renaissance. But, as he begins his diary, those days seem irrevocably over:

"Urbania, August 20th, 1885. I had longed, these years and years, to be in Italy, to come face to face with the Past; and was this Italy, was this the Past? I could have cried, yes cried, for disappointment. . . ."

Modern Urbania proves utterly dull, complacent, vulgar. Its supposed society beauties are fat and coarse, completely unlike Lucrezia Borgia, Beatrice Cenci . . . or Medea da Carpi. "Even before coming here," Spiridion confesses, "I felt attracted by the strange figure" of this last legendary enchantress. By the age of fourteen, Medea da Carpi had been affianced to three different men, one of whom kidnapped her and was later found stabbed in the chest by the hand of Medea herself. "He was a handsome youth only eighteen years old."

Two years later, the young woman's eventual husband, the duke of Stimigliano, is stabbed by his own groom. "Suspicion fell upon his widow, more especially as, immediately after the event, she caused the murderer to be cut down by two servants in her own chamber; but not before he had declared that she had induced him to assassinate his master by a promise of her love." Medea flees to the home of the elderly duke of Urbania, who in short order establishes the captivating widow in luxurious apartments. Before long, the lucky nobleman "suddenly, and not without suspicious circumstances," finds himself a widower. He weds Medea da Carpi "two days after the decease of his unhappy wife."

In due course, the duke himself dies mysteriously, but not before he wills his realm to Medea's infant son by her first husband. Those who question the succession are killed by an army loyal to Medea, commanded by "a certain Captain Oliverotta da Narni, who was rumoured to be her lover." Ultimately, however, Medea ends imprisoned in a mountain citadel, and her late husband's brother, a former cardinal, assumes the title of Duke Robert.

"It is said that she haughtily requested to see the new Duke, but that he shook his head, and, in his priest's fashion, quoted a verse about Ulysses and the Sirens; and it is remarkable that he persistently refused to see her, abruptly leaving his chamber one day that she had entered by stealth." Though now heavily guarded and watched over in a convent, Medea nonetheless somehow "contrived to send a letter and her portrait to one Prinzivalle degli Ordelaffi, a youth, only nineteen years old, of noble Romagnole family, and who was betrothed to one of the most beautiful girls of Urbania. He immediately broke off his engagement, and, shortly afterwards, attempted to shoot Duke Robert with a holster-pistol as he knelt at mass on the festival of Easter Day."

This time, church records explain, the duke determined to obtain proofs against Medea. The young man was tortured, brutally, then told he would be flayed alive and quartered, but "that he might obtain the grace of immediate death by confessing the complicity of the Duchess." Pressed by the nuns to save the poor wretch, Medea requested permission to stand at a balcony "where she could see Prinzivalle and be seen by him. She looked on coldly, then threw down her embroidered kerchief to the poor mangled creature. He asked the executioner to wipe his mouth with it, kissed it, and cried out that Medea was innocent. Then, after several hours of torment, he died."

This is too much for Duke Robert. Recognizing that "as long as Medea lived his life would be in perpetual danger," he has her "strangled in the convent, and, what is remarkable, insisted that only women—two infanticides to whom he remitted their sentences—should be employed for the deed."

Such then is the old story of this Renaissance siren, whom Spiridion feels, oddly enough, he understands. How else could a spirited woman make her way in the sixteenth century except through sex and assassination? Soon thereafter, the obsessed scholar discovers Medea's miniature, possibly the very one sent to the unfortunate Prinzivalle; he then stumbles across Duke Robert's peculiar safeguards taken after his own death, as if he feared meeting Medea in the afterlife; finally, the young Pole finds himself growing pale, feverish even, increasingly prey to disturbing hallucinations.

I'd better stop there. Let me just add that in her portraits Medea wears a necklace engraved with these punning words: "Amour Dure, Dure Amour." They can be loosely translated as "Love Endures, Cruel Love."

The original *Hauntings* contains only four long stories. In "Dionea" a young girl from a shipwreck is washed ashore at San Massimo. She speaks no recognizable tongue but through charity is brought up by the local nuns. Dionea turns into an enigmatic, solitary child. Pigeons swarm to her; the rose bushes she lies under bloom abundantly. As she grows older, Dionea also grows more and more dazzlingly beautiful. Yet no young man courts her, and the old women of the village think she possesses the evil eye—certainly her beauty inspires more awe than desire. Moreover, unexplainable and distressing things happen around her. Could she, for instance, have had anything to do with the suicide of a devout priest? There are worse fates in store for others.

In the novella-length "Oke of Okehurst," an artist—based on John Singer Sargent, a childhood friend of Lee's—visits an English country house to paint portraits of its squire and his wife. Okehurst appears a perfectly preserved Tudor manor, though its surrounding landscape can be disconcerting and mournful: "Outside, the mists were beginning to rise, veiling the park-land dotted with big black oaks, and from which, in the watery moonlight, rose on all sides the eerie little cry of the lambs separated from their mothers."

Oke, as his name suggests, is quite a sturdy, down-to-earth Englishman, but Mrs. Oke appears dreamy, romantic, strangely distracted. She has, apparently, adopted the fancy of dressing like an earlier Alice Oke, who—according to family legend—helped her husband murder the young poet who had become her lover. Why she helped is the mystery, even now, more than two hundred years later. The story of what happens at Okehurst is delicately brilliant, building toward a tragic finale with *Turn of the Screw*-like ambiguity. Is this a psychological study of a marriage breaking down? A depiction of madness, of a *folie à deux* or even *trois*? Or—as in "A Wicked Voice," the last tale in *Hauntings*—can the present truly call up the past and compel the supposedly long dead to walk again in the twilight?

In nearly all Vernon Lee's stories, love erupts as a destructive yet indestructible passion, forever entangled with violence and death. The late nineteenth century is, after all, the era of the Wagnerian *Liebestod*, of the Belle Dame Sans Merci, of goat-footed Pan and Ritter Tannhäuser. In these pages the old gods survive, and their daimonic power goes unrecognized until it is far too late.

Mario Praz's *The Romantic Agony* and Robert Graves's *The White Goddess* may serve modern readers as guidebooks to this erotic and darkly poetic world.

Most of Lee's stories are also celebrations of Renaissance Italy or, more accurately, of the intrigue-riven, larger-than-life Renaissance Italy of our imagination. They remind me of Stendhal's *Chroniques Italiennes* or John Webster's tragedies, tales where the stiletto or the poisoned kiss is always the best solution to any personal difficulty.

Little wonder that Vernon Lee was best known during her lifetime as an expert on Italian history, landscape, and civilization. Her books—*Euphorion, Genius Loci*, and a dozen others—were consulted as cultural Baedekers by English dowagers and their bored husbands. She herself spent most of her life in Italy, speaking perfect if slightly archaic Tuscan. As a young girl she was encouraged in her writing by a woman who had been loved by Shelley. During her lifetime she came to know the great English Italophiles—Walter Pater, John Addington Symonds, Bernard Berenson, Edith Wharton, Harold Acton. Her half brother told Henry James the story that led to *The Aspern Papers*.

Lee herself never married, was intensely puritanical and apparently incapable of expressing physical affection. She did enjoy passionate friendship with several women and felt noticeably betrayed when they left her, sometimes for marriage. Her stories can't help seeming like allegories of "the return of the repressed"—dammed-up erotic passions slowly seeping into the present with dire consequences.

But one shouldn't be reductionist about consummate artistry. Besides, Lee was herself exceptionally sensitive to psychology (and even popularized the word "empathy"). In her guidebook *The Handling of Words*, she insists that writing is the "the craft of manipulating the contents of the Reader's mind." Yet the ideal reader "must bring all his experience to the business, all his imagination and sympathy; he must enter deep into the Writer's work, help to make it live, and thus receive a strengthened and purified life in exchange." In Lee's various "hauntings" this is just what happens—people, often through reading or protracted study, find that they are making the past live again. And in return they do receive a strengthened and purified life—a vision or a feverish, mystical experience or the promise of all-consuming love. But after such transports, how can anyone return to, or even settle for, a merely ordinary existence?

Besides the quartet in *Hauntings*, Lee published a dozen or so other tales of the fantastic. The best are probably the touching "Prince Alberic and the Snake Lady," the ironic "Marsyas in Flanders" (marred by its giveaway title), the *Arabian Nights*–like adventure of Don Juan, "The Virgin of the Seven Daggers," and a superb *conte cruel*, "A Wedding Chest." In truth, most of Vernon Lee's strange stories are quite unforgettable, like the irresistible Medea da Carpi herself: "A curious, at first rather conventional, artificial-looking sort of beauty, voluptuous yet cold, which, the more it is contemplated, the more it troubles and haunts the mind."

Indeed it does.

July 29, 2003

POSTSCRIPT: The people who like English ghost stories—or the somewhat similar "club tale," in which a strange exploit is related over brandy when the fire has burned low—tend to like the genre a lot. To my mind, aside from the adventures of Sherlock Holmes and nearly anything by P. G. Wodehouse, such spooky narratives make for the best light reading in the world. I write about some of my favorites in *Bound to Please* (Vernon Lee, Algernon Blackwood, Robert Aickman), but hope readers will also look out for the work of Sheridan Le Fanu, M. R. James, Oliver Onions, A. M. Burrage, Saki, Lord Dunsany, Edith Wharton, John Collier, and Roald Dahl.

YOURS, PLUM:
THE LETTERS OF P. G. WODEHOUSE

Edited by Frances Donaldson

In 1935 P. G. Wodehouse was fifty-four years old, already the author of over fifty books, and the lyricist for more than forty musical comedies. He was shortly (in 1939) to receive an honorary doctorate from Oxford University and to be acclaimed by Hilaire Belloc "the best living writer of English." Both George Orwell and Evelyn Waugh, who agreed on virtually nothing else, admired him deeply; Waugh referred to him as the master and spoke of Wodehouse with a reverence he otherwise reserved only for the Catholic Church. At the same time, millions of ordinary readers of the *Saturday Evening Post* chuckled over his serials about Jeeves and Bertie Wooster, Blandings Castle, and the idiots of the Drones Club. He was beyond doubt one of the most successful authors in the world.

But also one of the most hardworking and unassuming. This very same year Wodehouse (pronounced Woodhouse) wrote to his old schoolfriend William Townend, "Ethel [PGW's wife] has been after me for years to write a play all on my own, so I said I would. It's the most ghastly sweat. But it does teach one a tremendous lot about construction." Teach? Construction? As these selected letters show again and again, no one could know more about plot construction than Wodehouse, or about any other aspect of authorship. By comparison, Flaubert seems a mere dabbler, Henry James a casual dilettante. Wodehouse's entire life—some ninety-three years—was given over to thinking up funny stories, working out their plots with drum-major precision, and setting down perfectly cadenced sentences of epigrammatic brilliance. Of these last there is seemingly no end, though every Wodehouse addict has his favorites:

"In the evening of his life his uncle Frederick, Lord Ickenham, still retained, together with a juvenile waist-line, the bright enthusiasms and the fresh unspoiled mental outlook of a slightly inebriated undergraduate."

"Like so many substantial citizens of America, he had married young and kept on marrying, springing from blonde to blonde like the chamois of the Alps leaping from crag to crag."

"Myrtle Prosser was a woman of considerable but extremely severe beauty. She . . . suggested rather one of those engravings of the mistresses of Bourbon kings which make one feel that the monarchs who selected them must have been men of iron, impervious to fear, or else shortsighted."

Wodehouse's best comic effects require some buildup—think of Gussie Fink-Nottle drunkenly presenting the school prizes in *Right Ho, Jeeves*—but he was also a master of the quick jab:

"He had just about enough intelligence to open his mouth when he wanted to eat, but certainly no more."

"He groaned slightly and winced, like Prometheus watching his vulture dropping in for lunch."

"Gussie, a glutton for punishment, stared at himself in the mirror."

Such random nuggets make clear why Evelyn Waugh marveled at Wodehouse's ability to come up with at least three fresh similes per page. Waugh, by the way, especially approved the phrase about "the acrid smell of burnt poetry."

Not surprisingly, these letters display only a glimmer of this wit, though Wodehouse can be sharp with the aperçu: "It's odd how soon one comes to look on every minute as wasted that is given to earning one's salary." In general, though, he was too much the professional to squander good material on friends. Instead, his correspondence focuses obsessively on the business and mechanics of his profession. Frances Donaldson, Wodehouse's authorized biographer, organizes the letters according to subject ("Work," "Dogs," "Hollywood"), but this hardly matters: Wodehouse's small talk nearly always turns into shoptalk. In writing to his stepdaughter Leonora he asks if she can give him "useful details" about her girls' school for a Jeeves story. He complains to his favored correspondents—his cronies Townend and Guy Bolton, both writers—that he can't think of any new plots. He reflects on the benefits and disadvantages of first-person narration. He reviews his material constantly, looking for ways to strengthen the "scenarios," speed up the action, make everything funnier. For anyone interested in how a writer thinks and works *Yours, Plum* deserves a place on the shelf near Henry James's notebooks, Trollope's autobiography, and Flaubert's letters.

"I believe the only way a writer can keep himself up to the mark," explains this genial teacher, "is by examining each story quite coldly before he starts writing it and asking himself if it is all right as a story. I mean, once you start saying to yourself, 'This is a pretty weak plot as it stands, but I'm such a hell of a writer that my magic touch will make it all right,' I believe you're done. . . ."

"Another thing is, what you want to put your stuff over is Action. . . . The more I write the more I am convinced that the only way to write a popular story is to split it up into scenes, and have as little stuff in between the scenes as possible. . . ." "I wrote a short story in 1947 for the *Cosmopolitan*. Subsequently writing a Jeeves novel, I needed what we call in the tayarter a block comedy scene, so I took out the middle part of the short story and bunged it into the book. A month or so ago I thought up a new middle and sold the new-middle story with the old beginning and end in England. And I have now devised a new beginning and end for the new-middle story and sold it over here [in the United States]. Quite a feat, don't you think?"

By doing nothing but writing—in France, Hollywood, and New York, almost anywhere but England, which in his imagination remained unchangingly Edwardian—Wodehouse settled into a life of sunny routine, eclipsed temporarily only by the death of Leonora in her early forties and by the brouhaha attending his World War II broadcasts. Interned by the Germans in 1942, Wodehouse quite innocently agreed to give five humorous radio talks about his life in a prison camp. He intended them simply as entertainment, directed toward his American readers, but they were used as German propaganda and wildly misinterpreted in Britain. The easygoing Wodehouse found himself vilified, his books withdrawn from libraries, his name anathema for quite some time, despite a stirring defense by George Orwell. Gradually, he came to realize that he had acted like one of his own silly-ass heroes, but the damage had been done: this archetypally English humorist lived his last thirty years on Long Island and never returned to the land of Wooster and Jeeves, not even in 1975 when he learned he had been knighted. By then, of course, Sir Pelham Grenville Wodehouse was ninety-three. Within a few months he was dead.

He died in the middle of a novel—published as *Sunset at Blandings*—with nearly a hundred other books to his credit. Probably none but the most fervent fan has read every one. Indeed, I wonder how much they are read at all these days. Wodehouse aimed to be an entertainer, bowed to editorial judgment as meekly as any novice, and himself admired pros of prose like Agatha Christie, Erle Stanley Gardner, and Henry Slessar (who wrote his beloved *Edge of Night* soap opera). Some popular writers—Dumas, Stevenson, Conan Doyle, Kipling—find that later generations transform their books into children's classics. Wodehouse, by contrast, seems to have lost his general audience and become mainly a cult author savored by connoisseurs for his prose artistry. Waugh predicted that this might happen—and welcomed it, in his typically snooty way.

For these readers, Wodehouse intuitively realized that literature is simply a construct of language; there is naturally no relation between his books and any reality, historic or otherwise. For all the author's attention to plot and storyline, one hardly cares what happens to his young men in spats, whether newt-fancier Gussie Fink-Nottle marries Madeline Bassett or whether the Empress of Blandings wins a silver medal in the Fat Pig division of the Shropshire Agricultural Show. What finally matters are those delicious sentences, with their zingy mix of slang and learned allusion: Lord Ickenham, on his way to take a bath, goes "armed with his great sponge Joyeuse." J. B. Priestley, of all people, was right: Wodehouse "has raised speech into a kind of wild poetry of the absurd."

Still, "Plum" Wodehouse would regret this view of his work. He was slightly perplexed by all this master and "Angelic Doctor" stuff; he thought himself a damn good comic storyteller. After all, his books constantly tease intellectuals, aesthetes, and writers. Who can forget the poetic bruiser Ricky Gilpin or Rosie M. Banks, esteemed authoress of "Mervyn Keene, Clubman?"

I think Wodehouse might have a wider audience again, but for the sheer volume of his work: casual readers simply don't know where to begin. The best advice is to start with his best work: among the novels, *Leave It to Psmith* (1923*), Right Ho, Jeeves* (1934), or *Uncle Fred in the Springtime* (1939). Several anthologies gather the best of the short stories, but everyone's favorites include the Mulliner tall tales "Strychnine in the Soup," "Honeysuckle Cottage," and "Mulliner's Buck-U-Uppo"; the Drones stories "Tried in the Furnace," "Fate," and "Uncle Fred Flits By"; the Lord Emsworth favorite "Pig Hoo-o-o-o-ey"; and that Jeeves masterpiece "The Great Sermon Handicap."

Of course, all these are utterly farcical and improbable tales of stolen heirlooms, mistaken identities, and love's cross currents. Mere piffle. But through their inimitable prose these silly, silly stories nonetheless bestow a small, but not insignificant, gift on anyone who reads them: pure unclouded happiness.

February 3, 1991

ALGERNON BLACKWOOD: AN EXTRAORDINARY LIFE

By Mike Ashley

If you were to ask readers of supernatural fiction to name the greatest story in the genre, the winner would almost certainly be "The Willows." Odds are that in the top ten you'd also find "The Wendigo" and "Ancient Sorceries." All three are by Algernon Blackwood (1869–1951), who lived, as Mike Ashley says, "an extraordinary life" and was an even more extraordinary writer. Just murmur some of his titles on a shadowy evening, and you'll begin to feel the shivers that he so wonderfully evokes and sustains: "The Listener," "The Camp of the Dog," "Secret Worship," "A Psychical Invasion," "The Man Whom the Trees Loved," "The Doll," "A Descent into Egypt." H. P. Lovecraft—who knew a thing or two about scary fiction—called Blackwood "the one absolute and unquestioned master of weird atmosphere," with an uncanny ability to evoke "an unreal world constantly pressing upon ours."

"Adventures come to the adventurous," Blackwood writes at the beginning of "The Insanity of Jones," "and mysterious things fall in the way of those who, with wonder and imagination, are on the watch for them; but the majority of people go past the doors that are half ajar, thinking them closed, and fail to notice the faint stirrings of the great curtain that hangs ever in the form of appearances between them and the world of causes behind." Our seemingly safe, ordinary world is but a veil beyond which lurk beings and matters far beyond normal human ken.

In "Ancient Sorceries," a meek Englishman named Vezin decides on a whim to stop in a small French town. As he gets off the crowded train, a fellow passenger murmurs something to him, a kind of warning, that ends with the words "à cause du sommeil et à cause des chats." Because of sleep and because of the cats. Vezin pays no mind and discovers a languorous, placid village, where he first feels oddly unwelcome, then surreptitiously but constantly observed. He is discouraged from going out after dark and soon notes that "something made him sleep like the dead." Gradually, he grows convinced that the real life of the town is somehow quite other than what is presented to his eyes. Increasingly ill at ease, he nonetheless finds himself unable to make up his mind to leave. And then he meets Ilsé: "He felt the presence long before he heard or saw anyone. Then he became aware that the old men, the only other guests, were rising one by one in their places, and exchanging greetings with someone who passed among them from table to table. And when at length he turned with his heart beating furiously to ascertain for himself, he saw the form of a young girl, lithe and slim, moving down the center of the room. . . . She moved wonderfully, with sinuous grace, like a young panther. . . . Something of red lips he saw and laughing white teeth, and stray wisps of fine dark hair about the temples; but all the rest was a dream in which his own emotion rose like a thick cloud before his eyes and prevented his seeing accurately, or knowing exactly what he did."

I'll say no more. Because of sleep and because of the cats.

Algernon Blackwood was born to an upper-middle-class English family—his father was high up in the postal service—and attended Wellington College, spent some school years studying with a strict Moravian sect in Germany, and in his early twenties traveled to Canada. He fell in love with that country, and as a young man tried to make a life there as a farmer and businessman. When his affairs foundered, he moved to New York, where he lived on the streets for a while before landing a job as a reporter for the *New York Times*. On one assignment he interviewed Lizzie Borden; on another, Sir Henry Irving, when he probably spoke with the actor's manager, Bram Stoker, not yet the author of *Dracula*. In New York, young Blackwood also posed for the artist R. W. Chambers, who himself went on to write that hauntingly titled supernatural classic *The King in Yellow*.

After these adventures in the New World—recounted in his memoir *Episodes before Thirty*—Blackwood returned to Britain, began the study of Theosophy, investigated haunted houses on behalf of the Society for Psychical Research, and became an initiate of the Hermetic Order of the Golden Dawn. Members of this last included the poet W. B. Yeats, the writer Arthur Machen (whose "The White People" is another leading candidate for finest supernatural tale of all time), and the Great Beast himself, Aleister Crowley. Later in life, Blackwood disparaged spiritualism, though he remained a pantheist, a man who had, in Ashley's phrase, "sold his soul to nature."

Meanwhile, largely for his own pleasure, Blackwood had begun to write stories. One day an old friend showed them, without permission, to a publisher. *The Empty House and Other Ghost Stories* appeared in 1906, and Blackwood's real career was finally launched at the relatively late age of thirty-six. During the next ten years, he was to produce nearly all his best short fiction.

Like so many Edwardian men of letters, Blackwood soon turned himself into a writing powerhouse. He generated novels about strange worlds "elsewhere and otherwise" (*Jimbo, A Prisoner of Fairyland*), speculative occult fiction such as *The Human Chord, The Centaur*, and *Julius Le Vallon*, and many children's books. He also created the psychic detective Dr. John Silence and the play about faery land *The Starlight Express*, for which Edward Elgar composed the music.

During the First World War, Blackwood took up spying, at one point reporting to John Buchan (author of *The Thirty-Nine Steps*). In the 1920s, he studied with the mystics P. D. Ouspensky and G. I. Gurdjieff. For more than thirty years, he also went skiing every year in Switzerland, where he met and was admired by Rilke. Stuart Gilbert—French translator and friend of James Joyce—even praised his work in *transition*, the famous experimental magazine of the 1930s. In *The Books in My Life*, Henry Miller called Blackwood's *The Bright Messenger* "the most extraordinary novel on psychoanalysis, one which dwarfs the subject." And in the 1940s, Blackwood gained further renown as a teller of tales, performing his work on BBC radio and even on television. Throughout his life, he owned virtually nothing, was apparently asexual, and looked, according to friends, like an "ancient Egyptian magician or a native American Indian." He died at eighty-two, following a series of strokes.

Mike Ashley is well known as an authority on popular fiction, editor of many anthologies (e.g., *The Mammoth Book of Historical Whodunits*), and author of *The History of the Science Fiction Magazine* and of *Who's Who in Horror and Science Fiction*. He certainly possesses the expertise to write a life of Blackwood. But, as a stylist he is no enchanter, his prose being at best serviceable: still, one can recommend this biography as a useful repository of facts and an informed guide to the work.

At the least, *Algernon Blackwood: An Extraordinary Life* should remind people about the existence of this magnificent storyteller, and one hopes that more of his fiction, long and short, will be reprinted. Over the course of a long January weekend during the national anthrax scare, I dug out my old copy of *The Tales of Algernon Blackwood* (1938) and reread a half dozen stories, including the gripping psychological shocker "Max Hensius," about an expert in "germs" stalking turn-of-the-century New York.

In "The Willows," two men spend the night on a small island in the Danube, and there find that they have . . . intruded. In an essay called "The Psychology of Places," Blackwood warns, in Ashley's words, "against camping on the edge of anything, because this is a frontier between forces. How would the guardians of that world treat us? What would they be like—powers beyond our comprehension, living at a different rate of vibration, and only discernible at the intersection of the two worlds." Algernon Blackwood's stories take us to those edges, to those cracks in time and space, and show us a glimpse of what lies beyond. Look if you dare.

February 3, 2002

TARZAN FOREVER:
THE LIFE OF EDGAR RICE BURROUGHS,
CREATOR OF TARZAN

By John Taliaferro

Surely everyone agrees that the most thrilling line in popular literature is "Mr. Holmes, they were the footprints of a gigantic hound!" (If you don't recognize this sentence from *The Hound of the Baskervilles*, you now know what to read on your next holiday.) That said, the final sentences of Edgar Rice Burroughs's *Tarzan of the Apes* are as perfectly noble, simple, and heartbreaking as—what? Hamlet's dying words? Plato's valedictory praise of Socrates at the end of the *Phaedo*? It seems ludicrous to suggest such comparisons, but they are the ones that come to mind.

Remember the situation: Even though Jane Porter loves Tarzan, she feels honor bound to marry William Cecil Clayton, nice-guy heir to the Greystoke title and fortune. At this moment, Tarzan receives an unexpected telegram from his friend D'Arnot: "Fingerprints prove you Greystoke. Congratulations." Clayton then appears. "Here was the man who had Tarzan's title, and Tarzan's estates, and was going to marry the woman whom Tarzan loved— the woman who loved Tarzan. A single word from Tarzan would make a great difference in this man's life." At which point, the cordially bluff Clayton suddenly asks, "If it's any of my business, how the devil did you ever get into that bally jungle?" To which comes the answer, the hushed last words of the novel: "I was born there," said Tarzan, quietly. "My mother was an Ape, and of course she couldn't tell me much about it. I never knew who my father was."

Curtain. Fade out. Notice though how deftly Burroughs makes you sense an ever so slight pause just before the last sentence. In that split second, we realize, Tarzan decides to sacrifice . . . everything. I can still remember how the tears ran down my twelve-year-old cheeks.

Do kids still care for the Tarzan books? Certainly for the fifty years after 1912, when the ape man first appeared in *All-Story* magazine, he must have been the most famous literary creation in the world, except for Sherlock Holmes. But it's been a long time since I heard a boy give a Tarzan victory yell. Everyone certainly knows about the Lord of the Jungle, and the movies with Johnny Weismuller and Maureen O'Sullivan live in our memories, but I suspect that the actual novels—*Tarzan the Terrible, The Beasts of Tarzan, Tarzan and the Lion Man*—are starting to seem as dated (and as little read) as books about Ruritania and Graustark. I had myself thought to reread some of these after finishing John Taliaferro's fast-moving, utterly engrossing biography of Edgar Rice Burroughs, but didn't quite dare to violate the memories of long-ago bliss. After all, Tarzan was the hero of my childhood. Everyone I knew yearned to have a pet like Jad Bal Ja, the golden lion. We all practiced swinging from tree branches and thumping our chests. And it was inevitably La, the nerve-tinglingly sexy ruler of Opar, who troubled my adolescent dreams. No, I wouldn't tempt fate.

In fact, as Taliaferro makes clear, it would be hard to read Burroughs today without feeling uncomfortable, to say the least, about his shoddy portrayal of Africans as barbaric subhumans, his xenophobic hatred of the Germans (World War I) and the Japanese (World War II), his enthusiasm for eugenics coupled with an undisguised horror of miscegenation, the repeated threats of brutal rape to his heroines, and an all-around gung-ho militarism. And yet, despite all these reprehensible attitudes, Burroughs comes across as a surprisingly attractive man. How can this be?

For one thing, he was no artsy prima donna. Like his hero Jack London, Burroughs experienced a lot of life before becoming a writer. Because he was born to a moderately well-to-do Chicago businessman in 1875, young Ed traveled east to spend a year at Phillips Andover, then transferred to Michigan Military Academy, and was eventually admitted to West Point—but failed the entrance exam. Undaunted, he enlisted in the army and was posted to the bloody Seventh Cavalry in Arizona Territory, where he briefly pursued Apache outlaws. Later he worked as a rancher and gold miner, then ran a stationery store and newsstand, temporarily joined his father's battery company, took a job as a railroad depot policeman, actually "sold electric light bulbs to janitors, candy to drug stores and Stoddard's Lectures from door to door," succeeded as head of the stenographic department at Sears, Roebuck but quit to start his own advertising agency, and finally found himself, on the edge of poverty, franchising a line of pencil sharpeners. At thirty-seven, hoping to earn a little extra money for his wife and children, this jack-of-all-trades discovered he was the master of one: he started writing a novel, *A Princess of Mars*, the first in his planetary romances about the swashbuckling adventures of John Carter on the red planet known to its inhabitants as Barsoom.

Amazingly, within a year and a half Burroughs followed this stunning debut with *Tarzan of the Apes* and *At the Earth's Core*, this latter the opening installment of his Pellucidar novels about a savage civilization, dominated by the reptilian Mahars, at the center of the earth. "Entertainment is fiction's purpose," asserted Burroughs, as he took his place among the world's great storytellers.

But as Taliaferro emphasizes, ERB hoped to be regarded as a Writer too, and before long was yearning to break out of the pulps into the glossy world of the *Saturday Evening Post* and similar magazines. Surprisingly, Burroughs never made it. Instead, he usually had to supply in crude quantity what he lacked in literary quality. So this talented hack churned out hundreds of thousands of words a year, producing realistic fiction about a Chicago tough (*The Mucker*), western stories (*War Chief*), semi-autobiographical novels about Southern California (*The Girl from Hollywood*), a series starring Carson of Venus and, of course, some twenty-four Tarzan books, eleven Barsoom novels, and a half dozen adventures set in Pellucidar.

Yet even while writing like a machine (or dictating to a machine, as he was later to do), Burroughs was simultaneously building a one-man multimedia empire. He incorporated himself. He demanded top dollar from magazine editors and skillfully played off one against another. He negotiated his own serial, reprint, and movie rights. He invested in various business ventures (airplane motors) and helped finance a movie company. At the height of his prosperity, he actually bought the palatial home of Harrison Gray Otis, the deceased editor of the *Los Angeles Times*, and with a flourish renamed this 550-acre San Fernando Valley estate Tarzana. For five years Burroughs flourished there like a Spanish grandee, but a lavish lifestyle, the occasional "breakout" book that never went anywhere, and poor investments eventually made him subdivide and sell much of his property. Despite his best efforts to free himself, Burroughs was forced to remain a slave to the typewriter almost until the end of his life.

Taliaferro describes all this with gusto, and often with considerable flair (of Chicago: "No other American city has inspired more eloquent metaphors of barbarism"). Not only does he discuss Burroughs's entire career; he also places the man and work in context. Kipling's Mowgli, the Wild Boy of Aveyron, a nationwide passion for physical culture, Victorian accounts of African exploration, the myth of Romulus and Remus, the science of evolution and the pseudo-science of racial superiority—all these, he shows us, contributed to the creation of Tarzan. And because Burroughs was as much a businessman as a mythmaker, Taliaferro discusses the writer's real estate adventures, his attempts to shape the movie image of Tarzan, and his marketing of Tarzan comics, radio shows, and souvenirs. Constant work was the law of his life—at least until his mid-sixties, when Burroughs suddenly left his overweight, alcoholic wife and took up with a beautiful blonde half his age. The couple moved to Hawaii, where the aging novelist tried surfing. As he used to say, "It's a great life if you don't weaken."

Burroughs never precisely weakened, but he quickly took to repeating himself, and his earliest books remain his most satisfying. As Taliaferro acutely remarks of *Tarzan and the Ant Men* (and by implication of many of the other ninety or so novels), "Burroughs is at his best at the beginning, plunging into a new world as if he himself is the one penetrating the thicket and discovering the next mysterious land. But once the stage is set, the actors costumed, and the curtain raised, his authorial excitement diminishes, and the drama settles into a churning sort of action, recycled and predictable. Capture, escape, capture again, rebellion, freedom. . . ." By 1923 "Burroughs, by his own accounting, had 'said all there is to say about Tarzan seven or eight times.' " Taliaferro adds dryly, "He would have shuddered then to know that he would do it at least a dozen times more."

When we study literature, we turn to the artists—Joyce or Fitzgerald, Proust or Ellison. But to understand storytelling, we must also honor another strain of writing, that represented by Zane Grey, Erle Stanley Gardner, Agatha Christie, Isaac Asimov, John D. MacDonald, Stephen King, Georgette Heyer. For half of the twentieth century Edgar Rice Burroughs was the lord of this jungle, and *Tarzan Forever* provides a first-rate guide to his colorful life and achievement.

April 11, 1999

CORNELL WOOLRICH:
FIRST YOU DREAM, THEN YOU DIE

By Francis M. Nevins Jr.

One night at age eleven Cornell Woolrich (1903–1968), later the author of such suspense classics as *The Bride Wore Black, Rear Window,* and *Night Has a Thousand Eyes,* looked up at the stars, realized he would some day die, and knew that no one cared. "I had that trapped feeling like some sort of a poor insect that you've put inside a downturned glass, and it tries to climb up the sides, and it can't, and it can't, and it can't."

Out of his despair that "men lived only while blind chance spared them," Woolrich eventually poured out more than a hundred terrifying short stories and two dozen novels, making himself one of the grandmasters of pulp fiction. But while Dashiell Hammett portrayed stoic and laconic tough guys and Raymond Chandler described political and personal corruption with sassy, street-smart wit, Woolrich plunged readers into a claustrophobic "city of subways, automats, movie palaces, cheap furnished rooms, cold stone streets, doorways thick with shadows," a netherworld of "people sick with terror, loving, clawing, killing, smoking too much, drinking too much, each one trying and failing to keep at bay the certainty of death."

As his biographer Francis Nevins emphasizes, "the dominant economic reality, even well into the forties," of Woolrich's fiction, "is the Depression. The dominant political reality is a police force made up largely of sociopaths licensed to torture and kill, the earthly counterpart of the savage powers above. The prevailing emotional states are loneliness and fear. Events generally take place in the hours of darkness, with a sense of menace breathing out of every corner of the night." Kafka meets Edward Hopper.

Surprisingly, this poet of desperation within and without started his career as a bright, witty novelist of the Jazz Age, whose model wasn't Poe but F. Scott Fitzgerald. A mediocre college student at Columbia, he began writing while recovering from illness; *Cover Charge* (chronicling complicated love affairs among the beautiful and damned) appeared in 1926 just after his twenty-second birthday. A year later *Children of the Ritz* (love between a rich girl and a poor boy) came out and was bought by Hollywood, with its young author hired as a scriptwriter.

In California, Woolrich got himself into a marriage he never consummated. According to Nevins, Woolrich was a thoroughly self-contemptuous homosexual, who liked dressing up in a sailor suit. Soon after his marriage was dissolved, Woolrich moved back to New York and into the Hotel Marseilles with his mother. For the next three decades he wrote for *Dime Detective, Black Mask, Argosy*, and other pulps, growing so prolific that he started using the pen names William Irish and George Hopley. When asked about his daily routine, he answered truthfully that "one day is exactly like another." He dedicated a novel to his typewriter.

Cadaverous, chalk white in complexion, alcoholic, shy, mother-obsessed, agoraphobic, homosexual, Woolrich needed only to look within to find the haunted world of the *contes cruels* he began to write in the early 1930s. With them he virtually established the "noir" sensibility, that mix of obsession, nightmare, and futility evoked by the subtitle of Nevins's biography: "First You Dream, Then You Die."

Consider some typically noir Woolrich stories. In "Three o'Clock" a crazed husband, who has planned to kill his seemingly unfaithful wife, finds himself trapped in the basement with his homemade bomb, while the minutes tick inexorably away. In "After-Dinner Story," a group of men enjoy a sumptuous meal, only to be told by their host that he has poisoned one of them—the murderer of his son. An antidote is placed on the table; whoever drinks it immediately reveals his guilt to all. As these suggest, nearly all Woolrich's tales are built on sexual obsession or revenge; the hero-victims race desperately against the clock, and usually they fail. Breathless prose—"soft-edged, verbose, full of vivid color, and brimming with emotion"—reinforces the feeling of emotions out of control, of characters on the edge of breakdown.

In 1940 Woolrich brought out his first and most celebrated suspense novel, *The Bride Wore Black*, a revenge thriller in which four men are murdered, one after the other, by an elusive and beautiful stranger who appears to each victim as his ideal woman. Four other "Black" novels followed, including the chilling masterpiece *Rendezvous in Black*, in which a man whose fiancée has been killed decides to seek revenge—not by murdering the people who caused her death, for that would be too kind, but by killing, one by one, the persons dearest to them. This stark vision of an unfeeling yet actively malevolent universe reached its apogee in *Night Has a Thousand Eyes*, in which the combined forces of law and rationality attempt to thwart a mystic's bizarre prediction that a New York millionaire will "at the stroke of midnight, on the seam between the fourteenth and fifteenth of June, meet death at the jaws of a lion."

Many of Woolrich's stories were made into radio dramas, television plays, and movies; they were perfect vehicles for programs like *Suspense* and *Alfred Hitchcock Presents*. The amnesiac who awakens from a blackout with the feeling that he did something dreadful which he cannot quite remember (*The Black Curtain*), the man whose beloved suddenly disappears and no one will believe she ever existed (*Phantom Lady*), the would-be suicide who trades identities with a dead woman who had every reason to live, discovers happiness, and then finds her past inexorably catching up with her (*I Married a Dead Man*)—all these Woolrich originals have been copied again and again.

Ideally, a new biography should reawaken interest in its subject. But *Cornell Woolrich: First You Dream, Then You Die* will appeal mainly to confirmed fans. Immensely long, it is in fact three books: a biography of what little can be found out about Woolrich; a 250-page catalog giving a précis of every last one of his stories, and thus destroying much of the pleasure of anyone who might want to read them; and another hundred or so pages devoted to listing every radio, TV, and movie adaptation of those stories.

Nevins doesn't lack critical sense—he talks perceptively about Woolrich's ability to make readers sympathize with, even root for, despicable characters—but he possesses the heart of a bibliographer, and seems more interested in publishing arrangements and film history than in criticism. He also sprinkles his prose with hyperbole, vulgarity, and cliché (one story "moves like a bat out of hell").

Oh well. Cornell Woolrich created a vastly impressive body of work, a bit dated now but at its best still powerful and disquieting. That's not such a poor legacy, after all, for the man who wrote, "I was only trying to cheat death. I was only trying to surmount for a little while the darkness that all my life I surely knew was going to come rolling in on me some day and obliterate me. I was only trying to stay alive a little brief while longer, after I was already gone. To stay in the light, to be with the living a little while past my time."

September 18, 1988

THE AVRAM DAVIDSON TREASURY

Edited by Robert Silverberg and Grania Davis

Avram Davidson (1923–1993) was one of the most original and charming writers of our time. So, it almost goes without saying, he was generally neglected and undervalued during much of his career. For the most part this bearded Orthodox Jewish autodidact wrote what one might call fantasy, of a sort, sometimes drifting into the starry realms of science fiction and sometimes into the wild gardens of the antiquarian essay (see the wonderful—and highly idiosyncratic—*Adventures in Unhistory*). Grasping fruitlessly for comparisons, his admirers have likened Davidson to Saki, Chesterton, John Collier, Lafcadio Hearn, Kipling, even I. B. Singer and S. J. Perelman. And you can see what they mean. I would add that he frequently reminds me of the *New Yorker* writer Joseph Mitchell: two similarly brilliant stylists with a compassionate interest in bohemians, losers, immigrant culture, New York, oddities, con artists, crackpot inventors, and the passing of humane, small-scale neighborhood life.

If people know any story by Avram Davidson, it's probably "Or All the Seas with Oysters," celebrated for what Guy Davenport calls "its crazily plausible concept that safety pins are the pupae and coat hangers the larvae of bicycles." Two of his other relatively well-known charmers are "The Golem," in which an elderly Jewish couple thwart a powerful android intent on destroying all mankind, and the hilarious "Help! I am Dr. Morris Goldpepper," wherein the executive board of the American Dental Association must save the earth from alien invaders. This last begins with delightful tongue-in-cheek portentousness:

> Four of the men, Weinroth, McAllister, Danbourge and Smith, sat at the table under the cold blue lighting tubes. One of them, Rorke, was in a corner speaking quietly into a telephone, and one, Fadderman, stood staring out the window at the lights of the city. One, Hansen, had yet to arrive.
>
> Fadderman spoke without turning his head. He was the oldest of those present—the Big Seven, as they were often called.

"Lights," he said. "So many lights. Down here." He waved his hand toward the city. "Up there." He gestured toward the sky. "Even with our much-vaunted knowledge, what," he asked, "do we know?" He turned his head. "Perhaps this is too big for us. In the light of the problem, can we really hope to accomplish anything?"

Heavy-set Danbourge frowned grimly. "We have received the suffrage of our fellow-scientists, Doctor. We can but try.

Davidson can often be funny, as here, but it would be a mistake to pigeon-hole him as a humorist. In a number of dark tales he describes the "sophisticated" Westerner's encounter with—and often exploitation of—an exotic or third-world culture. In "Where Do You Live, Queen Esther?" a repulsive, suffocating New York matron overworks her Caribbean maid, until one day the foolish woman actually dares to rifle through Queen Esther's coat pockets. In "Naples," as mysterious and unsettling as a Robert Aickman ghost story, a nameless traveler follows a shirtless guide into the bowels of the ancient city, on a quest for a certain "article," a "little something" that just might be death. About "Dagon," in which an American military officer acquires a Chinese concubine, with strange consequences, one can only say that Borges couldn't have written a better metaphysical horror story or Conrad a more haunting parable of colonial exploitation.

Still, no précis of a Davidson tale can do more than hint at the enchantment of his storytelling or the vast register of voices at his command: the high-toned diction of a nineteenth-century English remittance man, the mumblings of a crazy Hispanic inventor, the learned discourse of Dr. Engelbert Eszterhazy of Scythia-Pannonia-Transbalkania (it borders on Ruritania and Graustark), or the broken English of an old Slavic grandma: "In this one is chopped spleen stew with crack buckwheats. And in udder one is cow snout cooked under onions. Wait. I give you pepper." And who could ever forget the fast-talking market researcher T. Pettys Shadwell, "the most despicable of living men" ("The Sources of the Nile"), or that vile and legalistic southern slaver Mr. James Bailiss of "The Necessity of His Condition"?

A few of Davidson's stories close with an O. Henry–like snap (try that short-short classic "And Don't Forget the One Red Rose"), but some of the best remain tantalizingly imprecise. What does Dr. Eszterhazy detect when he phrenologically palpates the head of a sideshow impresario in "Polly Charms, the Sleeping Woman"? Is the title character of "Sacheverell" a talking monkey or not? The atmospheric "Manatee Gal, Won't You Come Out Tonight"—one of the Jack Limekiller adventures set in the Belize-like British Hidalgo—can be read again and again, just for its leisurely descriptions of a lush tropical littoral.

As Peter Beagle once noted, "Only in Avram's own sweet, sinister while do we come—far too late for our comfort—to the realization that those were not digressions at all, but coils. . . ."

The Avram Davidson Treasury carries the subtitle "a tribute collection," which means that each of the nearly forty stories in this handsome volume arrives with a short prefatory essay by a notable writer and Davidson fan. So Ursula Le Guin writes about "The House the Blakeneys Built" and Thomas M. Disch introduces "The Power of Every Root." Harlan Ellison and Ray Bradbury contribute more general appreciations, as does the editor Robert Silverberg. His coeditor, Grania Davis, is Davidson's former wife and sometime collabora-tor (she recently completed Davidson's dark fantasy novella, *The Boss in the Wall*). Though one may regret the absence of a few personal favorites—the very funny "Lord of Central Park," in particular—on the whole this collection really does collect its author's best. Not merely a treasury, it's a genuine treasure.

Having read and loved Avram Davidson's work for years, I've often thought about how to characterize his inimitable magic. The writer once said of himself, "I should like to have travelled slowly and leisurely throughout the odder and lesser-known corners of the world, writing of their history and ambiance." In a way, he did. He made himself into a prose laureate of "the Old Country." He celebrated vanishing cultures and foods and customs and places, most of them now absorbed in the homogenized tele-glitz of modern American mall life. There is no better sketch of the Slavic immigrant culture of my own youth—almost entirely gone now—than "The Slovo Stove," while the portraits of Jewish dentists and Hispanic cooks and old scholars from "Chairmany" and 1950s admen seem just as true and apt. Apparently Davidson spent much of his adult life in a series of rented rooms, enjoying the company of the raffish, the outcast, and the hardworking poor. Friends say he was a terrific raconteur, but from the evidence of his fiction he was an even better listener.

In his seventy years—too few, too few—Avram Davidson, born in Yonkers, served in the navy during World War II, fought with the Israeli army in the 1948 war for independence, spent long periods in Mexico and Belize, resided in California for a while, and ended his life in an old veterans home in Washington State. Though he never finished college, Davidson devoted him-self to arcane historical learning with an entirely rabbinical zeal. In just one instance, he filled twenty-five huge notebooks and generated more than five thousand file cards of background information for the Vergil Magus fantasies (based on the medieval legend that Vergil was not only a great poet but also a great sorcerer: see *The Phoenix and the Mirror*).

In his later years Davidson grew downright cranky, but didn't he have cause? He'd written some of the best short stories of his time, yet aside from a small circle of admirers he was virtually unknown and most of his work was out of print. *The Avram Davidson Treasury*, despite occasional misprints, is the kind of substantial hardback the man deserved instead of a lifelong series of mainly paperback originals. Some of its pages will carry you away to strange seas and shores, others will show you the marvelous within the seemingly ordinary, and just about all of them will take your breath away. But, then, that's what magicians do.

October 11, 1998

THE WINE-DARK SEA

By Robert Aickman

When winter approaches a reader's fancy naturally turns to mysteries and ghost stories. For many, that means an English country house whodunit or a sherry-and-spook tale à la M. R. James, the sort of cozy adventures just right for fireside and eiderdown. Before his death, Robert Aickman (1914–1981) was generally deemed the most accomplished writer of classic supernatural tales in English, and *A Wine-Dark Sea* might consequently seem an ideal holiday diversion. But let me offer a warning to the curious: these are not the ghost stories of an antiquary; these are enigmatic, disorienting spiritual journeys.

Aickman's "strange stories"—his preferred term—begin by lulling the reader with plain and unruffled prose, but they end by leaving him profoundly shaken. Most supernatural fiction aims to frighten or shock, or even gross out, but *The Wine-Dark Sea* inspires pity and terror, wonder and sadness; as in *Cold Hand in Mine* and *Painted Devils*, Aickman here relates Conrad-like tales of secret sharers and hearts of darkness with the dispassionate clarity of Kafka— and with the same sense of controlled but mounting panic.

Robert Aickman first began to publish during the early 1950s, establishing his reputation with what remains his best-known story, "Ringing the Changes." In that very adult chiller a middle-aged man marries a woman some thirty years younger than he; on their honeymoon they decide to stay at a seaside resort town, which has the unexpected tradition of ringing all its church bells on this one night a year, enough to wake the dead. This, it turns out, is meant quite literally. By the story's end, the marriage has been irrevocably stunted by the couple's discovery of the wife's fierce sexuality.

That kind of climax marks almost all of the eleven tales reprinted here, chosen from the nearly fifty Aickman wrote. Killer crabs don't come out of the sewers; no one is eaten (at least not usually). Instead lonely middle-aged people—out of step with our modern noisy world and already half in love with easeful death—meet seductive, charismatic figures and in their company gradually slip away to dreamlike realms, often associated with the woods or the past, and almost never find their way back.

The typical Aickman hero is Stephen Hooper in "The Stains," who recognizes—with unexpected consequence—"that, like everyone else, he had spent his life without living." Similarly, in "Never Visit Venice" the young Henry Fern yearns for the glamour and romance symbolized by a recurrent dream in which he floats along in a Venetian gondola in the embrace of a beautiful dark-haired woman. Late in life he finally travels to Venice, finds it horrible: vulgar tourists, loud motorboats, everything tawdry, venal, and kitsch. But on his last night he meets an aristocratic beauty, who invites him for a ride in her gondola and his dream is gradually realized in every detail. But only the most naive reader will fail to realize the identity of the enigmatic stranger.

Usually, though, few such certainties exist in Aickman's austere and unnerving stories. His great strength as a writer lies in his talent for building up a sense of disquiet and the uncanny, then leaving everything unresolved, unexplained, open-ended like life itself. In "The Next Glade" a young widow passes through a thicket and glimpses a huge pit filled with people typing, operating computers, performing all kinds of office work. Delirium? Or an unsettling vision of the world? In "Bind Your Hair" a newly engaged woman discovers a shallow-walled maze in which naked people crawl along on their bellies. This is chilling enough, but why do the women bind their hair? And what about the snuffling pigs? And how do these relate to the tensions Clarinda feels toward her fiancé and his family? Just as matters are getting truly weird, "Bind Your Hair" simply stops, like some of those old-style *New Yorker* stories, leaving us fearing greatly for Clarinda.

Aickman's stories often begin in childhood, when something uncanny—a dollhouse with an inaccessible hidden room, the death of a beloved mother at the appearance of a veiled stranger—blights or beguiles the main character. Years pass, and it is only in middle age that these preparatory traumas find their odd, yet profoundly right, fulfillment.

For Aickman deals less with horror than with peculiar psychic destinies, with how our deepest fears and deepest desires may be one. His characters resemble mental travelers through landscapes of the numinous, the holy and dreadful. Early in "Bind Your Hair," Clarinda meets a mysterious gypsy woman: "Altogether Mrs. Pagani gave an impression of unusual physical power, only partly concealed by her conventional clothes. It was if suddenly she might arise and tear down the house." So it is with *The Wine-Dark Sea:* despite their quiet openings, such stories as "Into the Wood" or "The Trains" suddenly do rise up and tear down the house.

In these dark prose poems of midlife crisis, dreams bring destruction, nothing good lasts, and the desire for love masks a preparation for death. Never well known in his lifetime, Aickman may be too bleak even now for readers reared only on Stephen King or Clive Barker. But to those whose taste includes William Golding or J. G. Ballard, *The Wine-Dark Sea* reveals a neglected master, a superb artist "concerned not with appearance and consistency, but with the spirit behind the appearance, the void behind the face of order." In that void, as Conrad's Mr. Kurtz knew, waits the greatest horror of all.

December 11, 1988

CHESTER HIMES:
A LIFE

By James Sallis

What is more common than for a writer to be acclaimed in his youth, then watch as his subsequent novels or poems are dismissed as failing to match the promise of that first, wonderful book? What can he or she do? The most serious novelists and poets simply keep on, digging ever deeper into themselves, restlessly trying out new forms. They may, as is only human, hope for further success, acclaim, even best-sellerdom, in short, that the world will appreciate and honor their work. But that remains secondary. Writing, after all, is not only the making of a verbal contraption or an illumination of the world around us; it is also—and perhaps primarily—a mode of self-inquiry.

Admittedly, that's a romantic, rather than classical, sense of the artistic vocation. But reading the life of Chester Himes (1909–1984) naturally provokes such thoughts. Himes's entire career consists of second acts, as he never stopped reinventing himself: middle-class black kid, halfhearted criminal, jailbird, dapper ladies' man, socialist, dockworker, roustabout, expatriate. But always and everywhere, a writer. In his twenties Himes started out with stories of prison life for *Esquire*, then brought out a socialist/proletarian novel of race and social change (*If He Hollers Let Him Go*), experimented with time and point of view in his most profound account of black and white relations (*The Primitive*, aka *The End of a Primitive*), and finally reconfigured the hard-boiled detective story in the phantasmagorical "Harlem Cycle," a series of absurdist thrillers about the formidable police detectives Coffin Ed Johnson and Grave Digger Jones. These last earned him a measure of fame—*Cotton Comes to Harlem* was made into a successful film—and are the books most people know, if they know any of Himes's works at all. There were also two volumes of raggedy autobiography, *The Quality of Hurt* and *My Life of Absurdity*. All in all, an impressive oeuvre, though Chester Himes appears destined to remain one of those writers whose novels are periodically rediscovered without ever quite growing canonical.

That may be a good thing in the long run. For years Himes clearly hoped to be the successor to Richard Wright, even if his nightmarish qualities more readily suggest the sardonic and surreal Nathanael West (*Miss Lonelyhearts, The Day of the Locust*). To my mind, though, Himes actually most recalls Philip K. Dick, the great visionary science fiction writer of the 1950s and 1960s. In their hyperbolic genre fiction, both broke free of the constraints of strict naturalism—(like Himes, Dick also wrote realist novels)—to explore the dark absurdities and contradictions of American life. Each blends gallows humor, speculation about the nature of identity (in Dick, what is it to be human?, in Himes, what is it to be black?), pulpy yet exciting storytelling, and a transgressive, druggy sense that anything can happen and probably will. James Sallis himself likens Himes to Ishmael Reed and Spike Lee, but doesn't stop there: "I'd begun seeing him simply as an extension of American crime fiction, one of the first great documenters of the inner city, but increasingly I came to perceive him as I do now: as America's central black writer."

A large claim. What of Langston Hughes, Ralph Ellison, Toni Morrison? Sallis explains: "Himes stood squarely at the crossroad of tradition and innovation, shaking together in his mix remains of the Harlem Renaissance, the energies of newly developing genre fictions, African-American tropes, and arealist storytelling styles, the found life of the streets about him. Again and again he told his story of great promises forever gone unfulfilled, of men who perish from hunger in the shadow of statues of plenty and perish from lack of thought in the shade of great ideas, creating a literature in its absolute individuality, in its strange power and quirkiness, in its cruelty and cock-eyed compassion, ineffably American."

That coloratura paragraph hints at some of the strengths and minor weaknesses of this exuberant biography. Periodically, Sallis's prose grows overemphatic, the similes just a tad ostentatious: "FDR jacked up the wreck our economy had become and started hammering out dents. . . ." Sallis also tends to repeat favorite insights: "Anything can keep you afloat if you grab it hard enough and hold on. . . . Antonin Artaud said that very little is needed to destroy a man; one has only to convince him that his work is useless." Brilliant observations both, but quoting them twice, then three times, first puzzles, then grates. In general, the biography possesses narrative dash and lots of personal enthusiasm but also feels a little rough-hewn: Sallis jumps around in time too much; an event may be mentioned on one page but the context presented only later; and I don't think the assertion about Himes's centrality as the African American writer is ever convincingly proven.

If that sounds harsh, let me point to abundant compensations, not the least being that these lively, jazzy pages are a lot more fun to read than, say, a

Serious Authoritative Life written in either high academese or no-nonsense journalese. Because Sallis summarizes critical opinion of Himes's various books (as well as proffering his own well-informed interpretations), he also provides a succinct introduction to a wide-ranging and uninhibited oeuvre. Moreoever, being himself a crime novelist, poet, and translator, and a man who has known hard times, Sallis occasionally reflects, movingly, about the nature of the writing life. Or about life itself: "The world is taken from us, as it was given, by degrees. We learn to close doors knowing we'll not come back to these rooms again. People, faculties, memories go away from us, and only slowly, with time, do we realize they are gone; only then do we begin to miss them. However he presumes to do so, a man can never sum up his life, as Chester tried to do, at the end; rather, he is summed up by it. But if he is a thoughtful man, a writer, [Ishmael] Reed's mystical detective, he has the privilege of being able to record the forces at work upon him both from within and without."

Such observations are likely to cause many readers to want to track down *The Long-Legged Fly*, *Moth*, and Sallis's other fiction.

Much of Chester Himes's early life remains shadowy. Born in Missouri, he grew up in Cleveland—what is it about Ohio, especially northern Ohio, that fosters black writers, from Paul Laurence Dunbar and Charles Chesnutt to Toni Morrison and Rita Dove?—and attended Ohio State for a year. Despite a middle-class family (albeit one roiled by his mother's ambitions), Himes fell in with low-life companions, got involved in petty crime, and ended up doing nearly eight years in the Ohio State Penitentiary for jewel theft. There he started writing stories and discovered his vocation.

Not that he ever settled down to a cautious life. He liked fine clothes, hard liquor, and white women. Through influential relatives, he did manage to receive small grants early in his career but never seems to have marshaled his funds thriftily. He spent time in New York and California, married a black woman but played around, worked on his fiction as an artist in residence at Yaddo. When the advances dried up, Himes would take jobs as a porter or at dockyards or in restaurants. By the late forties and early fifties, though, the writer came to believe that his books were being sabotaged by his publishers and decided to leave for France. He spent most of the last thirty years of his life there and in Spain.

In Paris he got to know Richard Wright and the rest of the black expatriate community. He lived with—and off—a number of lovers. (Always sympathetic to the plight of women—drawing analogies in his fiction between their oppression and that of African Americans—he also exploited them, for money, sex, and companionship.) At the request of a French editor, a dubious Himes typed up the first of his idiosyncratic crime thrillers, and these made his name more widely known in Europe. When he returned to the United States in the 1970s, he was feted as a major writer but by then had grown greatly enfeebled by arthritis, strokes, and other debilities. He died in Spain, in 1984, at the age of seventy-five.

Naturally, James Sallis fills out this rough outline, underscoring the themes of Himes's life and oeuvre: the egalitarian versus the patrician, his desire to force white America to confront the reality of black life, an artistic temperament that combined "repudiation and willfulness," an obsession with that all-American theme—the "dialogue between solitude and community." And always the nature and impact of racism. Though instinctively, and repeatedly, combative, Himes nonetheless regarded himself as primarily an artist. At the end of his life he wrote to his wife, Lesley, "Would you ... keep my books alive? I don't want to feel that I have lived without having accomplished something that's going to be remembered and I don't want to leave this world a common shade and I do so hope that my books will be read and that people will remember me."

More and more, it looks as though the shade of Chester Himes can rest easy: his works are in print and, thanks to feisty advocates like James Sallis, are likely to stay that way. *The End of a Primitive*, in particular, seems poised to take its place as a key American novel. Still, the Harlem Cycle will be hard to beat as Himes's most lasting achievement. Who else but Chester Himes would say, of a woman dressed in a flour sack, that her "breasts poked out of the top ... like the snouts of two hungry shoats"? Or that four nightclub dancers looked "as evil as housemaids scrubbing floors"? Or that a jazz pianist "was driving piles on the bass with his steady left hand while his right hand was frolicking over hot dry grass in a nudists' colony"? If such language makes you tingle with pleasure—and it should—go look for *A Rage in Harlem*, *The Heat's On*, or *Blind Man with a Pistol*. In fact, get going now.

February 19, 2001

SUSPECTS

By Thomas Berger

"You drive a lot, you store up information, like where they put the radar," explains Molly, a young trucker in *Suspects*. She is talking about long-distance driving to Lloyd, the moody hitchhiker who may have just slaughtered a mother and her angelic three-year-old daughter. "It's like any other job, probably. As you go along you keep learning and you get better at it."

Is this homespun wisdom always true? Or is it merely pretty to think so? The apprentice bricklayer methodically follows the directions on the bag of Quikcrete; an experienced mason runs his trowel through the mortar and knows it's right. Mechanics and plumbers, scholars and teachers, carpenters and seamstresses—the older, the better. When you're looking for real expertise, always go for the grizzled.

But what about novelists?

Certainly Thomas Berger (b. 1924) has mastered all the tricks of the writer's trade, and *Suspects* is a consummately readable and expertly entertaining book. From the very first pages, when an elderly widow discovers the slashed bodies of gorgeous Donna Howland and little Amanda, the storytelling grips the reader and never lets go. The cast of characters is itself pure Berger: the slobby, alcoholic cop; the shiftless and hot-tempered kid brother; a lonely young woman hungry for love; the crass, adulterous husband; a pair of grotesque neighbors. In plot, *Suspects* recalls a classic police procedural—who killed the Howlands, and why?—and it deftly reproduces the typical lingo of law officers and psychiatrists and nut cases; yet the overall tone remains slightly Olympian, irony tempered by wistfulness: gin and bitters. Admirers of *The Feud* or *Sneaky People* will recognize the voice.

So, do novelists get better as they grow older?

This is Thomas Berger's twentieth book and marks nearly forty years that he has lived as a professional writer (*Crazy in Berlin*, which inaugurated his acclaimed Carlo Reinhart saga, appeared in 1958). A just world would honor the reclusive Berger, in the Japanese fashion, as a Living National Treasure. He is, after all, the author of *Little Big Man,* one of the dozen or so best American novels since World War II. If Mark Twain had written Huckleberry Finn's further adventures, those that took place after he lit out for the territories, they could hardly better Jack Crabb's pungent recollections of the old west and the growing conflict between white and Indian cultures.

Several other books are nearly as fine, if less grandly conceived. In *Killing Time,* a wonderfully perverse tour de force, Berger creates a triple murderer who is also among the most winning and sympathetic figures in modern fiction: Forrest Gump as Raskolnikov. *The Feud,* with its escalating quarrel between two Depression-era families, feels as tightly plotted as a P. G. Wodehouse farce; and *Regiment of Women* depicts with brutal humor a future wherein once stereotypical sex roles have been thoroughly reversed: men dress in skirts, worry about their looks, and pout, while beefy women make catcalls and crude remarks whenever a cute young guy bends over or shows a little too much stocking.

In all his works of the sixties and seventies Berger displays an imaginative freshness, a disinclination to repeat himself, a young man's swagger and chutzpah. But since 1983, when *The Feud* was praised by Anne Tyler on the front page of the *New York Times Book Review,* the once tirelessly inventive writer seems to have settled into a niche: where he used to transform genres, now he seems content to work variations on them. Critics have greeted his recent retellings of the *Oresteia* and *Robinson Crusoe* (*Orrie's Story* and *Robert Crews*) as little better than the puns that inform their titles. Increasingly, reviewers praise the entire oeuvre, so as not to peer too closely at its latest addition.

Which, I see, is precisely what I've done here. Rather unfairly, especially if one is able to forget the earlier masterpieces. For *Suspects* really is a good, engrossing book, a bit meandering but smooth, professional, and better than any television police show it might resemble. In the aptly named detective Moody, Berger even seems to have drawn a partial self-portrait: an aging professional, dismissed by his colleagues as over-the-hill, troubled by the past, illness, betrayal, and the fallen ways of the world, but a man who nonetheless perseveres and, day after day, gets the job done.

As usual, too, Berger exuberantly mixes the vulgar with the ideal (some might say the sentimental), while his flair for replicating speech, whether the elegant diction of a grande dame, the joshing humor of cops on patrol, or the gibberings of a sex-crazed old man, reminds us that he was a master of the vernacular long before George V. Higgins and Stephen King. Not least, numerous sentences rustle with an almost imperceptible, low-keyed wit: "He had the kind of matter-of-fact voice that Moody once would have believed unlikely for a homosexual to produce, but it had got so in recent years that you were sure only that a man who spoke effeminately was almost certain to be straight." All this said, the conventionality of most of the characters and some of the generic action trouble me: the earlier Berger would have been more surprising.

So if *Suspects* isn't in the same class as, say, *Killing Time*, which it loosely resembles (and at times I wondered about deliberate self-pastiche), any Berger fan will still want to read the new book. Even when much is taken by time and age or habit and misjudgment, with a great writer like Thomas Berger much abides. We should be grateful. As Molly tells Lloyd at an interstate café: "Know what's good here? The pie." Then she adds, "It's not really homemade, but it's that kind that's like homemade." Sighing slightly, we know what she means. But let's not forget that the pie is still good.

September 29, 1996

SERGIO LEONE:
SOMETHING TO DO WITH DEATH

By Christopher Frayling

Once upon a time in Marseille I used to take the bus down to the Canebière, the main boulevard of this rowdy Mediterranean port city. In those days, 1970–71, I was living in a working-class district called St. Louis, teaching English, practicing my spoken French, and happy to be, finally, in southern Europe instead of northern Ohio. When I strolled around the Vieux Port— sporting a French cap and a navy blue sweater that buttoned dashingly across my left shoulder—it was with a quiet swagger. And why not? I was twenty-one and the world was full of sunshine.

On these bus trips to town, I regularly passed a cinema topped by a huge billboard advertising a movie entitled *Il Etait une Fois dans l'Ouest: Un Film de Sergio Leone*. Since my students kept on asking if I had seen *Once upon a Time in the West*, I eventually plunked down a fistful of francs to watch Charles Bronson, Jason Robards, Claudia Cardinale, and Henry Fonda (as the villain!) in one of the most spectacular westerns ever made. This wasn't any mere cowboy movie, I discovered; it was Greek tragedy in Monument Valley; not just a horse opera but an *opera seria* (with long close-ups of people's eyes functioning as silent but eloquent arias); not a shoot-'em-up but a threnody for the passing of a hard and violent age. Imagine a ritualistic dance of death, a ballet with bullets and bloodstains, a stereoscopic homage to the tough, solitary, and self-reliant.

And then there was the music: for long periods, lush, wistful melodies or jarring ululations, composed by Ennio Morricone, substituted for dialogue. Unnervingly quiet, the nameless hero, Charles Bronson, hardly bothers to speak more than a few sentences. Instead he plays a harmonica attached to a leather thong around his neck. Until the final showdown, he never even wears a sidearm. Yet whenever violence irrupts, Harmonica—as he is called—may drop a valise, or reach behind a wooden post, and his six-gun is somehow there. It's almost uncanny. But then much seems like legend or dark fairy tale in *Once upon a Time in the West.*

In the final reels, the picaresque bandit Cheyenne (Jason Robards) tells Claudia Cardinale—a Tunisian-Italian beauty with seriously troubling cleavage—that a man like Harmonica isn't going to stick around. "People like that have something inside . . . something to do with death." And indeed, at the very end, Bronson rides off into the desert, while Cardinale settles into a new life, no longer a costly New Orleans whore but a kind of nurturing earth mother, bringing water to the men who are building the railroad that will transform her farmhouse into a town. By now, we know that the West, or at least the mythic West as gladiatorial arena, is finished: no more will lean men test the firmness of their resolve and the quickness of their draw on dusty streets.

After seeing *Il Etait une Fois dans l'Ouest* I sought out Leone's other spaghetti westerns, including *A Fistful of Dollars,* which made Clint Eastwood a star; *For a Few Dollars More,* which introduced the steely Lee Van Cleef, "the man with the gunsight eyes"; and *The Good, the Bad, and the Ugly,* an epic dominated by Eli Wallach as the dirty, raggedy Tuco, an exemplar of pure appetite, but funny and human, especially compared with the laconic Eastwood and the malign Van Cleef. All these films also had those haunting Morricone soundtracks, a mix of voluptuous orchestration, whistled coyote howls, and mournful choral wailings. With their deadpan humor ("Get three coffins ready. . . . My mistake. Four coffins") and the Zen-like self-assurance of their heroes no matter how desperate the situation, Sergio Leone's westerns seemed less like celluoid melodramas than wish fulfillments, boyhood dreams realized. Is there a man alive who hasn't dreamed of being Clint Eastwood in a serape, with eyes narrowed and a cigarillo between his lips, as he reaches for the deadly Colt strapped to his thigh?

Christopher Frayling's new biography, *Sergio Leone: Something to Do with Death,* offers both a biography of the visionary director (1929–1989) who gave us these thrilling archetypes and an extensive commentary on the production and reception of each of his movies. It is a long, slow-moving book—not unlike a Leone film, in some ways—and one may need to be a fan to stick with Frayling for nearly 500 pages. For the exceptionally committed he provides a minutely detailed account of Leone's last project: the monumental gangster epic *Once upon a Time in America,* a complex and deliberately Proustian work set in three different time periods, which was ultimately butchered into dull simplicity because its American backers judged the plot too long and too confusing.

Sergio Leone was born into the movies. His father had been a minor film star and then a director; as a young man, he himself worked as a gofer or small-time actor with notable Italian moviemakers like Vittorio De Sica; he then spent years as an assistant director on all kinds of pictures, including kitschy sword-and-sandal epics such as *Hercules Unchained, The Colossus of Rhodes*, and *The Last Days of Pompeii*. All good training, of course, for anyone fascinated by heroic myth and lone avengers. Who can ever forget, try as one might, the posters for these Italian cast-of-thousands extravaganzas? "See the yawning jaws of the flesh-ripping alligator pit—the martyred Christians thrown to the gaping fangs of crazed lions. . . ."

Wonderful stuff, in its way, but Leone's destiny lay elsewhere. "The attraction of the Western, for me is quite simply this. It is the pleasure of doing justice, all by myself, without having to ask anyone's permission. Bang Bang!" By chance, though, the direct inspiration for his first real effort, *A Fistful of Dollars*, was Akira Kurosawa's *Yojimbo*. Leone reimagined this half-comic Samurai adventure as a western; because James Coburn wanted too much money and Henry Fonda and Charles Bronson were uninterested, he finally settled on Clint Eastwood to star. Today it's hard to imagine anyone else in the role of the enigmatic Man with No Name. (Leone did eventually get Fonda, Bronson, and Coburn to act in other films.) In fact, Eastwood seems to have helped reconceive the gunfighter he played: "I always felt that if the character explained everything as per the original script, we wouldn't have any mystery at all to him." As Frayling then adds, "Thus, Eastwood became one of the very few actors in film history to fight for fewer lines." As for the composer Ennio Morricone, whose melodies suffuse these films with yearning and melancholy, he turns out to have been a childhood schoolmate of Leone's in Rome.

Surprisingly, it took a while for *A Fistful of Dollars* to catch on. There were few reviews; overseas buyers weren't interested. But gradually word of mouth spread in Rome that there was this extraordinary movie. It rapidly grew into a cult film, followed by its sort-of sequels *For a Few Dollars More* and *The Good, the Bad, and the Ugly*. That last was promoted with a wonderfully over-the-top poster—"For Three Men the Civil War Wasn't Hell. It was Practice!"—and concluded with the best showdown in movie history: this trio of superior gunslingers, finally confronting each other, in a natural amphitheater in the center of a vast war cemetery. Who will shoot whom? And in what order?

The plump, bespectacled, and stingy Leone was a cinematic perfectionist to whom every detail in a film mattered: for *Once upon a Time in the West* he spent hours making Henry Fonda try on hundreds of hats before finding just the right one. He also chose Fonda to play the cold-blooded killer Frank because he wanted to cast him against type: the noble face, the clear, blue eyes, and the erect aristocratic carriage are used to mask an amoral, truly evil soul. Bronson, by contrast, was his physiognomy: "A sort of granite block, impenetrable but marked by life. . . . A man who knows just how long to wait." As for that epic's slow deliberateness—criticized by some critics—"the rhythm of the film . . . was intended to create the sensation of the last gasps that a person takes just before dying. . . . All the characters in the film, except Claudia, are conscious of the fact they will not arrive at the end alive. . . . And I wanted to make the audience feel, in three hours, how these people lived and died."

Despite occasional allusions in his interviews to Marx or Céline, Leone wasn't a thinker or a literary man, or even a particularly cultivated one, though he had a craftsman's liking for beautifully made objets (he collected antiques and paintings) and an encyclopedic recall of all kinds of films. In fact, much in his own work takes the form of postmodern quotation, often inverting elements from classics by John Ford or Howard Hawks. For instance, in the suspenseful "overture" to *Once upon a Time in the West* he reverses the central conceit of *High Noon*: here three pistoleros silently wait for the train that will bring the hero into town. This intricate intertextuality, as well as Leone's uncompromising artistry, deeply appealed to certain younger filmmakers, including Steven Spielberg, John Carpenter, and Quentin Tarantino. Who influenced whom in the case of Leone and Francis Ford Coppola and Sam Peckinpah remains open to argument.

Shortly after the debacle of *Once upon a Time in America*, its creator was diagnosed with heart disease. But Leone kept working, even planning a super-epic based on the siege of Leningrad, *Gone with the Wind* goes to Russia. But at the age of sixty, while watching a Robert Wise documentary called *I Want to Live!*, the filmmaker leaned his head against his wife's shoulder and said, "I'm sorry, I don't feel very well." Within a few seconds, writes Frayling, Leone was dead.

But his movies live on. I recently rented the videotape of *Once upon a Time in the West*, and Leone's buildup to the massacre of the McBain family—unexpected silences, frightened birds, the tables laden for the wedding feast—remains a masterpiece of filmic choreography; when the gunmen emerge out of the sunlit fields, they still seem ominous, unearthly, and yet strangely beautiful in their long tan dusters fluttering in the breeze; and when Henry Fonda finally draws his pistol to shoot the nine-year-old boy and thinly smiles, he still seems the coldest-hearted killer in all the world.

Anyone who cares for these violent and poetic films will want to take a look at Frayling's painstaking biography of their progenitor. Not only is it packed with useful insights into Leone, but it also tangentially chronicles much of the postwar Italian film industry. As Frayling concludes, "What Leone was trying to do was to re-enchant the cinema, while expressing his own disenchantment with the contemporary world and conveying the exhilaration he personally felt when watching and making movies. He was the first modern cineaste to make really popular films, a bridge between the 'art films' and popular cinema, and a deep confusion to the critics." Not to this one—I loved his movies when I first saw them long ago in France, and I love them still.

July 23, 2000

GRIEVANCE

By K. C. Constantine

No way. No way at all that a few hundred words are going to do justice to this deeply affecting novel. And I do mean novel—not mystery, whodunit, police procedural, thriller, or any of the other code words we use to slot a book into the genre ghetto. There's a murder, there are cops, there's a killer, but figuring out who put a bullet into the head of the wealthy J. D. Lyon merely precipitates the true investigation, one into the troubled soul of Detective Sergeant Ruggiero Carlucci. With the skill of an experienced millwright, K. C. Constantine neatly works through all the various, sorrowful implications of his title word: "grievance."

Constantine—a pseudonym, the author's real name being a long-preserved secret—has built his literary career by writing about crime in the decaying western Pennsylvania steel town of Rocksburg. You know this place: the slouching men in patched khakis carrying battered lunch boxes, the moun-tains of slag or coke next to the blast furnaces, the red-brick Our Lady of Sorrows on the hilltop, and behind the neatly painted garages the little plots overgrown with tomatoes and peppers. Early on in *Grievance*, Carlucci makes a list of eight foremen from the now closed steel plant, each a possible suspect in a murder: Steven W. Abramovic, Albert F. Bodnar, John J. Czarowicz, Regis A. Horvath, Edward T. Novotniak, Rudolph R. Shimkus, Paul J. Sroka, Luke J. Stefanko. We're not in Kansas, let me tell you. In Rocksburg even a name like Dirda doesn't seem the least bit unusual.

There are plenty of novels and memoirs about Jewish intellectuals and Gaelic charmers, about the African American experience and the legacy of the Civil War in the South, about drugged-out Gen-Xers, unhappy academics, Connecticut divorcées, and Washington bureaucrats who stumble upon global terrorist plots. But who today writes about working-class America? And by the working class I mean the Italians and Poles and blacks who do the real labor of the world, in foundries and factories, with lathes and diesel shovels and sweat.

I mean the people who need to stuff their dirty clothes in grocery bags and take showers in locker rooms before they go home at the end of an eight-hour shift. Sure, much of Rust Belt America is vanishing, but a lot remains, and one of its few laureates is K. C. Constantine.

His first books—*The Rocksburg Railroad Murders, The Man Who Liked to Look at Himself,* and a few others featuring the chief of police Mario Balzic—read like conventional police procedurals with lots of local, ethnic color. You might hear about stuffed cabbage, wine sipped from old jelly jars, the layoffs down at the mill, but solving the mystery was still the main engine of the plot. But in the 1990s Constantine grew increasingly didactic and polemical, so that a novel like *Bottom Liner Blues* settled into a series of rants about the government by a populist counterpart to Dostoevsky's Underground Man. For a while, it seemed to his admirers as if Constantine had lost his novelistic balance, merely using his fiction to vent rage and frustration.

The anger and the didacticism are still there in *Grievance*, but tempered by the humanity and distinctiveness of the characters, from the coldly superior Mrs. Lyon to the fatherly Mario Balzic, who puts in a cameo appearance. The novel actually opens with its hero, forty-six-year-old Rugs Carlucci, being punched in the nose by his mother. This might sound like a comic turn, but Mrs. Carlucci has grown seriously delusional, requiring constant supervision; Rugs has even installed hooks and eyes on the outside of the front and back doors, so that he can lock the old woman in when he has to leave her alone for a while. "Please," he tells himself "don't let there be a fire." Unfortunately, Mrs. Carlucci seems to be growing increasingly violent, and Rugs worries and worries about what to do. He can't afford to pay for a private nursing facility, and the County Home is a last resort.

Called to assist a state trooper named Milliron, Rugs finds himself investigating the shooting of J. D. Lyon, a corporate hatchetman who fifteen years ago soaked Conemaugh Steel for millions in stock options and then closed the mill, putting hundreds of men out of work. The foremen, in particular, lost everything, including their pensions, because of some legal chicanery blurring their status: they fell somewhere between management and labor, receiving benefits from neither. When John Czarowicz's wife gets cancer soon afterward, the ex-foreman and ex-Marine discovers that he makes just slightly too much for Medicaid assistance and ends up slaving at part-time minimum-wage jobs to pay off his bills. The young trooper Milliron, just dripping to make lieutenant by solving the Lyon murder, keeps getting confused about Medicaid and Medicare:

"Don't say it like there ain't no difference," answers Czarowicz, "there's a helluva big difference. You just ain't run up against it yet, so you don't know.

You think it's all one thing 'cause you don't need it yet, but you will. You'll need it some day, then I'll bet you'll be able to keep 'em straight."

The French novelist Raymond Queneau once said that the difference between fiction and nonfiction was that novels were about love and real life was about hunger. At least a few readers will identify with the agony of an honest, hardworking guy being dunned by collection agencies and forced to spend years working off doctor's bills, long after his cancer-ridden wife has died, following heartbreaking months of chemo and medication.

Of course, it wasn't supposed to be this way. None of it: Lost jobs. Law suits. Cancer. A spite-filled wife. Stupid, envious colleagues. A crazed mother. Murders. Wasted lives. All legitimate grievances.

Constantine's preferred structural device is the conversation. In particular, he likes to have somebody explain how something works—tax law, Medicaid, hospital protocol for the psychologically disturbed, a love affair. At his best, he keeps these monologues short, and he makes sure that they are spoken by sharply characterized men and women. For instance, here we meet again the shrewd alcoholic lawyer Mo Valcanas, who prefers to listen to jazz LPs in his underwear, and Howard Failan, the astute and unscrupulous DA who makes sure that others do his dirty work, and Franny Perfetti, third runner-up to Miss Pennsylvania and now the thirty-five-year-old social worker whom Rugs shyly dates and dreams about.

Of course, Constantine's greatest asset lies in his ear for spoken language, but since his characters tend to be cops, politicians, and factory workers, nearly every sentence includes the common vulgarism for sexual intercourse. Their exchanges are filled with hesitations, contractions, slang, and prejudice, as well as the strange poetry of profanity. Moreover, his people always speak with particular force because everyone, even the director of mental health at Conemaugh General Hospital, reveals some kind of grievance. Rugs asks why the director himself is filling out some legal forms, rather than a secretary. Dr. Moller explains, "We are woefully understaffed, and that's because we now serve, and have served, since the late eighties, all of us here in this building, at the pleasure of the insurance companies. Though it's gotten much worse lately. They, and by they I mean the insurance Nazis, they decide who gets what treatment, and when and where and how. So that's why I'm printing this information with a ballpoint pen instead of having it entered into a computer by a very competent woman whom we had to lay off more than a year ago."

I hardly believe that novels should deal only with "real" life. But if you're going to write about the way we live now, then you need to do it right. And this Constantine does perfectly. What's it like to live with a mentally deranged mother? How do you feel when you lose your job and can't find another? What do you do when your wife gets breast cancer? Why is it so complicated to check into a hospital, so demeaning to apply for government assistance? Is it right that leeches at the top keep driving their Porsches and avoid paying their taxes, while you push a broom and watch your life's savings get eaten up by medical bills? Why should they live, while you suffer?

Yes, Constantine understands how decent men and women worry and gripe and stoically endure and go to work and fall in love and die. And sometimes kill. He gets everything right in this novel. I know, because I grew up in a city just like Rocksburg, and these are, as they used to say, mine own people.

June 4, 2000

POSTSCRIPT: K. C. Constantine may call to mind three other contemporary novelists who have raised crime fiction to something more than a mystery or shoot-'em-up. Elmore Leonard is the master of tone—his prose being easygoing, artfully nonchalant, utterly cool, no matter how much violence threatens. George V. Higgins's early novels taught a generation the way real cops and criminals talked. One might say that half of contemporary crime writing comes out of *The Friends of Eddie Coyle*. Donald Westlake makes good writing look easy in both his smoothly ingratiating Dortmunder comedies and his hard, lean novels about the coldly professional thief Parker (written under the pen name Richard Stark). But Constantine is the least commercial and probably the most original of them all.

SECOND SIGHT

By Charles McCarry

The Spy Who Loved Me is probably the worst of the James Bond thrillers, but virtually all of Charles McCarry's superb espionage novels could rightly borrow some variation of that title. Secret Agent Paul Christopher is a man worn out by love—for family, friends, country, the truth—and his exploits point up the high cost of that most dangerous passion.

In the course of the five novels directly about him—McCarry's *The Bride of the Wilderness* (1988) and *The Better Angels* (1979) focus on other members of his family—Christopher loses almost everyone he cares about: his young mother sacrifices herself so that he can escape Nazi Germany; his spymaster father is murdered by Soviet agents in postwar Berlin; Cathy, his first wife, leaves him in part because of his undercover work; a girlfriend is killed in revenge for secrets he has uncovered; a beloved mentor turns out to be the most cunning of double agents. The entire Christopher Chronicle—for the various novels make up a tangled but single story—builds on a series of betrayals and deaths that culminates in Paul Christopher's ten years in a Chinese prison and quite possibly the destruction of the Outfit, the intelligence service to which he has devoted his life.

Such a grim scenario hardly seems the stuff that beach books are made of. But every one of McCarry's rococo thrillers, from *The Miernik Dossier* (1973) down to this latest, is airy, swift moving, absolutely exhilarating: nobody does it better. Consider the prose, for instance. McCarry can effortlessly buttonhole a reader, as in the opening of *Second Sight*: "It made no difference to David Patchen, the director of the Outfit, that his friend Paul Christopher had been out of the business of espionage for twenty years, or that he had spent more than half that time in a Chinese prison. He still told him secrets." Or notice the unexpected, perfect last word of this description: Maria Custer "had possessed these extraordinary breasts since she was in seventh grade, and she knew that no normal male could look at them without wanting to hold them in his hands and whimper."

Like a repertory drama troupe, McCarry's novels employ the same handful of larger-than-life players over and over. In some books they have walk-on roles, in others they become the principals. Fans learn to love their idiosyncrasies, to look forward to their reappearances—even if some ultimately turn out to be traitors. For example, *The Secret Lovers* (1977) revolves about Christopher's dazzling wife, Cathy, and the cultivated, worldly agents Otto and Maria Rothchild; all three make brief but crucial comebacks in *Second Sight*. Barney Wolkowicz plays memorable bit parts in several books, but steals the show in *The Last Supper* (1983). In an intelligence community dominated by blond Ivy League graduates, and in particular by the ultra-Waspy Hubbard-Christopher clan, Barney is an outsider, the son of a steelworker from Youngstown, a graduate of Kent State, unkempt, overweight, almost buffoonish. He is also, according to an implacable enemy, the most brilliant spy of his generation.

Besides the ability to write clean prose and create romantic characters, McCarry possesses the best gift of all: he can tell one hell of a story. As befits a former intelligence agent, he is devilishly brilliant at plotting. In *The Tears of Autumn* (1974), the linchpin of the whole sequence (and a high point in American espionage fiction), Paul Christopher apparently solves the greatest historical mystery of our time: why John Kennedy was shot in Dallas on November 22, 1963. (The answer is logical, astrological, and almost persuasive.) Just as ambitious in its plot complications, *Second Sight* unspools a dozen different threads—the random kidnapping of Outfit agents, a lost tribe of Israel, David Patchen's intelligence career, Cathy Christopher's unsuspected daughter, a Berber princess who can foretell the future, the Nazi Reinhard Heydrich's sexual obsessions, a terrorist group called the Eye of Gaza, several love affairs, and a long-planned revenge. All these disparate elements are wound together at a bloody climax, followed by a wistful diminuendo that brings this book and the whole Christopher Chronicle to a close.

What makes McCarry's work so broadly appealing is that he has managed to crossbreed the spy novel with the historical romance and the family saga. Paul Christopher can fire an Uzi or unearth a mole, but he is also every woman's dream: a soft-spoken and accomplished poet, the scion of a well-off New England family, and a bruised soul unable to forget those he has loved and lost. In fact, nearly all McCarry's people prove preternaturally talented, clever, beautiful, or traitorous, adept at witty conversation in Georgetown drawing rooms or at fighting their way through Burmese jungles. Such sterling characters are, of course, essentially wish fulfillments, twentieth-century versions of mythological heroes and Arthurian knights, but so what? In popular fiction we live out our daydreams, not our dingy daily lives.

Although *Second Sight* makes for terrific reading, it is not quite so fine as McCarry's other books. The story moves just a tad sluggishly, overemphasizes love affairs and family matters at the expense of intrigue and action, and by incorporating elements from several earlier books ends by feeling a bit diffuse. Though basically self-contained, *Second Sight* refers often and in such detail to old Outfit business that readers will constantly feel rushes of pleasure or annoyance: those who know, say, *The Last Supper*, will mentally fill in the details surrounding various allusions to it, while newcomers will rightly complain about learning the identity of that novel's traitor. Still, McCarry here shows his usual masterly command of the whole Jamesian bag of narrative tricks (minus the master's ponderousness): flashbacks, broken chronology, alternative interpretations of episodes, unreliable narration, neatly ambiguous statements, the probing of fine consciences, verbal leitmotifs.

To a great extent, McCarry constructs *Second Sight*—note the title—out of the gaps and sidelights of his previous books; an impressive trick, but McCarry has always been sensitive to such narrative legerdemain. His first novel resembled an intelligence dossier and ended squarely on the side of undecidability as to whether the bumbling Miernik was an innocent abroad or a consummate professional spy. Still, now that the Christopher books are behind him—in an appendix McCarry insists that this is the last one—I couldn't help wondering if he would ever go back and smooth out his saga's inconsistencies. Over the years he has proffered three different accounts of how Paul Christopher and David Patchen were recruited by the Outfit. In one novel Patchen's wife has left him, in another we are told that "no female would ever caress Patchen's scars," and in this one Patchen gets a devoted Quaker wife named Martha. Did the loathesome news commentator Patrick Graham sleep with the young Stephanie Christopher or not? Yes in one place, no in another. Most puzzling of all, a terrorist leader and his band are still active in 1995–96 (when *The Better Angels* takes place), long after this new novel has killed off the whole lot of them.

Some inconsistencies no doubt resulted when McCarry allowed his characters to grow and deepen—this is especially true of Barney Wolkowicz—but readers attentive to details, as espionage aficionados tend to be, will feel disturbed by easily avoidable anomalies. Not that they matter all that much. Committed McCarry fans will buy *Second Sight* right away; double agents armed with Sten guns couldn't stop them. But newcomers should probably start with the earlier books and work up to this grand finale. It's as much fun as a visit to le Carré's Circus. Indeed, Charles McCarry is as fine a novelist as the creator of George Smiley, and *The Tears of Autumn* and *The Last Supper* are every bit the equal in artistry to *The Spy Who Came in from the Cold* and *Tinker, Tailor, Soldier, Spy.*

June 30, 1991

NIGHT WATCH

By Terry Pratchett

Though he is arguably the leading comic novelist of our time, as well as a master of contemporary fantasy, Terry Pratchett hasn't been content with those enviable laurels. Until the advent of J. K. Rowling, he was also the best-selling author in Britain. The dust jacket on his previous novel, *Thief of Time*—published in 2001—notes that more than 21 million copies of his books have been sold worldwide. The jacket on *Night Watch* ups that figure to 27 million, meaning—if I retain my fifth-grade math skills—that he sold 6 million books in the last year or two. Recently, *The Amazing Maurice and His Educated Rodents* was awarded the Carnegie Medal as the best children's book of the year. His admirers, who are obviously legion, include such superb popular storytellers as Barbara Mertz (aka Elizabeth Peters) and Neil Gaiman, creator of the Sandman graphic novels (as well as Pratchett's collaborator on *Good Omens,* a comic fantasy about the end of the world). Not least, even highly browed intellectuals such as A. S. Byatt have called him "truly original" and "brilliant."

For some reason, though, Pratchett hasn't attracted the right attention in the United States. His work is seldom reviewed at length, and even the well-read haven't heard of him, or, if they have, their brains have lodged the Discworld series in the pigeonhole labeled "cutesy fantasy" and then dismissed it. In truth, Pratchett's work is almost impossible to describe without making it sound childish, sickly sweet, or twee. But there's nothing soft and cuddly about it: think *Monty Python* or *The Simpsons* rather than *Harry Potter;* satirical rather than silly.

The novels, approaching thirty at this point, take place on an Earth-like planet called the Discworld, where civilization, such as it is, blends the medieval and the modern (with touches of the Victorian)—i.e., swords and magic, robes and armor, but also a bustling, crowded capital (Ankh-Morpork) plagued by racial, religious, and political issues that we all recognize. Pratchett's various titles usually hint, often punningly, at their subtexts: *Jingo* is about political jingoism and war fever, *The Truth* about the role of the press in society, *Mort* about Death's new, rather bumbling understudy.

As the creator of an entire world, Pratchett has room to move about, to explore any theme that interests him, to call upon several different stock companies. There are novels in which Granny Weatherwax and various witches take center stage, others about the inept wizard Rincewind or the decrepit Cohen the Barbarian. Recently, *Thief of Time* introduced the Monks of History, a sect of Buddhist-like priests who seem harmless and dopey but are actually responsible for the temporal stability of the universe: they make sure that tomorrow happens. *Night Watch* itself slots into Pratchett's ongoing history of the metropolitan police force, the City Watch, a profession in the forefront of social change, since its coppers include trolls and dwarfs, a werewolf and even a zombie, as well as the rightful king of Ankh-Morpork (though no one quite realizes this). The force is headed by Sam Vimes, a onetime street urchin, whose leadership, courage, and urban smarts have won him the love of the aristocratic Lady Sybil, a fortune, and a ducal title.

The book opens with Sam awaiting the birth of his first child on, as it happens, a mysterious day of remembrance: several members of the Watch, including Sam, have pinned a sprig of lilac to their uniforms, as have the notorious Cut-Me-Own-Throat Dibbler (purveyor of street snacks you never want to touch, let alone eat) and the Patrician, Lord Vetinari, the courtly former Assassin responsible for the city's government. All of them, one gradually realizes, shared some great, doomed adventure thirty years ago, centering on a revered figure named John Keel, who lies buried in the cemetery of Small Gods: "This cemetery of Small Gods was for the people who didn't know what happened next. They didn't know what they believed in or if there was life after death and, often, they didn't know what hit them. They'd gone through life being amiably uncertain, until the ultimate certainty had claimed them at the last. Among the city's bone orchards, the cemetery was the equivalent of the drawer marked MISC, where people were interred in the glorious expectation of nothing very much."

Just as the reader is growing tantalized about the lilac blossoms and John Keel, the Watch is called out to track a sociopathic killer named Carcer. When Sam and the vicious, sweet-talking murderer start to grapple on the rooftop of the Unseen University's great library of magic, an electrical storm strikes, and they are both catapulted back in time. Carcer escapes, and Sam awakens to find himself being patched up by Doctor Mossy Lawn, a good-hearted medico who usually treats the city's "seamstresses," i.e., prostitutes.

To hide his true identity, Sam gives a phony name. John Keel has been on his mind all day, and so it naturally comes tripping to his lips. At this point, nearly any reader will have guessed what's bound to happen next. As Sam later remarks to Lu-Tze, a Monk of History usually known as the Sweeper, "I'm probably going to end up being the sergeant that teaches me all I know, right?"

Though Pratchett pays homage to many of the elements of time-paradox stories, at its heart *Night Watch* is less about the multiverse and metaphysical matters than about the nature of community, human rights, and our obligations to others. Pratchett's political views are apparently those of any reasonable man: all ideologies tend to dehumanize people and distort reality. At best we should accept the task before us, or as the Omnian religion stresses: "We are here, and this is now." One improvises, muddles through. The privileged and the powerful, no matter what their professed allegiance, should almost never be trusted. "One of the hardest lessons of young Sam's life had been finding out that the people in charge weren't in charge. It had been finding out that governments were not, on the whole, staffed by people who had a grip, and that plans were what people made instead of thinking."

Ultimately, *Night Watch* builds to a grand climax during which revolution strikes the city, an assassin moves silently through the darkness of the Patrician's palace, and the working-class citizens of Ankh-Morpork barricade their streets and declare themselves "The People's Republic of Treacle Mine Road," their clarion calls "Truth! Justice! Freedom!" and "Reasonably Priced Love!" As violence and confusion escalate, Carcer finds himself in his element, but so does Sam Vimes, aka John Keel, who desperately tries to keep the peace and save lives. For a while he seems to be coping pretty well. But then the military is called out, and a bloodbath threatens, despite the best intentions of the earnest, if somewhat irresolute, Major Mountjoy-Standfast. When the major "was a boy, he'd read books about great military campaigns, and visited museums and had looked with patriotic pride at the paintings of famous cavalry charges, last stands, and glorious victories. It had come as rather a shock, when he later began to participate in some of these, to find that the painters had unaccountably left out the intestines. Perhaps they just weren't very good at them."

There are laughs in *Night Watch*, much repartee and even observations borrowed from Sterne, Shaw, and the aphorist Chamfort. The book's rapid, cinematic pace—quick cutting, multiple plotlines slowly converging—never flags. Yet few readers would regard *Night Watch* as zany or even particularly comic. Like earlier satirists, Pratchett is, at least in part, a moralist and, because of his vast readership, one with clout. More and more, he's using his wit and brilliant talent for characterization and dialogue to attack every kind of intolerance, especially the imbecilities and cruelties of the modern nation-state. His oeuvre has deepened, even as it's grown more tendentious and less sheerly funny. But Pratchett wants to make us feel and think as well as laugh.

As a result, *Night Watch* turns out to be an unexpectedly moving novel about sacrifice and responsibility, its final scenes leaving one near tears, as these sometime Keystone Kops, through simple humanity, metamorphose into the Seven Samurai. Terry Pratchett may still be pegged a comic novelist, but as *Night Watch* shows, he's a lot more. In his range of invented characters, his adroit storytelling, and his clear-eyed acceptance of humankind's foibles, he reminds me of no one in English literature so much as Geoffrey Chaucer. No kidding.

November 24, 2002

CRITICAL OBSERVERS

VII

In my hot youth I yearned to become a scholar-critic, someone like Erich Auerbach, author of the magisterial and majestic Mimesis: The Representation of Reality in Western Literature. But my mind doesn't possess a flair for synthesis, or such easy mastery of European languages. My own practice as a book reviewer is, in fact, relatively simple: I pay attention, and try to understand both what things mean and what they really mean. The Cornell scholar Lane Cooper summarized my views in his Strunk-and-White-like advice about term papers:

"Careful reading should precede all writing. The object of each paper or report should be thoroughness and truth. Literary finish is desirable."

Not surprisingly, then, I reflexively bristle at any "discourse" that sounds needlessly highfalutin or pretentious. Yet back in the 1970s I did study the French structuralists (in French even), presented seminars on Walter Benjamin, and bought the books of now forgotten theorists like Lucien Goldmann. But, in the end, my model of the true critic derives from Schopenhauer, of all people:

"We should comport ourselves with the masterpieces of art as with exalted personages—stand quietly before them and wait till they speak to us."

These days I prefer a criticism based on facts rather than on fancies, and ideally the reflections of an actual maker on his craft. So in this section Vladimir Nabokov talks about the great European masters of fiction, Randall Jarrell discusses poetry, eminences such as Edmund Wilson and Elizabeth Bishop gossip about their friends, who just happen to be major artists and thinkers. When Harold Bloom surveys the Western canon, he finds in it a mirror to his own plangent self.

It may seem odd to find the New Yorker journalist Joseph Mitchell in this company. But if criticism may be regarded as an act of truly focused attention, then Mitchell brought this same gimlet eye to the mad artists, hellfire preachers, eccentrics, lowlifes, and misfits of New York. And his prose can be as mournful as Bloom's, and even more eloquent. To me, he raises journalism to a meditative art form, wistful, funny, and wise.

THEORY OF PROSE

By *Viktor Shklovsky*
Translated from the Russian by Benjamin Sher

Nowadays, no one of sound mind and body is ever likely to read a book of literary theory. You'd need to warm up with a general course in linguistics, a graduate seminar in Heidegger, and a serious crossword puzzle just to think of peeking into a volume by the deconstructionist Jacques Derrida. As the late Marvin Mudrick once observed, "When the French get heavy, they make the Germans look like ballerinas."

All this is really too bad, because people who read are constantly making judgments about books. Umberto Eco is dull; Umberto Eco is delightful. Well, which is it? Dick Francis and Robert Ludlum keep writing the same thriller again and again. So what—and is this good or bad? Who's better: Stephen King or Thomas Pynchon? Alice Walker or Toni Morrison? A mystery "falls apart at the end." What does this mean? A certain writer's novels aren't "true to life." Should they be? The reviewer for the *Times* loves a new biography, the critic for the *Post* hates it: Is one right and the other wrong?

These are typical questions with no easily agreed-upon answers. But there are a few books—Northrop Frye's *Anatomy of Criticism*, William Empson's *Seven Types of Ambiguity*—that will help an interested reader better understand the dynamics of a novel, a poem, or a play. Among the best is Viktor Shklovsky's *Theory of Prose*, first published in 1925 but only now translated in its entirety.

Shklovsky (1893–1984) was one of the leaders of the Russian formalists, an association of literary theorists who flourished in the heady decade just after the Bolshevik Revolution. To a degree, the members of Opojaz (the Russian abbreviation for Society for the Study of Poetic Language) are comparable to the Anglo-American New Critics: both groups concentrated on how works of art are made. It is this focus on construction, on the machinery of a poem or novel, that makes them so useful to ordinary readers.

In *Theory of Prose* Shklovsky begins with the function of art: quite simply, art aims—in a phrase made famous by Joseph Conrad—to make us see. Through routine and repetition the world has grown gray and dull: people who live near the seashore no longer hear the waves. Automatization, writes Shklovsky, "eats away at things, at clothes, at furniture, at our wives, and at our fear of war." "And so, in order to return sensation to our limbs, in order to make us feel objects, to make a stone feel stony, man has been given the tool of art."

Art's chief technique for lifting the scales from our eyes is what is called, in Russian, *ostraniene*. This has been variously translated as "defamiliarization" or "estrangement," though here Benjamin Sher prefers the more positive "enstrangement." Art makes the familiar strange so that it can be freshly perceived. To do this it presents its material in unexpected, even outlandish ways: the shock of the new. Literary theory studies these distortions, the divergences that create "literariness."

Most of *Theory of Prose* outlines the various devices that an author uses to counteract automaticized perception. Tolstoy never calls a thing by its name; he describes the world as though it were seen for the first time: to the young Natasha (in *War and Peace*) an opera performance appears as two fat people singing in front of some painted cardboard trees. Anything that slows our reading also increases our perceptiveness, makes us reconsider reality, gives density to the world. Shklovsky therefore focuses on such slo-mo devices as parallelism, digression, the displacement and violation of time sequence, simultaneous planes of action, step-by-step construction, framing and inset stories, and the "laying bare" of narrative tricks (this in a chapter in praise of that proto-postmodern classic *Tristram Shandy*.) Along the way, Shklovsky himself details the structure of *Don Quixote*, *Little Dorrit*, and Sherlock Holmes whodunits. Like the two older brothers in traditional fairy tales, Dr. Watson is necessary to impede the action, to delay the hero's triumph, by offering the wrong solutions to the mystery.

As one might expect from an aesthetic based on enstrangement, Shklovsky views art as artifice, the novel as a "cluster of compositional devices." He writes, "No more of the real world impinges upon a work of art than the reality of India impinges upon the game of chess." Even more strongly, "In art, blood is not bloody. No, it just rhymes with 'flood.' " In his view a novel should be an object of aesthetic contemplation, rather than the "catalyst" of any visceral emotion. This is, I think, somewhat overstated: we ought to suffer with characters, feel their hopes and fears, else we will miss the necessary enchantment of storytelling, that temporary loss of self that makes for reading bliss. Still, it is crucial to remember, after the last page is turned, that whatever else it may be, a novel is a fabrication, a machine designed to play with our perceptions. It offers not a slice, but a simulacrum, of life. Some readers—but few writers—may bristle at such a diagrammatic view; Shklovsky completes their disillusion by adding that "every novel assures us of its reality. It is a common practice for every writer to compare his story with 'literature.' "

A rambling, digressive stylist, Shklovsky throws off brilliant aperçus on every page. (He writes this way naturally: see *Zoo,* his charming half-factual, half-philosophical epistolary novel set among Russian émigrés in 1922 Berlin.) In *Theory of Prose* Shklovsky reminds us, for instance, of the crucial distinction between plot and story: the latter contains the events that need to be related, while the former is the arrangement of those events for particular artistic ends. He remarks on the "flickering" effect of watching drama, how we move between losing ourselves in the stage action and being aware of the audience around us (actually "flickering" also characterizes reading). When Shklovsky discusses the dynamics of literary evolution—and it is essential that fictional styles change, lest they too become "automatic"—he notes that the movement is "not from father to son but from uncle to nephew." By this striking phrase he means that a new writer will tend to reject dominating literary fashions and take up those that have been despised or neglected. So Dostoevsky's religious-philosophic novels are built on the pattern of sensationalistic crime thrillers.

Here Shklovsky reminds us of his Soviet heritage, for what is this theory of warring styles and techniques but an image of the dialectic working itself out in literary history? But as with most of his pronouncements he never really followed this up. Boris Eichenbaum, Yury Tynyanov, Boris Tomashevsky, and other colleagues elaborated and consolidated many of his insights. All of them, though, were neglected for decades, only being rediscovered in the 1960s when their ideas provided an anvil for the hammering out of early French structuralism.

Sixty-five years after it first appeared, *Theory of Prose* remains an exciting book: like an architect's blueprint, it lays bare the joists and studs that hold up the house of fiction.

July 22, 1990

KIPLING, AUDEN & CO.:
ESSAYS AND REVIEWS, 1935–1964

By Randall Jarrell

Readers of Randall Jarrell's three previous books of essays need to know only one thing about *Kipling, Auden & Co.*: it's here. No more scrounging through libraries for back issues of *The Nation*, no more shoving dimes into copy machines to preserve and carry home one more review by that unmistakable voice. Everything left uncollected is now available in a volume that anyone with an interest in modern poetry will not for a moment hesitate to buy.

Perhaps no American literary figure of the past fifty years has been so loved and admired as Randall Jarrell (1914–1965). His friends included the poet-critics Allen Tate and John Crowe Ransom, philosopher Hannah Arendt, storyteller Peter Taylor, poet Robert Lowell, translator Robert Fitzgerald, artist Maurice Sendak. In his heyday, the 1940s and 1950s, Jarrell told the world exactly why Marianne Moore and Elizabeth Bishop, Wallace Stevens and William Carlos Williams, were great poets—and the world listened; he helped discover such young unknowns as Lowell, Adrienne Rich, John Berryman; he reinterpreted the canon of modern poetry, uncovering the sexually knowing, dark side of Frost, brilliantly highlighting the best of Whitman, pointing up the odd attractiveness of Robert Graves. Besides poetry, he cherished short stories, especially those of Turgenev, Chekhov, and Kipling, and he kept recommending Christina Stead's then neglected masterpiece, *The Man Who Loved Children*, until it was finally reissued. Some of his own poems, especially those of the last two collections, *The Women at the Washington Zoo* (1960) and *The Lost World* (1965), will live as long as people read books. Without question, he was, until his death in 1965, the wittiest, cruelest, most caring and brilliant reviewer of poetry in the country.

What makes Jarrell so exciting to read, even now that the new books he chronicled have been forgotten or become classics, is his dramatic, almost histrionic, style. Once heard, his voice is never forgotten. Its characteristic liveliness, his innocent malice, crackles in the first piece of *Kipling, Auden & Co.*, a roundup of recent fiction of 1935, written when Jarrell was twenty-one: "You know Lucy Gayheart only in the way you might know yourself, if you were badly forgetful, and not very introspective." In a time when criticism was already turning professional and academic, Jarrell spoke as a reader, one who tried to convey his enthusiasm for or his disappointment in a book as sharply as he could manage. His essays channel Oscar Wilde's wit through the critical perceptiveness of a William Empson. Never does his writing sound like that academese he described in his celebrated diatribe "The Age of Criticism" (in *Poetry and the Age*): "A great deal of the criticism might just as well have been written by a syndicate of encyclopedias for an audience of International Business Machines. It is not only bad or mediocre; it is dull; it is, often, an astonishingly graceless, joyless, humorless, long-winded, niggling, blinkered, methodical, self-important, cliché-ridden, prestige-obsessed, almost-autonomous criticism." Blessedly, Jarrell never lived to see the rise of decon-struction, though he did comment on its practitioners: "The really damned not only like Hell, they feel loyal to it."

In all of Jarrell's work—and it includes, besides poems and essays, the wit-tiest American novel I know (*Pictures from an Institution*), children's books, translations, anthologies—there is an abiding affection for and glorification of childhood, "the lost world." Jarrell revered those poets of childhood Wordsworth, Rilke, and Proust; his favorite prose form was the fairy tale or folktale; even his preferred drink was reportedly "milk and cookies." To his crit-icism the poet brought similar childlike qualities—a serious attentiveness and startling freshness. If we could all respond to books with the passion, wonder, and enthusiasm we felt when first hunched over *The Jungle Books*, or *The Adventures of Sherlock Holmes*, or *The Count of Monte Cristo*, or *The Wind in the Willows*, we would read as Randall Jarrell.

That is, of course, provided we could support our enthusiasm with an almost unerring taste and a wide learning—like the devil, Jarrell can quote scripture, or anything else, to his purpose. What's more important, he could pick out every nuance of a poem—he was one on whom nothing was lost—and state his final judgment unforgettably: "After reading 'Under Sirius,' another poet is likely to feel, 'Well, back to my greeting cards.'" Even better, at least for those like myself who relish the wicked, he could deliver, with apparent ingen-uousness, a single phrase that killed: Pound "has taken all culture for his province, and is naturally a little provincial about it. . . . Nothing can make me believe that Mr. Berryman wrote this himself, and is not just shielding some-one. . . . If poetry were nothing but texture, Dylan Thomas would be as good as any poet alive. . . . Oscar Williams' new book is pleasanter and a little quieter than his old, which gave the impression of having been written on a typewriter by a typewriter. . . . True poets, so to speak, turn down six things and take the seventh; [Rolfe] Humphries always takes the fifth or sixth." A certain poet, he says, used to "crowd so many effects into every line that reading a stanza was like having one's mouth stuffed with pennies." Edith Sitwell's verses "are meant to have an apocalyptic grandeur, but they sound as if Madame Blavatsky (just after reading Yeats and the Prophetic Books and an anthology of Christian mysticism) had written them for a Society of Latter-day Druids."

Once started, it is hard to stop quoting. Some people have described such remarks, usually found in the verse chronicles, as "symbolic murders." (Jarrell is especially cutting with poets who treat traditional forms as mausoleums, enclosing within them their own dead sonnets and pastorals.) But Jarrell felt it his duty to Poetry not only to praise the good but to excoriate the bad. "This essay," he once wrote of a dreadful play, "is not intended to be a sympathetic or comprehensive analysis of *The Fall of the City*; I came to bury it if I could manage to." Jarrell defends this practice in an appreciation of B. H. Haggin's music criticism: "Taste has to be maintained (or elevated if it's at too low a level to make maintenance bearable) and there is no other way of doing it."

Two long polemics in this volume, "The Taste of the Age" and "Poets, Readers and Critics" (both appeared originally in *A Sad Heart at the Supermarket*), are especially impassioned, exaggerated, and even shrill pleas for standards—for more catholic reading, for a cultivated life amid the media debris, ultimately for an audience for literature in an age of the magazine article. "The trouble," as Jarrell's Bat-Poet sadly observes, "isn't making poems, the trouble's finding somebody that will listen to them." Jarrell's prose itself—awhirl with quotation, witticism, comparison, and anecdote—requires a shared heritage to be fully appreciated, sometimes even to follow the jokes. "Much of the wit or charm or elevation of any writing or conversation with an atmosphere," Jarrell believes, "depends upon this presupposed, easily and affectionately remembered body of common knowledge; because of it we understand things, we feel about things as human beings and not as human animals."

Throughout his career, this reviewer, lecturer, poetry consultant to the Library of Congress (1956–58), and teacher called upon the faithful (and the apostate) to read widely, to read not merely what is intellectually or socially fashionable but also the great and good books, poems, stories of the past. "Read at whim!" he entreats—which is what he himself did. (Only Jarrell could remark, casually, in passing, "after you have read Kipling's fifty or seventy-five best stories . . .") Hardly a Real Critic at all (he had no theories of literature except that modernism was a bastardized romanticism), Jarrell was just someone who loved to talk about books. Yet his conversation was such that it encouraged a complicity between himself and his readers, so that after finishing pieces on Kipling or Malraux's *Voices of Silence*, or on Housman, Frost, and so many others, one wants to go directly to the library shelf and just read, read, read. All of Jarrell's criticism can be summarized as a description of the joy he had found in reading, followed by the command "Go thou and do likewise."

Probably Jarrell's most characteristic phrase is "Anybody who cares about poetry will want to read"—*Paterson* or Auden, this book or that writer. Elizabeth Bishop's *Poems* and Robert Graves's *Collected Poems*, he tells us excitedly, "are worth a long walk through sand, worth reading by the light of a bottle of lightning bugs, worth more than anybody is ever likely to pay for them." By the time Jarrell is through evoking the riches and wisdom in even a flawed work like Dylan Thomas's *Adventures in the Skin Trade*, we want to run to the bookstore anyway: "If you like Grimm or Hoffmann or Kafka, you will like some of these stories, I think; and people who can really write something, really imagine something, are not so common that we can let even their odd or slight works go unread." Occasionally, Jarrell will hook us with a bit of autobiography that makes a long, seemingly abstruse text sound positively charming: "I began reading *A Study of History* on a cold, snowy Ohio evening in the year 1937, and I've been reading it, off and on, ever since. If reading Proust is the best of vocations, reading Toynbee is the most delightful of avocations." A line of Rilke's—from a poem that Jarrell translated— best particularizes his quality as a critic: "Whenever I saw something that could ring, I rang."

In order to help people with their reading, Jarrell, the good teacher, likes to make up lists. But what lists! He is himself, as he says of Kipling and Gogol, "one of those writers who can make a list more interesting than any ordinary writer's murder." In *Kipling, Auden & Co.* the reader is treated to Jarrell's recommended summer reading for 1955 (Kant's *Critique of Judgement* is on it— and he makes you want to take it along to the beach), a selection of Frost's best poems (in a review of *Steeple Chase* that is a kind of short version of the landmark "To the Laodiceans"), the best lines from otherwise forgettable poets, the chief characteristics of modernist poetry.

Most of *Kipling, Auden & Co.* is composed of reviews and verse chronicles, but there are also pieces on Jarrell's passion for sports cars, an attack on abstract art, essays on some favorite and flawed critics (Yvor Winters judges "not from his experience but from his standards"), and five selections reprinted from *A Sad Heart at the Supermarket*. In short, a treasure trove.

Through everything Randall Jarrell chose to talk about shines a sensitive, supple intelligence, an original wit, a learned sympathy for writing of any sort of excellence. These qualities once led Adrienne Rich to say, oh so rightly, "For many of us, if asked that old question, 'To what or whom do you address your poems?' the truthful answer would be: 'To the mind of Randall Jarrell.'"

July 20, 1980

LECTURES ON LITERATURE

By *Vladimir Nabokov*
Edited by *Fredson Bowers*

"A book is like a trunk," explained the robust, middle-aged professor to his class, "tightly packed with things. At the customs an official's hand plunges perfunctorily into it, but he who seeks treasures examines every thread." In *Lectures on Literature* Vladimir Nabokov (1899–1977)—for it is he who leans over the lectern—not only fingers every thread in some half dozen novels, but also appraises the weave of the narrative and the pattern of the imagery, and with the eye of one who knows, points out the fine buttonholing in the first sentence and the satisfying zippering of the last.

Given annually at Cornell University from 1948 to 1958, these lectures were designed to introduce undergraduates to "Masters of European Fiction." Long promised in book format, they are now presented—posthumously, alas—in two volumes, this one devoted to English, French, and German writers, and its companion, appropriately, taking up the great Russians. Because Nabokov never ironed out all the creases and wrinkles in his nearly 2,000 pages of manuscript, the lectures needed some smooth editing and this was supplied by the notable textual authority Fredson Bowers; the resulting book is something of a surprise.

After the success of *Lolita* (American edition, 1958) Nabokov moved to Switzerland, rented rooms at a Montreux hotel, and grew inceasingly curmudgeonly in opinion, Olympian in pronouncement. What these lectures accomplish, especially in conjunction with Peter Quennell's recent *Vladimir Nabokov: A Tribute*, is the restoration of humanity to a writer who seemed to have traded his flesh and blood for an ivory tower. This Nabokov, the one drawing his diagrams on the blackboard in Goldwin Smith Hall, is as much art's passionate enthusiast as its cold practitioner—the warmth of his own Timofey Pnin tempering the *petitesse* of the card-index commentator of *Eugene Onegin*.

Oddly enough, the exuberant expertise of the *Lectures on Literature* most reminds me of Ezra Pound's humorous, iconoclastic *ABC of Reading*. Pound, making brilliant critical statements in his best Ol' Ez style, advocated close attention to a few key works and a particular focus on form; similarly Nabokov exalts fine-tooth reading, coupled with "a poet's patience and scholiast's passion." For Nabokov a great writer requires a great reader, one who completes the text, paying vigilant attention to details and patterns, actively accompanying the author as he plants and nourishes his images, themes, and metaphors. Such a reader must feel "with his spine" the thrill of artistry, must be able to locate the single adjective that ignites a description.

In the analyses of *Mansfield Park*, *Madame Bovary*, or *Swann's Way*, Professor Nabokov properly, though a bit harshly, scorns the human tendency to identify with a book's characters or to find ideas in the narrative. These are false critical practices, leading at their worst to a Charles Kinbote, that comic apotheosis of the bad reader, who discovers in the lines of *Pale Fire* his own history and misadventures. To avoid this, one must instead "caress the details," so as to reconstruct exactly the world imagined by the writer. Nabokov consequently begins the discussion of a novel by correcting translation errors, drawing key diagrams on the blackboard (a beetle for Kafka's "The Metamorphosis," the plan of Dr. Jekyll's house), and by setting forth the principal images and themes. These outlines, illustrations, and corrections are among the most facinating pages of this facinating book, glimpses into the painstaking care behind the interpretive mastery.

Very little, it seems, got by Nabokov. He notes that Gregor Samsa's name is pronounced Zamza, and that Kafka's description suggests that the unfortunate young man is transformed into a domed beetle (not a cockroach). In 1904, he remarks, Leopold Bloom was one of only 4,000 Jews in an Ireland with a population of 4.5 million people; no wonder the hero of *Ulysses* felt lonely. How does Nabokov know these things? Quite simply because he has worked them out, or looked them up. He might well have called his critical method what he titled an essay on translation—"The Servile Path." Specific information, he once asserted, is "the highest and to me most acceptable literary criticism." Indeed, Nabokov's antagonism to all "isms" and general ideas derives from his conviction that "they distract the student from direct contact with, the direct delight in, the quiddity of individual artistic achievement (which, after all, alone matters and alone survives)." As he notes in his talk on *Mansfield Park*, even "the color of Fanny Price's eyes and the furnishing of her cold little room are important." Some may scoff that such "trifles are not worth stopping at"; but Nabokov answers that "literature consists of such trifles."

Not surprisingly, the stress on the precise detail led this Cornell prof to set rather peculiar examination questions; one student recalls being asked to describe the wallpaper in Anna Karenina's bedroom. Students who supported a critical point with an exact and apposite quotation received a bonus of two points. Of course, Nabokov's class knew what to expect of a teacher who could remark that its members had "almost a month to reread *Anna Karenin* twice before the midterm."

From their foundation in the factual, Nabokov's lectures gradually spiral upward. Style, the inner structure of a book, mattered most. Naturally, the author of intricate constructs like *The Real Life of Sebastian Knight* and *Pale Fire* could speak of novelistic technique with indisputable authority, expertly picking out levels of narrative complexity. For instance, in his *Bleak House* commentary Nabokov invents the term "perry" to describe a character whose sole purpose is to witness an event so that it can be written about. Later he explains that Flaubert developed more elaborate techniques, such as the "counterpoint" used in the celebrated county fair episode in *Madame Bovary*: Rodolphe's flattery of Emma alternates with the announcement of agricultural prizes. A further refinement occurs in the complex synchronicity of *Ulysses*, where some half dozen or more events are taking place simultaneously. In all three cases, Nabokov modestly points out the limitations and advantages of the varying techniques, linking them to other elements of artistry in these "great fairy tales."

Nabokov's enthusiasm for literature, as his students Hannah Green and Alfred Appel Jr. recall in the Quennell volume, renews the passion for reading—which also explains why nearly four hundred undergraduates might sign up for his course. Moreover, the famous verbal playfulness leavens the punditry. In *Bleak House* Nabokov savors the subtle progression from the reverential "My Lord" (spoken to the Lord High Chancellor) through a lawyer's quickly uttered "Mlud" to the "mud" that oozes from the book's opening paragraphs. Likewise, Nabokov casually alludes to Lady Dedlock's "deadish wedlock" and to the "I of the story, its moving pillar."

Such insights, though they may seem mere epigram or wordplay, nearly always illuminate a theme or character. Charles Bovary, observes the creator of so many lovelorn heroes, truly finds in his wife, Emma, all the romance and glamor that Emma yearns for in her dreams. Sometimes, too, almost in spite of his theories of aloofness, Nabokov interrupts a cool examination to exclaim, for instance, that Dickens's Jarndyce is "one of the best and kindest human beings ever described in a novel," that *Dr. Jekyll and Mr. Hyde* yields "a delightful winey taste," or that Bloom taking breakfast to his wife is among the greatest scenes in literature.

Nabokov's faith—that art resides in the details out of which the author constructs his imaginary world—helps to explain his loathing for symbol seekers and for "the Viennese quack," that butt of the introductions to his Englished Russian novels. Freudians, especially those who flourished in the 1940s and 1950s, often applied a standardized set of simplistic interpretations to the images of literature (a cigar equals a phallus); but as Nabokov reiterates, "the abstract symbolic value of an artistic achievement should never prevail over its beautiful burning life," a life rooted in a carefully tilled fictional field.

For the same reason Nabokov here dismisses the historical interpretation of literature, along with biographical "human interest." The Narrator of *Swann's Way* may be called Marcel, but his life is not Proust's. It is worth recalling, however, that Edmund Wilson, so much identified with the historical-biographical approach to literature, was at this time Nabokov's close friend and the man who persuaded him to add Jane Austen and Charles Dickens to his course list. (It seems oddly appropriate, too, that "Bunny" and "Volodya" should fall out over theories of translation, versification, and editing; and more than ironic that Fredson Bowers, arranger of this volume, was the guiding force behind the editorial practices excoriated by Wilson in "The Fruits of the MLA.")

Because Nabokov assumes familiarity with the books discussed, these lectures are less introductions than brilliant afterwords, combining "the precision of poetry and the excitement of science." They deserve to be read and reread as privileged, nourishing, irreplaceable meditations on the art of fiction.

October 19, 1980

POSTSCRIPT: Over the years I have written frequently about Nabokov, pegging later essays to collections of his letters, to the lectures on Russian literature and *Don Quixote*, to Brian Boyd's masterly two-part biography. For me, Nabokov and Evelyn Waugh are the two most fascinating monsters—and masters—of twentieth-century English prose.

THE WESTERN CANON:
THE BOOKS AND SCHOOL OF THE AGES

By Harold Bloom

Surely I am not the only admirer of Harold Bloom—distinguished Yale professor, theorist of literary influence, and arguably the best-read man of our
time—who finds his autobiographical asides and Emersonian aphorisms the
most appealing, indeed frequently touching, aspect of his work. In his most
daunting books, chiefly those of the 1970s expounding and illustrating "the
anxiety of influence," Bloom may blithely speak of precursors and ephebes,
refer to creative reading as misprision, and employ such rebarbative terminol-
ogy as "clinamen," "kenosis," and "apophrades" to describe the oedipal struggle
between poets and their forebears. But no one, I suspect, has ever really used
the "six revisionary ratios."

What readers take away from books like *Agon, Poetry and Repression,* and
Figures of Capable Imagination are their strikingly self-confident formulations:
"A poetic 'text' . . . is a psychic battlefield upon which authentic forces struggle
for the only victory worth winning, the divinating triumph over oblivion."
"Criticism is the art of knowing the hidden roads that go from poem to poem."
"Strong reading doesn't ever ask: Am I getting this poem right? Strong reading
knows that what it does to the poem is right. . . . If you don't believe in your
reading, then don't bother anyone else with it, but if you do, then don't care
also whether anyone else agrees with it or not. If it is strong enough, then they
will come round to it anyway."

Such assertions have been characterized by Bloom's detractors—and these
are legion—as hyperbole, bombast, or "brutal over-simplifications." Certainly,
the man displays a taste for superlatives—the opening of chapter 19 of
Huckleberry Finn "must be the most beautiful prose paragraph yet written by
any American"—but even these strike me as bookish challenges to the reader:
think of a more beautiful paragraph, a better poem, if you can. In recent years
Bloom's essays have grown increasingly stippled with fleeting confessional

details that lend to his writing an Ecclesiastes-like melancholy. In *The Western Canon*, his latest book and a kind of popular summa of his critical career, Bloom admits that he weeps with Esther Summerson, the heroine of *Bleak House*; he tells us that Tolstoy's late novella *Hadji Murad* "is my personal touchstone for the sublime in prose fiction, to me the best story in the world"; he confesses that "as I go into old age" Wordsworth's "The Old Cumberland Beggar," "The Ruined Cottage," and "Michael" "move me more than virtually any other poems, by their exquisitely controlled pathos and their aesthetic dignity in representing individual human suffering." He even writes, with his own controlled pathos, "After a lifetime spent in teaching literature at one of our major universities, I have very little confidence that literary education will survive its current malaise."

Bloom is in his midsixties now, and he projects throughout *The Western Canon* a sorrowful resignation, a sense that all that he has most valued in life, the quiet reading and rereading of great books, will soon be lost, sacrificed to technological razzle-dazzle and the clamorous ideology of "cultural studies." Against feminists and new historicists and others in what he calls the School of Resentment, he offers a brave and poignant gesture of defiance: "To read in the service of any ideology is not, in my judgment, to read at all. The reception of aesthetic power enables us to learn how to talk to ourselves and how to endure ourselves. The true use of Shakespeare or of Cervantes, of Homer or of Dante, of Chaucer or of Rabelais, is to augment one's own growing inner self. Reading deeply in the canon will not make one a better or a worse person, a more useful or more harmful citizen. The mind's dialogue with itself is not primarily a social reality. All that the Western canon can bring one is the proper use of one's own solitude, that solitude whose final form is one's confrontation with one's own mortality."

Such mournful authority is irresistible, and it is this unswerving defense of reading, of "hard" reading, that transmutes *The Western Canon* into a work of power and plangency. The book itself—in some ways an expansion of Bloom's *Ruin the Sacred Truths*—consists mainly of chapter-length essays on twenty-six major writers, starting with Dante, Chaucer, and Shakespeare and going up to Proust, Woolf, Joyce, and Beckett. There are only a few surprises among the chosen: chiefly, Goethe's phantasmagoric *Faust Part II*; the welcome inclusion of the remarkable Portuguese poet Fernando Pessoa; perhaps an overenthusiasm for Ibsen. Explaining his selections, Bloom reiterates, "One breaks into the canon only by aesthetic strength, which is constituted primarily of an amalgam: mastery of figurative language, originality, cognitive power, knowledge, exuberance of diction."

Shakespeare is, of course, the ultimate touchstone. Where an ordinary poet, novelist, or dramatist might look to some relatively minor literary figure as a precursor, the canonical writer nearly always challenges Shakespeare, attempts to rewrite, subsume, or contradict him (seldom with any real success). Besides Shakespeare, the other element common to canonical texts, according to Bloom, is their strangeness, "a mode of originality that either cannot be assimilated, or that so assimilates us that we cease to see it as strange.... When you read a canonical work for a first time you encounter a stranger, an uncanny startlement rather than a fulfillment of expectations."

In each of his essays Bloom zeroes in on an author's particular strength. Shakespeare, he notes, discovered "self-overhearing," which allows his characters to grow by listening to themselves talk. In *Paradise Lost* our guide points to the poem's sheer "weirdness," then dissects the character of Satan as a blend of Iago and Hamlet. He shows how Dante's relationship with Beatrice parallels that of Don Quixote with Dulcinea. In Chaucer's Pardoner he adduces the precursor to Iago and to Lear's evil Edmund ("a genius, as brilliant as Iago, but colder, the coldest figure in all of Shakespeare"), just as he finds the Wife of Bath a prefiguration of his beloved Sir John Falstaff. Montaigne shows us that all "experience is passage"; *Faust Part II* is "the grandest monster movie ever directed at us" (and, improbably, "the central work of European Romanticism"); and so forth.

At times Bloom fails to rise to his usual spirited originality—he doesn't really have much to say about Pablo Neruda, and his views on Jane Austen, George Eliot, and Dickens strike me as perfunctory (or extravagant: the simpering Esther he calls "the most formidable consciousness in all of Dickens, indeed in all of British literature of the Democratic Age"), but then what could you expect from a chapter entitled, like a Ph.D. dissertation, "Canonical Memory in Early Wordsworth and Jane Austen's *Persuasion*." By far his most demanding pages explore the simple-seeming Emily Dickinson, "the best mind to appear among Western poets in nearly four centuries." Though most of *The Western Canon* is addressed implicitly to the common reader, in this Dickinson portion Bloom unwarrantably starts discoursing to graduate students: the poet "begins before she begins, by the implicit act of unnaming she performs upon the Miltonic-Coleridgean-Emersonian blank, with her hidden Shakespearean substitution. She next unpacks the trope by restoring its diachronic aspect; she knows implicitly more than we do about the temporal inadequacy of metaphor...." Happily, such passages are few. After all, Bloom also gleefully informs us that "Goethe shares with Walt Whitman (unlikely duo) the oddity that they are the only major poets before the twentieth century to deal overtly with masturbation; Whitman celebrates it, and Goethe is ironical." After discussing *Song of Myself*'s threefold persona, about which it is hard to generate much interest, the Yale professor suddenly wins the reader over by adding, "When I am alone and read aloud to myself, it is almost always Whitman, sometimes when I desperately need to assuage grief."

In his essays on twentieth-century figures Bloom proposes a Shakespearean reading of Freud (rather than the other way around); posits that Leopold Bloom may be Joyce's representation of the man Shakespeare; discusses Borges and belatedness, rightly noting the short-story writer's principal weakness: "his best work lacks variety"; and analyzes Beckett's *Endgame* in terms of *Hamlet* and *Lear*. Following his "Elegiac Conclusion," Bloom appends a list of several hundred works, sans annotation, that he counts as the heart of the Western canon. Here too the choices are, for the most part, the recognized classics. Only the last section may rankle or surprise, as Bloom makes some shrewd guesses about the writers of today who may become canonical. To my eye a few entries on this contemporary list betray signs of friendship and private enthusiasm—but why not? A critic, as Bloom wrote twenty years ago about Walter Pater, "gives us a vision of art through his own unique sensibility." One values idiosyncrasy, as well as insight. Bloom reminds us that when he thinks of Samuel Johnson and the small handful of literary critics he most admires, what he recalls is not their doctrines but their "vehement and colorful personalities."

Though the overt antagonists of Bloom's canon are the currently vocal exponents of gender, cultural, and ethnic studies, the covert figure lurking in these pages is surely T. S. Eliot, the strong critical precursor. In his long career Eliot truly redefined the canon, promoting the metaphysical poets, downplaying Milton, dismissing Shelley, reevaluating the Elizabethan dramatists other than Shakespeare, espousing the mild doctrine of "tradition and the individual talent," emphasizing a quietistic religious sensibility. Against the Anglo-Catholic conservative royalist, Bloom, the Jewish Gnostic aesthete, has long done battle, countering nearly all of Eliot's judgments: championing the Romantic poets, especially Shelley and Blake; designating Milton as the defining influence on English poetry; revealing that "tradition" hides a psychic arena where new poets battle old masters to clear space for their own creative work; making Shakespeare, rather than Dante, the single key figure for Western literature; detailing the spread of Gnostic cults (what he has called "the American religion"); preferring the performing self to the austerely buttoned-down. Even in their choice of bookish diversion, these two differ, Eliot being a fan of detective stories, Bloom of fantasy and science fiction. Yet antithetical though they may seem, I sense that the two have more in common than Bloom would care to admit. But that's another story.

Certainly *The Western Canon* is an impressive work, uneven in places and repetitious, but also deeply, rightly passionate about the great books of the past. If only readers and teachers and scholars would take its plea to heart and turn away from the shiny, meretricious tinsel on the best-seller lists and in so many of our classrooms. But will anyone listen? Like Bloom, we should all be worrying about the fate of reading in our disjointed time.

September 25, 1994

POSTSCRIPT: See this book's Coda for "Classrooms and Their Discontents," which addresses some of these same issues about the study of literature in our time.

UP IN THE OLD HOTEL

By Joseph Mitchell

MY EARS ARE BENT

By Joseph Mitchell

Sometimes when it's a damp November in my soul, I pick up *McSorley's Wonderful Saloon* or *Old Mr. Flood* and read a few pages. They never fail to brighten my mood. Joseph Mitchell wrote most of his *New Yorker* profiles of outcasts, obsessives, and holy fools more than fifty years ago, but they provide a lot more than old-fashioned entertainment. In fact, Mitchell shows us how to endure and enjoy this heartbreaking world of ours.

"When I have time to kill," he wrote in a typical piece called "Hit on the Head by a Cow," "I sometimes go to the basement of a brownstone tenement on Fifty-ninth Street, three-quarters of a block west of Columbus Circle, and sit on a rat-gnawed Egyptian mummy . . . with Charles Eugene Cassell, an old Yankee for whose bitter and disorderly mind I have great respect. Mr. Cassell has Negro, French, Portuguese, and English blood. . . . About fifteen years ago, after he got too contrary to hold down a steady job, he took out some of his savings and opened a museum—Captain Charley's Private Museum for Intelligent People."

From the first, it seems, Mitchell was drawn to visionaries and pariahs whom the world had passed by and yet who managed to invest their lives with passion, generosity, hard living, and flamboyance. Gypsies, carnival freaks, panhandlers, evangelists of all sorts, watermen, calypso singers, deaf-mutes, Mohawk Indians, people who run seafood restaurants and old saloons, people who rake clams, live in caves . . . Most of them seem more admirable than anyone who has ever graced an issue of *Vanity Fair* or stood before the crowd at a political convention. They are not, Mitchell once warned, "little people": "They are as big as you are, whoever you are." Today they seem almost like figures from the Old Testament, men and women of power and majesty. As Mitchell says of the Gypsies, they "look like they've thought a lot about the way life is, they and their forefathers before them, and they don't see anything funny in it."

Up in the Old Hotel gathers nearly all of Mitchell's mature journalism—*Joe Gould's Secret* (1965), *The Bottom of the Harbor* (1960), as well as *Old Mr. Flood* (1948), *McSorley's Wonderful Saloon* (1943), and a few previously uncollected pieces. It makes such exhilarating reading that those new to Mitchell will hardly be able to turn the book's 700 pages fast enough. But it's also so good that anyone susceptible to Mitchell's bittersweetness—he might be called a stoic comedian—will want to linger over every one of those pages.

In most of Mitchell's early work New York appears as an enchanted realm, a Baghdad-on-the-Hudson of magic shops, haunted hotels, secret societies. The wandering reporter encounters beggar kings and Bowery queens, eavesdrops on prophets of doom, hears an unlikely bum recite "Hiawatha" in the language of seagulls, and even learns the secret of the elixir of life. He's like a wedding guest who keeps running into one Ancient Mariner after another.

Mitchell's plain prose unobtrusively employs every resource of art: symbolism (the saloon as womb and refuge), the precise recording of idiosyncratic speech, intricate time shifts, a mixture of high and low styles, lots of humor and pathos. In essence, Mitchell isn't simply a journalist doing a job; he's a romantic pilgrim, a walker in the city and along shorelines and through old cemeteries, like Leopold Bloom in one of his favorite books. He drinks at McSorley's, eats at the Fulton Fish Market, sits a spell with cranks and retired fishermen mainly for one reason: he likes these things, admires and even identifies with these people. Old Mr. Flood, for instance, suggests a semiautobiographical portrait of the artist as an old man, while the panhandler Joe Gould eventually grows into Mitchell's Dostoevskyan double.

From people so battered by time and fate comes the wisdom of experience, frequently punctuated by recollections of a lost golden age when, in the words of an old black bricklayer, "there were flowers in every yard, and rosebushes, and the old women exchanged seeds and bulbs and cuttings with each other. . . . People looked after things in those days. They patched and mended and made do, and they kept their yards clean, and they burned their trash. And they taught their children how to conduct themselves." A smart librarian would categorize *Up in the Old Hotel* as wisdom literature, like Ecclesiastes. Here, for example, Mr. Flood reflects on love: "I'm ninety-four years . . . and my mind is just a turmoil of regrets. . . . In the summer of 1902 I came real close to getting in serious trouble with a married woman, but I had a fight with my conscience and my conscience won, and what's the result? I had two wives, good, Christian women, and I can't hardly remember what either of them looked like, but I can remember the face of that woman so clear it hurts, and there's never a day passes I don't think about her, and there's never a day passes I don't curse myself. 'What kind of a timid, dried up, weevily fellow were you?' I say to myself. 'You should've said to hell with what's right and what's wrong, the devil take the hindmost. You'd have something to remember, you'd be happier now.' She's out in Woodlawn, six feet under, and she's been there twenty-two years, God rest her, and here I am, just an old, old man with nothing left but a belly and a brain and a dollar or two."

In the pantheon of *New Yorker* writers Joseph Mitchell is among the least widely known but, I think, the most haunting. There aren't many books that can make you reflective yet happy just to be alive, but this is one.

August 6, 1992

Eight or nine years ago, the late Joseph Mitchell brought out *Up in the Old Hotel*, an omnibus of his four major collections of *New Yorker* profiles: *McSorley's Wonderful Saloon*, *Old Mr. Flood*, *The Bottom of the Harbor*, and *Joe Gould's Secret*. To most people who work in what's been called, perhaps oxymoronically, literary journalism, that book is pretty much the equivalent of, say, Dashiell Hammett's mystery *The Maltese Falcon* or Alfred Bester's science fiction classic *The Stars My Destination*: a touchstone, the best in show, a work of art transcending, or even justifying, its genre. In New York's panhandlers and street evangelists, watermen and con artists, Mitchell discovered both an Old Testament grandeur and a no-nonsense acceptance of the world's fundamental bittersweetness.

Little wonder that Mark Twain and James Joyce were Mitchell's two favorite writers: all three possess a complex sense of humor, admiration for ordinary suffering humanity, perfect pitch for spoken English, a particular sympathy for the insulted and outcast, and a genius for making people come alive on the printed page.

Those who love Joseph Mitchell's writing—essentially anyone who's ever read one of his pieces—have always wished he'd written more. During the last thirty years of his long life, he never published anything. But the legendary reporter had produced one book not included in *Up in the Old Hotel*, never reprinted, and almost impossible to find: a collection of his youthful newspaper features from the *Herald Tribune* and the *World Telegram* called *My Ears Are Bent* (1938). Copies would occasionally surface in the used-book market and be snapped up for a couple of hundred dollars apiece. After years of searching, I finally found one on the shelves of the Duke University Library, checked it out, and spent an hour photocopying every blessed page.

But you won't have to do that.

This new issue of *My Ears Are Bent* reprints the original but also amplifies it by including a few related period pieces. True, this early reporting lacks some of the wistful, personal touches in Mitchell's mature journalism, and each mini-profile tends to end with an overly obvious flourish (usually some flashy comeback or pat statement), but the voice is still the same, as is the fascination with eccentrics, criminals, isolatos, and flamboyant characters in general. "Once I was working on a series of stories about voodoo and black magic in New York City. With an assistant district attorney, I had a long talk with a Negro streetwalker. From the vague story she told the Vice Squad detective who put her in the pokey the D.A. suspected that she had been used as an altar in a black mass. She wasn't much help because she saw nothing particularly unusual in her experience. Finally, exasperated, the D.A. asked her why she became a prostitute in the first place, and she said, 'I just wanted to be accommodating.'"

Throughout his career Mitchell practiced *ars celare artem*—the art that conceals art. He can make an ordinary sentence ache or surprise by choosing just the right word, and seldom a fancy one. Neither is he afraid to risk sentimentality. Take the time he and a group of reporters were bivouacked in a hotel in New Jersey, covering the trial of Bruno Hauptmann, who had been accused of kidnapping Charles Lindbergh's baby son. "One stormy night Thomas Benton, the painter, came out. He had been sent to make sketches at the trial by my newspaper. When he saw our oak fire he pulled off his shoes and sat down in front of it and talked until midnight about the beauty of the United States."

My Ears Are Bent offers sketches of legendary period figures like Father Divine, the burlesque queen Ann Corio, wrestling impresarios, voodoo cultists, the dapper cartoonist Peter Arno, the youthful William Steig (yes, the creator of *Shrek*, and still with us nearly sixty years later), and even George Bernard Shaw. In Mitchell's interview with an oyster-fishing boat captain, who eats dozens of oysters each day, one can detect some of the elements that went into the creation of his later fish fancier Old Mr. Flood. There's even a summer ode to New York's Depression-era East Side: "In front of all the grimy stationery-candy stores are little pot-bellied slot machines full of sunflower seed. And the pushcart men have pans full of sliced coconut meat. The white slices float in the ice water. And children jump into the concrete troughs at which truck horses are watered and cool themselves. And kids with shoe shine boxes slung over their skinny shoulders make their headquarters on the stoop of the Bank of the United States, at Allen and Delancey Streets. The windows are dusty, and papers are scattered about the floor inside, and the head bankers are in jail."

To read *My Ears Are Bent* is to relive the 1930s New York of newsreels and speakeasies and immigrant dreams. In its pages, Harlem is still in vogue and Coney Island crowded and the city itself an Arabian Nights realm of splendors and curiosities: "One after noon I went to see Mr. Jack Pfefer, an importer of freaks for the wrestling business. . . ." Joseph Mitchell, reporter, prose stylist, and observer of life, remains that vanished world's Scheherazade. It's good to see this book back in print.

June 10, 2001

ONE ART:
LETTERS BY ELIZABETH BISHOP

Selected and edited by Robert Giroux

Poets, those querulous and sensitive souls, can hardly agree about anything. Should a poem mean or be? Does inspiration come from the Muse or the news? Must a poet descend into the foul rag-and-bone shop of the heart or ought he to fashion monuments of unaging intellect? Can he do both? Here a poetic school espouses classical iambs, there another champions confessional "I am's." Some swear by John Ashbery, others swear at him.

Yet rising above these ancient dusty quarrels, there shines forth, like shook foil, the indisputed eminence of Elizabeth Bishop (1911–1979). No other post-war American poet is so generally admired, so deeply revered. Children study "The Fish," "The Man-Moth" has passed into myth, and at least a dozen Bishop poems are masterpieces, quiet miracles of rare device. In a noisy age Bishop's refusal of all grandiloquence even affords her a kind of holy power: after the whirlwind a still, small voice.

In tone Bishop always remains attractively dispassionate, her diction uncluttered and natural, her seriousness matched by a springlike freshness. With a deceptively simple phrase she may insinuate pages of meaning, hinting at emotions held in check just beneath the surface of her words: "We'd rather have the iceberg than the ship"; "Should we have stayed at home and thought of here?"; "The art of losing isn't hard to master." Bishop never wrote much—the last of her four volumes, *Geography III*, contains only ten poems, none long, nearly all perfect—and she was known to spend years getting every line right. She worked on "The Moose" for more than sixteen years. Little wonder that this shy and lonely woman now seems a kind of poetic Flaubert, an exemplary figure of artistic patience and mastery.

That Bishop is also a superb writer of prose—see the perfectly controlled panic and wistfulness of her story "In the Village" or the introduction to *The Diary of Helena Morley*—only adds to the pleasures of *One Art*, her selected letters. As a correspondent, Bishop sticks to the resolutely personal: she writes to close friends about her travels, reading (impressive and varied), asthma attacks, drinking. Her descriptions, especially, are marvels of evocative exactness. "Ships go by all the time, like targets in a shooting gallery, people walk their dogs—same dogs same time, same old man in blue trunks every morning with two Pekinese at 7 A.M.—and at night the lovers on the mosaic sidewalks cast enormous long shadows over the soiled sand."

But she also likes sharing amusing anecdotes and means for her letters to be enjoyable: "The local bookshop is run by an Englishman and his wife, who is about twenty years older than he, very cute really, with dyed bright pink hair. They play chess in the corner and very much dislike being interrupted by a customer. The other day a man I knew went in to buy a book and asked for it timidly. Hugh, the Englishman, said, 'Good Heavens, man! Can't you see I'm about to make a move?' "

A perfectionist as a poet, Bishop turns out to be similarly demanding of her publishers: for her first book she writes, with girlish excitement, "it seems to me that the Baskerville monotype 169 E, eleven-point, would be perfect—but eleven point might be too big—it might make too many run-over lines— maybe they could try and see." She also wonders if she might have "a glazed binding. And could it be dark gray? I think that quite a dark gray with a gilt *North & South* down the back would look nice, don't you—and if gilt is not possible maybe a dark blue lettering? Looking over the ms. as a whole it seems to me a slightly squarer than usual book would. . . ." Later, she complains about the lack of holiday advertising "since people do often give poetry for Christmas gifts, I believe." As she observes elsewhere in this volume, "I am quite fiendish about trivialities."

That's good advice for any would-be writer, and bits of inspirational shoptalk crop up periodically in these pages. "I can't tell a lie even for art, apparently; it takes an awful effort or a sudden jolt to make me alter facts." At her most passionate she even lays into her friend Robert Lowell when he alters and misrepresents his ex-wife Elizabeth Hardwick's correspondence (in his collection *The Dolphin*). "One can use one's life as material—one does, anyway—but these letters—aren't you violating a trust? If you were given permission—if you haven't changed them. . . . etc. But art just isn't worth that much." Obviously, Bishop's selected letters is the sort of book that's easy to pick up and hard to put aside. Read one page, and you'll want to read them all.

Robert Giroux, the poet's editor in her later years, supplies an excellent introduction that doubles as a compact biography. Reared by grandparents after her father died and her mother went mad, Bishop grew up a kind of orphan and in some ways remained one all her life. At Vassar she made friends with Mary McCarthy, began a long-term relationship with her classmate Louise Crane, and discovered the work of the poet Marianne Moore. After abandoning thoughts of either a medical or musical career, Bishop started to compose stories and poems, sending the latter to Moore for criticism. Relying on a trust fund, which gradually diminished as inflation increased, the young litterateur first traveled to Europe, then settled in Key West (1939–48). Her first book, *North & South*, garnered a rave from Randall Jarrell, and through him she met Robert Lowell (who years later confessed that he wanted to marry her). In 1949 Lowell smooth-talked Bishop into spending a melancholy year as the consultant in poetry at the Library of Congress. A happier time followed: in 1951, while on a trip to Brazil, Bishop unexpectedly fell ill and soon after fell in love. A wealthy Brazilian aristocrat, Lota Soares, whisked the American writer away to a villa an hour and a half from Rio and there, barring a few trips abroad, the couple passed the next fifteen years. Eventually, though, pressures of illness and overwork led to Lota's increasing irritability and an eventual breakdown. Following doctor's orders Bishop returned to New York. When Lota was finally allowed to visit, she seized the opportunity to commit suicide by taking an overdose of her medication.

After her beloved's death, Elizabeth Bishop slowly remade a kind of life, gradually finding new companions and eventually taking a series of teaching jobs to earn money for her old age. Having received the 1956 Pulitzer Prize (for *North & South* and *A Cold Spring*), the 1968 National Book Award (for *The Complete Poems*), and the 1976 Neustadt Prize for her life achievement, she stood high among the most honored and esteemed literary figures in America. Besides Moore, Jarrell, and Lowell, friends included the poets James Merrill, Frank Bidart (her literary coexecutor), and May Swenson (who at one time typed her manuscripts), as well as the pianists Robert Fizdale and Arthur Gold. Many of the letters in *One Art* are addressed to these distinguished artists. Yet Bishop also wrote faithfully throughout the decades to her elderly aunts and old college friends. She died suddenly of a cerebral hemorrhage in 1979 at the age of sixty-eight.

Letters reflect the soul, and Bishop's alternate between a restless need to travel and a desire for domestic security. But on the road or at home, reading is crucial to this self-described "minor female Wordsworth." She tells us that Defoe's "*Plague Year* and Bede are my two favorite books." Darwin is one of her heroes, and George Herbert an inspiration. No day without its book might be her watchword. "I have just started to read [Nietzsche's] *The Birth of Tragedy*— just the first chapter, which I like, but"—and this is the wonderful touch—"it is a little more popular than his other books, isn't it?" *Charlotte's Web*, she tells Marianne Moore, is just "so AWFUL," later recommending Huizinga's

Erasmus. To other friends she writes, "Didn't you like Robert Penn Warren—in spite of the accent? I've always been very enamored of that red hair and that blue glass eye, although I can't stand those novels with round-breasted heroines and wicked heroes—just like *Gone with the Wind* with metaphysical footnotes."

Down in Brazil she grouses that the airmail *New York Times* "only gives summaries of the lead reviews which, as you know, are always of books like *Republicanism—A Triumphant Conflict,* or something by John Steinbeck." She turns to George Saintsbury's three-volume history of prosody ("marvelous"), Paul Klee's journals, Chekhov's account of his visit to the prison island of Sakhalin. To Lowell she recommends "a superb book—but you probably know it—Marchand's *Memoirs of Napoleon?* If not, do read it immediately." In another letter she slyly suggests "a grim little book by Melanie Klein, *Envy and Gratitude.*" She devours the letters of everyone: Coleridge, Carlyle, Keats, Hart Crane, Millay. She also tries to stay up-to-date. "My publisher," she notes, "has now sent me all of Miss Sontag's works and I'm trying hard—think she knows too much for me, however—about Hegel and all the latest French Thoughts." In her last years she admires the work of Seamus Heaney and Derek Walcott. All of us should read so widely and so well.

Bishop once described herself as the loneliest person in the world. Maybe so. But she took her loneliness and put it to work—making airy, dreamlike poems about our common doubts and sorrows. These letters, funny, touching, and occasionally harrowing, remind us that this great poet was an altogether remarkable woman as well.

May 1, 1994

POSTSCRIPT: My taste in poetry tends toward the classical—I like wit, formality, polish, and clarity. W. H. Auden ranks high among my intellectual heroes. I haven't included reviews of contemporary poets in *Bound to Please,* because I was seldom able to write at any length about their books, being usually obliged to cover them in roundups. For what it's worth, I think the finest poets of the past forty or so years include Elizabeth Bishop, Anthony Hecht, L. E. Sissman, Howard Nemerov, Philip Larkin, James Merrill, and Geoffrey Hill. Oddly enough, it may seem to some, I also admire the New York school of Frank O'Hara, John Ashbery, James Schuyler, and Kenneth Koch: their wordplay and wit more than compensates for their occasional self-indulgence.

THE SIXTIES:
THE LAST JOURNAL, 1960–1972

By Edmund Wilson
Edited by Lewis M. Dabney

Like Virginia Woolf and the science fiction writer Philip K. Dick, Edmund Wilson (1895–1972)—critic, journalist, and man of letters—hasn't let death slow him down. Sure, twenty years ago at the age of seventy-seven he may have departed for that great Reading Room in the sky, but the old pro still manages to produce a book every few years. With a little help, of course. His widow, Elena, compiled his *Letters on Literature and Politics;* Leon Edel brought out his journals for the 1920s, 1930s, 1940s, and 1950s; Simon Karlinsky arranged his effervescent and eventually bitter correspondence with Vladimir Nabokov; and now Lewis M. Dabney—Wilson's authorized biographer—has edited *The Sixties,* the aged eagle's final diaries, memoranda, and travel notes.

For the general reader, these newly published journals, along with those of the 1950s, are probably Wilson's best. *The Twenties* humanized the Olympian critic by detailing his sexual life and preferences—he never met a foot he didn't like—but otherwise alternated between dull accounts of desperate pleasure seeking and even more tiresome pages of pointillist place description. In those early pages "Bunny"—the famous nickname he grudgingly learned to live with—hardly ever alludes to books or writers, reserving all his literary chatter and frequent chiding for his voluminous correspondence. But with the years Wilson's notebooks improve: as he grows famous, he continually seeks out those who are truly great, or at least interesting; and as he practices, with increasing efficiency, the journalist's rule of waste not, he relies more and more on his diaries as the draft material for his compact volumes of reportage and travel. *The Forties,* for instance, offers less polished, but sometimes franker, versions of the gossip and anecdotes of *Europe without Baedeker.*

Much of *The Sixties* was similarly plundered for *Upstate,* Wilson's admired record of visits to his family's old stone house in Talcottville, New York. As one of the last great representatives of the Wasp ascendancy, Wilson valued tradition, family, the puritan values of hard work and deserved accomplishment. As a result, the mind that grappled with the intricacies of the Dead Sea Scrolls also reveled in the small-town ways of a dozen or so Talcottville friends and relatives, many of whom readers will have trouble keeping straight. (Along with an exemplary introduction, Dabney provides a useful thirty-page biographical appendix, where, for instance, the Loomis sisters, Huldah and Gertrude, share a page with the poet Robert Lowell, the culture critic Dwight Macdonald, and the writer/ex-wife Mary McCarthy: Wilson, ever the embattled critic, would argue with the Loomises about "who had the best lady-slipper orchid or recipe for chocolate icing.") Among the Talcottville regulars only Mary Pcolar really stands out. The fat septuagenarian flirted shamelessly with this young married woman who taught him Hungarian, drove his car, and typed his manuscripts. Indeed, whenever two or three Wilson scholars are gathered together, the question will always come up: Did the author of *I Thought of Daisy* and "The Princess with the Golden Hair" sleep with Mary Pcolar?

If we can trust *The Sixties*, the answer is not quite. Once the pair fell into some serious petting on the sofa, but "when I told her that I wanted to see the rest of her body, she said with conscious humor . . . 'I'm perfectly beautiful, but no.'" Decades may have passed since the randy 1920s, but sex continues to play a major, even X-rated, role in Wilson's journals, second only to reading and conversation, slightly ahead of observations about gout, heart disease, and dentures. It is oddly impressive, if disconcerting, to learn that America's leading man of letters was still visiting porno movies and girlie shows in his seventies, applauding enthusiastically those acts that met his discriminating standards. At seventy-five, no less, Don Edmund initiates brief liaisons with two women identified here only as Z and O. Once, in bed with Z, he recalls, "We discussed pubic hair. What was it for? I suggested protection." (That earnest, investigative tone is characteristically Wilsonian.) Another time Wilson pleasures O with some remarkably intimate attentions in the deserted bar of the Princeton Club. At such moments you tend to feel as though Dr. Johnson were periodically transforming himself, before your wondering eyes, into his priapic alter ego, the lecherous Mr. Boswell.

In the diaries and essays, as seemingly in his life, Wilson prefers to stay on the surface of things, refusing those long looks within that might lead to despair, avoiding any semblance of soul-searching. He might be ravenous for learning, languages, and women; but the spiritual, except for natural beauty, is a closed book for him—he makes fun of the Canadian novelist Marie-Claire Blais's obsession with *angoisse* (angst), thinks Kafka overrated, can't understand the appeal of fantasy and mystery. Even with death stopping by for occasional chats—increased debility, shortness of breath, small heart attacks—he betrays no qualms about his atheism ("the story of Christ is to me a myth, and I have no clue at all in my own experience to the people who talk about loving God and God's love for the human race"). As a diarist he frequently resembles a camera attached to a pen, and excels at tart social observation: Cyril Connolly "has a queer mixture of lordly courtesy with boorishness and infantilism." Exactly right.

Not all that surprisingly, Wilson treats the books he reads as he does women: they are for use, solace, and amusement. Clearly, the force that through the green fuse drives the flower is the same that powers his pen. Yet this aggressive machismo is also Wilson's principal weakness as a critic: he can seem almost too strong a reader, and you sometimes wonder if he ever gives a book an even chance.

But this all sounds a bit too harsh. Edmund Wilson may not inspire warmth, but he does inspire. When in *The Triple Thinkers* he discusses John Jay Chapman or Henry James you know he's checked out everything in the library by or about the writer. Thousands of pages will have been smoothly filtered down into crisp paragraphs, and the paragraphs built up into an essay that is at once personal, entertaining, and authoritative. His longer books encompass larger matters with equal mastery and self-assurance: *Axel's Castle* defines modernism in guided tours of Yeats, Joyce, and company; *To the Finland Station* enshrines the heroic age of socialism, likening the death of Marx at his desk to that of a Roland at Roncesvalles; and *Patriotic Gore: Studies in the Literature of the American Civil War*, despite longueurs and a scanting of the issue of slavery, nearly is, as Alfred Kazin once called it, an American Plutarch's *Lives*.

When *The Sixties* opens, all these are behind Wilson. Now he works on a smaller scale, bringing out new editions of old books, settling unpaid taxes, reading for pleasure, suffering the indignities of age, remembering the past. He glances casually into a photo album belonging to the daughter of Scott Fitzgerald and at once "begins to feel pangs from way back. I remember how Scott, before he married Zelda, was telling me about her in New York. . . ." To the young director Mike Nichols he admits that, when doubtful about the quality of his work, he sometimes gets up "at four o'clock in the morning to read old reviews of my books." But, he notes elsewhere, when he looks into those books, "it seems to me that I am trying to reread a once favorite writer that I am beginning to see through."

Despite recurrent quarrels with his fourth wife, Elena, he declares "that making love to her has been the most wonderful thing in my life"—and then extolls her physical graces in embarrassing detail. Other embarrassments await: at a party "I had such an urgency to pee that I had to go to the back of the house and wasn't able to hold out till a spurt had partly wet my pants." Here is old age as it really is, though this incident is crowned by a grotesquely touching detail: "In the toilet was a young mouse desperately swimming around. I picked it up and put it on the brick walk." Increasingly, Wilson's own past life begins to grow mythic, fuzzy; "it is as if these things had never happened, and I have difficulty in believing they did." But he soldiers on. In an effort to seduce his dentist's wife—surely a mistake, from every viewpoint—he accompanies her to a roadside snack bar, where he drinks Ripple and orders an inedible sausage sandwich.

When Wilson finally gets his library in order, any fiction reader will know that the end must be near. As his heart condition worsens, the stubborn old goat refuses a pacemaker. He continues to drink a pint of whisky most nights, "drools" along in his diary, lustily eyes up every woman he meets. Fate being kind, he dies as he lived, with his worktable pushed up near so he could reach it from his bed, a volume of Housman's last poems at his side.

Once, when referring to a new study of the Dead Sea Scrolls, Edmund Wilson wrote, "I have bought the book and am going to read it." This might be the watchword of his life: he could well have been referring to almost any book, of any age. Imperfect in so many ways, Edmund Wilson was nonetheless a literary journalist who will last, an amazing man, and, of all the critics of his time, the wisest and justest and best.

July 4, 1993

POSTSCRIPT: To my regret, this essay was cut by about a quarter of its original length for space reasons—such are the exigencies of journalism. In the deleted (and now unrecoverable) paragraphs I spoke more expansively about the importance of Wilson as a critic, emphasizing his appetite for all kinds of books, his clear, forceful prose, and his emblematic position as a man of letters. While contemporary critics as insightful as Philip Rahv and Cleanth Brooks have already faded from canonical memory, Wilson survives—if just barely. But I own all his books, and they stand on a shelf next to those of William Empson, Northrop Frye, Hugh Kenner, Guy Davenport, and Cyril Connolly. I began reading Wilson as a freshman in college—see my memoir *An Open Book*—and continue to reread him to this day.

UNITED STATES:
ESSAYS, 1952–1992

By Gore Vidal

Whom the gods wish to destroy, observed Cyril Connolly, they first call promising. But in Gore Vidal's case the lords of Olympus have apparently been fast asleep at fortune's wheel. Over the years, nearly half a century now, the once precocious twenty-year-old author of *Williwaw* (1946) has triumphed in almost everything but electoral politics: his winning name may currently be glimpsed inside the envelope for best historical novelist (*Julian, Burr, Lincoln*), most exhilarating essayist, favorite talk-show guest (intellectual division), wittiest gadfly, and least appreciated Cassandra (political section). Even his artistic failures, mainly cinematic, have the stuff of legend in them (the *Myra Breckenridge* film, the X-rated epic *Caligula*). To such lavish plenty one should also add a loyal companion of many years, a circle of friends that loops from Paul Bowles to Paul Newman and, best of all, a book-lined apartment in Rome.

Surely, the gods must be crazy to have permitted this 1940s enfant terrible—not merely showered but soaked with looks, brains, and personality—to have grown up into so admired and envied a graying eminence. On the other hand, perhaps Zeus and company are simply repaying Vidal for services rendered. He has more than once scourged the "Christers," repeatedly set forth the logic and beauty of paganism, and faithfully lived according to the gospel of Petronius, that arbiter of Roman elegance who was both sensualist and satirist.

Like another noble Roman, Vidal has his gall and he divides his grandiosely titled collected essays into three parts: "State of the Art" focuses on books and their writers; "State of the Union" on politics and its discontents; and "State of Being" on matters autobiographical. In a note Vidal says that this imposing volume contains about two-thirds of the pieces he has published over the past four decades. (Those left by the wayside tend to be the more perfunctory early book reviews and play notices.) But even if you've wisely guarded your copies of *Homage to Daniel Shays* (1972), *Matters of Fact and Fiction* (1977), *The Second American Revolution* (1982), and *At Home* (1988), you'll still want this monument to an engaging intellect, if only for the new-to-hardcover essays on Ford Madox Ford, Montaigne, Orson Welles, and H. L. Mencken, as well as the "Reflections on Glory Reflected and Otherwise."

For those readers who have somehow missed Vidal as essayist—likely, I admit, only if your name is Rip Van Winkle—*United States* is spangled with glorious oldies like "The Top 10 Best Sellers" of early 1973, the almost too scholarly "French Letters: Theories of the New Novel," the devastating "American Plastic: The Matter of Fiction," the formerly scandalous account of the Kennedys entitled "The Holy Family," the still scandalous "Pink Triangle and Yellow Star" (about some gays and certain Jews), frequently unorthodox views of various American presidents (Adams, Lincoln, Grant, Teddy Roosevelt, Nixon, Reagan), and a whole series of lovingly thorough appraisals of once neglected writers: Dawn Powell, Italo Calvino, William Dean Howells, Logan Pearsall Smith, Paul Bowles, Thomas Love Peacock, L. Frank Baum, Louis Auchincloss, E. Nesbit, Frederick Prokosch. That some of these notables continue underappreciated only supports one of Vidal's leitmotif laments: that the age of the reader is passing and that we are living through its twilight's last gleaming.

Perhaps. Vidal is himself, though, nothing less than an old-fashioned bookman. He took the path to Rome, he claims, to be near its classical library when he was working on *Julian* (the Apostate). A long essay on Lincoln out-scholars the professors, refuting every doubt about the exactness of his knowledge of the president and his times. In fact, though our man may look like a movie star and have the name to match, he studies like a Cistercian. "I have now read all of Powell's novels and one of the plays." "During the last year, I have read Calvino straight through." "I have read all of Auchincloss's novels and I cannot recall one. . . ." Not since Edmund Wilson, maybe even George Saintsbury, has a nonacademic shown such bookish passion and purpose. Moreover, like these men of letters, Vidal believes that accurate and entertaining description should be the main function of criticism. Describe a novel properly and there's no need to trot out the demeaned adjectives of book chat, let alone the jargon-torn and syntax-tormented sentences of poststructuralism. Of course, Vidal nearly always manages to blend, seamlessly and semefully, just the right amount of wit, research, and conviction: "Like so many of today's academic critics, Barthes resorts to formulas, diagrams; the result, no doubt, of teaching in classrooms equipped with blackboards and chalk. Envious of the half-erased theorems—the prestigious signs—of the physicists, English teachers now compete by chalking up theorems and theories of their own, words having failed them yet again."

There it is, the famous Vidal style: witty, conversational, astringent, often highly personal, even gossipy. Never does one sense the ordinary book reviewer's rush to judgment: here are leisurely openings, a carefully contrived structural artlessness, enriching digressions, good talk. The sentences themselves buzz contentedly with half-veiled allusions, retooled clichés, quiet puns, unexpected juxtapositions.

Examples? Consider this wry mortaring of the hallowed and the hip: "Elsewhere in the Old Testament, the love that Ruth felt for Naomi was of a sort that today might well end in the joint ownership of a ceramics kiln in Laguna Beach."

Or this high-toned use of the low style: "Margaret Sullavan never simply kicked the bucket. She made speeches, as she lay dying; and she was so incredibly noble that she made you feel like an absolute twerp for continuing to live out your petty life after she'd ridden on ahead, to the accompaniment of the third movement of Brahms's First Symphony."

But now and then the allusions almost overwhelm the sense, as in this title-strewn sentence: "For Prokosch, each of the seven who flees is both generalized essence and specified ape, while the dark gravel-strewn Gobi beneath the sheltering sky that does not shelter is simply an extension of a shifting, living cosmos where man is all things that man observes; and the only constant is change—hence, the romantic's agony."

Yet Vidal can also be so plain you may think he's joking: "I date the end of the old republic and the birth of the empire to the invention, in the late thirties, of air conditioning." Before AC, Vidal explains reasonably, the politicians would abandon Washington in the summer; now they stay around all through the year, making mischief.

As an essayist, Vidal rises far above disinterestedness. He is frankly a provocateur and a partisan. When he writes on literary subjects or old friends, this makes for letter-perfect journalism; but when he turns to sex and politics the tone sometimes grows shrill, the humor heavy-handed, the message repetitive. (One sees this occasionally in his satirical novels too: even *Myra Breckenridge* seems more than a little sophomoric.) Again and again Vidal tells us that everyone is really bisexual in his impulses, that today's novels are written to be taught, not read, that the rich really control America, that we need to limit population growth, that certain intellectual Jews belong to an Israeli fifth column, that families are the chief means of keeping workers in their exploited place. Any or all of these things may be true and important, but sometimes you want to shout, "Gore, forget the blackjack. Use the stiletto."

Of course, Vidal might reply, with cool disdain, "Don't read so many essays all at once."

Still, I have not come to harry Caesar, but to praise him. Gore Vidal is the master essayist of our age, and we should thank the gods that we still have him to kick us around. Long may he flourish.

May 30, 1993

THE WAR AGAINST CLICHÉ:
ESSAYS AND REVIEWS, 1971–2000

By Martin Amis

Because Martin Amis looks snotty and supercilious as he glowers at the world from his dust jacket photos, it's always tempting to sneer back at him. Son of Kingsley Amis, holder of a first-class degree from Oxford, boy editor at the *Times Literary Supplement*, author of a really good first novel (*The Rachel Papers*) published when he was in his early twenties—what's not to hate? His autobiography, it was rumored, would be called "My Struggle." He was, as another wag had it, "nasty, British and short." People still frown because he disbursed some fabulous sum getting his teeth fixed (okay, but just price a couple of implants).

Alas, all this backstory is utterly irrelevant: the man's a genius with words, and there's an end to it. Some of Amis's books are masterly—*Money*, *Experience*—and some don't quite work, but how can you argue with electrifying sentences? He's on a par with Nabokov, Anthony Burgess, John Updike, Saul Bellow. The English language just begs and rolls over at his command. Should you happen to be a writer yourself, or—God help you—a literary journalist, you suddenly know, with numbing clarity, just how Salieri felt when Mozart sashayed into Vienna.

The War Against Cliché—a somewhat clunky title, but apt—showcases Amis the reviewer and essayist. Right off, one notices the literary and cultural *sprezzatura*, a sensibility duly appreciative of both the domestic authorial virtues of V. S. Pritchett and the promiscuous excesses of J. G. Ballard. About sex, masculinity, and Hillary Rodham Clinton, Amis can be skeweringly funny. If required, he can also be as learned as any Leavisite, whether inditing a paean to *The Adventures of Augie March* ("the great American novel. Search no further") or enumerating the dismal ineptitudes and phoniness of Thomas Harris's *Hannibal*. Though our lad may discourse on the tough-guy allures of poker and soccer, he writes with even deeper passion about chess, the game of kings and nerds. Like everyone else, Amis duly reveres Elmore Leonard for his sipping-smooth colloquial style, but who else has picked up on the Detroit master's habitual use of the present participle? Most important, whatever Amis chooses to say about a book or a writer seems just right—and lip-smackingly phrased. Note the gorgeous diction in this summary of Malcolm Lowry's sodden final years, the period when the author of *Under the Volcano* was so thirsty for anything alcohol-based that he once downed "a whole bottle of olive oil thinking it was hair tonic": "Towards the end, even Lowry's freak accidents and cluster catastrophes are assuming an air of the dankest monotony. An average hour, it seems, would include a jeroboam of Windowlene and Optrex, a sanguinary mishap with a chainsaw or a cement-mixer, and a routinely bungled attempt to guillotine his wife."

Perfection. But Amis can also employ a confidential, almost confessional plainness to equal effect: "Not many people know this, but on top of writing regularly for every known newspaper and magazine, Anthony Burgess writes regularly for every unknown one, too. Pick up a Hungarian quarterly or a Portuguese tabloid—and there is Burgess, discoursing on goulash or test-driving the new Fiat 500. 'Wedged as we are between two eternities of idleness, there is no excuse for being idle now.' Even today, at seventy, and still producing book after book, Burgess spends half his time writing music. He additionally claims to do all the housework.'

Amis, like all master word slingers, enjoys playing with catch phrases, overturning the familiar with the abandon of an S. J. Perelman or a forgotten Russian formalist. For instance, a reverse cliché superbly codifies the failure of Philip Roth's sexually overextended *Sabbath's Theater*: "Erotic prose is either pallidly general or unviewably specialized. Universality crumbles into a litter of quirks. After a while it provokes in the reader only one desire: the desire to skip. You toil on, looking for the clean bits."

As a critic, Amis is honest and patient: he opens an essay on *Don Quixote* by admitting how unreadable much of that classic is; he carefully charts the death toll in *Lolita* and notices just what the chiseling Humbert pays for preteen sexual favors; he points out that "no one has written more entrancingly about the rhythms and the furniture of daily life" than James Joyce. Not least, Amis can summarize a book or a writer's achievement with epigrammatical exactitude. *Under the Volcano* is the product of "drunkenness recollected in sobriety." The cosmopolitan Burgess possesses a "panoptic suavity." John Updike is all "lordly brilliance" (adding, "not for Updike the kind of prose that takes a vow of poverty"). "Hard-edged, pre-stressed, sheet-metalled"—such are Don DeLillo's tooled-up sentences. While Richard Rhodes's dreadful *Making Love: An Erotic Odyssey* is "a cataract of embarrassment," he regards

James Atlas's biography of Saul Bellow as even worse: "a moral disaster: hostile, inaccurate and ill written."

As one avidly turns page after page of *The War Against Cliché*, Amis deftly keeps the reader's excitement ratcheted up. For instance, you want to rush out for, or return to, the works he praises: Mailer's *Harlot's Ghost* ("prodigious—and prodigiously underrated"); Roth's *The Counterlife* ("a work of such luminous formal perfection that it more or less retired post-modern fiction"); Vidal's *Palimpsest* ("proud and serious and truthful"); Elmore Leonard's *Riding the Rap* ("This was bliss"); Updike's *Picked-Up Pieces*: "As a literary journalist, John Updike has that single inestimable virtue: having read him once, you admit to yourself, almost with a sigh, that you will have to read everything he writes."

In his introduction to this irresistible goody bag, Amis declares that "all writing is a campaign against cliché." (One cannot help recalling the theories of the Russian formalists—that the function of art is to defamiliarize, so that we may truly see the world.) Amis goes on, "Not just clichés of the pen but clichés of the mind and clichés of the heart. When I dispraise, I am usually quoting clichés. When I praise, I am usually quoting the opposed qualities of freshness, energy and reverberation of voice."

Those last half dozen words describe, of course, their author's own supremely assured prose, his own laid-back, jacked-up sound.

December 16, 2001

LOVERS, POETS,
AND MADMEN

 VIII

"To fall in love," wrote Borges, "is to create a religion that has a fallible god." In Western fiction love is a destructive passion, the basis of half our favorite romantic myths, from Antony bedazzled by Cleopatra, that serpent of old Nile, to besotted William Hurt manipulated by sultry Kathleen Turner in Body Heat. A guy's just going along, and suddenly—bam!—there she is, and nothing will ever be the same again. Those eyes, that hair, those curves to kill for! Before you know it, you're forsaking your country, betraying your wife, laughing at honor, even committing murder. But it's worth it. The soft touch of her lips, the passionate scratches of those red-lacquered fingernails. What's to regret? Nothing—until you have to fall on your sword in disgrace or wake up looking at iron bars and prison for life.

Adultery has been called the single great theme of Western fiction. Certainly romantic passion requires hindrances and delays to create intensity, and so prohibited or dangerous liaisons must necessarily be the most exciting. We play with the transgressive, pushing hard against the bounds of sense and safety. "The hind that would be mated to the lion," said Shakespeare, "must die for love."

One might have included in this section half the books mentioned in Bound to Please. But here I've concentrated instead on some older writers for whom love was central to their lives or to the lives of their characters. Colette portrays all the pleasures of the pure and the impure. Robert Graves devotes himself, body and soul, to Laura Riding, that avatar of the White Goddess. W. M. Spackman reveals the love affairs of elderly gentlemen of refined taste who educate—and are educated by—vivacious college girls. The novels of Dawn Powell show us not only the tragic but also the comic face of Eros, while Ben Sonnenberg's irresistible memoir chronicles a life of delicious hedonism. In general, though, one has to agree with Kenneth Clark: "Lives devoted to beauty seldom end well."

SECRETS OF THE FLESH:
A LIFE OF COLETTE

By Judith Thurman

As in life, Colette (1873–1954) continues to tantalize and vex her many admirers. Even now this great writer eludes easy definition, which may explain why she has been the subject of at least half a dozen significant biographies over the past thirty years. Yet this one by Judith Thurman will be hard to top, not only because it deftly summarizes the current state of "Colette scholarship"—how its subject would shudder at that phrase—but also because its prose is smoothly urbane, at times aphoristic, always captivating. Little wonder that Thurman's previous book, a life of Isak Dinesen (author of *Out of Africa* and *Seven Gothic Tales*), won a National Book Award. *Secrets of the Flesh* deserves similar prizes.

Say "Colette" and most readers will probably think of *Gigi*, the delightful story (later an equally delightful movie) about a young girl brought up to be a courtesan, or of *Cheri*, the darkly moving tale of the doomed love between a forty-nine-year-old cocotte and a callow boy half her age. To Americans these artful short novels, two parts of an erotic diptych, seem deeply, almost comically Gallic. We Yankees don't quite understand this French obsession with sex.

Marriage or adultery, sure. They're democratic. But the relentless examination of the human heart, careers of sensual pleasure, the often melancholy elucidation of "the mysteries and betrayals and frustrations and surprises of the flesh"—these are puzzling to us, vaguely troubling. Our Puritan heritage and our Protestant work ethic compel us to regard such hedonism as decadent, marginal, all right for jet-setters and gays, maybe, but not for your "normal" American. A job, a family, making millions from computers or litigation, any of these is patently far more important than the pursuit of luscious girls and sullen young men. Right? As Colette's second husband once complained to her, "Can't you write a book that isn't about love, adultery, semi-incestuous couplings, and separation? Aren't there other things in life?"

If nothing else, then, Colette always makes us uneasy. During her eighty-one years she blithely ignored all the usual boundaries. Just look at her various personae: tomboy, ingenue, wife, kept woman, lesbian, mime, music-hall performer, crime reporter, advice columnist, beautician, and one of the chief glories of modern French literature. Her first husband, Henry Gauthier-Villars, known as Willy, exploited her talent and took authorial credit for her first books, four spicy novels about the schoolgirl and young wife Claudine. This quartet still ranks as possibly the best-selling series in French publishing. Willy eventually introduced Colette to Marcel Schwob, Debussy, and other figures of the 1890s—and to threesome sex: to one woman friend she once wrote, "My husband kisses your hands, and myself all the rest." After her marriage soured, Colette turned mime and actress, appearing on stage in Oriental houri costume, exposing her left breast or passionately embracing her cross-dressing lesbian lover, the marquise de Morny, known as Missy. Around this time she was even glimpsed wearing a slave bracelet inscribed "I belong to Missy." We are talking, let me remind you, of a novelist admired by Proust and Rilke, interviewed by Walter Benjamin, compared by François Mauriac to Racine, a writer judged by her peers (in 1935) to be the finest French stylist alive.

But Colette's transgressions are hardly restricted to her youth. Though feminists have always tried to annex her, she once proclaimed, "You know what the suffragettes deserve? The whip and the harem." Just before World War I, this sexy vagabond/actress was assiduously courted by Henry de Jouvenel, a leading journalist who later became a major European diplomat. With their marriage the flamboyant social pariah emerged as the baronne de Jouvenel des Ursins. At forty she then had a baby daughter named Colette, whom she largely ignored, despite her own paeans in prose to her own mother, Sido. Soon after discovering her charismatic husband's infidelities, this fiftyish woman of letters boldly started a five-year love affair with her sixteen-year-old stepson, Bertrand.

Meanwhile, her novels brought increasing fame. When she covered the trial of Landru, that serial murderer of successive wives (and the inspiration for Chaplin's *Monsieur Verdoux*) recognized her and asked for an autograph. Alas, when she opened a beauty salon, featuring her own brand-name products, she failed dismally: Natalie Barney—the doyenne of Paris Lesbos— "noted that her clients came out looking twice as old as they went in."

Colette was always daring, unfettered in her writing as in life. In *The Pure and the Impure*, her study of "these pleasures which are lightly called physical" (and her favorite among her books), she opens with a description of a middle-aged woman faking an orgasm to please her dying young lover. (In a characteristically amusing sidenote, Thurman remarks that one of the novelist's closest friends, Paul Masson, committed suicide just before completing a survey in which he asked various literary folk, "What are the phrases, interjections, or onomatopoeic sounds which most habitually escape your lips at the moment of ecstasy?") When Colette was given the rosette of the Legion of Honor, she joked that it should have been a G-string. In the end this freest of spirits overcame her mild anti-Semitism to wed Maurice Goudeket, an unsuccessful Jewish businessman, fifteen years her junior, who just before their marriage had been reduced to selling used washing machines and deluxe toilet plungers. She called him her best friend. When Colette finally died, in 1954, the grande dame of French literature was denied a Catholic burial—Graham Greene protested—but was nonetheless granted a lavish state funeral. Thousands, most of them women, threw flowers on her casket. Her last coherent word had been, appropriately for one so observant of our sensual world, *Regarde*—Look!

Clearly, Colette's was a life in which, as her biographer notes, "the discipline of work sharpens the savor of pleasure." Throughout these 500 pages Thurman excels in chronicling both the work and the pleasure, and is particularly brilliant at pen portraits. Here she evokes the actress Polaire: "She was the original gamine, a prototype for Piaf and for other tiny, soulful, plebeian French vedettes who have pencilled their brows and belted out their love songs with fists on their haunches; whose memoirs are devoted to their love of lapdogs and thugs; who have been as sentimental about respectability as they were sexually profligate; and who—having put too much trust in fame and in their managers—have died broke and disillusioned."

There are similarly superb pages on Willy, who possessed the flair for publicity of a Hollywood producer; on the dashing and adventurous novelist Joseph Kessel, "who lived like a pasha, dividing his favors among a long-suffering wife and several grateful mistresses, each with her own establishment"; and on the novelist Rachilde, who, left in the shadows by her former protégée, once told a would-be novelist that the way to succeed was "to copy Colette and become a whore." At times Thurman's worldly wisdom matches that of her subject: "Her first much younger lover is a revelation no middle-aged woman whose senses have been numbed by rejection can ever forget. It is she who holds the power and maintains the detachment, at least in the beginning, and that novel inequality is as bracing—and as erotic—as the passion." "Colette respected those ambitious entrepreneurs of her own sex whose notion of bottom line would never be Virginia Woolf's five hundred a year and a room of one's own, but fifty thousand a year and a villa of one's own, with a great chef, a big garden, and a pretty boy."

When Proust once started to wax lyrical to Colette about her ethereal spirit, she abruptly interrupted him: "Monsieur, you're delirious. My soul is filled with nothing but red beans and bacon rinds." Colette always remained intensely down-to-earth, professional; she met her deadlines. She used to say, *La règle guerit tout*: Discipline cures everything. All in all, she composed sixty books (almost all of them written out with a Parker pen). Several of the best celebrate her childhood, the love of nature, gardens: *My Mother's House, Break of Day, Sido*. "Throughout my existence," she told a group of schoolchildren, "I have studied flowering more than any other manifestation of life." Indeed, she invariably demonstrated a freshness in her response to all experience, the "beginner's eye," and nothing was ever lost on her. Even her casual travel journalism, gathered together as *Prisons and Paradises*, could embrace "the gardens of Algeria; the despots and their dancing girls; the craggy splendors of the fjords; the desert and its flowers; reptiles; captive leopard cubs; perfumed dishes; the landscapes of Provence; depressed lions; heat and wind; magicians; roses; hidden springs; young wine; millionaires; white nights; beggars; the scent of dung and lilies; the smell of baked potatoes. . . ." This "sovereign vitality and attunement to nature" are, according to one critic, "the essence of Colette's greatness as a writer."

For Thurman, though, Colette's work is about the search for "an ecstatic experience of reunion, in which the split between two bodies, sexes, and generations is repaired," and she gives searching, if concise, analyses of the major books, often drawing on the work of Claude Pichois, the editor of the Pléiade edition of Colette, and frequently crediting insights to other biographers and critics. Thurman also salts her text with apt quotations revealing the sensuousness, elegance, and *esprit* of Colette's prose; when talking of love, the novelist sometime recalls Diderot in his philosophical dialogues or the aphoristic La Rochefoucauld: "Jealousy . . . is the only suffering that we endure without ever becoming used to it." At one point, Thurman does surprise with a highly critical reading of the hitherto much admired (by me, among others) *Julie de Carneilhan*, a short novel about a cast-off wife, a former husband, and a scam to blackmail the rich current wife. The biographer convincingly demonstrates that the text, composed during World War II, is marred by a more than implicit anti-Semitism.

As alien as her world of kept women, music halls, and Don Juans can seem at times, Colette's novels are, at heart, about the shifting balance between loss and gain, between hurt and self-knowledge, between the wisdom of the old and the vitality of the young. Today, works like *The Pure and the Impure, My Mother's House*, and *Break of Day* seem astonishingly modern: they dwell in the shadowland between memoir and fiction, play peekaboo with masks and the reversal of gender roles, emphasize the bond between mother and child, examine how a woman should come of age, and cope with its consequence. All very contemporary, indeed. Yet, as Auden said of this great writer, in her steady, clear-eyed understanding of the human heart, Colette most calls to mind only one other novelist: Tolstoy.

October 10, 1999

ROBERT GRAVES:
THE YEARS WITH LAURA

By Richard Perceval Graves

BETWEEN MOON AND MOON:
SELECTED CORRESPONDENCE (1946–1971)

By Robert Graves
Edited by Paul O'Prey

Has anyone in the twentieth century managed to write so many different kinds of books, and to write them so well, as Robert Graves (1895–1985)? His early autobiography, *Good-bye to All That* (1929), stands grimly as the classic memoir of the First World War. *I, Claudius* (1934) has been called—by the critic George Steiner, no less—the best historical novel of our time. And *The White Goddess* (1948), that quest for the secrets of a pre-Christian Muse who is the source of all true poetry, remains the cult book to end all cult books, one that actually reveals, along with many other oddities, exactly what song the Sirens sang and the name Achilles assumed when he hid himself among the women.

Need more proof of Graves's range? *A Survey of Modernist Poetry* (1927), written with Laura Riding (about whom much more shortly), is often credited with kicking off the New Criticism by its intensive analysis of a Shakespeare sonnet. Christopher Isherwood once chose "The Shout" (1928) as one of the dozen or so greatest modern English short stories; its vision of madness is certainly among the most terrifying. The two-volume *Greek Myths* (1955) and the translations of Suetonius, Apuleius, and Lucan remain school standards, despite their idiosyncrasies, while *The Reader over Your Shoulder* (written with Alan Hodge) overshadows virtually all other knuckle-rapping guides to the writing of forceful, clear prose. Besides these and a hundred or so other books,

Graves (1895–1985) also produced scores of essays, humorous pieces, and historical investigations—virtually all of them as entertaining as they are erudite.

Still, Robert Graves always counted his prose as little more than a means of subsidizing his poetry. He specialized in short lyrics, most of them about love, like this youthful charmer:

Love without hope, as when the young bird-catcher
Swept off his tall hat to the Squire's own daughter,
So let the imprisoned larks escape and fly
Singing about her head, as she rode by.

With the possible exception of "To Juan at the Winter Solstice," his ode to the White Goddess that opens, "There is one story and one story only / That will prove worth your telling," none of Robert Graves's poems is very well known or particularly quotable, yet dozens of them can be read with deep pleasure. Graves practiced a low-keyed but perfectly tuned poetry of wit, passion, and sheer loveliness, reminiscent of Robert Frost or E. E. Cummings. Poems, he maintained, should be inspired by and written for a single person, and the best should be invocations of the Muse, accounts of her awesome power to grant love or deliver death.

One would think that with so much literary production Graves must have had little time for anything but scribbling away with his steel-nibbed pen. By no means. In fact, this cranky, appealing man of letters led an exceptionally stormy life, and at its heart are his years of thralldom to Laura Riding.

In *The Assault Heroic*, the first installment of his three-part biography of Graves, Richard Perceval Graves suggested that the theme of his uncle's life was the need to be directed, to be taught and inspired, whether by his mother, an idealized schoolboy chum, or a genuinely heroic figure like his close friend T. E. Shaw, aka Lawrence of Arabia. That first volume naturally focused on early family life and the Great War, during which Graves was so badly wounded he was given up for dead (he was eventually able to read his own obituary in the *Times*). It concluded with an account of Graves's early married life with the feminist painter Nancy Nicholson.

The Years with Laura opens in 1926 as the poet, his wife, and four children set sail for Egypt, where Graves is to take up an appointment as an English teacher at the University of Cairo. With them is a young American named Laura Riding.

In her own right a hauntingly strange writer—the young Auden called her the "only living philosophical poet" and acknowledged her influence—Riding was briefly associated with the Southern Fugitives, in particular Allen Tate, with whom she had a short affair. (Years later, when asked about Riding, Tate callously remarked that she was all right "from the neck down.") Graves admired her poems and started a correspondence that eventually led to Riding's being offered a job as his secretary. As anyone might guess, this was a bad idea. Before long, the two poets were lovers, though Nancy didn't seem to mind much. A rocky marriage slowly turned into a sturdy ménage à trois.

From all accounts Riding possessed a charismatic, forceful personality, a superb mind, and a psychological acumen that permitted her to bend almost anyone to her will. She attracted both men and women (for a while she wore a medallion with Nancy's picture on it while she was sleeping with Robert). She was constantly coming up with utopian schemes to change the world, including a dictionary of "exact meanings" upon which she spent most of her life (it has never been published). At times she allowed herself to be regarded as a kind of world savior, even a god. Robert once remarked, "You have no idea of Laura's holiness."

Before long, though, the ménage turned into a menagerie: Riding invited a young Irishman named Geoffrey Phibbs to join the trio. But all too soon Phibbs ran back to his own wife, whom he had left in part because she was having an affair with the polymorphously priapic David Garnett, author of *Lady into Fox* and *Aspects of Love*. After a temporary reconciliation broke down, Phibbs sheepishly returned to Riding, but only to announce that he no longer loved her. In despair, Laura sipped some Lysol, tootled "Goodbye, chaps," and leaped out of a fourth-floor window. Robert immediately rushed down the steps; but realizing that his muse must surely be dead, he stopped on the third floor and jumped out a window after her.

Surprisingly, both survived, though Riding suffered spinal injuries that took years to heal. In the aftermath to this would-be *Liebestod*, symmetry, if nothing else, required Phibbs to take up with Nancy, which he did. Considerable name-calling followed, in the midst of which Graves nevertheless managed to write *Good-bye to All That* (in about three months). Soon thereafter, the two poets left England and, following the advice of Gertrude Stein, no less, settled on the Mediterranean island of Mallorca, near a village called Deya. Once installed, Laura announced that she had transcended sexual relations.

In the seven years following, Graves wrote his Claudius books, a bitter family comedy called *Antigua, Penny, Puce* (much savored by the poet Philip Larkin), and lots of poetry. He also worked on various projects with Riding—publications under their Seizin press imprint, political, literary, and feminist manifestos, and several failed potboilers. Anytime a halfway intelligent couple visited Deya, Riding would try to enroll them in her bizarre phalanstery. The young Jacob Bronowski and his then girlfriend joined the entourage briefly, as did a future editor of *Time* magazine, T. S. Matthews, and his wife. Both these couples, however, got away in time. Schuyler and Kit Chapin, friends of Matthews, were not so lucky.

After Franco came to power, Graves and Riding fled Mallorca for London, where Alexander Korda was producing a film based on the Claudius books (the never completed *Fool of Rome*, starring Charles Laughton). In 1939, though, the pair accepted an invitation to travel to America, where they lodged at the Chapin farm. No one likes to talk about the weeks that followed. In his memoir *Jacks or Better* Matthews recalls a hothouse atmosphere of increasing tension and dread, as Laura gave some kind of private instruction to Kit Chapin, whose mind gradually collapsed: the mother of four was finally taken away from the farm in a straitjacket and spent much of the next twenty years in mental hospitals. After purging the house of malefic influences, Riding started openly sleeping with Schuyler Chapin, and Graves found himself on a boat back to England.

One would think this would be enough insane passion for anyone outside of grand opera. But at this point the forty-five-year-old poet decided that the woman he truly loved was Beryl Pritchard, the young wife of his friend Alan Hodge. Before long, Beryl was pregnant with Robert's child and Alan was collaborating with him on *The Long Weekend: A Social History of England in the 1930s*. As Graves once observed, with notable understatement, "Funny life, ain't it?"

The Years with Laura ends in 1940; many of the subsequent high spots of Graves's career are indirectly chronicled in *Between Moon and Moon*, the second volume of Paul O'Prey's edition of Graves's often superb letters (the first was *In Broken Images*). During World War II Graves wrote many of his best love poems and began to be haunted, or hag-ridden, by the White Goddess; in 1946 he returned to Mallorca to become, in time, the island's grizzled Prospero. In the 1950s he helped in the rediscovery of hallucinogenic mushrooms, became fascinated with the notion that Jesus survived the cross, and—under the ambiguous influence of Idries Shah—came to admire Sufism. In these years he also grew enamored of four successive young women, incarnations, he felt, of the Goddess. Both O'Prey and Martin Seymour-Smith (in the latter's fine critical biography) vaguely sputter that these affairs were passionate but sexually innocent, with Beryl welcoming the women into the household. But several late poems suggest that Graves did more than worship at their feet. In matters of love, at least, the more things change, the more they stay the same.

For anyone with a taste for outrageous, deeply amusing literary scandal, books about Robert Graves and Laura Riding are quite unputdownable, though I find that Richard Perceval Graves's fact-filled life lacks sympathy for its subject and simply portrays Riding as an out-and-out witch; other reports credit her with considerable charm and even some humor. (But it is hard to argue with the view that Graves unconsciously used her as a model for Livia, the murderous mastermind of *I, Claudius*.) I also wonder why Riding hasn't been taken up more fully by women scholars, since she adopted a life of great unconventionality and, in her early years at least, wrote important poetry and some appealing fiction, especially her *Progress of Stories* (much admired by Susan Sontag, John Ashbery, and Harry Mathews). Admittedly, in later years her prose grew increasingly opaque and abstract, as she and Schuyler labored at their pet projects, her great dictionary, and his annotated edition of C. M. Doughty's alliterative epic, *The Dawn in Britain*.

In his peculiar way Graves also attempted to refeminize the world, though he certainly never saw woman as man's equal: she was his superior. "A main theme of Greek myth," he laments, "is the gradual reduction of women from sacred beings to chattels." And behind all the lovely crackpot speculations about secret alphabets, leafy quinces and other bits of *Golden Bough* folklore, *The White Goddess* properly insists "that the feminine has been so trampled as to make life artificial and intolerable for the whole of mankind."

To read late Robert Graves is to enter a strange world, like that of UFO believers, where the most extravagant impossibilities are set forth with Cartesian rigor and a seemingly irrefutable scholarship, all in the name of correcting history, of "getting it right." Still, even if you judge him a nut, the man's sheer liveliness, as thinker and writer, is quite irresistible.

And don't dismiss Graves's antiquarian speculations out of hand. After all, the first two editors who rejected *The White Goddess* committed suicide soon thereafter, while T. S. Eliot, who accepted it on behalf of Faber and Faber, within the year had received the Order of Merit, won the Nobel Prize, and seen his play *The Cocktail Party* acclaimed a Broadway hit. The goddess, after all, rewards her own.

December 30, 1990

THE LOCUSTS HAVE NO KING

By Dawn Powell

THE GOLDEN SPUR

By Dawn Powell

ANGELS ON TOAST

By Dawn Powell

Isaac Babel once remarked that there is no iron that can enter a human heart like a period in just the right place. He might have been describing Dawn Powell's novels: the killer aphorisms and sharp observations rain down like well-placed sniper fire. Turning the pages of these satiric group portraits of New York bohemians and Babbitt-like businessmen is like listening to, say, Gore Vidal at his most serenely malicious. Certainly it is no accident that Vidal has been Powell's champion—he calls her our finest comic novelist—and the efficient cause behind the republication of several of her books.

Dawn Powell (1897–1965) wrote thirteen novels and a couple of plays and was sometimes unkindly called the second Dorothy Parker. She spent most of her adult life in Greenwich Village, where much of her fiction takes place. Not quite period pieces, her novels are bittersweet screwball comedies, where the characters all drink like maenads at a bacchanal and the race under the table is always to the wittiest.

Powell's books typically take the reader on a tour of some glamorous, decadent locale, and feature dozens of characters. Sometimes there's a sympathetic central figure, but more often everyone is on the make, on a roll, or falling down drunk. She is exceptionally dazzling in her descriptions, often the dullest parts of modern novels. A young gold digger in a bar "was evidently proud of her extreme slenderness for her gray-striped green wool dress followed every bone and sinew snugly, and from the demure way she thrust out her high-pointed breasts you would have thought they were her own invention, exclusive with her."

This darling, Dodo by name, soon snuggles up to a public relations man who "might be engaged in the world's most degrading occupation but at least he was better at it than anyone else." Later she tricks the novel's hero, a medievalist named Frederick Olliver, into taking her to a soiree held by a rich but stingy publisher. Frederick eventually escapes her clutches to find himself "peacefully wandering around the Beckley library in the upper reaches of the house, looking at the glass cabinets of rare manuscripts, viewing the sumptuous canyons of books, the portraits of beagle-nosed Beckleys each firmly clasping an exquisitely bound book as if to keep the artist from stealing it."

All these quotations occur in the first 20 pages of *The Locusts Have No King* (1948), and the remaining 250 pages are just as wicked. Powell claimed that *The Satyricon* was her favorite novel, and she adopts very much its style in her own work: life as a sideshow; terrific party scenes; easy sexual liaisons; an atmosphere of brittle wit, desperation, and venality; an airy, tart prose; plot developments growing out of continual misunderstanding; mini-disquisitions about art, life, fortune. In truth, you don't so much read these satiric romances as look down into them from some quite lofty Olympian heights. Your friend Dawn merely points out the antic goings-on, as you both chuckle and weep and mumble, "What fools these mortals be!"

In *Locusts* Lyle Gaynor, who loves Frederick, is married to a creepy bedridden playwright. The invalid makes a pitch to go on a trip to the Southwest. "I could ride through the mountains," he explains, "and join up with the Penitentes, maybe, offer myself for crucifixion, really enjoy myself, for once." Hoping for some help with his career, Frederick meanwhile visits a book-chat wheeler-dealer named Tyson Bricker, who "beamed at Frederick with the honest affection one could feel toward a man who will never be a rival, a man one is sure will never be anything but a distinguished failure, a man one can praise freely and honestly without danger of sending him zooming up the ladder ahead of oneself."

As it happens, though, Frederick unexpectedly becomes a literary hot ticket and after a series of contretemps drifts away from his beloved Lyle; he then finds himself infatuated with Dodo. Powell is especially fine in describing love gone wrong, the birth of jealousy and the gray sorrowfulness that invades the soul. Frederick breaks Lyle's heart and then admires "the new pallor emphasizing the contrast of brown eyes and red-gold hair" while "the aura of secret sadness made her extraordinarily beautiful." Later, in a paragraph worthy of Proust, he gets on a bus to go back to his office, as Lyle crosses the street: "He caught a glimpse of her from his window and before he was conscious of it the old aching rush of love for her swept over him. He saw how thin she was, how sad her face, and as he watched she made a troubled gesture toward her eyes. He wanted to cry out to her, to beg her to wait, only wait—but for what? Tears came to his eyes as the bus carried him on."

Most of *Locusts* is powered by the various misunderstandings that prevent these two lovers from getting back together, but this simple device—straight out of French farce—allows the novel to embrace most of artsy New York during the late 1940s: Spanish poets, magazine editors married to Russian émigrés, ad execs, camp followers, night school litterateurs. Eventually Frederick starts to quarrel with Dodo; once while they are getting ready for bed, he shivers before "her slim body in the half unfastened purple jersey as taut as an arrow about to whizz through him." The affair finally over, Frederick finds himself "so exhausted that he could not trust his sense of relief. It was the relief of the tired mother when the baby stops crying at last; the realization of its death comes later." Anyone could write the first part of that last sentence; it takes genius to add the final chilling twist.

Superb as *The Locusts Have No King* is, its excellence is typical of Powell. *The Golden Spur*—her last book, published in 1962—is somewhat softer, kinder, in its portrait of New York ways. A young Candide comes to a bar called the Golden Spur seeking his real father among the New Yorkers his long-dead mother once hung out with. Naive, handsome, and winning, he soon attracts the attention of a pair of sophisticated young women who invite him to move in with them: Lize, with her close-cropped hair and boyish figure, "drew the interest of men of all sexes"; while Darcy seemed to exemplify midwestern practicality. In fact, her practicality "exhibited itself in tender little cries of 'But you'll be sick, honey, if you don't eat something after all that bourbon! You must eat! Here, eat this pretzel.' "

A classic innocent, Jonathan Jamieson changes the life—for the better—of everyone he meets. The faded lady novelist, the hack writer, the desperate art dealer, the legendary painter, the aspiring actress, the alcoholic professor, the haunted attorney, the world-famous novelist—all of them decide to be a mother, father, or lover to the young man. It's just like a fairy tale, as told by Scott Fitzgerald, with a suitable happy ending for Jonathan in the arms of a young girl in the back of a taxi heading for the Golden Spur.

Besides these forays into bohemia (another is *The Wicked Pavilion*), Powell's range also includes business satire à la John O'Hara or Tom Wolfe. In *Angels on Toast* she eviscerates a pair of two-timing businessmen who ride the night trains back and forth between Chicago and New York, balancing love affairs, wives, mistresses, elaborate schemes, and golden daydreams. As usual she sets up a full dramatis personae, shifting among its members to make her satirical thrusts. At one point, the two antiheroes encounter a pseudo-British, name-dropping sharpy named T. V. Truesdale. Powell captures him forever in a sentence:

"He paid for his beer very carefully from a frayed ancient pigskin wallet, and this too he fondled as he had his briefcase, as if these were all that had been rescued of his priceless treasures when the palace was destroyed."

Everything is wonderful in that sentence, from the balance of phrases to the simile that makes us smile. A writer as good as this merits more than redis-covery: she deserves readers. Lots of them.

March 18, 1990

POSTSCRIPT: And she has found those readers. Following the publication of her diaries and letters, as well as a fine biography by Tim Page, Dawn Powell is now enshrined in the Library of America.

A HOWARD NEMEROV READER

There's a lot to praise about *A Howard Nemerov Reader*, but let's start with the University of Missouri Press itself. In an era dominated by gimcrack, fast-buck publishing, it has produced, at a reasonable price, a real book, handsomely designed, bound in full cloth, and printed in a reader-friendly type on permanent paper. As to its contents, the selections from Howard Nemerov's poetry, short fiction, and essays could hardly be bettered. Best of all, this omnibus returns to print *Federigo, or the Power of Love*, a 1954 novel as sexy and fizzily delicious as any classic screwball comedy. In short, here is intelligent publishing, as it should be practiced.

These days Howard Nemerov (1920–1991) is known principally as a poet, the winner of a string of honors and awards, the nation's third poet laureate. But during most of the 1950s this multitalented writer alternated books of witty, elegant poems with books of witty, elegant prose. In 1955 Nemerov actually landed the *Kenyon Review* fellowship in fiction—and then turned around to serve for many years as that quarterly's regular poetry reviewer. He even nearly succeeded John Crowe Ransom as its editor (being Allen Tate's choice). The essays he wrote during these years are rightly admired for their shrewdness, honesty, wit, and range: Nemerov mulls over matters as various as the form of the short novel, the resemblances between poems and jokes, the nature of metaphor, and the work of Thomas Mann, Vladimir Nabokov, and the critic Kenneth Burke. Only a few years back he capped his criticism with one of the most useful and readable of all introductions to Proust, *The Oak in the Acorn*.

At his best—and this *Reader* shows him so—Nemerov proves quite irresistible. His poems are clear and musical, sometimes funny, sometimes religious, always engaging. Listen to the whingey grumbling of his poetic credo, "Lion & Honeycomb":

He didn't want to do it with skill,
He'd had enough of skill. If he never saw

Another villanelle, it would be too soon;
And the same went for sonnets. . . .

This is colloquial and looks easy, but it takes real mastery to give that fourth line just the right spin. For an even more virtuoso flight, admire this single sentence (from his early masterpiece, "Runes"), as neatly turned and balanced as anything in Pope:

> . . . There are still
> To be found, at carnivals, men who engrave
> The Lord's Prayer on a grain of wheat for pennies,
> But they are a dying race, unlike the men
> Now fortunate, who bottle holy water
> In plastic tears, and bury mustard seeds
> In lucite lockets, and for safety sell
> To be planted on the dashboard of your car
> The statues, in durable celluloid,
> Of Mary and St. Christopher, who both
> With humble power in the world's floodwaters
> Carried their heavy Savior and their Lord.

In one of his essays Nemerov calls himself a "respected minor poet," and it's hard to disagree with this general assessment. He is read, wins prizes, and probably fends off admirers, but he's never quite enjoyed the impact or the influence of his slightly older contemporaries Robert Lowell or John Berryman. Maybe his verse isn't gnarly or knotty enough; like Philip Larkin, he may be too accessible, too sheerly enjoyable to become an academic icon. Yet anyone who reads the forty pages of poetry in this *Reader* will be keeping an eye out for its author's *Collected Poems*.

Not surprisingly, this same imaginative playfulness, this shrewd naturalness, carries over into Nemerov's critical prose. One essay begins this way: "In books left by the old magician we find many things, things ill-assorted and not particularly well catalogued according to any scheme we are familiar with. . . . Here are the licenses and registrations of the self, its snapshots of single raindrops in distant towns, its myths of creation, spells which worked on one occasion only, receipted bills from Guatemala and the Waldorf, inventories, formulae, annotations on unidentifiable texts. . . ."

Could there be a better and more Stevens-spirited introduction to Wallace Stevens?

If Nemerov has a fault as a critic, it lies in his sharp, icy intelligence. Most of us look for information or entertainment from literary essays, while Nemerov requires a reader to slow down and think with him through some fairly complicated matters about language and poetics. But even in the midst of the highly theoretical he can be winningly down to earth, as when he admits of Harold Bloom's *The Anxiety of Influence,* "My trouble with the book may merely have been that it was too difficult for me." At other times, he will make a point with creative exuberance: "People read novellas, but they tend to live in novels, and sometimes they live there very comfortably indeed: Thus you have descriptions which are nothing but descriptions, thus you have philosophical excursions, set-pieces, summaries, double-plot, and full orchestration, not to mention that all the chairs are heavily upholstered and even the walls padded."

Naturally, then, Nemerov's own *Federigo, or the Power of Love* is a short novel, tautly encircling a handful of fine-conscienced characters, who undergo a round of erotic (or monetary) alliances and misunderstandings. One morning the thirty-six-year-old ad-writer Julian Ghent receives an anonymous note in the mail: "Sir—A word to the wise. Your wife, sir, is too much alone. And not always alone. Your friend, Federigo." As it happens, Julian himself has composed this friendly advice, out of boredom and a vague notion that it might justify his having an affair. He leaves the letter on the breakfast table where his wife, Sylvia, reads it—and before long matters get neatly out of hand.

Everything about this novel is delicious: the puckered sophistication of the prose, the opera buffa entanglements, the shrewdness of the psychological observation. How is it possible that so coolly perfect an entertainment has been forgotten? Even its minor characters are superb: the never-at-a-loss, banally evil psychiatrist, Dr. Mirabeau; the plump Mr. Ballou, who says, on taking Julian into his ad firm, "I pray you to remember . . . that our interest here is only money"; Mr. Bilsiter, the private detective, who "did not look as though he could detect eggs at Easter." And, of course, our hero's doppelgänger, the elusive, faintly effeminate Federigo himself. This is, in short, the sort of intricate and pleasing novel one looks forward to rereading every few years.

There's much more to *A Howard Nemerov Reader.* I haven't touched on the half dozen enigmatic, fantastic short stories that introduce professional dreamers, mysterious skywriters, stylized water ballets at the end of the world. I should, though, note a slight disappointment that Nemerov hasn't included a bit of his self-portrait of the artist as a blocked writer, *Journal of the Fictive Life.* I would also have enjoyed learning more about the man himself, his well-to-do parents, the sister who grew up to become the celebrated photogapher Diane Arbus. Still, these are only cavils. *A Howard Nemerov Reader* is a very good book, worth buying, reading, and keeping.

April 21, 1991

POSSESSION:
A ROMANCE

By A. S. Byatt

Critics are paid to offer informed, careful judgments, full of erudition or good sense or both, but sometimes all we really want to say about a book is "Wow!" A. S. Byatt's *Possession* is that kind of novel. You turn its last page feeling stunned and elated, happy to have had the chance to read it. At once highly traditional and eminently postmodern, this is a fiction for every taste: a heartbreaking Victorian love story, a take-no-prisoners comedy of contemporary academic life, and an unputdownable supernatural mystery that starts with an old book in a London library and ends on a storm-wracked night in a churchyard before an open grave. It is above all an uncanny work of literary impersonation, for Byatt re-creates the letters, journals, poems, fairy tales, and critical writings of a dozen characters, and interlaces them all with common leitmotifs, recurrent imagery, and other subtle connections. Imagine some impossible hybrid of Robertson Davies, Iris Murdoch, Anthony Burgess, and John Fowles, all writing at their very best, and you'll have an inkling of the pleasures of *Possession*.

"The book was thick and black and covered with dust." In this old volume (of Vico: a hint) Roland Mitchell, a young, somewhat dull textual scholar, stumbles upon the draft of a letter written to an unknown lady by the distinguished Victorian poet and model of marital propriety Randolph Henry Ash. "Dear Madam, Since our extraordinary conversation I have thought of nothing else," it begins. The sentences betray such unexpected emotion that Roland surreptitiously pockets the manuscript, telling no one of his discovery.

Internal hints in the letter soon lead him to Henry Crabb Robinson's voluminous diary, from which he figures out that the lady in question must be the reclusive poet Christabel LaMotte—who, it had been thought, never knew Ash. LaMotte is currently a hot property in academic circles, generally regarded as a lesbian and protofeminist, author of exquisite lyrics, some curious fairy tales, and an almost unreadable epic about the serpentine fairy Melusina. Pursuing his quest, Roland calls on the icy Maud Bailey, a leading expert on LaMotte (as well as the author of "Melusina, Builder of Cities: A Subversive Female Cosmogony"), and the two team up to piece together the clues of the mystery: What happened in the summer of 1859 between Randolph Henry Ash and Christabel LaMotte?

As these scholars sleuth their way through the library stacks and country houses of England, Byatt duly transcribes what they turn up: the documents in the case. In Lincolnshire the researchers uncover a cache of letters: "I read your Mind, my dear Mr. Ash. You will argue now for a monitored and carefully limited combustion—a fire-grate with bars and formal boundaries and brassy finials. . . . But I say—your glowing salamander is a Firedrake. And there will be—Conflagration." LaMotte's poems take on deeper meaning: "This is our doom / To Drag a Long Life out / In a Dark Room." And entries in Ellen Ash's unpublished journal point to further riddles: "Another letter from the mysterious and urgent lady. A matter of life and death, she writes. She is well-educated. . . . I put the letter by, feeling too low in spirits to decide about it."

R. H. Ash is modeled principally after Robert Browning, with touches from several other eminent Victorians (e.g., William Morris's fascination with northern mythology); Christabel recalls Christina Rossetti and Emily Dickinson. The gradual discovery of the two poets' secret relationship roughly mirrors George McLean Harper's reconstruction of Wordsworth's youthful love for Annette Vallon, but also owes something to the rumored passion of Christina Rossetti for the married poet-painter W. B. Scott.

But such is the power of Byatt's dossier—excerpts from the standard Ash biography, *The Great Ventriloquist*; feminist articles about LaMotte; even a footnote referring to a disparaging essay on Ash by F. R. Leavis—that a reader easily surrenders to the fancy that these two surely existed. They burn with such fire on the page as they speak of poetry, mythology, the condition of women, geology, evolution, spiritualism, love. Surely we overslept that day when Professor Altick lectured on them in English 401: Victorian Poetry; and no doubt Phyllis Rose really ought to have included a chapter on Ash and Ellen in her *Parallel Lives: Five Victorian Marriages*.

All this may sound like post-Nabokovian playfulness: inventive and inconsequential, but it isn't. Byatt, a former British academic as well as a novelist, aims to show how some literary professionals, obsessed with textual questions, Lacanian psychology or deconstruction, may blind themselves to the sheerly human, the actual feelings, in poems: they get the meaning and miss the poetry. Sometimes they even miss the meaning. In *Possession* the modern-day academics prove figures of fun, but never R. H. Ash and his Christabel. Their love is so incandescent, so right, that a reader hopes against hope for these two appealing, intelligent, doomed, long-dead people. "He remembered most, when it was over, when time had run out, a day they had spent in a place called the Boggle Hole, where they had gone because they liked the word. . . ."

But further mysteries abound in *Possession*. Maud and Roland, unknowingly, also visit the Boggle Hole, just for the fun of it. Maud and Christabel both buy the same kind of brooch. Parallels and echoes proliferate. Is there a supernatural affinity between the two poets and the two researchers? R. H. Ash once wrote to his wife, "If there is a subject that is my own . . . as a writer I mean, it is the persistent shape-shifting life of things long-dead but not vanished." As in some mythic ritual, the past seems to be repeating itself. But to what end?

Two love affairs—one Victorian and doomed, another contemporary and uncertain—thus make up the magnetic poles of *Possession*, but around these swirl wonderful subordinate characters. Blanche Glover, the desperate painter with whom Christabel has established a little civilization à deux. The baffling Ellen Ash. The young Breton Sophie, who dreams of becoming a writer and duly records a troubling visit from her English cousin Christabel. The phony medium Hella Lees, who inspires Ash to violence and to compose his satiric monologue "Mummy Possest." Each shares a rough counterpart in the present: the spinster Beatrice Nest, who is editing Ellen Ash's journals; Val, Roland's depressed lover; Leonora Stern, the American feminist critic, at once gaudy, vulgar, bawdy, and brilliant.

Naturally, Byatt also rings the changes on her meaning-laden title. Mortimer Cropper, custodian of the Stant Collection at the University of New Mexico, vows to possess every scrap of Ashiana. His rival James Blackadder will never quite let go of his great, long-awaited edition of Ash. Crusty Sir George Bailey hoards his manuscript treasures. Maud and Roland are both caught up in their quest for the truth, but also, it would seem, spiritually possessed by forces beyond their ken.

Throughout her romance, Byatt interweaves leitmotifs—key words, recurrent allusions, names—that gradually take on increasing significance: fountains, thresholds, the sunken world of Is, electric shocks, pale-golden hair, serpents, images of fire and whiteness, the fairy Melusina. With these she plaits together poems, lives, and scholarship. As the book proceeds, the achievements of Ash and LaMotte grow clearer, more personal, increasingly powerful. Appropriately one of the novel's climaxes leads to the proper reading of a poem and the discovery of a poetic vocation.

Possession is in every way an altogether magical performance, a prodigious act of literary ventriloquism. Still, the last words here must be those of

Randolph Henry Ash to his Christabel: "I shall forget nothing of what has passed. I have not a forgetting nature. (Forgiving is no longer the question, between us, is it?) You may be assured I shall retain every least word, written or spoken and all other things too, in the hard wax of my stubborn memory. Every little thing, do you mark, everything. If you burn these [letters], they shall have an afterlife in my memory, as long as I shall live, like the after-trace of a spent rocket on the gazing retina. I cannot believe that you will burn them. I cannot believe that you will not."

What a love story! What a book!

October 16, 1990

POSTSCRIPT: This review was published on the day my youngest son was born and so remains particularly special. A. S. Byatt invited me to lunch after it appeared, and we became friends. All very well—except that, as a result, I was never able to write about *Angels and Insects, Babel Tower,* or her other fiction. That's the downside of the literary life: should you get to know the people you admire, you can no longer review their books.

THE COMPLETE FICTION
OF W. M. SPACKMAN

Edited and with an afterword by Steven Moore

Talk about a dream world: in the novels of W. M. Spackman (1905–1990) lissome coeds ardently pursue courtly and seemingly irresistible bankers, painters, and professors, most of them Princetonians, nearly all of them past fifty, and every last one a lover of extraordinary sophistication and refinement. Picture George Sanders and Cary Grant at their most debonair. Not that Spackman ever actually describes the eiderdown frolics of his amorous couples. Instead he prefers to record "the ballet of coquetry," the musky, hothouse atmosphere of sexual attraction, the coy and knowing social comedy of wooing. His Jove-like heroes and lovesick nymphs gambol their summers away, sipping glasses of champagne, flirting through long, woozy lunches, clinging to each other on smoky dance floors late at night. In such a world, a love affair, preferably adulterous—so much more piquant—demands a delicate connoisseurship: how often the mature must instruct the unruly young in the proper forms and protocols! You may smile, but as Spackman observes and many know, "The scheduling of adultery in a college town is not an exercise for laymen."

W. M. Spackman's most famous novel appeared in 1978, and its title memorably announced its erotic ebullience: *An Armful of Warm Girl*. His third, *A Presence with Secrets* (1980), exuberantly detailed the affairs of an aging painter, frequently preyed upon by a series of delectable Smith undergraduates, beauties by turns "self-willed, flighty, ungovernably amorous, dithery, lawless, innocent, ruthlessly designing, demure, sly." Two other novels—*A Difference of Design* (1983) and *A Little Decorum, for Once* (1985)—provided further instances of the rich, handsome, and wellborn headily whirling along to the call of Pan's pipes. Of course, that sensual music was for Spackman more a stylized minuet than an orgiastic dithyramb. Even the most deeply smitten should, after all, preserve "a little decorum, for once."

Nearly everyone loves a love story, but Don Juanesque exploits would hardly be enough to establish an author as one of the most original writers of our time. A flair for epigram helps—"No doubt man's private pastime is feeling sorry for himself"—but there is, finally, no substitute for style. In his four major works Spackman's syntax cavorts and capers, breathlessly running away from the logic of grammar to achieve a higher fidelity to thought and feeling. Here is one example, cited and analyzed by Steven Moore in his masterly afterword to this omnibus of Spackman's complete fiction: "Mrs. Barclay being as it turned out late and Nicholas early, or as early anyway as a man in his right mind waiting for a pretty woman, he'd sat damn' near twenty minutes in Veale's unrecognizable bar, bolt-upright and presently glaring, before with a ripple of high heels in fluttered his angel in this breathless rush at last, blissfully gasping 'Oh Nicholas oh simply now imagine!' as he lunged up from the banquette with a happy bellow to grab her—though this act she parried, after one radiant flash of blue eyes, by seizing and tenderly pressing his hands while uttering little winded cries of salutation and reminiscence; and having let him merely peck at one heavenly cheek eeled out of his arms to the seat, onto which she at once sank, blown."

After pointing out this single sentence's velocity, conversational tone, careful choice of verbs, and its balanced sparring between Nicholas and Mrs. Barclay, Moore concludes that "most writers would have taken a page to convey what Spackman does here in a brief paragraph." Such streams of indirect discourse eddy regularly through these 600 pages, though Spackman can be quite plain when he wants: "As a summer project, she was reading Virginia Woolf entire. This, in a young wife as beautiful as Caroline, is an inscrutable omen." Soon, we realize, the lovely Caro will stoop to folly, or at least succumb to the hero's blandishments. More typically a young siren will mull over the pros and cons of seducing her host: "Because all this talk about honor, heavens! when I thought what if really I have only to stretch out my hand for him, wife of his guest or not? oh mon pauvre Alain how mean I could so easily be to you, I could be absolutely pétrie de méchanceté, goodness what lovely fun, shall I, or shall I?" Given the polish of his novels and their tone of upper-class nonchalance, it is little wonder that Spackman frequently laces his sentences with unitalicized French, Italian, and Latin. Rather, I suppose, like a sip of marc with one's after-dinner coffee.

All these—style, subject matter, foreign phrases—may be off-putting to the no-nonsense, just-get-on-with-it reader. But as a true artist, Spackman writes essentially to please himself or, more grandly, to realize his own vision. Born in 1905, this onetime professor of classics brought out his first novel, the rather conventional *Heyday* (1953), when he was nearly fifty; *An Armful of*

Warm Girl was published a quarter century later, when he was past seventy. Encouraged by ecstatic reviews, he produced his remaining books to comparable applause, and then died from cancer in 1990. Perhaps only an elderly man could write so vivaciously about the tingles and tangles of love, could evoke so achingly "the caress of transience." Besides the five known novels, this handsome volume also includes two short stories and the hitherto unpublished *As I Sauntered Out, One Midcentury Morning.* . . . Somewhat less intense in its prose, this last short book tracks the sentimental education of a young orphan, his affection for his cosmopolitan uncle, and the resolution of a family mystery. Happily, Spackman's passion for his *jeunes filles en fleurs* and his sense of romance remain undiminished: "But a girl saying good night to you in starlight is a lovely illusion. . . ."

In one of his essays (included in his 1967 collection *On the Decay of Humanism*), Spackman lists several of his favorite works of twentieth-century American fiction: Robert M. Coates's *Yesterday's Burdens,* Glenway Wescott's *The Pilgrim Hawk,* Tennessee Williams's *The Roman Spring of Mrs. Stone,* and Edmund Wilson's *I Thought of Daisy* and *Memoirs of Hecate County.* We also know he greatly admired the novels of Henry Green and Ivy Compton-Burnett (both of whom influenced his prose).

Sometimes books and authors such as these are fatuously dismissed as mere coterie favorites, outside the mainstream of literature. In fact, masterpieces are always outside the mainstream. They go their own way. W. M. Spackman is hardly a writer to every taste—some women readers, in particular, may find him objectionable—but he possesses what every writer yearns for: an unmistakable voice. "Now his and Nicholas's generation—well, take a leathery cousin of his own who when divorced had set up a showgirl in a little flat, perfectly normal showgirl, tendency to go to bed with outfielders; but all the same. . . ." Once heard, a voice like that is never forgotten. Nor should it be.

May 11, 1997

LOST PROPERTY:
MEMOIRS AND CONFESSIONS
OF A BAD BOY

By Ben Sonnenberg

Profligate, dissolute, promiscuous, and charming, Ben Sonnenberg has scarcely done a lick of real work in his life. Thrown out of ritzy prep schools in his teens, he skipped college and simply started to lah-de-dah his way through his father's sizable fortune, blithely acquiring expensive cars, clothes, and first editions, going to bed with dozens—make that scores—of attractive women, cozying up to the glamorous and the very pick of the chic, occasionally taking a stab at writing plays or spying for the CIA. In short, this "bad boy" has been a rake, a wastrel, a social parasite. And, it turns out, a brilliant autobiographer.

Actually, better than brilliant: irresistible. *Lost Property* stands up to comparison with the great romantic autobiographies, with Stendhal's *Life of Henry Brulard* and Musset's *Confessions of a Child of the Century,* with Cyril Connolly's aphoristic *The Unquiet Grave* and J. R. Ackerley's delicious *Hindoo Holiday.* Its style is just right: darting, anecdotal, slightly bemused, possessing a lilting irony that makes for compulsive readability. There's also something funny, sexy, or shocking on every page.

"I stole money from him"—he writes of his father, the public relations guru Benjamin Sonnenberg—"from when I was six to when I was in my twenties. He carried only new bills. A stack of these, to the thickness almost of a building block, lay on the marble counter of his dressing table, along with his keys and pocket watch. . . . Once, . . . early in my life of crime, I took six five-dollar bills. I was found out. Tell your father, my mother said. You have something to tell me? my father said. Never! I said, Prometheus preparing his defiance of Zeus. He'd taken off his jacket and was pulling off his shirt before lying down for his afternoon nap. Tell me, he said. My mother said, Tell your father. He took off his pants and underpants. Never! Naked, he hit me in the face. I said nothing. He hit me again, I was knocked to the floor. His belly swayed with the force of his blow. . . ."

This almost primal scene, which helped cement an early loathing for his parents, took place at 19 Gramercy Park, one of the finest private homes in New York. Its seven floors were furnished like a small but overtasteful museum, with English furniture and English butlers, with antiques and Old Masters and maidservants ("Is there a more erotic English word?" asks our man, who should know). Dinner parties featured corporate wealth and old money, anyone from the urbane Alastair Cooke to the savvy Abes Fortas and Ribicoff, a weekly crush of connoisseurs, aristocrats and kingmakers.

Unexpectedly, *Lost Property* portrays Sonnenberg père as a delightful man, shrewd, proud of his riches, possessed of "a wealth of vizier skills" but also pleasingly forthright. "I want it inscribed on my gravestone that poor as I sometimes was I never once took a nickel from Joseph Kennedy or Howard Hughes." To his scapegrace son he repeatedly quotes—or rather misquotes, using like instead of as—the famous sentence of Gibbon: "I sighed as a lover, I obeyed as a son." Naturally, young Ben turns out to be a faithless Don Juan and a fractious son.

At eighteen and no stranger to love's mysteries—he once got a girl into bed by telling her he was an associate editor of *Partisan Review*—Sonnenberg takes up with a prima ballerina. "I saw that, in time, with Nina, I would come to enjoy looking like a man living off the earnings of an older woman. Sallow, jealous and furtive, I'd order white-on-white shirts from Lew Magram ('Shirtmaker to the Stars'). I'd have a gold bracelet and wear a pencil mustache." Alas, our perfectly attired gigolo breaks off with his dancer after he meets Artemisia.

Who doesn't last long and is succeeded by Sabina, Pilar, Lynn, LeAnne, Katherine, and Siriol. Siriol tells him that Spike Milligan, the English comedian, "had a silver frame on his piano with an eight-by-ten glossy of Jesus Christ, signed 'To Spike, a swell guy. Love, Jesus.' " In Europe the cultivated, widely read Sonnenberg pals around with the pianist Glenn Gould, parties with the poets W. S. Merwin and Ted Hughes. He also enjoys the favors of Sally, Maria, Iope, and Gemma. Gemma "showed me exciting English country-house-party skills: how to make your bed look slept in when you spent the night somewhere else. 'Crease the sheets like this, press them down like that.' I used to leave her house before dawn. No one saw me. No one. But if they had, they'd have admired my luck, my grace, my stealth, my shoes, my shirt." He talks philosophy with Elias Canetti and music with the composer Elisabeth Lutyens, shares a joke with Samuel Beckett. But then it's on to Agnes, Atalanta, and Chloe. "I knew a number of households like Chloe's. Mother and daughter living together, luring men in, then stunning them and eating them up. The floors of Chloe's mother's house were littered with the casings of men they'd chewed up and spat out."

Finally, like some half-reformed Restoration rakehell, a thirtyish Sonnnenberg marries Alice, the seventeen-year-old sister of his former mistress Katherine. Naturally he'd also flirted with their mother, whose "kindness to me was reflected in numberless compliments, and in letting me sleep with her daughters of course." Soon the new husband is dandling a baby daughter and daydreaming about those lives "you see in Vuillard and Bonnard, rich, extravagant lives, innocent in their greed: calm lives but with a muted turmoil underneath." Back in New York, he pictures himself "sauntering into fame," perhaps as a playwright. Another daughter is born. Then Alice commits adultery and Sonnenberg takes up with the babysitter.

And so the carousel turns round and round—until one day this altogether winning but skirt-crazy thirty-four-year-old stumbles and falls on the street. A few months later, he falls again, and then again: multiple sclerosis. In a twinkling our dancing gold-hatted lover is using a malacca cane, two canes, a wheelchair. But the old charisma holds, as he meets Kate and then Sophie and eventually his current wife, Dorothy. After his parents die, Sonnenberg disburses his inheritance by founding a mildly leftish and very classy literary magazine, *Grand Street*. He becomes a superb editor, lynx-eyed in spying out new talent, intelligent, idiosyncratic, commissioning essays from scholars and polemics from journalists, as well as poems, reviews, appreciations, and translations. "For nine years, absorbed by *Grand Street*, even as I got sicker, I felt my life change for the better. I put out thirty-five issues at quarterly intervals. I printed only what I liked . . . and I stopped when I couldn't turn pages any more."

Now in his mid-fifties, Ben Sonnenberg is badly incapacitated; much of *Lost Property* could only be dictated. Nonetheless, he reportedly continues to work on literary projects, helped by his wife and various assistants. Is it too much to hope that some of these might be further essays and memoirs?

"Reading books, buying art, writing unproduced plays, seducing women: not much of a life." Oh, I don't know.

August 4, 1991

LICKS OF LOVE:
STORIES AND A SEQUEL,
"RABBIT REMEMBERED"

By John Updike

It's easy enough to grow blasé about John Updike. A serious mistake, of course, but understandable. After all, the beak-nosed virtuoso of American letters has been producing a substantial volume or two each year for more than four decades, alternating highly original fiction (*Of the Farm, Rabbit at Rest, Gertrude and Claudius*) with super-sized collections of essays (*Hugging the Shore, More Matter*) and occasional bursts of adroit and clever poetry. But such prodigiousness, I suspect, has led to a slight undervaluing of the writer's real genius. We have come to depend on an annual (or even semiannual) Updike just as we once looked forward to a "Christie for Christmas." To some, the books must consequently appear as merely slickly observant and streamlined, products of fancy rather than of imagination.

Still, any serious reader should resist such condescension. John Updike is our Flaubert, a word artist whose fifty and more books are all beautifully, carefully written: he may be the only major American novelist one could happily read just for his turns of phrase and handsomely tailored sentences.

Unfortunately, though, bespoke prose tends to be suspect in homespun America, and a simile that takes one reader's breath away may be dismissed by another as windy overwriting. A few critics have even argued that Updike's dash and flair not only detract from narrative urgency but should be regarded as little more than foppish verbal dandyism. Nabokov and Henry Green, two major influences on the young Updike, suffered the same disparagement. Yet fine novelists—not only murderers like Humbert Humbert—can possess fancy prose styles.

In the past, Updike was also knocked for his preoccupation with sex, generally adulterous and frequently oral; his lip-smacking descriptions of lovemaking have periodically been judged demeaning to women. *Couples*, in particular, brought him almost pornographic notoriety, though erotic yearning, indeed heartsickness in all its forms, pervades most of his books, particularly the four acclaimed novels about Harry "Rabbit" Angstrom.

Certainly, the wistful stories in *Licks of Love*—an allusion, by the way, to banjo picking as well as lingual sex play—keep mixing memory and desire. "In those days . . ." opens "New York Girl," and one can already hear the drawn-out sigh. Similarly, "His Oeuvre" starts with the irruption of the erotic past into a colorless present: "Henry Bech, the aging American author, found that women he had slept with decades ago were showing up at his public lectures." (I defy anyone to stop reading after such a hook.) The dozen subsequent pages chronicle four of Bech's lost loves, lingering over his youthful dreams and all the "rises and swales and dulcet shadowed corners" of feminine bodies. By contrast, in "The Women Who Got Away" the narrator finds himself thinking back to the women he failed to sleep with, who now "in retrospect, have a perverse vividness." With rue my heart is laden, sang Housman—just so does middle age plangently recollect heedless, glorious youth: "That was how it was, how it had been, the living moment awash with beauty ignored in the quest for a better moment, slightly elsewhere, with some slightly differing other, while the weeds grew in the peony beds, and dust balls gathered beneath the sofa, and the children, unobserved, plotted their own escapes, their own elsewheres."

Obviously, such effusions skirt close to the sentimental, yet even in this remain true to the largely maudlin inner life of those past fifty. First we are lovelorn, then forlorn.

Not that nostalgia is the only shock that older flesh is heir to. In "Metamorphosis" a man, grown obsessed with his plastic surgeon, notes a few of the indignities of age: "He was weary of the way whiffs of staleness arose to him from his lower regions, and of the way his crowned and much-patched teeth harbored pockets of suddenly tastable decay, as if all the deaths in the newspapers and all the years he had put behind him had been miniaturized and lodged in the crannies of his slimy mouth."

None of the stories in *Licks of Love* can be judged less than enjoyable, though I was especially touched by "Natural Color," in which a graying suburbanite glimpses a former lover after twenty-five years, and was slightly annoyed by the O. Henry–style trick ending of "Scenes from the Fifties." Yet the main reason to pick up this latest Updike is the nearly 200-page novella *Rabbit Remembered*. It is, of course, a kind of coda to the Rabbit tetralogy.

Some ten years after his death, Harry Angstrom can still overturn the lives of those who loved, hated, or envied him. One afternoon in September 1999, his widow, Janice, now remarried to his nemesis Ronnie Harrison, receives a visit from an unsuspected relation: Annabelle Byer, Rabbit's illegitimate daughter by Ruth Leonard. (See *Rabbit, Run* for details on their affair.) Ruth has recently died and on her deathbed told Annabelle the truth about her paternity. Before long, Rabbit's son Nelson, now working as a counselor at the Fresh Start Adult Day Treatment Center, finds himself drawn to the forty-year-old geriatric nurse: he is separated from his wife, Pru, unsure of his future, and lonely. Tensions build up and finally spill over at a Thanksgiving Day dinner, though matters aren't truly resolved until the last night of the millennium.

Nothing terribly dramatic happens in this novella—if one doesn't count close-ups of the quiet desperation in ordinary lives and scenes of the fraught, fragile relationships between fathers and sons, men and women. How unhappy people are! How much Time takes from us! Looking at her city, Janice recalls, with a pang, that "there had been a pet store here, and a music store run by Ollie Fosnacht." She "can scarcely believe so much is gone and she is still here to remember it."

Of course, the reader—as in Proust—aches over the same fictive past, as Updike reintroduces hot-blooded beauties now grown old, mentions the death from cancer of Charlie Stavros, Janice's former lover, shows the youthful coke-head Nelson now reformed, patiently trying to help a schizophrenic boy. Periodically, the novella also refers back to the drowning death of baby Rebecca, the burning of Rabbit's house (see *Rabbit Redux*), the improbable one night of sex between Harry and Pru. Again and again, Updike sharply distills "the heavy helplessness of blood" that "casts us into a family as if into a doom."

And yet against the "misery of the world . . . the pity of everything" Updike does proffer one compensation: love. Annabelle, explains Nelson to his mother, "wants what everybody wants. She wants love." Janice thinks that "she would never have believed in her teens what an innocent homely comfort it could be, after sixty, to have your bottom groped." Nelson misses his nerdy son Roy. Appropriately, the novella ends, like a Shakespearean romance, with a reconciliation and the likelihood of a marriage.

Halfway through *Rabbit Remembered* Nelson dreams about a shadowy figure in his backyard: "He goes to the window and sees out in the backyard a tall man practicing chip shots in the moonlight. The man is bent over and intent and a certain sorrow emanates from him in the gray-blue light. His back is turned and he doesn't turn his head to look up at Nelson. . . . Instead there is just that patient concentration, as if on a task he has been assigned for eternity— the little studied half swing, a slump-shouldered contemplation of the result, a disconsolate trundling another ball with the face of the club into position at the man's feet, and another studied swing. Nelson feels indignation that this mournful tall middle-aged stranger, in nondescript trousers and a long-sleeved blue-gray shirt, should have wandered into their yard. . . ."

It is, of course, his father, "discouraged," as always. "But dogged." Yet might it not also be Rabbit's golf-loving creator?

On every page Updike's details are wonderfully exact; he loves the *haecceitas* of things as much as Gerard Manly Hopkins did: "the purr of a zipper being unzipped"; "the four-screen cineplex" advertising "Blue Eyes Blair Witch Sixth Sense Crown Affair." And he can be funny. When the fourteen-year-old Roy discovers pornography online, his father reflects, "Who would have thought the Internet, that's supposed to knit the world into a shining tyranny-proof ball, would be so grubbily adolescent?"

At the close of the story "Licks of Love in the Heart of the Cold War," Updike daringly sets down a thesis sentence that sums up this entire collection, indeed his entire life's work: "You can go to the dark side of the moon and back and see nothing more wonderful and strange than the way men and women manage to get together."

Yes. But the very last word word in *Rabbit Remembered* even more compactly suggests the eager spirit in which this modern American master approaches all his writing, regardless of genre or subject matter. That final quickening word is "gladly."

December 10, 2000

MAGICIANS OF THE
WORD

Every reader learns to recognize his "fatal type," the writers to whom he automatically loses his heart. Mine goes out to those who play with language and attempt something new with form. The resulting books may be difficult to read, or seemingly unserious or gamelike, or even requiring decipherment. But these original artists are often the ones who matter most, who tend to be increasingly valued as time passes, while more steady, familiar talents gradually lose their magic. "Overambitious projects," said Italo Calvino (himself a noted example of this sort of artist), "may be objectionable in many fields, but not in literature. Literature remains alive only if we set ourselves immeasurable goals, far beyond all hope of achievement."

Indeed, as in old Ellery Queen mysteries, the books here sometimes present a "Challenge to the Reader." But virtually all the (supposed) edginess and originality of many young writers today can be found in the dazzling pages of Gilbert Sorrentino or Julian Rios.

By their practice such authors raise a key question about fiction: How much does a novel need to be linked to "real" life? My own liking for fantasy, science fiction, and adventure novels, as well as my late-romantic belief in "art for art's sake," may hint at my own take on this question: I don't believe we turn to fiction to understand the world better. Yes, novels may make us more sympathetic and sensitive to life's complexities, but this is finally only a by-product. What matters is aesthetic delight, the shape of sentences, the myriad arrangements of light and shade, black and white, architectonics. The notion that a serious work of fiction is an informed commentary on the way we live now, or an attempt to encapsulate in a single volume the zeitgeist of a nation, is to misjudge the deepest nature of art. A novel is a realm of words. As Nabokov proclaimed, "It is not the parts that matter, it is their combination."

SAINT GLINGLIN

By Raymond Queneau
Translated from the French by James Sallis

Here, then, is a novel with a big sunfish on its cover, translated from the French and titled *Saint Glinglin*. No doubt the fictionalized life of a particularly obscure Provençal saint, probably the celestial benefactor of Mediterranean watermen.

Not even close. But few people are likely ever to think of reading, let alone buying, *Saint Glinglin* unless they recognize the name of its author, Raymond Queneau (1903–1976). He is one of those writers, like his antic compeers G. K. Chesterton, Flann O'Brien, and Lewis Carroll, who inspire newsletters, fan clubs, passionate exegeses, and scholarly conferences. If you know *Exercises in Style* or *Zazie in the Metro* you may already relish the Quenellian sensibility with its "jocoserious" tone and mixture of the learned and lighthearted. If, however, Queneau is simply a name to you, and a rather strange one at that, don't worry: you have a lot to look forward to.

Officially, for much of his life Raymond Queneau was a high-ranking employee of the Gallimard publishing house, first the company's secretary-general and later founding director of its ambitious *Pléiade Encyclopedia*. One could hardly, it would seem, be more respectable. Yet what if—to choose Queneau's approximate American counterpart—Mortimer J. Adler, editor of the *Encyclopaedia Britannica* and Great Books guru, were actually Thomas Pynchon, had once belonged to *Monty Python's Flying Circus*, and still published poems under the name John Ashbery?

For within the bespectacled, gray-suited Gallimard executive there coexisted a major novelist and poet, a former surrealist, a Transcendent Satrap of the serio-zany College of Pataphysics, and the founder (with the mathematician François Le Lionnais) of the Ouvroir de Littérature Potentielle, the Workshop for Potential Literature, generally referred to by the haunting acronym OULIPO. This elite group, limited to thirty members, creates poetry and fiction according to self-imposed constraints—Georges Perec wrote an entire novel, *La Disparition*, without using the letter *e*—and employs mathematical permutations to generate strange new texts. Queneau's own *One Hundred Thousand Million Poems* (1961), for instance, consists of a booklet of bound paper strips, each containing a line of verse, that can be mixed and matched to create an ever-changing, virtually inexhaustible compendium of poetry.

Similar permutative playfulness animates *Exercises in Style* (1947), probably Queneau's best-known work. This tour de force retells exactly the same banal incident—little more than one passenger jostling another on a hot, crowded bus—in ninety-nine different ways. It's the verbal equivalent of Bach's *Art of the Fugue* or of Beethoven's *Diabelli* Variations—a display of sheer linguistic virtuosity. Consider the openings of three of the exercises, in Barbara Wright's justly admired translation. Abusive: "After a stinking wait in the vile sun I finally got into a filthy bus. . . ." Official Letter: "I beg to advise you of the following facts of which I happened to be the equally impartial and horrified witness. . . ." Reactionary: "Naturally the bus was pretty well full and the conductor was surly. You will find the cause of these things in the eight-hour day and the nationalization schemes. . . ."

Little wonder that an author of such supple ingenuity might also work up an essay on "the aerodynamic properties of addition" or compose a poem, "Le Chant du Styrène," that celebrates, in polished alexandrines, the fabrication of polystyrene. At one time Queneau even thought seriously of writing a biography of the fictional master criminal Fantomas, that archfiend of a thousand faces.

Raymond Queneau fell into composing fiction when he was struck by the notion of mixing Cartesian philosophy with the slangy French really spoken by Parisians. The result was *Le Chiendent* (*The Bark Tree*, 1933), an absurdist, somewhat Joycean masterpiece about a bank clerk's rise to self-consciousness. In one dizzying chapter a wedding party includes an abortionist-midwife, a concierge, a tavern keeper, a junk dealer, a professional soldier, and a magician. All one needs is an evil dwarf—and he appears a little later. Near the novel's end war unexpectedly breaks out between the French and the Etruscans (!), some of the characters discover that they are living in a book, and the entire story, ouroboros-like, loops back to its beginning.

Shortly after *The Bark Tree* came out (to such silence that the earth might have been deserted), Queneau began to study literary madmen for a projected "Encyclopedia of Inexact Sciences." Not surprisingly, no publisher wanted such a "reference" book, so Queneau inserted chunks of it into a novel (*Les Enfants du Limon*, 1938). Meanwhile, he was also solving chess problems, painting watercolors, taking notes (later published) on Alexandre Kojève's epoch-making lectures on Hegel, and writing a newspaper column called "Do You Know Paris?" in which he quizzed readers on their knowledge of the capital's geography and history. Novels like *Pierrot Mon Ami* (1942), centering on an amusement park, and *The Sunday of Life* (1952), about an unambitious shopkeeper who achieves a Zen-like oneness with the world, almost seem like fairy tales about particular Paris neighborhoods.

In 1947 Queneau produced a quite different fairy tale, the semipornographic *We Always Treat Women Too Well*. Brought out under a pseudonym, it describes a band of Irish revolutionaries, all named after minor characters from *Ulysses*, who seize a post office (not *that* post office) and discover to their shock that the hostage Gertie Girdle is by no means the decorous young lady she ought to be.

Philosophy, encyclopedias, pornography—even with all this, there's more to Raymond Queneau's almost infinite variety. He composed his autobiography in verse and topped it with a "cosmogony," an account of the world's history from its origins to the present day. One of his poems, a gather-ye-rosebuds lyric entitled "Si tu t'imagines," was set to music and sung by Juliette Greco, becoming France's number-one hit song. This genial polymath also found time to work up the French subtitles for Fellini's *La Strada* and to translate the Nigerian Amos Tutuola's *Palm-Wine Drinkard*. Queneau even lived to see his most famous novel, *Zazie in the Metro* (1959), reemerge as a minor film classic. Directed by Louis Malle, the movie, like the book, follows a worldly-wise and foul-mouthed little girl through a phantasmagoric Paris that is part Wonderland, part Arabian Nights and where no one is quite what he or she seems. Not even the ever-gentle Marceline. Or a certain obnoxious parrot.

Playful, ingenious, witty, Queneau's novels tend to focus on holy fools who participate in ordinary life with a kind of inner detachment that comes to seem like the deepest wisdom. All the books are strictly organized (but not always obviously). *The Bark Tree* is built around the number 7 and the artfully orchestrated deployment of various narrative techniques (letters, newspaper articles, a dog's consciousness, dreams, diary entries, etc.). *The Flight of Icarus* (1968) links its episodes to the several meanings of *voler* and *s'envoler* (e.g., to fly, to steal, to take off). Many of the books follow circular patterns, and *Saint Glinglin* (1948) is one of these.

An imaginary country enjoys perfect, unchanging weather, in part because of its annual Saint Glinglin festival, during which vast amounts of crockery are ritually smashed, and more directly because of its mysterious "cloud-chaser." The current mayor of Home Town is a powerful figure with three sons: Pierre, who grows into a death-haunted philosopher obsessed with understanding the meaning of life and racked with hatred for his "emasculating" father; Paul, who despises nature, maintains that the city is man's "natural" environment and eventually marries a star of the "cinematograph"; and Jean, who dwells as an ascetic and wanderer in the Bare Hills near the Home Town. In the course of the novel the sons discover that they have a beautiful but insane sister, who is exploited by their father, partly for her prophetic powers but perhaps sexually as well.

For a relatively short novel *Saint Glinglin* feels as tightly packed as an egg in its shell. The book's structure loosely follows that of the three kingdoms: animal, mineral, and vegetable. There are lots of bookish echoes—of Freud's *Totem and Taboo* (sons banding together to destroy their father); of Rilke's *Malte Laurids Brigge* (the meditative awakening of Pierre to life's reality while staying in a strange city); of Benji's monologue in Faulkner's *Sound and the Fury*; of elements from the Gospels and Old Testament (one section emulates long-lined biblical verse). The action, however, recalls some ancient tribal myth: the all-powerful father is transformed into a statue by a petrifying fountain; a period of never-ending rain sets in; each of the sons becomes mayor in turn; and finally fair weather is restored through human sacrifice. Imagine, then, an amalgam of the anthropological and the archetypal, leavened with sex, slapstick, wordplay, and philosophical investigations.

James Sallis's translation is deft and accurate, his English dotted with felicities. "Life, with all its seesaws, its alcohols, and its freaks." "He proceeded by small, measured steps, like one who has diarrhea." "The father came in struggling with delusions here and there, fore and aft, to the right, to the left." A dead grandmother is "wound in her finalest linen." In his brief introduction, Sallis also reminds American readers that "in French, when one says I'll love you till Saint Glinglin's, it means that his love will last forever. And when one says I'll do something-or-other on that fictitious saint's day, well, don't hold your breath: it'll never happen."

For a preliminary version of part of *Saint Glinglin*, Queneau once provided this dust-jacket comment: "Why shouldn't one demand a certain effort on the reader's part? Everything is always explained to him. He must eventually tire of being treated with such contempt." This novel will certainly repay readerly efforts—is it a vision of the end of history?—but none is required to enjoy its bizarre humor: fish swimming through flooded taverns while the drunks get drunker; an ethnographer, curious about local customs, suffering ritual kicks in the bottom; a satiric glimpse of foreigners who spend their lives in boxes; a movie queen who bathes nude and sexually arouses an entire town.

Rich as it is, *Saint Glinglin* is clearly only a core sample of Raymond Queneau's own amazing richness. Each of his books is original, each has its boisterous fans. (My favorites remain *The Bark Tree* and *The Sunday of Life*.) But all Queneau's novels share a spring-morning joyousness in transmuting the workaday into the wonderful. As one reads these philosophical fairy tales, they might almost seem inconsequential, light as air, but they linger in the memory and are made to last.

August 22, 1993

SURVIVING:
THE UNCOLLECTED WRITINGS
OF HENRY GREEN

Edited by Matthew Yorke

LOVING / LIVING / PARTY GOING

By Henry Green

NOTHING / DOTING / BLINDNESS

By Henry Green

"Anyway, the point is this," Evelyn Waugh once said emphatically to a friend, "Henry is a genius. I am not a genius." The author of *Brideshead Revisited* was quite sincere in his admiration for Henry Vincent Yorke (1905–1973), a manufacturer of distillery equipment who composed nine novels and a memoir under the name Henry Green. Moreover, Waugh was hardly alone, though certainly out of character, in his generous estimation of Green's talents. V. S. Pritchett once said that the author of *Loving, Party Going,* and *Doting* wrote "better than anyone living about sexual life." John Updike and Eudora Welty have long regarded Green with something approaching awe. W. H. Auden called him "the best novelist alive."

Green's books, often desperately labeled comedies of manners, all share certain characteristics: a highly dramatic structure, light punctuation and languid syntax, elusive symbols (birds, roses), a vaguely hallucinatory feel, and an uncanny ability to reproduce the way people—millworkers or millionaires—actually talk. The beauty that Green achieves through all this is hard to convey, but his "poetic" novels can be as sexually knowing as Restoration dramas, as serenely moving as Eliot's *Four Quartets*. Welty has said it best: here "the world is always right up against our eyes."

Still, if Henry Green is so good, why isn't he as famous as (Henry) Graham Greene? Of course, Green is known; he's even been dubbed "a writer's writer's writer." For general readers, though, his slender volumes with their gerundive titles may look a little airy-fairy and precious. This is unfair, as so much of Green's flavor derives from his belief that life is far more important than literature, "that over-blown trumpet." James Joyce's ideal artist was an indifferent god, paring his fingernails; by contrast Henry Green once said, "I write books, but I am not proud of this any more than anyone is of their nails growing." In fact, his best novels deal with quite ordinary people: factory workers, servants, firefighters, children. As Green believed that "simply everything has supreme importance, if it happens," so his books buzz with life while he takes up, time and again, the central human dilemma of love versus loneliness. Along the way he somehow manages to turn "the broken bottles our lives are" into art. In short, his is fiction for grown-ups, not kids.

Surviving, Green's uncollected writings as edited by his grandson, will find readers mainly among already confirmed Chlorophiles (John Updike's coinage). The most interesting pieces are the sections of an abandoned and overabstract novel from the late 1920s entitled *Mood*; a prose poem about lovers in a wood ("Fight"); several anecdotes of life with London's firefighters during the Blitz; and an essay on C. M. Doughty's *Arabia Deserta*, an acknowledged influence on Green's swirling, sinuous sentences. To buttress these fragments, playlets, and reviews, Updike contributes an appreciation, Sebastian Yorke an informative memoir of his father, and Terry Southern a very funny interview. In one notable exchange Southern asks the rather deaf Green about his work being "subtle"; the novelist coyly replies, "I don't follow. Suttee, as I understand it, is the suicide—now forbidden—of a Hindu wife on her husband's flaming bier. I don't want my wife to do that when my time comes— and with great respect, as I know her, she won't."

Green, like many of his famous Oxford generation (the novelist Anthony Powell, critic Cyril Connolly, travel writer Robert Byron, et al.), valued wit, and even his darkest books flash with humor. His first novel, *Blindness* (1926), completed before he was twenty though by no means a piece of juvenilia, tracks a young aesthete's spiritual growth after he is accidentally blinded when a boy throws a rock through a train window. At one point, the young hero fantasizes about revenge: "He would be apprehended for murder, and he would love it. He would make the warder read the papers to him every morning, he would be sure to have headlines: BLIND MAN MURDERS CHILD—no, TOR-

TURES CHILD TO DEATH. And underneath that, if he was lucky, WOMAN JUROR VOMITS, something really sensational."

Green's second novel, *Living* (1929), depicts life at a double of his well-to-do family's Birmingham foundry, where the Oxford dropout spent two happy years as a common laborer (his mates thought he was being punished by his father for some sexual misdemeanor). The book shifts back and forth between a group of workers and the upper-class Duprets, who own the mill, touching on contrasting love affairs. *Living* has long enjoyed notoriety because it uses virtually no articles in its descriptive sentences; "a," "an," and "the" appear only in conversation. Green has said that he wanted to pare the language down to give the book a stark and majestic, almost biblical quality: in one lovely scene a worker sings all day in Welsh, amid the din of heavy machinery, because "that night son had been born to him." Christopher Isherwood called *Living* the best novel ever written about working-class life; in an interview Green wondered how much Isherwood actually knew about working people.

After this quick start, Green—now a full-time factory executive—spent nearly ten years on his next novel, making its prose luxuriant and seductive. In *Party Going* (1939) he examines a group of rich young people—"my own crowd in London"—who are marooned by fog at a train station and take refuge in an adjoining hotel. Amorous intrigue, bitchy upper-class repartee, a vaguely threatening throng in the public rooms below, and an atmosphere rich in symbolism make *Party Going* a mix of Shakespearean romance and Kafkaesque disquiet. In the novel's opening scene a pigeon falls dead at an old lady's feet, and she carefully wraps it in brown paper. No explanation is offered. Later, an old servingman yearns for a kiss—and a beautiful girl suddenly appears from behind a trunk, kisses him, and vanishes, never to be glimpsed again. All the novel's characters seem caught up in this sensual music, especially the gorgeous and vain Amabel: "As she went over herself with her towel it was plain that she loved her own shape and skin. When she dried her breasts she wiped them with as much care as she would puppies after she had given them their bath, smiling all the time. But her stomach she wiped unsmilingly upwards to make it thin. When she came to dry her legs she hissed like grooms do."

Figuring that he would be killed in the coming war, the thirty-five-year-old Green adopted a fatalistic tone for his autobiographical *Pack My Bag* (1940). In this book he writes of family, fishing, Eton, his lazy Oxford routine (movies, drinking), the seriocomic discovery of sex and romance. "For a son there is a fatal ring to the words 'Her mother was an old friend of mine.'" Only briefly does he speak of his art: "Prose is not to be read aloud but to oneself at night, and it is not quick as poetry, but rather a gathering web of insinuations. . . . Prose should be a long intimacy between strangers. . . . It should slowly appeal to feelings unexpressed, it should in the end draw tears out of the stone."

Tears, and even more laughter, are certainly elicited in *Loving* (1943), Green's only near–best seller. Set in an Irish castle staffed, improbably, with British servants who worry constantly about the IRA and a possible German invasion, this modern fairy tale opens "Once upon a time" and ends with "they lived happily ever after." But here the frog-prince is a vulgar forty-year-old butler and the princess a young chambermaid with dark eyes "like plums dipped in cold water." Every scene is perfect: the hilarious moment when Edith discovers her adulterous mistress and the Captain tangled in bed together; Raunce the butler writing to his mother, first setting the words down in pencil, then carefully inking them in with a pen; Edith and Kate in a great empty hall "wheeling wheeling in each other's arms" to the music of a phonograph while the chandeliers reflect "in their hundred thousand drops the single sparkle of distant day, again and again red velvet panelled walls, and two girls, minute in purple, dancing multiplied to eternity in these trembling pears of glass."

During the war Green served, like several fellow writers, including Stephen Spender, as an auxiliary firefighter, an experience that provided the backdrop to his novel *Caught* (1945). ("On the pavement opposite Turtle's," says Evelyn Waugh naughtily in *Officers and Gentlemen*, "a group of the progressive novelists in firemen's uniform were squirting a little jet of water into the morning room.") In *Back* (1946) a returning soldier, who has lost a leg because he failed to notice "the gun beneath a rose," is obsessed with his dead beloved Rose. By the last page of this rose-haunted romance, our hero has, with difficulty, come to care for another woman—with whom Green informs us he will enjoy a happy life—but after their first lovemaking together the emotional strain is too great and he breaks down, tearfully murmuring, "Rose, Rose." Green immediately ends the novel with a poignant and beautifully constructed sentence: "And she knew what she had taken on. It was no more or less, really, than she had expected."

Party Going, Loving, Caught, and *Back* are basically love stories, but they also rank among the finest English novels about the impact of the Second World War. For some reason, though, *Caught, Back,* and *Concluding* (1948) have long been out of print in the United States. This is particularly regrettable in the case of *Concluding,* Green's autumnal masterpiece. In a vague socialistic future, an old scientist, living on the grounds of a state-run girls' school, worries about his granddaughter, who loves a young teacher; mean-spirited headmistresses conspire; two students disappear and one is found; the young girls, whose names all start with *M*, prepare for a dance; nature swarms and threatens in the background. The entire book also shimmers with a kind of verbal *sfumato*, and even Green's syntax is sexy. "At this instant, like a woman letting down her mass of hair from a white towel in which she had bound it, the sun came through for a moment, and lit the azaleas on either side before fog, redescending, blanketed these off again, as it might be white curtains, drawn by someone out of sight, over a palace bedroom window, to shut behind them a blonde princess undressing."

In his last two books, the brittle *Nothing* (1950) and *Doting* (1952), Green chose to tell his stories almost entirely in dialogue. Though somewhat lacking the old magic, the novels remain highly enjoyable: in *Doting*, for instance, a well-to-do father grows infatuated with a teenaged girl, while his wife, partly out of jealousy, takes up with his best friend. It's the stuff of farce and tragedy, but one also feels, with a voyeuristic frisson, that Green may here be somewhat too closely autobiographical, especially as some of the novel's details first appeared in *Pack My Bag*.

Green stopped writing in 1952, at age forty-seven, no one is entirely sure why, then retired from business in 1959. In these years before his death in 1973, he grew increasingly deaf and reclusive, even refusing to be photographed face-on; so Cecil Beaton took portraits of the author turned away from the camera. (A wag said, "I'd know that back anywhere.") Eventually, a time came when Green simply stayed indoors, drinking heavily and reading novels (one a day). With appropriate diminuendo, nearly the last piece of prose he ever published, "Falling in Love," concludes with the words "we are, all and each one of us, always and always alone." He might have called it "Finishing."

Henry Green's idiosyncratic, incomparable novels are not famous and probably never will be—alas. But those readers who care about the art of fiction will always and always, sooner or later, make their way to them. Start with *Loving*.

February 28, 1993

GEORGES PEREC:
A LIFE IN WORDS

By David Bellos

Italo Calvino, modestly passing over his own imaginative writing, maintained that Georges Perec's *La Vie Mode d'Emploi* (1978, translated as *Life A User's Manual*) was "the last 'real' event in the development of the novel so far." In one of the first essays in English on Perec's masterwork, Gabriel Josipovici dared to invoke not only Joyce's *Ulysses* for comparison but also Dante's *Commedia* and the Old Testament. Perec (1936-1982) himself privately hoped to write a book that could stand on the same shelf as *War and Peace* and *The Magic Mountain*.

Georges Perec? Georges . . . Perec? His is not precisely a household name here in the United States—to our loss. One can only hope that David Bellos's engaging and thoughtful, albeit somewhat overlong, critical biography may help redress matters. For Perec, his dense poetry apart, is exceptionally readable; *Life A User's Manual* resembles the ingratiating *One Hundred Years of Solitude* far more than it does the forbidding *Gravity's Rainbow*, to mention two contemporary books in its small class.

Bellos's life builds up to an account of the composition of Perec's *Life*, partly because that novel is one of those encyclopedic Big Books that draw on and surpass all of a writer's earlier work, and partly because the forty-six-year-old Perec died of cancer in 1982, a few years after completing it. To further organize his material Bellos has sought the secret engine of this French writer's imagination and found it in a pervasive, yet almost unspoken, Jewishness.

Born in 1936 to Polish Jews living in Paris, Georges Perec lost both his working-class parents to World War II: his father, Icek, died as a soldier early in the hostilities; his mother, Cyrla, was transported to Auschwitz and never heard from again. Fortunately, the young boy found himself taken in by well-meaning relatives, though he seems never to have truly fitted into the bourgeois family of his diamond merchant uncle. Bellos makes a strong case that the disappearance of his parents haunts all of Perec's fiction.

Consider, for instance, the notorious tour de force *The Disappearance (La Disparition,* 1969). I say notorious because the book appears little more than a lexical joke: not a word in this strange whodunit uses the letter *e,* a feat as extravagantly difficult in French as it is in English. In part, Perec adopted this form, called a lipogram, to demonstrate his bona fides as a new member of the French Workshop for Potential Literature (Ouvroir de Littérature Potentielle, or OULIPO), an elite group of mathematicians and writers devoted to exploring new methods of literary composition, especially the unexpected freeing of the imagination that accompanies the adoption of formal constraints. But Bellos emphasizes that Perec's alphabetic self-hobbling also incorporates deep feelings of personal loss and guilt. Each time a character in the novel is compelled to pronounce a word containing an *e,* he or she immediately dies. A mere letter, like a mere fact of birth, can result in extermination. In just such arbitrary fashion Perec's father and mother simply vanished. They are the true missing element in *La Disparition,* as in Perec's life. With a final flourish, Bellos reminds us that the letter *e* in French is pronounced the same way as the word for "them" (*eux*).

Though known for his unrivaled linguistic agility—Perec constructed the longest palindrome in the world (a 500-word story that makes a sort-of sense when read either forward or backward) and contributed weekly crosswords to *Le Point* magazine—this wild-haired, elf-like beatnik managed to invest everything he wrote with autobiography. His first novel, *Things (Les Choses,* 1965), which won the Prix Renaudot and became a surprise best seller, chronicles the obsession of Perec's generation with material goods; *A Man Asleep (Un Homme Qui Dort,* 1967) is a portrait of depression derived from its author's own bouts with melancholia; *W, or the Memory of Childhood (W, ou le Souvenir d'Enfance,* 1975) proffers a kind of fictive autobiography, alternating the tale of a country entirely devoted to sport with Perec's supposed earliest "memories" (many of which Bellos shows are slightly skewed); the two storylines intersect when the land of W gradually reveals its Nazi-like heart. Largely because of David Bellos and Godine, all three of these works, as well as *Life,* are available in English.

While growing up in Paris during the 1950s, Perec knew from an early age that he wanted to be a writer. But "Jojo" was no scholar and his academic career could be called checkered at best. To earn his living he became a glorified secretary/researcher for a medical laboratory, creating spectacularly efficient cross-indexes, card files, and record-keeping systems. While he looked like a disheveled bohemian in his old sweaters or Indian cotton shirts, and enjoyed partying with friends (drinking wine, playing cards or Go), Perec seems to have possessed the mind of a computer programmer and the soul of Lewis Carroll. He loved systematizing. During 1974 he kept a diary in which he noted down everything he ate; another year he recorded all his dreams. For one particularly ambitious work he developed a complicated algorithm, based on a magic square, that would allow him to describe again and again the same twelve places in Paris at the rate of two a month over twelve years; at the end of that time he would possess 288 sealed essays that would chronicle changes in his city, his life, and his memories.

Perec eventually gave up on this plan, mainly because he started to find it difficult to be in Paris at fixed times. Once established as a writer, he traveled frequently: to Germany, where he pioneered experimental radio programs (*Die Maschine*, 1972, is a kind of radio deconstruction of a famous Goethe poem), to America, for work on a film documentary about Ellis Island, and finally to Australia, where he became a writer in residence shortly before his death. Still, the aborted "places" series hovers behind that masterpiece of "multiplex constraint," *Life A User's Manual.*

Perec set forth on this book partly to demonstrate that OULIPian methods could be applied to an 800-page novel. *Life* relates, in a rather dispassionate, almost Olympian voice, the lives of scores of tenants in an apartment building at 11 Rue Simon-Crubellier. Each of the ninety-nine chapters zeroes in on one of the hundred rooms in the building (a certain corner storeroom is left out), describing the furnishings and relating the histories of past or current residents. The wealthy James Sherwood collects unique items and dispenses a considerable fortune to acquire the Holy Grail; the lexicographer Cinoc goes through dictionaries eliminating obsolete words to make room for new ones; Marcel Appenzell journeys to Sumatra to research an obscure tribe, which turns out to be surprisingly nomadic—because, he finally realizes, the people are trying to get away from him; sexy Ingeborg Skrifter works as a medium, who for a substantial fee can summon the devil for people willing to sell their souls.

These often fabulous stories—of bicycle racers and millionaires, of autodidacts and former movie stars—are in themselves as sheerly enjoyable as anything in *Ellery Queen's Mystery Magazine* or Jules Verne. But what makes *Life A User's Manual* so unforgettable derives from Perec's miraculous evocation of how "life goes on"—his favorite phrase—before and after major traumas, how crimes and scandal and heartbreak and the deepest sorrow are surrounded by decades of ordinary life. Such a revelation may surprise readers aware of the novel's elaborate scaffolding. As Bellos tells us, Perec began by constructing a grid of his imaginary apartment building; then established a system for moving among its hundred rooms based on a modified Knight's Tour (by which a knight covers a chessboard without ever landing on the same square twice). But that's only the beginning. Perec also created multiple sets of constraints, surreptitiously constructing each of the novel's chapters around elements from forty different categories; items from these ten-count lists (of authors, paintings, furnishings, activities, food, drink, etc.) are unobtrusively and systematically distributed, in various combinations, throughout the book. For instance, one of the literary works periodically alluded to is *Hamlet*: in one chapter the reader may glimpse the painting of "A Rat behind the Arras," in another the decorated plate entitled "A Bad Joke," which shows a man pouring some liquid into a sleeper's ear. To complicate matters further, this gleeful artificer even adopts extra constraints: e.g., buried in a list of the painter Hutting's works lie the names of all the members of OULIPO (here is the partially hidden Calvino allusion: "swimming to shore at Calvi, noting with pleasure . . .").

As it happens, Perec revealed only a few of his templates and methods to the public, so *Life A User's Manual* has been growing increasingly rich as critics gradually uncover its secret structures (and corny jokes, like the soloist Virginia Fredericksburg). Certainly it is the most carefully schematized book since *Ulysses*. Yet like Joyce's masterpiece, it remains, for all its hidden craft, extremely touching and exhilarating, both human and humane.

David Bellos's *Georges Perec: A Life in Words* illuminates all these matters and more. It is an ideal, if leisurely, introduction to Georges Perec's varied work, as well as a deeply engrossing biography of this troubled, unassuming, utterly unexpected genius of letters.

January 9, 1994

MULLIGAN STEW

By Gilbert Sorrentino

Let's begin with the essential: *Mulligan Stew* is outrageously dazzling. Its pedigree goes back not to the well-made novel but rather to the "anatomy"—those extravaganzas that sprawl across world literature, offering encyclopedic, and usually comic, views of life and its foibles. Like *Gargantua and Pantagruel* or *Tristram Shandy*, *Mulligan Stew* sustains a display of linguistic virtuosity that takes your breath away. It contains some of the best parodies since S. J. Perelman at his most manic, and perhaps the most corrosive satire of the literary scene since early Aldous Huxley. This is a novel with all the stops pulled out, Gilbert Sorrentino's masterpiece.

Gilbert who? Well you should ask. Born in 1929 in Brooklyn, Sorrentino began writing in the 1950s, founded a small magazine called *Neon*, and later became book editor of the influential critical magazine *Kulchur* in the early 1960s. He has written three previous novels—all neglected: *The Sky Changes* (1966), *Steelwork* (1970), and the searingly black-humored *Imaginative Qualities of Actual Things* (1971).

A mulligan stew can contain anything—and Sorrentino has said that he wanted to be able to put anything into his book. He has. Part of its pleasure is in its variety: there are morsels for every literary taste. Essentially, the book parodies—with enormous gusto—the degraded language of cheap fiction, bad poetry, academic criticism. To control, if only gingerly, a chaos of language, Sorrentino employs three interconnected, yet distinct, stories. The narrative lines may seem complicated in summary, but each is clearly labeled and a reader will have no trouble keeping things straight.

In the first, a writer named Antony Lamont is painfully composing an "absurdist" detective novel. He keeps a scrapbook in which he records his thoughts and plans for the book, as well as his correspondence with various people, among them his sister Sheila, who is married to a rival novelist, Dermot Trellis. In the second narrative strand, Sorrentino presents in toto each chapter of Lamont's novel, which unfolds the events that have led the publisher Martin Halpin to murder his friend Ned Beaumont. Beaumont had been in love with Daisy Buchanan ("haut monde her place, haute couture her love, haute cuisine her mundane fare") until he was bewitched by two mysterious temptresses named Corrie Corriendo and Berthe Delamode. For the third narrative plane, Sorrentino adopts a technique used by Flann O'Brien in *At Swim-Two-Birds*: all the characters in Lamont's novel are able to lead independent lives when the writer is away from his worktable. Halpin, for instance, keeps a detailed journal, recording Beaumont's gripes (about the sodden lout he must play) and both their opinions of the novel in which they appear.

Sorrentino, like his creation Lamont, obviously steals his players from other productions. Antony Lamont and Dermot Trellis (as well as the title to Trellis's pornographic classic, *The Red Swan*) are drawn from *At Swim-Two-Birds*. Ned Beaumont is the tough-guy hero of Dashiell Hammett's *The Glass Key*; Daisy and Tom Buchanan are from *The Great Gatsby*. Halpin, as he tells us, appears in Joyce, and several figures referred to in passing are the burned-out writers and artists of *Imaginative Qualities of Actual Things*. None of Sorrentino's characters is fleshed out; they remain—deliberately—caricatures, pegs on which to hang his prose.

Within each of the three narrative strands, which interact like a triple helix, Sorrentino works his kaleidoscopic inventions and parodies. Lamont's scrapbook, for instance, contains extracts from a number of his previous fictions. In one, Levenspiel monologizes from the pages of some archetypal "Jewish" novel: "My wife with the fur coats, the new dresses, the tight pants so you should see her whole body, I need this?" In another appears the weariest of world-weary detectives: "I crushed my glass in my hand. I didn't feel the pain except as part of the constant pain that was my whole bitter, shabby life."

Besides pastiche, Sorrentino has always delighted in lists, offering several in *Stew*. The best is a five-page epic catalog of the books and magazines in the cabin where Halpin is telling his tale of love betrayed. Their titles are wonderful (and subtly naughty): *Say Yes to Love*, by Molly Bloom; *Napalm and Its Role in World Peace*, by Maxwell Champagne, Lt. Gen. USAF (Ret.); *Golf Your Way to Sexual Fulfillment*, by Franz Godemiche; *Bridges: Poets Express Their Love*, by Horace Rosette, ed.; *A Layman's Guide to the Flies of North America*, by Rex Mattachine. Among the periodicals are *Gibraniana*, *Art Futures*, *Deep Image Quarterly*, and *The Fargo Catamite*. Nearly all these titles and authors are echoed elsewhere—the fictional Rosette, for example, apparently wrote the reader's report on *Mulligan Stew* for Grove Press.

Among the tastiest morsels of *Mulligan Stew* is an interview with a Nabokov look-alike named Thomas McCoy. "One wishes to create characters," says McCoy when questioned about his novelistic intent, "who will speak directly to the minds of comparative literature professors and intelligent book reviewers." Sorrentino, in his own way of course, does just this: the better read you are, the more jokes you get. Consider Lamont's arty allusions, always slightly off-center: "My favorite painter is the Picasso of *Blue Proles.*" There are numerous skewed borrowings from Eliot: "I wished that I might be a pair of ragged Moors battling to tear the drawers from nubile knees." Mallarmé cocktails contain "white crème de menthe and ocean spray."

Like Perelman, Sorrentino also relishes mixing metaphors and changing allusions in the middle of a sentence: "Autumn leaves while others stand and wait" or "French letters in the sand," or even "a shantih in old shantihtown." At times he comes out with home truths perfect in their perverse logic: "Pitchers are bad hitters because they think of the ball as their friend." "Those who do not follow trends are condemned to repeat them."

But this isn't all to this "soup of pleasures various." The notable critic Vance Whiteside introduces *The Red Swan* in perfect academese: "It is a kind of narrative in reverse, i.e., it does not so much unfold specifics as suggest alternatives to non-specifics. . . . What seems, on cursory reading, to be uncontrolled chaos atop chaos in this brilliant sur-fiction is revealed upon closer examination to be the continual stitching and unstitching of almost instantaneous metamorphoses. Things are not only not what they seem to be, they never were."

(This too is, beneath the jargon, a paradoxically close description of *Mulligan Stew* itself.) No less exact is the radio preacher style of Mrs. Ashby, the famed healer and seer: "Touch her radiant Body and her Power and Faith will flow into you." *The Sweat of Love*, a chapbook by Lorna Flambeaux, sings praises to love and the male sexual organ. Among her poems—all presented in their entirety—are "Hot Bodies," "Open to Your Pridehood: A Prayer," and "Summerfuck: A Dramatic Eclogue." (Flambeaux herself proves to be demurely puritan, shocked by Lamont's advances.)

The dual high points of *Mulligan Stew* are *Flawless Play Restored: The Masque of Fungo* and the orgy scene at the Club Zap. The first is a Joycean phantasmagoria—comparable to the Bloom in Nighttown section of *Ulysses*—with a cast of thousands, among whom are Susan B. Anthony and Barnacle Bill. The masque recounts the shortstop Foots Fungo's miraculous recovery of his ability for flawless play at baseball. The whole thing is a carnival of off-color jokes, puns, and burlesques, including a takeoff on Robert Herrick: "When as in scanties Betsy goes."

As should be clear by now, Sorrentino possesses a Rabelaisian bawdiness—some of his funniest jokes are not quotable here. After parodying every literary form going, he presents what he labels his "obligatory sex scene." Daisy and Halpin go to see Corriendo and Delamode at the Club Zap, in the hopes of freeing Ned Beaumont from their insidious clutches. Instead they are drugged and all four participate in a lovingly described orgy. Their various positions and swirling wisps of clothing are detailed in the tone of a leering fashion expert: ". . . her superbly crafted thighs tattooed with dainty lengths of insubstantially delicious straps that gently pinched the glossy tops of the navy sheerness that caressed her legs." The whole scene is ludicrous yet erotic.

One should bear in mind that all of these puns and witticisms are happening "with the rapidity of speed itself"—they never let up. Still, the scenes are sufficiently paced that the various stylistic acrobatics seldom pall—for example, a parodically dry paper on mathematical proofs thoughtfully prepares the reader for the luxurious orgy scene. Much of Sorrentino's brilliance and humor depend, too, on the gradual building of a situation and a language maniacally appropriate to it.

Mulligan Stew climaxes with the madness of Lamont, who, losing control of his novel, comes to believe it is being written by someone else. All his characters naturally abandon him. As Halpin prepares to leave he bids adieu: "To you other cats and chicks out there . . . a shake and a hug and a kiss and a drink. Cheers!"

Cheers, indeed—for Gilbert Sorrentino. One hopes that this brilliant tour de force will bring him the recognition he deserves, but I fear that, as he himself has written, "If you make a better book the world will build a mousetrap at your door."

June 17, 1979

POSTSCRIPT: This is the earliest review reprinted in *Bound to Please*. And I haven't changed my mind about Gilbert Sorrentino. He remains one of the most innovative and rewarding writers of his time. Who else would construct an entire novel—*Gold Fools*—as a series of questions? "Time in its Flight" is as fine a story as any by Scott Fitzgerald or John Cheever, one that lyrically relates a tale of young love while also undercutting its romanticism. *Imaginative Qualities of Actual Things* is not only shrewd about the artistic bohemia of the 1960s and 1970s but very, very funny. In everything he undertakes Sorrentino presses hard against the limits of conventional fiction.

RIDDLEY WALKER

By Russell Hoban

"HE WERE TALKING so many levvils at 1ce I dint all ways knows what he meant realy I wisht everything wud mean jus only 1 thing an keap on meaning it not changing all the time."

Many readers on opening *Riddley Walker*, Russell Hoban's extraordinary combination of quest romance, science fiction, linguistic experiment, and theological speculation, may feel the same confusion as its narrator-hero. For Hoban's is a complex story, being largely about how we interpret language and understand ourselves, "what the idear of us myt be." Suffused with melancholy and wonder, beautifully written, *Riddley Walker* is a novel that people will be reading for a long, long time.

The world, or rather what's left of it, has been bombed back into the Stone Age. At least 2,500 years after the "1 Big 1" (which occurred in 1997), people in England are still living in small groups, foraging across the burned-out land around Canterbury, once the location of a nuclear facility, and just beginning to farm again. Intelligence has declined, literacy persists only among certain shamans, man's most feared enemies are the dogs that roam in packs of forty or more, patiently waiting for the moment when they can rip throats and genitals. ("Whats a dog? Its some thing you can't get close to.") Even the weather seems to be uniformly bleak and desolate, either "a thin grey grizel" or rains "as took the hart and hoap out of you" and "made you feal like all the tracks in the worl wer out paths nor not a 1 to bring you back."

Virtually all knowledge of science, religion, and history has been lost.

Virtually, but not quite all. Shadows and shards of the past survive in songs, legends, and puppet plays. One troubling myth describes the fall from unity with nature when men and women grew "clevver." "Counting counting they wer all the time. They had iron then and big fire then had towns of parpety. They had machines et numbers up. They fed them numbers and they fractiont out the power of things. They had the Nos. of the rainbow and the

Power of the air all workit out with counting which is how they get boats in the air and picters on the wind."

The most pervasive myth, however, is the sacred Eusa Story. Hoban dextrously transforms the Christian legend of Saint Eustace—who was converted by a vision of Christ standing with arms outstretched between the antlers of a stag—into an allegory of atomic energy. According to the oral tradition, a scientist named Eusa "smaulert" himself so that he could track down the "the Little Shynin Man the Addom" and force him to reveal the number of the Master Chaynjis, the 1 Big 1. He accomplishes this, but only after tearing the Little Shynin Man in two, releasing vast power.

At the novel's beginning, twelve-year-old Riddley Walker becomes the new "connexion man" for his settlement after his father's death, his task being to interpret the semireligious puppet plays about Eusa performed by traveling showmen. Once initiated as a "connexion man," he grows increasingly sensitive to supernatural forces. After a series of omens, "blips and syns," culminating in the discovery of a disquieting hand puppet representing the unfamiliar figure of Punch, Riddley abandons his people and goes out "roading" into the storm and wilderness. Following the Black Leader of the Bernt Arse dog pack, he frees the imprisoned Ardship of Cambry, a blind, almost faceless psychic. With Lissener, as the Ardship is also called, Riddley finds himself involved in an attempt to rediscover the 1 Big 1, inadvertently bringing on a power struggle between the country's two most powerful chiefs, the Pry Mincer and Wes Mincer of Inland. That struggle ends with a bang when the components for gunpowder, the 1 little 1, are deciphered from an old riddle. Throughout this time, Riddley undergoes progressively more intense mystical experiences, gradually coming to realize "what we ben! And what we come to!"

What is marvelous in all this is the way Hoban makes us experience the uncanny familiarity of this world, while also making it a strange and animistic place, where words almost have a life of their own. "What ben makes tracks for what will be. Words in the air print foot steps on the ground for us to put our feet into." Hoban achieves this power largely through the book's transcription of Riddley's speech, at once degenerate modern English and a supple poetic tongue all its own, reminiscent of Anglo-Saxon in its rhetorical formality, rhythms, and music.

Consider "Fools Circel 9Wys," which at first seems only a children's rhyme, but gradually assumes increasingly disturbing significance:

Horny Boy rung Widders Bel
Stoal his Fathers Ham as wel
Bernt his Arse and Forkt a Stoan

Done it Over broak a boan
Out of Good Shoar vackt his wayt
Scratch Sams Itch for No. 8
Gone to senter nex to see
Cambry coming 3 times 3
Sharna pax and get the poal
When the Ardship of Cambry
comes out of the hoal

What does all this mean? The name of the rhyme suggests both a fool's circle and a full circle. Most of the capitalized words are the distorted place names of Kent, now known as the Dead Towns: Herne Bay, Whitestable, Faversham, Folkestone, Dover, Sandwich, Canterbury. Following a kind of folk etymology, they have lost their abstract quality and regained a new literalness, one appropriate to man's return to savagery. The Ardship of Cambry is both the hardship and the archbishop of Canterbury, a figure reviled and revered. "Vackt his wayt" breaks up a long word—evacuate—into simpler parts. Another common linguistic twist, the transposition of sounds, appears in "Sharna pax"—sharpen an ax.

This corrupt English, a language of compressed, unexpected power, gives the book its particular flavor and excitement. "Deacon terminations," "gallack seas," "party cools," "Saul and Peter" transform the forgotten into the familiar. Scientific jargon, such as "axel rating the Inner G," also crops up regularly: in his desperate search for the technological knowledge to help humanity get going "frontways" again, the Pry Mincer explains, "We've got to work the E qwations and the low cations we've got to comb the nations of it. . . . We ben diggin in the groun for it we ben spare the mending we ben tryl narrering for it we ben asking roun the circel for it."

"Asking roun the circel for it." After freeing Lissener, Riddley learns that "Fools Circle 9wys" describes an actual practice. It seems that following the catastrophe some of the "Puter Leat" (computer elite) employed by Eusa were kept alive as sacred monsters, lessons for the future: because they worked close to the Power Senter, they were the most genetically injured, such that all of their descendants are mutants and grotesques. Every twelve years the Ardship, leader of these Eusa Folk, ritually repeats a trek around the Dead Towns actually undertaken by Eusa during the "Bad Times." At each stop on that circuit he is questioned by the Pry Mincer about the Master Chaynjis—matter transformation, but also the spiritual ordering of the universe (with perhaps a hint of our Master Jesus); at journey's end, when the Ardship returns to Cambry, his head is chopped off, as was Eusa's in "time back way back."

Now Hoban has so contrived it that this circuit and return to the Power Senter reflects at once: (1) a children's ring game; (2) the "historical" travels of Eusa; (3) the actual trials of the Ardship of Cambry; (4) the anthropomorphized descriptions of a particle accelerated in a cyclotron and then shot back into a central core; and (5) the past and future movements of Riddley himself—he is the horny boy, who has rung the widders bel, inadvertently killed his father, etc. Yet only as the novel progresses do these meanings accrue, causing every word to shine out ever more brightly in several directions. The reader learns and solves the riddles along with Riddley.

Nearly all the important verbal elements of *Riddley Walker* undergo a similar crystallization. A key phrase like "Hart of the Wood" possesses a rich alchemical equivalence, meaning the stag of the forest (where Eusa discovered the Littl Shynin Man), the center of the stone wood at Cambry—apparently the pillars of Canterbury Cathedral—where Riddley experiences a spiritual awakening; the heartwood of a tree (used in making "chard coal" one of the three ingredients for the 1 Littl 1); the heart of the would, of "the wanting to be," that yearning for unity that appears on many levels throughout the novel (and much of Hoban's mature work); the hearth in the wood, where Riddley leads the blinded Pry Mincer after the explosion of the 1 Littl 1; and even perhaps the heart of the word—a simultaneous suggestion of Christ and the essence of language.

The power emanating from Cambry, around which the action like the characters revolve, is both atomic and religious, the two having become intertwined. In Riddley's climactic mystical vision, he falls to his knees, overwhelmed by the spiritual authority of Canterbury; there he feels how much humanity has lost, how much man still yearns for an end to "2ness," how much he needs to reunite the divided Addom: "Them as made Canterbury musve put ther selfs right. Only it dint stay right did it. Somers in betwean them stoan trees and the Power Ring they musve put ther selfs wrong. Now we dint have the 1 nor the other. . . . May be all there ever ben wer just only 1 minim when any thing cud be right and that minim all ways gone before you seen it."

At the book's end, Riddley Walker is still wandering, now a showman himself, not of Eusa, but of a rediscovered Punch and Judy. Punch he has learned, is the "oldes figger there is. He wer old time back way way back long befor Eusa ever been thot of. Hes so old he cant dy." Somehow Punch brings a new spirit into the world, as does, of course, the rediscovery of gunpowder. "Life aint qwite as simpl as it used to be."

Just as Riddley seeks to make connections, to find meaning, so readers of Hoban's book must explore the layering of its words and events. Back and forth goes the hermeneutic circle—Riddley and reader, each questing through a forest of symbols: "Walker is my name and I am the same. Riddley Walker. Walking my riddels where ever theyve took me and walking them now on this paper the same."

June 7, 1981

POSTSCRIPT: Except for Paula Fox, Russell Hoban is probably the only living American writer to have produced masterpieces for preschoolers, middle readers, and adults. His classic children's books include *Bread and Jam for Frances, How Tom Beat Captain Najork and His Hired Sportsmen,* and *The Mouse and His Child.* They are far simpler than *Riddley Walker,* but in their way just as good. Note, too, how Hoban's syntax in *Riddley Walker* anticipates email shorthand and even modern rap rhythms.

LARVA:

MIDSUMMER NIGHT'S BABEL

By Julián Ríos
Translated from the Spanish by Richard Alan Francis, with
Suzanne Jill Levine and the author

So you've spent the requisite twenty insomniac years on *Finnegans Wake*, worked out the knottier cruces of *The Divine Comedy*, and practically know *Gravity's Rainbow* and *Miss MacIntosh, My Darling* by heart. Umberto Eco holds no secrets for you; neither do Georges Perec, Arno Schmidt, and Joseph McElroy. But now, you ask expectantly, where are the fresh woods and pastures new of fiction, the writers worthy of your steel, the novels that you go into training for?

Heroic reader, *Larva* is the book for you.

It's got everything. It's translated—from Spanish (and has been acclaimed by Octavio Paz, Carlos Fuentes, and G. Cabrera Infante). Nearly every other word is a pun. There are five different "planes" of text: narrative on the right-hand page; footnotes on the left; explicatory "pillow notes" at the back; an index; and a set of photographs. And, best of all, it's only the first installment of five hefty volumes. When you've finished *Larva*, you can congratulate yourself on your stamina and then look forward to *Poundemonium, Auto de Fenix*, and two others as yet unwritten.

Such as it is, the main action of this tower of babble describes a phantasmagoric party held in London on midsummer's night. All the characters are masked or costumed; Don Juan is a principal figure, with guest appearances by harlequins, nuns, odalisques, amazons, and figures out of the *Arabian Nights* and Lewis Carroll. Periodically interrupting this gaudy spectacle, the book's "pillow notes" relate the adventures, most of them erotic, of Milalias (a thousand aliases), his beloved Babelle, his Belgian poet friend Rimbaudelaire and their mentor X. Reis. Neither of these two plotlines provides much narrative excitement beyond that of mild sexual titillation.

No, where *Larva* cracks open and takes wing is in its language, a kaleido-scopic display of linguistic excess that, like *Finnegans Wake*, starts with "the abnihilisation of the etym" and then turns the King's English into a "kinks English" of puns, palindromes, acronyms, and unruly garrulity. Imagine, again in Joyce's words, a crossmess parzel of plurabelle prose, a real mess of mottage.

Here's an example of what Julián Ríos is up to. Early on at the party Don Juan pursues Sleeping Beauty through a cluster of coupling couples. She sees "forming, gangling up, a naked nexus . . . nudes knotting in agreement. And farther back, in the weeds, amalgamating rituals." Eventually she comes upon a circle of witches and at their center "the Lecherous Goat from Goya's Witches' Sabbath, holding a big black book." A footnote here refers us to the opposite page where we read the following annotation: "Volume voluminous! Elephantiastique! Notre bouquin emissaire . . . [The scrapegoat and his defile cabinet. Summammary of his Magnum Opuss. The Black Book. The Book of Changes. The Wandering and the Book: Deambularvagabounding through London, reading on the run the book of their more or less imaginary lives. Or wandering blindly and randomly on his parodyssey, waylaid in search of adventures. His graphomanionianism made them err; airy erotic errata. Living the written and writing the relived was one of the paraphrasisyphean tasks of his Londonerous novel. They called it (w)rite to life, or writ(h)ing, without realizing they would ever overspend themselves in the undertaking.] Our old phony book. . . ."

After you catch your breath, you'll see that there are several kinds of word-play at work here. Simple sound repetition such as "volume voluminous." Portmanteau words à la Jabberwocky: "Elephantiastique," for instance, blends elephantiasis and the French *fantastique*. The next phrase takes the French slang word *bouquin* meaning book and attaches it to *bouc émissaire*, which is the French for scapegoat, and which in its turn echoes the Lecherous Goat. Note that "deambularvagabounding" incorporates the title "larva," as well as words for walking: "vagabond," "ambulate," "bound." I take the "deam" prefix to suggest dream, though I sense I'm overlooking something more.

"Parodyssey," a brilliant coinage, is another apt description of *Larva*, a book covered in black buckram as well as a book of (linguistic) changes. "Waylaid" slyly evokes the novel's sexual encounters. "Graphomanionianism" merges a mania for writing with the heresy of antinomianism, hence the "airy erotic errata." To compose *Larva* was certainly a "paraphrasisphyean task"—i.e., a Sisyphus-like labor of constant, never-ending paraphrasis. Writ(h)ing recalls Carroll's "reeling and writhing" while also suggesting the book's vitality, sexiness, and sinuous side-winding movement. "Overspend themselves in the undertaking" sets up a neat counterpoint. And "our old phony book" embodies *Larva*'s thickness and large number of characters, its humor, and even its utter artificiality.

This may all seem quite daunting written out, but a reader quickly picks up the knack of detecting and enjoying Ríos's multiple meanings. The best ones are often the simplest. "To each his onus." "Enemas and frenzies, I mean friends and enemies." "Quit your socrastination." "Harakyrieleison." "Don't count your chicks before they're laid." My favorite is "Sham Rock," the perfect name for a perfectly terrible Irish heavy-metal band.

Ríos, who's been working on *Larva* and its successors for more than fifteen years, loves every form of linguistic playfulness. Anagrams, such as "Silence gives license," sneak in repeatedly. A note on LSD says "Lysergic acid reinforces veiled arcana," which is a true-enough observation, but one whose initial letters also spell out "larva." Sometimes Ríos goes for pure sound effect: a porno moviemaker "screened his keen teen epicene dream to be seen in reams of obscene scenes." Allusions, literary and otherwise, abound: to undervalued writers like Jules Renard and the minnesinger Heinrich von Ofterdingen, to pop songs ("Help me, Rondo"), to Mr. Joyce from Dublin and Dr. Freud from Doblin. There's even a perfect two-line send-up, or put-down, of Swinburne, that by the addition of a single letter points out the kitschy quality of his most famous poem: "O sanguine and subtle Dolores . . . Our lady of Spain!"

Behind all this, of course, is Herr Narrator, "a sort of ventriloquacious nut who misproduces our voices. . . . A cunning conning cofounder and confounder." Behind him, in turn is Ríos, in back of whom are the astonishingly adept translators Richard Alan Francis and Suzanne Jill Levine—how did they ever manage to anglicize a daunting Spanish original? Nonetheless behind or before them all stand the readers who, by seeking the meanings in the book's extremes, become equal partners in its textual intercourse. Quite appropriately, the infinity sign becomes a key symbol in *Larva*, along with the four-leaf clover. A Ríos reader can use all the luck he can get.

Still, for all its oohs and awesome fireworks, *Larva* exemplifies associative wordplay more often than the true etymic fusion of *Finnegans Wake*. No doubt much is lost in even the most dazzling, dizzying translation, but in English the novel seems more an ingenious work than a work of genius. For some people, of course, it will hardly seem literature at all, more a sport of recreational linguistics or an example of what one might call—entering into the spirit of the thing—a punitive expedition into paronomasia minor. Or maybe a punishing workout? A pun-filled word-rout? A . . .

More pun-churner than page-turner, then, *Larva* nonetheless shows off the whirl within the word and reminds us that language can aim to be other than a transparent window, that one can sometimes have more gain with less pane. Painterly impressionism, incantation, musicality, rococo arabesque, multiple signification, sheer enchantment—these are Dionysiac qualities suppressed by the classical virtues of clear, efficient prose. A stern, schoolmasterly Samuel Johnson advised writers to give over their days and nights to the study of Addison; Julián Ríos, by contrast, rings the bell for recess and sends everyone, pushing and shoving, out to play.

February 24, 1991

LANDOR'S TOWER,
OR THE IMAGINARY CONVERSATIONS

By Iain Sinclair

Twenty years ago I was standing at one of the barrows in Farringdon Road, where George Jeffrey held the last remaining license to sell secondhand books on the streets of London. People often imagine the book trade to be a genteel business, but it isn't at all: runners—as the British call used-book scouts—are melancholy, sinewy men of indeterminate age, tough as rugby players, edgy as bike couriers. Come the end of the day or a sale, they will sip a beer, recall treasures lost and found, grow almost gregarious—but while the book fit is on them, they are ruthless, predatory, insatiable. A runner never rests until the last bookshop closes.

That Saturday morning my friend the science-fiction and fantasy collector John Clute introduced me to Iain Sinclair. I vaguely remember a slender guy in glasses, telling me that as a scout he specialized in the Beats and experimental literature. Later, I learned he'd published a few things himself, collections of verse mainly. When Peter Ackroyd's first big novel, *Hawksmoor*, came out, I read that it partly drew on Sinclair's long poem "Lud Heat."

Years went by, and Iain Sinclair eventually brought out his own novel, *White Chappell Scarlet Tracings*. It opens with a trio of scouts invading a provincial bookshop and one of them chancing on a *Beeton's Christmas Annual for 1887*, a volume then worth up to twenty thousand pounds—it contains the first appearance of Sherlock Holmes in *A Study in Scarlet*. Most people in the used-book world recognized the real-life originals of the three scavengers: Dryfield was the notorious Dryf, author of the scathing and hilarious *Grub's Guide to the Second-Hand Book Trade*; Nicholas Lane recalled the equally legendary Martin Stone, judged by many as the greatest all-around scout of his time. (I once visited Stone—jittery, skeletal, looking feverish—but with a council flat stuffed with some of the most fabulous books I have ever seen.) The narrator was apparently based on Sinclair himself.

White Chappell Scarlet Tracings alternates the misadventures of these three bookmen with a second story line, set in the 1880s, about Jack the Ripper. "Alternates" may not be the word: one story infects the other. Like Sinclair's subsequent novels, the book displays a kind of bipolar disorder, modulating between the real and the hallucinatory, the past and the present. One could see various influences on the style—William Burroughs, J. G. Ballard, Victorian shockers, noir fiction à la David Goodis—but Sinclair revealed a genius all his own. More about his prose in a moment.

After this debut, wildly acclaimed in the *London Review of Books*, Iain Sinclair gradually grew into something of a cult author in Britain. Essays, meditations on London (which he knows better than almost anyone else alive), more works of delirious semi-autobiographical fiction. One or two of these books were published in this country, with minimal notice. But now Granta has issued his latest novel, *Landor's Tower*, as an attractively designed hardback (with frenetic illustrations by Dave McKean), and brought out trade paperbacks of three works never before available on these shores: *Lud Heat and Suicide Bridge* (1975, 1979), *White Chappell Scarlet Tracings* (1987), and *Radon Daughters* (1994).

Such plenty is cause for celebration, though I fear the party is likely to remain a small one, mainly confined to those who like an author for the way he or she uses language. In his books Sinclair mingles learned wit, Welsh flyting, revved-up sentences, tall-tale exaggeration, paranoia, and keen observation, blending them all together in a style halfway between the cut-up humor of Wodehouse and the "cut-up" technique of William Burroughs. Sinclair incessantly packs in allusions to odd corners of English and American literature, throws in bits of occult lore, allows fictional characters to complain about his portrayal of them (shades of Flann O'Brien), views everything through the mad logic of a conspiracy theorist, and makes his rabid excesses as funny as Hunter Thompson on a good day in the early 1970s. Here, as a teaser, is a two-paragraph profile of a celebrated writer:

> Becky had motored from Hay with a golden youth (less young, more blusher-enhanced on close examination) who took everyone's eye by his gift of conspicuous modesty, being always on the drift—tensed, watchful. His steady gaze was blue-chip, money in the bank. Cretan lapis lazuli. The unacknowledged director of any scene in which he appeared: the mythologist Bruce Chatwin.
>
> Chatwin was adept at placing himself in positions, at the back of the crowd, where he could be effortlessly acknowledged by the notables, folk with country piles and A-list connections. Sunstreams, stained by their

transit through the mulberry windows of the church, followed him like a hot spot. You couldn't take a bad shot of the man. He did the concept of "used" with preternatural delicacy; shirts that looked as if they'd been borrowed from Stewart Granger, sandals that smelt, in the nicest way, of camel. Pernickety notebooks from a shop in the arcades nobody else knew.

The plot of *Landor's Tower* is both dizzyingly complex and simple: the narrator, Andrew Norton, has been commissioned to write a novel about the poet Walter Savage Landor but finds himself blocked. And worried: "My credit had long since run out. I bored critics who once patronised me as a rough-trade novelty act, a dirty walker. I had the potential, so they said, to become a W. H. Davies supertramp with a diploma in psychogeography; now I was damned for sticking too long to the same midden, riverine London. The next stage, I knew all too well, was oblivion. I'd be lucky to have my name misspelt in a Time Out round-up."

To help work through the blockage, Norton hires a conspiracy nut named Kaporal to videotape material relating to Britain's actual Jeremy Thorpe scandal (high-ranking politico, homosexual dalliance, dead dog). Meanwhile Norton himself travels to Hay on Wye, the famous Welsh book town, and there encounters a mysterious young woman who claims to have been the lover of the poet David Jones. En route we also run into the book scufflers Dryfield and Billy Silverfish, who hope to get their hands on some papers belonging to the Christian artist and sexual radical Eric Gill.

As the book progresses, it grows increasingly blurry, fuzzing real and unreal, now and then. Is there a murder? Why is Norton incarcerated in an insane asylum? Who is the enigmatic Prudence? What of this strange rock group and the spooky carpet-delivery van? As Norton/Sinclair observes, "I'd never had a problem cranking out labyrinthine fictions that tottered and tumbled under the weight of their conceits." Still, no one should read *Landor's Tower* for the ostensible thriller plot. Think of it as a meditation on books and writing (satirical jabs at Hay on Wye, a mini-essay about Ruth Rendell), as an original exploration of Wales and its creative spirits (Henry Vaughan, Francis Kilvert, Arthur Machen, Dylan Thomas, Vernon Watkins, as well as Gill and Jones), as paranoid history (political conspiracy, mystical ley lines, the author's childhood and its lingering power).

In brief, *Landor's Tower* is a highly showoffy tour de force, what the narrator calls a downloading of the trivia he carries in his head. Wonderful trivia, I might add. Not that everyone likes this sort of thing. One of the novel's filthy, drugged-out lowlifes periodically rounds on Norton/Sinclair:

" 'I've got to tell you, man,' Mutton yelled at my retreating back, 'you're copping out. My character has shifted from a Jungian fetch in your first novel, in *White Chappell*, to a shorthand cipher in *Slow Chocolate Autopsy.* Your prose is getting really slack, all those one-word sentences, the reliance on a narrow band of imprecise adjectives. Neglect the armature of grammar and the world loses definition. I have to say it, man, I'm sliding into caricature. Some days, I don't know if it's worth crawling out of bed to enact myself in such a shoddy cartoon. Where's your subtext? The authentic pain of childhood? The Polish part of my story? I go along with Terry Eagleton when he talks about the literature of a subject people taking refuge in linguistic showmanship, neologisms, farcical excess. I'll ring you soon to let you know how you're getting along. I'm working on a new chapter. You're plagiarising my existence, man.' "

Tales within tales, autobiography within fiction. "That's all we are in the end, any of us, a couple of dozen unreliable stories." But reading Iain Sinclair's sentences more than compensates for any narrative slackness: "He had the air of an abortionist fleeing from a house call that had gone badly wrong. . . . The worse the grub, the more lavishly it was presented. Descriptions of gourmet dishes were giddy with unpunctuated foreplay: lapin love-crushed on a bed of diced seaweed, crab smothered in a gush of colitic chocolate, antelope placenta sieved through a mesh of smoky fishnet. . . . Gayness was not obligatory for hanging out at the pool, but it didn't hurt to cultivate an air of sexual indecision, a wounded past. . . . Asking directions from a rural cyclist, he submitted his victim to a forty-minute rant on Baudrillard. When he found an audience, he made the best of it."

I hope Iain Sinclair finds more of an audience in America: he's an astonishingly original and entertaining writer.

September 16, 2001

EUROPEANS

One of the pleasures of middle age—there aren't many—lies in a growing appreciation for art that is urbane and refined. To be a man of the world is, in my mind, to be a courtly, music-loving intellectual living in Vienna or Prague during the final days of the Austro-Hungarian Empire. It is the last glimmering of a now vanished era when you could still find yourself standing on the field of honor with a raised pistol, or attending a masked ball where the mistress of the emperor, her eyes wide, her breasts heaving, might squeeze your hand and whisper "tonight."

During the past quarter century we've been lucky enough to enjoy new English translations of Rilke, Joseph Roth, and Sándor Márai, among others. Add Lampedusa and Yourcenar to this mix (though Italian and French, they are comparable spirits), and one gains an even greater sense of the civilization and douceur de vivre that has been lost to the cyberworld of the twenty-first century. Not that the books of these authors always portray the world as a chandeliered dinner table and a gentleman's library. Indeed not—look at Bruno Schulz or Paul Celan—but they know that civilization consists of human-scaled pleasures.

I suppose that of all the books mentioned in Bound to Please, those in this category are the ones I most hope people will go out to discover. The books are autumnal, wistful as well as witty, burdened by a deep sense of the past. They possess a seriousness about life that it is useful for Americans to know about. To be adult is to be, in some sense, European.

THE TALE OF THE 1002ND NIGHT

By Joseph Roth

Translated from the German by Michael Hofmann

Heavy, lugubrious, probably a little tedious—a bit, in fact, like Thomas Mann or Hermann Broch but with even fewer laughs: such was my vague impression of the dozen or so novels of the Austrian writer Joseph Roth (1894–1939). After all, Roth was a wandering Jew (and journalist) in between-the-wars Europe, an elegist of the tattered Austro-Hungarian Empire, and, not least, a dedicated alcoholic, who died at forty-five in Paris. There didn't seem much room here for Viennese gemütlichkeit, Lehar operettas, and prancing Lippizaner stallions.

Still, Roth was said to be a major novelist, by Nadine Gordimer and Joseph Brodsky, among others. So when an English translation of *The Tale of the 1002nd Night* was announced, I steeled myself for a gloomy political fable about, say, the sickening rise of fascism—and instead found myself utterly surprised. *The Tale of the 1002nd Night* (1939) is sexy, highly ironic, sophisticated, and funny. Even when sad, this entrancing book is sad in a cozy Chekhovian way. Moreover, it touches on congenial themes: how even the most experienced—a Middle Eastern potentate, a career army officer, a whore—may be fundamentally innocent; how a single impulsive act may echo through the years; how any of us can lose his way when life so often seems like a dream or a badly written play.

Roth opens and closes his novel with an *Arabian Nights* fantasy—the shah of Persia's two visits to fin-de-siècle Vienna in search of romance. On his first momentous trip, this sovereign finds himself utterly dazzled by the European women at a ball: "Thus far, the women he had known had been of two kinds: either naked bodies or arrangements of drapery. But here were both together, at one and the same time! A gown that seemed to want to fall of its own weight, and yet clung to a body: it was like a door that wasn't locked and wouldn't open. When the women curtsied to him, the Shah caught a glimpse of cleavage and then the downy hair on an exposed neck. And the split second in which the ladies raised their skirts with both hands before bending at the knee had something indescribably modest and at the same time fabulously indecent about it: it was like a promise that they had no intention of keeping. . . . How inexhaustible the amorous arts of the Occident must be!"

The shah is particularly drawn to a young blond countess. "She was," writes Roth, "one of those women who, in those bygone days, were revered and adored for no other reason than their sheer beauty. One looked on for a moment, and felt so richly rewarded one felt like saying Thank you." The imperious monarch beckons to his grand vizier and tells him that he wants the countess and he wants her that very night.

What to do? As it happens, one of the shah's advisers has come to know a Baron Taittinger, an army officer and local *bon viveur*. The answer is simple, says Taittinger to a worried contingent of Persian and Austrian officials. We simply find a lady of the evening who resembles the countess. And, as it happens, the baron knows just the woman—his own former mistress, Mizzi Schinagl, now working at Frau Matzner's brothel. So Mizzi is decked out in a ball gown, and the shah is led through the darkened corridors of what he thinks is a "fairy-tale Occidental castle"; a bliss-filled night fully convinces him "that the erotic arts of the West were considerably more sophisticated than those of his native land." (I love Roth's inversions of cultural stereotypes.) The next day the master of Persia orders his eunuch to deliver a gift to his "countess": an exquisite triple string of pearls.

At this point, Roth shifts the focus of the story to Mizzi and what she does with the pearls. Later, as in a round, he takes up the other morally flawed but very human figures touched by the sexual deception: the money-obsessed Frau Matzner; Taittinger, who finds that official Vienna shuns him as little more than a pander; and Lazik, a journalist desperate for a scandalous story to make his fortune. There is, eventually, a trial, a bankruptcy, an attempted murder, the opening of the World Bioscope Theater, and a suicide—as well as several beautiful descriptions: of listening to band music while sipping coffee with whipped cream, of arriving late at night in a provincial town:

"It was evening when he got in. A thin chilly boring drizzle was coming down gently and persistently, giving the dismal yellow oil lamps on the platform a damp halo. Even the first-class waiting room harbored an oppressive gloom, and the potted palm on the buffet let its heavy slender leaves droop as though it, too, were standing out in the autumn rain. Two gaslights, the newly acquired pride of the station, had something wrong with their mantles, and gave out a flickering greenish glow. They emitted, what's more, a plaintive buzz, a lamentation. The white shirtfront of Ottokar the headwaiter bore sorry stains of unknown provenance. The metallic glitter of the Captain of Horse made a victorious entrance into all this gloom. Ottokar brought a Hennessy 'to take the chill off,' and a menu. 'We have soup with liver dumplings today, Baron!' "

Discovering so much enchantment in *The Tale of the 1002nd Night*, in part for what the translator Michael Hofmann calls its strong "fabulistic" element, I couldn't help wondering how it compared to some of Roth's other novels. So I read three more of them. The early *Hotel Savoy* (1923) opens with a former soldier, newly released from a Russian POW camp, arriving in a gray, rain-swept industrial city somewhere in Central Europe. He checks into the local hotel, where he promptly falls in love with an unhappy exotic dancer, attends the deathbed of a vaudeville clown, becomes a millionaire's secretary, and eventually finds himself entangled in a fiery workers' insurrection. There's clearly a lot of period symbolism here, and the short novel possesses a tone both Kafkaesque and expressionist: the boorish rich man's son ends up with the beautiful, doomed Stasia; the unseen and all-powerful manager of the Savoy turns out to be, in fact, its elderly elevator operator.

About *The Radetzky March* (1932), generally esteemed Roth's masterpiece, one can hardly be temperate: it's one of the most impressive novels of the century. When a common infantryman saves the emperor's life at the battle of Solferino, he is elevated to the aristocracy and given the order of Maria Theresa. As a result, Captain Trotta feels alienated from his peasant father, and from his own true self. But he is locked into his new position, his new role—as will be his son, who becomes a government administrator, and grandson, who lives in the shadow of "the hero of Solferino."

The book is organized as a series of interlocking vignettes: young Carl Joseph's affair with the married Kathi Slama (who dies in childbirth); the destruction of a friendship and several lives by jealousy and the stupid code of military honor; the beautifully described death of an old family servant and its effect on the household's rigidly proper master. Reading these episodes, one murmurs, "Turgenev, Pushkin, Tolstoy," but where the Russians would have written entire novels or long stories, Roth compacts everything into a stunning chapter or two. Take, for example, the brilliantly controlled pages in which Carl Joseph calls to offer his condolences to the brokenhearted Sergeant Slama, who at the end of their awkward conversation shyly gives the young officer a small bundle: the lieutenant's love letters to the constable's dead wife. As in *The Tale of the 1002nd Night*, Roth presents a panoramic tableau of Austro-Hungarian society, from top to bottom. Interestingly, two minor characters in *The Radetzky March* are none other than Mizzi Schinagl—a fleeting passion of the civil administrator—and Baron Taittinger, an army colleague of young Carl Joseph.

I also read *The Legend of the Holy Drinker*, Roth's last major work (1939), in which a drunken vagrant, who normally sleeps under the Paris bridges, becomes the astonished recipient of a largish sum of money, which he is told must eventually be returned to Saint Therese. In the course of trying to repay his debt, Andreas meets a lascivious former mistress, a con artist, and various otherworldly figures, until an encounter with an innocent young girl leads him to fulfill his promise and find a happy death. It's a lovely tale, part Zola, part saint's life.

No doubt some of Roth's other novels—*Job*, for instance—deal more directly with his Jewish heritage. But in these particular books Jews are largely submerged in the ethnic goulash of the Austro-Hungarian Empire, a multilingual swirl of Ruthenians and Slovaks, Ukrainians and Galicians, Czechs and Serbs. One paragraph in *Hotel Savoy*, depicting the Jewish quarter of town, does provoke a tellingly mournful observation: "For thousands of years this race has been wandering in narrow alleys." But then Roth has a way with epigrammatic similes. The dancers at the Savoy "stood there, white and naked like young swans." In *The Radetzky March* there are dazzling descriptions of Cossack horsemen, of dismal outposts of empire, of sumptuous dinners, of bearded patriarchs and lustful wives. But throughout his work Roth reflects an appealing Central European suavity, a mix of the elegiac, ironic and drily humorous: "I remember this same sadness when I looked at a girl. We met in a train and I did not know whether I had slept with her or whether she had only ironed my laundry."

What a marvelous writer!

January 10, 1999

LIFE OF A POET:
RAINER MARIA RILKE

By Ralph Freedman
Lyrical verse translated from the German by Helen Sword,
in collaboration with the author

UNCOLLECTED POEMS

By Rainer Maria Rilke
Translated from the German by Edward Snow

Any fervent admirer of Rainer Maria Rilke (1875–1926)—regarded by many as the greatest European poet of the century—would do well to avoid Ralph Freedman's enormously detailed and scrupulously researched biography: on page after page it portrays one of the most repugnant human beings in literary history. As John Berryman so aptly put it, "Rilke was a shit."

Many writers may be eccentrics, isolatos, and obsessives, but they usually retain at least one or two admirable qualities aside from their devotion to art: think of Joyce's and Nabokov's love of family, Flaubert's stringent work ethic, Zola's political courage, James's kindliness. Even the most problematic moderns—such as Pound and Céline—can earn our sometimes grudging sympathy. But Rilke the man is hard to pardon or excuse.

Paradoxically, though, the author of the *Duino Elegies* and the *Sonnets to Orpheus* (both 1923) has long been viewed as a saint of modern art, a man who dwelt alone in a perpetual solitude of the soul, who made himself into a sensitive Aeolian harp for the shifting winds of poetry. Yes, he was ruthless to others as he was to himself, and yes, he shamelessly flattered rich aristos, but a poet has to live somehow. Isn't "Orpheus. Euridice. Hermes" worth a few broken hearts and a heap of rich women's gold?

A tricky question. Yet *Life of a Poet* makes clear that this hollow-eyed communer with angels, Greek torsos, and death was not merely a selfish snob; he was also an anti-Semite, a coward, a psychic vampire, a crybaby. He was a son who refused to go to his dying father's bedside, a husband who exploited and abandoned his wife, a father who almost never saw his daughter and who even stole from a special fund for her education to pay for his first-class hotel rooms. He was a seducer of other men's wives, a pampered intellectual gigolo, and a virtual parody of the soulful artiste who deems himself superior to ordinary people because he is so tenderly sensitive, a delicate blossom easily punished by a passing breeze or sudden frost.

In this long biography Freedman, author of a standard life of Hermann Hesse, chronicles scores of episodes in which Rilke callously shifts his allegiances, whether personal, financial, or political, solely for his own temporary advantage. Scarcely out of his teens, he permits his "fiancée" to use her savings to underwrite his first book, then dedicates the poems to a baroness and abandons the bewildered young girl. Yet for all his Uriah Heepishness, Rilke must have possessed undeniable charm—else how do you explain the veneration in which he was held by so many, from softhearted ladies to hardheaded publishers? "If the word magic," wrote Paul Valéry of his German counterpart, "has any meaning, I should say that the whole of his person, his voice, his look, his manners, everything about him gave the impression of a magic presence. You would have said that he had a way of giving to each word, as he spoke, the power of a charm." Of course, poets often possess the same rhetorical skills as con men. Once, in the midst of a love affair, Rilke actually persuaded the wronged husband to underwrite the rent for his errant wife's studio–love nest.

Rilke's poetry has always been easier to love than to understand. It is abstract, religiose, difficult to translate, solemn, obsessed with death, and sometimes unintentionally ludicrous. Only the most Teutonic soul would fail to laugh at the second line of the first sonnet to Orpheus: "O tall tree in the ear!" Any English major could interpret the phrase's significance—phallic imagery, echoes of the Annunciation, etc.—but the words themselves remain essentially ridiculous.

Perplexed by this strange yet powerfully seductive verse, many readers would welcome a reliable guide, one that would clarify Rilke's "passionate affirmations of life that must at once be denied." Freedman announces in his preface that he hopes to offer a critical biography that will interpret both the poems and their author. Alas, he doesn't quite deliver on this promise. He talks for instance about Rilke's experiences in Paris and their importance to his 1910 novel *The Notebooks of Malte Laurids Brigge*, but he never really explicates that sickly-sweet, death-centered text. He resorts to abstractions when discussing the poems, elaborating on their genesis or general meaning, yet without engaging very deeply with any of them. Most of the time Freedman is principally a recorder of events, laying out reams of research: one yearns to hear Rilke's voice in these monotone pages.

Still, the facts are all here for any who may want them. Freedman exhaustively chronicles the Prague childhood, the fruitful association with the remarkable Lou Andreas-Salomé, travels to Russia, Scandinavia, Egypt, and Spain, the apprenticeship to Rodin, the "interior marriage" to Clara, and every sycophantic encounter with the minor nobility of the *Almanach de Gotha*. For a guy who always wanted to be alone, Rilke seems to have known everyone: he visited Tolstoy (who snubbed him); encountered Gorky in, of all places, Capri; translated Valéry; received (anonymously) 10,000 Austrian kronen from Wittgenstein; hobnobbed with an aunt of the Mitford sisters; abandoned the painter Paula Modersohn-Becker (about whom he later composed a great "requiem"); persuaded his lover, the artist Clara Goll, to perform Salome's dance of the seven veils; corresponded with the poet Marina Tsvetaeva (who offered herself to him); and carried on a long affair with Dorothée Klossowska, mother of the notorious French novelist Pierre Klossowski and of the even more controversial painter Balthus. All this from a wasted valetudinarian, who—shades of Pope—once referred to "this long convalescence which is my life." Rilke obviously possessed the irresistible charisma of a guru, the hypnotic mind-clouding power of a cult messiah.

Though Freedman's biography may muffle Rilke's voice, it comes through like a ringing glass in *Uncollected Poems*, translated by Edward Snow, who over the years has given readers without German award-winning versions of *The Book of Images* (1905) and *New Poems* (1907–8). Snow is, with Stephen Mitchell and David Young, among the most trustworthy and exhilarating of Rilke's contemporary translators.

Despite the title, the hundred or so pieces here are hardly dregs. During the last fifteen years of his life, Rilke composed scores of poems for friends; but, being focused so intently on the *Duino Elegies*, he never bothered to gather this occasional material into a volume. Yet much of it is outstanding, including "The Spanish Trilogy," "To Hölderlin," and the Frost-like monologue "The Raising of Lazarus" (when Jesus lifts his hand and "no hand ever raised itself this slowly, with this much weight," for a moment he dreads "that all the dead might / come rushing back through the suction of that tomb . . ."). Memorable lines abound: "And here stands Death, a bluish distillate in a cup without a saucer." One couplet might be Rilke's apologia for cutting himself off from human attachment: "The transformed speaks only to relinquishers. All holders-on are stranglers."

A reader absolutely new to Rilke should start with Stephen Mitchell's edition of the *Selected Poetry* and his translation of *Malte Laurids Brigge*, followed by Snow's two-volume edition of *New Poems*. In these, if anywhere, is the achievement that justifies a life of remarkable egotism and caddishness. One can forgive much in exchange for "The Panther" ("It seems to him there are a thousand bars / and behind a thousand bars no world") or the "Archaic Torso of Apollo" ("You must change your life") or "The Bowl of Roses" or "Autumn Day":

> Whoever has no house now, will never have one.
> Whoever is alone will stay alone,
> will sit, read, write long letters through the evening,
> and wander on the boulevards, up and down,
> restlessly, while the dry leaves are blowing.

In reading Rilke, too often we focus on the tormented later poems, those explorations of inwardness with their relentless *Seelensprache* and talk of angels. Yet Baudelaire might have written "The Courtesan": "Who / has seen me once is jealous of my dog . . . / And boys, the hopes of ancient houses / Perish at my mouth as if by poison." Passages in *Malte Laurids Brigge* can be serenely beautiful: "The day began like spring, like spring in paintings." Despite their density, even the *Duino Elegies* pull us into their austere realm of Life-in-Death with their exhortatory music and gnomic utterances: "Who, if I cried out, would hear me among the angels' / hierarchies?" "Beauty is nothing but the beginning of terror." In the ninth, and I think greatest, of the elegies one even hears a voice like that of Eliot in the *Four Quartets* (a work somewhat analogous to the German masterwork):

> But because truly, being here is so much; because everything here
> apparently needs us, this fleeting world, which in some strange way
> keeps calling to us. Us, the most fleeting of all.
> Once for each thing. Just once; no more. And we too,
> just once. And never again. But to have been
> this once, completely, even if only once:
> to have been at one with the earth, seems beyond undoing.

Rilke stands among the greatest of those poets who use art as a means of knowing themselves, and who demand of their readers a corresponding receptivity, a willingness to delve into the pure ether of being. Sometimes Rilke would wait years for "a call from within" and then dash off thirty poems, several of them masterpieces, in a week. His work is so inward, so austerely removed from the quotidian, that it seems both vatic and ineffable. "There's an ancient hatred / between our normal life and the great work." To read the *Duino Elegies* is to feel that thought has become prayer, words music, the poet and the reader almost one.

Perhaps Rilke can be forgiven his human failures after all. Or . . . perhaps not. I still wish he'd been nicer to people, so that one could admire the man, as one does so many of his poems: unreservedly. "Who speaks of victory?" he once wrote pragmatically. "Enduring is everything."

March 31, 1996

EMBERS

By *Sándor Márai*
Translated from the German by Carol Brown Janeway

In a castle in Hungary, near a deep forest, the old General has been living alone with his servants, passing the days in reading Plato, overseeing his wine cellar, and turning over in his mind the events of a single day in 1900. As *Embers* opens, he receives a letter from his oldest friend:

> The General went into his room, washed his hands, and stepped over to his high, narrow standing desk; arranged on its surface of unstained green felt were pens, ink, and a perfectly aligned stack of those notebooks covered in black-and-white-checked oilcloth commonly used by schoolchildren for their homework. In the middle of the desk stood a green-shaded lamp, which the General switched on, as the room was dark.
>
> On the other side of the closed blinds, in the scorched, withered garden, summer ignited a last blast like an arsonist setting the fields on fire in senseless fury before making his escape. The General took out the letter, carefully smoothed the paper, set his glasses on his nose and placed the sheet under the bright light to read the straight short lines of angular handwriting, his arms folded behind his back.

For the General half a lifetime of waiting is nearly over. After forty-one years he will have his chance for revenge. But for what offense? And what kind of revenge?

While he methodically prepares for Konrad's visit that evening, the General wonders whether to wear his decorations: "As he held the medals of bronze, silver and gold in his hand and ran his fingers over them, he saw in his mind's eye a bridgehead over the Dnieper, or a parade in Vienna, or a reception in Buda's royal palace. He shrugged. What had life brought him? Duties and idle pleasures. Like a cardplayer absentmindedly gathering up his chips after a big game, he let the decorations slide back into the drawer."

Biblical scholars refer to books such as Proverbs and Ecclesiastes as wisdom literature. There is a subcategory of mainly European fiction to which one might also give this name. These are often short novels, marked by an autumnal forlorn air, purveying that knowledge of the world which comes only from heartbreak, disillusionment, and long experience, written in measured prose of high polish and urbanity. Think of Turgenev's *First Love*, Flaubert's *Sentimental Education*, Lampedusa's *The Leopard*, Mann's *Death in Venice*, Isak Dinesen's *Seven Gothic Tales*, Joseph Roth's *The Radetzky March*.

Embers takes its own place among this distinguished company. In a short space it covers a hundred years of Austro-Hungarian history, starting with the marriage of the General's ill-matched parents: "The General looked at the portrait of his mother. He knew every feature of the narrow, fine-boned face. The eyes gazed down through time with sad and somnolent disdain. It was the look with which women of an earlier era had mounted the scaffold, scorning both those for whom they were giving their lives and those who were taking their lives from them."

When the General was young, his old nurse once remarked to this same mother that someday Konrad would abandon his friend, who would suffer terribly: " 'That is our human fate,' said his mother. She was sitting at her mirror, staring at her fading beauty. 'One day we lose the person we love. Anyone who is unable to sustain that loss fails as a human being and does not deserve our sympathy.' "

It might be *die alte Marschallin* from Richard Strauss's opera *Der Rosenkavalier*.

Similarly, when the General reflects on his father and his father's comrades, he thinks, "A good generation, a trifle eccentric, not at ease in society, arrogant, but absolutely dedicated to honor, to the male virtues: silence, solitude, the inviolability of one's word, and women. If they were let down, they remained silent. Most of them were silent for a lifetime, bound to duty and discretion as if by vows."

That night, as the General finally sits over dinner with the friend who abandoned him, the two old men remember their youth together, that day of the last great hunt, and the General's long-dead wife, Krisztina. For a while Konrad talks about his years in the Far East, and how the tropics corrupts the westerners who flee to its plantations and jungles. He reveals that he returned to Europe to visit Vienna one last time but found, to his dismay, that the romantic city of his memory had vanished. He searched for the past and found only "change." For the most part, though, the General dominates their conversation, at one point raising a series of philosophical problems, which he proceeds to solve with stoic clarity: "One's life, viewed as a whole, is always the answer to the most important questions. Along the way, does it matter what one says, what words and principles one chooses to justify oneself? At the very end, one's answers to the questions the world has posed with such relentlessness are to be found in the facts of one's life. Questions such as: Who are you? ... What did you actually want? ... What could you actually achieve? ... At what points were you loyal or disloyal or brave or a coward? And one answers as best one can, honestly or dishonestly; that's not so important. What's important is that finally one answers with one's life."

After dinner, the two friends smoke cigars, sip brandy. They are courteous, even deferential, the General solicitous of his guest's comfort—nearly always a sign of dark cruelties to come. Are the old men waiting to duel at dawn? Or possibly hunt each other à la "The Most Dangerous Game"? Clearly neither feels any special urgency, as the conversation turns to music, soldiering, duty, the nature of friendship and, inevitably, love: "Passion," insists the General, "has no footing in reason. Passion is indifferent to reciprocal emotion, it needs to express itself to the full, live itself to the very end, no matter if all it receives in return is kind feelings, courtesy, friendship, or mere patience. Every great passion is hopeless, if not it would be no passion at all but some cleverly calculated arrangement, an exchange of lukewarm interests."

As the two seventy-five-year-old men sit in the darkness and reminisce long into the night, we wait impatiently to discover what happened on that day of the hunt forty-one years ago. The pair grew up together, shared quarters during their military service, were practically inseparable in the eyes of the world. But the General's family was rich, severe, of the noblest lineage, while Konrad was poor, musical, romantic, and, not least in importance, related through his mother to Chopin. Despite the parental sacrifices made to advance his career, he was hardly cut out for a soldier's life: "Deep inside you was a frantic longing to be something or someone other than you are," says the General. "It is the greatest scourge a man can suffer, and the most painful. Life becomes bearable only when one has come to terms with who one is, both in one's own eyes and in the eyes of the world. We all of us must come to terms with what and who we are, and recognize that this wisdom is not going to earn us any praise, that life is not going to pin a medal on us for recognizing and enduring our own vanity or egoism or baldness or our potbelly. No, the secret is that there's no reward and we have to endure our characters and our natures as best we can, because no amount of experience or insight is going to rectify our deficiencies, our self-regard, or our cupidity. We have to learn that our desires do not find any real echo in the world. We have to accept that the people we love do not love us, or not in the way we hope. We have to accept betrayal and disloyalty, and, hardest of all, that someone is finer than we are in character or intelligence."

Some modern readers may find this high style of conversation sententious. It is. But here an aging aristocrat and his equally aged friend are talking about life's vagaries and their lost dreams, and they are doing so as the world they grew up in is disappearing for good. How else should they speak, but with the seriousness of men? There are, besides, several mysteries in *Embers*: Did the General's mother have an affair with the Austro-Hungarian emperor? Why did Konrad abandon the General and Krisztina without a farewell and take off for the tropics, never to be heard from again? Why is Krisztina's portrait absent from the castle's walls? One dare say no more without marring Sándor Márai's expertly mitered narrative.

Sándor Márai? We learn from the dust jacket that he was born in 1900, became one of Hungary's leading writers during the 1930s, fled the communists in 1948, and committed suicide in San Diego in 1989. *Embers*—beautifully translated into English from a German version of the original—was first published in Hungary in 1942. It is as masterly and lovely a novel as one could ask for, evoking the memory of unspoken passions, the loss of illusions, the crumbling of an empire, and all the aching beauty of that which lasts but a moment and then is gone forever: "Snow kept falling, and coachmen drove pairs of lovers silently through the white air."

Knopf has promised that this is just the first of Márai's books to be translated into English. That's good news, though it will be hard to equal this compact masterpiece. Not since Overlook Press and Norton began reissuing the work of Joseph Roth has there been a European novelist who so merited rediscovery as Sándor Márai. *Embers* is perfect.

September 30, 2001

THE COMPLETE WORKS OF ISAAC BABEL

Edited by Nathalie Babel
Translated from the Russian by Peter Constantine

Sometimes publishers do get it right. In an era when vast sums are still being paid for subliterate thrillers, ignoble memoirs, and the evanescent speculations—on history, economics, or world affairs—of media whiz kids, *The Complete Works of Isaac Babel* appears almost coelacanthine: Aren't books as well produced as this one supposed to be extinct? Beautifully printed, authoritatively edited, bound so that the pages open flat, reasonably priced, and with a storage box to boot—this generous volume justifies an entire publishing season. Forget the best-seller list, Oprah, mega-movie deals with DreamWorks: here is a book that will last, that you will reread all your life and then pass on to your grandchildren. Or ask to be buried with.

Isaac Babel (1894–1940) is generally regarded as the finest Russian short-story writer since Chekhov. To the world at large he is probably best known for two sentences, one of them his last reported words: "I was not given time to finish," he is said to have shouted as he was being led away by the secret police in 1939. We now know that he was executed soon thereafter, though well into the 1940s there were hints that he might still be alive in some gulag or prison. The other celebrated sentence appears in his great short story "Guy de Maupassant." The youthful narrator, who has been invited to help a languorous Petersburg matron translate the French master, is discoursing about the nature of prose. "When a phrase is born, it is both good and bad at the same time. The secret of its success rests in a crux that is barely discernible. One's fingertips must grasp the key, gently warming it. And then the key must be turned once, not twice." That last phrase is itself quite wonderful but isn't the one that's famous. Our literary young man continues, first describing style as an army of words, deploying numerous weapons, then pronouncing that greatest of all syntactic truths: "No iron spike can pierce a human heart as icily as a period in the right place."

This is Peter Constantine's translation, approved by the author's daughter, Nathalie Babel, and presumably more accurate than the version I once copied into a notebook: "There is no iron which can enter the human heart with such stupefying effect as a period placed at just the right moment." I still prefer the rhythm of this formulation, even though there are yet others, for Babel has been much translated, even as long ago as 1929, when *Red Cavalry* appeared in the United States. Those stories—about the depredations and heroism of the Cossack army on the Polish border—were subsequently revised by Walter Morison, who added his own versions of the *Tales of Odessa* and the semi-autobiographical stories of childhood and youth: the result, the *Collected Stories*, appeared in 1955 with a substantial introduction by Lionel Trilling—and entered the literate public's heart with stupefying effect.

In the years since, Babel material has accumulated steadily in English, much of it overseen by Nathalie Babel (as her father wrote in a letter just after her birth, "Wise people say that a devoted daughter will provide for the old parents better than a lazy son"). *Isaac Babel: The Lonely Years 1925–1939* gathered some later stories (including that outrageous masterpiece "My First Fee") and the extensive family correspondence; *You Must Know Everything* added a score of lesser tales to the oeuvre, as well as seventy pages of essays and testimonials by contemporaries. In 1995 Yale published Babel's *1920 Diary*, edited by Carol J. Avins, describing day-to-day life with the Cossack army fictionalized in *Red Cavalry*; 1996 saw the appearance of *At His Side*, by A. N. Pirozhkova, a memoir by the woman with whom the writer shared his last years.

All these books are well worth owning, for they offer telling reminiscences, notes, letters, and photographs. Once you've read Babel, you'll want everything you can find by and about him. Though *The Complete Works* leaves out the correspondence, it does include the 1920 diary, preliminary sketches for many stories, reportage on life in Petersburg, France, and Georgia, two plays, and several movie screenplays—as well as a brief introduction by Cynthia Ozick, a foreword by Peter Constantine, a memoir-afterword by Nathalie Babel, and, not least, a detailed chronology, by Gregory Freidkin, of the writer's brief but crowded life (an important friendship with Gorky, literary celebrity, mistresses, illegitimate children). There's no stinting in this thousand-page volume, even if it seems likely that only the most Babel-obsessed will bother to read the film scripts and treatments.

What counts most, of course, are the stories: the brutal vignettes of the *Red Cavalry* cycle, sometimes reminiscent of Hemingway's *In Our Time*; the exuberant Odessa tales about Benya Krik the gangster (half Sholom Aleichem, half Damon Runyon); and the astonishing later examples of faux autobiography, starting with "The Story of My Dovecote," in which the narrator's grandfather is murdered during a pogrom, his father desperately abases himself to save the family store from looting, and the boy himself ends up covered with bird entrails when a beggar crushes a fluttering dove into his face.

Babel was both a patriotic Soviet citizen and a Jewish intellectual—one, to use his words, with glasses on his nose and autumn in his heart. Much of his work's energy derives from just this sort of polarity. Sensitive aesthetes find themselves thrust among crude and bloodthirsty Cossacks. Fathers kill sons and sons kill fathers. Vicious crime lords prove themselves models of courtesy and honor. Humor alternates with carnage. Art serves as a means to seduce women. As the critic Viktor Shklovsky observed, Babel could speak "in the same voice about the stars above and about gonorrhea."

But then Russia, especially Babel's Russia, is hardly a land of reason and moderation. Reality swiftly hurries toward fantasy. Who, for example, could be more typically Slavic than the doomed ship's captain Korostelyov? Babel calls him "a man ravished by drink, with lifeless flaxen hair. He was an adventurer, a restless soul, and a vagabond. He had traveled the White Sea on sailing vessels, walked the length and breadth of Russia, had done time in jail and penance in a monastery." When we first meet the captain, he is "sitting on the floor in a canvas shirt among green streams of vomit."

Or consider this scene from "Lyubka the Cossack." The plump and buxom Lyubka is a shady businesswoman, a trader in all kinds of goods, from liquor to whores. She is collecting merchandise from some sailors, one an Englishman named Mr. Trottyburn, another a drunken Malay: "Out of his bale he took cigars and delicate silks, cocaine and metal jiggers, uncut tobacco from the state of Virginia, and black wine bought on the island of Chios. Each item had a special price, and each figure was washed down with Bessarabian wine with its bouquet of sunshine and bedbugs. Twilight was already flooding the courtyard, twilight was flooding in like an evening wave over a wide river, and the drunken Malay, completely taken aback, poked Lyubka's breast with his finger. He poked it with one finger, then with each of his fingers, one after the other."

Who but a genius could write that amazing last sentence?

Grace Paley remarked that Babel's stories are, in fact, among the most rereadable in the world largely because of this steady rain of bizarre, yet unforgettable, images and phrases: the Jewish quarter of Odessa, the Moldavanka, is "crowded with suckling babies, drying rags, and conjugal nights filled with big-city chic and soldierly tirelessness. . . . The drunks lay like broken furniture in the courtyard. . . . The sun hung from the sky like the pink tongue of a thirsty dog. . . . His fat hands were moist, covered with fish scales, and reeked of wonderful, cold worlds."

But such snippets hardly give a sense of Babel's mastery. Here is a paragraph from a story called "Berestechko":

> I happened to be billeted in the house of a redheaded widow, who was doused with the scent of a widow's grief. I washed off the dirt of the road and went out into the street. An announcement was already nailed up on telegraph poles that Divisional Military Commissar Vinogradov would be giving a speech on the Second Congress of the Comintern. Right outside the house a couple of Cossacks were getting ready to shoot an old silver-haired Jew for espionage. The old man was screeching, and tried to break free. Kudrya from the machine gun detachment grabbed his head and held it wedged under his arm. The Jew fell silent and spread his legs. Kudrya pulled out his dagger with his right hand and carefully slit the old man's throat without spattering himself. Then he knocked on one of the closed windows.

"If anyone's interested," he said, "they can come get him. It's no problem."

But if violence is one face of Babel, then sex is the Janus-like other. At the opening of "My First Fee," the narrator is living in Tiflis: "I was renting a room in the attic from a newlywed Georgian couple. My landlord was a butcher at the Eastern Bazaar. In the room next door, the butcher and his wife, in the grip of love, thrashed about like two large fish trapped in a jar. The tails of these crazed fish thumped against the partition, rocking the whole attic, which was blackened by the piercing sun, ripping it from its rafters and whisking it off to eternity. They could not part their teeth, clenched in the obstinate fury of passion. In the mornings, Milyet, the young bride, went out to get bread. She was so weak that she had to hold on to the banister. Her delicate little foot searched for each step, and there was a vague blind smile on her lips, like that of a woman recovering from a long illness. Laying her palm on her small breasts, she bowed to everyone she met in the street—the Assyrian grown green with age, the kerosene seller, and the market shrews with faces gashed by fiery wrinkles, who were selling hanks of sheep's wool. At night the thumping and babbling of my neighbors was followed by a silence as piercing as the whistle of a cannonball."

Love and death—neither precisely laughing matters, yet Babel's portrayals of both are imbued with humor, the familiar Jewish lugubriousness and irony. When Benya Krik, just starting out on his life of crime, accidentally causes the death of an innocent clerk, he goes to apologize to the young man's mother: "Aunt Pesya . . . if you want my life, you can have it, but everyone makes mistakes, even God! This was a giant mistake, Aunt Pesya! But didn't God Himself make a mistake when he settled the Jews in Russia so they could be tormented as if they were in hell? Wouldn't it have been better to have the Jews living in Switzerland, where they would've been surrounded by first-class lakes, mountain air, and Frenchmen galore? Everyone makes mistakes, even God."

Yes, anyone can make a mistake. Though acquiring *The Complete Works of Isaac Babel* wouldn't be one.

November 25, 2001

MIKHAIL BULGAKOV:
A CRITICAL BIOGRAPHY

By Lesley Milne

Even as a kid who liked to read all kinds of things, I knew better than to bother with anything written after 1917 in the Soviet Union. Tsarist Russia produced masterpieces by the likes of Pushkin, Tolstoy, and Chekhov, but the USSR brought out touching love stories about a boy, a girl, and a tractor, novels with titles like *Cement*, and propagandistic tracts, disguised as fiction, that emphasized "positive" heroes and conformed to the tenets of "socialist realism." This was literature by committee, dull, lifeless, unimaginative, and all too politically correct.

As it happens, I couldn't have been more wrong, though I think my earlier impression of Soviet literature is probably widespread even now. In fact, during the 1920s Petersburg and Moscow seriously rivaled Paris and New York as literary storm centers. I envy anyone who has yet to read, for instance, Evgeny Zamyatin's *We* (1920)—the grimmest of all dystopian visions and a model for both *Brave New World* and *1984*—or the poet Osip Mandelstam's wonderful memoir of childhood, *The Noise of Time* (1922), or Viktor Shklovsky's exhilarating study of literariness, *Theory of Prose* (1925).

Of the writers who made their mark after the revolution, one of the most appealing is Mikhail Bulgakov (1891–1940). Born in Kiev to a middle-class family, Bulgakov spent his early twenties as a physician and probably fought with the Whites against the Bolsheviks. In 1920, though, he made the decision to adopt literature as his profession, with the aim of being nothing less than "brilliant" at it.

During the next ten years Bulgakov turned out sketches, short stories, novels, and a half dozen plays, nearly all of them comic or satiric. "The Adventures of Chichikov" imagines what might happen if the con-man hero of Gogol's *Dead Souls* were set down in the Soviet Union of the postrevolutionary New Economic Policy. The novella "The Fatal Eggs" lays out a kind of science fiction parable about a biologist who discovers a "red ray" that causes phenomenal growth; as the result of a bureaucratic bungle, the ray irradiates the wrong eggs, with 1950s horror movie results: snakes the size of oak trees overrun the provinces, herds of monster ostriches attack the army.

Enjoyable as his stories are, Bulgakov became truly famous for his plays. *The Days of the Turbins* (1926)—adapted from his first novel, *The White Guard* (1924)—proffers a sympathetic view of a bourgeois White family during the civil war in Kiev. Produced at the Moscow Art Theater, it became the most popular theatrical production of its day (at least in part because Stalin liked it; he was reported to have seen it fifteen times). Virtually simultaneously, Bulgakov had two other plays on the boards—the risqué *Zoya's Apartment* and the almost zany play within a play, *Crimson Island*. This last depicts a theater troupe's desperate attempts to take a draft of a new play and, with only twenty minutes' preparation, present it to the government censor for approval. As it happens, this drama about a revolution on a tropical island is perfectly awful, phoney art of the kind called *haltura* in Russian. In its critique of censorship and bad art, *Crimson Island* is at once troubling and hilarious, half Jean Genet, half Mel Brooks.

Following these successes, Bulgakov should have been set for life. Instead his public career was virtually over. After 1930 the arts were required to serve the revolutionary cause with May Day fervor, and there was no longer room for irony or social criticism. Bulgakov, finding his new plays banned, actually dashed off a letter to Stalin, asking to emigrate. The dictator telephoned one afternoon, the two chatted, and Bulgakov found himself under Stalin's compromising protection, though this didn't seem to help get his fiction published or his dramas produced. He was never permitted to leave the Soviet Union.

The 1930s slowly dragged on as a wasteland of failed projects. Then Bulgakov started to suffer from sclerosis of the kidneys; this led to blindness, followed by death at age forty-eight, in 1940.

And that might have been that. A significant career but not quite a stellar one—except that during his final decade Bulgakov had been secretly working on his "last, sunset novel," that dazzling, vastly entertaining, deeply moving, philosophical-satirical extravaganza, *The Master and Margarita*. This book—one of the high points of modern literature—sat in a closed drawer for twenty-five years until it was published in 1966–67. It has since enjoyed two English translations—the fuller is by Michael Glenny—and not long ago was named by Salman Rushdie as the primary literary influence on *The Satanic Verses*.

Sometime in the late 1920s the devil, under the name of Monsieur Woland, arrives in Moscow with his retinue: an enormous black cat called Behemoth, a murderous henchman named Azazello, a beautiful female vampire with an aversion to clothes, and a flashy con-man assistant nicknamed

Faggot. In the first chapter an official of a writers' union named Berlioz and a second-rate poet encounter Woland in a park, where the conversation takes an unexpected turn. When Berlioz announces that he knows precisely what he will be doing that evening, Woland contradicts him with an absurdity. This evening, he tells Berlioz, "Your head will be cut off! ... By a Russian woman, a member of the Komsomol." Berlioz insists that this is impossible, that he will be chairing a meeting at the MASSOLIT. But the foreigner insists, adding gnomically, "Anna has already bought the sunflower oil; in fact, she has not only bought it but has already spilled it." Woland's unlikely prophecy is fulfilled in every detail when Berlioz, hurrying to his meeting, skids on some spilled sunflower oil and falls into the path of an electric tram, driven by a woman, and is neatly decapitated.

After this startling overture Bulgakov goes on to relate the escapades of Woland and his followers, interspersing their carnivalesque antics with two other narrrative lines: an account of Jesus, here called Yeshua, from the viewpoint of the humane, though burned-out, civil servant Pontius Pilate, and the story of the beautiful Margarita's devotion to the unpublished writer known only as the Master. All three plot developments deftly mirror each other—Woland, Yeshua, and the Master show three faces of spiritual and artistic freedom—and include such sensational elements as a description of the activities of a secret agent in the time of Christ, the expansion of a small apartment into a gigantic palace existing in the fifth dimension, the creation of a vampire, the assassination of Judas, a vaudevillian magic show, the power of a suppressed book (about which subject Bulgakov was expert: "manuscripts," he once said, "don't burn"), and Satan's annual ball. Out of love for the Master, who is imprisoned in a mental hospital, Margarita agrees to transform herself into a witch and preside, naked, with Woland at his infernal orgy—all in the hope of being granted a single wish from this devilishly charming, shrewd, and finally rather kindhearted master of evil.

Readers of *The Master and Margarita* will certainly long to know more about Bulgakov. The standard biography in English, regrettably out of print, is by Ellendea Proffer, who (with her late husband, Carl Proffer) translated many of Bulgakov's plays and stories. This new "critical biography" by Lesley Milne covers some of the same ground and draws on some new post-Glasnost material, but focuses principally on detailed exegeses of the major works. The result is thorough and no doubt useful, but academic. Confirmed admirers of Bulgakov will nonetheless want to look it over; all others should first treat themselves to *The Master and Margarita*.

November 17, 1991

REGIONS OF THE GREAT HERESY:
BRUNO SCHULZ, A BIOGRAPHICAL
PORTRAIT

By Jerzy Ficowski
Translated from the Polish and edited by Theodosia Robertson

"My father," writes Bruno Schulz in a story about autumn, "was the first to explain the secondary, derivative character of that late season, which is nothing other than the result of our climate having been poisoned by the miasmas exuded by degenerate specimens of baroque art crowded in our museums."

Fall is caused by baroque art—who couldn't smile? This might be a sentence from an absurdist sketch by Donald Barthelme. However, Schulz (1892–1942)—one of Poland's greatest writers of the twentieth century—goes on in an increasingly gothic vein: "That museum art, rotting in boredom and oblivion and shut in without an outlet, ferments like old preserves, oversugars our climate, and is the cause of this beautiful malarial fever, this extraordinary delirium, to which our prolonged fall is so agonizingly prone. For beauty is a disease, as my father maintained; it is the result of a mysterious infection, a dark forerunner of decomposition, which rises from the depth of perfection and is saluted by perfection with sighs of the deepest bliss."

Reading the entire passage over, one shudders slightly at the reference to degenerate art—the label by which the Nazis condemned so much "Jewish" painting and music—and then pauses over this Poe-esque praise of fevers and delirium and infections and decomposition and the bliss and beauty of illness. What kind of imagination is at work here?

Jerzy Ficowski's *Regions of the Great Heresy*—the title denominates the imaginative realm that Schulz created—isn't so much a biography of the Polish-Jewish writer as a dossier. The book includes a long introduction by the translator Theodosia Robertson, Ficowski's groundbreaking biographical discoveries about Schulz with added chapters on the fate of his manuscripts and artwork, a detailed chronology (which supplies an orderly presentation of the life, as well as factual details not included in the main text), an appendix of important letters, and an abundance of explanatory and bibliographical endnotes. The result is a must-buy for Schulz admirers, but more casual readers expecting a conventional biography may be put off by Ficowski's sometimes florid pages of commentary.

Bruno Schulz published only two collections of tenuously linked stories in a pathetically abbreviated life: the 1934 *Cinnamon Shops* (titled *The Street of Crocodiles* in America) and the 1937 *Sanatorium under the Sign of the Hourglass*. Both might be loosely thought of as magic-realist evocations of his hometown of Drohobycz, where everything—furniture, the dead, tailor's dummies, the seasons, dreams, birds—pulsates with frenetic, unnatural vitality. Schulz himself maintained that he hoped to re-create the mysterious, sometimes surreal world that we actually perceive as children. So a few torn pages of advertising from a magazine or a child's stamp album open up entire universes— quite literally. The hero of many of these tales, Schulz's father, dies and is reborn again and again, sometimes shriveling up into dusty nothingness, at other times metamorphosing into a crustacean, and once, after his apparent demise, being restored to a kind of etiolated half-life by a sanatorium that controls time:

"You know as well as I," admits its director, "that from the point of view of your home, from the perspective of your own country, your father is dead. This cannot be entirely remedied. That death throws a certain shadow on his existence here."

Loose plots may be unearthed in a few of the stories, but narrative precision isn't really what Schulz cares about: he is a poet of metaphorical wildness. Descriptions of nature and the seasons, philosophical arias, crazed situations are yoked together to create dark carnivals, exhibits of bizarrerie. Wild animals, we learn, sport horns "to introduce an element of strangeness into their lives"; the citizens of Drohobycz go about listening to "the distant hum of the stars." As the contemporary Polish poet Adam Zagajewski has said, Schulz possesses "the wondrous ability to transmute the commonplace into the bewitching": "Enormous, heavy butterflies coupling in amorous frolics appeared. The clumsy, vibrating fluttering continued for a moment in the dull air. The butterflies flew past, as if racing one another, then rejoined their partners, dealing out in flight like cards whole packs of colorful shimmers."

Schulz's work sometimes recalls the feverish dream visions of Gérard de Nerval (in *Les Filles du Feu*) or the late supernatural tales of Maupassant. In "The Gale," Schulz writes, "There began the black parliaments of saucepans, those verbose and inconclusive meetings, those gurglings of bottles, those stammerings of flagons. Until one night the regiments of saucepans and bottles rose under the empty roofs and marched in a great bulging mass against the city." This could be the genesis of Maupassant's haunting short story "Who Knows?"—or a scene from a chilling picture book or noirish Disney cartoon.

Schulz possessed an intensely visual imagination, and it's little wonder that he taught art (to schoolchildren) for much of his life. Yet if his writing can be disorienting, his surviving prints and paintings—some used as illustrations for his stories—are far more disturbing. Bulbous heads on emaciated, twisted bodies call to mind photographs of concentration camp survivors, even though Schulz drew these images long before World War II. Other prints depict Blue Angel–like temptresses or indifferent nudes with the faces of twelve-year-olds, usually being worshiped by cringing, rodentine males, at least one of whom always resembles Schulz. The focus of this fetishistic masochism is usually the woman's foot or leg. As Stanislaw Witkiewicz—another great Polish author of the 1930s, best known for his novel *Insatiability* (wonderful title)—neatly observed, Schulz's "graphics are poems of pedal atrocity."

Schulz's work first came to the English-speaking world's attention in the 1960s, and he was initially regarded as another Kafka. Why not? He had written intensely strange stories—in one the father (rather than the son) is metamorphosed into a cockroach—and he was skinny, Jewish, sickly, the author of an incomplete masterpiece (*The Messiah*, now probably lost), obsessed with his father, etc., etc. But in this biographical portrait, Jerzy Ficowski, Schulz's great champion—somewhat analogous, paradoxically, to Kafka's friend Max Brod—staunchly contrasts the two writers: "Schulz was a builder of a reality-asylum that was a marvelous 'intensification of the taste of the world'; Kafka was an inhabitant and propagator of a world of terror, an ascetic hermit awaiting a miracle of justice that never came. Schulz was a metaphysician garbed in all the wealth of color; Kafka was a mystic in a hair shirt of worldly denials. Schulz was a creator and ruler of compensatory Myth, Kafka was the Sisyphean seeker of the Absolute. Schulz, the lavish creator of mundane Olympians, produced a metaphysics of an animate reality, while Kafka became the bookkeeper of the all-enveloping Abyss."

Ficowski can occasionally be even more highflown than this, but what he says in his ornate, rhetorical fashion is certainly true of Schulz (the characterization of Kafka is debatable). He also points out that Jozefina Szelinska, not Schulz, translated *The Trial* into Polish: the writer simply let his then fiancée "borrow" his better-known name.

Schulz spent most of his life in Drohobycz, so he relied on correspondence as a mode of creation as well as communication. In letters to the writer Debora Vogel, he worked up the stories later collected in *Cinnamon Shops*.

That book's critical success brought him the esteem of Witkiewicz and Witold Gombrowicz, among other notable Polish intellectuals. Schulz even composed a highly abstract article on the latter's famous novel *Ferdydurke*. But this timid, hunched-over introvert required long periods of quiet and time to create anything—while the need to support his relatives by means of his day job as a teacher kept him busy and exhausted. As a result, the later *Sanatorium under the Sign of the Hourglass* consists mainly of stories written before those of *Cinnamon Shops*. No one knows for sure how much he completed of *The Messiah*.

Once the Nazis invaded Poland, Schulz found himself interned, then pressed into service as an artist by a local Nazi commandant named Landau, who enjoyed shooting people from his bedroom window. Increasingly frail, Schulz finally decided to escape from Drohobycz with false papers—but a few hours before his departure, the local Nazis went on a rampage in reaction to a potshot at one of their own. Hundreds of Polish Jews were killed. A rival to Landau stalked Schulz, then shot him twice in the head, purely to spite the other Nazi.

None of Bruno Schulz's stories is about the Holocaust. Philip Roth once wrote that "Schulz could barely identify himself with reality, let alone with the Jews." And yet his pages are often elegiac and despairing, as if he had glimpsed the future horrors; the grayish dead dwell among the fanatical and the grotesque. But he leavens the horror with those lovely descriptions (of nature, of the dog Nimrod, of shop windows) and a self-mocking, deadpan humor— "One day my brother, on his return from school, brought the improbable and yet true news of the imminent end of the world"—and teasing hints at still hidden mysteries: "Every night I attend extremely important meetings at the Wax Figures Exhibition, meetings that must remain secret for the time being."

Were it not for the nearly fifty years of research and effort by Jerzy Ficowski, Bruno Schulz might well have been forgotten. Now he is unforgettable, though his imaginings remain elusive, tentative, and, as Ficowski writes, "too big and magnificent to be contained in mere facts. They are merely trying to occur, they are checking whether the ground of reality can carry them. And they quickly withdraw, fearing to lose their integrity in the frailty of realization."

December 8, 2002

THE LAST LEOPARD:
A LIFE OF GIUSEPPE DI LAMPEDUSA

By David Gilmour

An overweight bookish southerner, in a burst of activity just before death from cancer at age sixty, writes an old-fashioned historical novel about the impact of a civil war on the imperious owner of a great family estate. A major publishing house turns it down. The author dies. A few months later another publisher expresses interest in the manuscript, and the book is eventually published to rave reviews. Twenty years after the author's death it will have sold well over a million copies, gone through 121 printings, been translated into twenty-three languages, and—not least—been made into a greatly acclaimed film.

Gone with the Wind? Not quite, Scarlett, even though Giuseppe di Lampedusa's *The Leopard* (1958), the chronicle of an aging prince of Sicily presiding over the death of his world, has sometimes been compared to Margaret Mitchell's epic. The parallels are obvious. In 1860 Fabrizio, prince of Salina, struggles to protect his property and loved ones as the battles of the Italian Risorgimento swirl around him. After peace is reestablished, the prince must face up to a new order, where venal merchants grasp at power and beauty is bartered for a noble bloodline. To those who advocate change in the name of progress, he wearily maintains the aristocratic values of honor, loyalty, tradition, duty: "We were the Leopards and Lions; those who'll take our place will be little jackals, hyenas." When the prince dies, in a squalid hotel room near a train station, he looks back on his life—in one of the greatest death scenes in literature—and finds only "a few golden flecks of happy moments" amid an "immense ash-heap of liabilities."

No précis can convey the measured autumnal beauty of *The Leopard*, a novel as streaked with sun and shadow and dust as the labyrinthine palace of Donnafugata, where young lovers lose themselves in erotic games. It is a deliciously languorous book, evoking a time-honored round of early-morning hunting, afternoon prayer, formal dinners, and tales by firelight. With so much richness it is easy to overlook the novel's persistent low-keyed wit: an antique desk "was carved and decorated like a stage set, full of unexpected, uneven surfaces, of secret drawers which no one knew how to work except thieves." Still, *The Leopard*'s most thrilling moments may be its prose arias when the prince reflects on the movement of the indifferent stars, a garden's fragrance, the face of a dying animal, a momentary glimpse of a waltzing couple: "They were the most moving sight there, two young people in love dancing together, blind to each other's defects, deaf to the warnings of fate, deluding themselves that the whole course of their lives would be as smooth as the ballroom floor, unknowing actors set to play the parts of Juliet and Romeo by a director who had concealed the fact that tomb and poison were already in the script. Neither was good, each self-interested, turgid with secret aims; yet there was something sweet and touching about them both; those murky but ingenuous ambitions of theirs were obliterated by the words of jesting tenderness he was murmuring in her ear, by the scent of her hair, by the mutual clasp of those bodies destined to die."

Until now, most of the biographical information about the creator of *The Leopard* could be found in Archibald Colquhoun's lengthy "translator's note" in *Two Stories and a Memory*, the only other finished literary work by Lampedusa. David Gilmour's astute brief biography corrects a few errors and adds some useful detail, but in truth there's not a whole lot to the outward life of Giuseppe Tomasi, former duke of Palma, the last, almost penniless, prince of Lampedusa. He was born in 1896, traveled a bit to Paris and London as a young man, studied law for a while, lived with his domineering mother, eventually married a psychoanalyst (in a possibly sexless marriage), and never considered working for a living. For years he sauntered every morning to a café in Palermo where he would sip coffee, eat pastries, and read book after book after book. His personal library contained over 1,100 volumes of French history alone.

Reading was clearly the main focus of Lampedusa's every waking moment. Generally quiet and withdrawn, he came alive in talking about writers, especially his favorites, Shakespeare and Stendhal. He particularly loved "the pessimism and 'absolute moral nihilism' of *Measure for Measure*," that bitter comedy set in a ghostly Vienna "consisting of brothels, prisons and attics where abandoned women weep." He once aptly called Shelley, Coleridge, and Byron "a triad of the worst husbands of the world." Like André Gide, he thought Stendhal's *Chartreuse de Parme* the greatest novel in the world, admiring especially its "mellowness," a quality that he carried over into his own book.

The great catastrophe of Lampedusa's life arose from the destruction of his family's palazzo by American bombs during the Second World War. The resulting sense of personal devastation lingered for years, influencing the Proustian wistfulness of *The Leopard*. Gilmour speculates that Lampedusa finally commenced work on the novel partly out of pique that a cousin had received a poetry prize and partly from the example of the literary masterworks he was teaching informally to a few young people.

Though factually modeled after Lampedusa's great-grandfather, the prince clearly shares many of his creator's traits, especially "the problems of an outsider who has lost his way and can find no direction." Lampedusa's ultimate tragedy, of course, was "the coincidence of his physical decay with his brief period of artistic creativity." *The Leopard*, two stories, a lovely memoir of childhood, the start of a new novel ("The Blind Kittens"), and a thousand pages of literature notes were all written in his last thirty months of life, mostly by hand in blue ballpoint in school notebooks.

Gilmour briskly presents the facts of Lampedusa's world, offers fascinating chapters on his reading and good brief interpretations of *The Leopard* and the other works. I was surprised that he overlooked the apparent connections between the hero of the wonder-filled story "The Professor and the Mermaid" and his subject's cousin Lucio: both are learned in the classics, eccentric, believers in the supernatural, obsessed with finding a beautiful young girl. That very minor quibble aside, this is a fine short biography, entertaining in itself and likely to send many readers back to *The Leopard*, that ideal book for the end of any long hot summer.

August 18, 1991

PAUL CELAN:
POET, SURVIVOR, JEW

By John Felstiner

In the view of many critics, the redoubtable George Steiner chief among them, Paul Celan (1920–1970) is the finest postwar European poet. For most readers, even those with fluent German, he may be the most difficult as well. His verse is compact, elliptical, sometimes so personal as to be hermetic, deeply haunted by the Holocaust. In a Celan poem the words lie on the page like drops of blood.

Some poets may be enjoyed for their surface pleasures: a Robert Frost or an A. E. Housman can charm even a schoolchild. Not Celan. You don't read him for fun, or for his suavity and wit. He is a poet of anguish and remembrance, one of the few authors who doesn't seem vulgar or exploitative in making art—a sorrowful, torturous art—out of the death camps and the loss of European Jewish culture. In his most famous work, the early "Deathfugue," he interweaves Nazi callousness, music making in the camps, genocide, a blond Margareta, an ashen Sulamith, and some shocking, almost surreal imagery. Here are its opening lines:

> Black milk of daybreak we drink it at
> evening
> we drink it at midday and morning we
> drink it at night
> we drink and we drink
> we shovel a grave in the air there you
> won't lie too cramped
> A man lives in the house he plays with
> his vipers he writes
> he writes when it grows dark to
> Deutschland your golden hair

Margareta
he writes it and steps out of doors and
the stars are all sparkling
he whistles his hounds to come close
he whistles his Jews into rows has
them shovel a grave in the ground
he commands us play up for the
dance. . . .

In his later years Celan came to find this poem overly explicit, but there is no denying the power that has made it, for good or ill, an anthology piece: "Der Tod ist ein Meister aus Deutschland"—"Death Is a Master from Germany."

Readers of Celan, and not only new ones, generally welcome all the help they can get. As John Felstiner says, some of the later poems "are so cryptic as to seem like signals from another planet." One begins "Pour the Wasteland into your eyesacks" and doesn't grow any easier. Yet Celan himself insisted that he was "not in the least hermetic," because, in Felstiner's explanation, "if his poetry was seen as magically sealed off from understanding, that would relieve its readers of responsibility." For Celan, like some ancient, unwelcome prophet, carries a terrible burden: to bear witness to the unthinkable, to honor the dishonored, to resurrect through language a beloved and forever lost human presence.

John Felstiner's *Paul Celan: Poet, Survivor, Jew* takes the form of a "critical biography," that is, it focuses on the life chiefly as a means of elucidating the lifework. In this instance, we learn a fair amount about Celan's early days in Czernowitz, capital of Bukovina, part of Romania, on the eastern edge of the Habsburg empire, a crossroads of Central European culture. The young Celan—or rather Paul Antschel, as he was then called—gained proficiency in several languages, studied law in Tours, traveled to England, joined a communist youth organization, began to compose poems. Then everything changed. "What the life of a Jew was during the war years, I need not mention," Celan later noted with a reticence at once characteristic and heartbreaking. One night in June 1942, not long after the Germans had rolled into town, Celan's parents were simply deported to a labor camp; within a year his father had died of typhus and his mother had been shot as "unfit for work." Celan managed to avoid his parents' fate, though he spent much of the war in forced labor.

With the destruction of his world the young Jew from Czernowitz found himself an unhappy wanderer, settling briefly in Vienna and in 1948 permanently in Paris. During the next twenty-two years he was to marry a French graphic artist, become a lecturer in German at the Ecole Normale Supérieure, translate the poetry of Mandelstam, Shakespeare, Emily Dickinson, and Henri

Michaux (along with nearly forty others), and gain renown for his austere and demanding poetry. At the same time, though, Celan also fell prey to recurrent depression, endured hospitalization, never managed to shake an intense existential loneliness, and at forty-nine finally committed suicide by drowning himself in the Seine. Surprisingly little of this personal matter is reflected in Celan's poetry, yet I would have welcomed more information about his day-to-day life. Did he ever laugh? What did his students think of him? Is it true that his only son, Eric, became a magician? Such details would have humanized a saintly figure who seems almost too anguished to be quite real.

If Felstiner fails to satisfy human curiosity about the man, he excels at illuminating the poetry. He does have a program, however: virtually all Celan's poems must refer back to the Holocaust and embody strictly Jewish themes. In general, Felstiner is certainly right, yet other scholars—such as the translator Michael Hamburger and Amy Collin (author of *Paul Celan: Holograms of Darkness*)—suggest that some of Celan's work may be read in a less sectarian way. For instance, "The Vintagers" might be an *ars poetica*—a description of the poetic process—rather than an elegy to Holocaust victims.

The precise truth of these matters lies beyond my competence—though such disagreement suggests some of the sheer density of Celan's language. As a reader, I am simply grateful for Felstiner's careful and moving translations, his patient, often word-by-word analysis, and the wealth of biblical and linguistic expertise he brings to bear on so many otherwise enigmatic poems. Of course, some of this unique oeuvre's solemn energy must derive from the fact that Celan, the Holocaust survivor, must write in German, the language of his oppressors. It seems inevitable and almost natural that later poems move increasingly toward silence.

But there is more here than the homage of silence. Turn to any page of Celan, even his occasional prose, and lines shudder with moral truths and linger long in the memory: "The angels are dead and the Lord has gone blind in the region of Acra." "Whichever stone you lift— / you lay bare / those who need the protection of stones." "There was earth inside them, and / they dug." "Over all this / grief of yours: no / second heaven." "Landscape with urn-beings." "But where in great poetry is it not a question of last things?"

Poems, said Celan, are "gifts to the attentive." In *Paul Celan: Poet, Survivor, Jew* John Felstiner teaches us how to pay better attention to one of the most serious and rewarding poets of our time.

August 6, 1995

THAT MIGHTY SCULPTOR, TIME

By Marguerite Yourcenar
Translated from the French by Walter Kaiser,
in collaboration with the author

A writer has to be really sure of herself to burden a book, even a collection of essays, with a doorstop title like *That Mighty Sculptor, Time*. Not even Thomas Mann would have dared to be quite so august. But as admirers of *Memoirs of Hadrian* or *The Abyss* know, Marguerite Yourcenar (1903–1987) wrote prose with the kind of Olympian assurance that Jove himself might have envied. Like waves washing against a pebbled shore, her sentences soothe, then hypnotize; before long the sound of her voice—slightly weary, serenely wise—becomes that of Reason itself.

Like all philosophical novelists, Yourcenar is obsessed with mortality. The dying Roman emperor Hadrian ends his long letter to Marcus Aurelius by seeking to "enter into death with open eyes"; the sixteenth-century physician-alchemist Zeno (in *The Abyss*) travels the world in order, before his self-inflicted end, to make "at least the round of this, his prison"; even the fantasies of *Oriental Tales*, such as the exquisite "Last Love of Prince Genji," deal largely with death. One feels, after reading such fiction, a deep tenderness for man's lot, even a kind of spiritual consolation: "We are all alike, and the same fate lies in store for all of us." No wonder that these reflections on the human condition were literally the work of a lifetime: imagined in youth, then written, rewritten and polished, and finally published only decades after their conception.

Obviously Marguerite Yourcenar's somber sense of life will not appeal to everyone. But for those able to approach her as she deserves, she is likely to become a favorite author. One good introduction might be through her essays, nearly all of which are gathered in *The Dark Brain of Piranesi* and this new volume (very well translated, by the way: a spot check against the French original could turn up no gaffes). Together they display a moralist and critic of remarkable range and sympathy: in the earlier book are reflections on the late Roman emperors, the château of Chenonceaux (focusing on Henri III, "a prince so tragic, so futile, and so lucid"), the Italian artist Piranesi (best known for his vertiginous, Escher-like "imaginary prisons"), the Swedish novelist Selma Lagerlof (a writer I thought could be safely neglected until I read Yourcenar's appreciation), Thomas Mann, and the Alexandrian poet C. P. Cavafy. This "critical introduction" to Cavafy's historical soliloquies and love poems is, I think, one of the best pieces of criticism written in this century, at once learned, personal, and, above all, right: "The dry, flexible style [of Cavafy] makes no commitments, not even to concision; admirers of ancient Greek will recognize this smooth surface without highlights, almost without accents, which like certain modeling in Hellenistic statues reveals itself, when seen at close range, to be of an infinite subtlety and, one may say, mobility."

Yourcenar might be describing her own writing.

That Mighty Sculptor, Time emphasizes Yourcenar's more occasional journalism, much of it autobiographical, some of it quite impassioned. Being the first woman elected to the Académie Française was a matter of relative indifference to this crusader who raised her voice, long ago, against the "inhuman" methods of rearing livestock for food, against the slaughter of animals for their fur. Her causes, she has noted, are "overpopulation, cruelty to animals, crowded housing conditions, unhealthy working conditions, and most importantly, conservation and social justice." Yourcenar may have spent half her life on Mount Desert Island in Maine, but she never sequestered herself like some fustian Miss Havisham with a Belgian accent.

Other essays in the new collection, such as "Approaches to Tantrism" and "On Some Erotic and Mystic Themes of the Gita-Govinda," also remind us that Yourcenar sympathized with Eastern religions and believed, to some degree, in yoga, second sight, reincarnation, and mystical transcendence. In this light, her own fiction frequently seems the result less of imagination than of demonic possession, an attempt to listen for, then set down, faint voices from the past. Indeed, at times one can hardly distinguish her biographical essays from her fictional impersonations.

A few pieces here—"Sistine," "Festivals of the Passing Year," "Written in a Garden"—recall Yourcenar's occasional experiments in prose poetry (see the collection *Fires*). But the aphoristic interrupts even the most lyrical flights: Jesus is alone in an orchard "where everyone has forgot him except his enemies"; the true festivals, "those most deeply rooted in the human consciousness, are those we celebrate without knowing why"; and "Whoever carves statues only hastens, after all, the crumbling of mountains."

This tone of *memento mori* is firmly set by the opening meditation on a famous passage in Bede: there, we learn, the life of man can be likened to a sparrow that emerges from out of a winter's storm, flies through a fire-lit hall, and then disappears again into eternal night. For her title piece Yourcenar further reflects on how time and accident affect ancient works of art. Some, she notes, "owe their beauty to human violence: the push toppling them from their pedestals or the iconoclast's hammer has made them what they are. The classical work of art is thus infused with pathos; the mutilated gods have the air of martyrs." The longest essay, "Tone and Language in the Historical Novel," explains some of the stylistic decisions behind Yourcenar's own work—the ultra-dignified "style of the toga" in *Hadrian*, the polyphony of *The Abyss*.

For all its wisdom and beauty, *That Mighty Sculptor, Time* is not the book to pack for a sunny weekend at the beach. Save it instead for a quieter, more reflective season: after all, if summer comes, can autumn be far behind?

June 21, 1992

EXTINCTION

By Thomas Bernhard
Translated from the German by David McClintock

For years people have lavishly praised the fiction of the Austrian writer Thomas Bernhard (1931–1989), invoking for comparison such literary grandees as Borges, Musil, and Kafka. Once in a bookstore I opened a copy of Bernhard's *Correction*—in part, I was told, a meditation on Wittgenstein—and was immediately daunted by the forbidding appearance of the text: page after page without a single paragraph indentation, sentences that ran on and on, cobbled together with the loosest possible syntax, and all of it translated from the German. Somehow, *Correction* didn't look to be a fun way to spend an evening, and I went off to search for another Dawn Powell novel as fizzy as *The Locusts Have No King*.

To my surprise, however, I couldn't quite forget about Thomas Bernhard. The University of Chicago brought out a handful of his novels in its inviting Phoenix paperback line; and Knopf kept publishing newly translated work: *Wittgenstein's Nephew*, a semi-autobiographical account of Bernhard's friendship with Paul Wittgenstein; *Woodcutters*, which satirizes Austrian literary society; and, in 1991, *The Loser*, wherein a fictionalized Glenn Gould inspires the narrator's meditations on art, music, loneliness, and creativity.

All the reviews claimed these books were masterpieces. I wondered. At one point somebody gleefully told me that Bernhard's speech accepting the 1967 Austrian State Prize was so politically offensive that half the audience left in a rage, including the minister of culture. I liked the sound of that. I then read a congenially somber remark by Bernhard about literature—"Everything is ridiculous when one thinks of death." And, finally, I heard about Bernhard's will. "Whatever I have written, whether published by me during my lifetime or as part of my literary papers still existing after my death shall not be performed, printed or even recited for the duration of legal copyright within the borders of Austria, however this state identifies itself." By this time I was eager to try Bernhard again, and so jumped at the chance to read *Extinction*, the last novel he completed before his death at fifty-eight, of heart failure.

Extinction—it should hardly come as a surprise—proved to be exactly my kind of book. Some of the sentences may be long, but in David McClintock's smooth, convincing translation they are also perfectly balanced and continually interesting: each begins a small voyage of discovery. After a while, the eye quietly grows used to the lack of indentation. And indeed, for a book that is essentially a 300-page interior monologue, an exposition of a mind reflecting upon itself and various obsessions, there really is no artistic sense in breaking up the text into parts. Just ask Molly Bloom. But most important of all, Bernhard turns out to be an exceptionally ingratiating writer: the voice that rises from his prose is peculiarly, insidiously soothing: "On the twenty-ninth, having returned from Wolfsegg, I met my pupil Gambetti on the Pincio to discuss arrangements for the lessons he was to receive in May, writes Franz-Josef Murau, and impressed once again by his high intelligence, I was so refreshed and exhilarated, so glad to be living in Rome and not in Austria, that instead of walking home along the Via Condotti, as I usually do, I crossed the Flaminia and the Piazza del Popolo and walked the whole length of the Corso before returning to my apartment in the Piazza Minerva, where at about two o'clock I received the telegram informing me that my parents and my brother, Johannes, had died. Parents and Johannes killed in accident. Caecilia, Amalia, it read. Holding the telegram, I kept a clear head, walked calmly to my study window, and looked down on the Piazza Minerva, where there was not a soul in sight. . . . "

Extinction is divided into two halves. In the first—"The Telegram"—the middle-aged narrator, Murau, sits in his apartment, recalling his family and his upbringing. He plays with photographs of his parents, brother, and sisters, reflects upon each one's provincial conventionality, and summons up remembrances of things past, especially those relating to his unhappy childhood at Wolfsegg. Almost incidentally, he also reveals bits of information about his favorite people, chiefly a scapegrace uncle Georg, model for his own slightly sybaritic life; the urbane archbishop Spadolini, who had been his mother's lover; and, not least, his "anarchist" pupil Gambetti. Throughout, Murau is oppressed by the prospect of returning to Wolfsegg for the triple burial, and for a long while the reader suspects that he will never manage to do it.

But the second section of the novel—titled "The Will"—takes place at the estate and describes Murau's reactions to the elaborate preparations for the funeral service. He visits the Orangery, where the three coffins are laid out, talks briefly with his despised, worn-out sisters, observes the courtly Spadolini in action, and, while wandering around the house and park lands, ponders what to do with the ancient property that he has unexpectedly inherited. Here, Murau makes explicit his hatred (and Bernhard's) for Austria's Nazi past, its socialist present, and its Catholic culture.

The particular fineness of *Extinction* lies in its depiction of a consciousness in action: Murau, it turns out, can be weak, admirable, reprehensible, or mean-spirited, but his mind, as depicted on the page, seems absolutely true to life. Hypocrite narrator, one might say, *mon semblable, mon frère.* By comparison Dostoevsky's Underground Man—an obvious ancestor—sounds strung out, jumpy, more than slightly crazed. Murau is terribly serious about everything, observant, self-deluding, funny. "Human beings, it seems, exert themselves only for as long as they can look forward to idiotic diplomas that they can boast about in public." As one listens, he offers mini-disquisitions on photography, shopping, doctors and teachers, reading, the differing temperaments of gardeners and huntsmen, languages, mendacity, modern German literature, Austrian National Socialism, and the tyranny of three-ring binders. Here, for example, he notes "the superficiality of today's twenty-year-olds":

"When they were not dancing they stood around, stolid and humorless, visibly tormented by a deadly boredom that would afflict them all their lives because they had done nothing about it when there was still time. It's too late, I thought, for any of these young people to escape this deadly lifelong boredom; by now they're almost completely taken up with their fancies, their jobs, their girls and their women, totally absorbed in their perversely superficial concerns. Talking to them, one finds that they have nothing in their heads but this ghastly superficiality and think only about their trust funds and their cars. When I talk to one of them, I thought, I'm talking not to a human being but to an utterly primitive, unimaginative, single-minded show-off."

Alongside ferocious remarks about churchmen and Austrian culture, Bernhard brilliantly creates, in a language free of elaborate metaphor or stylistic fanciness, Murau's twisty paradoxical sense of himself. "When I take Wolfsegg and my family apart, when I dissect, annihilate and extinguish them, I am actually taking myself apart, dissecting, annihilating, and extinguishing myself." Murau repeatedly declares his rejection of his family and its estate, but through his obsessiveness unavoidably discloses his own constant and tortured love for these people, this past, even this country he intellectually loathes. Like the ideal unreliable narrator, Murau can neither be entirely trusted nor absolutely disbelieved: he can simply be experienced in all his introspective vitality.

While reading *Extinction* I found myself smoothing down page after page, deeply content to be listening to Murau comment on anything, in tune with a book that matched my own taste for worldly observation, self-pity, and wistfulness. I've never been to Austria and Murau is something of a creep, but so what? His inexorable volubility is quite irresistible, like a confession of strange sins or a declaration of hopeless love. Ultimately what I liked was Bernhard's anguished vision of things, his late-Beethoven-string-quartet sensibility. It is gratifying to know that there are at least seven or eight more Bernhard novels already translated into English. I think I'll look out for another copy of *Correction.*

October 8, 1995

AUSTERLITZ

By W. G. Sebald
Translated from the German by Anthea Bell

Few authors have won such widespread admiration and acclaim in so short a time as W. G. Sebald. And yet one could hardly have predicted this. After all, Sebald didn't start publishing until well into middle age—and he writes in German, in a single flow of words without paragraph indentations, largely about lugubrious, not to say tragic, matters: the burdens of the past and the aftershocks of the Holocaust in particular; his own nervous ailments and melancholia; the largely unvisited corners of literature and scholarship (Stendhal's memoirs, Kafka in Italy, Sir Thomas Browne, railroad station architecture, the theory of fortification). What's more, Sebald's four books—besides this one, they include *The Emigrants, The Rings of Saturn,* and *Vertigo*—blithely ignore genre boundaries: Are they novels? Memoirs? Essays? It's impossible to say where the factual leaves off and the fictional begins. Matters are further complicated by the author's practice of illustrating his narratives with poorly reproduced photographs. Are these the honest signposts of authenticity? Or a postmodern attempt to trick the naive into unwarranted belief? There's no sure way to know.

What holds all Sebald's work together, though, is his brokenhearted voice and his warmhearted personality. Even when a book is told largely through the words of another character, as in *Austerlitz,* we constantly feel Sebald's plangent presence. He is one of those endearing sad-sack figures we have come to know from Beckett: a stoic comedian, an observer of life when it falls into the sere and yellow leaf. In reality, W. G. Sebald may be a distinguished professor of German at the University of East Anglia and the former director of the British Centre for Literary Translation, but in his writing he is an unhappy wanderer through postwar Europe, a ghostly pilgrim, with a rucksack on his back and an ache in his soul, always encountering some shattered revenant from the shattered past. "In the second half of the 1960s I traveled repeatedly from England to Belgium, partly for study purposes, partly for other reasons which were never entirely clear to me, staying sometimes for just one or two days, sometimes for several weeks. On one of these Belgian excursions which, as it seemed to me, always took me further and further abroad, I came on a glorious summer morning to the city of Antwerp, known to me previously only by name."

Here, in the railroad station café, Sebald encounters Austerlitz, dressed in heavy walking boots, workman's trousers, and an outdated suit jacket. To his surprise, this apparent tramp turns out to be highly educated: "From the first I was astonished by the way Austerlitz put his ideas together as he talked, forming perfectly balanced sentences out of whatever occurred to him, so to speak, and the way in which, in his mind, the passing on of his knowledge seemed to become a gradual approach to a kind of historical metaphysic, bringing remembered events back to life."

In fact, *Austerlitz* proves largely a narrative about its eponymous hero's attempt to bring back to life his own forgotten past. As an old nurse tells him much later in the book, even as a boy he was always troubled by the nature of memory, of remembering: How do squirrels know where they have hidden their hoards when the ground is covered with snow? "Those were your very words, the question which constantly troubled you. How indeed do the squirrels know, what do we know ourselves, how do we remember, and what is it we find in the end?" The attempt to recover the past is, as readers of Sebald's other books know, one of his recurrent themes.

Austerlitz, it turns out, is a lecturer in art history, deeply afflicted in body and spirit. "No sooner did I become acquainted with someone than I feared I had come too close, no sooner did someone turn towards me than I began to retreat. In the end I was linked to other people only by certain forms of courtesy which I took to extremes and which I know today. . . . I observed not so much for the sake of their recipients as because they allowed me to ignore the fact that my life has always, for as far back as I can remember, been overcast by an unrelieved desperation."

Over the course of 300 pages, Austerlitz gradually unfolds his complex story to Sebald, touching on his suicidal impulses, his researches into architectural history, his vain attempts at love, and eventually his quest for the truth about himself.

As a boy, Austerlitz tells Sebald, he was brought up in Wales by stepparents, a stern minister named Elias and his wife, Gwendolyn: "It was the minister's unalterable custom to sit in his study, which had a view of a dark corner of the garden, thinking about next Sunday's sermon. He never wrote any of these sermons down, but worked them out in his head, toiling over them for at least four days. He would always emerge from his study in the evening in a state of deep despondency, only to disappear into it again next morning. But on Sunday, when he stood up in chapel in front of his congregation and often addressed them for a full hour, he was a changed man; he spoke with a moving eloquence which I still feel I can hear, conjuring up before the eyes of his flock the Last Judgment awaiting them all, the lurid fires of purgatory, the torments of damnation and then, with the most wonderful stellar and celestial imagery, the entry of the righteous into eternal bliss. With apparent ease, as if he were making up the most appalling horrors as he went along, he always succeeded in filling the hearts of his congregation with such sentiments of remorse that at the end of service quite a number of them went home looking white as a sheet. The minister himself, on the other hand, was in a comparatively jovial mood for the rest of Sunday."

Though reared by this religious couple, Austerlitz never feels at ease with them. And not only because of their coldness of heart. "At some time in the past, I thought, I must have made a mistake, and now I am living the wrong life." Everywhere he turns he finds a sorrow and despair that not even deep religious conviction can palliate. When Gwendolyn grows deathly ill, the minister cares for her devotedly: "On Christmas Day, making a great effort, Gwendolyn sat up in bed once more. Elias had brought her a cup of sweet tea, but she only moistened her lips with it. Then she said, so quietly that you could hardly hear her: What was it that so darkened our world? And Elias replied: I don't know, dear, I don't know."

Following his wife's death the minister loses his mind.

All this serves as prelude to the teenage boy's discovery that he is not, in fact, Dafydd Elias but Jacques Austerlitz, sent to England at five, by unknown parents, to escape the tightening grip of the Third Reich. Much of the second half of Sebald's book chronicles Austerlitz's stumbling, but persistent, quest for the truth about his parentage and childhood. That journey into the past eventually takes him to Prague and from there to Terezin and the darkness at the heart of our calamitous age.

This isn't, obviously, a cheerful book: ours is indeed a darkened world. Still, Austerlitz eventually unearths a great deal about himself and does find some kind of healing late in his troubled existence. Along the way, he enthralls us with his meditations on moths and the nonexistence of time, with reflections on Balzac's *Le Colonel Chabert* (that wonderful short novel about a Napoleonic soldier's return from the dead), and the organization of libraries and spas, with brilliant pages on the hatred of writing that frequently besets a writer, and how mankind's attempts to be rational so often lead to just the opposite. There are delicate aperçus about life, too: "Only now did she truly understand how wonderful it is to stand by the rail of a river steamer without a care in the world. . . . We take almost all the decisive steps in our lives as a result of slight inner adjustments of which we are barely conscious."

Yes, Sebald's is a crepuscular, autumnal world. Fortunately, his humanity and low-key gallows humor—smiling through the Apocalypse—help keep at bay the encroaching gloom, the spiritual weariness. If you're completely new to Sebald, you should probably start with his early masterpiece, *The Emigrants*, four accounts of lives stunted by exile; *Austerlitz* is, in a way, a fifth, fuller portrait, and similar in tone and character. Despite, or perhaps because of, their pervasive somberness, W. G. Sebald's are some of the most original and exhilarating books of our time.

October 14, 2001

POSTSCRIPT: In 2001 W. G. Sebald's death in an automobile accident unexpectedly cut short his brilliant late flowering. *Littera scripta manet.*

WRITERS OF OUR TIME

XI

As Howard Carter pushed through into the underground tomb of "King Tut" his colleagues eagerly shouted down after him, demanding to know what he was seeing. His answer was "Wonderful things." That sense of the fabulous—in both its senses—characterizes the contemporary books in this section of Bound to Please.

In the loosest sense, most of these books are highly polished literary fantasies, glimpses of dark worlds or magical realms, sometimes antiquarian romances or great fairy tales. See the pieces on Steven Millhauser, Ben Okri, Philip Pullman. Even those that are ostensibly realistic are linguistic dazzlements—William Gass's The Tunnel, Cormac McCarthy's Border trilogy, William Gaddis's A Frolic of His Own, Annie Proulx's Accordion Crimes. When Stanley Elkin starts his inimitable patter on the page, even a portrait of an old lady living in retirement in Florida is transmuted into something rich and strange. Similarly, there are few novelists more sheerly enjoyable than Robertson Davies, whose blend of patrician prose with a Dickensian taste for both melodrama and hocus-pocus can be irresistible.

But this is a section also loaded with regrets—the writers I admire, whom I never got to write about or couldn't address in depth when I did: James Salter, whose masterwork, Light Years, reminds me of Tender Is the Night in the beauty of its prose and its sorrowful evocation of a marriage breaking down; Alexander Theroux, whose sentences in, say, Darconville's Cat, crackle with nonstop erudition, invective, and stylistic bravura; Angela Carter, who died young, but still managed to write the enchanting Nights at the Circus and the Shakespearean Wise Children.

To my regret, the years have rolled by and I never found the right occasion to review Robert Stone, Toni Morrison, Saul Bellow, Tom Wolfe, and a dozen other important American writers. I also yearn to read or reread, then write about, the work of Eudora Welty, Flannery O'Connor, and William Faulkner and . . . One of these days.

I should add that all the books and writers here fulfill Willa Cather's injunction that "Every great story . . . must leave in the mind of the sensitive reader an intangible residuum of pleasure; a cadence, a quality of voice that is exclusively the writer's own, individual, unique."

What more can I say—except read them and see for yourself.

WHAT'S BRED IN THE BONE

By Robertson Davies

Robertson Davies is the sort of novelist readers can hardly wait to tell their friends about. Not that he's precisely unknown, even for a Canadian. A passionate fellowship exists among admirers of his Deptford trilogy: *Fifth Business, The Manticore*, and *World of Wonders*. Last year his urbane ghost story collection, *High Spirits*, even received the World Fantasy Award. When he lectures—as he did recently at the Library of Congress—the house sells out. With his out-of-date, high-buttoned suits, a handkerchief up his sleeve like a priest or a magician, and his imposing white beard, he calls to mind a genial sorcerer, an alchemical marriage of Prospero and Faust and Santa Claus.

His books reinforce this impression. If García Márquez practices "magic realism," then Davies specializes in what might be called "melodramatic realism"—his fiction mingles the supernaturalism of Le Fanu, the mystery of Wilkie Collins, the plummy richness and archetypal figures of Dickens. In *What's Bred in the Bone* he includes, to mention only a few, an idiot child, a bartered bride, a father-and-son spy team, several faked paintings, Nazis, Oxford communists, the Holy Grail, astrology, King Arthur's Tintagel, a dead dwarf, a millionaire art connoisseur, Bronzino's *Allegory of Time*, and a pair of angels. Being Davies, he weaves them all together so beautifully that a reader just sighs with pleasure as he turns the pages.

"What's bred in the bone comes out in the flesh": using this proverb, Davies traces the largely unhappy, though often comic, history of Francis Cornish, the eccentric Canadian art collector whose death provided the motor for his previous novel, *The Rebel Angels*. The new book addresses several large issues—the Jungian search for a completion of the self in love, the nature of biography, the working out of pattern and coincidence in life—but perhaps the most important is the growth of Francis's artistic understanding. The young boy, neglected by his parents, confused by his family's mixture of Anglicanism and Catholicism, picked on at school, finds solace in drawing and studying pictures. One day, hoping to learn anatomy, he persuades the local embalmer, a raffish character named Zadok Hoyle, to let him observe his work. The evenings that follow prove a revelation, determining—in several unexpected ways—the character of Francis's life.

Old McAllister was balding and scrawny. His face and hands were tanned a deep brown by sixty-seven years of Ottawa Valley weather, but the rest of him was a bluey-white. His legs were like sticks, and his feet fell outward and sideways. Zadok had cut off his underwear because Old McAllister, according to local custom, had been sewed into it for the winter. Francis knew all about that; most of the children in Carlyle Rural were so encased and they stank amazingly.

"A bath, for a starter," said Zadok. "First, though, a thorough swilling out. . . ." With a dribble from a short hose, and frequent dabblings of carbolic, Zadok washed Old McAllister; the water fell to the cement floor and vanished down a drain. He washed Old McAllister's hands, with plentiful lathering of yellow soap, and cleaned the nails with his jack-knife.

"Always a problem, this," he said to the busily scribbling Francis. "These fellas never clean their hands from Easter to Easter, but they have to have hands like a barber for the viewing. It's part of the art, you see. At the end they must look as they'd have looked on their wedding day, or better. Probably better."

He shaved Old McAllister with ample lather and hot water. "Lucky I had some experience as a valet. . . ."

Several delicate operations later. Zadok finishes Old McAllister's transformation. "He combed the hair with a left-hand parting, then quiffed the right-hand portion over his finger, giving Old McAllister a nifty, almost a dandified air. Quick work with the collar, the necktie; into the waistcoat, draping a huge silver watch-chain, from which the watch had been removed, over the sunken belly. On with the coat. A piece of card on the tip of which some white cambric was sewn was tucked into the breast pocket of the coat (Old McAllister had not used, or possessed, handkerchiefs of his own). The hands were folded on the breast, as if in Christian acceptance, and Old McAllister was a finished work of art."

Without undergoing the courteous attentions of Zadok Hoyle, over the past seventy-two years Robertson Davies has shaped his public self into a highly finished work of art. Born in 1913, Davies was the son of a newspaper publisher who eventually became a self-made millionaire. After schooling in Canada, he attended Oxford, where he wrote a thesis on the boy actors in Shakespeare, and subsequently joined the Old Vic acting company. He worked with its director Tyrone Guthrie from 1938 to 1940, married, and returned to Canada, spending the next twenty years as a literary journalist. He reviewed regularly (a special interest being Canadian culture), created a crotchety alter ego named Samuel Marchbanks, whose diary graced the pages of the *Peterborough Examiner*, and eventually became that newspaper's editor and publisher.

Throughout the 1940s and 1950s Davies focused his deepest creative energies on the theater, writing plays and drama criticism. In the early 1950s he did manage to produce three comic novels, frequently dubbed the Salterton trilogy (after their chief locale): *Tempest Tost* deals with intrigues and love affairs behind the scenes at a provincial production of *The Tempest*, *Leaven of Malice* with similar shenanigans at a university and newspaper, and *A Mixture of Frailties* with the education and fortunes of a singer.

By 1962 Davies had become a prominent and versatile Canadian man of letters. So it could hardly have been surprising when he began to teach nineteenth-century drama and melodrama at the University of Toronto. The following year he was elected master of Massey College, a position he kept until his recent retirement. Besides performing normal academic duties, Davies also established an eighteen-year tradition of reading an original ghost story at Massey's Christmas dinners. They were, he said, his attempt to inject a little magic and mystery into the new institution.

Davies's curious knowledge of the supernatural grew out of his passion for melodrama, with its archetypal villains and virgins, and was bolstered by his long study of Jung, an interest in saints' lives, much reflection on religion, insanity and evil, and virtually an adept's understanding of alchemy, astrology, the tarot, and conjuring. All these elements of arcane learning come together in the three Deptford novels, which trace the interlocking lives of several characters, chiefly the haunted schoolmaster Dunstan Ramsay, the millionaire Boy Staunton, and the magician known as Magnus Eisengrim. Their story has become a modern classic.

In an interview Davies has suggested that *What's Bred in the Bone* will be the middle volume of another trio of linked novels. *The Rebel Angels* focused on love among the learned, chiefly that of several professors for a beautiful gypsy graduate student named Maria Theotoky. In form the book resembled one of the "conversation" novels of Peacock or Aldous Huxley; an assembly of oddball characters quarrel and discourse about love, philosophy, religion, and other lofty matters before all ends happily in a marriage. *What's Bred in the Bone* portrays a kind man who enjoys triumphs as a painter and art critic, love affairs, Reilly-like spy adventures, and great wealth, but never finds reciprocated affection: of all the pictures in Francis Cornish's art collection the most important is a reproduction from his childhood entitled *Love Locked Out*, depicting a little boy weeping at a closed door. The third book, it can be surmised, will take up some other aspect of love, perhaps that of the married life.

For now Robertson Davies's fans will have to rest content with the world of wonders in *What's Bred in the Bone*, a book as laced with marvels, subterfuge, and melodramatic coincidence as *Fifth Business*. Its only flaw lies in the rather rushed account of Francis's years of fame; perhaps we will learn more of them in the future. I'm sure that the old magician has more than a handkerchief tucked up his sleeve.

November 17, 1985

POSTCRIPT: Robertson Davies (1913–1995) went on to write other good novels after this one—*The Lyre of Orpheus, The Cunning Man*—but this remains, in my view, his masterpiece. Over the years I've collected most of his books, and highly recommend his essays and letters, as well as his fiction. All his work displays a vast and desultory erudition supported by a shrewd understanding of the world and a showman's desire to entertain.

LITTLE KINGDOMS:
THREE NOVELLAS

By Steven Millhauser

"Reviews," finally concludes Steven Millhauser, "did not know which to praise more, the meticulous artistry or the haunting fantasy." Though Millhauser is talking about the animated feature *Dime Store Days*, the creation of the 1920s hero of his novella *The Little Kingdom of J. Franklin Payne*, the same words might also sum up the enthusiastic reception of his own best work. For no one alive, except perhaps James Salter or John Crowley, can write more beautiful prose. And no one since Borges and Calvino has composed such spellbinding literary fantasies. "The Barnum Museum," "Cathay," "August Eschenburg," "Eisenheim the Illusionist"—each is a little world made as cunningly, and as exquisitely, as a Fabergé egg.

And therein lies the common reservation about Millhauser. Aren't his tales—about an imaginary museum and the China of our dreams, about a fabricator of intricate clockwork automatons and a master magician—just a little precious and ethereal, aspiring, almost, to the condition of objets d'art? And isn't Millhauser himself somewhat obsessed with childhood and its sense of wonder? Certainly his early classic, *Edwin Mullhouse: The Life and Death of an American Writer*, uncannily evokes what it was like to grow up in the 1950s, but even its naturalistic exactness supports a playful Nabokovian romp in the schoolyard: the book purports to be a literary biography of the greatest novelist of our time, tragically dead at the age of eleven.

Millhauser will probably never shake the insinuation that he is merely a confectioner of trifles. His is, after all, an art that highlights rather than conceals itself. Instead of simply telling a story in which this happened and then, believe it or not, that happened next, Millhauser likes to re-create an artifact, often transmuting the throwaway—a guidebook, a catalog, a classic comic, even a game of Clue—into something rich and strange. Similarly, he may fragment a narrative into glittering shards, then scatter these shiny bits and pieces upon the page with seeming artlessness, where they await the sympathetic reader who will appreciate their beauty and piece together their meaning.

In fact, Millhauser's great strength lies in just this fanatical particularization (he has said that "one never forgives a work of art that is general and vague"). He can imbue his descriptive details with the evocative power and excitement of runaway narrative. *The Princess, the Dwarf, and the Dungeon*, in this new collection, delivers repeated shivers of erotic menace and violation— yet almost nothing sexual really happens. But then it doesn't have to: "Thus do we weave tales within tales, within our minds, when the tales themselves do not speak." Millhauser, without flourish, can simply make the tacit seem almost emphatic. Meanwhile, his actual sentences may shift from a Rabelaisian gusto and exuberance (see his underappreciated *From the Realm of Morpheus*) to a prose of such measured serenity and assurance that God himself might envy it: "Long ago these tales unfolded, long ago the prisoner escaped, the dwarf faded into darkness, the Princess closed her eyes. And yet even now we can sometimes see, in the high tower, a flash of yellow hair, we can sometimes hear, in the clear air, the sound of the prisoner cutting through rock. Ships pass on the river, bearing away copper bowls, armor plate, and toothed wheels for sawmills, bringing us spices, velvet, and silk, but under the river live trolls and mermaids."

This relationship or, as is usual, disparity between the life of the world and the life of the imagination has long been Millhauser's recurrent theme. It gnaws at the heart of the Romantic sensibility: there hath passed away a glory from the earth. I see not feel how beautiful they are. Heard melodies are sweet, but those unheard are sweeter. In such collections as *The Barnum Museum* and *In the Penny Arcade* we sometimes pierce the world's veil to find the numinous truth; at other times we lose our way in the madness of art. In the three wonderful (and woe-filled) novellas of *Little Kingdoms* Millhauser paints a triptych, demonstrating how the imagination enriches but may also trouble and destroy.

In *The Little Kingdom of J. Franklin Payne* a newspaper cartoonist grows obsessed with the laborious creation of short animated films. To create his thirty-minute masterpiece, *The Dark Side of the Moon*, requires some thirty thousand individual drawings. "Several critics complained," we learn, "that the deliberate rejection of studio techniques, the elaborate detail, the painstaking finish, set the cartoon so radically apart from its contemporary rivals that it existed in a world by itself." Payne, too, has always existed uneasily in our world, trying to balance the claims of domestic, personal, and professional life with those of his art. In the end he achieves an ambiguous triumph.

In *The Princess, the Dwarf, and the Dungeon* Millhauser counterpoints a tale of sexual jealousy, castle politics, and spiritual suffering with notes about the ordinary life of the townspeople across the river. The down-to-earth burghers—that is, most of us—need the high-flown romantic stories about the castle. "For across the sun-sparkling river, there on the far shore, we feel a heightened sense of things, and we dare for a moment to cry out our forbidden desire: for exaltation, for devastation, for revelation." Without art can we ever be fully alive? The close of this "fairy tale" opens onto multiple possible endings: "It is told how the Prince, longing for expiation, one day goes down to the margrave in the dungeon and insists on changing places with him, so that the margrave reigns in the castle while the Prince languishes in darkness. It is told how the margrave escapes from the dungeon after twenty-four years, and returns to defeat the Prince and marry the Princess, who in other versions dies in her tower after hearing a false report of the margrave's death."

Catalogue of the Exhibition: The Art of Edmund Moorash 1810–1846 is just that: historical notes on some two dozen paintings by a neglected American master. As the cataloger describes the slender output of this highly romantic artist—whose work incorporates Turner's atmospheric impressionism, Munch's existential angst, and Frank Auerbach's obsessively reworked canvases —a tragic story gradually emerges, almost like one of Moorash's own ghost paintings wherein the viewer only slowly makes out the figures in the darkness. Two sibling couples—Moorash and his sister Elizabeth, William Pinney and his sister Sophia—live near each other on lonely Black Lake in upstate New York. Inevitably, passion's cross-currents disturb friendship's placid surface. People grow forlorn, desperate, half in love with easeful Death. A careful reader will have noted early on that all the main characters die in the same year.

The melodrama, obliquely suggested by the paintings, reveals itself through deliberate Romantic excess: Moorash's canvases bear titles like *Clair de lune*, *Nachtstück*, *The House of Usher*, and *Totentanz*. They find some of their inspiration in Hoffmann, Poe, and Hawthorne; Elizabeth reads the Grimm fairy tales, Keats's "Eve of St. Agnes," Spenser's *Faerie Queene*; she plays Schumann's Fantasiestücke and Chopin on the piano. In Moorash's paintings, we are told, "it is impossible to make a neat distinction between the world of art and the world of nature, or the world of imagination and the world of experience. . . . It is as if Moorash had attempted to impart the experience of daydream itself, in which the boundaries between inner and outer grow uncertain."

Grouped together, the three novellas of *Little Kingdoms* subtly question each other about the imagination and its power. An artist's perhaps unhealthy bliss, the blessings and terrors of art, the blasted lives of those who love an artistic genius—each sounds a variation on this single, rather somber theme. Note, too, the sad names: Payne and Moorash. One hopes that Millhauser's own life is happier than that of his heroes, who hover, like him, in that uneasy limbo "between the realm of imperishable beauty and the world of decay."

September 5, 1993

POSTSCRIPT: Steven Millhauser went on to win the Pulitzer Prize for his short novel *Martin Dressler*, but he remains at his finest in the long short story or novella. See such collections as *The Knife-Thrower* and *The King in the Tree*. Over the years I've reviewed Millhauser's work again and again because every time he brings out a new book, I find myself drawn, yet once more, to the sound and beauty of his wistful, blissful sentences.

THE FAMISHED ROAD

By Ben Okri

"Our birth," wrote Wordsworth in a famous poem, "is but a sleep and a forgetting." Our souls, he explains, have fallen away from a spiritual realm of unity
with God and nature. But for Azaro, the young hero of Ben Okri's 1991 Booker
Prize–winning novel, *The Famished Road*, the ghostly world of preexistence is
all too close by and frighteningly real. His ghetto neighborhood, located
between a phantasmagoric city and a demon-haunted African forest, shimmers with spirits, talking rats, grotesque monsters, and the constant interpen-
etration of the Other World. It is visited by creatures with three or more heads
and by angels, but also by thugs, prostitutes, politicians, and beggars. Creepiest
of all is a blind old man who squeezes out repulsive, "evil" music on his accordion. All these visitants, supernatural and subhuman, are perceived through a
haze of heat and sun, frequently in fevers, nightmares, or half-drunken visions.

"To be born," notes Okri, "is to come into the world weighed down with
strange gifts of the soul, with enigmas and an inextinguishable sense of exile."
Azaro is, almost in spite of himself, a spirit child, an *abiku*, constantly pursued
by unearthly beings who hope to entice him back into their realm of the
unborn. One of their main portals into our human world, it turns out, lies in
the bar of the awesome Madame Koto, herself an ambiguous force for both
good and evil, crackling with power. Some whisper that she's a flat-out witch;
others hint, even more quietly, that she can manipulate reality itself.

Most of *The Famished Road* ostensibly chronicles the day-to-day life and
fever dreams of Azaro, his parents, and their neighbors. Mum—as this spelling
hints, the Nigerian Okri currently resides in Britain—circumambulates the
streets, trying to sell oranges and other provisions, with pitifully small success.
Dad unloads trucks, hauling heavy bags of cement, little more than a two-
legged beast of burden. At one point Azaro wanders deep into the city, escapes
some spectral predators, and spies his idolized father at work:

"And then I saw Dad amongst the load-carriers. He looked completely different. His hair was white and his face was mask-like with engrained cement. He was almost naked except for a very disgusting pair of tattered shorts which I had never seen before. They loaded two bags of salt on his head and he cried 'GOD, SAVE ME!' and he wobbled and the bag on top fell back into the lorry." The boy shouts out, "Dad, No!" His father looks around, and "when he faced my direction he stopped." Then "as the salt poured on his shoulder, tears streamed from his eyes, and there was shame on his face as he staggered right past me, almost crushing me with his mighty buckling feet."

Such anguish periodically brings *The Famished Road* back to earth when Azaro's adventures in anima-land, described in a dithyrambic prose that blends Revelation, almost Blakean symbolism, and African folklore, start to seem repetitive and even a little tedious. Nonetheless, Okri seems to be suggesting an analogy between the Other World and ours. The deformed beggars, for instance, who play an important role in the novel, look no different from the weird creatures that Azaro glimpses in the city or at Madame Koto's: "I shut my eyes and when I opened them again I saw people who walked backwards, a dwarf who got about on two fingers, men upside-down with baskets of fish on their feet, women who had breasts on their backs, babies strapped to their chests, and beautiful children with three arms. I saw a girl amongst them who had eyes at the side of her face, bangles of blue copper around her neck, and who was more lovely than forest flowers."

To all the human suffering and haunting strangeness in *The Famished Road*, politics adds its own macabre humor when the Party of the Rich battles the Party of the Poor in an election that never quite happens. Even though the Party of the Rich distributes free milk, which turns out to be bad and makes everyone sick, Madame Koto throws in her lot with its venal leaders, thereby gaining more and more power. Of all sorts, electrical as well as personal. Azaro has been in the habit of visiting Madame Koto—for a while she considers him a good luck charm—even though her patrons are demons more often than not and her bar an analogue to the intergalactic saloon in *Star Wars*. One afternoon the boy finds everyone dancing to mysterious music. "On the counter was an evil-looking instrument with a metal funnel that would have delighted the imagination of wizards. There was a disc which kept turning, a handle cranked round by a spirit, a long piece of metal with a needle on the whirling disc, and music coming out of the funnel without anyone singing into it. It seemed a perfect instrument for the celebration of the dead, for the dances of light spirits and fine witches."

Technology, it has been said, raised to a high enough level resembles magic.

As the novel progresses, Okri shifts his attention somewhat from the spiritual labors of Azaro to the growing political consciousness of his father. Dad's utopian vision of a more equitable and kindly Africa paradoxically arises out of violence. Frequently likened to a boxer, Dad eventually decides to train and actually become a fighter. He takes the name Black Tyger, gaining considerable local celebrity. Then late one night a shadowy figure in the darkness calls him out. Okri's description of the bare-fisted match between Azaro's father and Yellow Jaguar, a legendary but long-dead boxer, is one of the novel's most thrilling set pieces, comparable to the death struggle in the dark between Beowulf and Grendel, or the wrestling match by moonlight between the Icelandic hero Grettir and the monster Glaum. Seemingly invincible, Yellow Jaguar overpowers and wears down the living man—until Azaro suddenly cries out, "Black Tyger, USE YOUR POWER." Then, "with all the concentrated rage and insanity of those who have a single moment in which to choose between living and dying, Dad broke the chains of his exhaustion and thundered such blows on the man as would annihilate an entire race of giants." Death misses this victory.

Here, obviously, is a novel of vast ambition and equal achievement, alive with magic, allegory (is Madame Koto a symbol of Africa itself?), lyrical prose, recurrent road imagery, startling sentences ("She wore clothing that made the beggars ill"), and sly humor: at one point Azaro, while being stuffed into a sack by albinos, desperately calls for help, shouting, "Politicians! Politicians are taking me away!" Sometimes, though, Okri's prose poem teeters on the pretentious—"The world is full of riddles that only the dead can answer"—and there is a certain sameness to the supernatural encounters. Azaro and Madame Koto are virtually the only people with names; other characters are merely referred to as the photographer or the landlord. Though Azaro's supernatural journeys may derive mainly from folklore tradition and a taste for French or Francophone surrealism, their schizophrenic quality, complete with voices and visions, also recalls the more extreme novels of Philip K. Dick and even Julian Jaynes's controversial theories about human consciousness.

In its picture of corrupt politics, its oblique account of modernization in Africa ("It seemed that the trees, feeling that they were losing the argument with human beings, had simply walked deeper into the forest"), and its inspired use of ancient beliefs, *The Famished Road* suggests a fusion of the two most famous Nigerian novels, Amos Tutuola's fantastic, word-mad *The Palm-Wine Drinkard* and Chinua Achebe's soberly tragic *Things Fall Apart*. Still, Ben Okri's novel—he has previously been admired in this country only for his disorienting stories, *Stars of the New Curfew*—is a strikingly original piece of writing and a delicately nuanced picture of love between a child and his parents. After all the fighting ghosts, political violence, and mysterious strangers fade, what lingers most in the memory is the recurrent image of a family at night: the boy falling slowly asleep on his mat, listening to his mother's quiet breathing nearby while watching his tired father rock on a three-legged chair in the darkness. The terrors and attractions of the spirit world are finally no match for human tenderness.

May 24, 1992

ACCORDION CRIMES

By E. Annie Proulx

Annie Proulx's first two novels—*Postcards* (1992) and *The Shipping News* (1993)—walked away with virtually all the most glittering literary prizes, including the PEN-Faulkner, the National Book Award, the Pulitzer, and the *Irish Times* International Fiction Prize (big bucks). You would think Proulx would have the simple decency to make her third novel merely so-so, if only to let someone else grab a little limelight. No such luck. Born in 1935, Annie Proulx spent a lot of years learning her craft, selling articles to regional magazines, working on gardening books for Rodale, producing short stories (gathered in *Heart Songs*), as well as raising three sons. She now seems to know everything about writing. And a fair amount about life, too. After all, a young author may be accomplished, witty, or technically innovative, but no kid can ever match a middle-aged novelist for insight into everyone's favorite tragicomedy: the ravages of time and fate.

In *Accordion Crimes*, a group of eight linked stories, Proulx takes us on a panoramic tour (*d'horizon* and *de force*) of America's ethnic past. To accomplish this she creates a green button accordion—that most insulted and injured of musical instruments—which comes to be owned by a score or so working-class people during the hundred years of its knockabout existence. For these various family mini-sagas, set in Louisiana, Maine, Chicago, the West, and other regions, Proulx mimics perfectly the broken English, characteristic idioms, and keenly expressed prejudices of Italians, African Americans, Poles, French Canadians, Germans, Cajuns, and Hispanics. She vividly evokes, again and again, the exhausting lives and desperate pleasures of the poor: "He made her pregnant on their wedding night, and his life slipped into the ancient human groove of procreation, work, cooking, children's sicknesses and their little talents and possibilities. For the first time he saw he was no different than anyone else."

Many stories about immigrants in twentieth-century America tend to be uplifting, but not Proulx's. If one may criticize *Accordion Crimes* ever so mildly, it is only for its relentless existential bleakness. No one here gets out alive. Imagine the folksy tales of Lake Wobegon, retold by Dreiser or Richard Wright. An innocent Italian accordion maker is shot to death by an angry racist mob. A young girl lifts up her arms and has them sheared off above the elbow by a flying piece of scrap metal. A wheelchair-bound man is miraculously cured, then commits suicide.

Yet, grim as these events are, Proulx's sentences invest them with a sardonic lilt, like items from "News of the Weird." "A month later word came from Texas that Messermacher had dropped dead at his mailbox, the new Sears catalog open on his breast at the pages showing a selection of women's hair nets." A young Cajun girl watches her father almost burn her mother to a crisp: "The child directed a savage thought at her father, that he become small and weak. That night her father began to shrink. The process was agonizingly slow, but in ten years he was the height of a child, withered and tiny, his arms like hollow stalks, and when he finally died he was no larger than a loaf of bread. His scarred and ruined wife threw him into the yard for the hens to peck." Another character actually finds "a job for a few months delivering white ashtray sand to luxury hotels and apartment buildings."

Accordion Crimes beautifully re-creates the spicy, colorful, almost tall-tale side of American ethnic life. Tamonette joins a civil rights sit-in partly because her great-aunt "had gone to Paris in the 1920s as a white family's maid and there learned to fly an airplane, returned to the south as a crop duster until a white farmer shot her out of the sky in 1931; even then she went fiercely, aiming the diving fiery plane at the man in the field with the rifle, and got him, too." There are, not surprisingly, mouthwatering, high-caloric descriptions of food and feasts. Consider the cuisine of Mrs. Josef Przbysz:

"In her day she had cooked with passion and experience, a craftworker who needed no measuring cup or recipe, who held everything in her mind. She kept a garden in the handkerchief yard, tomatoes tied to old crutches she took from the Dumpster at the hospital, she made her own good sausage and sauerkraut." For her now dead son she regularly prepared a "snack of pierozki and the filling soup zurek with mushrooms and potatoes and fermented oatmeal and good sour bread . . . and for Sunday dinner golabki, the little cabbage rolls in a sweet-sour sauce, and always a fresh-baked round babka or two." Later, she mentions kolac nut rolls—unbeatable, by the way, with coffee. Proulx clearly knows the Slavic world of my own childhood.

But then she knows your childhood or your parents' too, provided you

come from an ethnic group that plays and loves the accordion in all its bellow-
ing, bleating oom-pah-pah glory. Mexican folk songs. Zydeco. Beerhall music.
Polkas. Proulx packs her pages with parties, dances, funerals, weddings, music
contests, nightclub acts—and she makes you hear the raucous chords, feel the
growing heat, see the manic sweating dancers. Still, my favorite of her many
musical soirees begins quietly when a trucker hires an accordion-violin duo to
play at a surprise birthday party:

"His wife was white with rage, had been truly and unpleasantly surprised,
for her birthday had come and gone unnoticed two weeks before; now, gripped
by savage menstrual cramps, both kids hacking with bronchial coughs, she had
been slopping around in a torn housecoat, the place a mess of strewn socks,
dirty dishes and dust kitties, when cars and trucks began to pull up and dis-
gorge strangers who wished her happy birthday, lit cigarettes and started to
drink." Matters rapidly go downhill.

All through her book Proulx sticks closely to her downtrodden and fated
protagonists, gradually disclosing their pathetic hopes for a better life and their
own recurrent prejudices: anti-German feeling during World War I, Polish
hatred for the blacks who are swarming into the old neighborhoods, Hispanic
loathing of Italians, the mutual disdain of cowboy and city slicker. In these
pages America's melting pot sometimes boils with rage but more often merely
simmers with unhappiness. While older immigrants dream, usually in vain, of
making it, getting rich, becoming American, their children or grandchildren
soon find themselves warped by ethnic pride or eager to reject all the old-
country ways or oppressed by a sense of loss, yearning for a vanishing culture
just beyond their grasp.

Though *Accordion Crimes* may at times seem like North American magic
realism, the book, with its admixture of representative types, gallows humor,
and overt symbolism, actually belongs to the underappreciated tradition of
naturalism. Its accordion leitmotif, for instance, calls to mind Frank Norris's
use of the birdcage in his classic *McTeague*. And in its grand ambition to portray the immigrant experience in this country, Proulx's novel might almost be
a condensed American version of Zola's Rougon-Macquart cycle. Like Zola,
Proulx knows life's extravagant bounty and wastefulness, loves a melodramatic
flourish: she deftly keeps the reader waiting hundreds of pages to see who
will discover the thousand-dollar bills hidden inside the green accordion.
From time to time, she also employs parenthetical flash-forwards to relate
the future of a child or minor character; very few people escape sad ends. But
then, who does?

And yet *Accordion Crimes* is by no means a depressing book. Instead it seems properly clear-eyed, even shrewd with peasant wisdom, about how the future is "crouching at a dark side road on the path of events" and seldom has any good in store for us. We must, it seems, find pleasure where we can, while we can—in food and drink, love, music, stories. All these, of course, *Accordion Crimes* supplies with exuberance and loving excess.

June 16, 1996

CITIES OF THE PLAIN
VOLUME 3 OF THE BORDER TRILOGY

By Cormac McCarthy

At the close of *All the Pretty Horses* (1992), the wonderful first volume in Cormac McCarthy's Border trilogy, the sixteen-year-old John Grady Cole slowly rode west through a barren country, then "passed and paled into the darkening land, the world to come." He has emerged out of 1949 Mexico, having survived boyish adventures, a spell in prison, a forbidden love affair with a wealthy rancher's daughter, the death of a companion, and near-mortal wounds from a savage knife fight. His rite-of-passage story—compared to *Huckleberry Finn* by critics, admired for its gravely lyrical prose, especially in the description of landscape—earned McCarthy (b. 1933) the National Book Award and sudden recognition as one of the finest living American writers.

Despite this best seller's undoubted mastery, some of McCarthy's long-term fans groused that *Pretty Horses* had unduly toned down the author's magnificent, occasionally grandiloquent, excess. Where was the incest, the necrophilia, the infanticide of his early southern gothic works, *Child of God* (1968) and *Outer Dark* (1974)? Even his just-previous novel, and first "western," *Blood Meridian* (1985), gloried in the sanguinary adventures of "the kid" with a company of scalp hunters in the Southwest and Mexico of 1849; in its pages there is no regeneration through violence, but simply an ecstatic anabasis of killing, a truly exultant savagery, and brooding religious mystery. Imagine the Old Testament book of Judges in Technicolor, and you will have an inkling of this feverish epic's gaudy violence and rhetorical grandeur. It is a great American novel.

In 1994 McCarthy brought out the next, rather longer installment of his trilogy: *The Crossing*. In general outline, the pattern of the second book resembled that of the first: young Billy Parham journeys three times into Mexico in the early 1940s, endures severe trials, including the death of his beloved younger brother, Boyd, and in the end finds himself on a barren stretch of road, utterly bereft, "while the right and godmade sun did rise, once again, for all and without distinction." The opening section of the novel—in which Billy captures a wolf and tries to return the displaced animal to its mountain habitat—is a starkly beautiful mini-epic of heroic endurance and disappointment. Alas, Billy's subsequent descents into Mexican hell are weakened by periodic encounters with philosophical revolutionaries, priests, and Gypsies, most of them given to overlong discourses about the meaning of life. Still, *The Crossing* displays so much hushed loveliness in its prose, and reveals so much sorrowful power in its telling, that most readers could hardly wait for the concluding volume of the Border trilogy.

In a rare interview the publicity-shy McCarthy was once asked about the relatively upbeat conclusion to *All the Pretty Horses*. "You haven't come to the end yet," he answered. "This may be nothing but a snare and a delusion to draw you in, thinking that all will be well." *Cities of the Plain* makes clear that the gods have so arranged our lives as to guarantee that nobody is happy very often or for very long. From the very moment John Grady Cole—now nineteen, working on a ranch in New Mexico with twenty-eight-year-old Billy Parham—falls in love with Magdalena, the frail and soulful teenaged prostitute of the White Lake brothel, you know that this couple isn't destined to live happily ever after. To add to the sense of imminent doom, the military is about to take over the ranch's land (for its base at Alamagordo), the ways of the cowboy are fast vanishing in 1952, and John Grady clearly possesses a soul too pure for the corrupt modern world. He is like the animals he trains. In a good horse "you can see what's in his heart. He won't do one thing while you're watchin him and another when you aint. He's all of a piece. When you've got a horse to that place you cant hardly get him to do somethin he knows is wrong."

In several ways *Cities of the Plain* feels quite different from the first two books of the series—more contemporary and urban, narrower in focus, at times overemphatic. For instance, the pimp Eduardo is circumscribed by his silk shirts, courteous gestures, thin cigars, and world-weary observations—we have seen him in a hundred movies and don't need to be told that he will never let Magdalena go and that only a fool would take him on in a knife fight. Of course, there are continuities, some subtle, with the previous volumes: Billy calls John Grady "bud" just as Lacey Rawlins used to in *Pretty Horses*, and the relationship between the two friends mirrors the earlier one between Billy and his brother Boyd. As usual, McCarthy eschews psychological interiority—we see what people do, rather than listen in on their thoughts. Conversations and descriptions take the place of the stream of consciousness.

In the Bible the cities of the plain were Sodom and Gomorrah, traditionally associated with homosexuality or sexual perversion. There's none of that here exactly—indeed the cities are El Paso and Juarez, where Magdalena is held in claustral captivity—but McCarthy does paint the timeworn round of cowboy life as a male idyll, a world of masculine camaraderie and skillfulness, one in which women may bring temporary happiness but ultimately only grief and regret. Mac, the widower ranch owner, still cries out his wife's name at night; an elderly, distracted father can't get the hang of his daughter's being dead; another cowpoke's revered brother dies because of a faithless woman; and from the beginning the protective Billy senses that John Grady's love for a Mexican prostitute is a prelude to disaster.

Conrad once wrote that a man who is born falls into a dream like a man who falls into the sea. *Cities of the Plain* is largely about our human propensity for such hopefulness and self-delusion. As Eduardo tells Billy, "Your friend is in the grip of an irrational passion. Nothing you say to him will matter. He has in his head a certain story. Of how things will be. In this story he will be happy. What is wrong with this story?" "You tell me." "What is wrong with this story is that it is not a true story. Men have in their minds a picture of how the world will be. How they will be in that world. The world may be many different ways for them but there is one world that will never be and that is the world they dream of." In an epilogue to the main story Billy patiently listens to an old Mexican recount an elaborate parable about life as a series of dreams, each embedded within the next like little Russian dolls. By this time Billy is seventy-eight years old and it is two years into the new millennium. The last novel of the Border trilogy closes with an old man restlessly dreaming about his long-dead younger brother.

To my mind the love affair at the heart of *Cities of the Plain* seems overly conventional, the sort of desolate tragedy commemorated in old pop songs: as much *West Side Story* as *Romeo and Juliet*. McCarthy's characters have often been types (e.g., "the kid"), but usually there was a compensating grandeur that lifted them into the mythic. At times John Grady recalls Billy Budd, Dostoevsky's Christlike Idiot or even Jesus himself ("All his early dreams were the same. Something was afraid and he had come to comfort it")—but one feels the strings being pulled. After all, how can the brokenhearted lover of Alejandra in *Pretty Horses* be so blind to the meretricious glamour of dreams?

Though the plot of *Cities of the Plain* may be slightly disappointing, its language, especially in the descriptions of men at work, still soars. Billy fixing an inner tube with a rubber-patch repair kit; John Grady cutting a calf out of a herd; the two of them roping wild dogs or rescuing some lost pups: one reads such passages as if they were poetry—and they are. There are superb scenes of men from the ranch studying the horses at an auction, trading stories of the old west, or just sitting around a kitchen table. And nobody since Hemingway has better evoked the clean, well-lighted place: "Socorro had gone to bed but there was cornbread in the warmer over the oven and a plate of beans and potatoes with two pieces of fried chicken. He carried the plates to the table and went back and got silver out of the dishdrainer and got down a cup and poured his coffee and set the pot back over the eye of the stove where there was still a dull red glow of coals and he took his coffee to the table and sat and ate. He ate slowly and methodically. When he'd finished he carried the dishes to the sink. ... The clock ticked in the hallway. The cooling stove creaked."

Of Cormac McCarthy's four western novels I think *Blood Meridian* and *All the Pretty Horses*—different as they are—deserve their reputations as masterpieces of postwar American literature. To my mind and ear, *The Crossing* is overburdened by its philosophical divagations, and *Cities of the Plain* feels too light with its thinner texture and familiar storyline. But even faulting, somewhat diffidently, these last two books, I would never have wanted to miss reading them. These are grave and majestic novels, resolutely focused on the heartaches of existence, but striated throughout with fatalistic joshing and sly humor. Turn to almost any page, and you will light upon sharply observed details, painterly descriptions, and the sound of real voices. Like the novelists he admires—Melville, Dostoevsky, Faulkner—Cormac McCarthy has created an imaginative oeuvre greater and deeper than any single book. Such writers wrestle with the gods themselves.

Near the end of *Cities of the Plain* Billy discusses some of life's mysteries with an elderly vagrant Mexican. He is himself homeless, itinerant, a lonesome wanderer across the modern Southwest:

Billy watched the light bring up the shapes of the water standing in the fields beyond the roadway. Where do we go when we die? he said.

I don't know, the man said. Where are we now?

The sun rose over the plain behind them.

May 24, 1998

POSTSCRIPT: Since I wrote this piece on McCarthy, I've come to regard *Blood Meridian* as one of the half-dozen greatest American novels since World War II, in the same company as *Invisible Man*, *The Recognitions*, *Catch-22*, and *Lolita*.

MRS. TED BLISS

By Stanley Elkin

"Death," the late Stanley Elkin once said, "is an education." Actually, that "once" is a considerable understatement: despite a stand-up comedian's timing for laughs and an authorial voice that could transmute advertising jingles, street slang, and Yiddish idiom into bel canto arias of gorgeous English prose, Elkin ranks high among the most death-obsessed writers of our time, right up there with Thomas Bernhard and Samuel Beckett.

Typically, Elkin's novels and short stories begin in this world, this junkyard of schlock and tinsel and the main chance, then wend their way slowly toward a vision of transcendence, some spiritual epiphany, at the very least a character's acceptance of his mortality. Often death waits just around the corner, when not already downstairs, comfortably stretched out on the davenport for a little visit. The great early story, "Criers and Kibitzers, Kibitzers and Criers," depicts the heartbreaking sorrow of a Jewish grocer for his son, dead at twenty-three; Ben Flesh, the glad-handing hero of *The Franchiser*, learns that he has a terrible degenerative disease; *The Living End* collects three novellas set in a shoddy afterlife (heaven as theme park); and *The Magic Kingdom* follows a group of dying children to Disney World.

For a time Stanley Elkin was labeled a humorist, a novel-writing Woody Allen. But, like Allen, he soon showed that many of the gibes and jokes were there to underscore the sheer awfulness of the human condition. "All books," Elkin affirmed with clear self-reference, "are the Book of Job," and solace is "art's and language's consolation prize." When in midcareer the mortality-minded novelist was himself diagnosed with multiple sclerosis, eventually becoming a wheelchair-bound "cripple" (his own word), he somehow found the will to keep on writing despite this bitter joke of fate and what must have been, at times, an immense despair: "All I've ever wanted, as I tell my friends, is to be rich and famous and to live forever without pain."

In a just world—Hah!—Elkin should have gotten his wish: the flat-out hilarious *The Dick Gibson Show*—about the career of a radio disc jockey— ought to have made him famous; the National Book Circle Award winner *George Mills* deserved to make him rich. Perhaps literary history will be more just to Stanley Elkin, who died this past June at age sixty-four, and his name will live forever as one of the best American writers of our time, which he was. Any doubters need only try *Mrs. Ted Bliss*, his latest and last novel, to see how language, keen observation, and a pervasive sense of the still, sad music of humanity may combine in a work of art that is also a tour de force.

Throughout most of his fiction, Elkin focused on fathers, sons, husbands—look at the very titles of the novels and stories: *A Bad Man*, "I Look Out for Ed Wolfe," "The Bailbondsman," *George Mills*. But here he enters the consciousness of an elderly Jewish widow, now residing in a Miami condo, whose entire life has been exclusively focused on her husband (a Chicago butcher) and children. The action follows Mrs. Ted Bliss from her early sixties to her early eighties, from the late 1970s through the 1990s, and almost nothing dramatic happens at all. For a while, just at the beginning, it looks as though Dorothy may be in some danger when she unknowingly sells her late husband's Le Sabre to a Latin American drug lord; for a while she grows friendly with a retired real estate lawyer named Manny; there are minor flare-ups with her grown-up children and painful memories of the terrible death of her eldest son from leukemia. In the very last pages Hurricane Andrew threatens. Still, that, on the surface, is pretty much it.

But sometimes death really is an education. Within this surprisingly innocent, often vulgar woman we observe the slow growth of a consciousness, as Dorothy comes to terms with the loss of her son and husband, understands more fully the complex dance of relationships between women and men, and finally learns that after everything falls away—family, friends, love—the self remains and that that is the most interesting thing of all.

Put so baldly, all this makes *Mrs. Ted Bliss* sound didactic, an inspirational fable about affirming life even in old age. But any hint of the earnest is swallowed up in the absolute rightness of observed detail and the rush of Elkin's language, an irresistible flood that a carnival barker might envy or a radio preacher emulate. Here the security guard, Louise Munez, offers the slightly deaf Mrs. Bliss some advice: " 'Your boy Frank,' " Louise said, 'the last time he was down here. You should have let him put up a signal light in your apartment that tell when someone at your door, or even if your intercom is buzzing. Those things are perfected now you know. They're state-of-the-art. If you're waiting will there be improvements down the line or will they come down in price, I can say to you that in my opinion there won't, and they'll never be no cheaper than they are right now either. It's your business, Mrs. Bliss, but who's Security here, me or you?' "

Elkin always takes the trouble to bring even such minor figures to blazing life. The elegant "importer" Tommy Auveristas is "not so much well groomed . . . as buffed, preened, shiny as new shoes. He could have been newly made, something just off an assembly line, or still in its box." Mrs. Bliss's auto mechanic grandson, Barry, invariably overdresses at family affairs and keeps his fingernails preternaturally clean—"it was terrible, she realized, the lengths to which he must have gone to rub away all the appearance of failure."

Though hyperbolic by instinct, Elkin can sometimes be as compact as a French aphorist: after describing the ethnic groups of Miami, he neatly concludes, "it wasn't a place, it was a pecking order." Still, Elkin is at his best when he can start a salesman's spiel, create a crescendo of sound. Listen to Mrs. Ted Bliss:

> "Girls, they tell you time heals all things? Time heals nothing. What, you think you're unhappy now? You think because your husband is gone this is the worst, the storm that breaks the camel's back, water in the basement and climbing the stairs, that it's up over the lip of the threshold and coming in under the door in the hall, that it's destroyed the linoleum and already lapping the wall-to-wall, licking high up the legs of the dining room chairs, the mahogany sideboard and credenza, that it's covered the tiles, and slipping down the side of the tub like dirty bathwater, is above the box spring and even with the mattress, is inside the chest of drawers with your things like stockings and underwear left to soak overnight in the bathroom basin.
>
> "Or that the final slap in the face is when the insurance claim comes back marked 'Sorry, not covered, act of God'?
>
> "You think?
>
> "Or from all that pile-on and pile-on of tsuris, the kids' bad grades and the death of friends, your own decline, the failure of beauty, of memory, incontinence, shortness of breath, the inability not just to climb steps but to cross the room without pain?
>
> "And that that's the *worst* that can happen, one by one, or served up like so many courses at a dinner. Or that *that* is?
>
> "You think, you think so? Well, all I can say is wait till *next* year!"

Democritus was sometimes called the laughing philosopher. Just so Stanley Elkin might be considered our laughing philosophical novelist. His amazing books can crack you up and make you cry and leave you marveling. He should have lived forever without pain.

September 10, 1995

THE TUNNEL

By William H. Gass

Long awaited. Eagerly anticipated. Thirty years in the making. Such siren calls have sounded before—most recently luring us to Harold Brodkey's misconceived *Runaway Soul* and Norman Mailer's *Harlot's Ghost*. Each time we wonder, could this be it? Our age's *Ulysses*? Our *Magic Mountain*? So we plunk down our cash, lug our shiny purchase home, swiftly read up to page 47 or 99—and then sigh. The great book, the masterpiece is, well, okay. No great shakes. Not bad really. But hardly the work of a god.

Doubtless we'd be less disillusioned if we didn't keep getting our hopes up so high. Because William H. Gass has been working on *The Tunnel* nearly half his life, I wanted the novel to be a transfiguring experience, the kind of book that blows readers away, creates acolytes, and strolls into the canon like a boulevardier into a café.

Sometimes, it would seem, hopes are, if not fully, at least partially fulfilled.

The Tunnel strikes me as an extraordinary achievement, a literary treat with more than a few shocking tricks inside it. For 650 pages one of the consummate magicians of English prose pulls rabbits out of sentences and creates shimmering metaphors before your very eyes. He dazzles and amazes. But be warned: he does so on his own terms, and some readers may be confused, bored, or repulsed.

First some background.

William H. Gass began work on *The Tunnel* back in 1966. He once told an interviewer, "Who knows, perhaps it will be such a good book no one will want to publish it. I live on that hope." Over the years a dozen sections of the novel appeared in little, arty, or even glossy magazines. During the same time, Gass established himself as a major essayist (the racy *On Being Blue*, 1976), a playful experimentalist (the even racier *Willie Masters' Lonesome Wife*, 1968), and a leading philosopher of fiction (three collections, most recently *Habitations of the Word*, 1985). All these built upon the reputation of a legendary debut novel,

Omensetter's Luck (1966), and a collection of short stories with a catchy title that has passed into the language: *In the Heart of the Heart of the Country* (1968). In his spare time Gass taught, mainly at Washington University in St. Louis, and read as intently as a Cistercian: he carefully parsed the prose of Gertrude Stein, aspired to the easy philosophical address of Valéry, worshiped before the achievement and example of Rilke.

And took his own sweet time with *The Tunnel*: "I hope that it will be really original in form and effect, although mere originality is not what I'm after." No speedy Updike he. "I write slowly," he once confessed, "because I write badly. I have to rewrite everything many many times just to achieve mediocrity." Yet in his essays and fiction, Gass's patient effort never shows, only a stylish perfection of tone and rhythm, along with a steady rain of unexpected simile. A meek professor's voice is "soft, soothing yet sugarless, deferential, low without sounding sexy, clear through, crisp enough, unaccented, unaffected, proper without being prim—in short, ideal if it were a telephone operator's, or if you wished to speak to the dying." Gass's prose doesn't need to aspire to the condition of music; it is music, meant to be sung, performed, listened to. The text itself becomes a score, the means to elicit hitherto unheard yet heavenly verbal melodies.

Not everyone, of course, cares for such bel canto splendor. A few pages into some of Gass's essay-arias, readers have been known to scream, "What's the point? Get on with it already." The late John "Moral Fiction" Gardner (who as an editor published Gass's first story) frequently debated his old friend, insisting that writing was more than rococo decoration. But Gass never wavered: words alone are certain good.

Or even beyond good and evil. The description of a girl being viciously beaten (from John Hawkes's *The Lime Twig*) is "impossible to overpraise. An example of total control." In *Under the Volcano*, Gass insisted, Malcolm Lowry is "constructing a place, not describing one; he is making a Mexico for the mind, where, strictly speaking, there are no menacing volcanoes, only menacing phrases." The folks who go to books for lifelike characters or plots "are really not interested in literature. They are interested in folks."

Given all this—the novel's abnormally long gestation, its author's Pateresque ideals, a high butter-fat prose—given all this, one might expect to find *The Tunnel* nothing less than a mining disaster. The sort of thing to inspire a folksong. Big Bad Bill. Instead the genial and ingenious Gass has created a cave of wonders. Barring a few deliberately dense, semiphilosophical sections, *The Tunnel* is by turns funny, lyrically beautiful, disturbing, pathetic, and perplexing enough to keep scholars busy for decades. Several of its characters— Uncle Balt, for instance, and Culp, who is writing a limerickal history of the world—are pretty clearly imaginary, projections of the narrator-hero's unhinged psyche. Throughout, Gass carefully smudges the line where the narrator's rhetorical exaggeration leaves off and a kind of real madness sets in. No doubt future graduate students will clarify these and other matters. For today's readers it is enough to pause, again and again, at such quietly perfect sentences as "I do the dishes in this house and so I care about the cleanliness of tines" or "A shoe is a poor swatter; it has no holes and advertises its coming."

Gass's prose invites admiration. Not so his hero, the historian William Frederick Kohler. A bigot and a Nazi sympathizer, this fat professor sexually exploits his students, mocks his colleagues, scorns his wife, and ignores his children. Kohler ("miner" in German) is the kind of guy who casually sets fire to insects and somehow manages to strangle a pet cat. As a boy he swipes pennies and bicycles, as a student in 1930s Germany he lobs a brick through a Jewish store window on Kristallnacht. He also serves up four-letter words with five-star mastery; few of his opinions even gesture toward the politically correct. Now middle-aged at the end of the 1960s, he feels washed up, despondent, self-pitying, and bitter. His sole interests have devolved to digging a tunnel in his basement and composing a preface to "Guilt and Innocence in Hitler's Germany," his "courageous revamp of the Third Reich and what it was." Unable to focus on his preface, he writes instead about himself and his unhappy, frustrating past.

What are we to make of Kohler? There lies the nub, the mystery of Gass's novel. At times Kohler enchants with his memories of boyhood reading, then repels us with what his lost mistress, Lou—her name a tribute, I suspect, to Rilke's beloved Lou Andreas-Salomé—once called his "loathesome" mind: he may casually refer to "jewspapers" or defend his father's hatred for Asiatic neighbors whose main crime lies in their not being the right kind of people. Then again Kohler can be heartbreaking as he depicts his sorrowful childhood—alcoholic mother, crippled dad, obsessive aunt. He can make us see and smell those old corner candy stores, ride along on a Sunday drive in the country, feel the anguish of a birthday party to which no one comes, taste the breakfast he makes for himself. For all his sheer awfulness it's hard to determine whether he is finally a man more sinned against than sinning. "My face simply serves as a place to put my palms."

Kohler, I think, represents that insulted and injured party that resides deep, sometimes not so deep, inside all of us. As he himself writes, "if we spoke emotion's language openly . . . then the child whose doll is broken would demand destruction for the world." He dubs this sentiment the "fascism of the heart." A bigot, Kohler says elsewhere, "is a person who has suffered an unmerited injustice, one which hasn't been put right, and woe to others if he ever has

WRITERS OF OUR TIME

a chance to get his own back." Even in his work on the Third Reich, the historian wants, as he notes with sickly humor, to put himself "in the villain's place,
to imagine the unimaginable." Which, of course, is just what William Gass is
triumphantly doing. In several senses, Kohler almost certainly descends from
Dostoevsky's bitter, self-contradictory Underground Man.

Kohler's character will provoke debate. Gass's trickiness—is our "hero"
actually constructing a tunnel or is he only digging into his past and self
through his writing?—will keep one balanced between uncertainties. In what
ways does it matter that Kohler's parents seem to mirror Gass's own? How
many different kinds of tunnel—womb, tomb, excretory tract, closet, trunk,
even the name Gass ("alley" in German)—can one spot in these 650 often close
and claustrophobic pages? There seem to be various chronological dispari-
ties—for instance, on one page Kohler's kids appear to be driving off to college,
at others they seem to be youngsters still living at home. There are also curious
repetitions—e.g., we are told twice about how Kohler's mother apparently lost
her rings, and he himself presents slightly differing accounts of what he was
doing on the day his bed-ridden father was taken to the hospital. Is there
artistry here? Or editorial oversight, the result of cobbling together a novel
from many short sections? Do we really need the book's occasional typographical tricks and illustrations? All interesting questions—for another day.

For now, let us rejoice in Gass's plenty—his language on the page. Here,
duly labeled, are some characteristic examples, though Gass's most delicious
effects arise in paragraphs and longer passages. As in a proper epic, Kohler
opens by asking for divine help: "Flounce from your stew, you sluttish Muse,
and bring me a pleasant subject." There are sly self-references: "Martha hates it
when I shape my sentences. She says it doesn't sound sincere." Wit: one of
Kohler's colleagues "is invariably prepared to grant you your point . . . after he
has blunted it." Capsule descriptions: "a smug moral look to him as if he'd
eaten oatmeal for breakfast." Sick humor: "my Brown Shirt rig (what an
unhappy Halloween that was)." Neat paradoxes: "You only hate what's going on
in the world because it interferes with your indifference." Memorable comparisons: "as useful as a jackknife in the hands of an Eagle Scout." Rhetorical
tricks: "Our party"—Kohler's imagined Party of Disappointed People—"shall
have planks, by god, planks we shall walk our enemies out on." Definitions:
causes, we learn, are "lies that advertise, lies that have fan clubs." Occasional
buried allusions: "it drizzles in my heart as it drizzles on the town." (Paul
Verlaine's "Il pleure dans mon coeur comme il pleut sur la ville.") Short stories
in a sentence: "Culp . . . claimed he went to work solely to summon the
strength, simply to find the courage (he said), only to gain time (he would
insist) to close the clasp on his briefcase and go home."

At one point, Kohler remarks that "the secret of life is paying absolute attention to what is going on." This is certainly how *The Tunnel* deserves to be read. It contains great beauty, as well as perversity and ugliness, much rage and a terrible sadness. "Never look beneath the surface of life," writes Kohler, "beneath the surface of life is the pit, the abyss, the awful truth." Perhaps Gass has managed, after all, to join his aestheticism to a moral fiction. By the end Kohler comes to seem a kind of fractured Everyman, broken by his past, his prejudices, his unfulfilled dreams. "I cannot complain," he says for all of us. "Yet I do. I do."

March 12, 1995

READER'S BLOCK

By David Markson

Sometimes you circle an author for years, slowly drawing closer and closer, waiting for the right book. Over the past two decades or so, I kept reading wonderful things about David Markson's fiction. William McPherson, my former boss at *Book World*, once praised Markson's *Ballad of Dingus Magee* (1965) as an "outrageously bawdy" and "brilliantly conceived" comic western. "Terribly funny" and "formidably intelligent," said my colleague Jonathan Yardley about *Springer's Progress* (1977), a zesty, semi-autobiographical novel, spilling over with wordplay, about a blocked writer's adulterous love affair. In 1988 Colin Walters, the urbane book editor at the *Washington Times*, even chose Markson's *Wittgenstein's Mistress* as his favorite book of the year. Told from the viewpoint of a woman who believes herself the last person alive on earth, the novel registers, in sentences, second thoughts, and sighs, its heroine's attempt to describe the world as she finds it. The result is a haunting portrait of a mind at the end of its tether. It should have won prizes.

David Markson, now approaching seventy, has obviously never been a writer content to repeat himself—or copy anyone else. But in *Reader's Block* he has actually come close to creating that ultimate novel dreamed of by the critic Walter Benjamin: one consisting entirely of quotations.

Markson imagines that a character called Reader is trying to draft a narrative about a Protagonist who is living either in a cemetery or on a beach. This tiny novelistic plot is then bejeweled with a series of literary anecdotes and lugubrious factoids, random lists and sorrowful observations that build up, through verbal pointillism, a picture of the artist's vocation as one of madness, deprivation, and early death. Since Markson requires the reader (lower case r) to pick up on all sorts of literary arcana, each page of this "novel of intellectual reference and allusion . . . minus the novel" offers a chance to test the breadth and depth of one's own reading. For many, the result will be quite unputdownable.

In what other book would one learn that "George Gissing's first wife became a prostitute. His second wife went mad" or that "the eulogy at Puccini's funeral was delivered by Benito Mussolini" or that "T. S. Eliot and William Burroughs's mother walked to dancing class together as children in St. Louis. Along the way passing Prufrock's Furniture Store" or that "Jackson Pollock once held a job cleaning bird droppings from statues in New York parks"? Alongside such pungent trivia, Markson inserts unattributed quotations, lists (Byron's mistresses, opera singers whose initials are ES), Latin tags, and Reader's changing thoughts about his Protagonist. In these last instances the reader's pleasure is often that of self-satisfaction, of sharing in Markson's culture, of knowing, for instance, that Skeres, Poley, and Frizer were the men who murdered Christopher Marlowe, that it was Paul Valéry who claimed "one does not finish a poem, one only abandons it," that Michael Ventris deciphered Linear B, and that Sheri Martinelli was a Greenwich Village heart-throb in the late 1940s and 1950s.

Obviously not everyone will respond to this "distant cousin innumerable times removed of *The Unquiet Grave*." Like Cyril Connolly's wistful classic, Markson's quotations sound a mournful taps for bookishness and deep learning: in Connolly's words, "It is closing-time in the gardens of the west." Still even those with only a mild literary bent will find much to enjoy in Markson's humor and provocations. "Can Protagonist think of a single film that interests him as much as the three hundredth best book he ever read?" "John D. MacDonald is by any standards a better writer than Saul Bellow."

Certain obsessive themes also emerge: famous writers who were anti-Semites; the sorrows of art—rejection, sickness, lost manuscripts, neglect, madness; roll calls of musicians and opera singers; the names of artists who committed suicide. In fact, *Reader's Block* gradually emerges as a kind of suicide note, a mournful litany proffering a cold and melancholy comfort. No intellectual despair is unique, the book seems to say; reflect on the suffering, despondency, and madness of those who were truly great. In his last entries, Reader imagines Protagonist as either drowning himself in the sea or turning on the gas in his little house by the cemetery. "In the end one experiences only oneself. Said Nietzsche."

Though death pervades *Reader's Block*, it never overwhelms the book's stoic and rueful gaiety (as Gilbert Sorrentino dubs it). Or the soul-satisfying pleasure of testing one's own literary connoisseurship. In these 200 pages the widely read will pick up on the opening sentences of Juan Rulfo's *Pedro Paramo*, Frazer's *Golden Bough*, Chekhov's *The Seagull*, and Sabatini's *Scaramouche*; there are unattributed quotations from Beckett, Gertrude Stein, Flaubert, Valéry, Dowson, Alexander Theroux, Melville, Celan, Malory, a couple of Roman emperors, Goethe, the Shakespeare scholar L. C. Knights, and Wyndham Lewis ("He doesn't come in here disguised like Westminster Abbey"—the blind and housebound Lewis on his old friend T. S. Eliot). At one point Markson even drops in the last sentence of *Wittgenstein's Mistress*—in French: *Quelqu'un vit sur cette plage*—"Someone is living on this beach."

Yet bookish expertise may also run from reader to Writer. Markson misspells Pausanias and gets the gender wrong of Valéry's Marquise who goes out at 5. Flaubert's and Baudelaire's most famous books were prosecuted not in the same year but in successive ones (1856 and 1857, respectively); neither did Samuel Johnson assert that no man ever wished *Robinson Crusoe* longer; he said this about *Paradise Lost*. Jacqueline du Pré played two Stradivarius cellos, not one; her favorite went to Rostropovich, the other to Yo-Yo Ma. Picky, picky: for where, of course, does erudition leave off and mere pedantry and one-upmanship begin? What really matters is that David Markson's "seminonfictional semifiction" is exhilarating, sorrowful, and amazing. Indeed, a minor masterpiece.

November 3, 1996

POSTSCRIPT: David Markson continues the adventures of Reader in two equally brilliant and plangent "semifictions": *This Is Not a Novel* and *Vanishing Point*. Don't miss them.

A FROLIC OF HIS OWN

By William Gaddis

How is it that the greatest fiction of our century has been so funny? Joyce and Proust, obviously; but think too of Evelyn Waugh, *Catch-22*, *Lolita*, much of *Invisible Man*, Pynchon, *The Master and Margarita*, Beckett, Borges. Nothing, it would seem, dates so quickly as the earnest. Really Serious Novels—by D. H. Lawrence, Hemingway, or Virginia Woolf—now sound tendentious, a bit histrionic, often downright embarrassing. Perhaps, to quote Lawrence himself, because ours is such a tragic age that we instinctively refuse to take it tragically. There's simply no other way to keep on going when the world is so clearly a hell of fraud, phoniness, and moral vacuity, a bloody arena of religious fanaticism, political bankruptcy, moneygrubbing, and personal betrayal. We laugh to keep from weeping.

As a guide to this fallen world, our world, no one is better, or funnier, than William Gaddis. To his bitter, exhilarating task he brings the savage indignation of a Swift or Gogol, an insider's command of the lore and lingo of specialized groups (artists, financiers, lawyers), a dramalike approach to storytelling, and a high modernist's cunning use of leitmotifs and symbols. Oh yes, and an unwavering, rigorous artistry. Gaddis's books can be quite long, but if you shake them nothing will fall out: They are made to last.

Since his youthful masterpiece *The Recognitions* (1955)—a near-legendary account of inauthenticity, the specter haunting so much postromantic writing—Gaddis has produced only three other novels, and that number includes this latest, *A Frolic of His Own*. A modern *Dunciad* striking out at the abuses of what we are obliged to call the law, it is, I think, the most accessible of all his books, vivid with comic characters, especially among its supporting cast. Take the randy and conspicuously wealthy Trish. She blithely cheats her shoe repairman, breaks her mother's will (thus impoverishing an old family servant), never pays her bills, and, in a particularly dizzying moment, hires one set of lawyers to bring a suit "for foetal endangerment and another set to defend her abortion." During the novel's most hilarious scene, a kind of updated Mad Tea Party, this amoral socialite opens an expensive picnic hamper, only to begin chattering that "they've put in these horrid little plastic forks you'd think we were Kurds or something." She's just awful—and just perfect. I could listen to her forever.

In fact, nearly any page of *A Frolic* will elicit a laugh, or more often a rueful smile. A white-shoe law firm lives up to its name of Swyne & Dour. A sensitive newspaper story thoughtfully begins a sentence, "Speaking on condition that he not be identified, Village official J. Harriet Ruth . . ." A bill before Congress promises to "restore the arts to their pristine decorative function."

Certainly *A Frolic of His Own* deserves lots of readers in Washington: it's all about civil suits, lawyers, greed, company loyalty, the proper and improper use of language, plagiarism, insurance scams, parental pressure, the thoughtless rich, venal evangelists, the relationship of the artist to society, the Civil War, the tensions between blacks and Jews, television, cornpone politicians, breast implants, and much, much more. Enriching the main narrative are judicial opinions, court decrees, depositions, and two-thirds of a rather high-minded play called *Once in Antietam*. You get a lot for your money. But, then, that's what the law's all about, isn't it? "It's the money," as the overworked lawyer Harry Lutz tells his wife, Christina, "it's always the money. The rest is nothing but opera."

The novel's plot incorporates three main lawsuits, all of them touching the idealistic and innocent, pitiably ineffective, part-time American history professor Oscar Crease. In the most complicated case, Oscar is bringing suit because his car—a Japanese Sosumi—accidentally ran him over while he was hotwiring its ignition. This whole affair grows increasingly byzantine—at one point Oscar seems to be suing the owner of the vehicle, who is of course himself; ultimately he is told that "you might almost say that this is a suit between who you are and who you think you are."

The central lawsuit of *A Frolic*, however, revolves around Oscar's case against the blockbuster Civil War movie *The Blood in the Red, White and Blue*, which he maintains knowingly plagiarized his unproduced drama about his grandfather's life. In the course of this action he retains a black lawyer named Harold Basie (who turns out to be more than he seems), suffers cross-examination by a veddy high-tone Anglo-Indian attorney (who addresses people as "old sport"), and ultimately discovers the sorts of truths that Dickens made famous in the case of *Jarndyce vs. Jarndyce* (in *Bleak House*). Against Oscar's two suits, Gaddis counterpoints an increasingly complex and far-fetched case, presided over by Oscar's father, ninety-seven-year-old judge Thomas Crease, in which a small dog is trapped inside a modern sculpture and cannot be freed. The village of Tatamount wants to destroy the artwork to liberate Spot; the sculptor vehemently protests. The result is some splendid judicial humor and legal wordplay:

"The court finds sufficent urgency in the main action of this proceeding to reject defendants' assertions and cross motions for the reasons set forth below and grants summary judgment to plaintiff on the issue of his motion for a preliminary injunction to supersede the temporary restraining order now in place." Who could argue with that?

In tone *A Frolic of His Own* ranges from cruel farce to deep outrage, from the accidental drowning of a born-again little boy undergoing baptism in the Pee Dee River at the hands of the unspeakable Reverend Ude to Oscar's frequent cris de coeur: "All this crime, greed, corruption in the newspapers, you think they're just part of the times we're living in today? that our great Christian civilization is breaking down here right before our eyes? It's just the other way around. . . . It's not the breakdown of our civilization that we're watching but its blossoming, greed and political corruption it's what America was built on in those years after the Civil War where it all got a start, so it's not whether corruption's a sign of decay but whether it's built into things right from the beginning."

Of course, high-tone Oscar himself succumbs to the lure of money; in fact, all the characters eventually fall prey to legal chicanery of one sort or another. "Justice?" the novel says in its opening lines. "You get justice in the next world, in this world you have the law." Alas.

As in his previous novel, *Carpenter's Gothic* (1985), Gaddis contrives to set most of his drama in a single locale, here a run-down old family house on Long Island, where Oscar is recuperating from his injuries. In its windy rooms he shuffles about, guzzles Pinot Grigio, watches television—news programs about starving children, interrupted by inane commercials for laxatives, or specials about nature (symbolically red in tooth and claw)—and generally exasperates his sister Christina, his brother-in-law Harry, his ditzy and well-endowed girlfriend Lily, all the while fending off insurance adjusters, attorneys, scam artists, realtors, and other undesirables. The effect is a little like *Dead Souls* or the more humorous sections of *The Possessed*, where everyone seems half crazy and no one ever plans to stop talking.

This dramatic quality is also reinforced by Gaddis's heavy reliance on dialogue (often unattributed and lightly punctuated), a technique first employed in his 1975 satiric masterpiece about America's obsession with money, *JR*, wherein an eleven-year-old kid wheels and deals from telephone booths, and by so doing creates the worldwide JR Family of Companies. Such polyphony may seem initially confusing, but one quickly learns to recognize each character's distinctive speech patterns and verbal tics. By his "authorial absence," Gaddis once explained, "the characters create the situation," adding "it was the flow that I wanted, for the readers to read and be swept along, to participate. And enjoy it. And occasionally chuckle, laugh along the way."

This last remark makes clear that William Gaddis—now in his early seventies—wants to be read and enjoyed, not simply revered by a cult; he has never thought of himself as experimental, avant-garde, or self-indulgently hermetic. Certainly *A Frolic of His Own* ought to earn him a wider audience, though impressed readers should go on, or rather back, to Gaddis's major works—*The Recognitions* and *JR*—which are just as enjoyable and even more ambitious in scope and accomplishment. There may be occasional longueurs to *A Frolic*—Oscar's play, for instance—and the book's last seventy-five pages seem a little anticlimactic, but on the whole this remains a superb comic novel, one in which you begin by laughing at the characters and end by caring for them deeply. Through them Gaddis reminds us that perhaps only art and love can counter both the madness of the modern world ("it can't go on forever, can it?") and the sorrows delivered by what he has famously called "the unswerving punctuality of chance."

January 23, 1994

THE AMBER SPYGLASS
BOOK 3 OF HIS DARK MATERIALS

By Philip Pullman

Genres are meant to be transcended, and our most ambitious writers and artists always push hard against the boundaries. This is as true for those who labor in children's literature—think of Alan Garner or Daniel Pinkwater—as for great science fiction and fantasy authors (Jonathan Carroll, Samuel R. Delany, Thomas M. Disch) and mystery and suspense novelists (Ruth Rendell, Iain Pears, K. C. Constantine). How much can be packed into a book before it bursts the conventions? What can be done that hasn't been done already? The two best credos for any creator are still Pound's "Make it new" and Beckett's complementary "Fail better."

Which isn't to say that a writer shouldn't strive to make his books formally perfect. Yet literature flourishes best, remains truly healthy, only when its practitioners sometimes go Too Far. Many grown-up readers of Philip Pullman's *The Amber Spyglass*, the earth- and heaven-shaking conclusion to the long story that started with *The Golden Compass* and continued with *The Subtle Knife*, are likely to bristle at its theological and ontological daring: this so-called young adult novel takes on the central religious tradition of the West and finds it wanting—not only wanting but downright evil. Think of this trilogy as a counterblast to C. S. Lewis's Christian science fiction and his celebrated chronicles of Narnia. Pullman is of the devil's party, William Blake's party, and he knows it. He has also written the best, deepest, and most disturbing children's fantasy of our time. By comparison, the agreeable and entertaining Harry Potter books look utterly innocuous.

In *The Golden Compass*—winner of the Carnegie Medal, Britain's equivalent of the Newbery—Pullman sets us down into a world reminiscent of late Victorian England, complete with steam locomotives, hot-air balloons, and Oxford colleges. But this isn't our earth, for here every person is connected to a visible demon, a totemic animal with which one's spirit remains inextricably entwined. In children the demon can change its shape at will; in adolescents it finally "settles" into a single animal. As it happens, experimental theologians (i.e., scientists) working for the church's ominous Oblation Board discover that the surgical separation of human and demon—intercision—releases a vast explosion of energy (similar to the splitting of the atom). Before long, street urchins start disappearing from London, spirited up to the north toward a place called Bolvangar.

When a kitchen boy named Roger turns up missing, his friend Lyra Belacqua resolves to rescue him. Lyra is no ordinary child but the outcome of a fateful liaison. Lord Asriel, her father, is a titanic Renaissance-style overreacher, a mixture of Dr. Faustus and Tamburlaine; Mrs. Coulter, her mother, a *belle dame sans merci* who can hold any man in her thrall and whose most gentle quality is ruthlessness. On the run from the authorities and her power-driven parents, the resourceful Lyra encounters a magnificent series of characters: the boat-dwelling "gyptians," a hot-tempered armored bear named Iorek Byrnison, the Texan aeronaut Lee Scoresby, and, my favorite, the wise and profoundly sexy Serafina Pekkala, clan queen of the witches of Lake Enara. Along the way, Lyra also learns that she possesses a fateful destiny, one somehow linked to her uncanny ability to read the alethiometer, a mechanical oracle that can answer questions and see a little into the future. A great deal happens in *The Golden Compass*, all of it thrilling, before the final pages when Lord Asriel unexpectedly opens a passageway between universes and disappears. Lyra vows to follow him.

In *The Subtle Knife* Pullman shifts the action to a strangely deserted Italianate city called Cittàgazze—and to bustling contemporary Oxford. The dramatis personae further expands to include angels and spirit-vampires called Specters; a theoretical physicist (and former nun) named Mary Malone, who is researching the nature of "dark matter"; a mysterious shaman known as Stanislaw Grumman; the sleekly threatening Sir Charles Latrom, who can move between worlds; and, most important of all, twelve-year-old Will Parry. At great personal cost Will acquires a mysterious knife of such sharpness that one side of its blade can shred iron as if it were paper. Yet the other edge is sharper still: it can cut holes in the fabric of space.

When *The Amber Spyglass* opens, Lord Asriel is continuing to build up his battalions for an all-out assault on The Authority (aka God) and Lyra has been smuggled away by her mother to a cave high in the Himalayas. There the young girl is kept constantly sedated, though in her dreams she finds herself communicating with the dead. Meanwhile, Will is befriended by two rebel angels who urge him to go to Lord Asriel and offer the Subtle Knife as a weapon in the battle against the Kingdom of Heaven. But Will is adamant: he will do nothing until he finds and rescues Lyra.

Alas, despite Mrs. Coulter's strategies, the Jesuit-like Consistorial Court of Discipline has already discovered the girl's whereabouts—and come to understand that all history is accelerating toward this sleeping beauty. To ensure its own survival, the church resolves to destroy Lyra, and so dispatches not only a great aerial flotilla but also a single lone assassin, remorseless and fanatically resolute. Fortunately, Lord Asriel has employed Gallivespian spies—a fiercely proud people the size of your hand—and so knows the church's plans: he sends gyropters under the command of his chief lieutenant, the African King Ogunwe, with orders to save the child at all costs.

As these two armies race across the skies toward Tibet, the scientist Mary Malone wanders by happy accident into still another world, a peaceful prelapsarian paradise inhabited by gentle wheeled creatures. Alas, this Eden is dying, for some primal essence keeps escaping from it at an ever-increasing speed. This conscious substance, Mary eventually concludes, is none other than her own Dark Matter, what Lyra's people call Dust. She resolves to find a way to stop this entropic drain on the universe. But how?

Let me stop there. To say much more about the action of *The Amber Spyglass* would certainly diminish the reader's pleasure in an expertly paced and orchestrated novel. Even those who judge his theology objectionable will find Pullman's sheer storytelling power sinfully irresistible. But make no mistake: this book views organized religion as repressive, life smothering, mendacious, and just plain wrong, right from the beginning of time.

"The Authority, God, the Creator, the Lord, Yahweh, El, Adonai, the King, the Father, the Almighty—those were all names he gave himself," explains the angel Balthamos. "He was never the creator. He was an angel like ourselves—the first angel, true, the most powerful, but he was formed of Dust as we are, and Dust is only a name for what happens when matter begins to understand itself. Matter loves matter. It seeks to know more about itself, and Dust is formed. The first angels condensed out of Dust, and the Authority was the first of all. He told those who came after him that he had created them, but it was a lie. One of those who came later was wiser than he was, and she found out the truth, so he banished her. We serve her still. And the Authority reigns in the Kingdom, and Metatron is his Regent."

In his acknowledgments Philip Pullman admits that he has stolen material "from every book I have ever read." Besides finding hints of *Paradise Lost* and Blake's poetry, the astute will pick up echoes of the following: Christ's harrowing of hell, Jewish Kabbalah (the legend of the godlike angel Metatron), Gnostic doctrine (Dust, our sleeping souls needing to be awakened), the "death of God" controversy, *Perelandra*, the Oz books (the Wheelers), Wagner's *Ring of the Nibelungs* (Siegfried's mending of the sword), Aeneas, Odysseus, and

Dante in the Underworld, the Grail legend and the wounded Fisher King, Peter Pan, Wordsworth's pantheistic "Immortality Ode," the doctrine of the hidden God and speculation about the plurality of worlds, situational ethics (actions, not people, being good or bad), the cessation of miracles, Star Wars, colonialist evangelizing, the fetch of British folklore, the seventeenth-century doctrine of sympathies (for the Gallivespian communication device, the lodestone-resonator), the popular mythology of the Jesuits as ascetic masterminds of realpolitik, superhero comics, and even Pullman's own early novel for adults, Galatea. Fans of science fiction and fantasy may also detect undertones of Ursula Le Guin's Earthsea books, Fritz Leiber's sword-and-sorcery tales of Fafhrd and the Gray Mouser, Jack Vance's elegant Dying Earth stories.

For the most part, Pullman transmutes all this disparate and often dark material, making it his own. But occasionally some passages sound like mere info-dumps, as in that Gnostic account of creation already quoted, or this series of questions by Mrs. Coulter: "Well, where is God if he's alive? And why doesn't he speak anymore? At the beginning of the world, God walked in the Garden and spoke with Adam and Eve. Then he began to withdraw, and he forbade Moses to look at his face. Later, in the time of Daniel, he was aged—he was the Ancient of Days. Where is he now? Is he still alive, at some inconceivable age, decrepit and demented, unable to think or act or speak and unable to die, a rotten hulk? And if that is his condition, wouldn't it be the most merciful thing, the truest proof of our love for God, to seek him out and give him the gift of death?"

This is heady stuff for a children's book. As is Lyra taking on the role of both Eve and Christ. Even the dead cry out from the depths that they were deceived about the afterlife, that there is no heaven, that they yearn to join their atoms to the great flux of the universe. "We'll be alive again in a thousand blades of grass, and a million leaves; we'll be falling in the raindrops and blowing in the fresh breeze; we'll be glittering in the dew under the stars and the moon out there in the physical world, which is our true home and always was."

The physical world: in the end, the Dark Materials trilogy is an ode to the joy of living in a physical world, a hymn to flesh, to exuberance, to the here and now, to free thought, imagination, and feeling, to nobility of spirit. By contrast, the followers of the Authority represent only fanaticism, brutal violence, lust, servitude, torture, and every kind of oppression, all of these justified as necessary means to a supposedly higher end. These ecclesiastics have no redeeming virtues. Yet how, really, does the passionate intensity of Father Gomez, the church-appointed assassin, differ from that of Lord Asriel and Mrs. Coulter, both cold-blooded murderers, who are nonetheless granted an opportunity for redemption?

Despite various flaws—too much overt moralizing, the unwarranted flip-flop in the fundamental character of Mrs. Coulter, not enough Serafina Pekkala—*His Dark Materials* is an overwhelming reading experience, brought to a sublime and touching close by *The Amber Spyglass*. This is a book that not so long ago would have made the Index, and in still another era gotten its author condemned to the stake as a heretic. Even now some concerned parents may judge that Philip Pullman has gone Too Far in his plainspoken critique of religious orthodoxy. But, as Blake said, you never know what is enough until you know what is more than enough. *His Dark Materials* is a novel of electrifying power and splendor, deserving celebration, as violent as a fairy tale and as shocking as art must be.

October 29, 2000

POSTSCRIPT: Children's literature counts as some of the most imaginative writing anyone could want. A lot of adults have read J. K. Rowling, but there are other novelists and storytellers just as good: Joan Aiken (whose Dido Twite books should be timeless classics), Daniel Pinkwater (author of *The Snarkout Boys and the Avocado of Death*), the prolific Diana Wynne Jones, William Joyce, William Mayne, Peter Dickinson, and the astonishing Alan Garner, who has blended myth and mystery to thrilling, sometimes horrific effect (see *The Owl Service* and *Red Shift*). Such artists deserve our appreciation and our thanks.

UNDERWORLD

By Don DeLillo

Don DeLillo's eagerly awaited new novel, *Underworld*, is extremely long, no question about it. But I'd have been happy if the book had been the length of *Possession, Atlas Shrugged*, and *Studs Lonigan* combined. That it recalls all these very different modern classics, as well as much of DeLillo's earlier work (*End Zone, Libra*), is a measure of both its ambition and its quite awesome achievement. This is a novel, after all, that draws together baseball, the Bomb, J. Edgar Hoover, waste disposal, drugs, gangs, Vietnam, fathers and sons, the comic Lenny Bruce, and the Cuban missile crisis.

And that's just for openers. It also depicts passionate adultery, weapons testing, the care of aging mothers, the postwar Bronx, 1960s civil rights demonstrations, populuxe culture, advertising, graffiti artists at work, Catholic education, chess, and murder. And still we're not through. There's a viewing of a lost Eisenstein film, meditations on the Watts Tower, an evening at Truman Capote's Black & White Ball, a hot-air balloon ride, serial murders in Texas, a camping trip in the Southwest, a nun on the Internet, reflections on history, one hit (or possibly two) by the New York mob, and an apparent miracle. Most amazingly, none of this seems jumbled or arbitrary: as DeLillo says and proves, "Everything is connected in the end."

Such richness. Think of *Underworld* as a great Victorian-style panoramic novel—*The Way We Live Now*, say—or even as a twelve-part miniseries, titled perhaps "Cold War and Remembrance." For DeLillo's masterpiece provides both a cultural history of America during the Bomb era and a suspenseful journey into the past.

The main character is Nick Shay, in the 1990s an aging waste-disposal expert but in his youth a teenaged dropout from the Bronx. Nick is the common element in several of the novel's principal obsessions. In his rowdy youth he takes up briefly with a neighborhood housewife, Klara Sax, who eventually remakes herself into a world-renowned artist, part Christo, part Georgia

O'Keeffe. Nick also comes to possess what may be—doubts remain—the legendary baseball, homered by Bobby Thomson, that unexpectedly gave the 1951 pennant to the Giants. As it happens, on that very same day, October 3, the Russians set off a powerful atomic blast, thus heating up the Cold War. And sometime in his youth, Nick seems to have committed a murder. Nuclear weapons, waste, the fate of that fateful baseball, and the destinies of an ordinary man and his loved ones plangently intertwine for 800 pages.

In an interview Don DeLillo once asserted, "I want to give pleasure through language, through the architecture of a book or a sentence and through characters who may be funny, nasty, violent, or all of these." *Underworld* delivers on every count.

Consider a few sentences. The moody stand-up entertainer Lenny Bruce resembles "a poolshark who'd graduated to deeper and sleazier schemes." In one performance he maniacally sums up every other Swedish art film of the 1960s: "Ursula Andress naked to the waist with a slain calf slung over her shoulder." When the formidable Sister Edgar is glimpsed, she is "diagramming a compound sentence, the chalked structure so complex and self-appending it began to resemble the fire-escaped façade of the kind of building most of the boys and girls lived in." After the Texas Highway Killer calls in to a news program to explain his crimes, he says, "I hope this talk has been conducive to understand the situation better. For me to request that I would only talk to Sue Ann Corcoran, one-on-one, that was intentional on my part. I saw the interview you did where you stated you'd like to keep your career, you know, ongoing while you hopefully raise a family and I feel like this is a thing whereby the superstation has the responsibility to keep the position open, okay, because an individual should not be penalized for lifestyle type choices."

Toxic waste-disposal experts, we learn, spread tales about a spectral ship, filled with unimaginably poisonous material, that can never come into port: *The Flying Liberian.* Advertising is dubbed, with a kind of Japanese aptness, "the industry of vivid description."

Underworld crackles with such memorable formulations. "A museum was empty rooms with knights in armor where you had one sleepy guard for every seven centuries." Marilyn Monroe, we learn, hated being Marilyn, but Jayne Mansfield loved it. Nick shrewdly observes "how people played at being executives while actually holding executive positions. . . . It's not that you're pretending to be someone else. You're pretending to be exactly who you are." Nick's brother Matt serves in Vietnam, "where everything he'd ever disbelieved or failed to imagine turned out, in the end, to be true." The original bomb heads, the scientists who worked at Los Alamos, flicker by as "all those émigrés from Middle Europe, thick-browed men, with sad eyes and roomy pleated pants." One Hispanic character has "the reflective head of an elder of the barrio, playing dominoes under a canopy while the fire engines idle up the street."

DeLillo can do voices—the Texas killer, a Jewish paranoid, Russian capitalists, artsy New Yorkers—as well as aphorisms. Here's a thrilling old black street preacher: "You see the eye that hangs over this pyramid here. What's pyramids doing on American money? You see the number they got strung out at the base of this pyramid. This is how they flash their Masonic codes to each other. This is Freemason, the passwords and handshakes. This is Rosicrucian, the beam of light. This is webs and scribbles all over the bill, front and the back, that contains a message. This is not just rigmarole and cooked spaghetti. They predicting the day and the hour. They telling each other when the time is come. You can't find the answer in the Bible or the Bill of Rights. I'm talking to you. I'm saying history is written on the commonest piece of paper in your pocket."

As should be evident, *Underworld* is rippled throughout with humor, from old ribaldries about Speedy Gonzalez to the guerrilla satire of the Terminal Theater. Just before the Black & White Ball, an earnest Clyde Tolson informs J. Edgar Hoover about a plot to steal the director's trash cans. "Confidential source says they intend to take your garbage on tour. Rent halls in major cities. Get lefty sociologists to analyze the garbage item by item. Get hippies to rub it on their naked bodies. More or less have sex with it. Get poets to write poems about it. And finally, in the last city on the tour, they plan to eat it. . . . And expel it . . . publicly." That night, at the ball itself, the guests do the twist "with all the articulated pantomime of the unfrozen dead come back for a day." Even Clyde dances with a provocative young masked woman who suddenly whispers, "If you kiss me, I'll stick my tongue so far down your throat . . . It will pierce your heart."

Formidable characters, themes, language—there's almost none of that icy detachment for which DeLillo has occasionally been faulted. Even his fascination with conspiracy and paranoia fits not only the times but also his novel's intricate architecture. After an opening prologue, set in 1951, the narrative leapfrogs to the early 1990s, and then gradually works its way back in time toward explosions of sex and death in the summer of 1952. An epilogue eventually returns us to the present. In effect, as we read, we penetrate beneath history's surface, gradually descending into the past, that underworld which shapes our lives.

Of course, DeLillo rings other changes on the meaning of underworld, associating it with crime, dreams, the afterlife, subway tunnels, and even that lost film masterpiece by Eisenstein, *Unterwelt*. Similarly, the novel creates numerous doubles and mirrorings: Moonman decorates subway cars, Klara paints old B-52s; Sister Edgar twins J. Edgar; a clip of a murder by the Texas

Highway Killer prefigures a viewing of the Zapruder film of the Kennedy assassination. Public and private intertwine; the half remembered fades into the wholly imagined. A nun in a burned-out ghetto screams at a busload of gawking foreign tourists: "Brussels is surreal. Milan is surreal. This is real. The Bronx is real." Periodically, DeLillo shows us our forgotten brethren, those who happened to live, figuratively or literally, downwind from the blast—the tortured damned of a Brueghel painting and the deformed experimental subjects in Eisenstein's movie, the lost souls of the barrio, the victims of atomic radiation in Kazakhstan.

But "everything's connected." Searching for the Thomson baseball, the obsessive Marvin Lundy examines old photographs and bits of movie film, enlarging details, patiently studying the very pixels. "All knowledge is available if you analyze the dots." Everything's connected: Nick's brother interprets photo data for the bombing runs of Chuckie Wainwright, who inherited a certain old baseball from his ad exec father, who once planned an orange-juice campaign similar to the one used on the billboard where the face of the martyred girl Esmeralda miraculously appears. One eventually discovers that *Underworld* operates as a kind of hypertext, a never-ending series of narrative links.

Of all these, the sections set in the early 1950s possess a particular magic. The opening sixty pages thrillingly re-create that final game of the 1951 pennant race. The account of Nick's cocky adolescence—cigarettes on the stoop, nights at the pool hall, sex in stolen cars, fights with outsiders—seems like the purest Americana, to use the word with which DeLillo presciently titled his first novel. Appropriately Nick's part of *Underworld* ends with a paragraph redolent of loss and desire, echoing Whitman, recalling *Gatsby*. Nearing retirement, enjoying a comfortable life and a successful career, Nick yearns for his youth: "I long for the days of disorder. I want them back, the days when I was alive on the earth, rippling in the quick of my skin, heedless and real. I was dumb-muscled and angry and real. This is what I long for, the breach of peace, the days of disarray when I walked real streets and did things slap-bang and felt angry and ready all the time, a danger to others and a distant mystery to myself."

Thomas Pynchon recently brought out *Mason & Dixon*. Now we have Don DeLillo's *Underworld*. Ambitious, imaginative fiction still flourishes. Let us read and rejoice.

September 28, 1997

PERFORMING SELVES

Diaries, memoirs, letters, revealing biographies—such books are the literary equivalent of Hollywood gossip. Who can resist wit, balanced between invective and bitchiness?

All the writers in "Performing Selves" are British, those masters of the barbed sentence, the casual put-down, the faux-naif, and the snootily sophisticated. But many of the authors mentioned elsewhere in Bound to Please—Gore Vidal, Ben Sonnenberg, Edmund Wilson—could readily match wits or anecdotes with them.

Given infinite space for this section, I would have added Ned Rorem, whose diaries are supremely intelligent, delicious, and mean; Janet Flanner, the great clearinghouse of Parisian news and gossip; the sexy M. F. K. Fisher, who chronicled a life of good food, love, and travel; and Quentin Crisp, an émigré from Britain who showed Americans that nothing was more important than style.

ACKERLEY:

THE LIFE OF J. R. ACKERLEY

By Peter Parker

J. R. Ackerley (1896–1967) has been called the greatest literary editor of our time and "one of the best writers of prose in this century." Evelyn Waugh, no less, proclaimed that it was "difficult to control one's enthusiasm and to praise temperately" Ackerley's touching and hilarious travel journal, *Hindoo Holiday*. Of its author's four other books, Christopher Isherwood observed that "each in its different way is a masterpiece."

Despite such praise, I suspect that Ackerley's highly amusing, neatly constructed books are destined to remain coterie favorites. Consider their topics. His best-known work, the posthumous *My Father and My Self*, reveals that good old dad was a bigamist in his maturity and probably a homosexual in his youth, that Ackerley himself liked to cruise gay bars in search of sailors and guardsmen, and that late in life he fell deeply in love with a German shepherd. A dog, not a man. The novel *We Think the World of You* and the slightly fictionalized *My Dog Tulip* both describe the writer's life with his beloved Queenie; the latter includes a chapter titled "Liquids and Solids," which is about just what you think.

In his letters and books Ackerley appears slightly bemused, absolutely frank, quietly funny. Peter Parker's biography perfectly captures that man, but also gives pleasure with its own low-keyed wit and stylishness. Take Parker's thumbnail description of the teacher S. P. B. Mais as "a man who genuinely liked boys (wisely rather than too well)." Above all, Parker possesses the biographer's greatest gift: he knows how to tell a story. A young medical student went to Copenhagen for treatment of his homosexual inclinations. "It was seriously believed that homosexuality could be 'cured' by removing one testicle and replacing it with the testicle of a heterosexual man. His professor at the medical school was prepared to carry out this extraordinary procedure, but whilst they were waiting for a donor—difficult to find, one imagines—

Johannes met Ackerley, became a great deal happier about his homosexuality and so decided against the surgery." Dashes have seldom been put to such nice effect.

"I was born in 1896," wrote Joe Ackerley in *My Father and My Self,* "and my parents were married in 1919." A well-off British fruit importer, his father, Roger Ackerley, was known as the Banana King and seems to have been a delightful man. Once Joe pretended to be visiting friends but was actually cavorting in Italy with his latest passion. While he was away, his father suffered a heart attack, and the worried son had to explain his surreptitious behavior. "It's all right old boy," Roger said. "I prefer not to know. So long as you enjoyed yourself, that's the main thing." Later, when a certain Dr. Wadd told Roger that if he gave up claret he could live ten years longer, the Banana King replied, "Thanks. I'd sooner have the claret."

Ackerley's mother was, in her way, just as much a charmer. A former actress, she would enter rooms "as if stepping before the footlights" and then deliver lines from drawing room comedies: " 'What a beautiful day! The air I should imagine is full of champagne.' " At the end of her life she became a secret tippler and kept a fly for a pet, feeding it daily with bread crumbs.

Then there was brother Peter, who had his head blown off in World War I. And sister Netta, a great beauty in early life, who entertained an incestuous passion for Ackerley. She did marry, but eventually abandoned both husband and son, sending the latter off to boarding school "clutching a model yacht, the only present he ever received from his mother." She spent most of her life sponging off others, living her last years with her brother and an aged aunt in a set of rooms at the Star and Garter apartments.

Shortly after World War I—in which Joe served in battle with distinction—the young dilettante composed his first major work, a play titled *The Prisoners of War.* Besides being a truthful account of life in a POW camp, it enjoyed notoriety for its homosexual undercurrents. At one point a Madame Louis tries to charm the hero, Conrad. "I have heard you do not like much the fair sex." "The fair sex?" Conrad replies. "Which sex is that?" About this time Ackerley also met an admiring E. M. Forster, and they became lifelong friends. In fact, some of Ackerley's letters from India, where he spent five months as the companion to a boy-crazy maharajah, helped the famous novelist complete *A Passage to India.*

In the late 1920s Joe Ackerley joined the staff of the *Listener,* a cultural periodical published by the BBC, and soon became its maverick literary editor. In the subsequent thirty years he commissioned pieces, largely unsigned and ill paid, by Forster, W. H. Auden, Christopher Isherwood, Virginia Woolf, Kenneth Clark, and many other famous names in modern British art and literature.

In *My Father and My Self* Ackerley never mentions the *Listener*, perhaps because his real life was focused on sex, friendship, and family. Ackerley's taste ran to heterosexual workingmen, whose favors he would buy, though he always hoped to find an Ideal Friend. That companion he finally discovered in the dog Queenie. For him she was always *the* woman, and he gave up his incessant sexual cruising for long romps *à deux* in the park. After she died, he gradually went into a decline, drinking more and more, writing cranky letters to newspapers about animal and homosexual rights. Always short of cash—partly because of his generosity and largely because he supported his sister and various hangers-on—Ackerley finally had to sell off his letters from Forster. In his last years he took to sitting in pubs and rereading his own books. He died in his sleep at seventy-one.

The latter third of *Ackerley* makes for sad reading. Seeing Joe and his sister, both sick and drunk, toddling down the street together, a neighbor was heard to murmur, "Charles and Mary Lamb." The humor, sorrow, and rightness in that allusion to the hard-drinking romantic essayist and his half-mad sister neatly characterize both Ackerley's odd life and this fine biography.

January 9, 1990

THE KNOX BROTHERS

By *Penelope Fitzgerald*

THE MEANS OF ESCAPE: STORIES

By *Penelope Fitzgerald*

"A masterpiece," proclaimed A. S. Byatt of Penelope Fitzgerald's last novel, *The Blue Flower*, an opinion seconded by scores of reviewers around the world. The National Book Critics Circle even awarded the book—about the German Romantic poet Novalis—its 1997 fiction prize (upsetting the champions of Don DeLillo and Philip Roth). By the time of her death, at eighty-three, Penelope Fitzgerald had swept the field as the literate reader's novelist of choice. *The Bookshop, Human Voices, The Beginning of Spring, Innocence*—none of these was much more than 200 pages, a length that made them seem all the more perfect: exquisite haiku fiction in a world of noisy epics.

Their oblique humor, perfectly cadenced sentences, and artful understatement also made them seem particularly English, part of that distinguished line that includes Ivy Compton-Burnett, Henry Green, Evelyn Waugh, Barbara Pym, Muriel Spark. Not for Fitzgerald the American rough-and-tumble, the I-go-at-life-freestyle-and-contain-multitudes approach to the novel, none of our straining after the bold personal experiment, our penchant for gaudy stylistic display: instead, her fiction possesses an almost uncanny stillness. So deeply felt is her vision of life and its travails that it verges on the sacerdotal. "I have remained true," she once confessed, "to my deepest convictions. I mean the courage of those who are born to be defeated, the weakness of the strong, and the tragedy of misunderstandings and missed opportunities, which I have done my best to treat as comedy—for otherwise how can we manage to bear it?"

For most American readers Penelope Fitzgerald came out of nowhere. After all, she never published, and probably never wrote, any fiction whatsoever until she was past sixty. She'd been a wife, mother, teacher. Anyone might easily assume that she'd simply bided her time during all those years, awaiting the wisdom that comes only with age, with having lived through enough weddings, christenings, and funerals.

Yes, of course, but just as important, this unassuming genius was born not a Fitzgerald but a Knox. Her father and her three uncles were among the most charismatic and witty, eccentric, and strong-willed personalities of the century. In *The Knox Brothers*, first published in 1977 but now brought out in a "corrected" edition, Penelope Fitzgerald relates the lives of these uncommon men with an affection and pride she makes no effort to disguise.

Nor should she. All the Knoxes possessed first-rate minds, an intense dedication to truth and duty, and an altogether enviable lovableness. Edmund (1881–1971), her father, became a leading Fleet Street journalist, exceptional light versifier (writing as "Evoe"), and editor of *Punch*; Dillwyn (1884–1943) devoted his energies to classical scholarship—and to top-secret government work as a cryptographer, being instrumental in figuring the "way in" to the Nazis' message-coding machine Enigma; Wilfred (1886–1950), the least known but most saintly, was ordained an Anglican priest and adopted an exemplary life of simplicity, poverty, and good works. Most famous of all was the baby of the family, Ronald (1888–1957): at Eton he was regarded as "the cleverest boy within living memory"; newspapers later dubbed him the wittiest young man in England; and throughout his life, his pen could, with equal assurance, produce mystery novels, lighthearted jeux d'esprit (such as his groundbreaking "Studies in the Literature of Sherlock Holmes"), scholarly works like *Enthusiasm*, in which he examines the emotional element in religion, and even a translation of the entire Bible into modern English. When Ronnie abandoned the Church of England to become a Roman Catholic, then a priest, his conversion was likened to Newman's—and with justice.

Not just a biography, *The Knox Brothers* provides superior literary entertainment, in part because Fitzgerald tends to leave out the boring bits (a technique she perfected in her fiction). When the reader begins to weary of Ronnie's social success among aristocratic Catholic ladies, the book will jump to Dilly the Cambridge agnostic, laboriously reconstructing the mimes of Herodas, then segue into an account of Wilfred at the Oratory of the Good Shepherd or Edmund badly cutting his hand just as the influential J. M. Barrie, who was deathly afraid of blood, is about to receive him. Throughout, the prose is deft and sonorous, but, like a proper gentleman's suit, never draws attention to itself. Except, perhaps, through its quotations and anecdotes.

One sickly Knox ancestor vividly remarked that she was "waiting till it was God's pleasure to dismiss her soul from its frail habitation." Another "had never looked up a train in his life, but simply went down to the station and complained to the stationmaster if one was not ready for him." A celebrated Rugby teacher could correct exams only to the sound of a barrel organ, "which he hired to play underneath his window." Describing the world of Edwardian journalism, Robert Lynd makes his immortal observation that he and his friends "were the sort of people our mothers warned us against." When the Knoxes' father, the bishop of Manchester, learned of his two younger sons' interest in Catholic ritual, he mournfully observed, "I cannot understand what it is that the dear boys see in the Blessed Virgin Mary."

There are splendid vignettes of the Knoxes' various colleagues and friends, too. Dilly's solicitor, for instance, was "the celebrated E.S.P. Haynes. Haynes had believed, until 1914, that a just world would prevail; since the loss of Grenfell, Lister, Guy Lawrence and their generation, he no longer thought so; he resigned himself to good living and to knowing everyone and everything, reminding his friends that 'to eat and drink with the wrong person is like intercourse with an inefficient prostitute.'" It was Dilly, too—my favorite of the brothers—who discovered that the drive from his house to the train station allowed him exactly enough time to recite the whole of Milton's "Lycidas." Even Ronnie, who hated modern technology, redeems his slightly too-too self when he maintains that his "idea of the last really good invention was the toast-rack." After his Bible translation received a critical drubbing, this friend of the waspish Evelyn Waugh also admitted that "on his deathbed, if he found he had no enemies left, he intended to forgive his reviewers."

Readers attuned to the Fitzgerald sensibility will particularly prize various small details in these pages: much of *The Gate of Angels*, set in Cambridge, seems to reflect Dilly's experiences there, from a bicycle accident to his loss of religious faith. As in Fitzgerald's fiction, a mere sentence can embody a universe of sadness: Dilly and his wife "loved each other for twenty years without being able to make each other happy." I particularly enjoyed the rare moments when Fitzgerald hints at a personal conviction behind a general truth: certain young people, criticizing Ronnie's affection for Lady Acton, "underestimated the amount of happiness necessary to someone of fifty." Speaking of Wilfred, she remarks, "A tenderness for the plants you have raised from seed and the earth you have turned over a thousand times seems one of the most allowable of earthly attachments."

There are a few blemishes, alas, in this charming book. Sherlockians, devoted as they are to the memory of Ronald Knox, will shudder when Fitzgerald wrongly refers to *The Sign of Four* when she means "The Five Orange Pips." There's an amusing typo, changing "underneath the window" to "underneath the widow." And did the *Times* crossword really spell the mahatma's name "Ghandi"?

If *The Knox Brothers* deserves a wide readership, *The Means of Escape* will interest mainly Fitzgerald completists. Most of the stories are generic fantasies: a *conte cruel* about an escaped convict and a young girl, a parable, a couple of ghost stories (one in the what-just-happened style of Robert Aickman, the other a modernized chiller about a forced retirement in the M. R. Jamesian mode); there's also an *Alfred Hitchcock Presents*-style suspense story, with a murderous final sentence, and a strange allegory about a music programmer visiting an old conductor on a Channel island. All of these read smoothly, even aphoristically: "Getting old is, of course, a crime of which we grow more guilty every day." However, several end in so low-keyed or mysterious a fashion one feels slightly cheated: we've had the experience but missed the meaning.

Barring a collection of letters or a diary, I suppose these are the last books we'll be seeing by Penelope Fitzgerald. Still, nine novels, a collection of stories, and three biographies (the other two are about the painter Edward Burne-Jones and the poet Charlotte Mew) make for just the right-sized oeuvre. Of course, Fitzgerald also shares a special gift with Turgenev and Jane Austen: her books, like theirs, can be read over and over, with ever-renewed delight.

October, 1, 2000

POSTSCRIPT: *The Afterlife*, a collection of Penelope Fitzgerald's essays and reviews, appeared in 2003, as did a two-volume collection of her fiction. Her reputation continues to grow. I feel honored to have once spoken with her on the phone.

COLLECTED TALES AND FANTASIES

By Lord Berners

The very title of Lord Berners's memoir of his early life, *First Childhood*, hints at the sly, compact wit that characterizes this multitalented English nobleman. Music lovers know Berners (1883–1950) as a playful, Satie-like composer— *The Triumph of Neptune* is probably his best-known ballet score—and fans of Nancy Mitford's novel *The Pursuit of Love* may remember that he provided the inspiration for the zany Lord Merlin. Recently, Mark Amory—editor of Evelyn Waugh's letters—brought out a well-received biography of this eccentric and attractive figure, but so far it hasn't acquired an American publisher. Perhaps Turtle Point can add it to its handsome Berners paperbacks, which include not only *First Childhood* but also the companion volume about Eton, *A Distant Prospect*, and—best of all—this omnibus collection of six short novels.

The artist Edward Gorey, an omnivorous reader of half-forgotten fiction, once chose Berners's *The Camel* (1936) as a neglected classic in a survey conducted by *Antaeus* magazine. This slender novel is probably a good test case to determine whether Berners's slightly fey, dry, and understated wit is to your liking. Just before dawn, as the Reverend Aloysius Hussey and his wife, Antonia, are asleep, they are awakened by a pounding at the door. To their surprise they discover a camel outside, and suspect that the animal must have escaped from some traveling circus. Soon Antonia grows attached to the creature and persuades her husband to let her keep it as a pet. What neither of them realizes is that the camel can understand English, and always tries to fulfill—surreptitiously—the wishes of its new mistress. This soon leads to misunderstandings and various disturbing incidents, some rather macabre. For example, Antonia's expressed yearning to see her dead pet dog just one more time results in the cadaver's reappearance on a silver serving platter during a dinner with the archbishop. Ultimately, matters take a tragic turn when the Reverend Hussey becomes convinced that his wife is carrying on with the church organist.

None of this on its own sounds particularly delightful. But one must imagine *The Camel* as roughly the novella equivalent to an Edward Gorey album, at once witty, slightly off-kilter, a bit camp, and perfectly pitched. To show what Berners can do, consider his capsule descriptions of various characters. The organist "Mr. Scrimgeour was a pale young man with weak knees and the expression of a tired fish." (the Reverend Hussey dislikes him, though there was "one good point that the Vicar was obliged to concede in Mr. Scrimgeour's favour. He took a great deal of trouble with the choir-boys.") The vastly rich Sir Solomon Bugle "preferred to live in London where, it was rumoured, he found plenty to keep him busy in the shape of a young lady whose acquaintance he had made at the Promenade of the Empire. Lady Bugle, who concealed beneath a majestic exterior a deeply sensitive nature, felt her husband's disaffection very keenly and whenever she had occasion to refer to him always spoke of him as though he were dead." Through some magic, this combination of deadpan prose, laced with mild Jamesian circumlocution, contrives to make *The Camel* a captivating work of light comedy.

In *Count Omega* (1941) Berners relates the disorienting adventures of a young composer who finds himself enamored of the gigantic but still magnetically alluring Gloria, the so-called ward of Count Omega, the "richest man in existence." With the help of the dressmaker Madame d'Arc—who believes she is the reincarnation of Jeanne d'Arc—Emmanuel manages to win Gloria's affection and to persuade the never-seen count to underwrite his long-projected symphony, *The Last Trump*. In it, Gloria will appear at the finale to sound a single note, of several minutes' duration, on her trombone. At the concert Berners describes the motley crowd in the entrance hall, including Gloria's duenna, who sports a gown specially designed by Madame d'Arc: "Her costume, as Madame d'Arc had said, was indeed a macabre caprice. Subtly, without actual definition, it suggested skeletons, tombstones and all the emblems of death. It gave her the appearance of a prison wardress lately arisen from the grave. A terrifying apparition that created a sensation in the crowd. On her face was a look of grim satisfaction with the consternation she was causing. . . . Prince Campo Santo, a diplomat suspected of necrophily, enquired eagerly of Mrs. Purdonium, 'Who is she? Do you know her?' Mrs. Purdonium, loth to admit her ignorance, moved away."

At such moments, one detects more than a soupçon of Ronald Firbank.

Still, my favorite of these novels is the last, *Far from the Madding War* (1941), a droll evocation of Oxford University life during the early years of World War II. The heroine, Emmeline Pocock, daughter of the warden of All Saints, "looked like a nymph in one of the less licentious pictures of Fragonard." This withdrawn young woman spends vast amounts of time alone, in a room sealed off from the hubbub outside. "Life," she says, "is so difficult to cope with that I find I can only do so by fortifying myself with long periods of respite from thought."

As it happens, though, Emmeline leads us to Mr. Jericho, a professor of the philosophy of history who is also a consummate gossip ("the most trivial, the most anodyne item of personal news was transformed by his exquisite artistry into a little masterpiece of psychological literature"); the romantic Mrs. Postlethwaite, who periodically "elopes" with unsuitable young men; Mrs. Trumper, whose "spartan temperament impelled her always to make herself uncomfortable and, incidentally, others as well"; and—an authorial self-portrait—Lord Fitzcricket, "always referred to by gossip-column writers as 'the versatile peer,' and indeed there was hardly a branch of art in which he had not at one time or other dabbled.... He had a collection of strange masks that he used to wear when motoring. He dyed his fantail pigeons all colors of the rainbow, so that they flew over the countryside causing bewilderment to neighboring farmers. He was always surrounded by odd animals and birds. When travelling on the Continent he had a small piano in his motor car, and on the strength of this he was likened in the popular press to Chopin and Mozart. Someone had even suggested a resemblance to Lord Byron, but for this he had neither the qualifications of being a poet nor a great lover."

Berners's novels are, then, subdued works of humor, soothing rather than hysterically funny, more Beerbohm or David Garnett (*Lady into Fox*) than Wodehouse. All of them seem to build, though, to some moment of bloody excess—murder, accidental death, and suicide bring the stories to a close. The other short novels in the *Collected Tales and Fantasies* include the *The Romance of a Nose* (1941, about Cleopatra), *Mr. Pidger* (1939, about a dog that ruins its owners' lives), and a youthful work, *Percy Wallingford* (1914, about a faultless English aristocrat). Like their companions, they are resolutely and perfectly minor, inconsequential, canonically unimportant—and extremely enjoyable.

As are those two memoirs, *First Childhood* and *A Distant Prospect*, which describe Berners's privileged background, his eccentric family (e.g., a half-mad grandfather confined to a darkened room and prey to alarming fits of cursing), and his life at Elmsley, one of those educational institutions presided over by an oily and sadistic headmaster and brightened by the shining presence of a beloved older classmate, the standard golden-boy athlete of English school memoirs. As he grows up, young Berners discovers some reliable pleasures—chiefly books and music—but his older self recalls only a few brief interludes of Wordsworthian joy: "Those who say that their childhood was the happiest period of their lives must, one suspects, have been the victims of perpetual misfortune in later years. For there is no reason to suppose that the period of childhood is inevitably happier than any other. The only thing for which children are to be envied is their exuberant vitality. This is apt to be mistaken for happiness. For true happiness, however, there must be a certain degree of experience. The ordinary pleasures of childhood are similar to those of a dog when it is given its dinner or taken out for a walk, a behaviouristic, tail-wagging business, and, as for childhood being care-free, I know from my own experience, that black care can sit behind us even on our rocking-horses."

That, I think, is a beautifully observed paragraph, and an indication that Lord Berners may have been a dilettante and a practical joker, but he was a wise man all the same.

June 20, 1999

CYRIL CONNOLLY: A LIFE

By Jeremy Lewis

There'll be no muted enthusiasm here—this is the most entertaining literary biography in years. And probably the funniest. Not only was Cyril Connolly (1903–1974) the leading English man of letters of his time, he was also a fat, moody, self-pitying, skirt-chasing bon vivant. "Lobsters he loved, and next to lobsters sex," observed the novelist Rose Macaulay; E. M. Forster complained that the Eton- and Oxford-educated critic actually "discredited pleasure." In *Who's Who* the sun-worshiping Connolly—who had an unfortunate penchant for flowery Hawaiian shirts—listed his hobby as simply "The Mediterranean," while elsewhere he proclaimed that his motto ought to be "Filez Sans Payer": Run off without paying. Unsurprisingly, this literary Artful Dodger died as he lived, with unfulfilled book contracts and over 27,000 pounds of debt ("Endless money worry, endless hack work, not a real writer but an unsuccessful businessman"). But Connolly also possessed a remarkable flair for friendship, and somehow somebody was always around to pick up the tab, whether at an expensive restaurant or a last stay in hospital. "Cyril," groused one loyal aristocratic chum, "is dying beyond my means."

A sponge, a lazy and unfaithful husband, an inveterate daydreamer, Cyril Connolly redeemed his buffoonery and sloth through brilliant writing. He could never manage that will-o'-the-wisp the Great Novel, but he displayed unrivaled virtuosity in the minor literary arts of parody, memoir, reviewing, and aphorism ("Whom the gods wish to destroy they first call promising"). Like most people, Jeremy Lewis tends to favor the earlier Connolly—the author of *Enemies of Promise* and that journal of a dark night of the soul *The Unquiet Grave*, as well as the satirist of "Where Engels Fears to Tread" and "Ninety Years of Novel Reviewing"—but the postwar book critic for the *Sunday Times* possesses an equal, if more discursive charm: a conversational, almost Horatian intimacy, the beguiling tones of a connoisseur of letters who is inviting you to share his memories and enthusiasms.

In truth, open any of Connolly's works—they tend to go in and out of print but can be found readily enough in used-book shops—and you will hear the same strikingly personal voice. It may be lyrical: "This is the time of year when wars break out, and a broken glass betrays the woodland to the vindictive sun." Or savagely funny: "Goosegrass or Cleavers," an imaginary first novel by a Miss Bumfiddle, "has genius, and not only is it a work of genius—of passionate intellectual sincerity and emotional directness—but it comes very near to being the best novel of the month, or at least the latter part of it." Not least, Connolly can be magnificently histrionic, as in this clarion call—from *Horizon*, the magazine he oversaw from 1939 to 1950—for a more serious wartime mentality: "We cannot afford the airy detachment of earlier numbers. We have walked through the tiger-house, speculating on the power and ferocity of the beasts, and looked up to find the cage doors open."

In all his writing Cyril Connolly explores, again and again, the ways artists create, or fail to create, masterpieces. He points out the snares of journalism and advertising, the sudden burn-out after youthful achievement, the distractions of marriage and family ("the pram in the hall"), the possible costs of government and personal patronage. These things matter. For Connolly, quite rightly, cannot imagine life without Watteau, Mozart, Flaubert (about whom he meant to write a book), Vergil, Montaigne, Congreve. "The human tragedy is almost unbearable but in the world of art, the kingdom of the page, we must acknowledge other standards. Here there is no tragedy except in the failure of great spirits to communicate their vision of the world before death or illness destroys them." Late in life, he lamented that the current generation was "coming to prefer the response induced by violent stimuli—film, radio, press—to the slow permeation of the personality by great literature." The slow permeation of the personality by great literature. What would such an elegiac temperament make of video games and MTV?

Jeremy Lewis forthrightly confesses to having written a book of almost Boswellian length and capaciousness. As with the *Life of Johnson*, this biography of a twentieth-century Cham of Literature bustles with flamboyant characters, for here are the famous and the raffish, grande dames and gold diggers. Connolly's best friend at St. Cyprian's school was Eric Blair, aka George Orwell (at age eleven, Orwell was already saying things like, "Of course, you realise, Connolly, that whoever wins the war, we shall emerge a second-rate nation"). At Eton or Oxford the future critic came to know the novelist Evelyn Waugh, the art historian Kenneth Clark, and such fastidious aesthetes as Brian Howard and Harold Acton—in short, all the "children of the sun." After Balliol (and a poor showing on his exams), Connolly took up a post as secretary apprentice to Logan Pearsall Smith, best known for his highly burnished maxims and mini-essays, *Trivia*. For Desmond MacCarthy—the affable and much loved Bloomsbury critic—the young man of letters composed his first book reviews in the late 1920s. At about the same time he was roaming around Europe, meeting Joyce, Hemingway, Bernard Berenson, and even Arthur Evans, hard at work excavating Knossos.

Still, these notables pale before some of the more glittering sexual adventurers that flash across these pages. Connolly's first wife, Jean, grew particularly close to the notorious Denham Fouts, called by Christopher Isherwood "the most expensive male prostitute in the world" (he died of a heroin overdose while sitting on the toilet). The biographer Peter Quennell, an exquisite, sometimes overexquisite prose stylist, actually published a book of poems at fifteen but then was expelled from Oxford for having an affair with a married woman; every time he appears, this dapper *coureur de femmes* sports a new and more beautiful wife or mistress on his arm. Quennell tells the story of the loyal *Horizon* assistant Sonia Brownell—she later married George Orwell on his deathbed—actually being chased into a pond by a drunken friend of Connolly's and then telling her rescuer, "It isn't his trying to rape me that I mind, but that he doesn't seem to realise what Cyril stands for." At times the sexual daisy chains can grow quite complex: Anne Dunn was the mistress of the painter Lucian Freud, who was at the time married to the novelist Caroline Blackwood, whom Connolly tried to seduce, and who subsequently married Robert Lowell. The *London Magazine* editor Alan Ross slept with both Connolly's second wife and his third—Barbara Skelton after she divorced Connolly and Deirdre Craven before she married him.

Of all these attendant figures the most electrifying is the free-spirited Barbara Skelton. Skeltie was, in Lewis's awed words, "a pantherine femme fatale with a sinuous body, tawny skin, golden hair, high cheekbones under lynx-like eyes, and a manner that was unnervingly both humorous and malicious, taunting and farouche." Though only glancing at her "raffish, turbulent and seemingly insatiable amorous career," Lewis does mention love affairs or marriages with the artist Feliks Topolski, Peter Quennell, King Farouk of Egypt, the millionaire publisher George Weidenfeld (Connolly discovers them in flagrante, "her dress pulled up over her shoulders"), the cartoonist Charles Addams, and the *New York Review of Books* editor Robert Silvers. Connolly fans have long cherished Skelton's memoir *Tears before Bedtime*, if only for her unsparing pen portrait of the *Sunday Times* book reviewer, lying in bed, utterly depressed, sucking on his blanket and murmuring to himself, "Poor Cyril, poor Cyril."

Over the years admirers have read Cyril Connolly's books again and again, partly because of their congenial wistfulness but also in the hopes of learning the secret of his lyrical yet aphoristic prose: "It is closing-time in the gardens of the West. . . ." "Life is a maze in which we take the wrong turning before we have learnt to walk." "As with Leopardi's peasants, the eve of the festival will always bring me more happiness than the Feast itself." In volumes like *Enemies of Promise* and *The Condemned Playground* (a collection of pieces from the 1930s that Philip Larkin called his "sacred book"), Connolly obviously transmuted into seductive art many of the life experiences that Jeremy Lewis shows to have been tawdry, petty, even reprehensible. A good biography, I suppose, can simultaneously cheapen and enrich its subject.

After this one, even more than after Clive Fisher's excellent but much shorter 1995 life, Connolly will never again be simply the regretful Palinurus of *The Unquiet Grave* or the precocious Eton schoolboy of "A Georgian Boyhood." He will also be the wild Irish lad "Tim" Connolly, running through the woods carrying an assegai, as well as "Mr. Smartiboots" (Waugh and Nancy Mitford), "that awful pimp Connolly" (Virginia Woolf), the Supreme Commander (Kenneth Tynan, like him in so many ways), and Pops (Barbara Skelton). I wish that this elegist and Epicurean had proved a more admirable human being, but *Cyril Connolly: A Life* ultimately reinforces Edmund Wilson's view of his opposite number as "a queer mixture of lordly courtesy with boorishness and infantilism." He was, in short, as much a Falstaff as a failed Flaubert, not only a man of letters but a Lord of Misrule.

Still, Connolly's books and essays remain, their magic intact, increased knowledge leading to deeper appreciation. Just as important, though, Jeremy Lewis has produced a biography that is also an anecdotal history of the Anglo-European literary/bohemian scene from the 1920s to the 1970s—even his footnotes will send you looking for items such as James Lees-Milne's *Another Self*, "possibly the funniest autobiography ever written." Lewis himself writes briskly, with infectious pleasure and a nice sense of comic timing: if ever a biography was a page-turner, this is it.

Even Connolly's funeral rouses an appropriately vibrant ghost: "It was a wet and windy day, and the church was crammed with mourners. . . . [A]t one point the porch door was flung open with dramatic effect and Duncan Grant—whose lurid murals are, perhaps, the best known feature of Berwick Church—staggered in, clad in an astrakhan hat, a duffle coat and bright red trousers." I'm sure Connolly would have smiled, as we do, at the brilliant entrance of the nearly ninety-year-old painter, among the very last survivors of Bloomsbury.

September 13, 1998

POSTSCRIPT: Over the years I've written a half dozen pieces about Cyril Connolly. To me he represents a last flowering of what one might call the critic as hedonist, seeking in literature both pleasure and consolation. I still reread *The Unquiet Grave* every year or two and, even though I recognize its occasional sentimentality and period flavor, continue to find it a mirror to my own heart.

THE LETTERS OF NANCY MITFORD

AND EVELYN WAUGH

Edited by Charlotte Mosley

The Letters of Nancy Mitford and Evelyn Waugh is quite simply the most amusing correspondence of our time. Strong readers will portion out the book in small servings so that it lasts for weeks and weeks; others—frail, fallen creatures like myself—will sybaritically gobble up these 500 pages, heedless of measure and propriety, forgetful of all but their own selfish pleasure. If they read any books on the island of the Lotos Eaters, this is bound to be one of them.

Here, for instance, is Evelyn Waugh (1903–1966), arguably the century's wittiest writer, describing a night on the town in 1946: "My little trip to London passed in a sort of mist. Did I ever come to visit you again after my first sober afternoon? . . . On the last evening I dimly remember a dinner party of cosmopolitan ladies where I think I must have been conspicuous. Were you there? I awoke with blood on my hands but found to my intense relief that it was my own. I sometimes think I am getting too old for this kind of thing."

And here is the slyly teasing Nancy Mitford (1904–1973), supposedly quoting her French lover on Waugh's acid satire *The Loved One*: "The Colonel says it's wonderful how you have brought out the best in American civilization."

Writes Waugh, "My daughter Teresa (age 11) has come back from school with a glowing report by her French mistress. . . . I asked her to name in French any six objects in the dining-room. After distressed thought she got five, four of them with wrong genders. I know of another girl who came back from another school with a special medal for swimming—a thing like the Garter with a great sash. Her parents put her in the pool and she sank like a stone."

Observes Mitford (who lives mainly in Paris), "Of course French children are different—somebody once said to me a French boy of 14 has a heavy moustache, 2 mistresses & a hoop."

Waugh: "I have been reading Proust for the first time—in English of course—and am surprised to find him a mental defective. No one warned me of that. He has absolutely no sense of time. . . ."

Mitford: "What to me is odd about Randolph [Churchill, who had lost a parliamentary election] is why he should think that anybody would ever vote for him? A man you wouldn't trust to post a letter for you—it makes no sense."

And on it goes for page after glorious page. Yet not only are the letters in this collection blissikins—to use a Mitford expression—but so are Charlotte Mosley's explanatory footnotes, invaluable for identifying members of the Brideshead generation and their numerous offspring. Here are a couple from page 205: "Hon. Pamela Mitford (1907–94). The least well-known Mitford sister. An expert on rural matters, especially rare breeds of poultry. Married to Derek Jackson, millionaire physicist and Grand National Rider, 1936–51"; and "Eugenie Sellers (1860–1943). An English classical archaeologist who lived in Rome. At the beginning of the century she was obliged to lecture from behind a screen because her beauty was so sublime that it distracted the students. . . ." Mosley could teach a graduate course on the art of the footnote.

To many Evelyn Waugh calls to mind a modern Samuel Johnson—moody, endlessly quotable, deeply religious, politically conservative, the center of a circle of brilliant, eccentric friends. But Nancy Mitford points out an equally apt comparison to Voltaire; *Decline and Fall* and *Vile Bodies* are as sparkling as *Candide* and *Micromégas*. Like the French *philosophe*, Waugh wrote a dry, delicious prose of utter clarity, relying on outrageous understatement and subtle, deadpan exaggeration to tease his friends and scourge the ever-growing legion of his enemies. Mitford succinctly defines her friend's writing talent as "your well known knack of one tap on the nail & in it goes, whereas the rest of us hammer & pound for hours." The aged, senile author Hilaire Belloc, notes Waugh, possesses "a noble look still, like an ancient fisherman in a French film." Tap and in it goes.

Not surprisingly, these letters allow Waugh to indulge fully his taste for grotesquerie. The novelist Henry Green arrives for a weekend: "Here in the country he looked GHASTLY. Very long black dirty hair, one brown tooth, pallid puffy face, trembling hands, stone deaf, smoking continuously throughout meals, picking up books in the middle of conversation & falling into maniac giggles, drinking a lot of raw spirits. . . ." (*Mon semblable, mon frère*: Except for the hair, the author of *The Ordeal of Gilbert Pinfold* could be describing himself.) Waugh visits Deborah Mitford, Nancy's sister: "I went to her slum & found her door surrounded by unemptied dustbins, dead flowers & empty bottles; all windows shut; a telephone ringing unanswered upstairs—plainly the scene of a sex-murder so I went away. . . ."

Frequent financial woes elicit this mock self-pity: "I am being sued for

3000 dollars which an American editor once gave me for a story I never wrote. There is no legal means of repaying him, as I willingly would, so I must go to prison soon. I shall write to Lady Mosley for advice about what to take."

The oblique humor of that last sentence requires a footnote: "Sir Oswald and Lady Mosley were interned in Holloway Prison during the war." Sir Oswald Mosley was the charismatic leader of England's fascist Black Shirts; Lady Mosley is Nancy Mitford's sister Diana (and editor Charlotte's mother-in-law). The slum-dweller Debo, the prettiest of the girls, eventually married Andrew Cavendish, who in due course became the duke of Devonshire, owner of the vast ancestral estate Chatsworth. Yet another Mitford, Jessica (known as Decca), joined the Communist Party, emigrated to America, and grew famous for her exposé of funeral homes, *The American Way of Death*. These three sisters flit in and out of the Waugh/Mitford correspondence. Yet another sister, Unity, fell in love with Hitler, shot herself, and died in 1948; brother Tom was killed during the war in Burma; and, as we know, Pam the poultry fancier was living quietly with her millionaire physicist husband—at least until he divorced her, remarried, and then ran off with his new wife's half sister, Angela Culme-Seymour, who . . . but one must stop somewhere. Clearly the Mitfords never lacked for dash and glamour.

There have been several memoirs and biographies of the clan, but for most readers the best introduction to Nancy Mitford's world remains her first novel about the "Radletts," *The Pursuit of Love* (1945). Waugh suggested the title, and Mitford eagerly turned to the established master for writing advice, though she soon recognized that her own talent was for a particular breeziness, what Harold Acton called "feline humor and lightness of touch": "My Uncle Matthew had four magnificent bloodhounds, with which he used to hunt his children." Based on Mitford's outdoors-loving father, Uncle Matthew grouses his way to comic immortality: "My dear Lady Kroesig, I have only read one book in my life, and that is *White Fang*. It's so frightfully good I've never bothered to read another." The sad ending aside, *The Pursuit of Love* remains an almost perfect light novel; little wonder that it sold 200,000 copies in six months and helped turn Nancy Mitford into a full-time writer.

Along with plentiful gossip about famous friends (Pamela Harriman, at that time Pam Churchill, is drooled over as "a very tasty morsel"), arguments about religion and politics, and complaints about health problems (Mitford's eyes, Waugh's misanthropy), the joys and financial agonies of the freelance literary life resound loudest through these pages. EW: "All my most valued books have been eaten by tiny spiders"; "No complaints about headaches. Revision is just as important as any other part of writing and must be done *con amore*";

"all Art is the art of pleasing"; "Jim Wedderburn has revived the Viscountcy of Dudhope (if we had invented that name customers would complain)." Both correspondents are avid readers, constantly recommending new authors and novels to each other: Muriel Spark's *Memento Mori*, Angus Wilson's *Hemlock and After*, P. H. Newby's *The Picnic at Sakkara*, Lampedusa's *The Leopard*, and—their most enthusiastic discovery—Sybille Bedford's *A Legacy*. Waugh also admires *Pale Fire*, though it's "too clever by half," and passes along this anecdote about Nabokov's other famous title: "The Turkish Ambassador said of *Lolita* (an indecent book that is enjoying a vogue in America) 'I don't like reading about such things. I prefer to see them.' " But, of course. Later, when Mitford inaugurates a craze over words that are U (upper-class) and non-U, Waugh complains that "the entire Burmese cabinet have adopted this damnable prefix." One needs to remember U Thant.

Toward the end of this book, the comedy inevitably darkens. Neither writer finds much to approve about an increasingly Americanized world. Waugh insures his life and hopes his airplane to Africa will blow up—"much the best thing for my poor children." He grows increasingly irritable, brutish, despondent. Just before his sudden, welcome death at sixty-two (on Easter, just after mass), he laments, "The state of my memory is such that I might never have lived at all." Some years earlier, on All Saints' Day, Mitford already writes, "We must think of Robert [Byron] and Tom [Mitford] today—those are the ones I miss the most. It will be nice to see them again, rather soon now." In 1969, after months of agony, she is operated on for a malignant liver tumour; the cancer nonetheless spreads to her spine; and this delightful woman passes the rest of her life in excruciating pain, which she endures "with characteristic courage and lack of self-pity." As a final insult, her much loved Palewski abandons her to marry another woman.

Yet even if she had foreseen these grim final years, I doubt that Nancy Mitford would have altered by a whit her optimistic, sensual outlook on life. Of her biography of Madame de Pompadour, she says "if my book has a message or meaning it is to proclaim the value of pleasure." Elsewhere she exults, with perfect seriousness, "The day one sets foot in France, you can take it from me, PURE happiness begins. . . . Of course I know it's partly that dear dear Colonel, but I don't see him all the time by any means & every minute of every day here is bliss & when I wake up in the morning I feel as excited as if it were my birthday."

By contrast, an incredulous Waugh once received a "letter from a group of American school girls asking me the Secret of Happiness. Me. I wrote back sharply that they were not meant to be happy but if they thought they were, you were the one to consult." Waugh's own dour views on life are more aptly summed up in this typical *cri de coeur*: "How I dread Christmas. The operating theatre & nursing home will come as a welcome treat after it."

The morose, blimpish Catholic Waugh, the cheerful, teasing Francophile Mitford—an odd couple but a pair of brilliantly funny correspondents. Just now this collection of their letters looks like the most entertaining book of the season.

April 13, 1997

BRUCE CHATWIN:

A BIOGRAPHY

By Nicholas Shakespeare

Stately, plump Cyril Connolly didn't much care for Bruce Chatwin. How could he?

Here was this blond, blue-eyed schoolboy—until the last few years of his life, Chatwin never looked more than thirty-five—who was not only good-looking; he was *Vanity Fair* gorgeous. You didn't even need to read the man's novels and collections of essays to hate him: one glance at his jacket photo would be enough. It just wasn't fair. How could anybody look this sexy in a khaki shirt or loden coat, so absolutely perfect, and at the same time be able to produce one of the most widely admired and imitated books of our time, *In Patagonia* (1977)?

It was, as usual, a matter of style. In the second of that travel classic's ninety-seven mosaic-like sections, Chatwin describes Argentina's capital: "The history of Buenos Aires is written in its telephone directory. Pompey Romanov, Emilio Rommel, Crespina D. Z. de Rose, Ladislo Radziwill, and Elizabeta Marta Callman de Rothschild—five names taken at random from among the R's—told a story of exile, disillusion and anxiety behind lace curtains." Such factual, mildly witty, two-sentence paragraphs—and *In Patagonia* is made of them—recall odd-shaped pebbles plucked up, one after another, from a cold mountain stream. There's nothing obviously flashy about them but, flecked with muted color, they feel smooth, solid, worth paying attention to.

Born in 1940, Bruce Chatwin may have been the last important writer in English brave enough to model his prose after Hemingway's. "By day the city quivered in a silvery film of pollution. In the evenings boys and girls walked beside the river. They were hard and sleek and empty-headed, and they walked arm in arm under the trees, laughing cold laughter, separated from the red river by a red granite balustrade." Such a style can easily lead to a kind of mannered starkness, and sometimes, as in *The Viceroy of Ouidah* (1980), his novel about Dahomey, Chatwin can sound sententious. But at his best and most alert, he is a consummate storyteller: "In Alice Springs—a grid of scorching streets where men in long white socks were forever getting in and out of Land Cruisers—I met a Russian who was mapping the sacred sites of the Aboriginals." Who would not stay to hear more about that Russian and his work?

Throughout this fine, if overlong, biography of Chatwin, notables as various as the travel writer Patrick Leigh Fermor, critic Susan Sontag, filmmakers Werner Herzog and James Ivory, memoirist Gregor von Rezzori, painter Howard Hodgkin, and novelists Sybille Bedford, Salman Rushdie, and Martin Amis stress that their friend was at his most dazzling in his conversation. This tow-headed faun possessed a talent not merely to amuse but to enchant. He paid for his room and board in Greece, Italy, and Manhattan by telling tales, some of which might be true, but not necessarily. Nicholas Shakespeare makes plain that all the major books, even though based on actual figures and places, are fictionalized, reimagined to make the best possible story, spruced up, Bruced up.

Many readers—myself included—were appalled to learn that *The Songlines* (1987) wasn't exactly an accurate, under-oath account of a visit to Australia. In fact, Chatwin fudged the facts whenever it made for a better narrative. Oh well. Rather than truth and fiction, Chatwin's constant artistic poles were his stripped-down yet dandyish style on the one hand and his philosophical and personal obsession with nomadism on the other. Above all else, he wanted to understand human restlessness. Wanderers, he once wrote, "allow themselves to be bowled along by the beauty and variety of the world."

Certainly, Chatwin's own life is marked by considerable beauty and even more variety. Its general outline is by now familiar to most of his fans, whether from his own testimony or from recollections by friends (see, in particular, his editor Susannah Clapp's superb memoir, *With Chatwin*: anybody not positively obsessed with "Bruce" will prefer its shapely account to Shakespeare's exhaustive dossier). The son of middle-class parents, an unexceptional student at Eton, young Bruce takes a job as a porter at Sotheby's auction house. There he learns that he possesses an "eye" for art and antiquities; rises quickly to become a director of the firm, with particular responsibility for Impressionist paintings; and then, at twenty-four, gets up one morning to discover that he is, temporarily, blind. Stress, says his doctor. Take longer views. There follow journeys to Africa, the Middle East, Central Asia.

Eventually, Chatwin abandons the art world to spend three years in Edinburgh studying archaeology, at which he excels in theory rather than in practice. This he chucks to accept a position as a staffer for the *Sunday Times* (of London) magazine, where he interviews André Malraux (an obvious role model), the German novelist Ernst Jünger, the fashion designer Madeleine Vionnet, Indira Gandhi. Then without warning, and here legend and biography roughly coincide, Chatwin lights out for Patagonia, intending to explore this tip of South America largely because he has been obsessed since childhood with a piece of brontosaurus skin sent home by his uncle Charley. (It turns out to be a bit of giant sloth.)

With the eventual publication of *In Patagonia*, Chatwin awoke, like Byron, to find himself famous. And increasingly restless, in every way. During his life he gradually visited six continents, had sex with African women and Australian men, sponged off rich friends, hung out with the photographer Robert Mapplethorpe's S&M crowd, read widely, and absorbed impressive amounts of unusual information: about human origins, Meissen porcelain, slave trading, the Greek Orthodox Church (which he joined just before his death), aboriginal art, and much else.

From the start, though, Chatwin was notorious for his name-dropping, for casual condescension, for the Shaker austerity of his rooms, and for never, ever picking up a dirty dish, let alone washing one. Throughout his gypsy years, he also stayed married to his American wife, Elizabeth, a paragon of understanding, patience, and devotion. In fact, many friends believe that Chatwin could cultivate a stripped-down nomad persona only because he knew that Elizabeth was back home in a proper English cottage whenever he needed her or it. Never publicly admitting that he had AIDS, Chatwin succumbed to the disease in 1989 at age forty-eight, just after completing *Utz* (1988), a short novel about an East European porcelain fanatic who discovers that love is more important than his Meissen collection or Czech politics.

If one can set aside the horror of his last years, it's nearly impossible not to envy Bruce Chatwin. He was a golden boy in just about everything that matters: art, scholarship, sex, friendship, writing. At times, he may strike some readers of this biography as a flake and poseur—he just had to buy special moleskin notebooks from a certain little shop in Paris, he could write only with a Montblanc, he couldn't pass a mirror without looking for crow's feet—and yet the testimony of his numerous friends is affectionate and sincere. Chatwin was obviously one of those galvanizing people who charge everything they do with magic. Dust-jacket photos don't always lie.

Sigh. Were he alive today the author of *In Patagonia* would be nearly sixty. Impossible to imagine. He seems the Jim Morrison of writing, living hard, dying young, and then growing positively mythic.

Nicholas Shakespeare's prose isn't particularly elegant, and he tends to tell us more than we want to know about everyone Chatwin meets, but his story never flags. There's plenty of gossip, a sensible presentation of the ideas about nomadism and human aggression, and no hesitation to point out the writer's flaws, mistakes, and prevarications. If you're a die-hard Chatwin fan—and his books inspire cultishness—you'll want to read every one of these 600 pages. Still, be warned: it will be difficult to worship quite as fervently at the cult of Bruce once you see how petty and petulant he could be. As even his wife, Elizabeth, once wrote, after an estrangement, "It's too bad really, but it's been a nice few years for him and as usual he had most things his own way."

February 13, 2000

THE DIARIES OF KENNETH TYNAN

Edited by John Lahr

Kenneth Tynan? One imagines many educated readers today murmuring "Tynan, Tynan," then confessing—like Pontius Pilate in Anatole France's short story, when queried late in life about Jesus Christ—"I cannot call him to mind." But ask anyone involved with the performing arts, and the name Kenneth Tynan will provoke sighs of admiration, caesuras of pure awe.

In the early and mid 1950s this young Oxford dandy made himself into the most formidable and witty drama reviewer in England. Later, he helped found England's National Theatre, devised the notorious erotic revue *Oh! Calcutta!* and then gradually smoked and drank his way to an early death at fifty-three, of emphysema. But in the course of a meteoric (here the adjective seems exact) career, Tynan managed to meet the most interesting "show people" in the world, and to write brilliant profiles of many of them. These included Miles Davis, Greta Garbo, C. S. Lewis (his tutor at Oxford), Humphrey Bogart, Tom Stoppard, Marlene Dietrich (virtual matron of honor at his second wedding), Mel Brooks, John Gielgud, James Thurber, Groucho Marx, Bertolt Brecht, and, not least, the silent film legend Louise Brooks: "The only star actress I can imagine either being enslaved by or wanting to enslave; and a dark lady worthy of any poet's devotion." A short life, then, and on the surface it would seem a glorious one, like Achilles'. After all, to have been recognized as the most brilliant theater critic since Bernard Shaw, to have enjoyed the friendship of the glittering and the gifted, to have helped shape the artistic culture of one's time—surely here is an earthly span of richness and fulfillment?

Not a bit. These diaries—which follow a monumental collection of letters a couple of years back, and a biography by his wife Kathleen Tynan a decade earlier—reveal a man of deep frustration, unhappiness, and anxiety. For the most part, the entries cover the 1970s—the years in which Tynan floundered after his early successes—and they memorialize the follies and dreams of a desperate man.

First, Tynan loses his job at the National Theatre when Laurence Olivier steps down as its director; then he can't quite nail down sufficient backing for an experimental erotic film; neither can he finish his study of the rogue psychologist Wilhelm Reich. Meanwhile, his debts mount and his health declines. Yet he continues to whirl through life with stylish abandon: leasing a Jaguar he can ill afford, maintaining a cook and nanny for his children, traveling and dining first-class, attending fancy parties with the assiduity of an Andy Warhol or a Truman Capote. In quieter moments he takes notes on his reading (Ronald Firbank, *This Side of Paradise*, a biography of Evelyn Waugh, Brecht's poetry), records his dreams, makes up puns, humorous poems and imaginary dialogues, recalls the women he's made love to. He also regularly visits a sweet young thing named Nicole for a little sadomasochistic sex, chiefly spanking and caning.

So given such a regret-laden, heartsick chronicle, why should anyone bother reading these sometimes bitter, even self-pitying diaries? Because they are, like the dazzling Tynan himself, quite irresistible. On October 10, 1971, our man attends a "writer's conference" sponsored by *Playboy* and there sights a famous guru of that era: "My favourite guest is the English-born philosopher Alan Watts, who has gone native for the past two decades in California, where he writes about Zen and the hippie life. Wearing a purple smock and sporting an out-thrust grey beard, Watts wanders through the conference inexplicably laughing to himself—whether because LSD and other drugs have conferred on him euphoria or brain damage it is hard to say. Turning a corner in the hotel, one sees him walking alone down an empty corridor, shaking with laughter. During the banquets at night, he grows restless and after the soup rises to his feet and passes among the other guests, pausing here and there to rest a kindly hand on people's shoulders and, bending down, to bestow on them some of his vast store of excess chuckle, which seems to come from inside him, like distant Sydney Greenstreet. He seldom speaks."

A week afterward, Tynan is back in England, enjoying "a late evening with the British journalistic intelligentsia, Anthony Sampson, Karl Miller, John Gross, David Caute etc., in their blue suits with their defensive, hedging, qualifying manner, as if all were in fear of being blackballed from some nameless club of which all aspired to be members. . . . I can talk about not writing with more passion than they talk about writing. They look about as vivacious as a group portrait of the Bulgarian chess team." That said, Tynan suffers no consequent illusions about his own freelance work: "I am perfectly aware that the function of a journalist is to draw readers' attention to the ads, and that when writing for *The New Yorker* (for instance) my primary duty is to sell vodka."

Such deft observations abound in these diaries. "Any actress with a deep voice is always hailed by male critics for her wit, shrewdness, intellectuality—simply because she sounds like a man. Example, Bacall, Kate Hepburn, Marlene—all of them nice women but by no stretch of the imagination mental giants." Reflecting on movies of the 1930s, he declares, "With the passage of time, the eternal things about them peel away, and only the basic trivialities remain to enchant us." He eventually formulates Tynan's Law of Responsible Cinema: "all films that seek seriously to diagnose the Contemporary Human Predicament are bad."

Even when writing primarily for himself, Tynan sees the world with the eyes of an ace reporter. He glimpses a White Russian actress "called Marie Britneva, attractive in a wild sharp-tooth way, like a very dashing stoat." When the director Michelangelo Antonioni arrives at a dinner party, he "turned up in a dark business suit looking grave and stricken, rather like Paul Lukas as a decent liberal in an anti-Nazi film." Hardly a page goes by without provoking a smile, at the very least: "Advice to anyone who would like to win the Grand National: buy and train carefully at Newmarket one of the wild horses that would not drag me to read Doris Lessing's new novel." Never shying from the tasteless, Tynan blithely imagines a British bomber crew's glee at the firebombing of Dresden: "Art gallery's bought it, sir, or I'm a Dutchman. I don't think Jerry'll be gloating over his ruddy Cranachs tomorrow morning."

And so the pages roll merrily along, though one slowly feels the deepening anomie. "I used to have a sign by my desk: 'Be light, stinging, insolent and melancholy.' But I am no longer any of these things, except melancholy." Tynan remembers pleading with a therapist to "please lighten the burden of guilt that now makes it impossible for me to leave my wife." He lists the celebrated lovers his second wife has taken during the past four years of their marriage. In California, where he lives while working on a series of *New Yorker* profiles (later collected in *Show People*), he grows ever more frail:

"Read a magazine quiz, compiled by experts on geriatric subjects, which purports to predict your life expectancy on the basis of your answers to questions about habits and general way of life. I answer with scrupulous accuracy and discover that I shall be dead in May."

When, one afternoon, Tynan detects a yellow discharge from his penis, he ruefully notes: "Bankruptcy, emphysema, paralysis of the will—and now this! Feel that God is making his point with rather vulgar overstatement." Eventually, the diarist finds himself in Puerto Vallarta, with debts in excess of $75,000 and his hands shaking so much he can barely write. For a while he amuses himself by imagining the ideal dinner party guests—Byron, Wilde, Shakespeare, Goya—but before long he is carefully choosing the music for his memorial service: "slow movement from Mozart's Clarinet Quintet, Adagio from Viviani's Second Sonata for Trumpet and Organ, The Beatles's 'A Hard Day's Night.' " Later he adds Dave Brubeck/Paul Desmond's "Take Five."

Still, even when he is truly dying, Kenneth Tynan never surrenders his passion for the theater—and for the theatrical: "2 December. Entranced by TV appearance of the eighty-nine year-old playwright Ben Travers. Very joyful old gentleman. He says that for him the hub of Edwardian London was the gents' lavatory in Leicester Square. He remembers it as entirely made of marble, with a plate-glass tank above each urinal. In every tank swam twenty goldfish. When the flush was released, the water-level would sink to a couple of inches. 'The fish would huddle together with consternation written all over their faces.' But then, as the tank refilled, 'You could see their relief—life was beginning again.' Travers says: 'I often think—isn't that a perfect image of human life as a whole? Disaster's about to strike, and then life goes on, and we all breathe again.' "

Breathing is, of course, just what people cannot do when suffering from advanced emphysema. Kenneth Tynan died in 1980.

But his writing lives on—or so one is supposed to say. But *Curtains, Show People*, and most of his other titles are out of print. Which is our loss. Few journalists can turn out such wickedly pleasurable sentences, and few critics can make you see the good and the bad in a performance you hadn't even attended. Oh well. Tynan's books will become available again someday. In the meanwhile, treat yourself to the diaries of this dashing, perverse, and stoical hedonist.

December 9, 2001

THE LETTERS OF KINGSLEY AMIS

Edited by Zachary Leader

Talk about one fat Englishman. This must be the most substantial single-volume collection of letters in publishing history: 1,212 pages. Not since the glory days of *The Stand* or even *The Rise and Fall of the Third Reich* has there been such an impressive brick of a book. One could pave courtyards with it, or build prison walls, or even heave it through the Garrick Club windows, come the revolution.

By comparison, the letters of Evelyn Waugh max out at 664 pages. Those of the poet Philip Larkin—Kingsley Amis's best friend and most frequent correspondent—halt at a paltry 791. Mere pikers, the two of them. But the author of the comic classic *Lucky Jim* and the Booker Prize–winner *The Old Devils* as well as a score of other novels proffers nearly twice as many pages of bawdry, comedy, outrageous opinion, and verbal histrionics. At less than three and a half cents a page, the book is also good value for money, not to mention a joy forever—provided you are, as they say, comfortable with a certain naughty laddishness.

Like what, you ask? In their Oxford days, Amis and Larkin tease each other with fantasies about lesbian schoolgirls (episodes in an ongoing collaborative story called "I Would Do Anything for You"), mail each other girlie pinups, compulsively distort names or spellings (the painter Pickarso; "the frigger in the cowpat"—Henry James's "the figure in the carpet"; WIRTE SNOO), and generally end their letters with the word "bum" attached to some trendy catchphrase: "You have to make up your mind whether you want me or bum. . . . Amis's world lacks among other things the inner dimension of bum. . . . Between Mr. Scott and myself there has never been the slightest question of bum." With his other close friend, the Sovietologist Robert Conquest, Amis trades conservative political opinions and dirty limericks (Conquest's—printed in footnotes—are unquotably brilliant). Throughout the correspondence with these friends, Amis swings between Benny Hill–like leers and a bluff, seriocomic literary Blimpishness: "I hope the Tatler asked you for your views on [Ronald] Firbank. I told them he summed up all the crappy things about novels that Saul Bellow left unsummed-up, though I didn't put it as elegantly as that. . . . By the way, could you reassure me about something? Ted Hughes is as ABSOLUTELY DEVOID OF ANY KIND OF MERIT WHATSOEVER as his late wife [Sylvia Plath] was, isn't he? I mean he is, isn't he? . . . Hey, and how does he mean, Ted? What does he blow? Mm? . . . P.S. Enclosed is by Seamus Heaney. Just a sample; there are 5 and one half more pages of it. . . . One doesn't just think, what blinding crap, but even more, what vociferously insincere ego-maniacal crap."

Many readers, like myself, will judge Amis dead wrong about all four of these writers yet still enjoy hearing the spluttering bile. For Amis hated any writing that seemed to him pretentious or overtly literary—and he mocks it repeatedly. Instead, he champions detective stories (especially the locked-room puzzles of John Dickson Carr) and science fiction, delivering a series of lectures on the genre at Princeton (later published as *New Maps of Hell*). His admiration for Ian Fleming leads to *The James Bond Dossier* and a novel about 007 (*Colonel Sun*). In later years, he can hardly read anything but the thrillers of Dick Francis and the Flashman adventures of George Macdonald Fraser.

But if you can forgive, allow for, or even approve much high-spirited incorrectness (political, sexual, and cultural) and put up with some tedious jazz-collecting talk in the early years, *The Letters of Kingsley Amis* offers wicked, wicked reading pleasure. And lots of it. I particularly relish Amis's mimicry, as here when he hits off a certain artsy, upper-class diction: "We thought we'd lay on a bit of a show for you since you don't come to London all that often. A cocktail party at about 5:30 with some of your admirers—George Steiner, Ian Hamilton, Arnold Wesker; Alvarez of course, and I hope A. L. Rowse, though I haven't heard from him yet. Then I've booked seats at Equus, which is really the most exciting thing to hit the stage for years, and after that a place I know with a marvellous group of young West Indiaaaaaaeeeeeoooghghggh."

That strangled gasp—frequently encountered in these pages—works as the verbal analogue to Jim Dixon's face making in *Lucky Jim*. As it happens, just as that novel comes out, Amis receives an unsolicited invitation to lunch with Anthony Powell, one of the eminences of modern English fiction. The young author fantasizes to Larkin: "I can imagine myself saying in fifteen years' time . . ." 'Yes, of course, that novel of mine was a pretty fair success. The first of the two, I mean.'—Oh really? 'Yes, I got to know Anthony Powell round about that time, I remember.'—Anthony Powell? 'Yes, the novelist. Died a couple of years ago.'—Oh yes. 'And I can remember him saying to me, Kingsley, you're the one we all look to to keep the English novel going when we go. Seems funny now, doesn't it?'—Yes, well I really must be going now Mr. Amis thank you for a most interesting would you mind letting go of my skirt please before I . . ."

These letters range from Kingsley Amis's undergraduate days till his death, and, despite the humor and verbal antics, they sometimes make for chastening reading. In a biography or memoir, a life is filtered through an authorial consciousness—and is thus toned down, made to fit an ongoing pattern, surveyed with a certain Olympian air. But letters are different. Here any experience feels immediate, more raw than cooked. Yes, a correspondence does encourage self-dramatization, but with close friends it also permits a distinctive immediacy and candor. Amis's early letters to Elizabeth Jane Howard, who became his second wife, ache with love and yearning and recollections of "sexual ecstasy" in room 238 of some hotel. But this happiness is short-lived, the marriage tense, then unhappy, finally hateful. Invariably, Amis and his pals turn to alcohol for solace, and in later life pay the price: "I am on my NAP (New Alcoholic Policy) again, 4–5 drinks a day, which means I can eat, sign my name at any time and follow films on TV at night. Just a few nightmares thrown in. . . . Of course it's not the booze you miss, you know. Not the booze as such. No no it's getting drunk and being drunk and going on being drunk and getting drunk again."

The final letters take up the misfortunes and indignities of age: "Barium enemas, Christ. . . . My own little bits of that have made me wonder why nobody tells you there are parts of life INCLUDING ITS END that are absolutely unlike the rest of it. . . . Philip in usual form. Writes, 'Can't think of anything but being old, then very old, then dead. If you're lucky, that is. May be just old, then dead, of course.'"

After Larkin succumbs to cancer at sixty-four, Amis is quietly devastated. As he writes to Conquest, Larkin was "something over and above friend and poet. I don't know; presence? Keep forgetting he's dead for a millisecond at a time: I must tell/ask etc. Philip—Oh Christ I can't. I didn't realise how often I must have thought of him. Every night I still read a few pages of the works before going to bed."

There are, of course, all sorts of other letters in this mammoth (behemoth? Leviathan?) collection: to academic friends like Paul Fussell, Edmund Keeley, and Dale Salwak, to wives, agents, fans, newspapers:

"Many thanks for your letter inviting me to sit for a portrait with my son Martin," writes Amis to the director of the National Portrait Gallery. "This is one of the most amazingly inept and tactless suggestions that has ever been made to me. Martin fully agrees with this judgment."

To the editor of a pedagogical journal, he waspishly opines, "Sir I read with interest your remarks about me in Teachers World. (By the way, shouldn't that name have an apostrophe in it somewhere? But I suppose it is safer to drop it if you aren't too sure where it should go.)"

He even tells readers of *Encounter*, "The Angry Young Man 'movement' " —of which he was the leading novelist—"was a phantom creation of literary journalists."

Originally trained as a scholar and teacher, Amis was always punctilious when editing anthologies (e.g., *The Oxford Book of Light Verse*) or commenting on grammar. At one point, for instance, he asks the critic Christopher Ricks just what Tennyson meant by the phrase "the moaning at the bar." And he kindly confesses to a fan his fundamental likes and dislikes: "I dislike men and women when they are cold-hearted (a reserved manner is okay), unpleasant to those who can't hit back (waiters, etc.), unable to allow others to finish a sentence, stingy, disinclined to listen to reason and fact, bad hosts, bad guests, affected, racialist, intolerant of homosexuality, anti-British, members of the New Left, passively boring."

Some of this litany is surprising, revealing a gentler and more compassionate soul than the splenetic, bibulous monster of publishing legend.

Allow me to say a little about Zachary Leader's exemplary editing of *The Letters of Kingsley Amis*. In a time when books are sloppily annotated, this is a masterpiece of intelligent footnoting. Amis often scribbled in a highly concentrated form, using abbreviations, phonetic spellings, and personal argot, so much so that there are times when he approaches the epistolary excesses of his bête noire Ezra Pound. But Leader clarifies all this arcana. He identifies people, poems, allusions, in-jokes, and anything else that might lead to a greater understanding and pleasure in the text. Without him, this book wouldn't be half as much fun as it is.

So, who then is the better letter writer, the volcanic Amis or the melancholy Larkin? I'd opt for. . . . No, the best way to find out is to read them both. And who knows? Robert Conquest still lives, and by the evidence of his exuberant limericks his letters should be something to look out for.

February 10, 2002

CODA

To round off these literary reflections, I'm appending an essay on education and multiculturalism that appeared in The Washington Post Magazine and another on the most influential prose stylists of the century that ran in the Post's Outlook section. The first sums up the implicit argument of this entire book—the need to read widely in the world's literature, regardless of time, geography, and genre. The second is, I think, a somewhat playful polemic, since my list includes some unexpected writers like H. P. Lovecraft and Georgette Heyer. Last, I'm also including three lightly annotated reading lists—books about the Renaissance, classics of religious thought, and representative high spots of modern science fiction.

CLASSROOMS AND THEIR DISCONTENTS

Some while back I planned to write an article about schools, with particular attention to multiculturalism and its impact. Naturally, I read a good number of books—from established classics of educational theory to contemporary polemics—and visited half a dozen area high schools, sitting in on English and history classes. I took detailed notes, talked to teachers and students, and, of course, reflected on my own experiences as a student, parent, and taxpayer. I accumulated lots of material.

When I came to write my essay, however, I felt utterly at a loss. Every day the paper carries news coverage and op-ed pieces about low SAT scores, playground violence, magnet programs, overcrowded classrooms, bureaucratic bungles, special-needs children, PTA shouting matches, banned books, national exams, the dumbing-down of standards, the impact of computers and the Internet, hand-wringing about why kids don't read, home schooling, burned-out teachers, voucher programs, the successes of Catholic schools, grade inflation, the impenetrable jargon of theorists and reformers, the nature of the canon, and dozens of other topics. How could one say anything new about education?

Above all, I had no interest in being one more shrill voice. Not that there weren't school issues that shocked and angered me. How could well-off Montgomery County, for instance, be other than ashamed of its crowded classrooms, its middle-school language courses without enough textbooks, its blatant favoring of some schools over others? Why did building Jack Kent Cooke Stadium seem far more important to our elected officials than improving the education of our kids? When did teachers—the most important figures in the lives of children, other than parents—cease to be looked up to as the equal of doctors, lawyers, or ministers and come to be subtly dismissed as second-rate drones?

The heart of the matter, I realized, is that no two people agree about what education should be. We want our kids to score high on standardized tests, but we pay only lip service to real learning. Where past cultures hoped young people would grow up to become heroes or philosophers or saints or gentlemen, we merely hope that Blair or Hakim will get into Harvard, marry well, make a lot of money, and live behind a gate in Georgetown. As our goals are superficial, so we look upon knowledge not as its own end but as simply a step toward a law degree or the means to a Mercedes.

Multiculturalism—the central education issue of our time—I found particularly inspiring and troubling. At times it seems as though one dream, as old as Socrates, is finally coming true: we are all becoming citizens of the world. But then one reads about ethnic strife in Eastern Europe, the rise of religious fundamentalism around the world, the popularity of nationalistic paramilitary groups in this country, the mythmaking of some Afrocentrist zealots. Certainly education should have nothing to do with fanaticism, prejudice, and xenophobia, yet how does one distinguish these from spiritual commitment, rugged individualism, and pride in one's heritage? Ideally, a multicultural program would stress, not the differences among the world's peoples, but the universal human need for art, ritual, and ethical standards. I would hope for a future time when nobody would be surprised that an African American man might turn to the poet Li Po for solace or a Hispanic woman become the leading authority on African carvings. Our schools should introduce young people to the world's cultural richness and variety, but then encourage them to follow their own tastes, no matter what their particular creed, color, or nationality.

Yet doesn't this merely license the so-called smorgasbord approach to learning? Don't we need a central core, a canon of some sort, to create a bond among us as Americans living on the cusp of the twenty-first century? But what should such a canon include? Personally, I've always felt that every child should be taught what used to be called the social graces: good manners, clear speech, the art of dinner-table conversation, sketching, singing, competence in playing a musical instrument, and even ballroom dancing. I'm not kidding. These make up a canon of polite learning that nearly everyone could agree about.

In truth, I think most teachers and school systems are successfully and thoughtfully enlarging the traditional canon. When I was in high school and college, it struck me as utterly absurd that literature classes hardly touched on the great books of the non-English-speaking world. Of course, much is lost when a student doesn't know a poem's or story's original language, but does that mean we should skip reading or teaching Plato's *Apology*, Saint Augustine's *Confessions*, the book of Job, the poetry of Tu Fu, the Grimms' fairy tales, Njal's Saga, Dante's *Commedia*, *Don Quixote*, Montaigne's essays, *The Arabian Nights*, *Crime and Punishment*, and even parts of Murasaki Shikibu's wonderful *Tale of Genji.* If works like these don't belong in the canon, then what titles do? Certainly today's children ought to learn some African or Asian folklore and mythology, as well as the adventures of the Norse gods. Schools really should take pains to include more work by women. Despite recent doomsayers, ours is an exhilarating period in literary scholarship, as we do in fact discover moving poetry and eye-opening fiction by hitherto neglected, if not altogether forgotten, writers.

And yet it is no shame to say that, for reasons of culture or blocked opportunity, Africa produced very little written literature before the twentieth century, that there are few eminent women composers of classical music, and that the best chroniclers of working-class life have come from the middle class. History should have nothing to do with fairness; its purpose is the pursuit of truth. One can't compensate for inequities by wishful thinking or fanciful scholarship. Cleopatra wasn't black—but Toni Morrison is.

This is not to dismiss literary or social criticism based on race, gender, class, or sexual orientation. To the contrary. The writings of W. E. B. Du Bois and Angela Carter, the novels of Dreiser and Harry Crews, Cavafy's poetry— all of these insist that attentive readers think about just such sociological matters. In the same way, knowledge that Walker Percy and Flannery O'Connor were devout Catholics—and Joyce a lapsed one—helps in our interpretation of their fiction. In truth, a good critic uses every kind of information he can get his hands on. But a work of art can never be diminished or dismissed because of the secondary factors of its production. Once made, art is primarily a matter of beauty, form, and truthfulness to human experience—a coming together of complex patterns of language or sound, color or design. Biography, politics, and sociology are ultimately only the servants of aesthetics.

Over the years education has been tugged back and forth between two opposing ideals: the need to impart certain kinds of knowledge deemed important to society, and the wish to allow the child to develop his or her own gifts. The crises in education are consequently of two types: (1) the students are not learning enough, or (2) the students' spirits (imagination, creativity, uniqueness) are being crushed. Both these extremes usually insist on curriculum reform, either a demand for higher standards, more homework, a return to the old ways, and increased testing, or a call for creative play, open classrooms, new, more up-to-date textbooks, and the abolition of grades. Since, ipso facto, no one is ever satisfied with the way our schools operate, American education lurches along, trying first one approach (progressive schools, tracking, new math), then another (whole language, mainstreaming, pass/fail).

At its most basic, the argument is whether children should be taught facts or how to think for themselves. Both, obviously. Various core knowledge and core curriculum groups believe that a common culture builds on common knowledge, hence they provide lists of what every schoolchild ought to know. The states establish standards, functional tests, and other measuring devices to be sure our students understand certain things: simple division, the definition of irony, the location of Hong Kong on a map, the dates for the Second World War, how to make inferences from given information. Of course, we now deliberately organize our classes around the standardized tests: English courses set quizzes that emulate questions on the SAT. As a result, we tend to force-feed data to kids who learn to spit it out a few months later. But how much sticks?

Children learn best what they love. We have all been amazed at ten-year-olds who can recite the batting average of every player in the American League or who can discuss and compare minor details in the various *Star Trek* series. The good teacher needs to inspire love for his subject; then all the rest will follow: children will learn the facts willingly, will read the books eagerly, because they will find them irresistible.

Easily enough said. But how can this be done, and done thirty times over in a classroom of sophomore English? There is only one way: the teacher must herself display such love for English that, like the nous of Neoplatonist creation, that love will overflow and enter into her pupils. Or at least a few of them. A true teacher, as the classicist William Arrowsmith maintained, embodies the subject he teaches: that is, a humanist should be learned, admirable, and humane; a mathematician ought to think clearly, display joyfulness in the very chalk strokes he makes in inscribing an equation on the blackboard. A teacher should be a living advertisement for his or her subject.

To encourage this process, we need to make a profound change in our society's attitude toward secondary school teachers. Teaching must again be regarded as a desirable and admirable profession. How can you love a subject if you have been tacitly taught to despise its advocate? We need to pay better salaries, attract top undergraduates to the field, and honor teachers in our community. T. S. Eliot once wrote that he had worked in a bank for many tiring hours, six days a week, but that by comparison with his stint as a schoolmaster, banking was one long vacation. Our educational system will remain mediocre until parents, especially well-to-do, successful parents, urge their brightest children to become high school math and history teachers.

And what do teachers want? I asked a group of English instructors at Wilde Lake High School in Howard County this question: If you could make one change to the school system as it now is, what would you wish for? All of them answered, "Smaller class size." In a class of thirty or more kids, now typical in many area schools, a teacher exhausts his energies simply keeping order; add one unruly dolt—every class has at least one—and a whole period can be wasted by his or her tantrums. But in a class of, say, sixteen or twenty, everything is more intimate, focused, and personal; the troublesome student cannot hide in a corner and must learn to participate; all the students can learn from one another.

I asked another group of teachers, at Albert Einstein High School in Silver Spring, to name the most important factor in determining how well a student would do in school. They all had the same answer: "Parental involvement." In the hard-hitting *A Black Parent's Handbook to Educating Your Children*, Baruti K. Kafele sensibly recommends that parents read their children's textbooks. A father or mother should check a child's assignments, making sure he or she understands what is being asked; the parent should then look over the homework to be certain it was done properly, with due attention to neatness. In every way, parents should hammer home that they value education.

After all, parents, not children, are responsible for the decline in national literacy. Even now many parents don't read aloud to their children—despite the widespread evidence that this is one of the best ways to foster a love of books in the young. Ideally, each child should be read to individually, and not just for a few minutes. The author Joan Aiken once asserted that people who weren't prepared to read to their children for an hour a day simply shouldn't have any.

But too many adults feel that they have done their part for literacy by turning the pages of a picture book with their toddler at bedtime—after spending most of the evening plumped in front of the television or computer. If you want your children to be readers, you must be a reader yourself. Do your kids see you sit down after dinner with a newspaper or novel? Do you frequently say, "Just a minute, I want to finish this chapter"? Is your house filled with books? Not law books or medical manuals, but works of history, fiction, poetry, philosophy? Do you have a bookcase? Do you and your family go to the library together? The bookstore?

The problems of education usually come down to such questions of values. What do we want from life? Instead of a desire for riches, power, and fame, education ought to impart—along with basic skills—certain kinds of noble ambition. To find a cure for multiple sclerosis. To compete in the Olympics. To discover a new star. To live a life of consequence. Thoreau said that he went to the woods "to live deliberately, to front only the essential facts of life," so that when he came to die, he would not "discover that I had not lived." The much maligned 1960s at least inspired young people to dream of and work toward a better, more egalitarian world. That kind of spirit should be encouraged in our schools again. We should be producing philosophers, discontented visionaries, obsessive scientists, and poets. We would do well for our schools to spend part of a semester studying Plutarch's *Lives of the Noble Grecians and Romans*.

Of course, multiculturalism raises numerous issues about the content of course work, the major one being this: Should a child be strongly grounded in a single national or ethnic tradition before being exposed to the world's diversity, or is it better to stress a global approach from the beginning? There is obviously merit to both arguments. The more narrow approach encourages depth (as opposed to breadth), fosters a strong sense of identity, and relies on familiar and incontrovertibly established and admired texts, the classics of the Western canon and, in particular, of the Anglo-American tradition. The great strength of this traditional curriculum lies in its integrated nature: over the years the great books have interacted with one another. Homer formed Vergil, who inspired Dante, who influenced Eliot. If one reads Homer, one gains an entry into hundreds of later poems, novels, and plays, from Joyce's *Ulysses* to Giraudoux's *The Trojan War Will Not Take Place* to Derek Walcott's *Omeros*. The educator Robert M. Hutchins once described the major authors of the Western world as being engaged in a great conversation.

The merits of multiculturalism are just as compelling. One should never, for example, underestimate the importance of freshness. A teacher may tire of talking year after year about *Great Expectations* or *Gulliver's Travels*; it can be exhilarating for him to read a new author, say, Yukio Mishima or Zora Neale Hurston. That excitement is sure to be passed along to his pupils. Work by contemporary authors may feel more accessible and relevant to many students; Alice Walker may speak more powerfully than *Antigone*. This doesn't mean that Walker is in the same class as Sophocles: There are different kinds of books appropriate to every age, taste, and experience. Contemporary texts may, in some instances, provide better teaching tools than older masterpieces.

Most objections to a multicultural curriculum presume that children will never read anything except what they have to read in class. Yet if we can hook kids on books by having them study Native American myths, slave narratives, contemporary science fiction, and the daily newspaper, they may become lifelong readers and go on to explore books of all kinds, with growing enthusiasm and sophistication. Many people who suffered through a traditional high school English curriculum can scarcely remember what they read, and recall the whole experience with distaste. Perhaps that's why so many grown-ups read nothing at all, or only the most obvious best sellers. It has long been a truism that the best way to kill a child's interest in a book is to make it a required school text. What was a locus of often illicit joy soon becomes the source of tedious homework assignments.

As in many things, the answer to the argument between the traditional and the multicultural curriculum should be pragmatic: teachers ought to use the books that work best with their particular students, always bearing in mind that certain texts are much richer than others. Any inflexible Western canon purist ought to reread "The Lottery," Shirley Jackson's chilling parable about an unthinking allegiance to tradition. But any ardent multiculturalist should also recognize that titles enter the canon not through some political hocus-pocus but simply because they are richer, denser, and more rewarding works than any others. I think it essential for all those engaged in education or the debates on education to bear in mind the distinction between great literature and effective teaching aids.

Most high school instructors are pretty sensible about these matters. They are genuinely eager to help all their students, not only those who are bright or whose religion or skin color matches their own. Extremists of whatever ilk don't tend to flourish in public schools: their playground is the university. A secondary school teacher can't afford to live in a never-never land of pure theory, whether that theory is feminism, deconstructionism, or Marxism. Every day a hundred or more children must be taught to read, write, interpret, calculate, think, express themselves, evaluate, and remember. Realpolitik is the name of this game.

In truth, most multicultural curricula are based on simple justice and common sense: our schools are heavily Hispanic, Asian, and African American. If we teach material relating to these cultures, we may capture the enthusiasm of these frequently disadvantaged students, as well as imparting some useful insights to kids from other backgrounds. Ultimately, anyone should be able to sympathize with the plights of Jane Austen's heroines or the feelings of Richard Wright's Bigger Thomas. After all, the essence of being human lies in that old phrase "our common humanity." Surely school should foster this universal ideal as much as any particular branch of learning.

In principle, an educated human being ought to be tolerant, civil, acquainted with the world's history, art, and literature, knowledgeable about modern science, an active citizen, thoughtful about philosophical and religious questions, able to express his views with clarity and force, devoted to family, conscientious in the performance of his work.

These are values that matter to me—but do they matter to you? What about a competitive spirit? Should teachers foster self-confidence, or introspection? Great thinkers, artists, and scientists seldom conform to this mild, humane model; neither do many business magnates, politicians, athletes, and movie stars. In fact, the world has been shaped not so much by sensitive nice guys as by obsessives, neurasthenics, madmen, and visionaries. We need Dionysus as much as Apollo.

Who, then, can we point to as our educational ideal? Jesus never laughed, Muhammad owned slaves, Socrates claimed to know nothing. A. E. Housman once noted that classicists—those masters of the traditional canon—were seldom better than other men in their personal lives: Richard Bentley, arguably the greatest classical scholar of all time, proved a venal and corrupt university official.

As I said earlier, once you start thinking about education, it grows increasingly difficult to assert anything at all. James Welton wrote, in a splendid article on education for the 1910 edition of the *Encyclopaedia Britannica*, "We may say with Plato that the aim of education is 'to develop in the body and in the soul all the beauty and all the perfection of which they are capable,' but this leaves quite undecided the nature and form of that beauty and perfection, and on such points there has never been universal agreement at any one time." Alas? Hooray?

Perhaps the finest historical account of that lack of agreement in this country is Richard Hofstadter's Pulitzer Prize winner, *Anti-Intellectualism in American Life* (1963), the one book—witty, scathing, and unashamedly intellectual—that everyone concerned with American education should read. For one thing, Hofstadter shows that the bitter issues dividing us today have recurred over the past two centuries with depressing regularity: "A host of educational problems has arisen from indifference—underpaid teachers, overcrowded classrooms, double-schedule schools, broken-down school buildings, inadequate facilities and a number of other failings that come from something else—the cult of athleticism, marching bands, high-school drum majorettes, ethnic ghetto schools, de-intellectualized curricula, the failure to educate in serious subjects, the neglect of academically gifted children."

Education. Sigh. I really don't understand it very well, and that worries me. Somehow, though, I hope our society continues to accomplish the one crucial goal of all schooling: in Bertrand Russell's words, "to rouse and stimulate the love of mental adventure." If we can do this, along with encouraging the quest for truth and fostering "the kind of tolerance that springs from an endeavour to understand those who are different from ourselves," we shall be all right. Can this be too much to ask?

November 9, 1997

THE DIRDA DOZEN

When a canon of one hundred great movies was recently announced, I—an inveterate daydreamer since childhood—started making up similar lists: the ten greatest pop songs ("Louie, Louie," "Shout," "American Pie," "Satisfaction," etc.), the world's finest opera (*Don Giovanni*), the painting I would most like to own (Vermeer's *The Little Street* or Watteau's *Embarkation for Cythera*), the most awesome comic book superhero (Green Lantern), the five best boys' adventure stories (*The Odyssey, The Count of Monte Cristo, Treasure Island, Journey to the Center of the Earth, King Solomon's Mines*), and the perfect food (pirogies, of course). When I started on the world's supreme muscle car (the 1964 Pontiac GTO) and the three days in my life I'd most like to relive, I began to see how deeply seductive list making can be.

Now, a book reviewer's fancy naturally turns to thoughts of literature, and modern literature in particular. One especially restless night, I found myself wondering which authors had been the most influential stylists of our century? Limiting myself to those who worked in English, these wouldn't necessarily be the "best" or the most important figures—James Joyce (like Shakespeare) being too various for imitation. Instead, I'd go after the men and women who created a presence on the page so singular, so memorable that they either founded genres or shaped the way prose is written in our time. Who were our most original voices?

There was never any question about my first selection: Ronald Firbank (1886–1926). "From the over-elaboration of his dress he suggested sometimes, as he did tonight, a St. Sebastian with too many arrows." Firbank died young and wrote only eight novels, all of them short, but each a masterpiece of camp humor. He created a voice—prissy, gossipy, and allusive—that has long characterized one sort of homosexual charm and that provided a starting point for such English comic novelists as Anthony Powell, Evelyn Waugh, and Nancy Mitford. He is particularly brilliant at conversation, and knows what to leave out, being a pioneer in the use of silences and ellipses. His characters bear deliciously silly names such as Miss Wookie, Mrs. Shamefoot, and Mrs. Paraguay, and they usually have a taste for finery and Catholic ritual. Just reciting Firbank's titles will convey a soupçon of his flavor: *The Flower Beneath the Foot, Inclinations, Concerning the Eccentricities of Cardinal Pirelli.*

Ernest Hemingway (1899–1961) represents the burly American counterpart to Firbank. It's fashionable now to denigrate Hemingway (macho, sexually confused, vainglorious), but half of modern fiction rests in his laconic, tough-guy shadow. The stripped-clean, emotion-free language; the willingness to repeat words and phrases to get things exactly right; the brilliant descriptions of men at work, war, or play; the ability to suggest depths of meaning without being overemphatic about it—such less-is-more qualities have characterized American writers from Dashiell Hammett to Raymond Carver and James Salter. "He started a fire with some chunks of pine he got with the ax from a stump. Over the fire he stuck a wire grill, pushing the four legs down into the ground with his boot. Nick put the frying pan on the grill over the flames. He was hungrier. The beans and spaghetti warmed. Nick stirred them and mixed them together. They began to bubble, making little bubbles that rose with difficulty to the surface. There was a good smell."

Such simplicity signaled the end of Victorian luxuriance and Biedermeier fustian.

For my next two selections, I could not resist the paramount fantasy writers of our century: Lord Dunsany (1878–1957) and H. P. Lovecraft (1890–1937). Dunsany dashed off—he was, lucky man!, a single-draft writer—nonfiction, poems, plays, and novels *(The King of Elfland's Daughter)*, but he is most original in his early short stories, collected in such volumes as *The Book of Wonder, Time and the Gods*, and *The Sword of Welleran*. The 1890s popularized gorgeous, purple prose, but Dunsany took this "Oriental" style and added a dry wit, a rhetorical grandeur not unlike that of the King James Version of the Bible, and his own flair for evocative names. "The Gibbelins eat, as is well known, nothing less good than man." "Toldees, Mondath, Arizim, these are the Inner Lands, the lands whose sentinels upon their borders do not behold the sea." In "The Fortress Unvanquishable Save for Sacnoth," Dunsany virtually founded the modern tale of sword-and-sorcery, and his influence extends from Clark Ashton Smith and Fritz Leiber to Jack Vance, Gene Wolfe, and Tanith Lee.

Of course, some readers choke on the clotted-cream style of Dunsany, just as others cannot bear the brooding portentousness of Lovecraft. I love them both. In some of his early work Lovecraft emulated Dunsany, but before long he unearthed the Elder Gods and great Cthulhu, opened that evil grimoire the "Necronomicon," and founded the haunted Miskatonic University. Listen to

the quiet opening of "The Dunwich Horror," and note the growing uncanni-
ness of the landscape: "When a traveller in north central Massachusetts takes
the wrong fork at the junction of the Aylesbury pike just beyond Dean's
Corners he comes upon a lonely and curious country. The ground gets higher,
and the brier-bordered stone walls press closer and closer against the ruts of
the dusty, curvy road. The trees of the frequent forest belts seem too large, and
the wild weeds, brambles, and grasses attain a luxuriance not often found in
settled regions. . . ."

There are few scarier stories in English than Lovecraft's, and his eldritch
shadow falls on nearly every writer of horror fiction in our time.

"I sent him groveling. In ten minutes he was back with a basket of appetizing fresh-picked grovels. We squeezed them and drank the piquant juice
thirstily." Puns, the metaphorical made literal, a razzmatazz vocabulary, and a
Groucho Marx leer—is there any doubt that here is the work of the wordsmith
and humorist S. J. Perelman (1904–1979)? In Perelman's essays and parodies,
the English language sails off into the stream of consciousness, and then
mutinies. "Thousands of scantily draped but none the less appetizing extra
girls milled past me. . . . Just one kiss, she pleaded, her breath hot against my
neck. In desperation I granted her boon, knowing full well that my weak
defenses were crumbling before the onslaught of this love tigree. . . . Our meal
finished, we sauntered into the rumpus room and Diana turned on the radio.
With a savage snarl the radio turned on her. . . ."

And so it blissfully goes. Woody Allen, Dave Barry, Fran Leibowitz, and
other modern humorists almost certainly keep a well-thumbed copy of *The
Most of S. J. Perelman* close at hand, if only as a holy icon.

I would have left William Faulkner (1897–1962) off this list, if I could
have. But, to paraphrase Flannery O'Connor, that would be like ignoring the
Dixie Limited when it comes roaring down the track. Faulkner embodies the
South: he knows all its secrets, all its voices. In *The Sound and the Fury* alone
he re-creates the thoughts of an idiot, the meditations of an old black servant,
the machinations of a venal modern businessman—and he sets down each
one's language with just the right sibilance and twang. The author of *Absalom,
Absalom!* and *Light in August* was once thought a minor regionalist, but these
days he has a good claim to be the greatest American novelist of the century,
and probably the most influential one as well. Virtually every Latin American
writer, for example, names Faulkner as a major influence on his work. That the
creator of Benji and Caddie and the Snopeses can be full of bombast and overt
symbolism and sentences that go on and on—well, you just have to accept that
some writers prefer glorious overabundance to careful stillborn perfection.

One other part of the country also discovered its laureate in this century.

Southern California hasn't wanted for novelists (Nathanael West, Ross Macdonald, Joan Didion), but the classic images of Los Angeles still belong to that bard of the hard-boiled, Raymond Chandler (1888–1959). "It was one of those clear, bright summer mornings we get in the early spring in California before the high fog sets in. The rains are over. The hills are still green and in the valley across the Hollywood hills you can see snow on the high mountains. The fur stores are advertising their annual sales. The call houses that specialize in sixteen-year-old virgins are doing a land-office business. And in Beverly Hills the jacaranda trees are beginning to bloom. . . ."

The weary, wisecracking voice of Philip Marlowe has echoed down the mean streets of American crime fiction for more than fifty years, from Lew Archer to Spenser, and in the last decade or so has been taken up by such tough-gal detectives as Sue Grafton's Kinsey Millhone and Sara Paretsky's V. I. Warshawski. Like Hemingway, Chandler is easy to parody—see Perelman's "Farewell, My Lovely Appetizer"—and he can be sentimental, making Marlowe, the tarnished knight, sound at times a little too noble and self-sacrificing. But at his best, Chandler writes some of the freshest prose you will ever read. As he himself once said, "I live for syntax."

Now, if you had to pick two twentieth-century godparents for contemporary children's literature, you could hardly do better than E. Nesbit (1858–1924) and J. D. Salinger (b. 1919). In Nesbit's work—for instance, *Five Children and It* or *The Enchanted Castle*—you find school holidays turned into a time of fantastic, yet cozy, adventure: into the ordinary world of childhood erupts *The Arabian Nights*, complete with sand fairies, mysterious amulets, flying carpets, dragons, treasure hunts, and statues that come alive. Nesbit is one of the first modern writers for children to avoid both didacticism and the killing tone of grown-up condescension. From her spring Edward Eager, Joan Aiken, Daniel Pinkwater, Roald Dahl, Diana Wynne Jones, Madeline L'Engle, J. K. Rowling, and all those fantasy stories in which magic intrudes to transform the quotidian. I have read that Noel Coward—that most consummate sophisticate—could find comfort only in E. Nesbit's books as he lay dying.

Is there a modern young adult novel that doesn't, in some way, play back the voice of Holden Caulfield? *The Catcher in the Rye* practically invented the YA genre. "If you really want to hear about it, the first thing you'll probably want to know is where I was born, and what my lousy childhood was like, and how my parents were occupied and all before they had me, and all that David Copperfield kind of crap, but I don't feel like going into it, if you want to know the truth." While Nesbit depicts the neverland of an ideal Edwardian childhood, *The Catcher in the Rye* mirrors the anxieties and swagger of everyone's adolescence. Much of twentieth-century literature has been occupied with celebrating the spoken language of the people, the street, the ghetto—and Salinger is the lucky one who found the sullen, uncertain voice of the teenager. Nobody who writes about young people can entirely escape his influence.

I wanted to include Georgette Heyer (1902–1974) on this list because her historical novels, largely set in the Regency, represent an entire literary duchy: that of romantic escape fiction, told with wit, an eye for period detail, and the requisite pull on the heartstrings. For the most part, Heyer's young women are willful, clever, and independent: Miss Taverner (in *Regency Buck*) "could not . . . admire her own beauty, which was of a type she was inclined to despise. She had rather have had black hair; she thought the fairness of her gold curls insipid. Happily, her brows and lashes were dark, and her eyes which were startlingly blue (in the manner of a wax doll, she once scornfully told her brother) had a directness and a fire which gave a great deal of character to her face."

Heyer is a superb historical novelist—Jane Aiken Hodge's excellent biography reminds us of how hard she worked to get the slang and fashions of her characters just right. She represents the deliberate recovery of an archaic style—roughly that of Jane Austen—and all those fictive acts of literary ventriloquism, from John Barth's *The Sot-Weed Factor* to A. S. Byatt's *Possession* to innumerable Regency romances, owe something to her virtuosity.

Though George Orwell (1903–1950) wrote two classic novels (*Nineteen Eighty-Four* and *Animal Farm*), he is most widely appreciated as our leading exemplar of the plain style. There are other candidates—Edmund Wilson, E. B. White—but Orwell possesses a directness and imaginative originality, coupled with attractive political convictions, that make these competitors seem like carpet-slippered men of letters (which, of course, they were). "In Moulmein, in Lower Burma, I was hated by large numbers of people—the only time in my life that I have been important enough for this to happen to me." That tone, at once personal, conversational, and slightly self-deprecating, is the model for most of the travel writing of the past thirty years, just as Orwell's reporting is the true progenitor for the New Journalism (see "Down the Mine" or *Down and Out in Paris and London*). Somehow, Orwell reduces the histrionics in his prose to a minimum, so that he always sounds as if he's saying exactly what he means. It is a rare gift.

For my last slot, I chose the writer who changed the way we look at the future: Philip K. Dick (1928–1982). If Heyer recaptures an elegant past, Dick shows us the next century—not a chrome-bright, spotless Tomorrowland, but a vast, overcrowded Hong Kong, an international ghetto, where the poor rent steps to sleep on, corporations sell us drug-induced dreams, and nothing works very well. This is the world of *Do Androids Dream of Electric Sheep?* (made into the movie *Blade Runner*) and *The Three Stigmata of Palmer*

Eldritch. But Dick is also a mystical writer—with a taste for infinite regression à la Borges, religious speculation, and philosophical inquiry: How does a man differ from a robot? What if the world around us were merely an illusion? In his most celebrated novel *The Man in the High Castle*, Dick shows us an alternative earth in which the Axis won World War II and only a few of his characters can imagine that it might have been the other way around. Dick is also consistently funny, and he sometimes seems the offspring of Kafka, the cousin of William Burroughs, and the scapegrace father of the cyberpunk William Gibson.

So, there's my list—and already I can hear the baying of enraged readers. What? No Virginia Woolf, no J. R. R. Tolkien, no Agatha Christie, no James Baldwin, no P. G. Wodehouse! Let me assure the frenzied and insulted that I admire these writers as much as they. My chosen dozen are merely those who seem to me the most influential and distinctive prose stylists of the century, the founders of schools of writing, if you will. But enough of these literary matters. On to pastures new. Who, for example, are the nine greatest baseball players of all time? And what are the three best desserts? And which is the funniest episode of *The Simpsons*?

July 5, 1998

A RENAISSANCE READING LIST

The Civilization of the Renaissance in Italy, by Jacob Burckhardt. Don't be put off by the magisterial title or the "classic" reputation: this long essay makes for enthralling reading, being chock-a-block with anecdotes, many of them scandalous. "Intrigues, armaments, leagues, corruption and treason make up the outward history of Italy at this period." Sounds like Washington. Typical quotation: "Insignificant and malicious, he governed with the help of a professor of jurisprudence and of an astrologer, and frightened his people by an occasional murder."

The Prince, by Niccolò Machiavelli. The breviary of realpolitik. Of some particularly dirty tricks, Machiavelli notes reprovingly, "it were far better to avoid them and live in obscurity than to reign as king by such methods." That's the high tone of the medieval moralist. But our man continues, in his quiet, snake-smooth voice (Henry Kissinger should do the audiotape): "Nevertheless, if a man wants to reign. . . ." He then proceeds to detail, with his trademark dispassion, how "reasons of state" may excuse a crime or why a ruler should prefer to be feared than to be loved.

Renaissance and Renascences in Western Art, by Erwin Panofsky. What do we mean by a renaissance? And was that of the fifteenth and sixteenth centuries unique? What about the tenth-century Carolingian Renaissance and the twelfth-century Renaissance in France? Panofsky's is the most scholarly treatment of these questions, but is also a fount of amazing scholarship. A flabellum, we learn, was "a liturgical fan used to keep the flies away from the priest when saying Mass." Panofsky neatly encapsulates the difference between the Middle Ages and the Renaissance by noting the etymology of two names: Dante's Beatrice "suggests the redemption granted by Christ" and Petrarch's Laura evokes "the glory bestowed by Apollo."

The Renaissance, by Will Durant. Not profound, but filled with good stories, this engaging narrative history of the Italian Renaissance is built around the biographies of its leading figures. John Addington Symonds's *The Renaissance in Italy* (frequently found in secondhand shops as a two-volume Modern Library Giant) also makes for entertaining browsing, but Symonds relegates some of the juiciest scandals to untranslated footnotes. We learn that Bandello, who wrote 214 novellas, occasionally attempted the tragic chord, "as in the ghostly story of Violante, who revenged herself upon a faithless lover by tearing him to pieces with pincers, or in the disgusting novel of Pandora, or again in the tale of the husband who forced his wife to strangle her lover with her own hands." Alas, these tantalizing morsels are all that Symonds gives us.

Lives of the Artists, by Giorgio Vasari. Anecdotal accounts of the great painters and sculptors of the period. Many editions. Typical story: when Pope Boniface VIII, planning to commission a major art project, sent an emissary to bring back some proof of Giotto's talent, the preoccupied, somewhat annoyed painter took out a blank sheet of paper, picked up a brush and, with one stroke, drew a perfect circle. Now that's chutzpah.

Early Renaissance and *High Renaissance,* both by Michael Levey. Published in a Penguin series called Style and Civilization, these two volumes offer approachable, elegant, and beautifully written accounts of Renaissance art. Intended for the general reader, the books possess a freshness and vivacity, not to mention brevity, missing from standard art-history textbooks, such as Frederick Hartt's *History of Italian Renaissance Art* or the minutely detailed volumes in the admirable Yale/Pelican history of art.

The Renaissance, by Walter Pater. Sometimes dismissed as a "mere" impressionist, Pater is in fact a superb critic, as well as one of the great prose poets of the English language. He describes the figures in Botticelli's paintings as being "like angels, but with a sense of displacement or loss about them—the wistfulness of exiles." About any artist—and in these pages he treats Leonardo, Giorgione's followers, and several others—he tries always to answer the question "What is the peculiar sensation, what is the peculiar quality of pleasure, which his work has the property of exciting in us, and which we cannot get elsewhere?" It was Pater who talks of the Botticelli Venus's sorrow at the thought of love, while his description of Mona Lisa is an anthology piece: "She is older than the rocks among which she sits; like the vampire, she has been dead many times, and learned the secrets of the grave; and has been a diver in deep seas, and keeps the fallen day about her. . . ."

Those interested in the intellectual history of the Renaissance should turn first to the works of Paul Oskar Kristeller, especially the essays collected as

Renaissance Thought and Its Sources. Some of the most eminent contemporary historians and scholars of this period include Anthony Grafton, Peter Burke, Hugh Trevor-Roper, John Pope-Hennessy, and J. R. Elliott—all of whom can be read with pleasure by the nonspecialist. The masterpiece of the *Annales* school of history, Fernand Braudel's *The Mediterranean* minutely focuses on every economic aspect of life in the sixteenth century, while the controversial New Historicists, led by Stephen Greenblatt, examine the ideological and socioeconomic underpinnings of the period. To understand the Renaissance one should, of course, know its literary classics; especially recommended are Montaigne's *Essays*, Thomas More's *Utopia*, Erasmus's *Praise of Folly* (dedicated to More, with its Latin title punning on his name, *Moriae Encomium*), the works of Rabelais, and the plays of the Elizabethan dramatists, particularly Christopher Marlowe's *Dr. Faustus* and John Webster's *Duchess of Malfi.*

August 14, 1994

JOURNEYING TOWARD GOD:
TEN CLASSICS OF FAITH AND DOUBT

This is a very short list, but I include it because religious classics have long interested me as works of solace and as guides to living. Some day I hope to write a book about wisdom literature and the moral essay.

The Confessions of St. Augustine—the model for all spiritual autobiographies.

The Book of Common Prayer—"In the midst of life we are in death."

John Bunyan, The Pilgrim's Progress—"As I walked through the wilderness of this world."

George Herbert's poetry—"Love bade me welcome; yet my soul drew back / Guilty of dust and sin."

Pascal's Pensées—"The eternal silence of these infinite spaces terrifies me."

Gerard Manley Hopkins's poetry—"Not, I'll not, carrion comfort, Despair, not feast on thee."

Dostoevsky, The Brothers Karamazov—especially the "Grand Inquisitor" chapter in which Christ returns and is condemned to death by the church.

Tolstoy, "The Death of Ivan Ilych"—the last days of an ordinary man.

T. S. Eliot, Four Quartets—"At the still point of the turning world."

The Habit of Being: The Letters of Flannery O'Connor—very funny, deeply devout, and inspiring.

A SCIENCE FICTION READING LIST

Despite movies, television, and assorted high-tech games, science fiction is still mainly a reader's universe. There are books for every taste, from the sophisticated to the schlocky, from artful masterpieces to political tracts and soft-core porn. The following reading list—a baker's dozen presented in chronological order—emphasizes the best sf of the past.

The Time Machine, by H. G. Wells (1895). In the far future mankind has split into two races: the gentle Eloi and the Eloi-eating Morlocks. Among other things a fable of class warfare, this short, beautifully written novel is charged with a twilit sadness, especially in the Time Traveller's glimpse of the earth's last days. All of Wells's early science fiction is worth reading.

Last and First Men, by Olaf Stapledon (1930). Future history on a cosmic scale. This novel, with a time span of 2,000 million years, chronicles the future evolution of man, especially his biological mutations, alterations, and adaptations, as he travels across the solar system out into the universe. Imagine Gibbon writing about the future instead of the past—such is the grandeur of this book.

More Than Human, by Theodore Sturgeon (1953). Many rank Sturgeon among the best American writers of short stories. (See his collections, *Not without Sorcery, The Stars Are the Styx.*) This novel, his masterpiece, describes how an adult idiot, two neglected little black girls, a mongoloid baby, and other outcasts of society come together to form a single gestalt, or superbeing. The opening section is told from the viewpoint of the idiot and nearly rivals the Benji section of Faulkner's *The Sound and the Fury.*

The Stars, My Destination, by Alfred Bester (1956). Imagine the revenge plot of *The Count of Monte Cristo.* Add a cast of grotesques who would be at home in a Fellini film. Tell the story in quick march time, with lots of fireworks. Together, these make up Bester's swashbuckling adventure novel, a book more exciting than *Star Wars* and *Raiders of the Lost Ark* combined. Here's the novel that will make a kid of all but the most jaded adult.

Citizen of the Galaxy, by Robert A. Heinlein (1957). Truth to tell, Heinlein is at his best as a writer of tightly controlled short stories and young adult novels. Avoid the bloated best sellers of his later years. The early stories "By His Bootstraps" and "All You Zombies" are probably the most dazzling time paradox tales ever told. But Heinlein's flair for entertaining, cliff-hanging adventure is best seen in *Red Planet, Starman Jones, The Star Beast,* and this book—all intended for teenagers, though any adult can read them for pleasure. In *Citizen of the Galaxy* he takes up a classic sf theme—the passage from childhood to adulthood—as he recounts the life of Thorby, by turns a slave, beggar, soldier, businessman, and galactic magnate. The book opens with a grabber sentence: " 'Lot 97,' the auctioneer announced, 'a boy.' " This is just the book for a youngster beginning to be interested in sf.

A Canticle for Leibowitz, by Walter M. Miller (1959). Excepting only Stephen Vincent Benet's short story "By the Waters of Babylon," this is the finest of all portraits of society after a nuclear holocaust. Scientists, blamed by survivors, have been massacred during the age of "Simplification"; the world has reverted to savagery. Only in a few monasteries does civilization linger, especially in that of Brother Francis Gerard, who discovers fragments of writing—a shopping list, a blueprint, a racing form—ascribed to the Blessed Leibowitz. Slowly, mankind lifts itself from its new dark age—until nuclear war once again looms. But this time the powerful order of Saint Leibowitz has made plans.

The Best Short Stories of J. G. Ballard, (written in the 1960s–1970s). Widely admired outside of sf (his novel *Empire of the Sun* nearly won the Booker Prize), Ballard employs all the techniques of modern fiction (he deeply admires William Burroughs) to depict a world slowly running down. Images of empty and cracked swimming pools, low-flying aircraft and car crashes mark his work, especially in the demanding, often horrific "condensed novels" of *The Atrocity Exhibition*. Ballard takes a lot of chances but usually hits the jackpot, as in such somber stories as "The Voices of Time," "The Drowned Giant," and "Billennium."

The Three Stigmata of Palmer Eldritch, by Philip K. Dick (1964). Since his death a few years ago, Dick has increasingly come to be regarded as the most important sf novelist of the past forty years. For Dick, the high-tech future resembles a decaying and desperate Youngstown. Out of this bleakness, he nonetheless generates a wonderful black humor: in one novel, Mars is controlled by the president of the plumbers guild; in another, animals are so scarce that a man's greatest dream is to own a sheep. This novel is Dick's darkest, most paranoid vision: colonists on a desolate Mars need the hallucinogenic drug Can-D in order to maintain their sanity. But suddenly a new drug appears, Chew-Z, brought by Palmer Eldritch from beyond the galaxy and with frightening properties. Its hallucinatory effects may be permanent—indeed, it may truly alter reality, whatever that is.

The Left Hand of Darkness, by Ursula K. Le Guin (1969). Upon the strength of this novel, her fantasy trilogy (*A Wizard of Earthsea* and its sequels), and the political novel *The Dispossessed*, Le Guin was for many years the most highly regarded artist in sf. The inhabitants of the planet Winter undergo biological cycles, periodically assuming either male or female sexuality. On this framework Le Guin builds an intricate and austerely beautiful study of friendship, love, and sexuality.

Warm Worlds and Otherwise, by James Tiptree Jr. (1975). Generally regarded as the finest writer of short fiction to emerge in the 1970s, Tiptree stunned the sf community when it was revealed that he was a she, Dr. Alice Sheldon of McLean, Virginia. This collection, his (her?) second, includes one of the finest "feminist" stories ever written: "The Women Men Don't See." It's a stunner—especially the climax: a pair of American women, on vacation in Yucatán, encounter some stranded humanoid aliens, establish contact, and eventually blast off with them in their repaired ship, having decided that life among aliens has to be an improvement over that with men on earth. Other stories here include "Love Is the Plan, the Plan Is Death" and "The Girl Who Was Plugged In." Quirky, chilling, funny, open-ended, brilliant fiction. Readers interested in women's sf—and many of the best contemporary sf writers are women—should also seek out the work of Joanna Russ, especially the polemical classic *The Female Man* and the stories gathered in *The Zanzibar Cat*.

Little, Big, by John Crowley (1981). In *Little, Big*, Crowley recounts an American family's long involvement with the realm of faerie, along the way embracing everything from the tarot to television, from Thornton W. Burgess's animal fables to poignant love stories. Confirming, and surpassing, the artistry of his earlier novels—*The Deep, Beasts*, and *Engine Summer*—this superb book established its author as a master of lyrical fantasy, equal in ambition and accomplishment to Le Guin and Russell Hoban. Utterly assured and beautiful, it is the greatest fantasy novel so far written by an American.

The Book of the New Sun, by Gene Wolfe (1980–83). Published in four volumes—*The Shadow of the Torturer, The Claw of the Conciliator, The Sword of the Lictor, The Citadel of the Autarch*—this long novel has been acclaimed one of the richest, and most complex, novels in the whole sf genre. If Proust, while listening to late Beethoven string quartets, had written *I, Claudius* and set it in the future, the result might resemble this measured, autumnal masterpiece. Ostensibly, the books recount the adventures of an apprentice torturer—as in much sf, the world has again grown medieval in appearance—who sets out on picaresque adventures, discovers his parentage, and gains an unexpected reward. This is a masterpiece that can stand comparison with the best fiction of our time.

Neuromancer, by William Gibson (1984). This first novel won all the major sf awards everywhere. As a result, it soon became the spearpoint of the "cyberpunks," sf writers with a 1980s sensibility in tune with high technology, drugs, and a punk lifestyle. Gibson's prose bristles with neologism, computer technology, and nonstop energy, as the hero Case hooks himself into a vast computer matrix to help his lover Molly, a street samurai with special fighting skills, defeat some very decadent people and a nearly sentient computer. Old-time adventure, but state-of-the-art fiction.

The Science Fiction Hall of Fame, edited by Robert Silverberg et al. (1965–85). For readers in a hurry, the four volumes of this anthology reprint much of the best shorter work in modern sf. The first volume, choosing the finest stories (pre-1964) in the eyes of the Science Fiction Writers of America, includes Isaac Asimov's "Nightfall" (once regarded as the most popular sf tale of all time), Cordwainer Smith's unforgettable "Scanners Live in Vain," and Daniel Keyes's heartbreaking "Flowers for Algernon." Subsequent volumes focus on novellas, among them Algis Budrys's existential thriller *Rogue Moon* and characteristically elegant work from Robert Silverberg, Jack Vance, James Blish, and many others.

Beyond these hardly disputable classics, I would personally recommend the work of science fiction's best satirist, John Sladek, especially his masterly novels *Tik-Tok* and *Roderick: The Education of a Young Machine*. Who could resist the tale of a robot named Tik-Tok, like the mechanical man of Oz, who blithely murders a little girl—more exactly, who murders a *blind* little girl—and from this mild impropriety builds himself a career that leads to the threshold of the presidency? Or a stylist who regularly writes such original sentences as this one: "The history professor looked at his watch. Another minute had passed into his domain." John Sladek was one of the most imaginative and versatile writers I have ever known, and he should have been famous.

ACKNOWLEDGMENTS

I couldn't have written these essays without the support, informed criticism, and back talk of my colleagues during the past twenty-five years at *The Washington Post Book World*. Let me name them here: William McPherson, Brigitte Weeks, Curt Suplee, Alice Reid, Michele Slung, Robert Wilson, Reid Beddow, Nina King, Francis Tanabe, Dennis Drabelle, Jonathan Yardley, Marie Arana, Elizabeth Ward, David Nicholson, Brian Jacomb, Zofia Smardz, Ednamae Storti, Mary Morris, Jabari Asim, Chris Lehmann, Jennifer Howard. Our copy aides and news aides were important to me too, especially Joe Caruso, Anne Laurent, Deirdre Donahue, Margaret Camp, John Allison, Teresa Moore, Carolyn Ruff, Katie Gardner, and Chris Schoppa.

I want to thank Andy Solberg, fellow member of the Baker Street Irregulars, for lending me his vacation home as a retreat in which to organize the initial draft of *Bound to Please*. My friend Elizabeth Ward bravely read through the entire manuscript. Marian Peck Dirda and our sons, Christopher, Michael, and Nathaniel, actually put up with me during the years I was writing about all these books.

At Norton my steadfast and insightful editor, Robert Weil, deserves all praise, as do his colleagues Brendan Curry, Tom Mayer, Elizabeth Riley, Louise Brockett, Georgia Liebman, Bill Rusin, Jeannie Luciano, Nancy Palmquist, and many others. It is an honor to be published by such people at such a publishing house.

As always, my agents Glen Hartley and Lynn Chu, and their associate Catharine Sprinkel, have worked tirelessly on my behalf.

Not least, I want to thank *The Washington Post*, and especially its CEO, Donald Graham, for allowing me to reprint these pieces and for having given me the opportunity to write them in the first place. I don't think any other newspaper in the country would have granted me the space and latitude to talk about so many different kinds of writers and books.

ABOUT THE AUTHOR

Michael Dirda, a longtime staff writer and editor for *The Washington Post Book World*, received the 1993 Pulitzer Prize for criticism and is the author of *Readings: Essays and Literary Entertainments* and the memoir *An Open Book*.

8328077R0

Made in the USA
Lexington, KY
24 January 2011